O9-AHW-496

Managerial and Supervisory Principles for Physical Therapists

SECOND EDITION

Senior Acquisitions Editor: Pamela Lappies
Managing Editor: Anne Seitz
Marketing Manager: Mary Martin
Project Editor: Caroline Define

Designer: Doug Smock
Typesetter: Lippincott Williams & Wilkins
Printer: Quebecor

351 West Camden Street
Baltimore, Maryland 21201-2436 USA

530 Walnut Street
Philadelphia, Pennsylvania 19106

The publisher is not responsible (as a matter of product liability, negligence or otherwise) for any injury resulting from any material contained herein. This publication contains information relating to general principles of medical care which should not be construed as specific instructions for individual patients. Manufacturers' product information and package inserts should be reviewed for current information, including contraindications, dosages and precautions.
Printed in the United States of America

Library of Congress Cataloging-in-Publication Data
Nosse, Larry J.
Managerial and supervisory principles for physical therpists / Larry J. Nosse, Deborah G. Friberg, Peter R. Kovacek ; contributor, D. Kathleen Lewis. -- 2nd ed.
p. ; cm.
Includes bibliographical references and indexes.
ISBN 0-7817-4261-1
1. Physical therapy--Practice. 2. Physical therapy--Management. I. Friberg, Deborah G. II. Kovacek, Peter R. III. Lewis, D. Kathleen. IV. Title.
[DNLM: 1. Physical Therapy (Specialty)--Organization & administration. 2. Practice Management, Medical. WB 460 N897ma 2004]
RM713.N674 2004
615.8'2'068--dc22
2004040849

The publishers have made every effort to trace the copyright holders for borrowed material. If they have inadvertently overlooked any, they will be pleased to make the necessary arrangements at the first opportunity.

To purchase additional copies of this book, call our customer service department at **(800) 638-3030** or fax orders to **(301) 824-7390**. For other book services, including chapter reprints and large quantity sales, ask for the Special Sales department.

For all other calls originating outside of the United States, please call **(301)714-2324**.

Visit Lippincott Williams & Wilkins on the Internet: http://www.lww.com. Lippincott Williams & Wilkins customer service representatives are available from 8:30 am to 6:00 pm, EST, Monday through Friday, for telephone access.

05 06 07 08 09
1 2 3 4 5 6 7 8 9 1

Managerial and Supervisory Principles for Physical Therapists

Second Edition

Larry J. Nosse, MAPT, PhD.
Associate Professor
Department of Physical Therapy
Marquette University
Milwaukee, WI
President, LJN Therapy, S.C.
Wauwatosa, WI.

Deborah G. Friberg, PT, MBA
Senior Vice President WakeMed/Executive Director
WakeMed Rehab
Raleigh, NC.

Peter R. Kovacek, PT, MSA
President and Chief Executive Officer
Kovacek Management Services, Inc.
Harper Woods, MI.

Contributor:

D. Kathleen Lewis, MAPT, J.D.
Associate Professor
Department of Physical Therapy
Wichita State University
Wichita, KA.

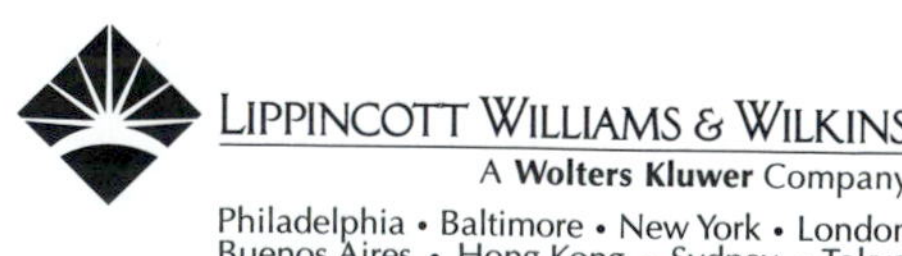
LIPPINCOTT WILLIAMS & WILKINS
A Wolters Kluwer Company
Philadelphia • Baltimore • New York • London
Buenos Aires • Hong Kong • Sydney • Tokyo

Preface to the Second Edition

In the few years since the first edition of *Management and Supervisory Principles for Physical Therapists* was published, much has changed. There have been numerous political, legal, economic, and educational events that have impacted the profession of physical therapy. Some of the notable events that have occurred since 1999 include:

- The weathering of the untoward effects of the Balanced Budget Act of 1997 on the physical therapy workforce
- Greater then ever increases in healthcare costs for everyone—providers, recipients, and payers
- The formation, approval, and dissemination of the American Physical Therapy Association's 2020 Vision statement and an associated rapid development of doctor of physical therapy education programs
- The estimate that by 2004 approximately half of the physical therapist educational programs will have taken steps to move to the clinical doctorate level of education
- Continued successful legislative efforts at the state level to allow patients to access physical therapists directly
- The leaders of at least two of the largest healthcare organizations in the country have been investigated for a variety of offenses
- The Health Insurance Portability and Accountability Act came into effect
- 9/11

These legislative, professional, and educational examples are among the reasons a new edition was needed. To deal with contemporary issues in management and supervision, we have added 19 chapters and significantly revised the remaining 15 chapters to produce an up-to-date, introductory, healthcare-oriented book for future physical therapist managers.

We have chosen again to write for physical therapists–to–be and physical therapists who are early in their professional development and who have little or no formal background in business. Our reasons for focusing on a single professional group were philosophical and practical. Philosophically, we believe that most physical therapists have the innate attributes to satisfactorily handle managerial responsibilities. We chose to do what we can to help physical therapists with the desire to grow in important knowledge and skill areas that facilitate the delivery of direct patient care. Growth in these areas can lead to advancement in organizational influence or to ownership of a physical therapy business. Simply put, we wish to contribute to the advancement of physical therapists and physical therapy as a profession in realms that complement direct patient care, e.g., life-long career development, community leadership, and legislative and organizational influence. The practical reason for writing to physical therapists is because that is what we are, physical therapists. In addition to having clinical experience, we also have experience as educators, supervisors, and managers of physical therapists.

Our Frame of Reference

We give high priority to actions that benefit patients. In support of this priority, we address moral, ethical, and legal matters as they relate to the management of healthcare organizations and clinical service departments. We also recognize that the delivery of healthcare is a business. Like any business, it is right that good service and the provision of appropriate products be paid for. No business can continue to function if it does not have the money to operate. To help assure that excellent care is provided, and healthcare organizations that provide quality care succeed financially, physical therapists must have the knowledge, skill, and disposition to help such organizations to flourish. To contribute to the success of a healthcare organization requires more than good patient care skills. It requires management knowledge and skills.

Management is responsible for providing the environment for quality care to be delivered. In many cases, the management structure of healthcare organizations has placed more responsibility in the hands of those closest to where services are delivered. Physical therapists, with and without a managerial title, are making some decisions that formerly were exclusively for managers to make. First-level managers (supervisors) or work teams made up of staff members are making management decisions. Today, managers need staff members who have good clinical skills, who understand the bigger picture of healthcare organizational operation, the influence of external events on healthcare, and who have the knowledge and skill to achieve goals through the efforts of others. This expanded view of the needs of the physical therapists of today and tomorrow is consistent with that of the American Physical Therapy Association's Section on Administration, now the Section on Health Care Policy and Administration (http://www.aptasoa.org/lamp/htm).

In 1998, the Section on Administration invited a select group of members to form the Task Force on Leadership, Administration and Management Preparation (LAMP). The Task Force's purpose was to examine and develop a position on professional education related to LAMP. The Task Force ultimately produced a framework for the study of the LAMP processes and content priorities for continuing education based on LAMP. Subsequently, four LAMP Summit Conferences were held at Marquette University from 2000 through 2003, and formal research on the management knowledge and skill needs of student and practicing physical therapists was carried out (Lopopolo, Schafer, Nosse, 2004). The LAMP document, LAMP summit conferences, and the related research heavily influenced the content of this edition.

About the Title

The title of the book includes the words management and supervision but not administration. This is because we perceive management as the general term for getting work done through the efforts of others and supervision as the first level of management. All managers supervise someone; therefore, supervision is an important topic to address. Administration is a term we associate with the upper levels of management. It is most likely that readers will become supervisors. Therefore, the title of the book reflects management as the core topic and supervision as a level of management and a general management responsibility. The word principles is also in the title. Principles are fundamental or general truths (when there is supporting data) or rules of thumb (when experience provides the best evidence) to guide efforts to achieve a specific end. In this book, some principles of both types are presented.

Organization of this Edition

There are 34 chapters in this edition, allocated in 6 parts with 4 to 8 topically related chapters per part. The part titles and their general content are:

- I The Big Picture—Background information about healthcare, law, values, and ethics
- II Understanding Business and Management—Organization and management fundamentals
- III Managing Human Resources—Developing and dealing with people in the workplace
- IV Service Marketing—Marketing principles applied to healthcare services
- V Managing Money—Healthcare economics, accounting, budgeting, and reporting
- VI Measuring Up and Getting Paid—Outcomes, accreditation, risk management, and consultant help

The progression of information from foundational concepts of government and business related to healthcare to outcomes and hiring consultants is rational, yet there are accommodations for reading the various parts in any order.

User Friendly and Flexible

In organizing this edition, much thought was given to making the book user friendly for readers and instructors. From our personal teaching experience, we recognized that management courses for physical therapist students vary in their content, credit hours, and placement in the general educational schema. We felt that this book had to allow flexibility in meeting these different needs. Therefore, chapters were written to allow the reader and instructor flexibility. To accomplish this, we adopted a planned redundancy strategy. By design, we often included the same core concepts within related chapters, i.e., the same information was repeated in several places. This redundancy makes each chapter semiautonomous, i.e., each has unique information as well as being linked by common terminology and concepts to other chapters. By reiterating core concepts in a common language, readers and instructors have flexibility in choosing the order in which chapters are read and which chapters are assigned. To support flexibility in the assignment of readings and selective reading on specific topics, every chapter has multiple cross-references. When being introduced to a new body of knowledge, it is helpful to provide readers with a schema to show how the component parts are related and the order that they will be presented.

To facilitate envisioning the interrelationships between the parts of the book, a consistent figure was used at the start of each part of the book to show what content will be addressed and how this information relates to the other book parts. The same format was used for each chapter under the assumption that this consistency would help readers know where certain information would be in any chapter.

Active Learning Exercises

Adult learners make efforts to learn what they think they can use in the near future. The near future for many readers will include their first physical therapy staff position or their first supervisory position. To encourage engagement with the material, scenarios appropriate to readers in these situations are presented in two case studies in every chapter. One case study is for an individual to complete, and the other is to be completed in groups. The intent of these cases is to stimulate thought and discussion on an individual or group basis. The discussion of the cases is expected to lead to a deeper understanding of the principles gained through personal involvement, reflection, and feedback.

Broad Coverage of Topics

A final comment about this edition is its breadth of content. Most physical therapy educational programs provide at least one course in management that usually includes some content on health policy, healthcare legislation, legal aspects of healthcare, and laws related to physical therapy, and professional or career development. No book that we are aware of has substantively addressed management principles plus all of these topics. This edition does.

Larry J. Nosse

ACKNOWLEDGMENT

We are extremely thankful for the efforts of the exceptional, dedicated reviewers who helped us sharpen our focus and the clarity of our writing. The reviewers were:

Barbara Billek-Sawhney, PT, EdD
Graduate School of Physical Therapy
Slippery Rock University

Sam Coppoletti, MPT
Physical Therapy Assistant Program
Shawnee State University

Diane V. Jewell, PT, MS, CCS
Department of Physical Therapy
Virginia Commonwealth University

Ann Noonan, EdD, PT
Department of Physical Therapy
Northeastern University

Their thoughts influenced the content of the book for the better.
LJN, DGF, and PRK
June, 2004

CONTENTS

Part I The Big Picture

Part II Understanding Business and Management

Part III Managing Human Resources

Part IV Service Marketing

Part V Managing Money

Part VI Measuring Up and Getting Help

Part I

The Big Picture

PART I (Ch 1-6)
The Big Picture

PART II (Ch 7-13)
Understanding Business and Management

PART III (Ch 14-20)
Managing Human Resources

PART IV (Ch 21-25)
Service Marketing

PART V (Ch 26-30)
Managing Money

PART VI (Ch 31-34)
Measuring Up and Getting Help

CHAPTERS

Chapter 1

Health Care Social Philosophy, Public Policy, and Legislation

Learning Objectives

1. Define the main elements of a generic system.
2. Analyze the core features of a health care system.
3. Examine social philosophy and public policy regarding health care underlying the Soviet, selected continental European, United Kingdom, Canadian, and U.S. health care systems.
4. Use the concepts and terminology associated with the first three items on this list to compare and contrast the health care systems in terms of control, access, funding, and selected outcomes.
5. Compare and contrast the major health care systems in terms of the benefits and deficits from the point of view of consumers, physical therapist clinicians, managers, and yourself as a taxpayer.

Key Words

Canada Health Act (CHA), Canadian health care system, capitalism, centralized, communism, comprehensive health care system, distributive justice, entrepreneurial health care system, federalist, gross domestic product (GDP), justice, National Health System (NHS), policy, private health care, public health care, public policy, selected continental European (SCE) countries, social philosophy, social policy, socialism, solidarity, Soviet health care system, system, United Kingdom (U.K.), United Kingdom health care system, United States (U.S.) health care system, welfare health care system

Introduction

The focus of this chapter is health care systems. A **system** is the integration of a number of interrelated parts that work in concert to produce a service or product that is more than the sum of the parts considered separately (Shelton, 2000). The general purpose of this chapter is to stimulate thinking about the major health care systems around the world. To meet this purpose this chapter does the following:

- Provides the reader with a rationale for investigating health care systems worldwide
- Presents sufficient background information on each system to allow making important comparisons
- Relates the information to physical therapy practice and management

As will be detailed later, the management of any business requires an understanding of the major external variables that affect the business (Chapter 11). Social, political, and economic factors affect the availability of health care and how it is paid for. Managers who understand the various health care systems have a greater chance of assessing the effects of projected changes on the system they work in. This chapter presents an international perspective of health care systems. The discussion includes immigration, emigration, clinical practice and management applications, and comparisons of major health care systems on control, financing, access, choice, and payers.

Immigration, Emigration, and Physical Therapy

Immigration brings people from different countries to the United States. The most recent U.S. census estimated that 11.5% of the U.S. population was foreign born. Most (52.2%) of this segment of the population were born in central America or Mexico (U.S. Census Bureau, 2003). Some immigrants will be our clients. Immigration also brings in physicians and physical therapists who were not trained in the United States. Some of these individuals will be sources of patients sent to physical therapists and some will be our coworkers. It is likely that many physical therapists will work with colleagues who were born and educated outside of the United States. This likelihood has increased in recent years because some physical therapist educational programs outside of the United States have sought and earned accreditation from the Commission on Accreditation for Physical Therapy Education (CAPTE). CAPTE is the same agency that accredits entry-level U.S. physical therapy educational programs (American Physical Therapy Association [APTA], 2002a). In 2002, this organization accredited 20 foreign physical therapist educational programs (APTA, 2002b). In 2003 three foreign institutions, one each in Canada, Ireland, and Scotland, had CAPTE accreditation (APTA, 2003a).

Why Learn About Health Care Systems?

At least five practical positive outcomes can be reached when physical therapist clinicians and managers know about other countries' health care systems and act on this knowledge. Anticipated outcomes:

1. Acceptable customer satisfaction ratings from nonnative individuals
2. Desirable levels of intradepartmental and interdepartmental communication
3. Reduced risk of lawsuits
4. Adherence to professional behavior guidelines
5. Fostering of professional development

Customer Satisfaction

A general understanding of the health care systems immigrants are accustomed to can harmonize expectations and minimize misconceptions and misunderstandings. Immigrants include patients, nonprofessional staff, physical therapists, and physicians. People in these categories are potential consumers of physical therapy services (Chapter 21). Understanding the general differences between the U.S. health care system and the systems of other nations can contribute to customers' belief that they have received good care. Customers who are treated with respect and understanding are generally tolerant of imperfect conditions. This may reduce the risk of a suit (Chapter 33). When an organization's workforce includes recent immigrants, cordiality may be fostered if there is some understanding of differences between health care systems from the standpoint of both patients and providers of care. This kind of understanding may be considered one aspect of being culturally competent. The final reason physical therapists should understand other health care systems comes from two statements in the APTA Guide For Professional Conduct (APTA, 2003b). Principle 1.1A indicates that physical therapist association members are to respect and respond to individual patients' differences. Honoring this principle includes understanding the broad perspective of a patient's health care experiences. Similar considerations apply to interactions with nonnative colleagues. Principle 11.2 notes that physical therapists should not undermine professional relationships, and principle 11.3 cautions against disparaging other health care providers. Understanding the differences in health care systems may help the practitioner follow both of these principles.

An understanding of other nations' health care systems can also benefit U.S.–trained physical therapists who venture beyond the borders of the United States to practice. There is an increasing variety of international volunteer (APTA, 2002c) and some employment opportunities available outside of the United States. (APTA, 2000). Student physical therapists also have international opportunities (Bergman, 1998; Scheuing, 2003). Another component of professional development is reading journals and books. Information based on clinical interventions applied to patients in another country must be interpreted by the reader within the context of the health care system in the country where the work was performed. The impression that what works elsewhere, in the United Kingdom for example, must be tempered by the understanding that the delivery of physical therapy there occurs in the context of a health care system unlike that of the United States.

Everyone Is Concerned About Health Care

Individual governments and multinational organizations, such as the Organization for Economic Cooperation and Development (OECD) and the World Health Organization (WHO), also study similarities and differences between health care systems. The 30 OECD member countries (Fig. 1.1) have for years collected and shared comparative data on access, expenditures, outcomes, and other areas. The geographical locations of OECD members are shown in Figure 1.1.

Issues

Most industrialized nations are facing the same issue: how to meet health care needs under the constraints of finite and often unpredictable revenue sources (Wimberly and Thai, 2002). The study of health care system innovations and their results is also useful because it provides an evidence-based database to guide decision making.

The next sections contain an overview of health care–related social, political, and economic philosophical principles, reflections on differences in health care policy and legislation, and multiple comparisons of the key elements of health care systems in five general sociopolitical conditions. The international comparisons made in this chapter are important background to the more detailed discussion of the U.S. health care system presented in Chapter 2.

Important Questions to Address Worldwide

Government officials in most nations are concerned about the health of the people of their country. How to meet the health care needs of their constituencies is an issue that government leaders spend much time debating. These are important common questions that are debated during consideration of health care for a country's population:

- Who should receive health care?
- Who should pay for it?
- How much care to provide?

The answers to these questions vary because of national differences in history, social philosophy, available resources (economics), beliefs about health care, cultural priorities, and the health status of people (Daniels and Sabin, 2002; Reagan, 1999; Roemer, 1993; Shi and Singh, 2001).

Social Philosophy, Public Policy, and Legislation

Discussions about who should get health care is philosophical and political. In complex systems, such as managing the health care of a nation, questions of rights and **justice** are commonplace. These discussions focus on

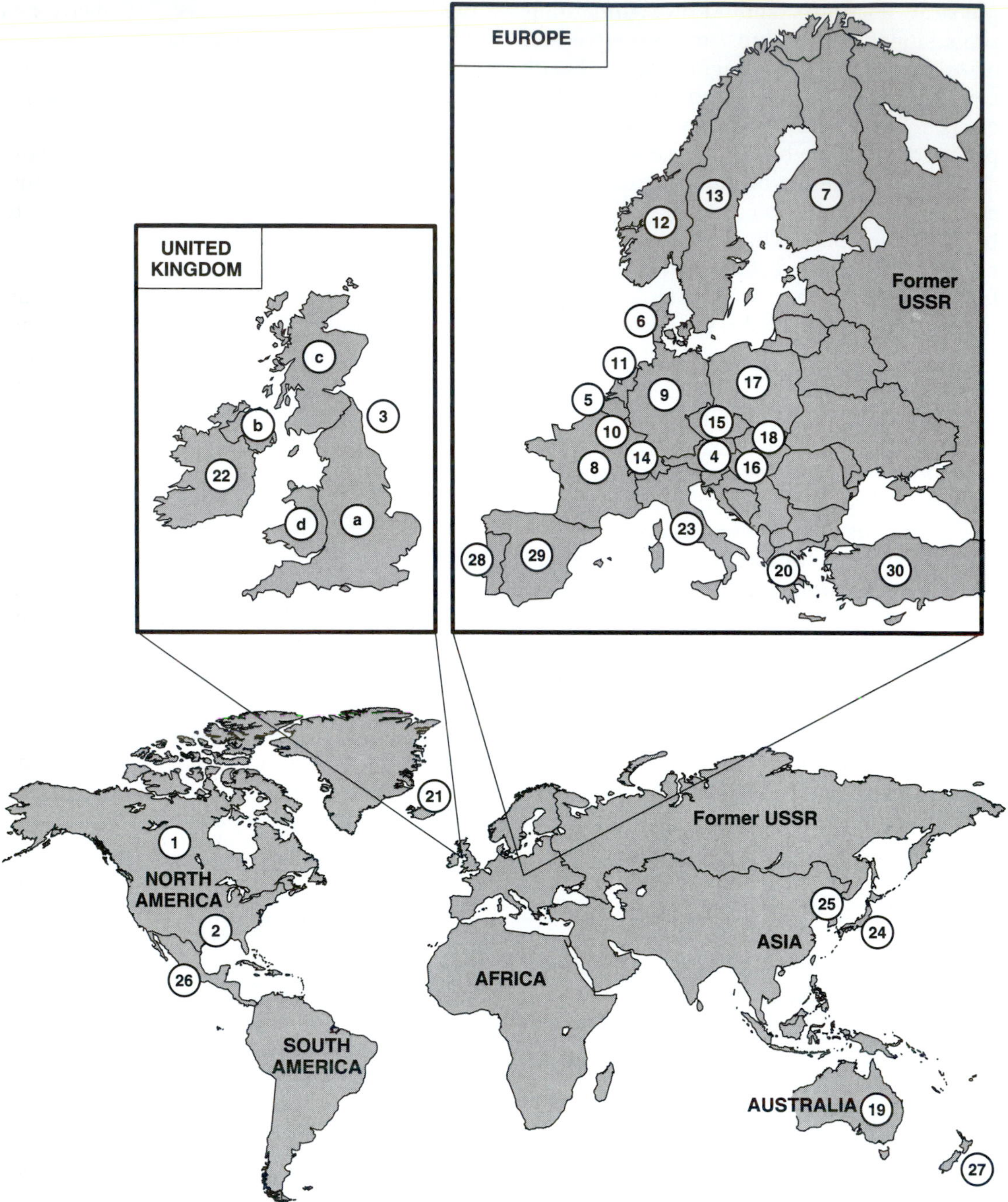

Figure 1.1. Members of OECD in 2000 listed in alphabetical order within their geographical regions. North America: 1, Canada; 2, United States; 3, United Kingdom; a, England; b, Northern Ireland; c, Scotland; d, Wales. Continental Europe, selected members: 4, Austria; 5, Belgium; 6, Denmark; 7, Finland; 8. France; 9, Germany; 10, Luxembourg; 11, Netherlands; 12, Norway; 13, Sweden; 14, Switzerland. Former Soviet Bloc: 15, Czech Republic; 16, Hungary; 17, Poland; 18, Slovak Republic. Others: 19, Australia; 20, Greece; 21, Iceland; 22, Ireland, Republic of; 23, Italy; 24, Japan; 25, Korea; 26, Mexico; 27, New Zealand; 28, Portugal; 29, Spain; 30, Turkey.

weighing available options. The weighing and actions finally taken are subject to political influences (Loewy, 2001). Therefore, the interests of those in political power and their political ideology do affect major issues like what a health care system looks like, how it operates, and whom the system serves. This intermingling of influences that affect public policy merits further discussion.

A **policy** for this discussion is defined as a broad statement containing goals, objectives, and means that form a framework for organizing specific activities. **Public policies** are the results of decisions made by an authoritative branch of government (in the U.S. they are the executive, judicial, and legislative branches; in some other countries it is the ministry or department of health) that are intended to influence the use of resources, including political power (Shi and Singh, 2001). Public policy discussions, overtly or otherwise, entail deliberations grounded in ethical principles according to various social philosophies. Taking guidance from a **social philosophy** entails the formal or informal adoption of ethical concepts to form a moral backdrop against which decisions about the allocation of relatively scarce resources are played out. Ethical concepts relevant to fair access to health care in general focus on justice and in particular on issues of social and distributive justice (Austin, 2001) (see next section and Chapter 6). The ethical concepts that are adopted provide the context for discussions that are part of the process used to develop public policy.

Social philosophy relates to a wide range of social matters. Assistance programs for the poor, for women and children, for people with disabilities, for people beyond a certain age, and for indigenous peoples are all examples of social welfare programs that benefit many members of society. While there may be desire to do more for people with real needs for the right reasons, there is the general constraint of limited resources and of course varying political philosophies that also influence final decisions. These interacting forces place various proposals and programs in competition for funding. Recent examples of competitive health care issues in the U.S. are the need to increase efforts to counter bioterrorism and the need to improve drug benefits for people eligible for Medicare. Health care is only one of many competing programs on the agenda that government officials and elected legislators must consider when they exert their influence to shape policies and make laws. In democratic countries public policies indirectly reflect voters' wishes. Voters vote to help get candidates of their choice elected. Once this is accomplished, constituents can engage in dialog with their elected officials to express their views on issues of importance to them. Chapter 2 includes more discussion about involvement in the legislative process.

The core philosophical issues related to access, allocation, and rationing health care services relate to fairness or justice. In its most general sense justice deals with moral oughts. In health care this can be translated as concerns about who ought to get what, or **distributive justice** (Daniels, 1985). Health care managers confront distributive justice issues when they allocate funds for one program over another or close a facility and direct resources to others. While there is no consensus on the principles of distributive justice (Austin, 2001; Daniels and Sabin, 2002) in public policy discussions, distributive justice is at the core of arguments for health care services being a right and justification for entitlement programs. In the context of this chapter this all boils down to determining "how to meet health care needs fairly under resource constraints" (Daniels and Sabin, 2002). Resources have costs; therefore, economic considerations of any program a policy advocates must include a parallel discussion of how the program will be paid for. Given the capitalistic free-market economic philosophy of the U.S., the economic cost of health care influences decisions along with consideration of moral oughts. In economic terms health care services can be perceived as a commodity, that is, something to buy and sell in the marketplace (Part IV and Chapter 26). In an open market (Chapter 26) those who can afford services can buy them. Those who cannot buy standard services find less costly alternatives or do without. The ethical discussion of health care includes reasoned debate about whether access to adequate health care is a right of all members of a society. Among the industrialized nations of the world, all but one, the U.S., have determined that their residents have a right to health care. These countries allocate resources to ensure universal or nearly universal access to adequate health care at little or no out-of-pocket cost to residents.

General Comparison of Health Care Systems

A system was defined earlier as several parts working together such that their interaction produces something greater than could be produced by the individual parts working independently (Shelton, 2000). A useful approach to compare health care systems is to categorize systems based on the relative degree of governmental involvement in the planning, financing, and control of health care for a nation's residents (Grogan, 1993) and then do a more specific analysis where there are meaningful commonalities (Roemer, 1993). Figure 1.2 and Table 1.1 integrate these thoughts. The figure shows the relative amounts of governmental and private control of health care under the different systems. The table shows a general progression in degrees of central government control over health care under different sociopolitical and economic philosophies and how the systems differ in terms of financing, payers, access, and freedom of choice.

The communism column refers to the health care system developed by the Soviets and implemented throughout the former Soviet bloc countries (see example countries in Fig. 1.1). Russia's health care system is the prime example of this system. The communism column is first because is represents the system with the most government (public) control over health care and the least availability of alternative (private) health care. While the system has not existed since approximately 1990, it does merit discussion:

- It represents one extreme in the ways health care can be systematized.
- Thousands of people in the United States, Canada, Eastern Europe, Israel, and elsewhere were cared for under this system.
- Vestiges of the system remain in Russia and the former Soviet bloc countries (Bourhanskaia, Kubataev, Paterson, 2002; Evetovits, 2002).

Politically and socially, the Soviet bloc was communistic. **Communism** does not recognize the right to private ownership (Loewy, 2001). All resources belong to the government as the caretaker of society (Brinton, Christopher, Wolff, 1967). Under the **Soviet health care system** very little private-pay health care was available (Roemer, 1993). Responsibility for all aspects of health care, including planning, education, research, financing, and delivery, resided with the central government. The central government owned the health care system and related resources and employed all personnel (Roemer, 1993); that is, everyone was a government employee. The central government also recognized health care as a right of citizenship. Citizens of the Soviet Union have been entitled to free health care paid for by the government for decades; however, basic medical and acute care for most citizens was not realized until the 1980s (Bourhanskaia et al., 2002). Care for the general population was provided through regional general and specialty hospitals and ambulatory care centers. While medical services were free, medications were only conditionally free. Most drugs had to be purchased from government-owned pharmacies. However, drugs considered critical to one's well-being were commonly provided at no charge (Roemer, 1993). As in most countries, facilities and services were more widely available in populated areas than other areas. In addition to usual medical and nursing staff, care was provided by feldschers, a combination nurse practitioner and physician's assistant. Interestingly, physical therapy, along with other services typically provided by health professionals other than physicians, were provided by medical doctors (Bourhanskaia et al., 2002). Some especially well-

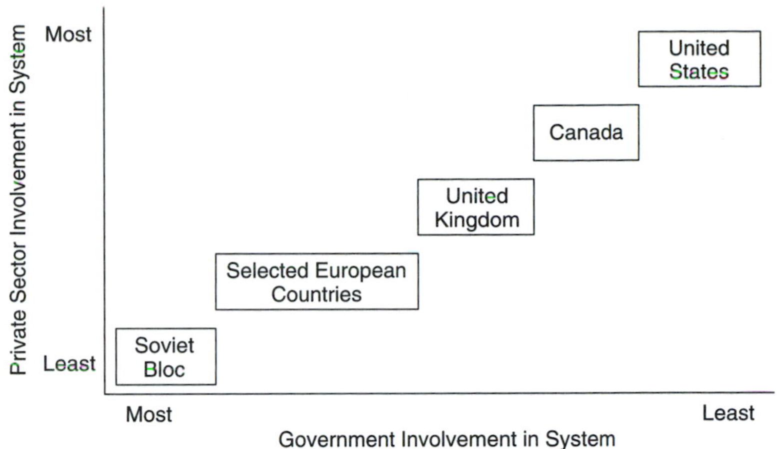

Figure 1.2. Comparison of five health care systems showing the relative amount of government and private sector involvement.

equipped and well-staffed hospitals and clinics were reserved for "important persons" (Roemer, 1993). Near its end the tightly controlled Soviet health care system approached its goal of meeting the medical needs of most of its constituents at government expense. The recipients, however, had few choices as to where they were treated or by whom, as they were assigned by home address to local care facilities.

At present there is turmoil in the former Soviet bloc nations as they struggle to move from totalitarian socialistic government toward more democratic government, as privatization evolves and market economies begin to flourish. The most adequate description of the state of health care in the Russian Federation and the former Soviet bloc nations is that they are in transition (Bourhanskaia et al., 2002; Evetovits, 2002; Roemer, 1993).

The socialism column in Table 1.1 exemplifies the health care systems of Germany and Sweden (Fig. 1.1). Both countries employ elements of socialism in their approach to the health care of their respective populations. ***Socialism*** is sometimes used interchangeably with *communism*. This is incorrect. Socialism recognizes the right to limited private ownership. Communism does not (Loewy, 2001). What they have in common is that social conditions are associated with the economic system (Brinton et al., 1967; Rodwin, 1999). Socialism is a system based on the view that certain services, products, and institutions benefit the whole of society (Brinton et al., 1967). Because these resources represent a good to be used by the greater community of citizens, these assets should be controlled by the central government so they can be put to use to benefit the community (Loewy, 2001). Health care is considered one of these community assets. From a socialist viewpoint a health care system must be under governmental control to ensure equitable distribution of this asset. A related unique feature of socialist health care systems is the concept of social solidarity. **Solidarity** can be described as a stance taken by a civic community (including those with historically similar ethnic and social backgrounds [Kovner and Jonas, 1999]) that socially beneficial programs, such as health care, should be "evaluated on more than a materialistic and monetary standard; economic actions are not separated from social morals and actions of society" (Morton, 2001, p. 140). The concept of social solidarity recognizes both shared benefits and shared responsibilities (Churchill, 1994). Membership in unions, trade associations, and professional associations is bolstered by the solidarity concept. Such organizations have benefited their members by negotiating good benefits from employers. Solidarity is clearly exemplified in Germany, where almost all res-

Table 1.1 General Comparison of Important Elements of Health Care Systems Based on Social, Political, and Economic Philosophy

	Communism	*Socialism*	*Comprehensive*	*Welfare*	*Entrepreneurial*
Example countries	Russia; former Soviet bloc, e.g., Czech Republic, Hungary	Germany, Sweden	United Kingdom[a]	Canada	United States
Control	Central government owns all resources, employs all providers, plans for and finances all aspects.	Varying degrees of central government control to ensure access. Control through legislation for national insurance tax, mandatory work-related insurance, availability of private insurance. Actual control can be legislated to local authorities.	Extensive central government control to ensure access to quality care. NHS plans for comprehensive health care throughout U.K. to be delivered by local authorities, which arrange for and authorize comprehensive care at the local level. Local accountability is mandated.	Extensive central control. Legislation to support care in part by federal government. Provinces and territories may offer and pay for unlegislated services. Delivery of services is in hands of private sector, e.g., hospitals and physicians. Local accountability is mandated.	Central government plans and legislates for varied levels of care for specified segments of population. State and local governments do same. Most resources are owned and controlled by private entities who operate within legal statutes.
Financing levels	Federal taxes for specialized care. State payroll taxes and insurance funds to provide care for the employed, territorial taxes for others.	Taxes, public and private insurance funds. Minimal patient out-of pocket payments.	Taxes, public and private insurance funds, minimal patient out-of-pocket payments.	Taxes, public and private - insurance funds. More out-of-pocket payment as more private services become available.	Taxes, public and private insurance funds, variable levels of patient out-of-pocket payments, charity.
Payers	Government	Government > private	Government > private	Government > private	Government < private
Patient choice	None for most people	Extensive	Access to hospital and specialists controlled by local general practitioner.	Limitations regarding elective procedures, access to specialists, special diagnostic tests.	No restrictions to very restricted. Depends on care plan and ability to pay.

[a]England, Northern Ireland, Scotland, Wales.

idents, citizens or not, have health insurance (Swami, 2002) and by the historic and expensive reunification of East and West Germany in 1989. The essence of this example is that solidarity may buffer economic arguments in socialistic countries as new health care policies are brought forward.

Typically the central government of socialist countries assumes the responsibility to do **central** health care planning. Planning is done for areas that are necessary to ensure that universal health care is available free of direct charge for citizens and, in some cases, for noncitizens. Socialist-oriented governments finance health care through various combinations of general and special tax revenues, special public and private insurance funds, and small user fees. In Germany the government manages the system in a less centralized fashion than some of its near socialist neighbors (Grogan, 1993) but exerts more control than socialist-oriented Sweden (Kaati, 2002). The German government neither finances nor pays for health care services. It ensures health care coverage by legislation two ways. The first is by requiring employers, trade associations, and professional associations to maintain sickness funds that cover health care for their respective members. About 90% of the population is covered by sickness funds. The second is to exert price controls on drugs. Private health insurance is available to individuals who wish to opt out of the sickness funds. Payment to providers is negotiated fee-for-service. Another feature of the German health care system is that doctors are limited as to where they treat patients. Doctors who work from their private office are not permitted to see patients in the hospital. Similarly, hospital-based doctors are salaried employees who see only hospitalized patients. Supply and demand work to foster competition for patients. Admission to German medical schools has been available to all who meet qualifications. Over time this has produced an oversupply of physicians (Swami, 2002).

In terms of outcomes, socialistic health care systems, when adequately funded, have met most of the basic health care needs of nearly all of their constituents (Roemer, 1993; Swami, 2002). While there is little or no out-of-pocket cost to service users, health care is not free; it is paid for through taxes or contributions to special insurance funds. At present, there is generally a high degree of satisfaction with the socialistic health care systems along with a deep concern about their sustainability (Thai, Wimberley, McManus, 2002). From a management perspective, getting payment is relatively uncomplicated. There are two payer sources, the sickness fund and private insurance. The paperwork is standardized for billing. This simplification results in low administrative costs. In Germany hospitals spend about 40% as much as U.S. hospitals on administrative expenses (Swami, 2002).

The third type of system in the continuum is called comprehensive (Table 1.1). This system is unique to the **United Kingdom**, that is, England, Wales, Scotland, and Northern Ireland (Fig. 1.1). The **U.K. health care system** is also a socialist model (Bloor and Maynard, 2002), but it differs significantly from the continental European models. First, it is considered a **comprehensive health care system** (Roemer, 1993). The hallmarks of this system are:

- A great deal of central planning and overall management of local government health authorities
- Less governmental control than in several continental socialist systems
- Universally available health care through government-provided services plus private health care services
- Availability of private insurance to cover elective procedures (Bloor and Maynard, 2002).

Under the U.K. version of a highly centralized comprehensive health care system, the entire national populations of multiple countries are entitled to complete health care. A recent estimate of how health care services and products are paid for found 86% came from general taxes, 12% from payroll taxes, and the remainder from users who received dental services and prescription drugs (Bloor and Maynard, 2002). Administratively, the Department of Health is the central governmental agency overseeing the health care. The coordinating link between the central government and the **National Health System (NHS)** are the strategic health authorities. These authorities are charged to help local NHS staff develop strategies for quality care. Local hospital trusts actually employ health care and related professionals and staff. Everyone is a salaried government employee. The government periodically reviews salaries through independent review boards and makes adjustments in the salary schedules. Services are provided at NHS facilities as well as in homes. However, because "Every...citizen has the right to be registered with a local GP and visits...are free" (National Health Service, 2002, p. 3), local groups of primary care physicians are the portals of entry into the care system. This places general practitioners in a gatekeeper role because it is up to them to decide whether there is to be a referral for specialist or hospital treatment (Bloor and Maynard, 2002). Services are "free" in the sense that a relatively small financial exchange takes place directly between the care recipient and the care provider. Payment comes mostly from taxes the recipients have paid.

The U.K. system is under scrutiny worldwide for good reasons. It is apparently cost and outcome effective, and it provides comprehensive care for everyone. In outcomes it is ranked near the middle of OECD and other major industrialized nations in key measures. User satisfaction levels for selected aspects of the system are apparently adequate. A 2002 Department of Health user satisfaction survey sampled a large number of patients throughout the U.K. from 1998 to 2001. Depending on location, it was found that 81 to 91% of patients were satisfied with their experience; that is, they did not consider complaining or actually complain (Department of Health, 2002). And finally, the U.K. system functions at a relatively low cost to the government (Bloor and Maynard, 2002). A contributing reason for relatively low cost is that the NHS pay scale is set through periodic negotiation for all NHS health care providers.

The fourth column in Table 1.1 is labeled as a welfare health care system. Canada is the unique representative of this system. Its location in the table reflects less central government and more private involvement in health care than the systems discussed thus far. The major point in common with the other health care systems is accessibility.

In the Canadian **welfare health care system**, residents have universal access to care (Roemer, 1993). Canadian universal health care insurance is called Medicare (Romanow, 2002). This Medicare program is for all ages and differs from the age and disability limitation requirements of the U.S. Medicare program. The **Canadian health care system** is based on a social philosophy that holds health care as a right. In this system health care for citizens is a shared responsibility of the federal and provincial governments.

The dual responsibility for health care is clearly stated in the **Canada Health Act (CHA)**, passed by Parliament in 1984. This act was formulated to ensure that all Canadian residents would have access to prepaid necessary health care by establishing criteria and conditions for the provinces and territories to satisfy to qualify for their full share of federal funding (Canada Health Act, 2002). The actual role of the central government in health care is indirect (Kluge, 2001). The CHA made the federal government responsible for setting and administering health care standards and assisting with the financing of the health care programs of Canada's 10 provincial and 3 territorial governments. The act mandates that provincial and territorial governments be responsible for managing, delivering, and securing additional tax and other revenues to ensure that all residents receive all medically necessary hospital, physician, and allied health services and some drugs. Provinces and territories have the option to offer benefits beyond those mandated by the CHA, and local ministries of health define what services are medically necessary. This means there is variation in health care services and other benefits. Canadian Medicare covers about 70% of health care spending (Romanow, 2002).

To meet a broader scope of health care needs, increasing numbers of Canadians are purchasing private health insurance (PriceWaterhouseCoopers, 2003). Because there are waiting lists for some diagnostic tests and access to specialists usually requires a wait averaging more than 16 weeks (Walker and Wilson, 2002), some Canadians come to the U.S. for services. Their public insurance pays for care given outside of Canada at the prevailing Canadian rate. This rate may be less than is usual and customary in the U.S., but it is acceptable to some U.S. providers, who are happy to have patients for whom payment is guaranteed.

Means of sustaining the Canadian system are under investigation. The Commission on the Future of Health Care in Canada is in dialog with a wide range of stakeholders, representatives of other socialist health care nations, and international organizations to determine how the Canadian government can sustain a system that will continue to fulfill a core Canadian value, providing health care for all residents according to need (Romanow, 2002).

The final column in Table 1.1. is labeled entrepreneurial. This is the unique **U.S. health care system**. The entrepreneurial model of health care incorporates two components. One component is tax supported. The other component is privately supported. Excepting the communist system, other health care systems do have public and private health care. The difference is the relative importance in terms of financing and the numbers of people covered by private sources of funding. In the U.S. the private component dominates (Fig. 1.2). In recognition of the magnitude of influence of private health care in the U.S., the system has also been tagged an **entrepreneurial health care system** (Roemer, 1993). An entrepreneur is one who risks personal assets to start and run a business with the intent of earning a profit (Olsen, 1999). Historically, the private entrepreneurial health care component flourished for the most part because of a fee-for-service payment method that paid for services a la carte (Roemer, 1993). These introductory comments are important to the following short interpretive review of the history of the U.S. political process and the characteristics of U.S. economic system and national characteristics. These areas constitute the necessary background for understanding why and how the two-component U.S. health care system is unique.

The United States has a **federalist** form of government in which there is delineation in the authority of local, state, and federal government and a tendency to favor decentralization of health care (Grogan, 1993). U.S. political ideology is linked to **capitalism**, an economic philosophy that espouses a market orientation, that is, a free-market economy and competition (Kronfeld, 1997; Reagan, 1999; Shi and Singh, 2001) plus an orientation favoring individual efforts to succeed. Individuals engaged in self-advancing actions are expected to ultimately benefit society (Kronfeld, 1997). Individual rights are fervently upheld. These economic, political, and orientation factors have led to the development of parallel health care system components. In short, one component is public, tax based, and reflects the social philosophy that government has a responsibility to provide access to health care, especially for those in most need. The other system is privately managed and funded, market related, and entrepreneurial.

The **public health care** component evolved to care for the poor, disabled, and other needy segments of society. The social philosophy underlying the public health care system reflects recognition of responsibility to the greater community to ensure access to health care of specified segments of the community, that is, those least able to meet this need on their own. Many proposals to extend health care benefits to all members of society have been offered, but they have come and gone without advancing to reality (Morton, 2001; Reagan, 1999; Shelton, 2000; Shi and Singh, 2001). The prevailing political view has been that the responsibility for securing health care coverage generally lies with the individual, that is, secure a job with health care benefits or self-pay. The general public may not agree with this. In a poll taken in 1996, respondents were asked if it were appropriate for government to ensure universal access to health care; 84% responded yes (Reagan, 1999).

Like any other business, to survive, a health care entity has to make more money than it spends (see Part V for fiscal information). The main payers in the **private health care** component include employers providing health care insurance as a benefit of employment or offering health care themselves, individuals who pay for their own health insurance or pay cash, and philanthropists (including charity and pro bono care). Private individuals and organizations providing health care thrive in a system based on fee-for-service; that is, each unit of service has a separate charge. The private component exemplifies many aspects of a market-based economy along with the U.S. character as described earlier. These two points in the context of private health care providers include the ideas of the right of individuals to do something to better the human condition, the right to provide charity care, and of course, the right to meet demand for health care as an entrepreneur and make a profit. For consumers, the private system provides an alternative to publicly funded health care, the right to choose where they obtain services, and the right to choose from among competing providers.

In comparison to the other 29 OECD countries (Fig. 1.1), the public component of the U.S. health care system is different in that the government does not ensure that all of its citizens have access to health care (Shi and Singh, 2001). This means the government does not pay for most health care costs of its citizens (Centers for Medicare and Medicaid Services [CMS], 2002; Levit, Lazenby, Braden et al., 1996). (This assertion will be challenged later.) The government does not run the health care system (Shi and Singh, 2001; Swami, 2002). For example, in the category of payment for health care, estimates from 2001 data determined that for every $1 spent on health care the private sector paid $0.66 and the U.S. Department of Health and Human Services (HHS) paid $0.33 (Department of Health and Human Services, 2002). Another analysis of data from 2000 estimated that 55% of health care financing came from private sources: insurance (34%), patient's pocket (15%), and charity care and philanthropy (6%) (CMS, 2002).

Compared to other OECD member countries (Fig. 1.1) the U.S. federal and state governments contribute the least to cover the overall health costs of their constituents (Oxley and MacFarlan, 2002). This is true because of the predominance of private payers. Recently, the HHS estimate of the portion of health care–related costs it pays has been challenged as being underreported and conservative. The crux of the argument is that HHS reporting does not recognize tax deductions employers and others are allowed for health care as a tax subsidy, that is, a deduction from tax revenue, which is a cost to the government. Neither do HHS estimates consider expenditures made from public funds for private health insurance purchased for government employees. If the identified items and some other costs were included as part of the tax-supported contribution to health care, the government estimate would be approximately 15% higher than the 45% it identifies (Woolhandler and Himmelstein, 2002).

In any business it is common to examine the cost to produce a service or product (Chapter 27). Health care in the United States is mostly provided by businesses, so it should be assessed this way and compared to the less expensive alternative systems of the world. For global economic comparisons the amount spent on health care for each person in a country and the relationship between health care expenditures and the **gross domestic product (GDP)** are commonly used. The GDP is the total value of all services and goods produced by labor in a country (Bureau of Economic Analysis, 2002). Table 1.2 shows a comparison of selected OECD countries based on per capita total money spent and total health care expenditures as a proportion of GDP. The table clearly shows that on economic criteria the U.S. health care system ranks at the top. It is the most expensive system in the world.

Numerous international organizations, for example the WHO and OECD, compare the

Table 1.2 Rank Order Comparison of OECD Countries That Spent Over $1000 per Person on Health Care in 2000

Rank	Country	Spending per Capita	Rank	% of GDP Spent on Health Care
1	United States	$4,631	1	13.0
2	Switzerland	3,222	2	10.7
3	Germany	2,748	3	10.6
4	Iceland (Luxembourg)[a]	2,608	6	8.9
5	Canada	2,535	5	9.1
6	Denmark	2,420	8	8.3
7	France	2,349	4	9.5
8	Belgium	2,269	7	8.7
9	Norway	2,268	18	7.5
10	Netherlands	2,246	12	8.1
11	Australia	2,211	8	8.3
12	Austria	2,162	14	8.0
13	Italy (Sweden)[b]	2,032	12	8.1
14	Japan	2,012	16	7.8
15	Ireland	1,953	21	6.7
16	United Kingdom	1,763	19	7.3
17	Finland	1,664	22	6.6
18	New Zealand	1,623	14	8.0
19	Spain	1,556	17	7.7
20	Portugal	1,441	11	8.2
21	Greece	1,399	8	8.3
22	Czech Republic	1,031	20	7.2

Reprinted from OEDC Health Data 2000.
[a]2000 data not available. Ranking in 1999.
[b]2000 data not available. Ranking in 1998.

health of the population of many countries. Different measurement tools and different outcome criteria have been used. This hinders interpreting findings. However, in some of the commonly compared areas, such as life expectancy at birth and infant mortality, the United States has not been the leader (Pohl, 2002; WHO, 1999). In other words, "there is no conclusive evidence that health outcomes are better in the United States than in other industrialized nations" (Blumenthal, 2001). On the positive side, the consensus is that the U.S. health care system is the most responsive, that is, has less wait time for nonemergency care than systems in other wealthy nations employing more governmental control of health care (Anderson and Hussey, 2002).

There is no perfect health care system. All systems exclude some constituents and leave some users unsatisfied with timeliness of access, outcomes, and costs.

Globally, all systems are evolving to find a better balance between resources and needs. A major issue regarding the entrepreneurial bent of the U.S. system, with its foundation based on the ability to pay, is that it contributes to "an ever widening gap between rich and poor" (Institute for the Future, 2000, p. 192). In terms of health care, the poor include people who have inadequate health insurance as well as those who have none. Even though the U.S. health care system has been the most expensive to operate for decades, it has excluded too many people. Between 1997 and 2001 14 to 15% of the population under 65 years of age has been uninsured (Centers for Disease Control, 2003). Because the U.S. system has no central planner, no single owner, and no single payer, some have questioned whether it should be called a system (Shelton, 2000; Wimberley and Rubens, 2002). Nonetheless, the two-component U.S. entrepreneurial health care system has been superb in developing medical technology and techniques (which increases costs) and new drugs (which also increases costs), has produced a sufficient well-educated and well-trained workforce, and has sufficient physical facilities along with many other wonderful attributes and innovative programs (Blumenthal, 2001; Pohl, 2002; Roemer, 1993). On the other hand, for all its resources and expenditures, the U.S. system does not serve everyone, nor does it produce outcomes on some basic health measures that are as good as those of other wealthy industrialized nations. In line with entrepreneurial thinking, when something made in the United States costs more to produce, and the local product does not perform better in important measurable outcomes than comparable foreign products, innovation has to occur. The point is that there are lessons to be learned from other health care systems. All health care systems continue to evolve as they seek means of balancing the influences of social responsibility and finite resources. Payers, providers, and consumers need to be vigilant when proposed changes are under discussion. Part of the strategy for vigilance is to investigate what has occurred in health care systems that have already implemented similar changes. Health care personnel at all levels must be vigilant. Health care managers and staff members need to know about potential effects of proposed health care system changes so they may work for or against changes that they perceive would benefit or harm their stakeholders, respectively.

Student Notes

The U.S. health care system is unique in its dual driving forces: government and private enterprise. You have the opportunity to treat only patients whose treatment is paid for by the government by working as a government employee in a government-owned facility. Alternatively, you can work in a privately owned environment and treat patients who have private insurance or who pay out of their own pocket. In most cases, you will treat patients whose payment comes from public or private sources. This is why a fundamental understanding of the motivations underlying each component of the U.S. system will be useful as you learn to deal with the idiosyncrasies of each component. Your understanding of the main differences among health care systems will help in your efforts to assess future proposals to alter the public component and plans to control the private component.

Summary

This chapter paints a broad picture of health care systems by defining systems and presenting criteria for cross-nation system comparisons. Using primarily seven criteria, that is, socioeconomic philosophy, accessibility, organization, management, financing, satisfaction, and to a lesser extent, health-related outcomes, five general health care systems are defined, compared, and contrasted. Four of these systems provide nearly universal care for their constituents. The system with the most central government control was the former Soviet model. It had essentially all aspects of health care under governmental control. There was a negligible private health care presence. Socialist systems, particularly those in continental Europe, are typified as having tax-financed health care programs controlled in varying degrees by the central government. While some private health care programs and services are available in these countries, most service users are covered by government programs. A comprehensive health care system is described as a unique socialist-oriented model developed in the U.K. The system has central government control with strong local representation, as the facilities and the providers are government owned and government employees, respectively. This national health system has been cost effective in meeting most of residents' health care needs. A relatively small number of individuals choose to purchase additional private health care insurance.

Canada also has a health care system that provides universal health care access. The central government ensures health care ac-

INDIVIDUAL CASE STUDY

How might you respond to the statement that the federal government ought to stay out of health care? Think about it. Discuss it. What are the implications for you as a physical therapist if there were more federal government involvement in the payment for and delivery of health care in the United States? What are the implications for you as a physical therapist if there were less federal government involvement in the payment for and delivery of health care in the United States?

cess by providing financial support to local governments and coupling it with standards of coverage. Local (provincial and territorial) governments can offer more than minimal health care benefits, and they have the right to raise taxes to fund the locally determined health care needs. Providers are not governmental employees. Payments are "socialized," as providers get a negotiated fee-for-service rate and in some localities physician incomes are capped. Services are provided on a medical necessity basis. Private insurance or out-of-pocket payment is required for other procedures. Increasingly, Canadians are buying insurance to get quicker care and access to certain procedures.

The U.S. health care system is described as the one most reflecting a free-market socioeconomic policy. It has two components, one publicly funded and one privately funded. The U.S. system is the most expensive in the world, most decentralized, mostly (but arguably) privately funded, and the only wealthy country not providing for equal access to health care. Instead, selected citizens, that is, those least able to afford health care, are insured by the government. Others typically have private health care insurance through their employer or personal purchase. Estimates suggest that 14 to 15% of the U.S. population has been uninsured.

GROUP CASE STUDY

Form small groups to discuss the following questions and your findings. Select a spokesperson to report to the group at large.

Choose a national health care issue related to physical therapists. An excellent place to start is http://www.apta.org/Advocacy or /reimbursement. There will be a number of issues to consider. Review the issues.

- What issue or issues most interest you?
- Why?
- How will you find out more about it or them?
- What is the likely effect on patients?
- Does any group of individuals lose or gain anything?
- Do you as a soon-to-be-licensed or licensed professional benefit in some way?
- What can you do to support your chosen point of view?
- If you chose a regulation issue, how will you find out who your legislative representatives are? Who is your APTA affiliate legislative representative? How do you find out whom to contact in the APTA? How do you find out whom to contact at the APTA section level?

The broad and comparative view of the U.S. health care system presented in this chapter will be very useful when the system is analyzed in more detail in Chapter 2. Building on the two-component framework, underlying perspectives, and health care system options, the next chapter focuses on how the dual components of the U.S. system operate: sometimes separately, sometimes in partnership, sometimes as adversaries. Physical therapists work with both components of the system, making it necessary to understand how to work with each for the benefit of patient—no matter who pays the bill. Of the more than 300 programs operated by the HHS, discussion will be limited to the major programs. Discussion of the private system will focus on types of health insurance and managed-care delivery systems. Governmental and private entities pay for care in the same types of settings and can both pay a portion of a person's medical costs. As will be seen, such overlaps are a source of much consternation on the part of care providers.

REFERENCES

American Physical Therapy Association. International opportunities in physical therapy. Alexandria, VA: American Physical Therapy Association. 2000.

American Physical Therapy Association. CAPTE. Available from http://www.apta.org/education/accreditation. Accessed 8/12/02a.

American Physical Therapy Association. Evaluative criteria for accreditation of education programs for the preparation of physical therapists. Available from http://www.apta.org/education/accreditation. Accessed 8/12/02b.

American Physical Therapy Association. International affairs. Available from http://www.apta.org/advocacy/internationalaffairs. Accessed 8/12/02c.

American Physical Therapy Association. Accredited Physical Therapy Programs: Foreign schools. Available from http://www.apta.org/Education/accreditation/dir acc PT ed prog?process=1&foreign=1. Accessed 9/17/03a.

American Physical Therapy Association. APTA guide for professional conduct. Available from http://www.apta.org/pt practice/ethics pt/pro conduct. Accessed 9/17/03b.

Anderson GF, Hussey PS. Multinational comparisons of health systems data 2000. Available from http://www.cmwf.org/publist/publist2. Accessed 8/22/02.

Austin SE. Medical justice: A guide to fair provision. New York, NY: Peter Lang. 2001.

Bergman R. Theology in the pit of the stomach. Creighton University Window. 1998;15(1):16–21.

Bloor K, Maynard A. Universal coverage and cost control. The United Kingdom National Health Service. In Thai KV, Wimberley ET, McManus SM, eds. Handbook of international health care systems. New York: Marcel Dekker. 2002:261–286.

Blumenthal D. Controlling health care expenditures. New England Journal of Medicine. 2001;344: 766–769.

Bourhanskaia EA, Kubataev A, Paterson MA. Russia's health care system: Caring in a turbulent environment. In Thai KV, Wimberley ET, McManus SM, eds. Handbook of international health care systems. New York: Marcel Dekker. 2002:59–78.

Brinton C, Christopher JB, Wolff RL. A history of civilization 1715 to the present, Volume Two, 3rd ed. Englewood Cliffs, NJ: Prentice-Hall. 1967.

Bureau of Economic Analysis. BEA news release. National income and product accounts second quarter 2002 GDP (advance) revised estimates: 1999 through first quarter 2002. Available from http://www.bea.doc.gov/bea/newsrelease. Accessed 8/20/02.

Canada Health Act. Purpose and requirements. Available from http://www.oag-bvg.gc.ca/domino/reports.nsf/html/9929xe02.html. Accessed 8/20/02.

Centers for Disease Control. Fact book 2000/2001. Available from http://www.cdc.gov/maso/factbook/fact%20book.pfd. Accessed 3/10/03.

Centers for Medicare and Medicaid Services. The nation's health dollar: 2000. Available from http://www.cms.hhs.gov/statistics/nhe/historical/chart/asp. Accessed 8/20/02.

Churchill LR. Self-interest and universal health care. Cambridge, MA: Harvard University Press. 1994.

Daniels N. Just health care. New York: Cambridge University. 1985.

Daniels N, Sabin JE. Setting limits fairly: Can we learn to share medical resources? New York: Oxford University. 2002.

Department of Health. Patient care experience in the NHS. Available from http://gov.uk/public/stats1. Accessed 8/20/02.

Department of Health and Human Services. Overview of program management, and financial performance. Available from http://www.hhs.gov/of/reports. Accessed 8/20/02.

Evetovits T. Reforms in the Hungarian health care system. In Thai KV, Wimberley ET, McManus SM, eds. Handbook of international health care systems. New York: Marcel Dekker. 2002:29–58.

Grogan CM. Federalism and health care reform. American Behavioral Scientist. 1993;36:741–759.

Institute for the Future. Health and health care 2010: The forecast, the challenge. San Francisco: Jossey-Bass. 2000.

Kaati PG. Sweden's health care system. In Thai KV, Wimberley ET, McManus SM, eds. Handbook of international health care systems. New York: Marcel Dekker. 2002;287–331.

Kluge EHW. Health care as a right. A brief look at the Canadian health care system. In Loewy E, Loewy RS. Changing health care systems from ethical, economic, and cross-cultural perspectives. New York: Kluwer Academic. 2001;29–48.

Kovner AR, Jonas S, eds. Jonas and Kovner's health care delivery in the United States, 6th ed. New York: Springer. 1999.

Kronfeld JJ. The changing federal role in U.S. health care policy. Westport, CN: Kraeger. 1997.

Levit KR, Lazenby HC, Braden BR et al. National health expenditures, 1995. Health care Financing Review. 1996;18:175–214.

Loewy E. Health care systems and ethics. In Loewy E, Loewy RS. Changing health care systems from ethical, economic, and cross cultural perspectives. New York: Kluwer Academic. 2001:1–14.

Morton LW. Health care restructuring: Market theory vs. civil society. Westport, CN: Auburn House. 2001.

National Health Service. The NHS explained. Available from http:// www.nhs.uk. Accessed 8/15/02.

Olsen D. Ownership and private practice physical therapy. In Nosse LJ, Friberg DG, Kovacek PR. Managerial and supervisory principles for physical therapists. Baltimore: Lippincott Williams & Wilkins. 1999:278–298.

Oxley H, MacFarlan M. Health care reform, controlling spending and increasing efficiency. Available from http://www.oecd.org/pdfM0001000/M0001088.pdf. Accessed 8/19/02.

Pohl CM. The United States health care system. In Thai KV, Wimberley ET, McManus SM, eds. Handbook of international health care systems. New York: Marcel Dekker. 2002;99–133.

PriceWaterhouseCoopers. Healthcare. Available at http://www.pwcglobal.com. Accessed 3/10/03.

Reagan MD. The accidental system: Healthcare policy in America. Bolder, CO: Westview Press. 1999.

Rodwin VG. Comparative analysis of health systems: An international perspective. In Kovner AR, Jonas S, eds. Jonas and Kovner's health care delivery in the United States, 6th ed. New York: Springer. 1999:116–151.

Roemer MI. National health systems throughout the world. American Behavioral Scientist. 1993;36: 694–708.

Romanow RJ. Interim report 2002. Shape the future of health care. Available from http://www. healthcarecommission.ca. Accessed 8/18/02.

Scheuing KM. International service learning program connects communities abroad and on campus. Marquette, the Magazine of Marquette University. 2003;21(3):20–25.

Shelton MW. Talk of power, power of talk: The 1994 health care reform debate and beyond. Westport, CN: Praeger. 2000.

Shi L, Singh DA. Delivering health care in America—A systems approach, 2nd ed. Gaithersburg, MD: Aspen. 2001.

Swami B. The German health care system. In Thai KV, Wimberley ET, McManus SM, eds. Handbook of international health care systems. New York: Marcel Dekker. 2002:333–358.

Thai KV, Wimberley ET, McManus SM. Healthcare financing. A comparative analysis. In Thai KV, Wimberley ET, McManus SM, eds. Handbook of international health care systems. New York: Marcel Dekker. 2002;543-572.

U.S. Census Bureau. Foreign-born population in the United States: March 2002. Available from http://www.census.gov/prod/2003pubs/p20-539.pdf. Accessed 9/19/03.

Walker M, Wilson G. Waiting your turn, 11th ed. Available from http://www.fraserinstitute.org. Accessed 8/18/02.

Wimberley ET, Rubens AJ. Like plugging the holes in a colander. Health policy and provision in the United States circa the millennium. In Thai KV, Wimberley ET, McManus SM, eds. Handbook of international health care systems. New York: Marcel Dekker. 2002:135–206.

Wimberley ET, Thai KV. Introduction to international health care systems. Themes and variations on themes. In Thai KV, Wimberley ET, McManus SM, eds. Handbook of international health care systems. New York: Marcel Dekker. 2002:1–28.

Woolhandler S, Himmelstein DU. Paying for national health insurance—And not getting it. Health Affairs. 2002;21:88–98. Retrieved from ABI-INFORM database 8/20/02.

World Health Organization. The world health report 1999. Available from http://www.who.int/whr/1999/en/report.htm. Accessed 8/21/02.

MORE INFORMATION RELATED TO THIS CHAPTER

For a candid pro and con approach to health care issues see Health Care. Opposing viewpoints (Toor JD, ed.

San Diego, CA: Greenhaven Press. 2000). An interesting narrative analysis of the U.K.'s plans for change in the 21st century is available at http://doh.gov.uk/nhsplan shiftinggears. A similar discussion is ongoing in Canada (http://www.health carecommission.ca). The legislative affairs section of the APTA Web site (http://www.apta.org) has current issues of relevance to physical therapists, as does the section on health policy and administration. To be among the first to know about federal discussion about health care, check the Federal Register (http://www.access.gpo.gov/ sudocs/aces/aces). Information on Mexico based on 1994 to 1997 data can be found at http://paho.org/English/SHA/prfmex.htm and http://www.americas.health-sector-reform.org/ English/Mexican.pdf.

Chapter 2

U.S. Health Care System

Learning Objectives

1. Discuss the traditional social, political, and economic philosophies that have influenced the development of the public and private segments of the U.S. health care system.
2. Using ownership, access, service options, and outcomes as comparative criteria, compare and contrast the U.S. health care system to other health care systems.
3. Recognize and correctly use common terms and abbreviations associated with the public and private segments of the U.S. health care system.
4. Explain the financing of the public and the private segments of the U.S. health care system from the perspective of the main stakeholders, that is, the consumer, the payer, and the provider.
5. Examine and contrast direct care and management incentives and disincentives inherent in providing physical therapy under a variety of payment methods, such as prospective payment, capitation, fee-for-service, and diagnostic related groups.
6. Analyze the concepts of managed health care and commercial indemnity insurance plans in terms of cost, access, and scope of services.
7. Summarize important direct care and management implications of providing physical therapy under the main public and private health care plans.

Key Words

assignment of benefits, beneficiary, capitated, Centers for Medicare and Medicaid Services (CMS), CHAMPVA, coinsurance, copayment, deductible, Department of Health and Human Services (HHS), enrollee, Federal Employees Health Benefits Program, federal medical assistance percentage (FMAP), fee-for-service (FFS), for-profit (FP), gatekeeper, Health Care Financing Administration (HCFA), health care industry, health maintenance organization (HMO), health maintenance plan, indemnity health insurance, in-network, insured (person), managed care, managed care organization (MCO), managed care plan, managed care product, Medicaid, Medicare, Medicare Part A (hospital insurance), Medicare Part B (physician services), Medicare + choice/Medicare + C (managed care option), Medigap, Medicaid, not-for profit (NFP), outlier, out-of-network, out-of-pocket, panel, per member per month (PMPM) fee, point of service (POS) plan, preferred provider, preferred provider organization (PPO), preferred provider plan, State Children's Health Insurance Program (SCHIP), self-insured, third-party payer, Tricare, uniformed services, Family Health Plan, workers' compensation

Introduction

The broad and comparative view of the U.S. health care system presented in Chapter 1 will help you understand the system as it is analyzed in more detail in this chapter. Building on the framework of the already familiar public–private health care system, this chapter details the ways the dual components of the U.S. system operate. Attention is drawn to important points for those beginning their career along with points relevant to managers. Health care in the U.S. is a business. To clarify the system, some basic business terms are introduced.

Health care in the U.S. is delivered in both public and privately owned settings. Physical therapists work in both settings. They treat patients covered by insurance from either or both parts of the public–private system. To ensure that patients get what they are due and the provider of service gets paid, therapists should have a general knowledge of their patients' health care plans. These are the main governmental and standard commercial plans. Managers have the responsibility of ensuring that payment is received. In all settings managers are ultimately responsible for ensuring that all staff members have sufficient knowledge and understanding of the requirements of different payers so that when bills are submitted, payers pay.

To understand the unique U.S. health care system it is helpful to discuss history. This will reveal why there is such a wide spectrum of health care services, so many service locations, numerous major payers, and a variety of types of public and private insurance. As new graduates read the material, they will find possible sources of employment mentioned. For managers there are points of interest about potential markets to increase patient volume, revenue, and benefits and challenges of meeting demands of multiple payers.

Scope of the Health Care Industry

In the broad sense, the **health care industry** includes anything and anyone related directly or indirectly to health promotion, injury or disease prevention, and diagnosis or treatment of mental or physical pathologies, impairments, and functional limitations. In addition to the obvious direct care by professionals and technicians, this broad definition includes faculty who teach health care–related personnel and provide for their clinical training; facility architects and construction companies; manufacturers and vendors of equipment and supplies; and support personnel, such as security, sales clerks, cooks, and volunteers. The industry also includes an array of consultants, including accountants, attorneys, insurance and risk management representatives, and technical experts (Chapter 34), along with continuing education presenters, job placement agents, lobbyists, members of volunteer organizations, publishers, and accreditation agencies. Given the scope of the U.S. health care industry, the following discussion is necessarily selective. The abbreviated accounting focuses on the following:

- The scope of patient care services
- Where health care services are provided
- Ownership of health care delivery services
- Sources of payment for health care services and products
- Physical therapy in the private segment of the U.S. health care system
- Physical therapy in the public segment of the U.S. health care system

The Scope and Continuum of Patient Services

Health care in the United States is available throughout the lifespan, from preconception, that is, genetic counseling, to beyond death, that is, cryogenics. Services are provided anyplace from the site of an accident to highly specialized care settings to video communication between distant locations. Figure 2.1 is a representation of the U.S. health care system based on three general levels of care with seven sublevels listed as a continuum of care possibilities.

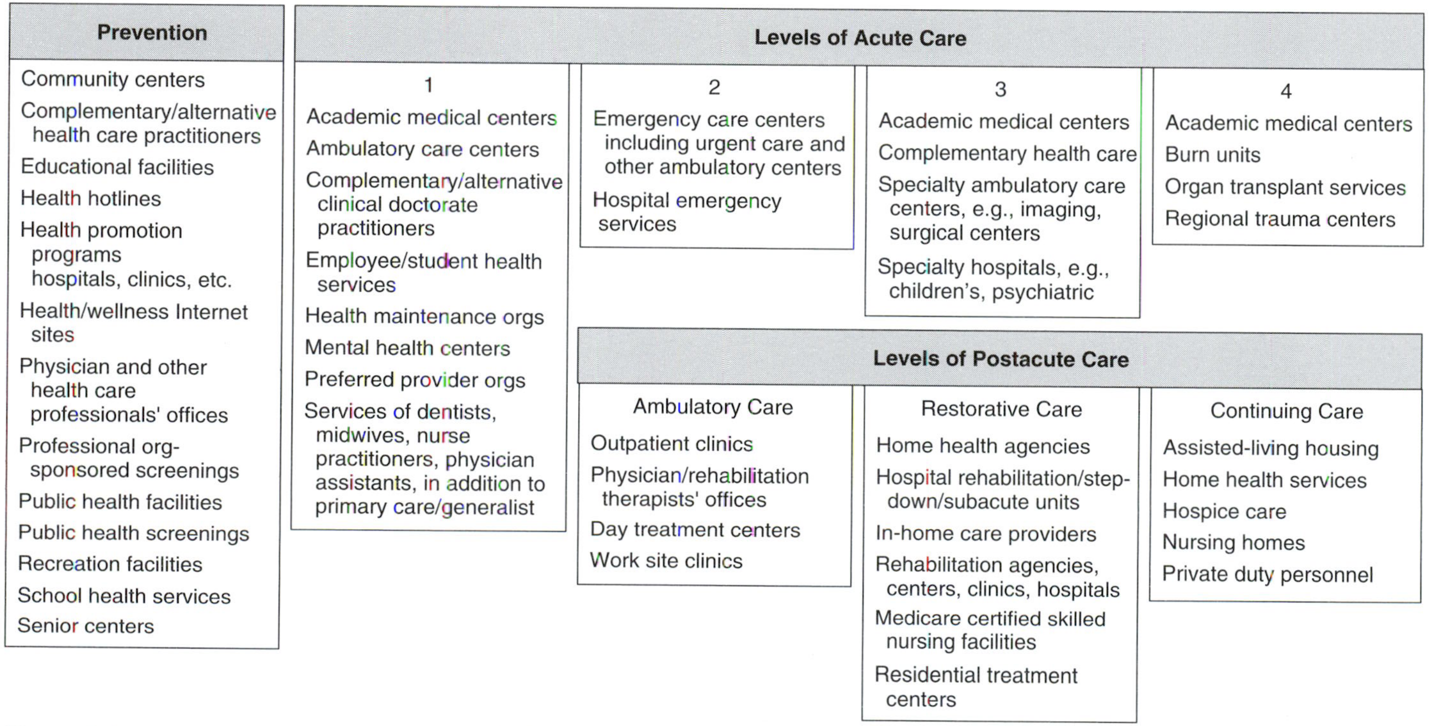

Prevention

- Community centers
- Complementary/alternative health care practitioners
- Educational facilities
- Health hotlines
- Health promotion programs hospitals, clinics, etc.
- Health/wellness Internet sites
- Physician and other health care professionals' offices
- Professional org-sponsored screenings
- Public health facilities
- Public health screenings
- Recreation facilities
- School health services
- Senior centers

Levels of Acute Care

1

- Academic medical centers
- Ambulatory care centers
- Complementary/alternative clinical doctorate practitioners
- Employee/student health services
- Health maintenance orgs
- Mental health centers
- Preferred provider orgs
- Services of dentists, midwives, nurse practitioners, physician assistants, in addition to primary care/generalist

2

- Emergency care centers including urgent care and other ambulatory centers
- Hospital emergency services

3

- Academic medical centers
- Complementary health care
- Specialty ambulatory care centers, e.g., imaging, surgical centers
- Specialty hospitals, e.g., children's, psychiatric

4

- Academic medical centers
- Burn units
- Organ transplant services
- Regional trauma centers

Levels of Postacute Care

Ambulatory Care

- Outpatient clinics
- Physician/rehabilitation therapists' offices
- Day treatment centers
- Work site clinics

Restorative Care

- Home health agencies
- Hospital rehabilitation/step-down/subacute units
- In-home care providers
- Rehabilitation agencies, centers, clinics, hospitals
- Medicare certified skilled nursing facilities
- Residential treatment centers

Continuing Care

- Assisted-living housing
- Home health services
- Hospice care
- Nursing homes
- Private duty personnel

Figure 2.1. U.S. health care system categorized by level of care with selected examples.

Preventive Health Care Services

The purposes of preventive health care services are fourfold: (1) reduce the likelihood of incurring an injury or developing a disease, (2) increase the likelihood of early identification of injuries or diseases, (3) reduce the likelihood of exacerbating an existing health problem, and (4) reduce the likelihood of secondary problems occurring during and after care (Shi and Singh, 2001). Physical therapists may be involved at all levels of prevention. Health promotion activities that involve physical therapists at the primary level of prevention include screenings through which such problems as balance deficits, scoliosis, and unsafe housing conditions may be identified. During treatment for one condition, another may be identified. For example, treatment for lower limb weakness may lead to findings such as loss of leg hair; decreased sensation at the posterior thigh, leg, and sole; and prolonged capillary filling of the great toe. A referral to a physician for a medical diagnosis is the judicious response to such circumstances. In-home treatment of a patient with emphysema and a stroke may lead to observation of alcohol, tobacco, and self-purchased medication use. This may lead to a referral to a nurse or case manager for follow-up. Finally, the treatment program for a patient who is functionally dependent usually includes a positioning program or arrangements for obtaining a pressure-reducing mattress. Physical therapists are often involved in these tasks in rehabilitation and long-term care settings.

Acute Care

Acute care refers to initial medical care for injury or mental or physical illness that on average is less than 30 days in duration (Longest, Rakich, Darr, 2000). Acute care is provided in multiple locations by a variety of personnel, from emergency medical technicians to physicians. Four levels of acute care are identified in Figure 2.1. Some categories of facilities are listed in more than one level of acute care. This is because several levels of health care can be offered by a single provider organization. For example, many academic medical centers offer services across the continuum. The progression of degrees of intensity and sophistication of medical care are called primary (1), or entry into the care system; secondary (2), tertiary (3), and quaternary (4) levels (Sandstrom, Lohman, Bramble, 2003). An example of the four levels of care might start with a visit to a physician's office (primary care) that results in admission to hospital (secondary care) followed by laboratory and imaging tests (tertiary care) and eventual transfer to a regional organ transplant center (quaternary care).

The role of physical therapists in acute care is longstanding in hospitals, academic medical centers, specialty care units, and ambulatory care settings. Involvement of civilian physical therapists in emergency departments (Woods, 2000) and triage are evolving areas (Waldrop, 2002). In 2002 fewer than 17% of the physical therapists who were members of the American Physical Therapy Association (APTA) worked in acute-care hospitals (APTA, 2002a). With more emphasis being placed on differential diagnosis in educational programs, and the vision of the APTA to have physical therapists provide patient care at all levels (APTA, 2002b), physical therapists may aspire to do more at the primary care level.

Postacute Care

Postacute care differs from acute care in duration and types of conditions treated. Postacute care, also called long-term care, is on average care given longer than 30 days for illnesses or mental or physical conditions considered chronic. Chronic conditions may be progressive or permanent and may cause residual disability (Shi and Singh, 2001). Treatment of patients with chronic conditions may be continuous or periodic, depending on changes in the patient's status (Sandstrom et al., 2003). Most physical therapist members of the APTA work in postacute care settings. Approximately half work in ambulatory care settings and nearly 20% work in restorative care (APTA, 2002a).

System Ownership

In law an owner is a person who has ownership, control, or proprietorship (Nolan and Nolan-Haley, 1990). As discussed in Chapter 1, ownership of health care businesses can be classified several ways (Fig. 2.2). The public pays taxes to governmental agencies. Facilities owned by the government are known variously as governmental, public, or tax supported.

Privately owned facilities likewise have several designations; however, there are major differences between private entities. The first distinction is based on the Internal Revenue Service requirements for being classified as a **for-profit (FP)** or a **not-for-profit (NFP)** entity (Chapter 7). FP entities pay taxes. A FP entity is formed to make a profit. The owner or owners of a FP organization may take the profit for their own use. Shares of stock in some FP corporations are offered for sale to the public through stock exchanges. Such corporations are said to be publicly traded. Owners of shares are stockholders. Stockholders buy shares with the expectation that they will earn dividends while they own the shares and a profit when they sell their shares. Taxes are paid by corporations and by the individuals who gain from the operation of FP businesses. Some private businesses also provide health care for their employees and their employees' dependents, for example Quad Graphics of West Allis, Wisconsin.

In the private sector, some health care organizations are classified as NFP. Many charitable (for example, Shriners) and religious groups (for example, the Roman Catholic Church) are NFP. NFP associations or corporations are formed for reasons other than for making a profit (Internal Revenue Service, 2002). These reasons usually are associated with meeting the needs of a particular community or constituency (Nolan and Nolan-Haley, 1990). To advance and improve their offerings to their constituents, NFP businesses must make more money than they spend, just as FP businesses do. The difference between FP and NFP entities is that in an NFP the revenue that exceeds expenses is put back into the organization rather than being distributed to owners, as is done in a FP business. NFP entities are

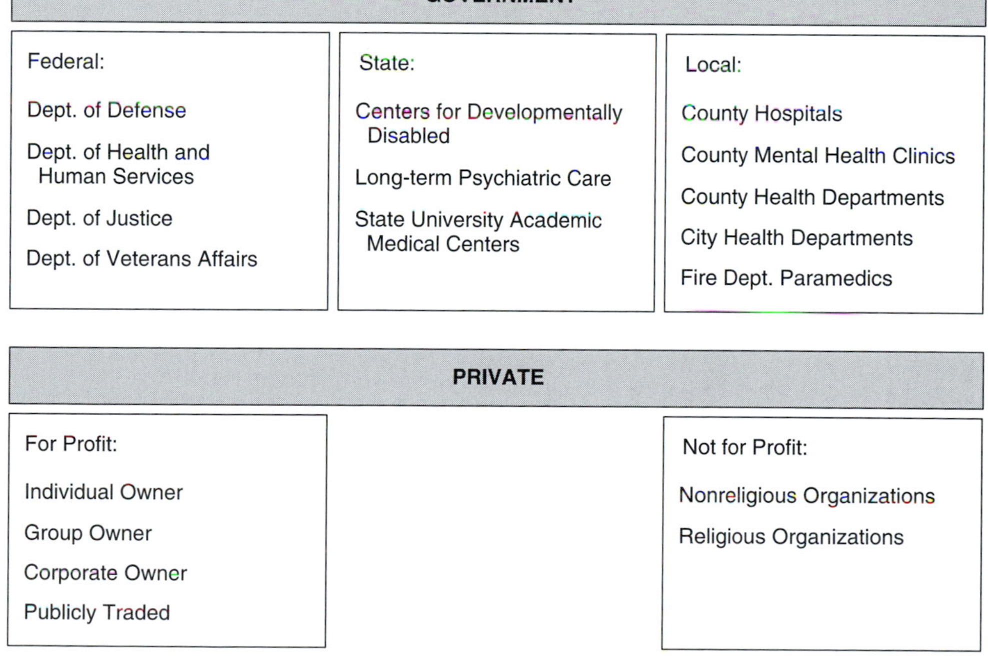

GOVERNMENT
Federal:
Dept. of Defense
Dept. of Health and Human Services
Dept. of Justice
Dept. of Veterans Affairs
State:
Centers for Developmentally Disabled
Long-term Psychiatric Care
State University Academic Medical Centers
Local:
County Hospitals
County Mental Health Clinics
County Health Departments
City Health Departments
Fire Dept. Paramedics
PRIVATE
For Profit:
Individual Owner
Group Owner
Corporate Owner
Publicly Traded
Not for Profit:
Nonreligious Organizations
Religious Organizations

Figure 2.2. U.S. health care system categorized by ownership with selected examples.

tax exempt (Chapter 4). Some NFP organizations, such as hospitals, offer health care for their employees and their dependents.

Payment

There are six sources of payment for health care in the United States:

1. Commercial insurance (for example, indemnity plans purchased by employer or individually)
2. Employment benefit (for example, managed care plan for employees and dependents)
3. Income taxes (general revenue from which the government pays for health care)
4. Employment taxes (for example, Medicare, social security, workers' compensation)
5. Philanthropy or charity (for example, Shriners, free drugs from manufacturers, charges reduced based on ability to pay)
6. Self-pay (for example, copayments, deductibles, individual commercial health insurance policy, out-of-pocket cash)

U.S. Multiparty Payer System

A health care delivery transaction includes a person receiving service and a service provider. When it comes to paying for health care services, the recipient may or may not be the person paying the provider, notwithstanding copayments and deductibles, which will be discussed shortly. Payers other than the service recipient are called third parties or **third-party payers** (Nosse, Friberg, Kovacek, 1999). Figure 2.3 presents the interconnections between patients who pay from their own pockets, third-party payers, managed care purchasers, and managed care organizations.

The service recipient can pay cash or can purchase an individual commercial health insurance plan or a managed care plan. Many such individuals are self-employed or are not working. Those who have left a job can buy into a prior employer's health care insurance plan for up to 18 months after leaving (see COBRA in Chapter 3). At present, the usual case is that recipients have health insurance through their employer. This is where the third-party payer becomes involved. The employee and employer usually each pay a portion of the insurance premium. The employer chooses the health care plan that will be available to employees. The options for the employer are to self-insure or purchase insurance. The types of plans available in the commercial sector are insurance indemnity plans, which cover what is written into the policy, and managed care plans, which control some aspect of use.

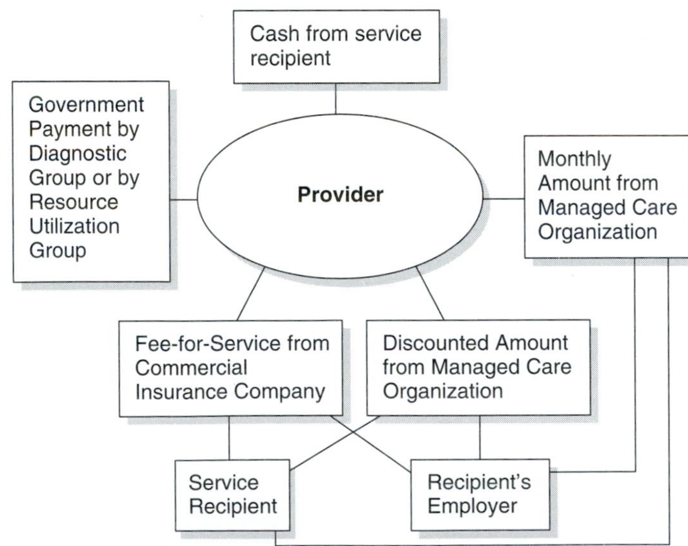

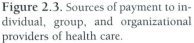

Figure 2.3. Sources of payment to individual, group, and organizational providers of health care.

Commercial Health Insurance

Health care, like other services and goods in a free-market economy (Chapter 26), is available for a price. Health care services, products, and payment are linked. Someone has to pay for desired as well as necessary health care. The menu of health care services available in the United States is extensive. To use the full menu is costly. Individuals who have health care insurance with relatively few exclusions or limitations, that is, commercial **indemnity insurance plans**, or who have resources to pay treatment costs themselves, known as paying **out-of-pocket**, have the luxury of picking and choosing from the menu.

A person covered by indemnity insurance plans is called **an insured**. Insureds can pay for services and be reimbursed by the insurance company or they can have payment sent to the provider. This latter arrangement is known as **assignment of benefits**. Indemnity health insurance plans cover the costs of care incurred by the insured up to the dollar limit of the policy. Choice of providers and payments to providers are essentially unrestricted.

Compared to other health care insurance plans, indemnity plans are the most costly for insurance companies. This makes them the most costly for purchasers. The method of payment associated with indemnity plans is known as **fee-for-service** (**FFS**). Under this method of payment the provider may charge a fee for each individual service. The payer is billed the sum of the individual fees. Many commercial indemnity health insurance plans have a preset payment schedule for each item of service. The amount paid to the provider is called the usual and customary rate. Some providers accept this amount as full payment, that is, they accept the payer's fee schedule. Insureds pay nothing. If a provider does not accept the payer's fee schedule as full payment, the insured is responsible for charges above those covered by the payer (Nosse et al., 1999). Understandably, physical therapists in independent practice, hospitals, and other providers are delighted to have customers who are covered by FFS indemnity insurance plans. An unintended downside of freedom of choice of providers is that the individual providers may not interact. In such cases, the patients may carry much of the responsibility for managing communication between health care providers and coordinating their own care.

Managed Care

The majority of U.S. citizens are enrolled in **managed care** insurance plans rather than in traditional indemnity insurance plans (Fox, 2001). Managed care entails controlling access to care. This means that access to some providers and services is restricted. These limitations are strategies intended in part to control costs. Such plans allow **enrollees** access to specified parts of the health care menu. How much of the overall menu is made available depends on the plan's details. Many managed care plans require some out-of-pocket payment for specified parts of the menu. The common out-of-pocket costs are as follows:

- *The deductible*: the amount the individual must pay each year before the health care plan begins to pay according to the plan's coinsurance stipulations
- *Coinsurance*: a proportion of the cost paid by the individual after the deductible has been met, with the remainder paid by the insurer, called a **managed care organization** (**MCO**); for example, after a $300 deductible is paid, 25% is paid by the individual and 75% is paid by the MCO (plans set a maximum after which they will pay 100%)
- *Copayment*: the amount the individual must pay each time services are used or prescription drugs are bought

For most people less than 65 years of age, health insurance typically is a work-related benefit that is fully or partially paid for by employers. Employers purchase insurance from a commercial insurance company, a MCO, directly from health care providers, or they pay for health care costs for employees from set-aside company funds. This last method is called **self-insurance** or self-funding. In these cases, the employer assumes the risk for covering medical costs rather than purchasing health insurance (Kongstvedt, 2002). The employer collects premiums and uses this pool of funds to pay health care expenses. These plans are exempt from state insurance laws and from paying premium taxes, and they accrue interest on the funds (Sultz and Young, 1997). See ERISA in Chapter 3.

Managed Care Organizations and Health Care Plans

Managed care, or managed health care, means a health care delivery system that links service and financing in ways that allow the payer to control access to services, costs, and quality (Kongstvedt, 2001). A MCO is a business entity that is a health care provider, a health care insurer, or both and that provides or arranges for services under a philosophy of managing care as defined earlier (Kongstvedt, 2002; Marcus and Thomson, 2001;Rodwin, 1999) A MCO may develop, market, and sell one or more **managed care plans**, also called products, to individuals or to employers to cover groups of employees (Marcus and Thomson, 2001).

It is estimated that more than 75% of employed individuals receive their health care through one of the forms of managed care (Gentry, 2001). The main elements and concepts associated with managed care are depicted in Figure 2.4.

A MCO arranges and pays for the delivery of care through its own providers; through contractual arrangements with individuals, groups, or organizations; or through both (Gentry, 2001). Those selected to be providers in a managed care environment are called **panel** members. When the managed care plan pays for care provided only by approved providers, the panel is known as a closed panel or **in-network** provider (Gentry, 2001). The plan does not pay for services outside of the approved panels. Closed-panel providers treat only enrollees of the MCO (Kongstvedt, 2002). An organization that provides for the overall health care of a defined population of enrollees under the closed-panel model is usually called a traditional **health maintenance organization (HMO)**. An HMO can also have open-panel

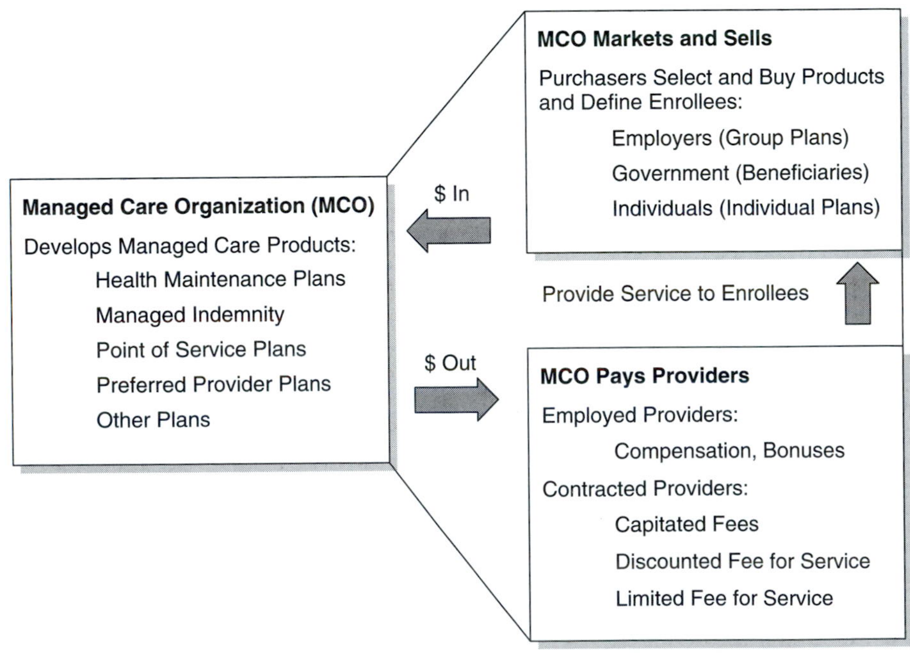

Figure 2.4. The components of managed care: the business entity (MCO), the customers, and common payment arrangements.

plans. In this model, if certain conditions are met, enrollees can have access to providers outside of the plan's panel. The most common incentive to seek care from the closed panel is cost. Going outside of the HMO's closed panel, that is, **out-of-network**, results in additional out-of-pocket cost to the enrollee. Open-panel members, also known as preferred providers, are individuals or groups of specialists who treat enrollees from the perspective of their specialty rather than managing the overall health care of enrollees as is typical in a HMO.

The **health maintenance plan** caption in Figure 2.4 refers to a managed health care plan that has the following characteristics aimed at controlling costs and providing quality care:

- It provides services to maintain health along with usual medically necessary care in case of illness or injury.
- Enrollees must see their assigned primary care physician.
- The primary care physician, sometimes called the **gatekeeper**, is responsible for allocating medically necessary health care resources, such as access to specialists, including physical therapists, special tests, and so on, and coordination of enrollees' care.
- Care is provided only by a specific group of providers, that is, a closed panel.
- Means of determining the ongoing cost of fulfilling the obligations are set out in the plan.
- Means of determining the quality of care delivered under the plan are spelled out.
- Payment from a managed care entity or from an employer who has contracted directly with the provider is a fixed (**capitated**, or capped) amount paid monthly per member; it is known as the **per member per month (PMPM) fee** (Nosse et al., 1999).

Physical therapy under health maintenance plans is a specialty service that is available through referral from a patient's primary care physician. Under a capitated payment arrangement, the incentive for providers is to treat efficiently, that is, do what is necessary, quickly and as inexpensively as possible. Payment is the same no matter how much or how little service is provided. This can be an incentive to undertreat.

A **preferred provider plan** differs from a health maintenance plan in two important ways: (1) It offers a choice of providers. (2) Its method of payment is different. A preferred provider plan is a managed care plan that allows enrollees to seek care from a variety of approved providers (Gentry, 2001). A choice of providers allows an enrollee to manage his or her own health care. A **preferred provider organization (PPO)** is an individual, group, or organization that accepts a contract from a MCO to be an approved provider, that is, a **preferred provider**, of services to a specified population of enrollees. In contrast to a health maintenance plan, payment to the PPO is usually a discounted FFS, that is, there is a usual and customary fee schedule for each item of service, and each individual item of service is a charge (Chapters 27–29). In exchange for a potential increase in patient numbers, PPO managers negotiate a discounted FFS rate for services provided to MCO enrollees and their dependents (Chapter 28). The enrollees may or may not need to have the services preauthorized. A contract with a MCO may require the PPO to function as a closed panel, that is, it may prohibit them from treating patients from competing MCOs. Physical therapists may become preferred provider panel members. While utilization review for quality and cost are not usual requirements in PPO contracts (Longest et al., 2000), such information can be useful when seeking and keeping managed care contracts in a competitive market (Chapters 11 and 23). Tracking outcomes (Chapter 31) and costs is important (Chapters 27–29) because PPO payments increase when more service is provided. MCOs develop profiles of panel members to identify **outliers**, those whose payments are more and less than the norm and whose outcomes are above and below the norm on selected criteria. These data are considered when contracts are offered or up for renewal. To negotiate contracts with MCOs, groups of physical therapists form associations whose members may pool their outcomes, provide group outcome data, and share administrative and other costs to reduce general operating expenses (Chapters 27 and 28).

A variation that combines the lower cost of a health maintenance plan and the option of seeing providers other than those on the panel is a PPO **point of service (POS) plan**. This is a managed care product that operates much like an HMO except that it offers the option of choosing providers other than members of the HMO's panel of providers. For an additional cost, that is, a higher premium than for a traditional health maintenance plan and higher out-of-pocket payment, an enrollee can receive care from providers outside the panel. Some plans require authorization for services outside the panel to control costs. For the enrollee a POS offers access to the HMO panel providers for usual care and the option of accessing others for special purposes, for example, second opinion or specialty services.

Health care insurance products continue to evolve. Today, the distinctions between the various managed care plans, that is, health maintenance, preferred provider and point of service health care insurance plans are blurred (Kongstvedt, 2001). Competition for market share (Chapters 11 and 21–23) has produced a spectrum of managed care products. These plans mix various aspects of the basic managed care products in new ways to balance cost controls with choice of providers. The view of the primary care physician also is evolving. The primary care physician is being reframed as an integrator of care. This means the primary care physician coordinates care across the spectrum from prevention through treatment while giving due consideration to the patient's psychosocial as well as physical needs (Shi and Singh, 2001).

Tax-Funded Health Care

The federal government is also a third-party payer because it allocates funds to cover health care for a variety of federal departments, bureaus, and offices and targeted segments of the general population (Chapter 4). The major federal and other government related entities that employ (e) physical therapists or pay (p) for services provided by civilian physical therapists are as follows:

- Department of Defense (DOD)
  - Tricare (p)
  - Uniformed Services Family Health Plan (p)
  - Uniformed services medical or military treatment facilities (e)
- Department of Veterans Affairs
  - Veterans health care facilities (e)
  - Contracted services (nursing homes) (p)
- Department of Justice
  - Federal Bureau of Prisons (e)
- Office of Personnel Management
  - Federal Employees Health Benefits Program (p)
- Department of Health and Human Services (HHS)
  - Health Resources and Services Administration (HRSA)
  - Public Health Service (e)
  - Indian Health Service (e, p)
  - Centers for Medicare and Medicaid Services (CMS)
    - Medicare (Title XVIII) (p)
    - Medicaid (Title XIX) (p)
    - State Children's Health Insurance Program (Title XXI) (p)
- State and local government programs
  - City and county hospitals (e)
  - Mental health facilities (e, p)
  - Workers' compensation (p)

Federal funds allocated to the Department of Defense are used in part for the health care of active duty and retired military personnel and dependents of deceased members of the military. Current and former members of the military and their dependents receive care from three sources: **Tricare**, **Uniformed Services Family Health Plan**, and uniformed services military medical treatment centers. Through Tricare, HMO, PPO, and FFS plans are offered through civilian MCOs. Civilian physical therapists provide care under these plans. Care under Tricare can also be obtained at uniformed services military medical facilities as space is available. Uniformed Services Family Health Plan is a network of primary care physicians and hospitals in seven regions of the United States that is paid on a capitated basis. Uniformed services military medical facilities are located worldwide to care for military personnel during peace and conflicts. Physical therapists who are active members of the military provide care at many of these facilities (Tricare, 2002a, b).

Veterans' health care facilities are under the control of the Department of Veterans Affairs (VA). The VA system is an integrated health care system of hospitals, clinics, and nursing homes. The priority patient populations are veterans with service-related illnesses and disorders and poor veterans. Other veterans and nonveterans are also served as resources permit. The VA shares the cost of covered health care services for specific groups associated with veterans through a program known as **CHAMPVA**. This health care benefits program is for the dependents of veterans who are totally and permanently disabled, veterans with non–service-related conditions, and dependents of veterans who were killed in action or died of service-related conditions (Shi and Singh, 2001; VA, 2002a, b). The VA health care system cares for more than 6 million veterans (VA, 2002b), many of whom are 70 years of age and older. Physical therapists working in the VA system are civil service employees, that is, civilian employees. They usually see the full spectrum of medical conditions from acute to chronic, and they provide care in various locations from hospitals to home care.

The Federal Bureau of Prisons is a division of the Department of Justice. It is responsible for the health care of prisoners in federal penal facilities, including community-based programs. It employs various health care professionals, including physical therapists. It also uses community consultants and external specialists. It operates four advanced-care facilities for federal prisoners (Bureau of Prisons, 2002a). Physical therapists are among the health care providers who work in federal prisons through the Commissioned Corps of the Public Health Service. Internships and externships are also available for health care students, including student physical therapists (Bureau of Prisons, 2002b).

The health care of approximately 8 million civilian employees of the federal government is administered by the Office of Personnel Management (Office of Personnel Management [OPM], 2002a). The **Federal Employees Health Benefits Program** offers preferred provider and health maintenance plans for federal employees and their dependents (OPM, 2002b). Private preferred providers, contract groups, and employees associated with these plans include physical therapists. Federal employees who are injured, disabled, or killed on the job are covered by the Department of Labor's workers' compensation programs (OPM, 2002c). Federal laws also cover interstate railroad employees, members of the Merchant Marine, longshoremen and harbor workers, and miners with pneumoconiosis (Shi and Singh, 2001).

The **Department of Health and Human Services (HHS)** is responsible for five direct health care service divisions. These divisions are administered by three components of HHS. These components are the Health Resources Services and Administration, the Indian Health Service, and the Centers for Medicare and Medicaid Services. The Health Resources Services and Administration oversees the Public Health Service. The mission of the Public Health Service is the management of the health of populations rather than individuals. The direct care arm of the service is the Commissioned Corps, the uniformed service of the Department of Health and Human Services. Members of the corps serve medically underserved populations, serve some federal beneficiaries, promote health in the general population, and participate in health care in times of national emergency, including war (U.S. Public Health Service, 2002a). Physical therapists are among members of the Commissioned Corps (U.S. Public Health Service, 2002b). More will be said about the corps in the following discussion.

The Indian Health Service maintains the Indian health care system (Indian Health Service, 2002). This system is the primary source of care for nearly 2.5 million American Indians and Alaskan Natives, most of whom live near or on reservations in 35 states. The staff of the Indian Health Service includes the usual breadth of health care professionals necessary to operate hospitals, health care centers, residential treatment centers, clinics, and urban Indian health care centers. Indian Health Service personnel are mostly Indians and members of the Public Health Services' Commissioned Corps. Physical therapists are among the corps members who serve in the Indian Health Service. Contracted private providers are also used to meet care needs. These individuals, including physical therapists, are paid on a FFS basis. Of interest to Indian physical therapy students are the Public Health Service Commissioned Officer Student Training and Extern Program discussed earlier. In June of 2001, the **Health Care Financing Administration** (**HCFA**) was restructured and renamed the **Centers for Medicare and Medicaid Services** (**CMS**). CMS is the world's largest purchaser of health care services, with nearly 70 million people covered just by the Medicare and Medicaid entitlement programs in 2001 (CMS, 2002a). The centers oversee and pay for services for Medicare, Medicaid, and the **State Children's Health Insurance Program** (**SCHIP**) beneficiaries. Individual centers are devoted to managing these benefit programs. The names of the three centers and examples of their functions are:

1. *Center for Medicare Management*: focuses on the traditional FFS Medicare A program.
2. *Center for Beneficiary Choices*: focuses on providing comparative information on traditional Medicare and three other Medicare programs. (1) **Medigap** insurance, which is self-purchased health insurance to cover costs not paid by Medicare; (2) Medicare Select, which is similar to Medigap insurance except that is it less expensive because enrollees are required to use designated hospitals and physicians; and (3) **Medicare + Choice**, which is the Medicare managed care option offered on an individual rather than group basis. This option generally offers greater benefits and lower or no deductibles or coinsurance than the original medicare plan.
3. *Center for Medicaid and State Operations*: focuses on federal and state programs that include SCHIP and insurance regulation.

Medicare (original, traditional, or FFS) is a two-part federal government–sponsored health care program for those who are at least 65 years of age, who are permanently disabled, or who have kidney disease requiring dialysis or transplant. Traditional Medicare coverage consists of **Medicare Part A**, also known as hospital insurance. Part A is financed by social security payroll taxes. The deduction is listed as the FICA deduction (Chapter 27) of 1.45% of wages on a pay stub. Employers contribute an equal amount. Self-employed individuals are taxed at 2.9% of net earnings. Part A covers hospital inpatient services, skilled nursing facilities, and home health and hospice care. Physical therapists provide services to beneficiaries in these settings. There is an annual deductible and a daily coinsurance for extended hospital and skilled nursing facility stays. In general, Part A covers approximately 50% of a **beneficiary's** total health care costs (Longest et al., 2000). The costs, benefits, options, and other core aspects of Medicare change yearly. At present a referral from a physician is required for a physical therapist to treat and be paid for services provided to Medicare beneficiaries. Consult the Medicare Web site (http://www.medicare.gov) for additional and current beneficiary information. The second part of Medicare is **Medicare Part B** (physician services). It is also known as supplemental medical insurance, physician insurance, or the voluntary part of Medicare. Most people 65 and older are eligible for Part B, but not everyone is covered by this insurance. In contrast to Part A, one must pay a monthly premium to be enrolled in Medicare B. In addition to the monthly premium there is an annual deductible and a coinsurance (20% paid by enrollee, 80% paid by Medicare). This insurance mainly pays for physician visits, hospital outpatient services, outpatient rehabilitation services including physical therapy, home health services not covered under Part A, diagnostic and laboratory services, prosthetic devices, some durable medical goods, medical supplies, emergency department services, ambulance services, and some preventive services. Physical therapists care for patients with Part B insurance. A physician referral is necessary for payment. Payment for services provided to patients with Medicare insurance requires additional discussion because payment methods for Part A and B differ. Payment will be addressed in depth in Part V, Chapters 27 to 30.

Medicaid is a joint federal and state government medical assistance program for individuals with low incomes and limited resources who meet state-determined eligibility criteria (Chapter 4). In recent years, this program has been tied in with eligibility for cash assistance programs to expand health care for pregnant low-income women, poor children, and some poor Medicare beneficiaries (CMS, 2002b). Approximately 12% of the U.S. population receives medical assistance through Medicaid. In 2002, more than half of Medicaid beneficiaries were under 21 years of age, and approximately 11% were 65 or older (CMS, 2002c). Medicaid is a matching fund program in which each state receives funds from the federal government for a percentage of the administrative costs in addition to an annually determined percentage of what the state pays for the care of the targeted populations. The federal government contribution is known as the **Federal Medical Assistance Percentage** (**FMAP**). The percentage is derived by a formula that compares the state's average per capita income level with the national average. The law requires that the FMAP be between 50% and 83% of the national average (CMS, 2002b). The lower a state's per capita average, the higher the FMAP. States have some latitude in how they manage their Medicaid program, for example, what services it offers, the cost to users, and other areas. This means that Medicaid programs vary somewhat between states. To receive federal medical assistance funds the states must provide minimum services to the categorically needy population. These include medical, dental, inpatient outpatient hospital, and nursing facility services to those over 21 years of age; home care, early and periodic screening, diagnosis, and treatment for those under 21 years of age; and health center and ambulatory care services.

Each state administers its own program. This means eligibility, type, amount, duration and scope of services, and rate of payment for services are unique to each state. The conditions required for eligibility and payment can change at any time. Payments for services are made directly to the provider. Physical therapists provide treatment to patients with Medicaid benefits in inpatient, outpatient, and skilled nursing facilities and in patients' homes. Payment for physical therapy requires a physician's referral. To facilitate being paid for medically necessary services, providers need regular contact with their state medical assistance department. Those who practice in more than one state have to deal with different Medicaid conditions. Contact information for all states can be found at http://www.cms.gov/medicaid/mcontatct.asp.

The SCHIP program is administered by CMS and the Health Resources and Services Administration. SCHIP provides matching funds to assist states to expand health care coverage for uninsured children. As with the Medicaid program, individual states set eligibility and coverage standards, and there are broad federal guidelines. General eligibility guidelines are low income, no health insurance, and ineligible for Medicaid. However, SCHIP funds can be used to expand Medicaid eligibility for health assistance to additional low-income children not otherwise covered by Medicaid. States that choose to make care available through MCOs must ensure that services are at least equivalent to preferred provider health care plans offered in the commercial market by Blue Cross/Blue Shield or the health maintenance plan offered by the largest HMO in the state (CMS, 2002d). Physical therapy is covered in both of these types of plans.

Individual state and local governments are engaged in a variety of health care activities. All 50 states have public health authorities. The focus of local public health agencies is on the health of populations. Interventions typically include disease prevention and education programs and plans for dealing with epidemics and other emergencies. There are also state-run health care institutions for individuals with developmental disabilities or psychiatric problems and for prisoners. At the local level there are tax-supported community health centers, clinics, and city and county hospitals for the care of eligible residents. Physical therapists work at the state and local government levels as consultants, managers, and direct care providers.

Health care for employees injured on the job is covered by workers' compensation programs. There is a separate set of workers' compensation laws in each state to cover nonfederal employees. These laws are designed to do the following:

- Deal with payment of wages lost because of incapacitation
- Deal with payment for medical treatment
- Ensure that employees who are injured or disabled in job-related events are awarded a fixed number of dollars in lieu of suing
- Ensure that dependents of workers who die of work-related illnesses or accidents receive death benefits

Each state develops its own workers' compensation laws, which produces variations in the dollar amount of awards and other areas. No state law covers all workers. Among the groups excluded are domestic employees and farm workers (Clarkson, Miller, Jentz, Cross, 1994). The cost of a workers' compensation program is born by employers. Employers can buy insurance by contributions to a state fund, purchase insurance from commercial sources, or self-insure. Depending on the state, employers may have all three options. Injured workers covered by workers' compensation are often treated by physical therapists, for example work-hardening programs post surgery. For more detailed information on a particular state's workers' compensation statutes log on to http://www.law.cornell.edu.

Student Notes

For the foreseeable future managed care will be the dominant method of packaging and delivering health care in the United States. You will be providing care under the following general conditions:

- Limited number of authorized treatments
- Increasing costs to patients (copayment, coinsurance, additional cost for going out of network)
- Rising insurance costs (for employers and other purchasers)
- As a provider of direct care, the expectation that you will be very efficient and effective (high level of productivity, minimal use of resources, positive outcomes)
- Progressively do more and better and with fewer resources

Regardless of the circumstances, the number one job is to meet patients' needs. One of these needs is to do what is best for the patient given his or her ability to pay and/or within any insurance restrictions. This means that sometimes, that is, when very few treatments are authorized, it may be best to spend more time teaching the patient to be his or her own caregiver than treating the patient directly. It may also require spreading the treatments over a number of weeks to see how the patient is progressing rather than giving the allowed treatments several days in a row. In the interval between treatments you may have to request authorization of a reasonable number of additional treatments if you believe they are necessary. This is an example of being an advocate for your patients. Advocacy can extend to being active in the support of legislators who have demonstrated through their actions that they have the best interest of patients in mind when they vote.

Federal health care programs, particularly Medicare and Medicaid, continue to evolve just as commercial products do. Additional changes in Medicare can be expected. Any change in these programs has a tidal wave effect on all components of the U.S. health care system, from the beneficiaries to the medical equipment manufacturers to the providers in hospitals, outpatient facilities, and nursing homes. You would do well to follow health care policy discussions. Your future may be negatively affected by the stroke of a pen. Be an active advocate for your patients, your profession, and yourself by becoming involved with the grassroots committees of your state component of the APTA.

Summary

Selected important components of the private and public U.S. health care system were identified and compared in terms of the groups they serve, how they are organized, payment methods, and other features. The involvement of physical therapists in both systems was addressed. The discussion included the traditional core types of health care services based on progressive specialization of services, that is, primary, secondary, tertiary, and quaternary care. These types were discussed along with newer types of ambulatory, outpatient, and day surgery services that may provide care at lower cost than hospitals. The common ways patients gain access to health care services and the ways that bills get paid were presented. The U.S. third-party payer system was defined as a payer of services for a service recipient. Commercial indemnity health care insurance was distinguished from other types of insurance as a FFS plan without restrictions on choice of providers. Managed care as a concept was introduced as a health care–related system that combines the insurance for care and the delivery of care in ways that allow managing utilization and thus costs. Managed care insurance products include health maintenance plans, which pay providers on a capitated basis; preferred provider plans, which pay providers on a discounted FFS basis; and a combination of both plans called point-of-service plans. Federal and state government health care insurance was addressed. In particular, Medicare, Medicaid, SCHIP, Tricare, Uniformed Services Family Health Plan, American Indians and Alaskan natives, veterans' health care, health care for federal government employees, and special groups were covered. At the state level the joint state–federal Medicaid program was discussed. Included in the discussion was the optional relationship between Medicaid and SCHIP. The workers' compensation program, a program for employees injured, disabled, or killed on the job program, was different in each state. Employers pay the costs for workers' compensation insurance through several means. Other state, county, and city health care programs, such as public health, facilities for the care of special populations, and city hospitals were also discussed.

The federal government programs discussed in this chapter exist because of legislation. Federal programs are the result of laws. Laws at the state level also affect health care organizations and direct care providers.

INDIVIDUAL CASE STUDY

Assume you practice in a state that allows patients to come to you directly, that is, without a referral from a physician, dentist, chiropractor, podiatrist, physician's assistant, or nurse practitioner. However, at publication time, payment for providing care to patients without a referral who have government-funded insurance is unlikely. This restriction has been brought to the attention of legislators (APTA, 2002c), but no action has been taken as this book goes to press. What do you think would happen if CMS dropped the referral requirement? How do you feel about being an entry point to the health care system? If you look ahead to Chapter 5, you will see that the issue is complicated by state licensure laws.

GROUP CASE STUDY

This case should be done in pairs. It is good but not necessary for both members to be from the same state. Later, pairs will join to form larger groups.

Situation

Congratulations. You passed the licensure examination and are now a licensed physical therapist in ______________ ____________ (name your favorite state). You have accepted a position in large health care organization that is a preferred provider for six managed care plans and a certified Medicare and Medicaid provider, and it will be a contracted health maintenance provider within a month. You are new to the state and want to get up to speed as fast as possible. You have a couple of days before you start work. Being a conscientious person (that is part of why they hired you) and having a strong desire to learn, you begin to inform yourself about the benefits, limitations, and idiosyncrasies of the various insurance plans your anticipated patients will have. You begin with ____________ (name the insurance plan) because __________________ (state your reasoning). The first source of information you consult is __________________ (make your choice). What did you find out? Review and discuss your strategy, rationale, and findings. Are you satisfied with your effort and results? What will you do next? Now form a larger group and discuss your responses, methods, findings, and plans to deal with the issue addressed in this case.

Only a few of the federal laws that regulate health care relevant to the practice and management of physical therapy services have been discussed. Chapters 3 and 4 address many others. Governmental oversight of health care is extensive. Patients, employees, managers, and owners alike are affected by regulations associated with payment and eligibility to employment practices and record keeping. There is a need to discuss the government agencies that oversee the health care of a large percentage of the U.S. population. Chapter 3 introduces the spectrum of governmental departments, agencies, and offices that facilitate the implementation and enforcement of the health care laws. Attention is given to the role of government in overseeing the health care of those in government-paid programs. An understanding of the role of government in health care oversight, important regulations, and the consequences of not complying with the law is essential to practice ethically and legally and to manage according to a variety of laws.

REFERENCES

American Physical Therapy Association. Type of facility in which members practice. Available from http://apta.org/rt.cfm/Research/survey_stat/pt_demo/pt_fac. Accessed 10/12/02a.

American Physical Therapy Association. APTA house of delegates endorses a vision for the future. Available from http://apta.org/news/news_archives/visionstatementrelease. Accessed 10/12/02b.

American Physical Therapy Association. Government affairs. Available from http://www.apta.org/advocacy/govt_affairs. Accessed 11/23/02c.

Bureau of Prisons. Inmate programs and services: Health care facilities. Available from http://www.bop.gov. Accessed 11/15/02a.

Bureau of Prisons. PS 6021.03 Commissioned officer student training/extern program of the Public Health Service. Available from http://www.bop.gov. Accessed 11/15/02b.

Centers for Medicare and Medicaid Services. Factsheet. Available from http://www.cms.gov. Accessed 11/16/02a.

Centers for Medicare and Medicaid Services. Medicaid services. Available from http://www.cms.gov/emicaid/mservice.asp. Accessed 11/16/02b.

Centers for Medicare and Medicaid Services. Statistics. Available from http://www.cms.gov/reseracjers/

pubs/CMSSstatisticsBlubook2002.pdf. Accessed 11/16/02c.

Centers for Medicare and Medicaid Service. Balanced Budget Act of 1997. Available from http://www.cms.gov/schip/kidssum.asp. Accessed 11/16/02d.

Clarkson KW, Miller RL, Jentz GA, Cross FB. West's business law, 6th ed. Minneapolis/St. Paul, MN: West. 1994.

Fox PD. An overview of managed care. In Kongstvedt PR, ed. Essentials of managed health care, 4th ed. Gaithersburg, MD: Aspen. 2001:3–16.

Gentry C. Managed care and integrated organizations. In Shi L, Singh DA. Delivering health care in America: A systems approach, 2nd ed. Gaithersburg, MD: Aspen. 2001:312–361.

Indian Health Service. About the Indian Health Service. Available from http://ihs.gov. Accessed 11/15/02.

Internal Revenue Service. Tax-exempt status for your organization. Available from http://www.irs.gov/pub/irs-pdf/p557.pdf. Accessed 11/08/02.

Kongstvedt PR, ed. Essentials of managed health care, 4th ed. Gaithersburg, MD: Aspen. 2001.

Kongstvedt PR. Managed care: What it is and how it works, 2nd ed. Gaithersburg, MD: Aspen. 2002.

Longest BB Jr., Rakich JS, Darr K. Managing health services organizations and systems, 2nd ed. Baltimore: Health Professions Press. 2000.

Marcus G, Thomson JC. Sales and marketing in managed health care plans: The process of distribution. In Kongstvedt PR, ed. Essentials of managed health care, 4th ed. Gaithersburg, MD: Aspen. 2001:535–554.

Nolan JR, Nolan-Haley JM. Black's law dictionary. St. Paul, MN: West. 1990.

Nosse LJ, Friberg DG, Kovacek PR. Managerial and supervisory principles for physical therapists. Baltimore: Williams & Wilkins. 1999.

Office of Personnel Management. Home page. Available from http://www.opm.gov/insure/03 html/brochure.asp. Accessed 11/15/02a.

Office of Personnel Management. 2003 guide to federal employee health benefits plans for federal civilian employees. Available from http://www.opm.gov/insure/03/guides/70-1.pdf. Accessed 11/15/02b.

Office of Personnel Management. Work-related injuries and fatalities. Available from http://www.opm.gov/asd/pdf/ri84-002.pdf. Accessed 11/16/02c.

Rodwin VG. Comparative analysis of health systems: An international perspective. In Kovner AR, Jonas S, eds. Jonas and Kovner's health care delivery in the United States, 6th ed. New York: Springer. 1999:116–151.

Sandstrom RW, Lohman H, Bramble J. Health services. Policy and systems for therapists. Upper Saddle River, NJ: Prentice Hall. 2003.

Shi L, Singh DA. Delivering health care in America: A systems approach, 2nd ed. Gaithersburg, MD: Aspen. 2001.

Sultz HA, Young JM. Health care USA: Understanding its organization and delivery. Gaithersburg, MD: Aspen. 1997.

Tricare. Tricare Factsheet. Available from http://www.tricare.osd.mil/factsheet. Accessed 11/15/02a.

Tricare. Tricare your military health plan. Available from http://www.tricare.osd.mil/beneficiary. Accessed 11/15/02b.

U.S. Public Health Service. Mission of the commissioned corps. Available from http://www.hhs.gov/html/mission.html. Accessed 11/15/02a.

U.S. Public Health Service. Therapists. Available from http://www.hhs.gov/html/ therapist. html#work. Accessed 11/15/02b.

Veterans Affairs. Health Administration Center. Available from http://www.va.gov/hac. Accessed 11/16/02a.

Veterans Affairs. Fact Sheet: 2002 Facts about the Department of Veterans Affairs. Available from http://www.va.gov/pressrel/vafacts.htm. Accessed 11/15/02b.

Waldrop S. Physical therapists' vital role in disaster management. PT Magazine. 2002;6. Available from http://www.apta.org/PTmagazine. Accessed 11/17/02.

Woods EN. The emergency department: A new opportunity for physical therapy. PT Magazine. 2000;8. Available from http://www.apta.org/PT-magazine. Accessed 11/17/02.

More Information Related to This Chapter

The constant change in Medicare, Medicaid, and other federal programs requires that information be made available to the public and providers as quickly as possible. Internet transmissions meet this need. Http://www.cms.gov is the Web site for the Centers for Medicare and Medicaid Services. The Medicare tutorial is updated several times a year. Medicare forms are available through this site. Useful sites for finding the most current information include http://cms.gov/regulations; http://cms.gov/glossary; and http://cms.hhs.gov/providerupdate. The Federal Register is the official text of the government. It can be accessed at http://access.gop.gov/su_docs/aces/aces140.html. Inexpensive government publications on Medicare and other programs can be ordered on line at http://www.gpo.gov. but they will be dated, as will textbooks. *PT Magazine* and *Rehab Manager* are two publications that deal with current topics of interest to physical therapists. The APTA Web sites http://www.apta.org/govt_affairs and http://www.apta.org/reimbursement have timely information for members of the association.

Chapter 3

Oversight of Health Care Organizations and Providers

Learning Objectives

1. Define oversight and examine the implications for health care providers.
2. Define regulations and examine the implications for health care providers.
3. Become efficient in accessing the full text of timely health care information from governmental Web sites to verify what is said from original sources.
4. Become familiar with the names, acronyms, purposes, and general authorities of governmental agencies, centers, and departments with responsibility for regulation of health care organizations and/or providers.
5. Correctly define and use common government health care agencies' terminology in oral and written communications.
6. Compare and contrast the purposes of the most common government agencies that physical therapists are likely to have contact with on behalf of their patients.
7. Identify the most common government agencies that managers of physical therapy services are likely to have contact with on behalf of their organization.

Key Words

Administration for Children and Families (ACF), Administration on Aging (AoA), Agency for Health care Research and Quality (AHRQ), Americans with Disabilities Act (ADA), Antitrust Division of the Department of Justice, Centers for Medicare and Medicaid Services (CMS), Centers for Disease Control and Prevention (CDC), community standards, Comprehensive Drug Abuse Prevention and Control Act of 1970, Controlled Substances Act (CSA), Department of Education (DOE), Department of Health and Human Services (HHS), Department of Justice (DOJ), Department of Labor (DOL), Drug Enforcement Administration (DEA), Environmental Protection Agency (EPA), Federal Accounting Standards Advisory Board (FASAB), federal antitrust and consumer protection laws, Federal Trade Commission (FTC), Financial Accounting Standards Board (FASB), Food and Drug Administration (FDA), fraud and abuse, General Accounting Office (GAO), Health Resources and Services Administration (HRSA), Indian Health Service (IHS), Internal Revenue Service (IRS), managed behavioral health care organizations, Medicare Payment Advisory Commission (MedPac), National Council on Disability, National Institutes of Health (NIH), National Labor Relations Board (NLRB), Occupational Safety and Health Administration (OSHA), Office of Diversion Control, Office of the Inspector General (OIG), Office of Special Education and Rehabilitative

Services (OSERS), oversight, participation agreement, regulatory compliance, Solid Waste Disposal Act, State Children's Health Insurance Program (SCHIP), Substance Abuse and Mental Health Services Administration (SAMHSA), Veterans Health Administration (VHA), Waste Tracking Act

Introduction

A government regulation is a rule that carries the same weight as a law (Finkler and Ward, 1999) (Chapter 5). The scope and breadth of the U.S. health care industry and the numerous government health care programs (Chapter 2) have resulted in health care being one of the most heavily regulated industries in the U.S. This scrutiny of health care comes from the government's obligation to protect the health and well-being of its citizens. To meet this obligation government has made laws designed to prevent illness or injury, provide access to health care services, and ensure the availability and quality of health care services. The enforcement of the law is delegated to one or more governmental agencies, bureaus, departments, or offices. These government groups in turn formulate the rules or regulations to enforce the law. This enforcement is **oversight**. Health care providers and product manufacturers are subject to oversight by government at all levels. Oversight is carried out in many ways, for example by supervisors, management, direct control, and surveillance. In addition, since the creation of the Medicare and Medicaid Programs, the federal government has become the largest purchaser of health care services in the U.S. (Chapter 2). It should not be surprising that when government assumed this financial burden, its interest in how health care is delivered, to whom, and at what cost increased dramatically.

New clinicians are often surprised by the number and diversity of the regulations with which health care organizations and providers must comply. As with any law, it falls to the individual health care organization and/or provider to know and to follow all applicable regulations. The penalty for noncompliance can be significant. In order of severity, the main penalties include the following:

- Loss of credentials to provide health care services
- Payment of one or more fines
- Imprisonment

More will be said about legal penalties and physical therapists in Chapter 5.

It is unfortunate that the health care regulatory landscape seems to change faster than the seasons. The number, diversity, of and frequent changes in regulations make compliance a real and costly challenge. Compliance starts with knowledge about the regulatory landscape. Ignorance of the law is unacceptable as a defense against a legal action.

In addition to government regulation, health care organizations and providers often voluntarily subject themselves to oversight from professional associations and accrediting organizations. This topic is specifically addressed in Chapter 32. Meeting governmental mandates, that is, **regulatory compliance**, is the first step toward preparing for voluntary accreditation.

Note 1. Given the rapidly changing regulatory environment and geographical and organizational differences, it is the organization's or provider's responsibility to identify and comply with all applicable regulations. For updates see the section More Information Related to This Chapter.

Note 2. Most of the material in this chapter comes from various Web sites that you can access on your own. However, even with experience using key words and advanced searches, finding pertinent information is time consuming. We have done weeks of work to put basic information on health care oversight in one place to guide your searches. As is discussed in Chapter 11, investigation of the political landscape is part of an external environmental assessment that management conducts to develop plans to advance the organization.

Government Departments and Agencies

Therapists who spend most of their time treating patients are responsible for knowing the essence of the regulations that apply to their patients, because it is they who are dealing directly with the patient. Managers are responsible for knowing the regulations in more depth for several reasons:

1. To guide those whose work they oversee so they practice lawfully
2. To help ensure the continued flow of patients for whom payment is likely to be received
3. To help the department, and ultimately the organization, to meet financial goals
4. To contribute to meeting the health care needs of the segments of the population the government has identified needing assistance in paying for health care services

Health care providers have historically been subject to external oversight. Oversight has come in the form of government regulatory compliance and voluntary accreditation reviews (Chapter 32). Regulatory compliance reviews are performed by federal, state, and local governmental agencies or their representatives. Regulatory reviews can occur as a condition of participation in government-funded health care programs such as Medicare and Medicaid. They can also occur as a condition of continued licensure, operation, and/or reimbursement as a health care provider approved by a state or local government. Continued operation may require annual reviews for facility safety inspections or compliance with state licensure requirements for medical professionals such as nursing.

The purpose of health care regulation is to protect the interests of the public. Independent professionals and organizations who deliver health care services are held accountable to the public through the enactment and enforcement of regulations that set **community standards** for health care service. Government regulations affect most of the service delivery, payment, and operations of health care providers, including the following:

- Organizational structure
- Business and financial management practices
- Patient accounts management
- Service documentation
- Service evaluation
- Personnel practices
- Facility design, construction, and operation

Full cooperation with the regulatory review process is mandatory. Failure to participate and/or cooperate can result in cancellation of a provider's **participation agreement** for government-funded health programs or loss of licensure to operate. Several departments of the federal, state, and local governments administer health care regulation. For example, at the federal level, the most notable is the Centers for Medicare and Medicaid Services (CSM) (formerly the Health Care Financing Administration, or HCFA) (CSM, 2003). The Office of the Inspector General is responsible for policing Medicare fraud and abuse (Chapter 5). At the state and local level, one or more departments of the government are responsible for health care oversight. For example, a state's physical therapy licensure board is responsible for oversight of physical therapy practice.

Federal Government Departments and Agencies

The **Department of Health and Human Services (HHS)** is the federal government's principal agency for protecting the health of and providing essential human services to all Americans, especially those least able to help themselves. According to HHS, the department provides a broad range of services, including more than 300 programs. The wide scope of HHS shows in its organizational chart (Fig. 3.1) and a sampling of the many programs it oversees (Table 3.1).

HHS works closely with state, local, and tribal government agencies, often working through these nonfederal government agencies or private sector contractors to deliver its services and for regulatory enforcement. HHS is also the largest grant-making federal

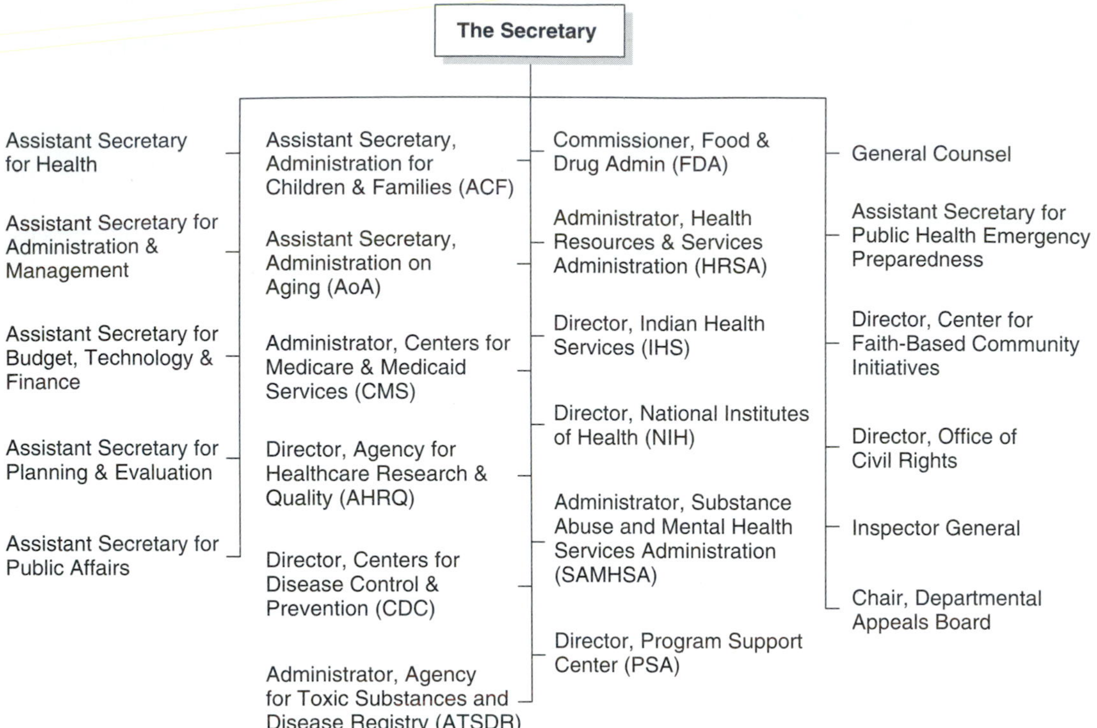

Figure 3.1. Main elements of the organizational chart of the U.S. Department of Health and Human Services (2003).

agency, providing 60,000 grants per year. Medicare makes HHS our nation's largest health care insurer, handling more than 900 million claims per year. HHS also collects national health data. In 2002, HHS employed more than 65,000 people and had a budget of $460 billion (HHS, 2003).

Table 3.1 Notable HHS Programs and Services

Medical and social science research
Preventing outbreak of infectious disease, including immunization services
Ensuring food and drug safety
Medicare and Medicaid
Financial assistance and services for low-income families
Improving maternal and infant health
Head Start (preschool education and services)
Preventing child abuse and domestic violence
Treatment and prevention of substance abuse
Services for older Americans, including home-delivered meals
Comprehensive health services for Native Americans

Source: http://www.hhs.gov

HHS administers its programs through 11 operating divisions that include eight public health service agencies and three human service agencies (Fig. 3.1). Physical therapists and managers of physical therapy services who treat government beneficiaries are likely to be interested in consulting the information provided online by these agencies:

Administration for Children and Families
Administration on Aging
Centers for Medicare and Medicaid Services

National Institutes of Health (NIH) is a medical research organization that supports more than 35,000 research projects for diseases like cancer, Alzheimer's, AIDS, arthritis, and heart ailments. NIH includes 18 separate health institutes, the National Center for Complementary and Alternative Medicine, and the National Library of Medicine.

According to NIH (2003), its mission is science in pursuit of fundamental knowledge about the nature and behavior of living systems and the application of that knowledge to extend healthy life and reduce the burdens of illness and disability. In 2002, NIH employed 17,471 people and had a budget of $20.9 billion (HHS, 2003). NIH goals:

1. Foster fundamental creative discoveries, innovative research strategies, and their applications as a basis to advance significantly the nation's capacity to protect and improve health.
2. Develop, maintain, and renew scientific human and physical resources that will ensure the nation's capability to prevent disease.
3. Expand the knowledge base in medical and associated sciences to enhance the nation's economic well-being and ensure a continued high return on the public investment in research.
4. Exemplify and promote the highest level of scientific integrity, public accountability, and social responsibility in the conduct of science.

The **Food and Drug Administration** (**FDA**) has the responsibility to ensure the safety of foods and cosmetics and the safety and efficacy of pharmaceuticals, biological products, and medical devices. These products represent 25% of U.S. consumer spending. In 2002 FDA employed 9,989 people and had a budget of $1.3 billion (HHS, 2003).

The **Centers for Disease Control and Prevention** (**CDC**) work with state and local government and other partners to provide a health surveillance system for the following:

- Monitor and prevent disease outbreaks (including bioterrorism)
- Implement disease prevention strategies
- Maintain national health statistics
- Provide for immunization services
- Provide for workplace safety
- Provide for environmental disease prevention
- Guard against international disease transmission

CDC's mission is to promote health and quality of life by preventing and controlling disease, injury, and disability (CDC, 2003). Some examples offered by the CDC include the use of innovative "fingerprinting" technology to identify a food-borne illness, evaluating family violence prevention programs, training partners in HIV education, and protecting children from preventable diseases through immunizations. In 2002 the CDC employed 8,627 people and had a budget of $3.7 billion (HHS, 2003). The CDC director also oversees the Agency for Toxic Substances and Disease Registry, which help prevent exposures to hazardous substances from waste sites considered to be a priority by the Environmental Protection Agency. The **Indian Health Service** (**IHS**) operates hospitals, health centers, school health centers, and health stations in rural and urban areas that provide services to nearly 1.5 million American Indians and Alaska Natives of 557 federally recognized tribes. IHS services include about 69,000 hospital admissions, 7 million outpatient visits, 4 million community health representative client contacts, and 2.4 million dental services annually. In 2002, IHS employed more 14,000 people and had a budget of $2.9 billion (HHS, 2003).

The **Health Resources and Services Administration** (**HRSA**) provides access to poor and uninsured people living in rural or urban areas where health care is scarce. HRSA-funded health centers provide primary and preventive medical care serving 9 million patients each year at more than 3000 sites nationwide. HRSA also works in partnership with state and community organizations, supports healthy mothers and children programs, and provides support services for people fighting HIV and AIDS (HHS, 2003). In 2002, HRSA employed more than 2,000 people and had a budget of $6.5 billion (HHS, 2003).

The **Substance Abuse and Mental Health Services Administration** (**SAMHSA**) was established to improve the quality and availability of substance abuse prevention, addiction treatment, and mental health services. It provides federal block grants to states to support and maintain substance abuse and mental health services. SAMHSA provides funding for hundreds of programs nationwide to increase the use of proven prevention and treatment methods through Knowledge Development and Application grants. In 2002

SAMHSA employed 600 people and had a budget of $2.9 billion (HHS, 2003).

The **Agency for Healthcare Research and Quality (AHRQ)** supports research designed to improve health care quality, reduce cost, improve patient safety, reduce medical errors, and improve access to essential services. AHRQ-sponsored research provides evidence-based information on health care outcomes; quality; and cost, use, and access. Health care policy makers, leaders, providers, and patients can use this information to make well-informed decisions about health care services. An example of AHRQ efforts was the introduction of the standardized Hospital Consumer Assessment of Health Plans (CAHPS, H-CAHPS) survey to be used in a HHS initiative to measure and publicly report patients' experiences of care in the nation's hospitals (National Research Corporation, 2003). This hospital patient survey was requested by the Centers for Medicare and Medicaid Services as a way to provide comparison information for consumers who need to select a hospital and as a way of encouraging accountability of hospitals for the care they provide (AHRQ, 2003). In 2002, AHQR employed 294 people and had a budget of $91 million dollars (HHS, 2003).

The **Administration for Children and Families (ACF)** has responsibility for 60 programs that promote the economic and social well being of families, children, individuals, and communities, including the state–federal welfare program and Temporary Assistance to Needy Families. ACF also administers Head Start, provides funds to assist low-income families in paying for child care, and supports state programs to provide for foster care and adoption assistance and to prevent child abuse and domestic violence. In 2002, ACF employed 1,537 people and had a budget of $44.6 billion (HHS, 2003).

The **Administration on Aging (AoA)** is the advocate agency for older persons and their concerns. The AoA administers federal programs, mandated under various titles of the Older Americans Act, that help vulnerable older persons remain in their own homes. AoA funding provides supportive services, including nutrition programs such as home-delivered meals (Meals on Wheels) and health enhancement programs. The AoA works with state and local agencies on aging to develop, plan, and coordinate community services that meet the needs of older persons and their caregivers. In 2002, AoA employed 124 people and managed a budget of $1.3 billion (HHS, 2003).

The **Centers for Medicare and Medicaid Services (CMS)** (formerly the Health Care Financing Administration) administer Medicare and Medicaid. Medicare provides health insurance for the elderly and some disabled individuals (Chapter 2). It serves more than 39 million Americans. Medicaid is a joint federal–state program that provides health coverage for low-income elderly and children (Chapter 2). CMS also administers the new **State Children's Health Insurance Program (SCHIP)** in collaboration with HRSA via state-based plans (Chapter 2). SCHIP is expected to provide health care coverage for 10 million uninsured children. CMS is particularly important to health care organizations and providers because it is the nation's largest health care payer. In that role it sets many of the standards for health care delivery. CMS also regulates all laboratory testing (except research) performed on humans. CMS's stated mission is to ensure health care security for beneficiaries. In fiscal year 2002, CMS employed 4500 people and had a budget of $374.7 billion (HHS, 2003).

In administering the Medicare, Medicaid, and SCHIP programs CMS:

- Ensures that these programs are properly run by its contractors and state agencies
- Establishes payment policies for health care providers
- Conducts research on various methods of health care management, treatment, and financing
- Assesses the quality of health care facilities and services
- Takes action to enforce its regulations

The mission of the **Department of Justice (DOJ)** is to "enforce the law and defend the interests of the United States according to the law, to provide federal leadership in preventing and controlling crime, to seek just punishment for those guilty of unlawful behavior, to administer and enforce the nation's immigration laws fairly and effectively, and to ensure fair and impartial administration of justice for all Americans" (DOJ, 2003). Two DOJ initiatives have specifically affected health care organizations and providers. The first is a joint initiative between the **Antitrust Division of the DOJ** and **Federal Trade Commission (FTC)** related to the enforcement of antitrust regulation in health care (FTC, 2003). The second is the DOJ focus on enforcement of federal regulations related to health care charge setting and billing practices. According to Mintz and associates (2003) the DOJ has targeted health care **fraud and abuse** as an enforcement priority. Health care organizations and providers have paid billions in restitution, penalties, and fines as a result of governmental and private enforcement. And the number of enforcement actions continues to increase.

The **Department of Labor (DOL)** "fosters and promotes the welfare of the job seekers, wage earners, and retirees of the United States by improving their working conditions, advancing their opportunities for profitable employment, protecting their retirement and health care benefits, helping employers find workers, strengthening free collective bargaining, and tracking changes in employment, prices, and other national economic measurements" (Department of Labor, 2003). In carrying out this mission, the DOL administers a number of federal labor laws related to workers' rights to safe and healthful working conditions; a minimum hourly wage, overtime pay, employment discrimination, unemployment insurance, and other income support. Health care organizations and providers are subject to the regulations administered by the DOL.

The **Drug Enforcement Administration (DEA)** has a mission "to enforce the controlled substances laws and regulations of the United States and bring to the criminal and civil justice system of the United States, or any other competent jurisdiction, those organizations and principal members of organizations, involved in the growing, manufacture, or distribution of controlled substances appearing in or destined for illicit traffic in the United States; and to recommend and support non-enforcement programs aimed at reducing the availability of illicit controlled substances on the domestic and international markets" (DEA, 2003).

The DEA is responsible for enforcing the United States controlled substances laws and regulations. These are examples of DEA responsibilities that pertain to health care organizations and providers:

- Enforcement of the provisions of the Controlled Substances Act as they pertain to the manufacture, distribution, and dispensing of legally produced controlled substances
- Investigation and preparation for the prosecution of major violators of controlled substance laws
- Investigation and preparation for prosecution of criminals and drug gangs

The DEA's **Office of Diversion Control** is responsible for the diversion of controlled pharmaceuticals and controlled chemicals. In enforcing the **Controlled Substances Act (CSA)**, Title II of the **Comprehensive Drug Abuse Prevention and Control Act of 1970**, the DEA is involved in the regulation of the manufacture and distribution of opioids, stimulants, depressants, hallucinogens, anabolic steroids, and chemicals that could be used in the illicit production of controlled substances.

The **Environmental Protection Agency (EPA)** has a mission "to protect human health and to safeguard the natural environment—air, water, and land—upon which life depends" (EPA, 2003). The EPA works with hospitals and biotech firms to do the following:

- Reduce waste, including mercury use
- Encourage product stewardship
- Evaluate waste management rules and policies that affect health care facilities

Another example of the EPA's role in health care is the production of materials to encourage health care professionals to educate patients on the safe disposal of sharps (lancets, needles, and syringes) in hard plastic or metal containers with screw-on or tightly secured lids. In addition, the **Waste Tracking Act** of 1989 amended the **Solid Waste Disposal Act** to require the EPA to promulgate regulations for the management of infectious waste.

The **Federal Accounting Standards Advisory Board** (**FASAB**) promulgates accounting principles for federal government reporting entities (Chapter 27). The board's Web site provides access to all publications issued by FASAB, including exposure drafts, the volume of original pronouncements (codification), newsletters, minutes, and meeting agendas. Specific questions about state and local governmental entity accounting may be answered by visiting http://www.fasb.org.

The FTC is responsible for the enforcement of **federal antitrust and consumer protection laws**. The FTC seeks "to ensure that the nation's markets function competitively, and are vigorous, efficient, and free of undue restrictions and works to enhance the smooth operation of the marketplace by eliminating acts or practices that are unfair or deceptive" (FTC, 2003). Simply stated, FTC efforts are directed toward stopping actions that threaten consumers' opportunities to exercise informed choice. The FTC's antitrust authority comes primarily from the Federal Trade Commission Act and the Clayton Act. The FTC's antitrust arm, the Bureau of Competition, seeks to prevent business practices that restrain competition. Competition results in lower prices and greater availability of products and services. As noted earlier under the DOJ, both the FTC's Bureau of Competition and the Antitrust Division of the DOJ enforce antitrust laws.

The FTC Bureau of Competition has developed expertise in a number of industries important to consumers, such as health care, other professional services, and other areas of consumer interest. As part of its consumer protection role, the FTC publishes a variety of consumer advisories on health care topics, such as tips for buying exercise equipment, diet and fitness, aging, health clubs, weight loss, and sources of information about health care products and services.

The **General Accounting Office** (**GAO**) is the "audit, evaluation, and investigative arm of Congress. GAO exists to support the Congress in meeting its Constitutional responsibilities and to help improve the performance and ensure the accountability of the federal government for the American people" (GAO, 2003). GAO examines everything from the use of public funds to the performance of federal programs and activities. The GAO operates FraudNET for the reporting of allegations of fraud, waste, abuse, or mismanagement of federal funds, including Medicare and Medicaid funding.

The **Internal Revenue Service** (**IRS**) administers the Internal Revenue Code enacted by Congress. The IRS is the nation's tax collection agency. Its mission is to "provide America's taxpayers with top quality service by helping them understand and meet their tax responsibilities and by applying the tax law with integrity and fairness to all" (IRS, 2003).

The **Medicare Payment Advisory Commission** (**MedPac**) is an independent federal body that advises Congress on issues affecting the Medicare program. MedPac is made up of 17 members who have diverse expertise in health care financing and delivery. The members meet publicly to discuss policy issues and formulate recommendations to Congress on improving Medicare policies. MedPac publishes its recommendations twice annually and in other reports periodically mandated by Congress. Some examples of publications and opinions are the Medicare Hospital Outlier Payment Policy (December 20, 2002) and MedPacletter on skilled nursing facility coverage in Medicare + Choice plans (December 19, 2002). MedPac seeks and accepts input from professional and advocacy organizations on topics of current interest.

The **National Council on Disability** (**NCD**) is another independent federal agency. The NCD makes recommendations to the president and Congress on issues affecting Americans with disabilities. NCD is composed of 15 members who are appointed by the president and confirmed by the Senate. It was an NCD proposal for a civil rights law for people with disabilities that led to the signing of the **Americans With Disabilities Act** (**ADA**) in 1990. The purpose of the NCD is to "promote policies, programs, practices, and procedures that guarantee equal opportunity for all individuals with disabilities, regardless of the nature or severity of the disability; and to empower individuals with disabilities to achieve economic self-sufficiency, independent living, and inclusion and integration into all aspects of society" (NCD, 2003). NCD has undertaken a multiyear study on the implementation and enforcement of civil rights laws, including the Americans With Disabilities Act.

The **National Labor Relations Board (NLRB)** is an independent federal agency that administers the National Labor Relations Act (NLRA), the primary law governing relations between unions and employers in the private sector. The NLRA gives employees the right to organize and bargain collectively with their employers or to refrain from all such activity. The NLRA applies generally to all employers involved in interstate commerce other than airlines, railroads, agriculture, and government. According to NLRB publications it has two principal functions:

1. To determine by secret ballot the free democratic choice of employees, whether they wish to be represented by a union in dealing with their employers and if so, by which union.
2. To prevent and remedy unlawful acts, called unfair labor practices, by either employers or unions.

The NLRB does not act on its own but reacts to charges of unfair labor practices and petitions for employee elections that are filed with one of its offices.

The **Occupational Safety and Health Administration (OSHA)** has a mission to save lives, prevent injuries, and protect the health of America's workers. OSHA does this through the administration of the Occupational Safety and Health Act of 1970 working in partnership with state and local governments, workers and employers (OSHA, 2003).

With more than 200 offices throughout the country, OSHA and its state partners have inspectors, investigators, engineers, physicians, educators, standards writers, and other personnel who establish and enforce protective standards. OSHA also offers technical assistance and consultation programs to employers and employees (OSHA, 2003).

There are 57 **Offices of the Inspectors General (OIG)** in 59 federal agencies (Nuclear Regulatory Commission, 2003). The HHS OIG has local offices in every state; Washington, DC; and Puerto Rico (Health and Human Services Office of the Inspector General, 2003). This is a reflection of the amount of oversight focused on federally funded health care. The specific purpose of the HHS OIG (Fig. 3.1), as mandated by Public Law 95-452, is to "protect the integrity of HHS programs, as well as the health and welfare of the beneficiaries of those programs" (OIG, 2003). The OIG reports on program and management problems and recommendations to correct them to both the secretary of HHS and Congress. The OIG's duties are carried out through audits, investigations, inspections and other related functions.

The **Office of Special Education and Rehabilitative Services (OSERS)** is part of the **Department of Education (DOE)** (DOE, 2003). It is committed to improving results and outcomes for people with disabilities. OSERS's mission is to "provide leadership to achieve full integration and participation in society of people with disabilities by ensuring equal opportunity and access to, and excellence in, education, employment and community living" (Office of Special Education and Rehabilitative Services, 2003). It achieves this mission through support of programs that benefit children, youth, and adults with disabilities. OSERS is composed of three program components: the Office of Special Education Programs (OSEP), the National Institute on Disability and Rehabilitation Research (NIDRR), and the Rehabilitation Services Administration (RSA). OSERS programs provide support to parents, educators, and states in special education, vocational rehabilitation, and research.

The **Veterans Health Administration (VHA)** is a division of the Department of Veterans Affairs. VHA provides a broad spectrum of medical, surgical, and rehabilitative care to enrolled and eligible veterans (Chapter 2). It is the stated goal of the VHA to share information about these benefits and services to

Table 3.2 California Health and Safety Agencies

Healthcare services	Department of Pesticide Regulation
Mental health services	Department of Rehabilitation
Substance abuse programs and services	Department of Social Services
Hospitals and health facilities	Department of Toxic Substances Control
Emergencies	Department of Justice
Safety	Department of Veterans Affairs
Public safety	Division of Occupational Safety and Health
California health and safety laws and regulations	Emergency Medical Services Authority
California health and safety policy sources	Environmental Protection Agency
California health and safety agencies	Health and Human Services Agency
Board of Prison Terms	Highway Patrol
Board of Registered Nursing	Managed Risk Medical Insurance Board
Department of Aging	Office of Emergency Services
Department of Alcohol and Drug Programs	Office of Traffic Safety
Department of Corrections	Youth Authority
Department of Forestry and Fire Protection	Medical Board of California
Department of Health Services	Office of Statewide Health Planning and Development
Department of Justice, Office of the Attorney General	State Fire Marshal
Department of Managed Healthcare	Youthful Offender Parole Board
Department of Mental Health	

Source: California Web Home Page at http://www.ca.gov/state/portal

make it as easy as possible for eligible persons to receive the care (Veterans Administration, 2003). The VHA serves veterans through a health system that includes medical centers and outpatient care clinics. The Veterans' Healthcare Eligibility Reform Act of 1996 allowed the way for the creation of the Medical Benefits Package, a health benefits plan generally available to enrolled veterans. Like other standard health care plans, the Medical Benefits Package emphasizes preventive and primary care, offering a full range of outpatient and inpatient services. Most non–service-connected veterans and noncompensable service-connected veterans need to complete a means test annually or they must pay the VA an applicable copayment. The means test is based on their income and net worth. Based on the means test, veterans may be required to make copayments for VA medical services. Veterans must also provide health insurance information so that the VA can submit claims to insurance carriers for treatment provided for all non–service-connected conditions (VA, 2003).

State and Local Government

State and local governments also regulate the activities of health organizations and providers. Because each state government has unique structure, the many roles of state government in the regulation of health care is best demonstrated by examples. Table 3.2 is a listing of California health and safety agencies, and Table 3.3 is a listing of San Francisco health and social services. These examples clearly demonstrate that health care oversight comes from many sources at the state and local levels. Again, it is up to health care organizations and providers to identify and comply with all applicable governmental regulation.

Table 3.3 San Francisco Health and Social Services

Aging and Adult Services
Office on the Aging
Veterans Service office
Public administrator/public guardian
Mental health conservator
Child Support Services
Department of Children, Youth and their Families
Department on the Status of Women
Department of Human Services
Immigrant Rights Commission
Mayor's Office on Disability
Mental Health Board
Public Health Department
Veterans Affairs Commission

Source: San Francisco Government Home Page http://www.ci.sf.ca.us/

To learn more about specific state and local agencies, go to http://www.firstgov.gov.

Student Notes

Compliance with governmental regulations and nongovernmental standards is a basic part of health care professional practice. It is incumbent on every health care provider to be familiar and compliant with all applicable regulations. The risks of noncompliance vary but can be as significant as loss of credentials, fines, and/or legal prosecution. A portion of workplace orientation information should include a review of how to practice within the laws of the state (Chapter 5) and federal government in that particular setting. Prior experiences, good and bad, provide employers with the appropriate background to choose what to emphasize. Given the breadth of governmental oversight and the volume of governmental regulations, new graduates may expect continual education regarding government involvement in health care. Most health care organizations provide ongoing employee education that addresses regulatory requirements as well as the organization's policies and procedures aimed at regulatory compliance. The topic of corporate compliance plans will be explored further in Chapter 4. Government Web sites provide the most readily available information at no cost.

Summary

Health care providers have historically been subject to external oversight. Oversight has come in the form of government regulatory compliance reviews and voluntary accreditation reviews. Regulatory compliance reviews are performed by federal, state, and local governmental agencies or their representatives. Regulatory reviews can be a condition of participation in government-funded health care programs, such as Medicare and Medicaid. They can also be a condition of continued operation as a state or local government–approved health care provider. Annual reviews for continued licensure, facility safety inspections, or compliance with state licensure requirements for medical professionals such as nursing may be a condition of continued operation.

The purpose of health care regulation is to protect the interests of the public. Several departments and agencies of the federal, state, and local government are responsible for the administration of health care regulations and oversight of the health care industry. Independent professionals and organizations involved in the delivery of health care services are held accountable to the public through the enactment and enforcement of regulations that set community standards for health care service. Government regulations affect

INDIVIDUAL CASE STUDY

Government oversight should not be a new concept to you. You may have been graduated from a state-supported educational institution. Part of your educational costs may have been paid through government programs. You can practice as a physical therapist in private settings only if you have been granted a license to practice by a state. If you treat Medicare patients on your own, you must obtain a Medicare provider number. These several examples highlight some of the many interrelationships between the practice of physical therapy and government agencies, centers, and departments. These interrelationships are such that you will have to devote time and effort to finding information on oversight, dedicate time to reading the information, and seek consultation from others to practice as required from multiple levels of government.

GROUP CASE STUDY

This case requires three people to work together. Group members will look at federal regulations related to Medicare.

Situation

The Centers for Medicare and Medicaid Services will have great impact on you if you work for an employer who is authorized to provide services to Medicare or Medicaid beneficiaries. In time, you may consider treating patients in your spare time outside of your workplace. Currently there are regulations that need to be followed if you intend to do this. One of the regulations is that a physical therapist in private must have their own Medicare provider number in order to be reimbursed for services to Medicare beneficiaries. Assuming that you want to look into this as a future option for yourself, what additional information would you like to have now? As a group, collaborate on the basic issue, i.e., how to get a Medicare provider number. What does the number allow you to do? How do you use the number? Start with an Internet search.

most of the operating practices of health care providers, including organizational structure, business and financial management practices, service documentation, service evaluation, personnel practice, and facility design. Full cooperation with the regulatory review process is mandatory. Failure to participate and/or cooperate can result in fines, cancellation of a provider's participation agreement for government-funded health programs, and/or loss of licensure to operate or practice (Chapter 5). In addition to health care regulations, general business laws apply to health care organizations and individual service providers. It is important that health care managers understand the major business laws that affect health care facilities. These laws are the focus of Chapter 4.

REFERENCES

Agency for Healthcare Research and Quality. Available from http://www.ahrq.gov. Accessed 2/01/03.

California. Web home page. Available from http://www.ca.gov/state/portal. Accessed 2/01/03.

Centers for Disease Control and Prevention. Available from http://www.cdc.gov. Accessed 2/01/03.

Centers for Medicare and Medicaid Services. Available from http://cms.hhs.gov. Accessed 2/01/03.

Department of Education. Available from http://www.ed.gov. Accessed 2/01/03.

Department of Health and Human Services. Available from http://www.hhs.gov. Accessed 2/01/03.

Department of Justice. About DOJ. Available from http://www.usdoj.gov. Accessed 2/01/03.

Department of Labor. Available from http://www.dol.gov. Accessed 2/01/03.

Drug Enforcement Administration. Available from http://www.dea.gov. Accessed 2/01/03.

Environmental Protection Agency. Available from http://www.epa.gov. Accessed 2/01/03.

Federal Trade Commission. Promoting competition, protecting consumers: A plain English guide to antitrust laws. Available from http://www.ftc.gov/bc/compguide/index.htm. Accessed 2/01/03.

Finkler SA, Ward DM. Essentials of cost accounting for health care organizations, 2nd ed. Gaithersburg, MD: Aspen. 1999.

General Accounting Office. GAO. Available from http://www.gao.gov. Accessed 2/01/03.

Internal Revenue Service. Available from http://www.irs.gov/irs/index.html. Accessed 2/01/03.

Mintz, Levin, Cohn, Ferris, Glovsky, and Popeo, P.C. Fraud and abuse. Available from http://www.mintz.com/pcgroup/FRAUDABS.htm. Accessed 2/01/03.

National Council on Disability. Available from http://www.ncd.gov. Accessed 2/01/03.

National Institutes of Health. Available from http://www.nih.gov. Accessed 2/01/03.

National Research Corporation. Report 2003. Available from http://www.nationalresearch.com/news/releaseH-CAHPS.html. Accessed 2/01/03.

Nuclear Regulatory Commission. Office of the Inspector General semiannual report to congress (NUREG-1415, Vol. 14, No. 2). Available from http://www.nrc.gov/reading-rm/doc-collections/nuregs/staff/sr1415/v14n2/#exec-sum. Accessed

8/25/03.

Occupational Safety and Health Administration. Available from http://www.osha.gov. Accessed 2/01/03.

Office of the Inspector General. Available from http://oig.hhs.gov. Accessed 2/01/03.

Health and Human Services Office of the Inspector General. Available from http://www.oig.hhs.gov/reading/history/ighistory.pdf. Accessed 8/25/03.

Office of Special Education and Rehabilitative Services. Available from http://www.ed.gov/offices/OSERS. Accessed 2/01/03.

San Francisco Government. Departments and agencies. Available from http://www.sfgov.org/site/mainpages_index.asp?id=7695. Accessed 2/01/03.

Veterans Administration. Available from http://www.va.gov/health_benefits. Accessed 2.01/03.

MORE INFORMATION RELATED TO THIS CHAPTER

Murer C. Corporate compliance: Establishing leadership and compliance programs to prevent health care fraud. Rehab Management. 1998. December/January.

Up-to-date information about the various federal government Internet sites noted in this chapter may be found at these sites:

ACF http://www.acf.gov.
AHRQ http://www.ahrq.gov.
AoA http://www.aoa.gov.
CDC http://www.cdc.gov.
CMS http://cms.hhs.gov.
DOL http://www.dol.gov.
FDA http://www.fda.gov.
FTC http://www.ftc.gov/ftc/consumer.htm.
HRSA http://www.hrsa.gov.
IHS http://www.ihs.gov.
IRS http://www.irs.gov.
MedPac http://www.medpac.gov.
NCD http://www.ncd.gov.
NIH http://www.nih.gov.
NLRB http://www.nlrb.gov.
OSERS http://www.ed.gov/offices/OSERS.
OSHA http://www.osha.gov.
SAMHSA http://www.samhsa.gov.
VHA http://www.nlm.nih.gov/medlineplus/veteranshealth.html.

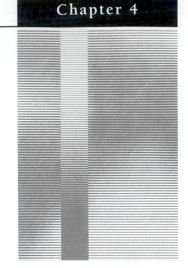

Chapter 4

LAWS RELEVANT TO HEALTH CARE BUSINESS

Learning Objectives

1. Examine the implications of major laws relevant to management of health care organizations and direct care providers.
2. Contrast laws and regulations.
3. Analyze the main elements of important laws and regulations that are of particular interest to physical therapist managers.
4. Analyze the main elements of important laws and regulations that are of particular interest to physical therapy staff members.

Key Words

Best Pharmaceuticals for Children Act, Bioterrorism Act of 2002, business associate, Centers for Medicare and Medicaid Services (CMS), compliance plan, Substances Act, Department of Health and Human Services (HHS), Department of Labor (DOL), Dietary Supplement Health and Education Act of 1994, Drug Enforcement Administration (DEA), electronic transaction and code set, Employment and Training Administration, enrollee, Environmental Protection Agency (EPA), Federal Food, Drug, and Cosmetic Act, federal minimum wage, fee-for-service, fiduciary, Food and Drug Administration (FDA), Health Care Fraud and Abuse Control Program (HCFAC), Health Resources and Services Administration, Health Insurance Portability and Accountability Act (HIPPA) Title I, Health Care Access, Portability, and Renewability, HIPAA Title II, Preventing Health Care Fraud and Abuse, Hospital Insurance (Part A), Medical Liability Reform Administrative Simplification, Limited English proficiency (LEP), Local Emergency Planning Committee (LEPC), Mammography Quality Standards Act (MQSA), Material Safety Data Sheet (MSDS), Medical Device User Fee and Modernization Act (MDUFMA) of 2002, Medical Insurance (Part B), Medicaid Program (Title XIX), Medicare Program (Title XVIII), Occupational Safety And Health Act (OSH Act), Occupational Safety and Health Administration (OSHA), Office of Labor-Management Standards (OLMS), Office of Minority Health (OMH), overtime pay, Pension and Welfare Benefits Administration (PWBA), personal health information (PHI), Prescription Drug User Fee Act, privacy, regulation, Ryan White Care Act, Securities and Exchange Commission (SEC), security, self-regulatory organization (SRO), State Children's Health Insurance Program (SCHIP) (Title XXI), Superfund Amendments and Reauthorization Act (SARA), Americans With Disabilities Act (ADA), Black Lung Benefits Act, Comprehensive Omnibus Budget Reconciliation Act of 1985 (COBRA), Davis-

Bacon Act, Disadvantaged Minority Health Improvement Act, Emergency Planning and Community Right-to-Know Act (EPCRA), Employee Polygraph Protection Act, Employee Retirement Income Security Act (ERISA), Energy Employees Occupational Illness Compensation Program Act, Fair Labor Standards Act (FLSA), Family and Medical Leave Act (FMLA), Federal Employees' Compensation Act (FECA), Federal False Claims Act, Federal Food, Drug, and Cosmetic Act (FFDCA), Freedom of Information Act (FOIA), Health Insurance Portability and Accountability Act of 1996 (HIPAA), Immigration and Nationality Act, Investment Advisers Act of 1940, Labor-Management Reporting and Disclosure Act of 1959, Longshore and Harbor Workers' Compensation Act (LHWCA), McNamara-O'Hara Service Contract Act, National Environmental Policy Act of 1969 (NEPA), Omnibus Budget Reconciliation Act of 1989, Omnibus Reconciliation Act of 1993, regulation, Pollution Prevention Act (PPA), Sarbanes-Oxley Act of 2002, Securities Act of 1933, Securities Exchange Act of 1934, Social Security Act, Uniformed Services Employment and Reemployment Rights Act, Walsh-Healey Public Contracts Act, Waste Tracking Act (MWTA), Worker Adjustment and Retraining Notification Act (WARN), Veterans' Employment and Training Service (VETS), Wage and Hour Division of the Employment Standards Administration, Waste Tracking Act (MWTA) of 1989 amended by the Solid Waste Disposal Act, whistle blower

Introduction

Federal laws are formulated by the U.S. Congress. This process is depicted in Figure 4.1. Many influences that affect Congress are not shown (Chapter 2). When a law is enacted, it must be implemented and enforced. This is accomplished through regulations. A **regulation** is a rule issued by a federal or state agency (Nolan and Nolan-Haley, 1990) or independent regulatory body (Longest, Rakich, Darr, 2000) that has the force of law. There are many regulations for businesses. Health care is a business. This means that health care organizations and providers are subject to many business regulations in addition to health care–specific regulations (Chapter 2). These are

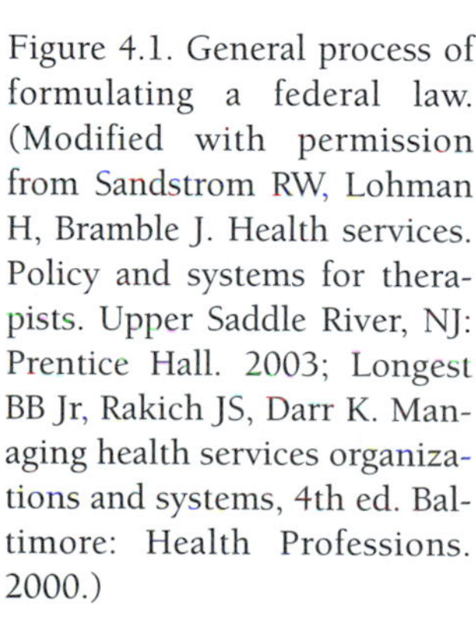

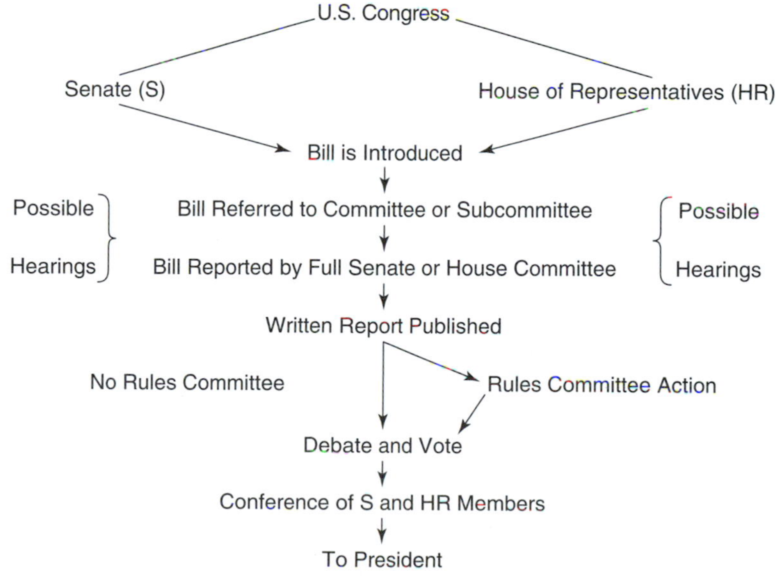

Figure 4.1. General process of formulating a federal law. (Modified with permission from Sandstrom RW, Lohman H, Bramble J. Health services. Policy and systems for therapists. Upper Saddle River, NJ: Prentice Hall. 2003; Longest BB Jr, Rakich JS, Darr K. Managing health services organizations and systems, 4th ed. Baltimore: Health Professions. 2000.)

among the regulated areas of interest to health care managers:

Employment practices (e.g., hiring, promoting)
Financial management (e.g., accounting, fraud)
Manufacture, labeling, handling, sale, and use of food, drug, and medical equipment (e.g., sale of products, administration of unusual physical agents)
Handling and disposal of materials used in the delivery of health care services (e.g., handling of materials used to clean up body fluids, cleaning of equipment)
Operations and clinical practice (e.g., control of employees' behavior, checking on credentials)
Fraud and abuse (e.g., coding, restraint of patients)
Reporting practices and compliance (e.g., infection rate, medical record security)

In fact, health care providers do very little that is not affected by regulatory considerations in some way. This chapter provides just a sampling of pertinent laws that will affect staff and managers of physical therapy services in their daily work in both large and small settings. This chapter provides a starting point for physical therapists new to the practice and business of physical therapy. The chapter deals first with regulations applicable to most employers regardless of their type of business. Health care–specific regulations follow.

Note. The regulatory requirements that apply to businesses, especially health care businesses, change daily. All providers and managers need to make a deliberate effort to stay current with regulatory requirements throughout their career. In addition to independent study, participation in a network of other knowledgeable managers and professionals in law, accounting, and human resources is highly desirable. Clinical managers must know the general regulations and where to find expertise within their organization. Large organizations have experts on staff or as consultants who provide legal counsel, human resources, risk management, compliance, and accounting expertise. An examination of the legislative and regulatory requirements to operate a health care business is part of the continual environmental assessment necessary to protect and advance the organization (Chapter 11).

This chapter provides the background information about business law to assist in practicing according to law and to engage in discussion with a variety of individuals with specific areas of legal expertise.

Employment Regulation

The **Department of Labor** (**DOL**) is responsible for the administration of several federal laws related to employment and employee compensation, benefits, safety, health, and welfare. Many DOL-administered laws affect health care organizations and their employees. According to the DOL (2003a), these include the following:

The **Fair Labor Standards Act** (**FLSA**) sets standards for wages and overtime pay that affect most private and public employers. The FLSA requires employers to pay covered employees who are not otherwise exempt at least the **federal minimum wage** and **overtime pay** of 1.5 times the regular rate of pay. It also restricts the hours that children under age 16 can work and forbids employment of children under age 18 in certain jobs deemed too dangerous for nonagricultural operations. For agricultural operations, it prohibits the employment of children under age 16 during school hours and in certain jobs deemed too dangerous. The FLSA is administered by the **Wage and Hour Division of the Employment Standards Administration**.

The **Immigration and Nationality Act** enforces labor standards provisions that apply to aliens authorized to work in the United States under certain nonimmigrant visa programs. These standards may apply to the recruitment and employment of physical therapists and other difficult-to-recruit professional staff from other countries.

The **Occupational Safety and Health Act** (**OSH Act**) regulates the safety and health conditions in most private industries. This also covers public-sector employers. Employers have a general duty under the OSH Act to provide a workplace and work free from recognized serious hazards. Employers must comply with the regulations and the safety and health standards promulgated by the **Occupational Safety and Health Administration** (OSHA). OSHA uses workplace inspection and investigation, compliance assistance, and cooperative programs as enforcement mechanisms. An example of how OSHA affects health care workers is in the requirements for **Material Safety Data Sheets** (MSDSs). MSDSs provide information on hazardous components, management of spills, and accidental exposure to chemical substances. The operators of health care businesses are required to prepare or have available to their employees MSDSs for any listed chemical found in the workplace.

The **Federal Employees' Compensation Act** (FECA) establishes a comprehensive and exclusive workers' compensation program that pays compensation for the disability or death of a federal employee resulting from personal injury sustained while in the performance of duty. The FECA provides these items:

- Wage loss compensation for total or partial disability
- Schedule of awards for permanent loss or loss of use of specified members of the body, related medical costs, and vocational rehabilitation.

In addition to the FECA, the **Black Lung Benefits Act** provides monthly cash payments and medical benefits to coal miners totally disabled by pneumoconiosis (black lung disease). The **Longshore and Harbor Workers' Compensation Act** (LHWCA) provides for compensation and medical care to certain maritime employees. The **Energy Employees Occupational Illness Compensation Program Act** provides lump-sum payments and medical benefits to employees (or certain of their survivors) of the Department of Energy, its contractors, and subcontractors for cancer caused by exposure to radiation and for certain illnesses caused by exposure to beryllium or silica incurred in the performance of duty.

The **Employee Retirement Income Security Act** (ERISA) regulates employers who offer pension or welfare benefit plans for their employees. Title I of ERISA is administered by the **Pension and Welfare Benefits Administration** (PWBA). ERISA deals with **fiduciary** matters, that is, the duty of trustees to act primarily for another's benefit (Nolan and Nolan-Haley, 1990). It imposes a wide range of fiduciary, disclosure, and reporting requirements on fiduciaries of pension and welfare benefit plans and on others having dealings with these plans.

The **Comprehensive Omnibus Budget Reconciliation Act of 1985** (COBRA) has several parts. It mandates that employers allow for the continuation of employee health care provisions (insurance) after termination of employment. The law does not address who pays the cost.

The **Labor–Management Reporting and Disclosure Act of 1959** (also known as the Landrum-Griffin Act) deals with the relationship between a union and its members. It requires labor organizations to file annual financial reports; requires union officials, employers, and labor consultants to file reports regarding certain labor relations practices; establishes standards for the election of union officers, thus protecting union funds; and promotes union democracy. The act is administered by the **Office of Labor-Management Standards** (OLMS).

The **Employee Polygraph Protection Act** bars most employers from using lie detectors on employees, permitting polygraph tests only in limited circumstances. The Wage and Hour Division administers this law.

The **Family and Medical Leave Act** (FMLA) applies to employers of 50 or more employees. It requires employers to allow up to 12 weeks of unpaid job-protected leave to eligible employees for the birth or adoption of a child or for the serious illness of the employee or a spouse, child, or parent. While this law has been a great benefit to employees, it can create a significant financial and operational hardship on employers, who must often allow for the use of earned sick leave benefits or work short-handed. The Wage and Hour Division of the Employment Standards Administration administers the provisions of the FMLA.

The Immigration and Nationality Act requires employers who want to use foreign temporary workers (less than a year) on H-2A visas to get a labor certificate from the **Employment and Training Administration** certifying that there are not sufficient, able, willing, and qualified U.S. workers available to do the work. The provisions of this act must be met when recruiting physical therapists or other health care professionals from foreign countries. There are also visas for those who want permanent residency to work in the United States. The Wage and Hour Division of the Employment Standards Administration enforces this law.

The **Davis-Bacon Act** requires payment of prevailing wages and benefits to employees (laborers and mechanics) of contractors on federal government construction projects. This applies to recipients of government contracts, grants, or financial aid.

The **McNamara-O'Hara Service Contract Act** sets wage rates and other labor standards for employees of contractors furnishing services to the federal government. This applies to recipients of government contracts, grants, or financial aid.

The **Walsh-Healey Public Contracts Act** requires payment of minimum wage and adherence to other labor standards by contractors. This applies to recipients of government contracts, grants, or financial aid.

The **Worker Adjustment and Retraining Notification Act** (WARN) requires that employees receive early warning of upcoming layoffs or plant closings. Employees must be provided with severance pay that covers the required notice period if notice is not given. WARN is enforced through the federal courts.

The **Uniformed Services Employment and Reemployment Rights Act** grants certain persons who serve in the armed forces, such as those called up from the reserves or National Guard, the right to reemployment with the employer they were with when they entered service. As with FMLA, this law is designed to protect the employee but may cause a significant impact on the employer and/or coworkers, who may have to work short-handed while the protected employee is away. The **Veterans' Employment and Training Service (VETS)** administers this Act.

The **Americans with Disabilities Act (ADA)** has four sets of provisions: (1) employment, (2) communications, (3) public accommodations, and (4) transportation (Americans With Disabilities Act, 2003). These various areas are enforced by several federal agencies, including the Equal Employment Opportunity Commission, Department of Justice Civil Rights Division, Federal Communications Commission, and Department of Transportation. Of particular importance to employers are the provisions that prohibit discrimination against a qualified person with a disability when the discrimination is attributable to the individual's disability. Also, an employer is required to make reasonable accommodation to facilitate the employment or continued employment of a qualified applicant or employee, respectively (Engel, Calderone, Lederman, et al., 1996).

Finance and Securities

All businesses, including health care organizations, are subject to regulation of their financial management and reporting practices. Ownership and legal structure (Chapter 7) will determine how regulations affect a health care organization. These are the major laws governing financial management and reporting:

The **Securities Act of 1933** applies to for-profit health care corporations whose stock is publicly traded and whose ownership is legally separate from its owners (Chapter 7). Ownership or a percentage thereof is represented by stock (securities) that can be bought and sold to investors through the stock market. This law has two objectives:

1. To require that investors receive financial and other significant information concerning securities being offered for public sale.

2. To prohibit deceit, misrepresentations, and other fraud in the sale of securities.

The **Securities Exchange Act of 1934** created the **Securities and Exchange Commission** (**SEC**). It authorizes the SEC's broad authority over all aspects of the securities industry. Its authority includes "the power to register, regulate, and oversee brokerage firms, transfer agents, and clearing agencies as well as the nation's securities **self regulatory organizations** (**SROs**). The various stock exchanges, such as the New York Stock Exchange, and American Stock Exchange are SROs" (SEC, 2003). The act also dictates acceptable and unacceptable conduct in the stock markets. It provides the SEC with disciplinary powers over regulated entities and persons associated with them and gives the SEC the power to require periodic reporting of information by companies with publicly traded securities.

The **Investment Advisers Act of 1940** (amended in 1966) regulates investment advisers. This act requires advisers who have at least $25 million of assets under management or who advise a registered investment company to register with the SEC.

The **Sarbanes-Oxley Act of 2002** was enacted in response to events that led to allegations of misdeeds by corporate executives, independent auditors, and other market participants, undermining investor confidence in the U.S. financial markets (Aguilar, 2002; Waggoner and Fogarty, 2002). This act effects sweeping corporate disclosure and financial reporting reform.

Food and Drug Regulation

The U.S. **Food and Drug Administration** (**FDA**), with enforcement through efforts of the **Drug Enforcement Administration** (**DEA**), is responsible for the administration of several statutes. According to the DEA (2003), these include the following:

The **Federal Food, Drug, and Cosmetic Act** (as amended by the FDA Modernization Act of 1997) regulates such things as definitions, standards, packaging, and labeling for food, food supplements, drugs, medical devices, and cosmetics. Additional information is provided in the environmental regulation section.

The **Best Pharmaceuticals for Children Act** amended the Federal Food, Drug, and Cosmetic Act to improve the safety and efficacy of pharmaceuticals for children.

The Bioterrorism Act of 2002 was enacted to improve national preparedness for bioterrorism and other public health emergencies through the following provisions:

- Enhancement of government control over dangerous biological agents and toxins
- Protection of the security and safety of the food, drug, and water supply

The **Controlled Substances Act** provides the authority to control as well as set standards and schedules for all controlled substances.

The **Dietary Supplement Health and Education Act of 1994** amended the Federal Food, Drug, and Cosmetic Act to establish standards for the labeling, and safety of dietary supplements.

The **Mammography Quality Standards Act** (**MQSA**) establishes regulations and national quality standards for mammography services.

The **Medical Device User Fee and Modernization Act** (**MDUFMA**) **of 2002** establishes user fees for premarket FDA reviews for approval of new devices and technologies. The revenue obtained from these user fees allows the FDA to provide patients with earlier access to safe and effective technology and to provide more interactive and rapid review to the medical device industry. Fees may be reduced for small businesses.

The **Prescription Drug User Fee Act** establishes a user fee for premarket review for FDA approval of drugs and drug supplements.

Health Care

While many laws affect health care organizations and providers, those administered by the agencies of the **Department of Health and**

Human Services (HHS) generally have the greatest influence on health care access, operations, clinical practice standards, and payment. The listing of HHS-administered laws is extensive. These laws may be of particular interest to health care consumers, organizations and providers (HHS, 2003a):

The **Social Security Act** established three health care insurance programs to guarantee access to health care for the young, the elderly, and the poor. The combined enrollment of these health insurance plans, including the **Medicare Program (Title XVIII)**, **Medicaid Program (Title XIX)**, and the **State Children's Health Insurance Program (SCHIP) (Title XXI)** has made the federal government the largest provider of health care insurance in the nation (CMS, 2003) (Chapter 2). Run by the **Centers for Medicare and Medicaid Services (CMS)**, the **Medicare Program** covers nearly 40 million Americans at a cost of just under $200 billion. According to CMS (2003) the Medicare Program provides health insurance to these groups:

- People aged 65 or older
- Some people with disabilities under age 65
- People with permanent kidney failure requiring dialysis or a transplant

Medicare is divided into **hospital insurance (Part A)**, which helps pay for inpatient hospital services, skilled nursing facility services, home health services, and hospice care, and **medical insurance (Part B)**, which helps pay for doctor services, outpatient hospital services, medical equipment and supplies, and other health services and supplies. Medicare **enrollees** and **beneficiaries** may have the choice of enrolling in the original Medicare **fee-for-service** plan, a Medicare managed care plan, or a private fee-for-service plan, depending on what is available in their geographical area (Chapter 2).

Medicaid is a health insurance program for certain low-income people. It is funded and administered jointly by a state–federal partnership. As a result of this partnership approach, states are required to follow broad federal requirements for Medicaid but have a wide degree of flexibility to design their program. States must cover these services:

- Inpatient and outpatient hospital services
- Laboratory and radiology services
- Skilled nursing and home health services
- Doctors' services
- Family planning
- Periodic health checkups
- Diagnosis and treatment for children

States may establish eligibility standards, decide what benefits to offer and services to pay for, and set payment rates. According to CMS (2003), 36 million people are eligible for Medicaid, including certain low-income families with children; certain low-income people who are aged, blind, or disabled; certain low-income children and pregnant women; and people who have very high medical bills.

School Children's Health Insurance Program (SCHIP) is run by CMS, along with the Health Resources and Services Administration (HRSA) and is designed to help states expand coverage to uninsured children. As with Medicaid, states must follow broad federal guidelines but have the authority to determine eligibility and coverage. In all cases enrollees must be low income, uninsured, and ineligible for Medicaid. Not all states participate in the SCHIP program. States that do participate must cover these services:

- Inpatient and outpatient hospital services
- Doctors' surgical and medical services
- Laboratory and radiology services
- Well baby and child care, including immunizations

The **Health Insurance Portability and Accountability Act of 1996 (HIPAA)**, administered by CMS, is intended to "improve portability and continuity of health insurance coverage in the group and individual markets, to combat waste, fraud, and abuse in health insurance and health care delivery, to promote the use of medical savings accounts, to improve access to long-term care services and coverage, to simplify the administration of health insurance, and for other purposes" (HHS, 2003b). There are two parts to HIPAA. **Title I, Health Care Access, Portability, and Renewability**, addresses the portability and continuity of health care insurance. **Title II, Preventing Health Care Fraud and Abuse; Administrative Simplification; Medical Liability Reform**, targets administrative simplification, waste reduction, fraud control, and privacy.

Title I, Health Care Access, Portability, and Renewability, protects health insurance coverage for workers and their families when they change or lose their jobs. According to CMS (2003) this may help consumers in these ways:

- Increase their ability to get health coverage when starting a new job
- Lower the chance of losing existing health care coverage
- Maintain continuous health coverage when changing jobs
- Buy health insurance coverage personally if coverage is lost

HIPAA does this by limiting the use of exclusions for preexisting conditions, prohibiting group health plans from discriminating in coverage decisions based on past or present poor health, guaranteeing certain small employers and individuals the right to purchase health insurance, and guaranteeing that in most cases employers or individuals who purchase health insurance can renew the coverage regardless of any health conditions of individuals covered under the insurance policy.

HIPAA Title II, Preventing Health Care Fraud and Abuse; Administrative Simplification; and Medical Liability Reform, sets requirements intended to reduce the costs and administrative burdens of health care. This is accomplished by making possible the standardized electronic transmission of many administrative and financial transactions. Health information privacy is also a requirement of administrative simplification. Title II has had the greatest impact on health care organizations and providers in terms of time and resources. Rules to implement Title II have been categorized into three topic areas: (1) **security**, (2) **electronic transactions and code sets**, and (3) **privacy**, thus:

- The standards for the security of electronic health information published in the Federal Register specify "a series of administrative, technical, and physical security procedures for covered entities to use to assure the confidentiality of electronic protected health information. The standards are delineated into either required or addressable implementation specifications" (CMS, 2003).
- The rule for electronic transactions and code sets for electronic health information establishes national standards that must be followed by all health care providers (including insurers) except retail pharmacies (CMS, 2003). The goal is to establish a universal electronic language and a standardized information system that allows for the improved flow of information within and between organizations and thereby reduces the administrative costs of health care. The adoption of this rule affected all health care providers, health plans, and health care clearinghouses that use electronic transmission for billing, collection of accounts, and/or communications involving health care information.
- The rule adopting standards for privacy applies to health information created or maintained by health care providers, health plans, and health care clearinghouses that engage in certain electronic transactions. These standards require covered entities to protect the privacy of individually identifiable health information, called **personal health information (PHI)**, that applies to all entities. PHI is defined as all medical records and other individually identifiable health information held or disclosed by a covered entity in any form, whether communicated electronically, on paper, or orally. Generally, the use of PHI is limited to health purposes only. General PHI use guidelines published by the **Office for Civil Rights** (**OCR**) advises that PHI can be

used or disclosed by a covered entity only for purposes of health care treatment, payment, and operations. PHI disclosures must be limited to the minimum necessary for the purpose of the disclosure. This does not apply to the transfer of medical records for purposes of treatment. For nonroutine disclosures of PHI, patient authorization must be truly informed and voluntary. To ensure that these requirements are met, covered entities are required to do the following:

- Adopt written privacy procedures to include who has access to PHI, how it will be used within the entity, and when the information may or may not be disclosed
- Designate a privacy officer
- Establish grievance processes as a means for patients to make inquiries or complaints regarding the privacy of their records
- Take steps to ensure that their **business associates** protect the privacy of PHI
- Train all employees to understand the new privacy protections procedures

The standards not only seek to control the flow of sensitive patient information but also to establish real penalties for the misuse or disclosure of this information. This latter rule gives patients new rights to understand and control how their personal health information is used. The OCR is responsible for implementing and enforcing the privacy regulation. According to the OCR (2003), the privacy rule has given patients these rights:

- To be educated about their rights related to privacy protection. Health care providers and health plans are required to provide all patients with a written explanation of how they can use, keep, and disclose their health information. A signed acknowledgment of receipt of this privacy notice by the patient or an authorized representative must be kept on record. The process enables the patient to take the following actions:
  - Get copies of and request amendments to his or her records
  - Get a listing of all releases of the PHI. Covered entities must keep records of and be prepared to release information about most disclosures of a patient's PHI
  - Give consent in writing before PHI is released. Health care providers are required to obtain the patient's consent before releasing PHI for treatment, payment, and health care operations
  - Give consent specifically for nonroutine uses and most non–health care purposes
  - Give consent in a manner free from coercion for nonroutine disclosures
  - Complain to covered entities or the authorities about violations of any provision of the privacy rule

Under HIPAA, covered entities that misuse PHI are subject to civil and federal criminal penalties.

The **Freedom of Information Act (FOIA)** provides specifically that "any person can make requests for government information" (DOL, 2003b; Environmental Protection Agency, 2003). Persons requesting information are not required to identify themselves or explain why they want the information. All branches of the federal government must adhere to FOIA provisions. There are some restrictions for work in progress (early drafts), enforcement confidential information, classified documents, and national security information. FOIA applies to government documentation related to health care facility licensure and quality-of-care reviews performed under the authority of the CMS. That means that any sanctions or performance deficiencies that are identified during government-authorized facility or provider reviews or surveys are available to the public upon request.

The **Disadvantaged Minority Health Improvement Act** requires the **Office of Minority Health (OMH)** to enter into contracts to increase the access to health care of persons with **limited English profi-**

ciency (LEP) by developing programs to provide bilingual or interpreter services. Some states also require providers to offer language assistance to LEP persons in many service settings (Office of Civil Rights, 2003).

The **Omnibus Budget Reconciliation Act of 1989** placed limits on self-referral, barring referral of Medicare patients to clinical laboratories by physicians who have or whose family members have a financial interest in those laboratories. The **Omnibus Reconciliation Act of 1993** expanded this self-referral ban to 10 additional health services (HHS, 2003c):

1. Durable medical equipment and supplies
2. Home health services
3. Inpatient and outpatient hospital services
4. Occupational therapy
5. Orthotics, prosthetics, and prosthetic devices and supplies
6. Outpatient prescription drugs
7. Parenteral and enteral nutrients, equipment, and supplies
8. Physical therapy
9. Radiology services
10. Radiation therapy services and supplies

The 1993 law also applies the referral limits to Medicaid and clarified exceptions. Self-referral laws are self-enforcing in that the existence of an improper financial relationship is subject to loss of Medicare payment or a civil fine. This creates an incentive for health care providers to comply with the law through due diligence.

The **Ryan White Care Act** provides HIV and AIDS primary health care treatment and support for low-income individuals. It includes programs that provide medications to fight HIV. Ryan White funds go to eligible local communities hit hardest by HIV.

Environmental Regulation

Several major laws form the legal basis for the authority of the **Environmental Protection Agency** (EPA). Many of these specifically affect health care organizations and providers (EPA, 2003):

The **National Environmental Policy Act of 1969** (NEPA) establishes national policy to "encourage productive and enjoyable harmony between man and his environment; to promote efforts which will prevent or eliminate damage to the environment and biosphere and stimulate the health and welfare of man; to enrich the understanding of the ecological systems and natural resources important to the Nation; and to establish a Council on Environmental Quality" (NEPA, 2003).

The **Emergency Planning & Community Right-To-Know Act** (EPCRA), also known as Title III of the **Superfund Amendments and Reauthorization Act** (SARA), is the national legislation on community safety. EPCRA was designated to help local communities protect public health, safety, and the environment from chemical hazards. Broad representation on **Local Emergency Planning Committees** (LEPCs) by emergency response personnel, health officials, government representatives, community groups, industrial facilities, media, and local emergency managers ensures that all necessary elements for effective planning are represented. LEPCs have been increasingly active as part of the federal initiatives to improve homeland security.

The Federal Food, Drug, and Cosmetic Act (FFDCA) regulates such health care activities as the use of investigational drugs and devices, clinical trials involving humans, pharmaceutical compounding, patient access to unapproved therapies and diagnostic procedures. This law also requires dissemination of information about unintended uses of drugs and devices.

The **Pollution Prevention Act** (PPA) regulates pollution issues related to medical waste tracking and disposal along with related health issues.

The **Medical Waste Tracking Act** (MWTA) of 1989 requires the EPA to disseminate rules on the management of infectious waste.

Health Care Fraud and Abuse

Control of claims fraud and abuse has become a hot topic among health care regulators and providers alike. There are several laws that are used by government departments and agencies to combat fraud and abuse. These include:

The **Federal False Claims Act** has been used by federal law enforcement to fight alleged cases of health care fraud. According to the American Medical Association (AMA), the False Claims Act provides for treble damages and mandatory fines of $5,000 to $10,000 per claim and can result in payments of millions of dollars. Under the False Claims Act prosecutors do not have to prove intent to defraud federal programs (Reardon, 1997).

HIPAA, discussed earlier, represents a consolidation of government efforts to fight health care fraud and abuse. HIPAA established a comprehensive program to combat fraud committed against all health plans, both public and private. The legislation required the establishment of a national **Healthcare Fraud and Abuse Control Program** (HCFAC). The HCFAC is under the joint direction of the U.S. attorney general and the secretary of the Department of Health and Human Services acting through the department's inspector general (HHS, 2003d). The HCFAC program is intended to coordinate federal, state, and local law enforcement efforts to stop health care fraud and abuse.

State and local laws regulate organization and professional licensure, facility design and operation, and many other matters (Chapter 5).

Compliance Planning

It is evident that health care organizations and providers must comply with a multitude of laws. Many of the federal laws reviewed in this chapter have **whistle blower** protections and rewards for employees who complain about violations of the law by their employers. These whistle blower provisions are designed to encourage employees to report any suspected violations of regulations. A **compliance plan** can prevent inadvertent violations, such as incorrect charge coding. In addition, having a compliance plan can act as evidence that any violations were truly inadvertent. Reardon (1997) recommends that a compliance plan include the following elements:

- *Commitment.* There must be a clear commitment on the part of the organization to know and comply with all applicable standards and regulations. This includes a plan to take action when violations are recognized.
- *Compliance officer.* The organization must designate a compliance officer who has the authority to direct regulatory compliance policy and practices.
- *Training.* Organization-wide training should define employee's roles and responsibility for regulatory compliance. Training should make compliance understandable.
- *Monitoring.* Compliance monitoring should include a well-publicized method for employees to internally report any suspected fraud or abuse.
- *Communication plan.* Communication regarding the compliance plan should be highly structured, consistent, and ongoing.
- *Enforcement.* Organizations should make provisions to investigate and take corrective as well as disciplinary actions when necessary.
- *Prevention.* Anytime a compliance violation is identified, the organization must take steps to prevent similar violations. Prevention efforts should be documented.

Given the huge amount of regulation that health care organizations must follow, compliance would be virtually impossible without a formal compliance plan.

INDIVIDUAL CASE STUDY

Clinical practitioners in many settings need intimate knowledge of regulations for treating patients covered by Medicare, Medicaid, SCHIP, and workers' compensation. Clinical managers need to know more about these programs to teach others; they must also know about ERISA, FOIA, HIPAA, OBRA, wage and hour employment standards, compliance plans, OSHA requirements, and other regulations. The regulations discussed in this chapter in one way or another were formulated to protect the rights of specified groups, for example, beneficiaries, employees, retirees, job seekers, and people injured on the job. Adhering to law is an ethical as well as a legal obligation (Chapters 5 and 6). Choose one of the specified groups that are eligible for government health care assistance. Identify the criteria for assistance and summarize what you find out about physical therapy coverage for this group.

Student Notes

Whether a new graduate chooses to become an employee or to enter private practice, regulatory compliance is a key element in the broad picture of professional practice. In most settings, physical therapy facilities produce inpatient billing on a daily basis. Patient billing is an activity fraught with risk for inadvertent fraud and abuse. Even inadvertent errors are considered fraudulent. Charging for the wrong services or too much service, using the wrong charge code, or charging under the wrong date of service may be construed illegal acts. Charging without supporting documentation may also be viewed as fraud. Be careful to get charges right (Chapter 30) and ensure that professional documentation in the medical record supports the billed charges each and every time.

GROUP CASE STUDY

Pair up to work on this case.

Situation

In the course of reading this chapter you decided to seek clarification on fraud and abuse at http://www.hhs.gov/asl/testify/t970626c.html. What you found about coding was shocking.

You discovered that you and a colleague misunderstood the procedure for billing Title VXIII patients. Both of you were assigning billing codes (see Chapter 30) for a specific type of treatment based on information provided to you by your employer. As a result of this misunderstanding, you estimate that the two of you have overcharged at least fifty patients over the past several months by assigning codes for treatment that have higher payments than for the code you should have used. You check and find that all of the bills have been paid. What do you do now? Discuss where to get more information, the electronic and human resources you will consult, options you have, and how to protect yourself. After you and your partner formulate your answers, discuss them in small groups and then report on the discussion to the group as a whole.

Summary

This chapter focused on federal regulations relevant to health care organizations and providers. These regulations have the force of law. The regulations cover the general rules of business as well as specifics for health care entities. Health care organizations and providers are therefore subject to many regulations that cover a variety of topics. The areas of regulation that are of particular interest to clinical health care managers are employment practices; financial management; food and drug manufacture, labeling, handling, and sale; handling and disposal of materials used in the delivery of services; fraud and abuse; operations and clinical practice; and reporting and compliance practices.

To comply with regulatory requirements, health care providers must become familiar with major laws relevant to health care organizations and providers. Physical therapists must access and use resources provided by governmental regulatory departments and agencies, external consultants (Chapter 34), and experts internal to an organization to learn about legal requirements. Knowledge of regulatory requirements must be applied to daily practice–related activities from obtaining consent through the billing process to ensure compliance. Failure to comply can result in loss of license to practice, exclusion from participation in government-financed health care programs, or fines.

The influence of state government in the practice of physical therapy is continued in the next chapter. One's license to practice is issued by his or her individual state. Licensing-regulations and related laws are presented in Chapter 5.

REFERENCES

Aguilar L. Scandals jolting faith of investors. Denver Post, June 27, 2002.

Americans With Disabilities Act. A guide to disabilities rights laws, August, 2001. Available from http://ada.gov/cguide.htm. Accessed 3/08/03.

Centers of Medicare and Medicaid Services. Programs. Available from http://www.cms.hhs.gov. Accessed 2/01/03.

Department of Health and Human Services. Department of Health and Human Services organizational chart. Available from http://www.hhs.gov/about/orgchart.htm. Accessed 2/01/03a.

Department of Health and Human Services. Public Law 104-191. Available from http://aspc.dhhs.gov/adminsimp/Pl104191.htm. Accessed 2/01/03b.

Department of Health and Human Services. Testimony on physician self-referral regulations by Kathy Buto. Available from http://www.hhs.gov/asl/testify/t9905/3a.html. Accessed 2/01/03c.

Department of Health and Human Services. Office of the Inspector General. Report on health care fraud and abuse control program (HCFAC). Available from http://oig.hhs.gov/publications/hcfac.html. Accessed 2/01/03d.

Department of Labor. Major laws. Available from http://www.dol.gov/opa/aboutdol/lawsprog.htm. Accessed 3/09/03a.

Department of Labor. Freedom of Information Act. Available from http://www.dol.gov/dol/foia/main.htm. Accessed 3/09/03b.

Drug Enforcement Administration. Available from http://www.dea.gov. Accessed 2/01/03.

Engel DA, Calderone BJ, Lederman BG, Wesolik CJ, Warnick MP. Human resources issues. In Health Insurance Portability and Accountability Act of 1996 Public Law 104-191 Aug. 21, 1996. Available from http://aspe.dhhs.gov/admnsimp/pl104191.htm. Accessed 2/01/03.

Environmental Protection Agency. Freedom of Information Act. Available from http://www.epa.gov/foia. Accessed 2/01/03.

Longest BB Jr, Rakich JS, Darr K. Managing health services organizations and systems, 4th ed. Baltimore: Health Professions. 2000.

National Environmental Policy Act of 1969 (NEPA); (42 U.S.C. 4321-4347) available from http://ceq.eh.doe.gov/nepa. Accessed 2/01/03.

Nolan JR, Nolan-Haley JM. Black's law dictionary, 6th ed. St. Paul, MN: West. 1990.

Office of Civil Rights. Available from http://www.hhs.gov/ocr/hipaa/bkgrnd.html. Accessed 2/01/03.

Reardon TR. Health care fraud and abuse update: Report of the board of trustees of the AMA 25-I-97. 1997. Available from http://www.ama.org. Accessed 2/01/03.

Securities and Exchange Commission. Available from http://www.sec.gov/. Accessed 2/01/03.

Waggoner J, Fogarty TA. Scandals shred investors' faith: because of Enron, Andersen and rising gas prices, the public is more wary than ever of corporate America. USA Today, May 5, 2002.

MORE INFORMATION RELATED TO THIS CHAPTER

Up-to-date information about the various federal government Internet sites noted in this chapter may be found at the following sites:

CMS http://cms.hhs.gov.
DOL http://www.dol.gov.
FDA http://www.fda.gov.
FTC http.://www.ftc.gov/ftc/consumer.htm.
HRSA http://www.hrsa.gov.
NCD http://www.ncd.gov.
OSHA http://www.osha.gov.

For physical therapy–specific information on selected legal matters see the Web site of the American Physical Therapy Association (http://www.apta.org), practice and governmental affairs links.

An overview of visa information may be found at http://www.usaimmigrationservices.org. A course on Medicare and Medicaid fraud and abuse can be downloaded from http://www.cms.hhs.gov/medlearn/CBT-frau.asp. Information about state and local health care regulation is available through official government Web sites that can be located through http://firstgov.gov.

Chapter 5

General Legal Requirements and Principles

Contributed by D. Kathleen Lewis, MAPT, JD

Learning Objectives

1. Discuss the relevance of health care regulation to clinicians, support personnel and department managers.
2. Describe responsibilities of licensees, managers, licensing boards, and legislators relative to practice acts and rules and regulations.
3. Discuss legal concepts and principles.
4. Distinguish liability when actions are intentional from liability when actions are unintentional.
5. Apply legal concepts and principles to hypothetical cases.
6. Explore various consequences that may result from one incident or event and support your key points with information presented in this chapter.

Key Words

Assault, battery, breach, causation, censure, consequences, continuing competence, criminal law, damages, defamation, defendant, discovery, duty, emotional distress, expert witness, false imprisonment, Federated State Boards of Physical Therapy (FSBPT), fraud, infliction of emotional distress, intentional tort, invasion of privacy, lawsuit, libel, malpractice, multijurisdictional practice, National Practitioners' Data Bank (NPDB), negligence, plaintiff, practice act, professional liability insurance, revocation, rules and regulations, settlement, sexual misconduct, slander, statute of limitations, sunset laws, suspension, temporary license, tort, triggering event

Introduction: How Important Is the Law to Health Care?

Health care consists of six salient ingredients: law, ethics, evidence-based decision making, skillfully delivered services, education, and management. Historically, each of the six ingredients has been inherent in health care; however, the legal aspects have not always been as prominent as they are today. Figure 5.1 depicts the changing emphasis of these six ingredients over the past few centuries. A brief historical review of health care in the United States (U.S.) indicates that the primary ingredients change over time, depending on a variety of influencing factors.

For centuries, the dominant ingredient was clinical skill to treat the most acute conditions for survival. For example, malaria threatened progress along the Santa Fe Trail, as evidenced by Sir Ronald Ross's exclamation, "Malaria fever is important not only because of the misery it inflicts on mankind, but also because of the serious opposition it has always given to the march of civilization. No wild deserts, no savage races, no geographical

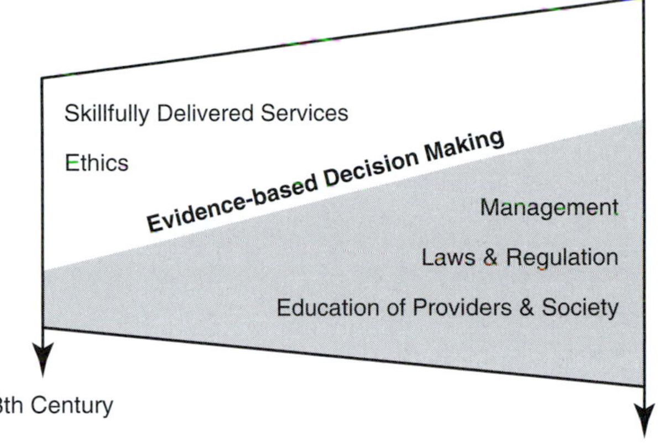

Figure 5.1. Graphical representation of changes in health care landscape. (Adapted with permission from D. Kathleen Lewis, Wichita, Kansas.)

difficulties have proved so inimical to civilization as this disease" (Hall, 1971, p. 82). Preventing death from disease and physical hazards was the utmost concern for pioneer health care providers. Since knowledge was limited, equipment was crude, and the number of trained care providers was meager, many medical successes may have been due to sheer luck. Survivors were thankful to be alive, with or without loss of limbs, vision, or hearing. Later, the focus of medicine turned to research for prevention and treatment of diseases. Successes in research resulted in a knowledge explosion, development of high-tech equipment, and advancements in clinical skills. Soon, education of providers and patients began taking center stage. During the 1966 Surgeon General's Workshop on Prevention of Disability From Arthritis, experts declared that too often patients had been advised by their care providers that nothing could be done for their disease; subsequently, most of them passively went home and regressed (U.S. Department of Health, Education and Welfare, 1966).

A primary recommendation from the surgeon general's workshop to increase funding for research and education on prevention of disabilities may have been a major turning point toward emphasis on research, education, and prevention of disabilities. In the mid 1960s, the health care industry began an era much like the Industrial Revolution, significant changes with many successes and failures. The Health Care Revolution Age continues to the present. At the beginning of this era, the importance of management, legal considerations, and education rapidly increased. Although some people claim the increasing emphasis on legal aspects has been related to an increasingly litigious society, research does not support this claim. According to the Harvard Medical Practice Study (Bodenheimer and Grumback, 2002), only 2% of patients who are injured as a result of medical malpractice actually file malpractice claims, and only half of those receive some compensation for their injuries. Legal considerations have become a major ingredient of health care as a result of government, politics, economics, demographics, technological advancements, the digital age, changes in health problems, and consumer advocacy. These influencing factors have resulted in a proliferation of regulation in health care for organizations and individual providers. The following list of primary changes is not exhaustive; it is but a sample of major regulatory changes.

1. Proliferating regulation of health care providers from only 13 licensed disciplines in all states in 1970 to more than 1,000 regulated in all states by early 1990s (Schmitt and Shimberg, 1996).
2. Increased socialized medicine with corresponding regulation, for example Medicare and Medicaid.
3. Rapid increases in health care costs, leading to increased state and federal regulations to control costs.
4. New and changing forms of business, for

example managed care, resulting in complex contractual arrangements.

5. Increased emphasis on individual rights, resulting in regulations to prevent discrimination, for example Americans With Disabilities Act, equality of care for those with cultural differences, and privacy of health records.
6. Ethical issues related to rationing health care, right to life, and technological advancements in genetic mapping.
7. The struggle to define quality of care, resulting in increased accreditation requirements, peer review, performance review of individual workers, continuing education, and specialty certifications.
8. Computer technology facilitating the ability to track organizations and individuals who provide poor quality of care and those who have committed fraud and abuse. Consequently, government funding has been increased to enforce existing laws, laws and regulations have increased, and published factual reports are readily available through the Internet.
9. The constant struggle between states' rights and federal regulation of health care matters, causing political conflict and sometimes confusion.

Today, health care may be one of the most regulated industries in our society. Practitioners simply cannot afford to ignore their legal responsibilities. The law ingredient for health care is a primary, essential ingredient, and juries or judges will not accept ignorance of the law as a defense for violations. This chapter will spotlight the more common legal aspects: licensure, negligence, malpractice, intentional torts, and some criminal law. Information in this chapter is not intended to be used for legal advice. Specific concerns should be addressed by seeking counsel from an attorney who is qualified to practice in the individual's jurisdiction.

Overview of the Legal System

As the health care landscape has changed (Fig. 5.1), practitioners are increasingly exposed to legal issues that affect the future of their profession and care of their patients. A general understanding of legal aspects is a *must learn* topic to prepare practitioners for meeting ethical and legal responsibilities. The connection between ethics and law is clear in the American Physical Therapy Association (APTA) Code of Ethics, Principle 3. This principle says that a physical therapist shall comply with laws and regulations governing physical therapy and shall strive to effect changes that benefit patients or clients (APTA, 2001a) (Chapter 6). The Guide for Conduct of the Affiliate Member, Standard 4 says that a physical therapist assistant shall comply with laws and regulations governing physical therapy (APTA, 2001b). Before exploring particular legal concepts, it is necessary to understand the basics of the legal system.

Figure 5.2 shows the primacy of constitutional laws. The U.S. Constitution and the state constitutions supersede all other laws and regulations. The U.S. court system is divided into three sections: criminal law, civil or tort law, and administrative law. Criminal charges are brought against individuals or groups by the government, federal or state. Civil or tort (French for wrong) law claims are brought by individuals, groups, or the state to recover damages when a tort has been committed against a person or property. Administrative law claims are brought against individuals or groups by administrative agencies, for example licensing boards, which were created by the government to administer and enforce a particular set of statutes. Criminal, civil (tort), and administrative law violations can coexist with any one set of facts (Fig. 5.3). For example, a practitioner who has been charged with fraud and abuse of Medicare may face civil, criminal, and administrative charges.

This practitioner may be found legally accountable in one or two of the charges but not a third. How can this happen? First, the burden of proof in a criminal case, where one's liberty and perhaps one's life are at stake, is much greater than when one's finances and license are at stake. In criminal cases the burden of proof is beyond a reasonable doubt, whereas civil and administrative cases require

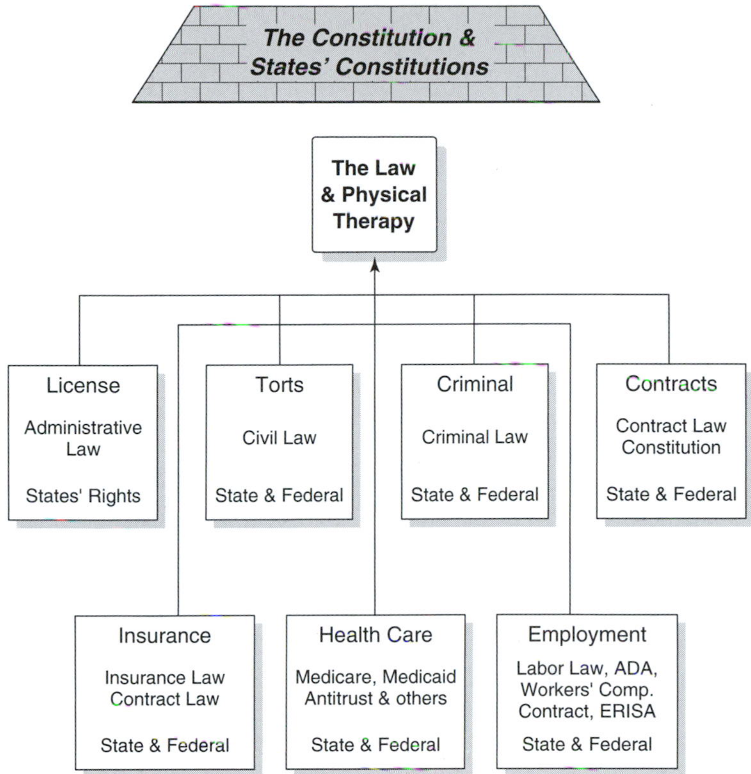

Figure 5.2. Constitutional laws supersede all other laws and regulations. (Adapted with permission from D. Kathleen Lewis, Wichita, Kansas.)

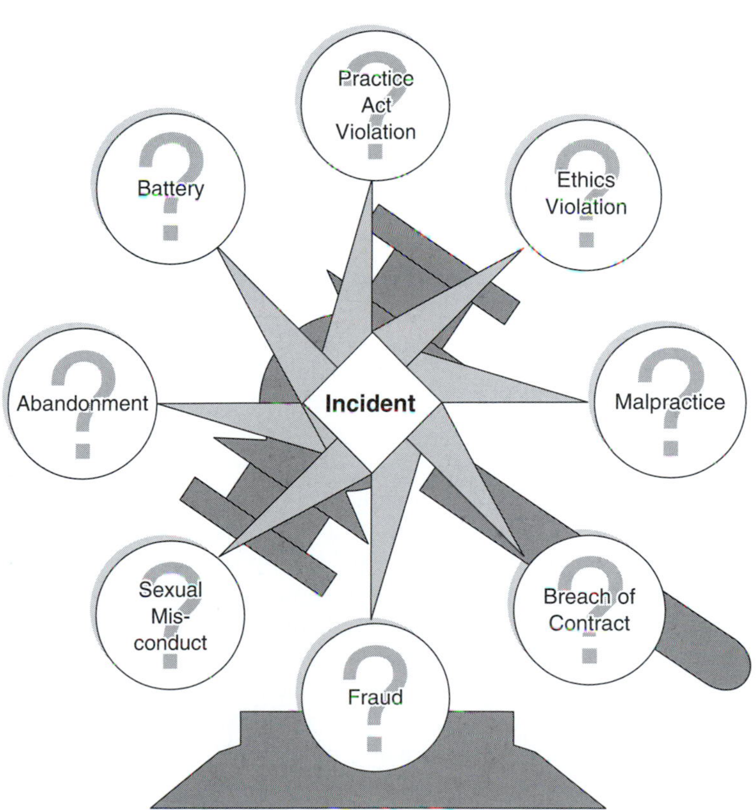

Figure 5.3. One incident, multiple legal concerns. (Adapted with permission from D. Kathleen Lewis, Wichita, Kansas.)

only a "preponderance of" or "substantial" evidence. If death is a result of negligent care, it is possible for a practitioner to be charged with negligent homicide or manslaughter (criminal, for loss of liberty), malpractice (civil, for monetary damages), and licensure violations (administrative law, for limited or loss of practice privileges).

Administrative Law: Licensure, a Fundamental Requirement

With few exceptions, health care providers must be licensed to provide reimbursable clinical services. A license is evidence that the state has given qualified individuals a privilege to practice within certain parameters as written in the state law (**practice act**). No one is guaranteed a license; qualified individuals must apply for a license and show evidence that they have met the state's qualifications. (Unless otherwise stated, use of the terms *license*, *licensed*, and *licensee* in this chapter include state-granted registration and certification). After a license has been granted, a licensee must meet his or her responsibilities as stated in the practice act and corresponding regulations. When a licensee fails to meet those responsibilities, the privileges to practice may be limited, temporarily suspended, or permanently withdrawn (revoked).

Practice Acts: Enactment and Enforcement

Each state reserves the right to pass laws for protection of residents within the state (constitutional provisions for states' rights). Licensure laws are enacted through each state's legislative process to protect residents within the state from incompetent and unscrupulous health care practitioners. Health care providers may influence laws that govern their respective practices by persuading legislators to sponsor legislative changes or defeat unfavorable bills. However, legislators, as the lawmakers, ultimately control changes in the law by voting for or against licensure bills. Typically, a governing board is granted authority in the practice act to issue and renew licenses to qualified individuals, discipline licensees who have not complied with the practice act, and adopt **rules** and **regulations** necessary for administration of the practice act. Rules and regulations have the same effect as the law (practice act); therefore, these should be reviewed and followed with as much diligence as the practice act.

Enforcement of practice acts is unlike civil and criminal law procedures, in which either a jury or a judge decides the case. The state boards follow administrative law procedures, which allow decisions to be made by a hearing panel, generally composed of health care professionals and public representatives. Administrative law procedures do not provide the same degree of protection for the accused party: strict rules of evidence are not required; courts will not overturn a board's decision unless the hearing panel has violated fundamental rights or the regulation may be unconstitutional; and the accused licensee may waive appeal rights simply by failing to submit timely responses.

Responsibilities of Licensees

Licensees are responsible for reading and understanding the practice act, rules, and regulations. Table 5.1 may be copied and answered for easy reference to frequently needed detailed information. Practice acts for all jurisdictions and some regulations may be accessed at http://www.fsbpt.org, http://www.apta.org. http:///or http://www.washlaw.edu. Both the practice act and regulations must be studied for accurate and thorough completion of Table 5.1.

Although practice acts vary dramatically among jurisdictions, these are common responsibilities for individual licensees:

- Practice within parameters of the law (practice act and corresponding regulations)
- Send written notification to the board when personal mailing address changes
- Renew license by the specified deadline whether or not notice of renewal has been received

Table 5.1 A Quick Reference to Licensure Details Of Your Jurisdiction

Name of licensing board
Address of licensing board
Telephone and fax numbers of licensing board
URL of the board's Web site
Licensure renewal date
Renewal requirements: number of continuing education units and time frame; jurisprudence examination, fees
Direct access: special requirements and limitations
Required supervision ratio of PTs to PTAs
Type and definition of supervision requirements for PTAs
Type of supervision requirements for aides and other ancillary personnel
Type and definition of supervision requirements for special circumstances, e.g., temporary licenses, graduate students
Practice privileges with additional requirements or limitations, e.g., 2 years' experience to supervise one who has a temporary license or proof of additional training for electromyography
Specific required clinical responsibilities, e.g., examination of patients performed only by physical therapists
Specific limitations or exclusions
List grounds for denial or disciplinary actions
Other important information

PT, physical therapist; PTA, physical therapist assistant.

- Meet requirements for licensure renewal and submit evidence per board requirements
- Pay required application and renewal fees
- Be truthful to the licensing board

Responsibilities of Department Managers

The department manager should not assume that employees have complied with licensure requirements. Managers should implement procedures to ensure that personnel they are responsible for are practicing in accordance with licensure requirements of accrediting agencies, third-party payers, other regulating agencies, and the organization's own policies. With numerous requirements and deadlines, the task can be onerous. Table 5.2 provides a general checklist for broad assessment of a department's tracking and use of licensure information.

Responsibilities of the Licensing Board

All licensing boards are responsible for protecting the public against incompetent and unscrupulous practitioners. They are granted statutory authority to deny a license when an applicant does not meet the required qualifications and take disciplinary action against licensees who have violated the practice act or rules and regulations. These are examples of disciplinary actions and corresponding sanctions:

1. The board suspended a physical therapist's license for 30 days because the board found that the therapist had falsified patient records (Texas Board of Physical Therapy Examiners, 2001).
2. Several physical therapists who were working in unregistered facilities had their licenses suspended for several months (Texas Board of Physical Therapy Examiners, 2001).
3. When the board found evidence that a physical therapist allowed aides to treat patients without supervision, the therapist's license was suspended for 45 days, and the therapist was required to take a number of tutorial education hours (Texas Board of Physical Therapy Examiners, 2001).
4. In separate cases, a board determined that a physical therapist and a physical therapist assistant had practiced in a manner detrimental to public health and welfare when their respective patients were burned

Table 5.2 Licensure Checklist for Managers

Criteria	*Yes*	*No*
All physical therapists have a valid license from the jurisdiction of the clinic.	☐	☐
All physical therapist assistants have a valid license from the jurisdiction of the clinic (if licensure is available in the state).		
All temporary personnel, e.g., contract therapists, have provided a copy of a valid license and appropriate measures have been taken to verify authentication of the license.	☐	☐
Copies of all departmental licenses are displayed in a public place. (Essential if required by the practice act or an accrediting agency. Advisable for marketing if not required.)	☐	☐
Job descriptions for PTs and PTAs are congruent with the jurisdiction's practice act. It is recommended that the job descriptions include limitations as well as responsibilities.	☐	☐
Job descriptions for ancillary personnel (for example, aides, massage therapists, athletic trainers, exercise physiologists) are congruent with the jurisdiction's practice act. It is recommended that the job descriptions include limitations as well as responsibilities.	☐	☐
There is a mechanism to track licensure renewal requirements.	☐	☐
Performance appraisal instruments and mechanisms are congruent with licensure requirements and limitations.	☐	☐
Other.	☐	☐

by negligent application of modalities (Texas Board of Physical Therapy Examiners, 2001).

5. When the **State Boards of Physical Therapy (FSBPT)** learned about widespread cheating efforts by physical therapy students in preparation for taking the licensure examination, two individuals were denied access to sit for the National Physical Therapist Examination and a third individual's license was withheld pending further investigation. Others may be implicated subsequent to findings throughout the investigation (Federation of State Boards of Physical Therapy, 2002).
6. In one jurisdiction where the law limited the number of times an applicant could take the licensure examination, the board refused to allow a physical therapist assistant who had failed the licensure examination three times to sit for the examination a fourth time. The board's decision was upheld by this state's appellate court (American Health Lawyers Association, 2002a).

Regulating Professional Conduct

Although practice acts may change slowly, grounds for disciplinary actions eventually change as the health care industry and society change. Examples of these changes over several decades are regulation of moral conduct, advertising, consumer rights to information about practitioners, and licensees' rights throughout investigations, hearings, and appeals. In the early 1900s, practice acts had strict codes of moral conduct. About mid to late 1960, moral conduct outside the workplace came to be considered personal, and many references to such personal matters were stricken from regulations. In recent years, society has recognized problems with **sexual misconduct** by health care practitioners (Chapter 33). In response to societies' dismay and concern, practice acts and codes of professional conduct have been revised to prohibit sexual relationships and activities between practitioners and their clients. These are some examples of regulations about professional conduct:

- APTA Guide for Professional Conduct 2.1.C, Patient/Physical Therapist Relationship. A physical therapist shall not engage in any sexual relationship or activity, whether consensual or nonconsensual, with any patient while a physical therapist/patient relationship exists (APTA, 2001a).

- APTA Guide for Conduct of the Affiliate Member 2.1.E. A physical therapist assistant shall not engage in any sexual relationship or activity, whether consensual or nonconsensual, with any patient entrusted to his/her care (APTA, 2001b).
- Texas Practice Act: §322.4, Practicing in a Manner Detrimental to the Public Health and Welfare. Engaging in sexual contact with a patient/client as the result of the patient/client relationship.
- Arizona Practice Act, Section 10. Engaging in sexual misconduct. For the purpose of this paragraph "sexual misconduct" includes: (a) Engaging in or soliciting sexual relationships, whether consensual or nonconsensual, while a provider–patient relationship exists. (b) Making sexual advances, requesting sexual favors ***or*** engaging in ***other verbal conduct*** or physical contact of a sexual nature with patients. (c) ***Intentionally viewing*** a completely or partially disrobed patient in the course of treatment if the viewing is not related to patient diagnosis or treatment under current practice standards.
- California, Section 2660.1. A patient, client, or customer of a licentiate under this chapter is conclusively presumed to be incapable of giving free, full, and informed consent to any sexual activity which is a violation of Section 726. The commission of ***any act of sexual*** abuse, misconduct, ***or relations*** with a ***patient***, ***client***, or ***customer*** constitutes unprofessional conduct and grounds for disciplinary action for any person licensed under this division, under any initiative act referred to in this division and under Chapter 17 (commencing with Section 9000) of Division 3.
- During the past 2 decades, society has influenced legislative changes related to use of drugs and alcohol. Professional licenses are affected by these regulatory changes, and boards are acting accordingly. When a licensee has a driving under the influence (DUI) felony conviction, the Texas Physical Therapy Board has suspended licenses for approximately 30 days, with 5 to 6 years' probation (Texas Board of Physical Therapy Examiners, 2001). In February 2002, the California Court of Appeals upheld the Medical Board of California decision to revoke a physician's license. The court stated that the two misdemeanor convictions for reckless driving involving alcohol were conclusive evidence of unprofessional conduct. Furthermore, the court found substantial legal authority that conduct occurring outside the practice of medicine may reflect on a licensee's fitness and qualifications, thus forming the basis for disciplinary action (American Health Lawyers Association, 2002b).

Additional Consequences to Licensure Disciplinary Investigations and Actions

Reverberations of a complaint against a licensee (Fig 5.3) may result in additional predicaments ranging from effects on future employment to criminal investigations. Sometimes additional legal concerns arise when a board's investigation reveals issues other than those described in the initial complaint against the licensee. In Cohan versus Duncan-Poitier, a patient complained to the Dental Board of New York that Cohan, a dentist, refused to provide the patient with his treatment charts and x-ray films. In addition to finding evidence to substantiate the patient's complaint, the board's investigation revealed that the dentist had submitted false and fraudulent insurance claims and had failed to retain patients' records for the legally required time.

Another reverberation is the impact from laws other than the practice act requiring licensing boards to report certain information about licensees. In response to consumers' demand for easy access to information about licensed professionals, a few states passed laws requiring boards to post licensure and disciplinary actions on the Internet. The type and amount of information about licensees is quite different from state to state. In the near future, more states will probably be posting licensure information on the Internet. Although the legislative intent for posting licensure information is to protect the public, practitioners should be proactive when their state is considering legislation to provide profile information to the public. In particular, the legislation should include procedures for ensuring that information is accurate and mechanisms are available to correct errors. To see what a few states currently post about licensed physical therapists and physical therapist assistants see these sites:

- Massachusetts at http://www.state.ma.us/reg/boards/ah/
- Florida at http://www.doh.state.fl.us/mqa/
- New York at http://www.op.nysed.gov/pt.htm
- Texas for licensure verification at http://www.ecptote.state.tx.us/

Current and Future Changes to Licensure Regulation

Numerous external and internal factors are likely to result in licensure regulatory changes of physical therapists, physical therapist assistants, and other health care providers. Some jurisdictions will be affected sooner than others, so practitioners who are observant about legislative changes and trends in other jurisdictions will be prepared to advocate for effective legislative changes and to oppose less effective legislative changes in their respective jurisdictions.

- **Temporary licenses**: Since licensing boards have been able to expedite issuance of licenses with the advent of electronic administration and scoring of examinations, the FSBPT is encouraging all jurisdictions to eliminate temporary licenses. Some states have eliminated temporary licenses, while many others are waiting for more favorable times before opening their practice acts.
- Continuing education versus **continuing competence**: Proponents of continuing education requirements for licensure renewal claim that continuing education is the best available method to ensure that practitioners make use of current research and technology. Jurisdictions that require continuing education for licensure renewal have not been able to show conclusive evidence that passive learning activities is sufficient evidence that practitioners remain competent in their respective areas of practice (Finocchio, Dowen, Blick, Gragnola, 1998). Continuing competence is a topic that most people agree is important for every health care provider; however, few agree on a fair, valid assessment method because the topic has an abundance of onerous issues (Swift, 1999).
- **Sunset laws**: Some states have sunset laws that require state regulatory bodies to provide convincing data that the actual function of the regulatory body is a benefit to the public. Generally sunset laws have provisions to eliminate boards that cannot provide convincing evidence that they are effectively protecting the public from incompetent practitioners. Boards and state APTA chapters who have undergone sunset review face the review with trepidation. In the mid 1980s, the physical therapy board in Colorado underwent intense scrutiny when it was reviewed by the legislature. Some regulatory changes resulting from Colorado's sunset review include changes in board structures, establishment of an oversight body, more aggressive disciplinary activities, and increased budgets to provide boards with adequate support to improve effectiveness (Douglas, 1999).
- National licensure or **multijurisdictional practice**: When licensees move to another jurisdiction, getting a new license is often cumbersome, time consuming, and expensive. Numerous influential people and organizations suggest that defects in the licensure system could be remedied by some type of national oversight or national legislation to facilitate professional mobility and practice across state lines (Puskin, 1999; Pew Commission, 1998). There have been numerous attempts at the federal level to allow practice across state lines, particularly to provide services to residents in remote geographical areas (Puskin, 1999). The National Council of State Boards of Nursing has successfully lobbied for states to enact legislation for mutual recognition compacts. These compacts allow nurses to have one license to practice in member states of the compact. By January 2002, 14 states had enacted compact laws for nurses and 5 states had pending legislation. On

July 18, 2002, Senate Bill 2750 was introduced in the 107th Congress to *"encourage and facilitate the adoption of State provisions allowing for multistate practitioner licensure across State lines."*

Other professions are also studying this issue. In January 2001 the California Supreme Court appointed an advisory task force on multijurisdictional practice to assess whether and in what circumstances attorneys licensed to practice in other jurisdictions should be permitted to practice law in California. In the final report of January 7, 2002, the task force recommended that two categories of out-of-state attorneys be allowed to practice law in California through a special registration process (California Supreme Court, 2002). The American Bar Association and state bar associations have established committees to study multijurisdictional practice (National Council of State Boards of Nursing, 2002). State laws are distinctly different from one state to another, whereas standards for health care are arguably approaching national standards. If state bar associations eventually allow multijurisdictional practice under certain circumstances, will health care regulatory bodies do likewise?

- **Practitioner profiles**: Among regulatory policy changes suggested by University of California, San Francisco Center for the Health Professions, report cards on individual practitioners should be made public by allowing boards to cooperate with public and private organizations in collecting data to identify a standard health personnel data set (Gragnola and Stone, 1997). Third-party payers have been collecting profile data on health care providers for several years; however, data from these various resources have not yet been merged to one common data set.
- **Professional liability insurance** for licensure renewal: In 2002 at least one state (Pennsylvania) passed a law requiring physical therapists to carry professional liability insurance. A few other states are considering this as a requirement for licensure.

These are only a few of the changes on the horizon about regulation of health care providers. Only one prediction can be made from these points: regulatory changes will continue to occur in the near and distant future.

Civil Law: Torts

Society protects individuals from wrongful acts of others by allowing those who are wronged to file lawsuits and collect monetary awards as compensation for the damages or seek other remedies as permitted by law. There are two general types of **torts**: negligent and intentional.

- **Negligence**: Negligence is defined as omission (or commission) of an act that a reasonable prudent person would (or would not) do under given circumstances. Professional negligence, also called ***malpractice***, occurs when the alleged wrongdoer is a professional and the requisite action is within the scope of practice, thus requiring the knowledge and skills of a professional.
- **Intentional tort**: An intentional tort is defined as an act that is intentionally committed knowing that harm is a likely result. These are some common examples of intentional torts:
  1. **Assault and battery**: Assault is a threat to touch another without consent; battery is intentional touching of another without his or her consent (Chapter 33). Touching without consent includes touching tangible items that are considered to be an extension of the person, for example a patient's clothing, crutches, or wheelchair.
  2. **False imprisonment**: confinement of a person to the extent that there is no reasonable exit and physical restraint is not necessary. There are special regulations on use of restraints, and most organizations have policies and procedures about use of restraints which should be heeded. The Nursing Home Reform Law (OBRA) of 1987 and Medicare and Medicaid regulations 42 CFR §483.13(a) (1990) prohibit use of restraints (chemical and mechanical, for example vests,

belts, mitts, geriatric chairs, gates, and side rails) for purposes of discipline or convenience.

3. **Defamation**: communication to a third party or parties that holds a person up to scorn and ridicule. Oral defamation is **slander**; written defamation is **libel**.
4. **Fraud**: intentional misrepresentation in a manner that could cause harm.
5. **Invasion of privacy**: intentional deprivation of one's right to be left alone.
6. **Infliction of emotional distress**: intentional actions or omissions that would cause a reasonable person to suffer emotional trauma.

Examples of negligence, intentional torts, and criminal violations are listed in Table 5.3.

Other chapters in this book (Chapters 6 and 9) discuss the importance of ethical conduct and organizations' policies and procedures that strive for quality of care (Chapter 10); they will also help avoid claims such as those represented in Table 5.3. Each of the potential causes of action in Table 5.3 requires a litigant to prove specific elements, although there may be sufficient overlap that one incident may provoke a litigant to file several causes of action in one suit (Fig. 5.3) and to file suit against all potential defendants.

Negligence: Malpractice and Ordinary Negligence

Negligence consists of four elements, each of which must be proved by the party filing a negligence claim.

- **Duty**: There was a *duty* owed to a person. A legal duty is established whenever a

Table 5.3 Legal Actions And Examples

Legal Actions	***Examples***
Ordinary negligence	After removal of an ice pack from a patient's neck, water from the bag drips on the floor, leaving a slippery area. While getting dressed, the patient slips on the water, resulting in exacerbation of neck pain.
Malpractice (professional negligence)	Hot packs are applied to a patient with impaired circulation and sensation. No additional precautionary measures are taken. The hot pack burns the patient.
Product liability	Treadmill stop switch fails to function properly, causing a patient to fall and fracture an ankle. An investigation reveals that the product is defective in design or manufacture.
Premises liability	The railing on the steps of a pool stops short of the last two steps into the pool. While entering the pool, a patient slips on the last step, resulting in a back injury.
Battery	A patient is persistent in refusing treatment, but the physical therapist or physical therapist assistant proceeds to stretch the patient's hamstrings. The patient does *not* suffer any physical harm.
Invasion of privacy; negligent intentional infliction of emotional distress	A patient is a plaintiff in a lawsuit about an automobile accident. A health care facility releases all medical records of the plaintiff to an attorney for the defendant. Among the released records are several pages marked "Confidential. Do NOT release without specific authorized consent." These confidential records disclose positive results of the patient's HIV test and have no relevance to the auto accident case.
Defamation	A health care provider writes in a patient's record that another health care provider did not return a call (libel). A health care provider indirectly or directly advises a patient that his or her physician was incompetent (slander).
Fraud	A health care provider promises that a care plan will cure a patient but knows that it will not (intentional tort). A health care provider knowingly bills Medicare or another third-party payer for services to a group of patients although those services were never rendered, nor was there any intention to render those services (criminal).

health care facility or provider undertakes care or treatment of a patient. A claimant must be able to demonstrate that there was an active patient–therapist relationship at the time of the alleged incident. Employers of health care providers have a duty to supervise employees, hire qualified employees, and monitor employees' performance. Courts reasoned that these duties and the fact that employers can recover costs of lawsuits by increasing the price of goods and services would better serve public policy than having injured plaintiffs who may receive nothing for their damages. Two legal theories, respondeat superior (let the master answer) and corporate liability, were created from the courts' reasoning to allow an injured plaintiff to file suit against employers and supervisors.

- **Breach**: The duty was not met, either by failure to act (an omission) or by failing to meet the standard of care for the circumstance at the time. The standard of care is determined by what a reasonable professional would have done under like or similar circumstances. The Guide to Physical Therapist Practice (APTA, 2001a), classical textbooks, research that was known at the time, the organization's policies and procedures, and documentation about the patient's care are all scrutinized to determine whether the standard of care was met.
- **Damages**: The party who was owed a duty incurred damages. Damages are generally divided into direct, indirect, and punitive. Direct damages include lost earnings and current and future medical expenses. Indirect expenses may include a value for pain, emotional distress, and loss of consortium (services performed by a domestic partner, for example companionship, homemaking). Punitive damages may be added to an award when a provider's conduct was intentionally harmful or so grossly negligent that it was wanton and willful disregard for the standard of care.
- **Causation**: The breach of duty caused injury or there was a causal connection between the breach and the damages. Proving that there was a causal connection between the breach and damages can be tricky; however, a sympathetic jury may base its decision on some minor association.

Malpractice is a special type of negligence that occurs when the actions in question require the knowledge and skill of a professional. The same four elements are required for proof in a malpractice case; however, expert testimony is required because the ordinary person is not capable of determining what the professional standard of care should be. However, professional negligence (malpractice) *is NOT*:

- A bad result
- Choice of one treatment when another is available
- Failure to cure
- An error in judgment (hindsight is always 20:20)
- Intentional harm

The four elements are easier to understand if you review a hypothetical case (Table 5.4) that is based on an actual case.

In this case, Mrs. D., the **plaintiff** (the party who sues), bears the burden of proving all four elements. If she fails to prove any one of the elements, the defendant or defendants will prevail and avoid liability. Table 5.4 suggests that breach and causation are the primary elements on which the physical therapist's attorney, in collaboration with the defendant physical therapist, should focus defense efforts. The physical therapist will attempt to prove that he or she did not breach the standard of care by presenting thorough, timely, objective documentation supporting the therapist's claim that the interventions were appropriate for this patient in the given circumstances (for example the patient's rate of recovery and tolerance to the treatment regimen). Evidence provided by an expert witness for the physical therapist should be easy for the jury to understand; the expert's testimony should be credible; and information provided by the expert should indicate that the standard of care provided by the therapist was within acceptable professional standards for this patient at the time of the incident and considering all circumstances at the time care was rendered. The physical therapist's testimony must be credible, for example demeanor confident but not

Table 5.4 Malpractice Case Example

Case facts: Mrs. D. and her husband, H. D., were seriously injured in a motorcycle accident. Dr. B. repaired Mrs. D.'s femoral shaft fracture by inserting a rod and stabilizing the rod with a plate and screws. Mrs. D. was discharged from the hospital and received physical therapy at home. About 8 weeks after surgery, she appeared to be progressing with a normal course of recovery. Dr. B. advised the physical therapist to be "more vigorous" with therapy. Shortly thereafter, during one of her therapy sessions, Mrs. D. heard a loud pop when the physical therapist was forcefully bending her knee. Later it was discovered that the rod broke when Mrs. D. heard the pop. She had to undergo another surgery when the surgeon removed the broken rod and replaced it with a larger rod.

Duty	Both the doctor and the physical therapist owed Mrs. D. a duty as soon as the patient–provider relationship was established. *Duty for the doctor and physical therapist is not an issue in this case. Duty for employers of the doctor and physical therapist may be an issue.*
Breach	Dr. B. may have breached his duty by performing substandard surgical procedures. The physical therapist may have breached his or her duty by performing substandard physical therapy. (In this case, the amount of force, the direction of force, the duration of force, and location of stabilization may attribute to substandard care.) *Breach of a duty and who breached a duty are issues in this case.*
Damages	As a result of the rod breaking, Mrs. D. had to undergo a second surgery, which resulted in a significantly greater recovery time. *The fact that Mrs. D. had damages is not an issue in this case; however, the amount of damages will be an issue if Mrs. D. prevails in her lawsuit.*
Causation	Since rods do not ordinarily break, the manufacturer of the rod may have produced a defective product, or the design of the rod may have been defective. If so, Mrs. D. could not prove that any possible breach by either Dr. B. or the physical therapist caused the rod to break. If the surgical procedure was substandard, for example insertion of a rod that was too small for the patient, Dr. B.'s breach may be the cause of the rod breaking. If the physical therapist did not meet the standard of care when applying force to Mrs. D.'s leg, the therapist's breach may have been the cause of damage to Mrs. D. A battle of the experts during trial may convince a jury that more than one defendant (Dr. B., the physical therapist, and/or the product manufacturer) were partially at fault. *Causation is an issue in this case.*

arrogant, testimony consistent with documentation and his or her deposition, the testimony truthful and reflecting that the therapist is competent. If the therapist can prevail at proving the standard of care was met, Mrs. D. will have failed at proving one of the four elements (Fig. 5.4, second small diagram showing the missing breach element). If, however, the therapist did not meet the standard of care, this is not yet a lost cause. For example, fractures can occur as a result of osteoporosis or in this case a defective rod or a negligent surgical procedure, so the therapist should also focus on causation of Mrs. D.'s damages.

If the physical therapist does not present clear and convincing evidence that the standard of care was met, a huge challenge remains to avoid liability. The therapist will need to prove that breaching the standard of care did not cause Mrs. D.'s damages. Many jurisdictions today will prorate fault when there are multiple defendants and each of those defendants contributed to the damages. In this case, the physical therapist may be found 51% at fault, the surgeon found 49% at fault, and the manufacturer not at fault for a $200,000 award. Some jurisdictions will prorate the damages based on the percentage of fault, the physical therapist owing $102,000 and the surgeon owing $98,000.

Some jurisdictions will allow the prevailing plaintiff to collect all damages from a defendant who is 50% or more at fault (called joint and several liability). In this example, if the therapist had liability insurance in excess of the award but the surgeon was underinsured or had no insurance, Mrs. D. may collect the entire award from the physical thera-

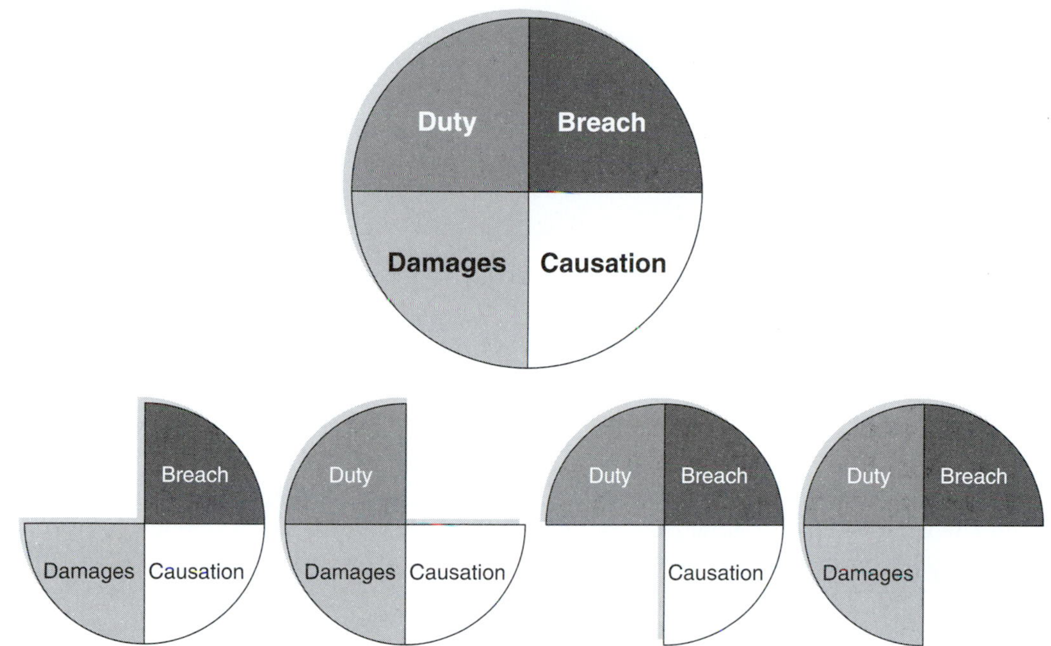

Figure 5.4. Elements that a plaintiff must prove to prevail in a negligence or malpractice case. If a defendant is able to disprove any one of the four elements, the defendant will prevail and avoid liability. (Adapted with permission from D. Kathleen Lewis, Wichita, Kansas.)

pist. The surgeon would remain liable, but the physical therapist would have to file a claim against the surgeon to collect the $98,000. Providers should be cautious about purchasing excessive limits of liability insurance, particularly in jurisdictions with joint and several liability laws (Lewis, 1994).

In jurisdictions with contributory negligence laws, a finding that a plaintiff who contributes 50% or more fault will be barred from receiving any damages. The most credible and strongest resource of evidence when contributory negligence is an issue will be the patient's record; therefore, care providers should accurately and objectively document information such as missed appointments or other evidence indicating that the patient may contribute to damages.

Anatomy of a Malpractice Suit

Every **lawsuit** begins with a triggering event. The trigger may be as simple as a misunderstanding, a dissatisfied client, an unusual sign or symptom, an accident, or a clearly defined injury resulting from substandard care. The course of events in a lawsuit are depicted in Figure 5.5; however, additional events, such as appeals, lawsuits evolving from the original suit, and licensure or other regulatory investigation, can follow trial court decisions. From beginning to end, a lawsuit can last for 7 years or more, which often seems like an eternity to the involved parties. Clearly, good practice and good ethics are worthwhile objectives for any health care provider, but even the best cannot be certain that they will never be sued. Some actions can detour lawsuits or decrease liability. As you read about the course of events in a lawsuit, consider dissecting a hypothetical case.

A Case Example

A month after diskectomy, a 39-year-old man reported to physical therapy for examination and treatment. Interventions were

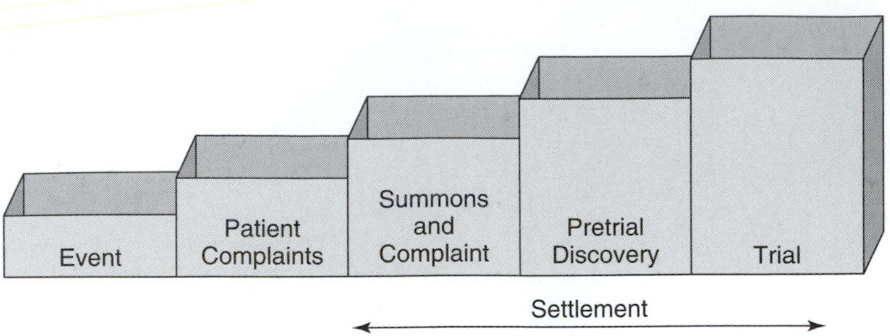

Figure 5.5. Anatomy of a lawsuit: As the suit progresses through these stages, legal costs increase, personal and professional stresses often increase, and more facts that may or may not be favorable are discovered. (Adapted with permission from D. Kathleen Lewis, Wichita, Kansas.)

range-of-motion exercises, manual therapy, treadmill work, and instructions on a home exercise regimen. Three days after his fourth visit, the patient called the clinic with concern about low back pain and radicular symptoms. The physical therapist advised him to discontinue the exercises and contact his physician. The patient filed suit against the physical therapist, alleging severe disc herniation secondary to physical therapy interventions that were "contraindicated."

The Event

As soon as an event occurs, the care provider should take immediate action to remedy the situation. Research shows that only 2% of patients who are injured as a result of malpractice actually file a claim, and only half of this 2% receive compensation for injuries (Bodenheimer and Grumback, 2002). Dissatisfied clients are more likely to file a lawsuit than satisfied clients, and satisfied clients are more likely to return for care than dissatisfied clients. Taking appropriate actions immediately after an event is not only good risk management, it is good business.

In this case, the physical therapist should have documented specific objective information about the patient's reported complaints and advice to the patient. Subsequently, the therapist should have telephoned the patient's physician with this information and followed up with a written memorandum to the physician (Lewis, 2002). The care provider should notify the clinic's risk manager and the provider's liability insurance carrier when (1) a patient voices concern about an event; (2) the patient, a family member, or an attorney places a phone call after treatment or after dismissal from care; or (3) the patient, a family member, or an attorney sends a letter to the clinic about the event.

Summons and Complaint

A lawsuit is formally initiated when two specific legal documents (a summons and a complaint) are filed with the court by the patient or his or her attorney. The summons names the defendant (or defendants), the plaintiff, the jurisdiction of the lawsuit, and when and where the named defendant should appear. The complaint gives detail about the case against the defendant and outlines the basis of the suit, including how the elements were fulfilled. Both the summons and complaint must be given to the defendant and filed in a court in the jurisdiction where the alleged malpractice occurred. Generally, these documents are delivered (called service of process) to defendant by a sheriff or other law official. The deadline (statute of limitations) for filing the summons and complaint varies from state to state but is generally within 2 years from the date of the negligent action or omission and may be 3 years from the date of an intentional tort. Special circumstances, for example if the patient is a minor or the plaintiff could not have known that he or she was a victim of malpractice within the 2-year time limit, extend the statute of limitations.

Upon receipt of the summons and complaint, the defendant feels fear, worry, mental and physical fatigue, and embarrassment. It is important to avoid allowing these emotions to control decisions and actions. The defendant should immediately:

1. Notify his or her insurance carrier and employer
2. Review all records
3. Preserve all records

The time limit for responding to the complaint, generally about 30 days, is not long considering that the defendant must meet with legal counsel and the attorney must prepare a response with plausible defenses. The defendant *should* NOT:

- Distribute original records without advice from legal counsel
- Make changes in the records
- Converse about the case with colleagues, family, or friends

The plaintiff's attorney can depose (take testimony) from anyone who knows about the case. Therefore, defendants who talk about the case with others risk the opponent getting access to unintended or misconstrued admissions or inconsistent statements.

Pretrial Discovery

During pretrial **discovery**, both parties to the suit (defendant and plaintiff), research relevant facts to be presented to the court. Discovery consists of oral depositions, written depositions (interrogatories), and requests for production of records, including medical records, office calendars, diaries, correspondence, and personal notes. Oral depositions are taken under oath in the presence of a court reporter. The plaintiff's attorney will attempt to gather admissions and inconsistencies that support the plaintiff's case. The deposed party will be given a transcript of the deposition to review, correct any errors, and sign. Once the transcript is signed, the document is sworn testimony.

Physical therapists and their assistants may be deposed as fact witnesses as well as when they are named defendants in a lawsuit. It is important to be cautious about etiquette and demeanor during depositions and the trial. That is, be well groomed, alert, and professional. The legal process is adversary: opposing counsel often attempts to catch the defendant off guard by creating a particular emotional state to elicit responses. It is important that defendants avoid getting angry, show respect for the opposing attorney, always answer questions honestly, answer only the question being asked, and follow advice from his or her attorney.

The Trial

The trial begins with opening statements by attorneys for the plaintiff and defendant. These statements outline the case and respective arguments. The trial is adversarial, with each side trying to persuade the jury in its favor. Credibility of the parties and witnesses throughout presentation of the evidence can result in crucial turning points for or against the parties. If judgment is in favor of the plaintiff in a malpractice case, the defendant may face several consequences:

- **Financial** consequences: direct damages to the plaintiff for lost earnings and current and future medical expenses; indirect damages for pain, emotional distress, and loss of consortium; punitive damages if the defendant's conduct was gross negligence. Punitive damages may not be covered by malpractice insurance.
- **Employment** consequences: unusual carelessness, intentional actions, or gross negligence may result in disciplinary action or dismissal.
- **Licensure** consequences: licensure boards may investigate and take disciplinary action, for example, **censure**, **suspension**, or **revocation**.
- **National Practitioners' Data Bank (NPDB)**: The Health Care Quality Improvement Act (HCQIA) of 1986, which established the NPDB, requires that health care entities, insurance carriers, and state licensing boards report certain information to the NPDB (Chapter 3).

Settlement

Settlement is an option until a case goes to trial. The defendant may fear settling a case, thinking that settlement is an admission of fault. A settlement is not an admission of fault. There are two primary advantages of settlement: (1) It is less expensive than paying for attorneys, expert witnesses, and court costs throughout a lengthy process. (2) A settlement amount may be significantly less than a jury might award, particularly when there is a sympathetic plaintiff and/or the jury does not view the defendant's evidence as credible.

Differences Between Intentional Torts and Malpractice

Malpractice suits often draw more attention from the news media and health care practitioners than intentional torts. Newscasters focus on newsworthy reports, for example multimillion dollar malpractice awards, a plaintiff who is considered attention-grabbing, or a case that represents a social issue. Health care practitioners should avoid devising practice decisions and actions based solely on these featured stories. Those who do will tend to practice defensively and overlook other legal responsibilities. In many respects, the hazards and consequences of intentional torts are more detrimental than those of negligence. These are some differences between intentional torts and negligence:

- **Statute of limitations**: In many jurisdictions, the statute of limitations is longer (approximately 1 year longer) for an intentional tort claim than for negligence. If a potential litigant failed to file a malpractice claim within the statute of limitations and the facts could be construed to be an intentional tort, the statute of limitations cannot be used as a defense.
- **Liability insurance** coverage: While professional liability insurance may cover legal costs to defend an intentional tort, the insurance carrier generally has the right to recover defense costs if the insured is found to have committed the intentional tort, and the policy will not cover any damages awarded to a prevailing plaintiff. The party who committed the intentional tort will eventually be liable for all legal costs and awards to the prevailing plaintiff.
- **Expert witness**: Juries are presumed to understand issues that relate to an ordinary person's standard of care, whereas expert witnesses are required to present evidence about the professional standard of care. Expert witnesses are expensive, so the cost for a malpractice suit is substantially greater for both parties.
- **Employers**: Although an employer may be named as a defendant in an intentional tort claim, the employer may not be held liable for intentional acts of employees *unless* the employer knew or should have known about the intentional acts and failed to take remedial actions with the named employee. Employees who commit intentional torts in the course of their employment are subject to disciplinary action and possibly dismissal.

Criminal Law

Criminal laws protect society from egregious acts or acts that are considered as violating strong public policy. Criminal charges are brought against individuals or groups by the federal or state government. When the government files a criminal charge against a group or individual, it is not considered double jeopardy if the victim or victims of the crime file civil suits to recover damages. Criminal acts discussed earlier in this chapter include assault, battery, driving under the influence, substance abuse, sexual misconduct, and fraud. Any criminal act, for example theft, elder abuse, intentional failure to report abuse, will affect the future of a health care provider.

Today, many health care employers require background checks to identify criminal records of potential employees. Some clinical affiliation sites require background checks on students. Licensure boards may refuse to issue licenses or may take disciplinary action against licensees who have been convicted of a felony.

Georgia's practice act is similar to those of many other states with the definition of conviction, explicitly stating that the criminal offense need not occur in the licensee's or applicant's jurisdiction: "...been convicted of a felony or crime involving moral turpitude *in the courts of this state, the United States, or the conviction of an offense in another jurisdiction* which if committed in this state would be deemed a felony. For the purpose of this Code section, a '*conviction*' shall include a finding or *verdict of guilty, a plea of guilty, or a plea of nolo contendere* [Latin for I will not contest it] in a criminal proceeding regardless of whether the adjudication of guilt or sentence is withheld or not entered thereon pursuant to the provisions of Code Sections 42-8-60 through 42-8-64, relating to first offenders, or any comparable rule or statute..."

Michigan's adult abuse law, like many other states' laws on abuse, recognizes the vulnerability of patients relative to health care provider's superior control. Michigan Adult Abuse Statute: §28.342A(n)(2) states, "caregiver or other person with authority over the vulnerable adult is guilty of vulnerable adult abuse in the second degree if the reckless act or reckless failure to act of the caregiver or other person with *authority over the vulnerable adult* causes serious physical harm or serious mental harm to a vulnerable adult."

Fraud and abuse in health care have been in the headlines since the False Claims Act (FCA) was significantly strengthened in 1986 to impose liability when one *submits or causes the submission of false or fraudulent claims* with "*reckless disregard*" or in "*deliberate ignorance*" of the truth or falsity of the claim. Congress has significantly increased the Office of Inspector General's budget to support investigation and prosecution of those who commit fraud and abuse in health care (Chapter 3). Those who are convicted of Medicare or Medicaid fraud and abuse are excluded from participating in these programs, are subject to fines, and may be incarcerated. Because fraud and abuse have been so prevalent in health care, the federal government advises Medicare and Medicaid beneficiaries to recognize or suspect fraudulent activities. Current federal law allows private persons (known as relators) to file *qui tam* claims against health care providers. *Qui tam* is a Latin phrase meaning *one who sues for the king* as well as for himself. Rewards to relators include attorney fees plus as much as 30% of the government's ultimate recovery, which in some cases amounts to several million dollars (U.S. Department of Justice, 1998).

Risk Management

Risk management (Chapter 33) is accepting the responsibility for recognizing, identifying, and controlling exposures to losses or injuries created by activities of the organization. Because risks vary from one practice setting to another, it is impossible to make one risk management plan to fit all. Therefore, an intelligent approach is necessary. The approach involves objective identification of risks, appraising the probability of loss due to them, establishing methods for controlling them, implementing selected methods for treating them, and assessing effectiveness of the risk management plan.

What should a provider do when an incident occurs? First and foremost, take immediate actions to render emergency medical care. Preserve evidence of what may have caused the incident until the area or equipment can be inspected and conditions recorded. As soon as possible, record all facts while they are still fresh in your mind: date, time, place; names of those in the immediate area; objective description of any injury, loss, or damage; and actions that were taken. Never admit liability; to do so may jeopardize insurance coverage. Immediately notify a representative from the risk management department.

Student Notes

An easy way to remember the standard of care that must be met in a malpractice case is to think about your practical examination evaluations. What were the minimal requirements for you to pass? The minimal requirements to

INDIVIDUAL CASE STUDY

Last week you attended a workshop where the presenter introduced a new manual therapy technique that involved applying high-velocity strong forces to spinal structures. The presenter clearly stated that this technique was not substantiated by research and might harm patients. You have a patient who has not responded to any interventions for the past 2 months. If you decide that your patient might benefit from this new technique, what basis would you use for your decision? What legal concerns would you have about using this new technique?

GROUP CASE STUDY

The cast and the environment in this scenario include the following:

- A physical therapist assistant (an employee of a home health agency that is owned by a hospital)
- A surgeon
- A home health agency manager (a hospital employee)
- A hospital manager (the supervisor of the home health agency manager)
- A physical therapist (a pool therapist who works in all of the hospital's facilities, including home health)

Each of the group members takes one of the roles. Ad lib any information that you need to protect yourself.

The Situation

The patient in this situation is a 58-year-old who had a total knee arthroplasty and was discharged from the hospital to home for home health physical therapy. The surgeon ordered physical therapy to begin with "toe-touch weight bearing." The hospital's discharge instructions were translated as "weight bearing as tolerated." The home health agency admission assessment stated that the patient was "non–weight bearing." The physical therapy treatment plan, developed by the physical therapist employee of the home health agency, did *not* indicate that the knee prosthesis was uncemented and did *not* indicate that the patient was "non–weight bearing."

The physical therapist assistant (PTA) saw the patient 3 times a week for approximately 3 months. Not realizing that the patient's prosthesis was uncemented, the PTA followed the protocol for a cemented total knee. Within the first 6 weeks the patient was walking without assistive devices and doing standing-pivot transfers and standing squats for strengthening. The patient complained of swelling and pain throughout the treatment period; however, the regimen remained unchanged.

Subsequently, the physician noticed that the patient was not making any progress, and a second surgery was performed, after which the knee became infected. A third surgery was performed to remove the prosthesis and implant a third device.

Questions to Discuss

- Who owed a duty to this patient?
- Who may have breached the duty?
- What was the standard of care that was breached?
- Did the patient suffer damages?
- Speculate on the amount and type of damages.
- Was the breach of any party the cause of this patient's damages?
- Which party or parties could the patient sue for malpractice?
- Did either the physical therapist or the physical therapist assistant violate your state's practice act? If so, in what respect?

pass your practical examinations are the same as or similar to the minimal requirements needed to defend a malpractice claim. Instructors often fail students when any part of their performance was unsafe, even when all other elements of the performance were well done. *Safety first* and *first do no harm* are good mottos in the classroom and in the clinic. There is a major distinction between the minimal standard of care and quality of care. Think of the minimum as the floor and quality care as the ceiling. You will try to reach the ceiling, but you will encounter trouble if you go below the floor.

Summary

Legal aspects of the health care landscape have dramatically increased in the past 4 decades, and practitioners are becoming progressively more accountable for learning their legal responsibilities. Licensure laws, as a fundamental regulation, either implicitly or explicitly incorporate most legal and ethical responsibilities. Individual licensees, licensing boards, department managers, and employers have responsibilities to protect the public from incompetent or unscrupulous individuals.

Federal and state health care regulations include civil, criminal, and administrative laws. When a practitioner is faced with a legal action (civil, criminal, or administrative) the consequences can permanently or temporarily paralyze his or her professional life. Responsible practitioners incorporate legal principles in their day-to-day clinical decision making as part of their best-practice standards. Lawsuits, however, can happen to anyone at any place and at any time. Thus, each practitioner and each clinic should manage risk while simultaneously striving for quality care.

In a hierarchy of obligations, law is the moral baseline set by society to regulate selected aspects of human behavior and business practices. Ethics, the study of morality, provides means of analyzing morality matters and making moral choices between options. From these comments it is clear that more must be said about the relationships between law, values, mortality, and ethics. The next chapter builds on the legal information presented in this chapter with an integrative focus that places the attention on the relationships between law, values, morality, and ethics.

REFERENCES

American Health Lawyers Association. Missouri appeals court holds that statute barring candidates from taking PT assistant exam after three failed attempts applies retroactively. State Bd. of Registration for the Healing Arts v. Boston, No. WD 59989, 2002 WL 522631 (Mo. Ct. App. Apr. 9, 2002). Health Law Digest. 2002a;30(June).

American Health Lawyers Association. California appeals court says state law that defines physicians' convictions involving alcohol as unprofessional conduct is constitutional. (Griffiths v. Medical Bd. of Cal., No. B143674, 2002. WL 307761 Cal. Ct. App. Feb. 28, 2002). Health Law Digest. 2002b;30(May).

American Physical Therapy Association. Guide to physical therapist practice, 2nd ed. Physical Therapy. 2001a:81:697–700.

American Physical Therapy Association. Guide to physical therapist practice, 2nd ed. Physical Therapy. 2001b:81:701–702.

Bodenheimer TS, Grumback K. Understanding health policy: A clinical approach, 3rd ed. New York: Lange Medical Books/McGraw-Hill. 2002.

California Supreme Court. Advisory Task force on Multijurisdictional Practice. Final report and recommendations. Sacramento: California Supreme Court. 2002.

Douglas B. Board and governance structure. Paper presented at the National Summit on State Regulation of Health Professionals in the 21st Century. Atlanta: Council on Licensure, Enforcement, and Regulation. 1999.

Federation of State Boards of Physical Therapy. Internet cheating: Physical therapist students. Federation News Briefs. 2002;4:1.

Finocchio L, Dower C, Blick N, Gragnola C. Strengthening consumer protection: Priorities for health care workforce regulation. Taskforce on Health care Workforce Regulation. San Francisco: Pew Health Professions Commission. October 1998.

Gragnola C, Stone E. Considering the future of health care workforce regulation. San Francisco: University of California San Francisco Center for the Health Professions. 1997.

Hall TB. Medicine on the Santa Fe Trail (Limited Edition to 1000 copies ed.). Dayton, OH: Morningside Bookshop. 1971.

Lewis K. Professional liability insurance: Are you covered? PT Magazine of Physical Therapy. 1994;2:49–54.

Lewis K. Do the write thing: Document everything. PT Magazine of Physical Therapy. 2002;10:30–33.

National Council of State Boards of Nursing. Nurse licensure compact. Available from http://www.ncsbn.org/ Accessed 8/24/02.

Pew Commission. Strengthening Consumer Protection: Priorities for health care workforce. University of California, San Francisco. October 1998.

Puskin D. Board and governance structure. Paper presented at the National Summit on State Regulation of Health Professionals in the 21st Century. Atlanta: Council on Licensure, Enforcement and Regulation. 1999.

Schmitt K, Shimberg B. Demystifying occupational and professional regulation: Answers to questions you may have been afraid to *ask*. Atlanta: Council on Licensure, Enforcement and Regulation. 1996.

Swift R. Continuing competence. Paper presented at the National Summit on State Regulation of Health Professionals in the 21st Century. Atlanta: Council on Licensure, Enforcement and Regulation. 1999.

Texas Board of Physical Therapy Examiners. Disciplinary actions. Communiqué. 2001;Spring:4.

U.S. Department of Health, Education and Welfare. Report: Surgeon General's workshop on prevention of disability from arthritis. 1966. Available from http://www.sgreports.nlm.nih.gov/NN/B/C/H/O/ /nnbchq.pdf. Accessed 8/8/02.

U.S. Department of Justice. Health care fraud report fiscal year 1998. Available from http://www.usdoj.govwww.usdoj.gov/03press/03_1_1. Accessed 10/23/98.

MORE INFORMATION RELATED TO THIS TOPIC

A standard law dictionary is Black's (Nolan JR, Nolan-Haley JM. Black's law dictionary, 7th ed. St. Paul, MN: West Group. 1999. Legal matters of specific interest to physical therapists may be found by checking the index of PT Bulletin at http://www.apta.org/publications/ptmagazine. Textbooks focused on legal considerations for physical therapists include the following: Scott RW. Legal aspects of documenting patient care, 2nd ed. Gaithersburg, MD: Aspen. 2000; Scott RW. Health care malpractice. A primer on legal issues for professionals, 2nd ed. New York: McGraw-Hill. 1999; Swisher LL, Krueger-Brophy C. Legal and ethical issues in physical therapy. Boston: Butterworth-Heinemann. 1998. Liability insurance information for student and licensed physical therapists can be found at http://www.hpso.com and http://www.mcginnis-ins.com.

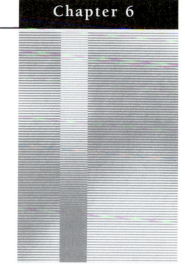

Chapter 6

Value, Moral, and Ethical Matters Matter

Learning Objectives

1. In your own terms define and contrast the terms values, moral, morality, ethics, and ethical as they are presented in this chapter.
2. Explore your personal value priorities.
3. Analyze and evaluate your personal values hierarchy, and based on your experiences, provide examples that reflect your value hierarchy.
4. Analyze the code of ethics of a professional organization and extract the ethical principles that each part of the code represents.
5. Evaluate scenarios with direct care content for values, ethical principles, and morality content and then compare and contrast your appraisal with that of your peers.
6. Evaluate scenarios with management content for values, ethical principles, and moral issues, and then compare and contrast your appraisal with that of your peers.

Key Words

Balanced consideration, common value goal, ethical, ethical principle, ethics, ideal, morality, morals, moral ideal, moral obligation, moral ought, moral rule, principle, stakeholder, values

Introduction

Ideally, laws reflect the shared values of most of the people who are affected by them. Laws are the minimum guides to good behavior (Chapter 5). Laws do not define ideal behavior (Hall, 1996). **Ideals** speak to a higher than minimal level of behavior, that is, desirable goals, intended to foster social harmony, peace, and other socially beneficial ends. This means that a person, a profession, or an organization seeking to be held to the highest social standard has to do more than obey the law. The person or entity must behave toward others in moral ways. Terms like values, moral, and morality refer to intangible psychological concepts. Such terms are given reality by what people say and do. Throughout this chapter the following definitions are used:

- *Values*: consciously chosen needs-based goals that vary in importance and function as guiding principles when making choices from among competing options that are expected to fulfill priority-ordered goals (Feather, 1992; Ros, Schwartz, Surkiss, 1999)
- *Morals*: specific behavioral guidelines formed by society to foster social interactions and sustain societal values (Purtilo, 1993)

- *Morality*: all of a society's morals; generally refers to assumptions about what is good and right (Kurtines and Gewirtz, 1995) and duties and obligations (Omery, 1989); how people ought to act to preserve peace and harmony (Purtilo, 1993)
- *Ethics*: a branch of philosophy focusing on morality as an ideal (Hall, 1996); systematic means of evaluating competing moral theories of rightness or wrongness (Veatch and Flack, 1997)
- *Ethical principles*: values-derived means to guide arriving at decisions (Hall, 1996) in the face of conflicting moral obligations to other interested parties (Veatch and Flack, 1997)

When there are options and choices must be made, values are involved. Choices are made in identifying what is right, wrong, good, bad, and important. Whenever conscious decisions are made, personal values are involved. Understanding this point makes it logical to initiate this discussion with values before moving on to ethics and ethical principles. Values and ethics, as they apply to management and patient care decisions, will be addressed. Physical therapists may be considered a unique culture with their own values reflected in a code of ethics. Therefore, professional ethics are included in this chapter (also see Chapter 5).

Point of View

The organization of this chapter flows from the view that acting in ways that are in one's best interest should not be a knee jerk response. In health care, serving one's own interests should be balanced by considering what is in the best interest of others. To help identify and clarify moral matters, determine appropriate solutions, and make choices that are good for all parties, the application of ethical principles can be very useful. This is not to say that moral decisions cannot be based on experience rather than formal systematic analysis; that is, practice makes perfect. However, for new practitioners, rules help (Hall, 1996). Ethical principles help to resolve conflicts of obligation, but the decision to analyze the conflicts is up to the person making the decision. The decision to consider the moral implications in human interactions depends on how important acting morally is to the personal identity of the decision maker (Nisan, 1995), that is, the degree to which being moral is valued. To show how values and ethics interrelate and how they influence organizational culture, managers, supervisors, and staff, we start the discussion as if the world were a perfect place. We begin with the ideal, or gold standard, for making balanced decisions. Once the ideal is described, we can move on to talk about applying the standard in clinical settings.

Ideal Health Care Environment

We visualize an ideal health care environment as one in which group and personal decisions are made after **balanced consideration** of moral obligations, possible consequences of chosen actions, and interests (values) that are being served. Our approach in this chapter is to emphasize what should be rather than what is. We take this idealistic approach without losing sight of the fact that everyone in health care has multiple obligations, with the greatest of them being meeting patients' needs. However, for a business to continue, the bills have to be paid (Chapters 7, 9, 27–30). To guide balanced consideration of what it means to be good, our ideal is expressed in Figure 6.1. This figure reflects our belief that for managers to run a good health care business, they have to ensure that the care given is technically good, that obligations to others are given full consideration in deliberations, and that actions taken are legal. These tasks require managers to go beyond meeting mandated legal obligations and be moral exemplars.

Good for Whom?

In health care environments two general categories of interaction require behavioral guidelines. The first interaction is usually related to the business of providing health care

Figure 6.1. Three goods associated with an ideal business.

services (Chapter 7); for example, a new patient has to declare who will pay for the services. The second interaction is the treatment aspect, that is, examination and therapeutic exercise. In this business–care interaction many kinds of decisions must be made by managers and staff members. Each time a decision is made, there is a possibility that someone will gain something and someone else will lose something. Those who have something at stake when decisions are made are called **stakeholders**. The principal stakeholders in health care are patients. Patient–stakeholders are at risk for losing in the business sense, perhaps because they did not know what their insurance does and does not cover. They are liable for payment of uncovered costs. Front office staff or admissions personnel need to seek out coverage information and inform the patient of any potential liability. In the therapeutic situation most patients lack the background to make informed decisions about treatment techniques. Unless treatment options, expectations, alternatives, and other relevant information are presented in language appropriate to the patient's background, the patient is at risk for giving permission for the therapist's favorite treatment rather than one supported by research. The concept of stakeholders is broad, as it includes everyone with whom we have substantive interactions. Stakeholders include clinic owners, other employees, equipment vendors, and colleagues in similar professions (Chapter 25). Competitor organizations and non–physical therapist health care professionals are considered stakeholders because they also have an interest in what happens in the industry. Given the trend for organizations to consolidate through mergers and outright purchases and for the provision of comprehensive therapeutic services, today's competitor could be tomorrow's associate. The point is, there are many stakeholders. This makes it difficult to arrive at decisions that reflect balanced consideration of self-interests and obligations to key stakeholders. To facilitate clear thinking in the complicated matter of giving balanced consideration of options and the anticipated consequences of each option requires pointed discussion of values, moral rules, and ethics.

A Theory of Values

According to recent psychological literature, values are consciously chosen "desirable goals, varying in importance, that serve as guiding principles in people's lives" (Sagiv and Schwartz, 1995, p. 438) when a choice between conflicting options has to be made (Schwartz, 1996). Desirable goals arise from three basic requirements (Schwartz, 1992):

1. Biological
2. Individual social interaction
3. Group or institutional coordination

Another way to think of the constructed term values is that values provide a psychological stimulus or motivation to initiate behaviors that are consistent with one's view of oneself (Feather, 1995; Rokeach, 1973). Said succinctly, actions supporting self-interests spring from values.

The standard ways of determining what people value are to ask them or see what they exert their efforts for (Super, 1995). A theory of values based on the above three general human needs proposed 10 common goals that most people seek to fulfill (Schwartz, 1992).

In addition, the theory proposed that these **common-value goals** should be organized in a logical set of relationships. Through survey research that used 44 individual value items known to have similar meanings across cultures, the theoretical relationships among the

Table 6.1 Ten Nearly Universal Ends Served by Individual Values (Schwartz, 1994)

Motive Terms	*Definitions*
Universalism	Appreciation, tolerance, understanding, and protection of the welfare of all people and nature. Example value: broad-mindedness
Benevolence	Enhancement and preservation of the welfare of people with whom one is in requent contact. Example value: forgiveness
Conformity	Restraint of actions and impulses likely to upset or harm others and violate social expectations or norms. Example value: self-discipline
Tradition	Acceptance, commitment, and respect for the customs and ideas that traditional culture or religion provide. Example value: moderation
Security	Harmony, stability, and safety of self, relationships, and society. Example value: social order
Power	Prestige and social status, control over resources and people. Example value: wealth
Achievement	Personal success earned by demonstrating competence according to social standards. Example value: success
Hedonism	Sensuous gratification and pleasure for oneself. Example value: enjoyment of life
Stimulation	Challenge, excitement, and novelty in life. Example value: A varied life
Self-direction	Independent thought and action. Example value: creativity

Modified from Nosse et al, 1999.

common-value goals have empirical support (Sagiv and Schwartz, 1995; Schwartz, 1994). The theoretical common goals exemplified by the 44 cross-culturally recognized values are defined in Table 6.1. Figure 6.2 presents the theorized relationships among the common-value goals.

The steering wheel figure shows the common value goal relationships organized according to the logical compatibility or incompatibility of the various goals. The organizational logic is that the pursuit of different value goals can be compatible or incompatible. Compatible common goals can be achieved with little psychological conflict. Incompatible goals are difficult to fulfill concurrently because they call for oppositional actions (Schwartz, 1994). The relationships are shown in Figure 6.2. The wedges enclosed by the spokes of the wheel that are next to one

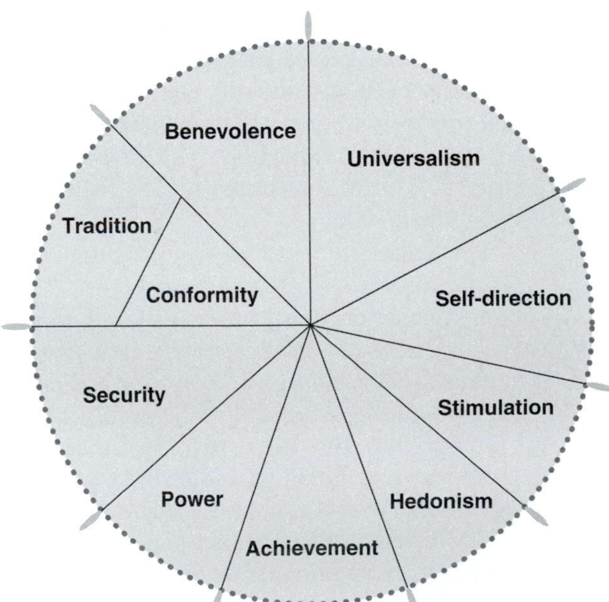

Figure 6.2. Common-value wheel showing the continuous relationships between value goals. (Adapted with permission from Larry Nosse, Wauwatosa, WI.)

Table 6.2 Compatibilities and Conflicts Among Common-value goals

Common-value goals That Are Compatible
Values associated with the goal of benevolence, for example forgiveness, loyalty, helpfulness
Values associated with the goal of universalism, for example broad-mindedness, equality, social justice
Common-value goals in Conflict With Those Above
Values associated with the goal of achievement, for example capability, success, ambition
Values associated with the goal of power, for example authority, wealth, social power

Value examples from Schwartz, 1992.

another represent compatible common-value goals. The distance from a particular wedge in either direction around the wheel represents a progressive decrease in common-value goal compatibility. For example, values that have the common goal of benevolence or universalism are compatible, as their commonality is that they reflect great concern about the welfare of other people, ideas, and the environment in general (Table 6.2). The pursuit of these common-value goals is least compatible with values with the goals of achievement and power because these goals focus on self-enhancement.

The common goal values theory has been used to study student and licensed physical therapists in one state (Nosse, 1998; 2000; Nosse and Sagiv, 2000). These studies showed the organizational structure of physical therapists to be similar to the prototypical model shown in Figure 6.2. Table 6.3 describes and compares the common-value goal priorities of these groups.

The rank order of the relative importance of the common-value goals shows much consistency. The same relative importance was given to the two most important and the least important common-value goals. All three groups rated benevolence (doing good for close others) and self-direction (independent thought and action) more important than the other common-value goals. These priority-ordered common-value goals are appropriate for those who make professional judgments

Table 6.3 Comparison of Importance Rankings of Common-value goals for Wisconsin Physical Therapist Students, Staff Physical Therapists, and Physical Therapist Managers and Supervisors

	Student Rankings		***Staff Rankings***		***Manager Rankings***		***Findings***
Common value goals	***(n = 209)***	***Mean****	***(n = 258)***	***Mean****	***(n = 265)***	***Mean****	***Significant @ P > .01***
Benevolence	1	6.01	1	6.05	1	5.99	
Self-Direction	2	5.38	2	5.28	2	5.30	
Conformity	5	5.07	3	5.21	3	5.22	
Achievement	3	5.35	4	5.05	4	5.19	Students > staff
Hedonism	4	5.17	5	5.04	5	4.77	Both > managers
Universalism	6	4.73	6	4.91	6	4.72	
Security	7	4.45	7	4.58	7	4.65	Managers > students
Tradition	9	4.08	8	4.17	8	4.24	
Stimulation	8	4.30	9	3.89	9	3.69	Students > both
Power	10	2.69	10	2.38	10	2.85	Managers > staff

*Based on a rating scale of 1, not important, to 8, supremely important.

Reprinted with permission from Nosse LJ. Predicting a physical therapy career working with elderly patients. [dissertation]. Milwaukee: Marquette University. 1998.

in the service of others. The groups also agreed on the least important common value goal: power (prestige and social status, control over resources and people). These findings are logical, since the theory places benevolence and power opposite one another; that is, they are oppositional (Fig. 6.2). Statistical analyses of the value importance ratings showed seven significant differences among common value goal priorities (Table 6.3). Student physical therapists prized stimulation values more than both of the other groups and achievement values more than did staff physical therapists. Physical therapists with management titles rated hedonism values less important than the other groups, security values more important than did students, and power values more important than did staff physical therapists.

These findings provide a new perspective on self-understanding and possible ways for a manager to deal with conflict in the workplace. To summarize, the values theory provides the manager with these tools:

- A set of definitions to facilitate communication and understanding about personal values in terms of common-value goals
- Empirically supported logic and structure for understanding staff members' values (motives) as a system rather than as individual unrelated constructs
- A basis for gaining insight into behavioral choices and the possibility of predicting behavior better than if values are not directly considered
- A foundation for analyzing underlying causes for conflicts in the workplace, that is, differences in common value goal hierarchies (Chapter 16)
- An additional perspective on how solutions to conflicts in the workplace can be resolved (Chapter 16), for example, exploring ways that common-value goals can be fulfilled

Management and Values

The discussion focuses on individuals rather than health care organizations for good reason. Sometimes the term *organizational values* is used to express what is important to those associated with the organization (Chapter 9). An organization is a business entity, an inanimate object. It is the people associated with the organization who have values, not the organization per se (Stackman, Pinder, Connor, 2000). It is more accurate to say that organizational values are those espoused by the upper levels of management. While organizations are made up of people who have the same values, people order them differently. These differences are due mostly to variations in exposure to social influences (Brown, 1996; Laupa and Turiel, 1995) and are individualized as cognitive interpretations of these experiences (Lent, Brown, Hackett, 1996). The challenge organizational leaders face is how to bring about an alignment of value priorities between their core values and those of the other members of the organization. When alignment occurs, everyone's efforts are focused on achieving the same common-value goals with nearly the same priorities (Chapter 9).

Moral Rules, Ethics, Morals, and Morality: Related Terms but Different Concepts

The discussion of values extends to the next section, on moral and ethical matters. It is necessary to add more construct terms from philosophy and psychology. Identifying which values are most important is a critical component of any discussion of morals and ethics. Morals and ethics include rules for human interaction. The bottom line is that these rules require making choices. To make choices, one must hold some values more important than others.

Moral Rules

Societal values are represented as important rules for guiding interpersonal behavior so that peace and harmony prevail (Purtilo, 1993). These values are embodied in **moral rules** (Gert, 1992). Moral rules are so critical to sustaining what society holds as important that there is a field of study dedicated to their interpretation and analysis known as ethics

(Roth, 1994). Judgments and choices are also influenced by life experiences (Hall, 1996) and by the physical and psychological impact of these experiences (Lent et al., 1996; Pelaez-Nogueras and Gewirtz, 1995). Psychological fulfillment or satisfaction is in part a result of engaging in behaviors compatible with one's self-image (Rokeach, 1973). In practical terms, if acting in accord with moral rules is important to sustaining self-image, then following moral rules is a priority. The schema in Figure 6.3 brings together several of the terms discussed thus far, for example, legal, value, moral, and ethical concepts.

Morals are the individual guidelines set by society to guide social interactions and sustain what society values. Taken together, the morals of a society define its morality: the ways people ought to act to preserve peace and harmony (Purtilo, 1993). In its most general form, morality involves assumptions about what is good and right (Kurtines and Gewirtz, 1995) and duties and obligations (Omery, 1989). Moral obligations to act toward others in a certain way are universal (Laupa and Turiel, 1995). Moral rules apply to every person who is rational and responsible for his or her own actions (moral agents) (Gert, 1992). All social contexts and situations have moral obligations (Pelaez-Nogueras and Gewirtz, 1995). Moral obligations are also not contingent; that is, there are no exceptions: they are absolute (Berkowitz, 1995). Moral obligations have the same compelling rightness or wrongness for everyone. Members of boards of directors, corporate executives, departmental managers, professional staff members, and other staff members are all obligated to follow the same moral rules. Moral rules are applicable whenever:

- The welfare of an individual or group is in question (Berkowitz, 1995)
- When justice or fairness is a concern (Veatch and Flack, 1997)
- When rights are in question (Purtilo, 1993)

Moral rules are often expressed as prohibitions, or *do nots* (Gert, 1992). Table 6.4 lists five important moral *do nots* and five more that have the potential to exacerbate the severity of consequences of breaking one of the main rules.

Moral rules are obligatory. A moral person obeys moral rules because doing so helps sus-

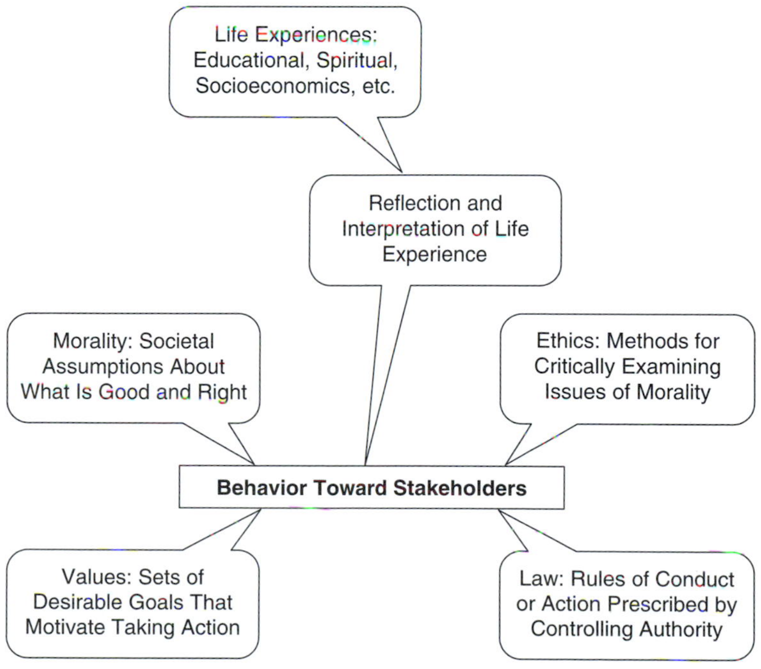

Figure 6.3. Integration of variables on behavior toward stakeholders.

Table 6.4 Example Moral Rules to Prevent Harm to Stakeholders

Universal Moral Rules	*Extension Moral Rules*
Do Not	And Do Not
Cause physical or mental pain	Break laws
Deprive one of pleasure (as long as the other rules are followed)	Cheat
Disable physically or mentally	Deceive
Kill	Make false promises
Restrain freedom or opportunity	Neglect social or professional duties

Based on Gert B. Morality, moral theory, and applied and professional ethics. Professional Ethics. 1992;1:5–24.

tain a fair and just society (Purtilo, 1993). A quick examination to determine whether a matter is one with moral elements can be accomplished by asking whether an impartial, knowledgeable person would advocate that the act under consideration be publicly allowed (Gert, 1992). A yes answer means the matter is not likely to involve a moral issue. That is to say, everyone in society could engage in the behavior without harming others. Common matters without moral implications include those involving social conventions, preferences, and interests. Moral rules are more important to sustaining social values than social conventions without moral implications (Gert, 1992), such as insisting on being called doctor in the clinical environment. A more thorough examination of moral matters entails application of the principles of ethics.

Ethics and Ethical Principles

The discussion thus far has been about personal values and doing the right thing when interacting with others. Doing the right thing implies that an act is done for the right reasons. The right reason means that the act is morally defensible. The study of morality is the focus of moral philosophy or, as it is commonly called, ethics (Murphey and Berg, 1988). The right reasons are determined by reflection guided by the application of ethical principles to moral matters.

The various theories of ethics set priority orders for values through the application of principles for comparing moral options (Hall, 1996). Ethical principles therefore reflect socially prized values, and they provide ways of resolving conflicts of obligations to stakeholders that are morally justifiable. Table 6.5 identifies and defines ethical principles commonly associated with moral matters involving health care managers and staff members.

Ethical principles reflect moral values. As has been discussed, from values spring actions. Ethical principles are tools for systematically analyzing moral matters to determine the core issues, weight them, and make morally defensible choices from competing options. Ethical principles allow justification of courses of action on the strength of the particular value or values they fulfill. For example, restoration of joint range of motion can rarely occur without some discomfort to the patient. Several moral rules listed in Table 6.4 may apply here. One says do not restrain

Table 6.5 Ethical Principles

Principle	*Definition*
Autonomy	Respect the rights, decisions, and dignity of competent stakeholders
Beneficence	Do what is in the best interest of stakeholders
Fidelity	Keep explicit and implicit promises
Justice	Maintain fairness in allocation of goods as well as harms
Nonmaleficence	Avoid harming stakeholders
Respect for life	Refrain from acts that will likely end a life
Veracity	Tell the truth when it is known

freedom (of choice). Another says do not cause physical pain. An extension rule says do not neglect professional duties. Yet another says do not disable. Taken together, there are at least four moral obligations: (1) avoid making a decision without the patient's input, (2) avoid doing something that is likely to cause unnecessary pain, (3) avoid doing something that has little benefit in cases like this, and (4) avoid doing something that may cause further limitations. Ethical principles that apply here include autonomy, beneficence, justice, and nonmaleficence (Table 6.5).

A moral issue may arise if the therapist is skilled in manual therapy (a professional interest) and believes this to be the appropriate treatment, but the patient claims to have so much pain as not to want to be touched. The main conflict lies between autonomy (of the patient as well as the therapist) and beneficence. Also, the choice of treatment depends on some management responsibilities. For example, the manager must be sure that the therapist is competent, that is, has current technical knowledge and skill. Management also is responsible for providing suitable equipment and other resources and sufficient numbers of staff so that therapists have enough time to meet each patient's needs. Personal values are involved when important decisions about alternatives are considered. They affect one's perspective in making judgments about viable alternatives. The point is, to make moral choices requires a commitment to taking actions that are likely to benefit key stakeholders at the expense of enhancing oneself. Therefore, in moral conflict, the examination of one's value priorities should be incorporated into the resolution process. Hall (1996) offers a clinically useful ethical analysis that incorporates this recommendation:

- Think about personal values: what is personally important to you in this situation?
- Recognize that conflicts are based on value priority differences
- Consider what is important (personal values) to the stakeholder
- Separate personal values and professional interests from stakeholder values
- Consider the desired means and outcome from the perspective of the stakeholder
- Consider the desired means and outcome from your perspective
- If there are differences, seek to determine whether the conflict is related to a moral rule or an ethical principle
- If the matter relates to a moral rule or ethical principle, determine, with help if needed, which principle is to be honored
- Review your choice to ensure impartiality throughout the process
- Act in accord with the outcome of the analysis

Professional Ethics

Ethical principles commonly applied to health care professionals focus on the ideal (Hall, 1996). Meeting moral ideals is in addition to meeting the absolute universal moral obligations stated as *do not* rules discussed earlier. Professional ethics identify what shall be done as well as what should be aspired to or what one should strive to attain (Gert, 1992). Professional codes of ethics therefore contain a blend of **moral oughts** and **moral ideals** (Gert, 1992). Failure to meet moral oughts results in professional condemnation (expulsion) because the obligations are universal for members. Not so for moral ideals. The moral ideals of a professional association are applicable to its members and reflect special concerns for the welfare of stakeholders to which most members agree (Hall, 1996). The attainment of moral ideals is encouraged. However, failure to fulfill an ideal does not result in public punishment (Barker, 1992). For physical therapists the moral oughts and ideals are contained in the Code of Ethics of the American Physical Therapy Association (APTA) (APTA, 2002a) and elaborated upon in the Guide for Professional Conduct (APTA, 2002b). Table 6.6 brings together the author's interpretation (L.N.) of the values, moral oughts, ideals, and ethical principles evident or inferred in the Code of Ethics.

The culminating application of the core concepts developed in this chapter and presented in Table 6.6 show that even when there are standardized definitions of terms,

Table 6.6 Values, Moral Rules and Ideals in the APTA Code of Ethics

Principle 1: ...respect the rights and dignity of all individuals...provide compassionate care	
Common-value goals	Benevolence, universalism
Moral rule	Do not cause physical or mental pain, restrain, neglect professional duties
Moral ideal	None
Ethical principles	Autonomy, beneficence, justice
Principle 2: ...act in a trustworthy manner...in all...aspects of...practice	
Common-value goals	Benevolence, universality
Moral Rule	Do not deceive or make false promises
Moral Ideal	None
Ethical Principles	Fidelity, veracity
Principle 3: ...comply with laws...strive to effect changes...	
Common-value goals	Conformity, tradition, security
Moral rule	Do not break laws
Moral ideal	Strive to effect changes
Ethical principles	All principles (see Table 6.5)
Principle 4: ...exercise sound professional judgment	
Common-value goals	Achievement, benevolence, conformity, security, self-direction
Moral rules	All rules (see Table 6.4)
Moral ideal	None
Ethical principles	All principles (see Table 6.5)
Principle 5: ...achieve and maintain professional competence	
Common-value goals	Achievement, benevolence, security, self-direction
Moral rules	Do not cause physical or mental pain, disable, break laws, neglect professional duties
Moral ideal	None
Ethical principles	Beneficence, fidelity, nonmaleficence
Principle 6: ...maintain and promote high standards	
Common-value goals	Achievement, benevolence, security
Moral rules	Do not cause physical or mental pain, disable, neglect professional duties
Moral ideal	Promote high standards in practice, education, research
Ethical principles	Autonomy, beneficence, nonmaleficence
Principle 7: ...seek only such remuneration as is deserved and reasonable...	
Common-value goals	Benevolence, conformity, universalism
Moral rules	Do not cause mental pain, break laws, cheat, deceive
Moral ideal	Reasonable remuneration
Ethical Principles	Beneficence, fidelity, justice
Principle 8: ...provide and make available accurate and relevant information to clients...public	
Common-value goals	Benevolence, power
Moral rules	Do not break laws, deceive, make false promises
Moral ideal	Inform public (other than clients)
Ethical Principles	Autonomy, beneficence, fidelity, veracity
Principle 9: ...protect public and profession from unethical, incompetent, illegal acts	
Common-value goals	Achievement, benevolence, conformity, security, universalism
Moral rules	Do not cause physical or mental pain, disable, deceive, break laws, neglect professional duties, restrain from opportunity
Moral ideal	Protect the profession
Ethical principles	Achievement, beneficence, conformity, tradition, security
Principle 10: ...endeavor to address the health needs of society	
Common-value goals	Benevolence, universalism
Moral Rule	None
Moral Ideal	Endeavor to...
Ethical Principle	None
Principle 11: ...respect the rights, knowledge, and skills of colleagues and other...professionals	
Common-value goals	Benevolence, security, universalism
Moral rules	Do not cause mental pain, restrain opportunity
Moral ideal	Respect knowledge and skills of other professional
Ethical principles	Autonomy, beneficence, justice

For full text of code, see American Physical Therapy Association. APTA code of ethics. Available from http://www.apta.org/pt_practice/ethics_pt/code_ethics.

INDIVIDUAL CASE STUDY

Review Table 6.6. Select any Code of Ethics principle that interests you (http://www. apta.org/pt_practice/ethics_pt/code_ethics). Now go to the Guide for Professional Conduct (http://www. apta.org/pt_practice/ethics_pt/pro_conduct). Analyze the guide content associated with your code principle. For your analysis use the same four criteria that were used in Table 6.6. Compare and contrast your analysis with the analysis in the table. Discuss with a nearby classmate your findings and impressions of what you learned from this task.

there remains a great deal of subjectivity in determining which values, rules, and principles apply to a statement. Table 6.6 reflects the author's common-value goal priorities, which in turn affect the choice of references consulted and the choice of people asked to evaluate the concept, format, and content of the table. At the very least, the table examines the APTA Code of Ethics in an integrative manner as it puts to use the key concepts examined in this chapter.

Student Notes

Know thyself (your values hierarchy). This is an essential requirement for making consistent choices in like situations so progress is made toward your most cherished goals. Know thy society (moral rules). This adds to the difficulty of determining and pursuing what is gratifying, for it requires one to take into consideration how the accomplishment of your goals affects others. Develop an integrated problem-solving style (values, rules, principles). Think broadly. Consider personal goals and their impact on close and peripheral others, on your educational institution, on your employer, and on your profession. Well-thought-out choices lead to fulfillment of desirable goals through actions that are legal and morally defensible based on analysis using ethical principles.

Summary

This chapter provides comparative information about personal values, moral obligations, and ethical analyses. The concept of a stakeholder is introduced. A theory for understanding the role of personal values in influencing choices is presented. Personal values affect whether moral obligations are

GROUP CASE STUDY

Form a small group to discuss the following case. Situation: The client has passed the acute stage of a medial elbow sprain. Your assessment of the client is that joint mobilization, strengthening, soft tissue work, and relaxation training are indicated. You have some skill in ________________(fill in the blank) and very little skill in ______________ (fill in the blank). Use the ethical decision making process that starts with "Think about personal values" (a bulleted list on page 95). As a group determine what you would do in this case. Be prepared to justify your decision. Form a larger group to discuss your answers. Pay particular attention to variations in choice of value priorities and ethical justifications for proposed actions.

important to the decision maker. The chapter describes how values, morals, morality, and ethical principles interrelate to influence decision making that benefits stakeholders. Processes for value assessment and analysis of moral matters are described along with examples pertinent to physical therapists.

Values and ethics continue to be addressed throughout the book, albeit in less theoretical terms. You can develop more skill in the next part of the book, when the business side of health care takes the spotlight. The stakeholder concept continues to be part of the discussion, as do values, morals, and ethics, but the latter concepts are often kept in the background. The examples also change from the individual to groups. Part II begins with business basics, which address what it means to be in business and the functions of managers in organizations. Different kinds of businesses and levels of managers are compared. The implications of these differences for clients, staff, supervisors, and managers are addressed.

REFERENCES

American Physical Therapy Association. APTA code of ethics. Available from http://www.apta.org/pt_practice/ethics_pt/code_ethics. Accessed 8/01/02a.

American Physical Therapy Association. APTA guide for professional conduct. Available from http://www.apta.org/pt_practice/ethics_pt/pro_conduct. Accessed 8/01/02b.

Barker SF. What is a profession? Professional Ethics. 1992;1:73–99.

Berkowitz MW. The education of the complete moral person. Aberdeen, Scotland: Gorden Cook Foundation. 1995.

Brown D. Brown's values-based, holistic model of career and life-role choices and satisfaction. In Brown D, Brooks L and associates. Career choice & development, 3rd ed. San Francisco: Jossey-Boss. 1996;337–372.

Feather NT. Values, valences, expectations, and actions. Journal of Social Issues. 1992;48:109–124.

Feather NT. Values, valences, and choice: The influence of values on the perceived attractiveness and choice of alternatives. Journal of Personality and Social Psychology. 1995;68:1135–1151.

Gert B. Morality, moral theory, and applied and professional ethics. Professional Ethics. 1992;1:5–24.

Hall JK. Nursing ethics and law. Philadelphia: Saunders. 1996.

Kurtines WM, Gewirtz JL. Moral Development: An introduction and overview. In Kurtines, Gewirtz JL, eds. Moral Development: An Introduction. Boston: Allyn & Bacon. 1995:1–25.

Laupa M, Turiel E. Social domain theory. In Kurtines WM, Gewirtz JL, eds. Moral development: An introduction. Boston: Allyn & Bacon. 1995:455–473.

Lent RW, Brown SD, Hackett G. Career development from a social cognitive perspective. In Brown D, Brooks L, and associates. Career choice and development, 3rd ed. San Francisco: Jossey-Boss. 1996:373–421.

Murphey MG, Berg I. Introduction. In Murphey MG and Berg I, eds. Values and value theory in twentieth-century America. Philadelphia: Temple University. 1988:3–11.

Nisan M. Moral balance: A model for moral choice. In Kurtines WM, Gewirtz JL, eds. Moral development: An introduction. Boston: Allyn & Bacon. 1995:475–492.

Nosse LJ. Predicting a physical therapy career working with elderly patients. [dissertation]. Milwaukee: Marquette University. 1998.

Nosse LJ, Sagiv L. Value structures of Wisconsin physical therapists and student physical therapists. Physical Therapy. 2000;80(5) Supp.: S67.

Nosse LJ. Values and job satisfaction. The Resource. 2000;30(1):21.

Nosse LJ, Friberg DF, Kovacek PR. Managerial and supervisory principles for physical therapists. Baltimore: Williams & Wilkins. 1999.

Omery A. Values, moral reasoning, and ethics. Nursing Clinics of North America. 1989;24:499–508.

Pelaez-Nogueras M, Gewirtz JL. The learning of moral behavior: A behavior-analytic approach. In Kurtines WM, Gewirtz JL, eds. Moral development: An introduction. Boston: Allyn & Bacon. 1995:173–199.

Purtilo R. Ethical dimensions in the health professions, 2nd ed. Philadelphia: Saunders. 1993.

Rokeach M. The nature of human values. New York: Free Press. 1973.

Ros M, Schwartz SH, Surkiss S. Basic individual values, work values, and the meaning of work. Applied Psychology: An International Review. 1999;48:49–71.

Roth JK ed. Ethics. Pasadena: Salem. 1994:283.

Sagiv L, Schwartz SH. Value priorities and readiness for out-group social contact. Journal of Personality and Social Psychology. 1995;69:437–448.

Schwartz SH. Universals in the content and structure of values: Theoretical advances and empirical tests in 20 countries. In Zanna M, ed. Advances in Experimental Social Psychology. 1992;25:1–65.

Schwartz SH. Are there universal aspects in the structure and contents of human values? Journal of Social Issues. 1994;50:19–44.

Schwartz SH. Value priorities and behavior: Applying a theory of integrated value systems. In Seligman C, Olsen JM, Zanna MP, eds. The psychology of values: The Ontario symposium, Vol. 8. Mahwah, NJ: Lawrence Erlbaum. 1996:1–24.

Stackman RW, Pinder CC, Connor PE. Values lost: Redirecting research on values in the workplace. In Ashkanasy NM, Wilderom CPM, Peterson MF, eds. Handbook of organizational culture and climate. Thousand Oaks, CA: Sage. 2000:37–54.

Super DE. Values: Their nature, assessment, and practical use. In Super DE, Sverko B, Super CM, eds. Life roles, values, and careers: International findings of the Work Importance Study. San Francisco: Jossey-Bass. 1995:54–61.

Veatch RM, Flack HE. Case studies in allied health ethics. Upper Saddle River, NJ: Prentice Hall. 1997.

More Information Related to This Chapter

The Winter 2000 issue of the Journal of Physical Therapy Education was dedicated to ethics in the context of physical therapy. Triezenberg reported on the current ethical issues determined by members of the American Physical Therapy Association's Judicial committee (Triezenberg HL. The identification of ethical issues in physical therapy practice. Physical Therapy. 1996;76:1097–1107). This article provides many examples from which to develop scenarios to evaluate for ethical content. For a perspective on values that distinguishes between moral and non-moral values see Rokeach M. Beliefs, Attitudes and values: A theory of organization and change. San Francisco, CA: Jossey-Bass. 1980. Seven values that reflect professionalism in physical therapy were identified, defined, and translated into clinical behaviors at a consensus conference in July, 2002. See the document titled Professionalism in physical therapy: core values produced by the APTA Department of Education (undated).

Part II

Understanding Business and Management

PART I (Ch 1-6)
The Big Picture

PART II (Ch 7-13)
Understanding Business and Management

PART III (Ch 14-20)
Managing Human Resources

PART IV (Ch 21-25)
Service Marketing

PART V (Ch 26-30)
Managing Money

PART VI (Ch 31-34)
Measuring Up and Getting Help

CHAPTERS

Chapter 7

Business Basics: Forms of Business Organizations

Learning Objectives

1. Contrast the various common legal structures available to health care business organizations and individual professionals.
2. Differentiate the liability assumed by business owners under various legal structures of health care business.
3. Contrast the tax burdens on owners under the various common legal structures.
4. Analyze the main similarities and the main differences between for-profit and not-for-profit health care organizations.
5. Evaluate your beliefs about making a profit from the delivery of health care services.

Key Words

Articles of incorporation, board of directors, board of trustees, C corporation, corporation, costs, dividend payments, entity, expense, for-profit (FP), general partnership, governing body, governmental ownership, gross revenue, incorporation, jointly and severally liable, legal entity, legal structure, limited liability company (LLC), limited partner, limited partnership, National Securities Commission (NSC), net revenue, not-for-profit (NFP), operating or configurational structure, organization, organizational structure, organizing, owner's equity, partnership, partnership agreement, pass through, personal service corporation, private ownership, profit, public ownership, restructuring, return on investment, S corporation, shares, sole proprietorship, stock, stock exchange, structural or operating configuration, tax status

Introduction

An organization's success depends on its leader's ability to motivate others toward maximum performance (Chapter 8). Managers must put into practice the values of the **organization**, creating an organizational culture that will support and guide all employees in the performance of their work (Chapters 9 and 12). The **structural** or **operating configuration** adopted by an organization is a reflection of its legal structure, ownership, vision, and mission and its leader's assumptions about employee behavior and performance. By definition, an organization is an administrative or functional structure with defined relationships between organizational parts and members (Nosse and Friberg, 1992). **Organizing** is the act of applying systematic planning and a united effort to the arrangement of independent elements into an interdependent whole (Weltman, 1997). Knowledge of organizational structure and work design is particularly important to health care managers. The rapid rate of change in the external environment of health care organizations can be readily observed. Management efforts to accommodate external change have left many health care organizations in a state of continual restructuring.

Characteristics of Business Structures

There are many ways to approach a discussion of **organizational structure**. Several structural terms are commonly used to describe health care organizations, including legal structure, tax status, and operating or configurational structure. These references define the organization in different ways. **Legal structure** defines some elements of ownership, the relationship between owners, the type of business, and/or the purpose of the organization. **Tax status** helps define the organization's purpose and relationship with its owners and with other individuals and organizations. The operating structure provides insight into the organization's response to all of the internal and external factors that influence its success. This chapter concentrates on the legal and tax aspects of structure. Operating structure is covered in Chapter 10.

Legal Structure

An organization can be formed under any of various legal structures. The best legal structure for a business is determined by its objectives and by consultation with experienced attorneys and accountants (see Chapter 34). **Incorporation** is the process by which a business venture receives recognition as a **legal entity** separate from the individual owners or trustees (Clarkson, Miller, Jentz, Cross, 1995). An **entity** is an organization recognized as existing apart from its stockholders or owners (Nolan and Nolan-Haley, 1990). Incorporation is desirable if the business owners wish to separate the organization's legal and financial affairs from their personal ones.

This section provides an overview of the main forms of business that health care practitioners may form: sole proprietorship, partnership, corporation, and limited liability company (Table 7.1).

These are structures common to health care businesses. The authors' intent is to provide a general understanding about the variety of options available. This information should not be applied to any specific situation. Choosing an appropriate form of business requires careful consideration of issues and expert advice (Chapter 34). When considering starting a business, you should consult legal, financial, and tax advisers in the state in which they expect to provide services.

Table 7.1 General Comparisons of Legal Forms of Businesses Commonly Found in Health Care

Legal Name	*Liability*	*Federal Taxes*	*Example*
Sole proprietorship	Personally liable	Individual tax rate	One-owner private clinic
General partnership	Personally liable	Individual tax rate	Two-owner private clinic
Limited partnership			
General partner	Personally liable	Individual tax rate	Two-owner private clinic
Limited partner	Proportionally liable	Individual tax rate	Two-owner private clinic
Corporation			
C corporation	Owners have limited liability	Graduated corporate tax rate	Large regional corporation
S corporation	Owners have limited liability	Individual tax rate	Home health agency
Personal corporation	Personally liable	Flat 35% on corporate profit	Two or more physical therapists
Limited liability company	Limited liability	Individual tax rate	Any mix of the above could become a limited-liability company

The Sole Proprietorship

A business run by an individual or family that does not adopt a formal business structure is by default a **sole proprietorship**. This designation applies to any unincorporated business, including a professional private practice of lawyers, accountants, or therapists. In a sole proprietorship, the business and the person are legally one and the same. The owner may be required to register the sole proprietorship with a government office. A sole proprietorship is easy and inexpensive to form because you can do it yourself. The owner has full control and takes all of the profit. For tax purposes, business profit is treated as the owner's personal income.

Disadvantages of a sole proprietorship include unlimited personal liability. The owner is directly liable for all of the debts and expenses of the business. That means the owner's personal assets, such as savings and house, are at risk. The only protection is through insurance and managing risks (Chapter 33). A sole proprietorship cannot provide tax-free benefits, such as health or life insurance, to the owner. A sole proprietorship may also have more difficulty borrowing money for capital investment than other types of business organizations (Weltman, 1997).

The Partnership

A **partnership** is a simple business structure with more than one owner. There are no legal requirements to forming a partnership. When two or more persons come together to do business, they are considered partners from both a legal and tax perspective. This is known as a **general partnership**. Local government may require a partnership to be registered.

Like the sole proprietorship, a general partnership is easy and inexpensive to form because you can do it yourself. The partners share control. Profit is divided between the partners. For tax purposes, business profit is treated as personal income. Partners pay taxes on their share of the profit at their own tax rate, even if the partners have different rates.

Disadvantages of a general partnership include unlimited liability. The partners are directly liable for all debts and expenses of the business. Each partner's personal assets are at risk. Partners are **jointly and severally liable**. This means that all partners are liable for the full extent of any liability, even if it resulted from the actions of another partner (Wood and Spudis, 2001). Shared liability applies to all aspects of business operations. In the case of a physical therapy practice, any potential liability, such as a malpractice claim (Chapter 5), would be the responsibility of each and every partner regardless of the partner or employee at fault. The only available protection is through insurance and risk management. As with a sole proprietorship, a partnership may have some difficulty raising capital. A partnership cannot provide tax-free benefits such as health or life insurance to the partners.

A second type of partnership that limits liability for one or more partners is a **limited partnership** (Porter, 2001). This type of business entity allows some partners to limit their liability to the amount of their investment in the partnership. Partners with limited liability are called **limited partners**. At least one partner, the general partner, is at full risk, with unlimited personal liability. The limited partners are "silent" in that they cannot be involved in the day-to-day management of the partnership. The general partner or partners have complete control of the business, hence the liability for debts and other obligations of the partnership (Wood and Spudis, 2001). Even though it is generally not required, it is advisable to have a **partnership agreement**. This agreement can delineate the purpose, structure, and membership of the partnership. It can address funding, management structure, distribution of profits or losses, partnership termination, and other operating arrangements. It should delineate what each partner will do and how he or she will be compensated. Partners sometimes disagree strongly about some aspects of the business. To fully protect a business and its partners, a qualified attorney should draw up the partnership agreement (Weltman, 1997).

Corporation

When it is desirable to legally separate a business from its owners, the business can incorporate. Every **corporation** is governed by an elected **board of directors** who as a group control the corporation. The board appoints the corporate offices to manage operations (Clarkson et al., 1995). The three types of corporations to be considered are the C corporation, the S corporation, and the personal service corporation (PC or SC).

A **C corporation** is a legal entity distinct from its owners, and must be formed under state law. This option is more expensive than the others, in part because of incorporation fees. An attorney is not required but is usually advisable. The advantages of incorporation include limited personal liability. The corporate structure offers ease of ownership transfer, and the corporation can continue to exist without the initial owners. Corporations have the easiest time raising capital.

As legal entities, corporations are subject to income tax on profits. If the after-tax profits are distributed to the owners, the distributed funds are subject to a second tax paid at the owner's income tax rate. This double tax can be costly. Other disadvantages of a C corporation include more regulation and more legal restrictions than with partnerships and sole proprietorships. Shareholders are considered passive investors and not liable for the actions of corporate officers (Porter, 2001).

The **S corporation** offers both limited personal liability and **pass-through** tax treatment for federal income tax purposes. Pass-through means that corporate taxes are avoided because all of the business's income passes directly to the owners (shareholders) as a distribution of the profits. The owners are taxed only once, at the personal income tax rate (Clarkson et al., 1995). The S corporation is the only option for a one-person company looking for limited liability without corporate taxes. Other advantages include continuity of existence without the original owner and ease in raising capital. Disadvantages are similar to those of the C corporation, including high regulation and legal restrictions. The S corporation also has two ownership restrictions. Shareholders are limited to a maximum of 35 individuals, who must be U.S. citizens or resident aliens (Weltman, 1997).

Members of professions, such as consultants, physical therapists, physicians, and attorneys, can form a **personal service corporation**. Some states use the designation personal corporation (PC) or service corporation (SC) for personal service corporations. A PC or SC is for individuals who are both the owners and the providers of the services. A husband and wife who are physical therapists may incorporate as whichever type their state law allows. The tax advantage of a PC or SC is that benefits such as health care costs can be deducted as expenses from the corporation's income. Computer equipment, mileage to and from work, continuing education expenses, and other business expenses may be deductible, as are salaries. All income can be spent on business expenses and salaries, leaving no corporate tax to pay. Taxes are paid at the personal income rate. This form of business is easy to form, and formation costs are generally modest.

The PC or SC has several disadvantages. First, all owner–service providers must be members of the same profession. Second, there is no personal liability protection. As with a general partnership, each owner is liable for the acts of the other owners. Taxwise, when there is a profit, the corporate rate for a PC or SC is a flat 35%. This differs from C corporations, for which there is a graduated rate that starts at 15% (Porter, 2001).

The Limited Liability Company

Over the past 2 decades, a flexible form of business entity with the best features of some of the other structures has gained popularity. This is the **limited liability company** (LLC). The LLC gained popularity following a 1988 Internal Revenue Service ruling (revenue ruling 88-76) regarding the taxation of LLC profits. Members of the company govern and own this type of corporation and are called a members committee. The members are essentially shareholders. For federal tax purposes, a LLC is taxed like a partnership and not like a C corporation. A LLC is therefore an unincorporated business form that is regulated in every state (Wood, 2001) and the District of Columbia (McCray and Thomas, 2003). Like a corporation, the LLC is a separate legal entity from the owners, but for tax purposes it is like a partnership (Northwestern Mutual Financial Network, 2003). This type of business is a hybrid that operates somewhat like a partnership, a limited partnership, and an S corporation. A LLC has the profit pass-through feature of all three of these business forms. Profit is divided between the members and treated as personal income for tax purposes. The double tax associated with a C corporation is avoided. A LLC also has in common with a limited partnership limited liability for the limited partner. In a LLC, members' liability is limited to the amount of their investment. Another advantage is that it is not limited as to the number of shareholders, as is an S corporation (Clarkson et al., 1995). One person can form an LLC in all states but Massachusetts (Aresty International Law Offices, 2003). The LLC has three disadvantages: (1) lack of uniformity in state laws regarding them, (2) their newness, which means there has been relatively little legal testing of issues associated with them, and (3) more complexity, more formality, and more cost to set up than a partnership.

Tax Status

A business can be either **for-profit** (**FP**) or **not-for-profit** (**NFP**). Tax status is determined by two factors, the purpose of a business and how the business uses its profits (Chapter 2). The need to make a **profit** is fundamental to all businesses. Money is required for a business to sustain itself and achieve its purpose. To grow and prosper, a business must earn more than it spends. When money is earned through the sale of services and products, interest on investments, or contributions from external sources, it is called **gross revenue**. When money is spent, it is an **expense**. Gross revenue minus expenses is **net revenue**. When net revenue is positive, the business has made a profit. Profit increases the value of the business. A negative net revenue or loss decreases the value of the business (see Chapter 27).

The nature of the business and how profit is used determine tax status. Does money provide the means to achieve a purpose? Is making money the purpose itself? For example, clinic A makes money by providing services to patients with the means to pay for care. The money is used to pay the expense of providing care to those who cannot pay and to provide an up-to-date outpatient facility for all residents of the community. Clinic B makes money by providing services to patients with the means to pay for care. The money is used to provide an income for the owner–operator. Both of these businesses provide high-quality care. What distinguishes clinic A from clinic B is purpose and what happens when operations produce a profit. In this example, clinic A will likely qualify for tax-exempt status, while clinic B probably will not. A not-for-profit corporation allows its representatives to arrange for the corporation to own property and form contracts without exposing the representatives to liability (Clarkson et al., 1995).

The For-Profit Business

The for-profit (FP) business provides goods and services to make money for its owners. Both private and publicly traded businesses can be FP. A FP business pays taxes on its profits. It is also subject to local taxes, such as property and sales tax. Profits remaining after taxes can be used to improve the financial position of individual owners. The FP business may choose to distribute the remaining profit directly to its owners through **dividend payments**. Alternatively, it can retain the money to increase the value of the owner's holdings, also called **owner's equity** (Chapter 27). In some legal structures an owner may claim profit as personal earned income. This is done so the profit can be taxed at the owner's personal income level. Otherwise, the profit would be taxed first at the corporate level and then again as earned income.

Many health care businesses are FP. Therapy and other private practices are often FP. National publicly traded for-profit health care corporations operate hospitals, long-term care facilities, ambulatory surgery centers, home health agencies, therapy contract services, and more.

The Not-for-Profit Business

A not-for-profit (NFP) business is designated as tax exempt; that is, it is exempt from all forms of federal, state, and local taxes, including income tax, property tax, and sales tax. A business must apply to the Internal Revenue Service for a tax exemption. Exemptions are granted to businesses whose primary purpose is some form of community service.

NFP businesses may not provide financial benefit to any private individual or FP business. The payment of reasonable compensation to an owner–employee, other employees, or corporate owners does not fall under this restriction. NFP businesses are required to retain and reinvest excess revenue in the business to support its mission to a community (Chapter 2). The Internal Revenue Service (2002) lists the following examples of businesses that are frequently designated as tax exempt:

- Charitable organizations
- Churches
- Community service organizations
- Government-operated businesses
- Health care organizations
- Professional associations
- Religious communities

Over the past few years, increasing attention has been paid to the public cost of tax-exempt organizations. The public cost is a combination of lost tax revenues and the expense of government services, such as fire and police protection, used by tax-exempt organizations at public expense. Many NFP businesses, including health care providers, are being challenged to demonstrate that the community benefit equals or exceeds public cost. As communities face an increasing financial burden for health and social services to the poor, the demand for accountability is likely to increase. Health care organizations risk the loss of their tax-exempt status if they fail to provide a reasonable level of community service.

Ownership, Purpose, Values, and Vision

The three basic types of ownership are **private**, **public**, and **governmental** (Chapter 2). All three types of ownership arrangements are used in the health care industry. Private ownership implies that an individual, a group of individuals, or another privately owned business solely owns the business. The owners have the right to establish the purpose of the

INDIVIDUAL CASE STUDY

You are the manager of a rehabilitation services department at one of three local hospitals. Your employer is a private NFP corporation. The city newspaper just reported that your hospital made $10 million last year. In the same article it stated that your hospital's chief executive officer received a salary of $390,000 plus a $50,000 bonus. Your neighbor, Joe, was recently seriously injured when he was hit by a car. The driver was uninsured. Luckily, Joe has fully recovered, but he has an unanticipated $7,000 of out-of-pocket hospital and physician expenses to pay off. The hospital has offered to set up an extended payment plan. Because Joe can pay, the hospital will not fully forgive Joe's bill. After reading the article, Joe is furious. He can't believe that the hospital charges so much and is allowed to make millions off the suffering of the sick and injured. He knows you work at the hospital and has just confronted you at a neighborhood cookout. He wants an explanation! How do you respond? How do you feel about the salary and bonus?

GROUP CASE STUDY

Form a group of eight people. Make role assignments: two members of the board of directors, two physicians, two community members, and the heads of the physical therapy and nursing departments. You are all at a meeting to discuss a possible change of ownership.

Situation

A rural community, population 65,780, receives most of its primary health care services from the local community hospital and a single private-practice medical group. All of the physical therapy is done at the hospital. The hospital is a private NFP organization. The hospital participates in Medicare and state Medicaid in addition to providing a growing amount of charity care. The closest alternative hospital is a regional tertiary-care medical center 60 miles away. There is a longstanding referral relationship between the community hospital and the regional medical center. Both organizations consider the relationship beneficial and make an effort to collaborate to bring new services to residents of the community. The medical group serving the community is proud that it has been able to attract and retain a sufficient number of family practice physicians to meet the community's needs. It generally pays its physicians more than they would make in larger communities to counter the issues of lifestyle related to practice in a rural setting. This group has historically provided care regardless of a patient's ability to pay. This business practice is becoming harder to support as expenses increase in the face of declining government and private payer reimbursement. The community places a high value on its hospital, and most of the residents have been patients of the medical group since birth.

For the past 5 years the local government has been providing the hospital with an annual subsidy. Without the subsidy the hospital would be losing money and would not be able to keep its doors open. The hospital's operating deficit is growing as the community's ability to pay the subsidy declines. The hospital's board of directors believe that the circumstances require that the option of selling the hospital to a new owner must at least be investigated. The board's investigation has yielded a great deal of interest and controversy. The board has received three offers to purchase. The regional medical center, a private FP hospital chain, and surprisingly, the local medical group have all indicated a serious interest in owning their hospital. In fact, the local medical group is so concerned about the potential transfer of ownership as to say that if they are not the successful bidder, they are not sure they can continue to meet the needs of the community. Some of the physicians are threatening to leave the community.

In addition to the value of local control, what should the board consider when evaluating the offers from prospective buyers? Discuss this specific question; then meet as a class and discuss the various groups' perspectives.

organization. The owners' purpose may be anything—provision of a financial return, personal employment, meeting a community need by supporting a special philanthropic interest. An owner may be involved directly in the management of the business or rely totally on employed managers. Public ownership implies that the **stock** representing an ownership interest is traded to members of the public on a **stock exchange**. A publicly traded business is owned by a group of diverse individuals who have elected to invest in the business through the purchase of stock. They are the stockholders. Managers of a publicly owned business are accountable to their stockholders to provide a return on investment. Local, state, or federal government can also own a business, for example a county hospital. These businesses are usually are tax exempt and NFP.

Student Notes

The matter of legal structure or tax status may seem like a topic far from treating patients. In health care, however, they affect both how care is delivered and what happens to the money collected from services that you and other employees provide. The legal structure relates to the owner or owners of a FP business or the trustees of a NFP business. If you work for the former, the profit you help generate goes to private individuals. It can be shared with you if the owners care to do so. The owners can also buy more equipment, redecorate, provide additional perks, and so on—or not. A NFP organization is more restricted in how it distributes the revenue that exceeds expenses. The trustees can approve many of the same expenditures noted for a FP entity, but they must spend money to improve the community in which it operates. Better equipment, more locations, and special programs are all examples of expenditures that are congruent with the community service missions the NFP health care organizations are obligated to fulfill to retain their tax-exempt status. The question is not which type of tax status is better for patients or employees, but rather a question of differences in the purpose of the organization.

Summary

Several key features define an organization: its legal structure, its tax status, and its operating structure. Ownership and the owner's vision, mission, and goals for the organization determine how an organization will or can be structured. Structure in turn will affect the strategic goals of a business. Any and all of the legal structures described in this chapter can be found in the health care industry. Some structures are common to specific types of health care businesses. For example, it is common for hospitals in the United States to be privately owned NFP entities, while the typical physician practice is a privately owned FP business. There is, however, no "right" organizational structure for a health care business. The best structure for any organization is determined by it business objectives. The development of business objectives is the responsibility of the formal leadership of an organization. Managers are expected to lead and to supervise others so the organizational objectives are met. Chapter 8 addresses these three important interrelated topics.

REFERENCES

Aresty International Law Offices. Limited liability company FAQ. Available from http://www.lawguide.com/aresty/guideview.asp?layer=3&article=340. Accessed 5/4/03.

Clarkson KW, Miller RL, Jentz GA, Cross FB. West's business law: Text cases, legal, ethical, regulatory, and international environment, 6th ed. St. Paul: West. 1995.

Internal Revenue Service. Tax-exempt status for your organization. Available from http://irs.gov/pub/irs-pdf/p557.pdf. Accessed 11/08/02.

McCray RA, Thomas WL. Limited liability companies. Available from http://www.irs.gov/pub/irs-tege/topich00.pdf. Accessed 4/28/03.

Nolan JR, Nolan-Haley JM, eds. Black's law dictionary. 6th ed. St. Paul: West. 1990.

Northwestern Mutual Financial Network. Limited liability companies (LLCs). Available from http://ww2.northwesternmutual.com/tn/netserve—business—limited_lab_co_pg. Accessed 5/04/03.

Nosse LJ, Friberg DG. Management principles for physical therapists. Baltimore: Williams & Wilkins. 1992.

Porter DB. Legal liability considerations in choosing a form of a business. In Wood RW, ed. Limited liability companies: Formation, operation, and conversion, 2nd ed. New York: Panel. 2001:17–36.

Weltman B. The big idea book for new business owners. New York: Macmillan Spectrum. 1997.

Wood RW. Preface. In Wood RW, ed. Limited liability companies: Formation, operation, and conversion, 2nd ed. New York: Panel. 2001.

Wood RW, Spudis BC. Limited liability companies: An introduction. In Wood RW, ed. Limited liability companies: Formation, operation, and conversion, 2nd ed. New York: Panel. 2001:1–16.

MORE INFORMATION RELATED TO THIS CHAPTER

For information on setting up a business:

Jackson RM. The entrepreneur's reference guide to small business information, 3rd ed. Business Reference Services. Science, Technology, and Business Division, Library of Congress, Washington, DC 1999 at http://www.loc.gov/rr/business/guide/guide2.html.

The Small Business Administration at http://www.sba.gov/bi/bics/referencematerial.html
The Library of Congress Business Reference Services at http://www.loc.gov/rr/business/.

For more information on forms of business:

http://sos.state.ia.us/business/sole.html
http://www.mycorporation.com/llcclear.htm
http://www.ianr.unl.edu/pubs/consumered/nf253.htm
http://www.quickmba.com/law/sole-proprietorship.

An additional type of corporation not discussed in this chapter but available to physical therapists in some states, including California, is a professional corporation. It has some similarities to a regular corporation and some to a partnership. For a quick summary of professional corporations access http://www.sos.state.ia.us/business/professcorp.html

Chapter 8

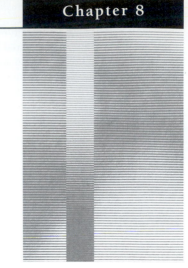

Management, Supervision, and Leadership

Learning Objectives

1. Compare and contrast management, supervision, and leadership in terms of organizational power, scope of influence, and personal attributes, skills, and knowledge.
2. Assess the knowledge, skills, world view, and values of managers at the upper, middle, and lowest levels of management.
3. Analyze the similarities and differences between the relative strengths of a midlevel manager and an appointed team leader.
4. Assess your own management, supervision, and leadership knowledge and skills.
5. Examine the results of your self-assessment, interpret them, and identify areas you wish to explore further for your own development.

Key Words

Administration, administrator, chief executive officer (CEO), cross-functional team, direct report, executive, first-level manager, follower, functional category, functional operating team, leader, leadership, leadership process, management, manager, network, productivity, self-managed work team, staff, supervise, supervisee, supervision, supervisor

Introduction

In all types of organizations (Chapter 10) those who have formal power and responsibility for achieving work related goals through the efforts of others are called **managers** (Caroselli, 2000). To facilitate the completion of the quantity of work (**productivity**) at the desired level of quality, managers **supervise** the work of others. **Supervision** involves direction, instruction, constructive feedback and other means intended to have a positive influence on work related behaviors. **Supervisees** or **staff** are said to report to their manager. This means they are responsible to their manager for the work they do. In business the term **direct report** is used to denote this relationship (Yukl, 2002).

A traditional business hierarchy has three tiers of management: upper, middle, and first-level (Table 8.1). In the hierarchy in Table 8.1 upper management reports to a board of trustees (who own the assets) or directors (who do not own the assets) or the owner or owners (Clarkson, Miller, Jentz, Cross, 1995). Middle management reports to and is supervised by upper management, and **first-level managers** are supervised by and report to middle managers. First-level managers are sometimes called **supervisors** (Umiker, 1998; Dunn, 1998). In health care settings first-level managers supervise front line staff, that

Table 8.1 Comparison of Health Care Managers: Frame of Reference and General Duties

Upper-Level Management

Frame of reference: the organization
- Vision, values, mission
- Coordination organization-wide
- Integration
- Dealing with the external environment
- Long-term goals

Middle-Level Management

Frame of reference: various clusters of work groups and related work groups
- Coordination of groups
- A variety of operations
- Short-term goals

First-Level Management

Frame of reference: personnel in a department and functionally related departments
- Coordination of individuals
- Direct-care operations
- Short-term goals

is, those who serve clients directly and are not managers.

Core management knowledge and skills are similar at each organizational level. Differences lie in what knowledge and skills are used most frequently. An expectation of employees at all levels is that management is able and willing to make timely decisions and take actions that will bring about desirable results.

Sometimes managers ask those who report to them to take certain actions that have not been tried before. This makes the anticipated outcome less than a sure thing. There are also times when little information is available and actions have to be carried out on faith. Actions that require seemingly major changes, involve significant risk, require extra effort, or necessitate formulating a solution for problems that are incompletely understood are circumstances that cause discomfort for those expected to carry them out. In such out-of-the-ordinary circumstances pooling of thoughts, commitment to finding a solution, and critical discussion of relevant points of view can help develop solutions and commitment to specific actions. The person or persons who move the discussion toward a solution that results in new thoughts and actions, that is, influence those who are working to meet an objective, can be called the **leaders**. Often management is separated from leadership to focus on the skills needed by managers in different situations. Table 8.2 lists situational differences between management and leadership.

Table 8.2 Comparison of a Managerial and a Leadership Frame of Reference

Management	***Leadership***
Solve operations-focused problems	Solve change-focused problems
Short-term goals	Long-term goals
Predict tangible results	Offer a vision of the future
Maintain order	Communicate the vision
Establish structure	Establish strategies for change
Monitor results	Motivate and inspire

Leader is not an official title in an organization. A leader is often a manager, but leaders are not limited to managers. Others can lead by influencing others to bring about solutions through formal and informal communications.

This chapter addresses management, supervision, and leadership. The knowledge, skills, abilities, values, and other characteristics associated with management, supervision, and leadership are discussed with emphasis on the lower levels of management. This emphasis is appropriate for three reasons. First, health care organizations today have few middle managers; that is, they are flat organizations and getting flatter (Chapter 10). When management positions are eliminated, they often come from the middle level. The work done by middle managers is shifted downward to the remaining first-level managers (McConnell, 2002). Second, this book is directed at those who are early in their career. Within the next few years you will likely have the opportunity to move from direct patient care to first- or middle-level management. Third, the stance of the American Physical Therapy Association's Section on Administration (now the Section on Health Policy and Administration) is that new graduates should have a basic understanding of and skills in management and leadership (Section on Administration, 2003).

Some of the information in this chapter is general and discussions short. Additional depth on management responsibilities, organizational structure (Chapters 9–11), and other management topics are covered in other chapters.

Management

Management is the allocation of responsibility and provision of resources for others so they can do the work that fulfills organizational objectives. Managers are officially responsible for the work outcomes of others and base their choices on a variety of sources of information to fulfill organizational objectives and goals. Management is about efficiency in the routine operation of an organization (Bennis and Nanus, 1985) (Table 8.2). Much of this efficiency in health care is associated with the cost of labor, that is, salaries and related costs (Chapters 17 and 20). A desirable situation is to manage employees so they are highly productive. Productivity at the front line means that staff physical therapists treat many patients well without the need to hire more staff or use per diem contractors even when the volume of patients increases periodically (Chapter 29). The success of management is therefore measured indirectly as the outcomes produced by their staff (Umiker, 1998).

The essential concepts related to the management of an organization deal with the distribution of responsibilities, scope of influence, and power. These concepts are briefly introduced here and expanded in Chapters 10 and 11.

Management in Terms of Responsibility, Scope, and Power

Responsibility, scope and power are best described in the context of a traditional bureaucratic hierarchy (Chapter 10). This hierarchy has three levels of management, upper, middle, and lower, or first level (Table 8.1). An organization of this type has a small number of managers at the upper level. This upper management has the overall responsibility for the welfare of the organization, the widest scope of influence, and therefore the most organizational power. Upper management deals with a variety of external parties and middle management within the organization. Upper-level managers select and supervise the level below. They are supervised by and report to a board of directors or similar body. Middle management has operational responsibilities for segments of the organization. The term operations refers to the day-to-day activities of an organization, such as financing and service product development (Nosse and Friberg, 1992). Middle management reports to and is supervised by upper management. The scope, influence, and power of middle managers are intermediate. Much middle-level managerial work is with first-level managers. In health care, first-level management typically has responsibility for supervising those who provide services directly to patients and other customers. This level of management reports to and is supervised by middle management. At this lowest level of management, the scope of organizational influence and power is limited in a traditional tall hierarchical structure (Chapter10). Conversely, when an organization has few levels of management, the managerial work is passed downward, resulting in more responsibilities at the first level.

Management is not necessarily synonymous with ownership (Chapter 7). A physical therapist who owns a private practice and has at least one employee is both the management and the owner. A **chief executive officer (CEO)** of a not-for-profit health care organization is at the top level of management, but he or she is an employee. Many health care organizations have boards of directors or trustees. The board members hire upper management to run the organization to the board's satisfaction (Chapter 10).

Managers

Managers have official responsibility for achieving organizational goals through the efforts of those they supervise. Thus, the essential job of a manager is to develop people through work so the manager and ultimately the organization meet objectives and fulfill goals. This means that the success of a manager is measured to a large extent on the outcomes derived from the work of others (Umiker, 1998). In addition to the general levels of management a number of titles are used to differentiate among managers. Common titles assigned to managers at the upper, middle, and first level of management, respectively, in a traditional bureaucratic health care organization include chief executive officer, director of rehabilitation services, and manager of physical therapy services. Other titles that may be used at the upper management level include **administrator**, executive director, and president. Alternative names for middle or first levels of management include director, coordinator, supervisor, and team or group leader. The responsibilities of each level vary in the influence of their decisions and the number and jobs of the people they supervise. The consequences of an upper manager's actions can affect every aspect of the organization, including its continued existence. At the next level down, what a middle manager does affects the department under his or her direction, for example, whether to expand service locations and how they will be organized and coordinated. At the first level of management the work involves supervising the efforts of staff. The actions of first-level managers directly affect the fewest employees, that is, the members of his or her department. In health care this is where the patient or customer is dealt with face to face. Management at this level is critical to the success of any organization whose existence depends on how well the needs of customers and potential customers are met (Dunn, 1998) (Chapter 21).

Functional categories of managers include the following:

- *Administrative managers* are generalists who understand most of the functional areas of management as opposed to having specialized knowledge.
- *Financial managers* deal with an organization's financial resources and are knowledgeable about accounting principles, cash management, and investments.
- *Human resource managers* are responsible for the hiring and development of employees, salary and benefits, and educational programs to adhere to employment laws.
- *Marketing managers* develop and promote an organization's products and services.
- *Operations managers* are responsible for creating and overseeing the systems that produce the organization's products and services.
- *Specialized managers* are skilled in areas of special need, for example, public relations, law, and risk management.

Even though there are differences in responsibilities, scope, and influence of actions, common knowledge, skills, and attributes are associated with managers at all levels throughout the organization. These variables are discussed next within the context of the responsibilities and roles of managers.

What Managers Do

For decades the literature on organizational management has often dealt with Fayol's (1949) concept of what managers do, for example, control, coordinate, organize, and plan (Mintzberg, 1975). Refining efforts to define the responsibilities and roles of managers were made by Yukl (2002), Mintzberg (1973, 1975), and Mintzberg, Quinn, and Voyer (1995). Yukl (1994, 2002) discussed nine areas of managerial responsibilities supported by survey data gathered over 11 years from more than 10,000 managers in 20 countries. Mintzberg (1973) and Mintzberg et al. (1995) melded information from management literature on the work of managers at all organizational levels with his own observations of five executive officers of small businesses. He identified 10 roles managers fulfill. For comparison, Table 8.3 presents these two lists of what managers do. The lists of the generic responsibilities of managers are aligned to indicate which terms have similar intent. Thus, several terms in the Mintzberg list are matched with Yukl's descriptive terms.

To *administer* means to carry out activities such as formulating policies, analyzing data, and maintaining records. An *administrator* is a person at the upper level of an organizational hierarchy. The *consult* responsibility includes acting as a sounding board for others, maintaining current competence in technical areas, and offering expert advice (Chapter 34). To *coordinate* means to share information with and bring about cooperative efforts among individuals who may not be directly under the control of the manager. *Control* over the delivery of services and production of goods requires analysis, scheduling, budgeting, and quality control. The responsibility of *decision maker* requires quick determination of what to do with resources and when to do it and resolving disagreements in the face

Table 8.3 Summary of Manager Responsibilities

Based on Mintzberg et al., 1995	*Based on Yukl, 1994*
Make decisions	**Make decisions**
When critical unplanned events occur	Quickly
When changes are needed	In unpredicted conditions
When resources are to be allocated	When resources are to be allocated
When negotiations must be carried out	When negotiations must be carried out
	When to stretch boundaries
Inform others	**Inform others**
About state of internal environment	About internal and external environment
External to the organization/department	External to the organization/department
About matters they would not usually know about	By sharing information
Interact with others	**Interact with others**
As representative of organization/department	As representative of organization/department
External to organization/department	External to organization/department
To motivate, inspire, lead	Administer
	Policies, analyze data, record systems, etc.
	Develop subordinates
	Supervise, train, set performance objectives, etc.
	Coordinate
	Efforts of others; solve problems, mediate, etc.
	Consult
	With others, for others, regarding new methods, etc.
	Control
	Schedules, quality, effectiveness, etc.
	Organize and plan
	Operational policies, procedures; short-, long-term plans, budget, etc.

of unique and unpredicted circumstances. All manager responsibilities require decision making. The *monitor* function is keeping an ear to the ground regarding the internal and external environments and assessing them in terms of their being threats to the organization or department or opportunities to be seized upon. Monitoring involves developing broad networks and equitably exchanging information among network members. A manager must *organize* and *plan*. These responsibilities include making budgets, assessing outcomes, determining resource utilization, and setting objectives and goals. Managers *represent* the organization or department to external stakeholders and others in ways that project a positive image toward the organization or department. To *supervise* others involves assisting them to assess what they do well and what they need to do to improve, providing technical training for them to meet their job requirements, and assessment of their performance relative to defined objectives and goals. More will be said about supervision later. Decision making and influencing could have been added alongside each of the responsibilities and roles (Table 8.3) to indicate that managers are always engaged in decision making (Longest, Rakich, Darr, 2000) and opportunities to influence others (leadership) are ever present (Mintzberg et al., 1995).

A closer look at the identified responsibilities and roles of managers suggests that some condensing of the many terms used to describe what managers do is possible. Based on a review of the literature, Yukl (2002) concluded that most manager activities fostered at least one of four general processes:

1. Building and maintaining relationships
2. Exchanging information
3. Making decisions
4. Influencing others

Similarly, Mintzberg et al. (1995) related their 10 manager roles to three higher-order categories:

1. Decision making
2. Informing
3. Interacting

Table 8.4 shows the comparative descriptions of these general categories of managerial activities.

Of particular interest to new graduates and licensed therapists early in their career is what to expect in the near future in terms of management responsibility and how to prepare for these responsibilities. The usual initial transition is from direct patient care only to direct patient care plus management responsibilities. The initial transition may also be to a first-level management position with infrequent or no direct patient care responsibilities. Yukl's (1994) description of management in terms of four general processes, that is, relationships, information exchanges, decision making, and influencing others, is useful to synthesize what first-level managers do and how to prepare to become a manager.

Table 8.4 Comparative Lists of the Responsibilities and Roles of Managers

Responsibilities (Yukl, 1994)*	*Roles (Mintzberg et al., 1995)*
Administrate	Monitor
Consult	Liaison
Coordinate	Disseminator, negotiator, liaison
Control	Resource distributor
Make decisions	Problem solver
Monitor	Monitor
Organize and plan	Entrepreneur, resource distributor
Represent	Figurehead, spokesperson
Supervise	Leader

* Based on Page R. The position description questionnaire. Unpublished paper. Minneapolis, MN: Control Data Business Advisors. 1985. Cited in Yukl G. Leadership in organizations, 5th ed. Upper Saddle River, NJ: Prentice Hall. 2002.

First-Level Manager: Relationships

Formal supervisory responsibility over former peers changes relationships from "one of us" to "one of them" (Umiker, 1998). Physical therapists value being benevolent toward their patients or clients more than they value control over people and resources (Nosse, Friberg, Kovacek, 1999) (Chapter 6). They want to help their patients and clients. The authors have had conversations with students, clinicians, and faculty who held the opinion that moving away from direct patient care and into a management position was akin to leaving the profession. We disagree with this outdated view. Undoubtedly, a physical therapist should first and foremost have the knowledge, skills, psychosocial attributes, and supervised experience to treat patients competently. While highly important, direct patient care is only one aspect of a successful health care department or clinic. Measuring customer satisfaction (monitoring), having responsibility for the work of nonprofessionals (supervision), being productive (planning and organizing), attending a variety of interdisciplinary meetings (communicating), and presenting positive aspects of the department or clinic, organization, and profession (representing) are important for the welfare of the organization. If the organization does not strive to do well in all of these areas, how can patient care be what it should? Ideally, today's competent clinician should be able to treat patients well and to manage the immediate and external environments related to patient care (Section on Administration, 2003). Managers need to be competent in dealing with the broader departmental and external environmental issues as well as foster the development of those that report to them so department and organization expectations are at least met and preferably exceeded.

Based on the thoughts of other authors and our own experiences, these are important skills, knowledge, and strategies for first-level managers in relationship building:

- Professional technical competence (Umiker, 1998): be respected as an experienced, clinically competent physical therapist
- Standard managerial knowledge and skills (Dunn, 1998): know how to organize and plan and be able to communicate the plan
- Commitment to working hard on behalf of staff and upper-level management (Dunn, 1998): make consistent efforts to present the organization's views to staff and staff views to those higher in organizational hierarchy
- Able to lead (McConnell, 2002): inspire others to do more and do it better than they thought possible
- Facilitate team building (Umiker, 1998): prepare staff to make autonomous and semiautonomous decisions and empower them to make decisions in specified cases
- Accessible (Nosse and Friberg, 1992): keep an open door, be seen often, and make time to listen as often as possible
- Listen (Nosse and Friberg, 1992): give full attention to those who come to express needs, feelings, or ideas
- Keep staff informed (Nosse and Friberg, 1992): let staff know why they are being asked to do things, what they are to do, and how they are progressing
- Play fair (Nosse and Friberg, 1992): strive for win-win solutions, be just, consistent, and ethical (see Chapter 6)
- Create opportunities for staff (Nosse and Friberg, 1992): develop a work environment with opportunities to fulfill a variety of changing sets of needs
- Give recognition (Nosse and Friberg, 1992): publicly and privately reward staff for a job well done
- Know the staff as individuals (Nosse and Friberg, 1992): learn each staff members' strengths and weaknesses and enough about their background to be able to match them with growth opportunities that are fulfilling for them and beneficial to the department

First-Level Manager: Exchange Information

Official information exchanges within an organization take place at multiple levels of the organization (up and down) as well as between managers at the same level (horizontal). First-level managers are intermediaries between middle managers and staff. The information flow is bidirectional. The information exchange is up and down. The concerns of management are brought to staff members through the first-level manager, and the first-level manager carries the concerns of staff members to the next level of management. Managers often exchange information with other managers at the same level. The exchange of information at the same level of the organization, that is, horizontally, is extremely important to facilitate cooperation and to implement processes that affect more than one department. The first-line manager therefore needs to exchange information with his or her manager (upward), staff (downward), and peers (horizontally). In informal information exchanges managers are encouraged to develop personal **networks** of people within and external to the workplace to exchange information with on a wide range of topics (Yukl, 1994). Networks can provide emotional support, new information about the organization, new external influences, consultation, education, and guidance (Yukl, 2002). Personally beneficial contacts that can develop into networks can come from a variety of interactions, such as serving on cross-functional teams (Chapter 17), serving on committees, joining civic groups, and attending local, state, and national professional conferences (Yukl, 2002).

Most of the information exchanges managers engage in are short and unplanned, cover multiple topics, and occur at a fast and unpredictable pace (Yukl, 1994). Middle and first-level managers have been reported to spend 27 to 82% of their time in oral communications (Yukl, 2002). First-line managers frequently exchange information with staff members on a one-to-one basis. Information exchanges that are done face-to-face require an understanding of word phrasing and the effect of tone, voice, and nonverbal expression on message receivers (Chapter 16). Information exchanges that are written, such as e-mail, letters, and reports, may be better received if etiquette is followed, the composition is interesting and logical, words are spelled correctly, and standard formats are used (Chapter 16).

Discussion is necessary for an exchange of information. Discussion allows the parties to determine the extent of mutual understanding and gives opportunities to influence one another's thinking and gauge the degrees of agreement, disagreement, and commitment to alternative strategies. When there is no exchange, communication is one way. While one-way communication is time efficient, it denies opportunities to clarify, extend, relate, affirm, or challenge. In essence, the message gets delivered without a receipt being obtained.

Oral communication requires effective expression and attentive listening on the part of the information sender and receiver (Chapter 16). People differ in abilities and desire to express their thoughts, listen, or read the thoughts of others (Chapters 17 and 18). These differences may be related to variations in value priorities (Chapter 6), culture (Chapter 1), level of stress, or preferred psychological coping strategies.

Here are some suggestions to foster useful exchanges of information between first-level managers and others in internal and external work environments:

- Know the time constraints.
- Be prepared to share information and present it concisely.
- Actively listen, not just hear what is being said.
- Contribute to the discussion by offering reactions, opinions, and clarifications; rephrase as you understand the issue; help weigh options.
- Recognize nonverbal signs of interest, disinterest, belief, disbelief, sincerity, disgust, anxiety, and anger.
- Know your own nonverbal reaction tendencies when you are interested or uninterested, accept or reject an idea, are sincere, anxious, or angry
- Redirect unintended or undesirable reactions to reestablish a context for the information exchange to continue.
- Be genuine.

First-Level Manager: Make Decisions

All intellectually capable persons make decisions and have been doing so since they were old enough to reason. In health care, managers and staff make decisions. Some are made out of habit. Such decisions deal with matters that come up routinely. Experience therefore is useful for making routine decisions. Experience also allows ready identification of deviations from expectations. Experience, knowledge, and creative thinking contribute to what we will call intuition, or gut feeling. Managers use intuition to make some decisions, especially when there is no compelling information to help choose one option over another. Another consideration in decision making is time. There are degrees of urgency associated with decision making. When there is extreme pressure for an immediate decision, personal knowledge of the salient circumstances, experience in dealing with similar circumstances, intuition, and creativity come into play (Umiker, 1998). A clinical example can illustrate these points: A patient who appears to be about to lose his or her balance is rescued by a student physical therapist before the patient actually loses balance. In the same situation a physical therapist might have quickly moved closer to the patient and increased the size of the base of support in anticipation of giving support but not making actual contact. The physical therapist used experience, which indicated that the patient was not yet falling. The therapist allowed the patient to face a greater challenge to balance than did the student.

Some decisions are less constrained by time. When time is available to make a decision, additional information can be obtained from a variety of sources. In this situation more data can be used to analyze and inform one's experience, intuition, and creative thinking. In the example of the student physical therapist, the student might have told the patient to stop, told the patient that he was leaning to lessen the immediate urgency, and gained time to consider alternative actions. These might include review of instructions for the patient, recruitment of a second person to help guard, or a call for a wheelchair. The appropriateness of the decision can be determined by student and supervising therapist. A similar decision-making process can be identified for first-level physical therapist managers. The sequential actions and related guiding questions in decision making are as follows:

- Determine the issue. What is the problem?
- Identify the degree of urgency for making a decision. How much time do you have to respond?
- Collect data. What kind of information is needed, who has it, and how much is necessary, given time limitations?
- Analyze data. What is most useful? What are the limits of the information? What is lacking? What does the information suggest?
- Identify the options. What does the information suggest? What does experience suggest? What does your gut feeling say about the options?
- Compare alternatives in terms of their expected outcome and cost. Is there enough information to decide? What does experience suggest? What does your gut feeling say about the comparison?
- Implement the decision. Why must we do this now?
- Follow up. Can the decision-making process be improved? How?

Additional comments and strategies for decision making can be found in Chapters 6, 11, 22 and 25.

In several common situations a decision may be delayed or none made. First-level managers have a defined scope of influence. Decisions that are outside of this scope, such as about those who work for another manager, should not be made. Emotional reactions such as anger and fear can hinder clear thinking. When you or others display emotional reactions and seem to cloud perceptions of the issues, it is better to take a break or reschedule a meeting than to make a decision. Some times the shoe does not fit. If you are not the best person to make a decision, delegate the authority to the appropriate person in your department. A common situation is that the information is inadequate, incomplete, irrelevant, or not interpretable. Do not make a significant decision if there is not enough relevant information. The converse of this situation also exists. Seldom does one have all of the data one would like to have by the time decision deadlines have arrived. Do not delay a significant decision if some relevant information, together with your experience and intuition, allows you to feel comfortable with a decision.

First-Level Manager: Influence Others

To influence the beliefs and actions of others generally defines the term **leadership** (Yukl, 2002). This discussion addresses whom a first-level manager influences and the manager's areas of influence. The section that follows deals with leadership.

To identify the individuals a first-level manager influences, consider a physical therapy department in a rehabilitation center. In accord with his or her formal organizational status, a manager interacts with direct reports, that is, those whose work they are responsible for. A first-level manager's direct reports commonly include office staff, on-the-job-trained aides, physical therapist assistants, regular staff physical therapists, senior staff therapists, the coordinator of clinical education, part-time therapists, and contracted therapists. The first-level manager in turn is supervised by and reports to a middle manager who may or may not be a licensed health care provider. If the middle manager is a licensed clinician, he or she may be a member of another profession. Functional relationships, also called horizontal or lateral relationships, are likely to include managers in nursing, speech and language pathology, social work, medical records, and housekeeping. Downward, upward, and lateral interactions hold opportunities for reciprocal influencing. Whenever discussion takes place (Chapter 16), participants have the potential to influence each other. Therefore, first-level managers are in a position to influence and be influenced by their supervisor, their professional and nonprofessional staff, and their manager peers. Yukl (2002) has identified the following areas as those in which managers exert their influence on others:

- Interpretation of internal (departmental or organizational) events
- Interpretation of external events (events in the community and beyond)
- Processes for decision making
- Establishment of trust
- Enlistment of support from lateral and external entities
- Development of skills important to the department and organization
- Choice of objectives, goals, and strategies
- Organization of the work to be done
- Motivation to achieve at a level above current personal expectation

The discussion to this point has been on what managers, particularly first-level managers, do and how to prepare to assume manager responsibilities and roles. Since management is working through others to achieve desired goals, it is necessary to have a deeper discussion of how to ensure that goals are met. This leads to consideration of supervision.

Supervision

To function as a manager requires overseeing others to ensure that a certain quantity of work is completed at an acceptable level of quality. The relationship between performance and the components that influence performance for can be expressed as:

> **Employee performance = (knowledge + skill + ability × motivation (value priorities) + (resources + empowerment)**

Stated in words, this formula suggests that to have high levels of job performance a manager should hire the right people (knowledge, skill, and ability [Chapter 14]); meet their priority psychological needs (Chapter 6); provide the necessary tools, supplies, and systems to do the job (resources); and prepare people to accept responsibility and delegate appropriately (empower [Chapters 15 and 16]).

Supervision entails maintaining or improving the performance of direct reports by assisting them to develop the knowledge and skill to assess their own strengths and weaknesses and by making available resources and opportunities for growth (Yukl, 2002). What this means for the first-level manager is addressed next.

First-Level Manager: Supervision

The distinguishing feature of first-level management is that the direct reports are not managers (Umiker, 1998). Commonly these direct reports include receptionists, clerks, secretaries, phone operators, and volunteers, as well as direct care staff. In health care settings non–patient care staff is often the first to be contacted by the public, including customers, their family members and friends, and vendors. The core purpose of providing health care services is to meet customers' needs and expectations (Chapter 21). This places the first-level manager in an exceptionally strategic position relative to the success of a department or organization (Dunn, 1998).

To get the job done with and through others, the first-level manager needs to know the jobs of direct reports. It is advantageous for a first-level clinical manager to be recognized as a competent clinical practitioner by the therapists, because it intimates knowledge of their job and a tacit assumption that the welfare of patients will be a priority in the department. These qualities are helpful for getting the job done through others:

- Self-understanding, that is, knowledge of the values that shape one's world view (Bennis, 1994)
- Some knowledge of each direct report's value priorities (Chapter 6)
- Knowledge of the dynamics of small groups (Langfred and Shanley, 2001)
- Knowledge of the principles of human behavior, work motivation, social learning theory, and conflict resolution (Locke, 2001; Rahim, 2001; Rainey, 2001).

Formal background in these areas is most likely to aid a manager to develop direct reports when the knowledge is coupled with opportunities for skill development and feedback from others on his or her performance.

Feedback

Knowledge of results is feedback on performance. Feedback includes criticism and praise, or negative and positive feedback, respectively. Feedback is usually taken to heart if it relates to an important goal of the individual whose behavior is being assessed (Locke, 2001). In the workplace the first-level manager sets departmental goals in accord with organizational goals (Chapter 9). Direct reports have to have mechanisms to know how they are doing relative to departmental goals. So to maximize performance to achieve goals, the goals must be paired with feedback on performance. The goal is the targeted end result. The feedback is the degree of progress made toward to the goal. Some opportunities to provide feedback are as follows:

- Chance meeting
- E-mail
- Formal face-to-face meeting
- Group meeting
- Memo
- Phone call
- Post comparative data with personal identification numbers
- Reports
- Video conference

The choice of method depends on urgency, previous feedback, availability, personal preference, previous interactions with the person, and other variables. While electronic means of communication are frequently used today, for the first-level manager, e-mail is likely to be used for communicating with peers and middle managers. Communication with direct reports is most likely to be spontaneous face-to-face encounters.

An understanding of a person's global level of self-esteem and self-efficacy, or task-specific confidence (Bandura, 1997), are invaluable in deciding the contextual aspects and content of the feedback session. Individuals with low self-esteem are often overwrought by feedback they consider negative (Wexley and Latham, 1991). Individuals with high self-efficacy for certain tasks will set high personal goals for that task, will pursue the goal with vigor, and are persistent in the pursuit of specific goal achievement because they believe they have the ability to do what it takes to be successful (Peterson and Smith, 2000). A high level of self-efficacy may be developed by exposure to role models, mentor relationships, and public and private positive feedback. Feedback should be provided as soon as possible after a performance, or at least within an interval that allows a clear connection between the behavior and the outcome. The comments should be specific and the volume of comments appropriate to the knowledge, skill, and experience of the direct report. New staff members usually benefit from the essential information, while experienced staff members are often appreciative of the bigger picture.

In Table 8.2, the list under management reflects a point of reference that targets the here and now compared to the leadership list, which contains items that reflect a future of change. Change is inevitable. For managers in health care change is frequent, often unanticipated, and fraught with novel problems. In short, there are many opportunities to influence others in positive ways to deal with change. Those who influence lead.

Leadership

Leadership, management, and supervision have not been defined so narrowly that there is no overlap between them. This is understandable, because managers lead, manage, and supervise others. To focus closely on the leadership aspect of management, it is helpful to consider two points: (1) Influence is the essence of leadership. (2) Leadership is not a single entity; it is a process. Leadership entails at least two parties voluntarily discussing some kind of change. In the interaction one party or a group, that is, the leader (or leaders), desires to influence or change the thinking, and eventually the behavior, of another party or group, that is, the **follower** (or followers). This leader–follower relationship is situational and impermanent, because in different circumstances the roles can change. Managers often assume the role of leader; however, the leader role is not limited to those with the official title of manager. A leader may have the formal title of manager, but staff can lead in some situations. Another condition of leadership is that the followers voluntarily accept or reject the situational legitimacy of the leader. Leaders do not coerce followers. Followers voluntarily choose to accept the influence of the leader. Given these introductory conditions, the definition of the **leadership process** can be stated to be a process in which the leader intentionally exerts influence to facilitate, guide, and structure actions and interactions of willing followers (Yukl, 2002).

Managerial leadership is an expectation in organizations. When it occurs at lower levels, for example within units or individual work groups, the organization has a competitive edge (Chapter 10). For example, a receptionist may notice a patient acting strangely in the waiting room. She may check to see what other appointments the patient has had (undesirable reaction?). She may let a colleague know that she is going out into the waiting area to talk with the patient and to keep an eye on her and request that the colleague locate the patient's therapist, the manager, or another therapist in case help is needed. Spontaneously, the receptionist assumed the leadership role to deal with a problem. In doing so she fulfilled the common health care organization value of advocating for the welfare of each patient.

Leader characteristics other than official title also come into play; these include ability to communicate, vision, and persuasiveness. Leadership potentially exists at all levels of an organization (Charan, Drotter, Noel, 2001). New issues that affect patient care, caregivers, and the success of the organization arise daily. An admissions clerk, a nurse, a physical therapist assistant, and others may be the first to recognize a threat and take action to deal with the matter. If an organizational culture empowers its members to take the lead in dealing with unusual circumstances and it supports leadership and provides leadership training, the organizational environment is set to transform leadership potential into practical leadership skill. This view recognizes that leadership training should be as much a part of an employee's overall development scheme as continued development of technical skills (Chapters 14 and 20). With respect to physical therapists, the Task Force on Leadership, Administration and Management Preparation (LAMP) targeted the need for development of management and leadership skills to complement direct care skills (Section on Administration, 2003).

Leader Attributes

Leader attributes or traits, including psychological needs, personality characteristics, temperament, and values, have been studied for decades. These attributes have not been found to be useful in predicting who will be a leader. The study of attributes has therefore moved away from prediction and toward identifying traits and skills associated with successful leadership (Yukl, 1994). Reviews of the literature on leadership traits by Stogdill (1974) and Kirkpatrick and Locke (1991) identified 18 traits associated with successful leadership (Table 8.5).

In addition to leaders' traits, Stogdill (1974) noted that various authors identified qualities of successful leaders:

- Ability to conceptualize
- Ability to organize
- Cleverness
- Creativity
- Fluent speech
- Strong knowledge of the task at hand
- Persuasiveness
- Social skills
- Tact

Table 8.5 Major Traits and Skills Frequently Associated With Successful Leaders

Stogdill (1974)	*Kirkpatrick and Locke (1991)*
Adaptability	Cognitive ability (intelligence)
Ambition	Drive
Assertiveness	Desire to lead
Cooperation	Honesty, integrity
Decisiveness	Relevant knowledge
Dependability	Self-confidence
Dominance	
Energy	
Persistence	
Self-confidence	
Social awareness	

Individual leaders have their personal mix of skill strengths and weaknesses. However, none of these skills have been found to be absolutely necessary for success as a leader. Even so, having strong skills in some areas enhances the probability that a leader will be effective (Yukl, 1994). As this chapter emphasizes first-level management, the discussion of leadership should include leadership of small numbers of people.

Small Teams and Leadership

The organizational complexity of many health care organizations, such as acute-care hospitals, skilled nursing facilities, and multiservice outpatient and home health enterprises, has led to increasing dependence on small numbers of people on teams to make meaningful decisions. For the following discussion a team consists of up to 12 members (Hiebert and Klatt, 2001).

Teams may be formally empowered to make decisions that used to be made by some level of management (Cohen and Bailey, 1997). Because of this empowerment, membership on a team offers opportunities to develop and fine-tune leadership skills. Among a number of different types of teams, three generic types are the **functional operating team**, **cross-functional team**, **and self-managed work team** (Yukl, 2002). These types of teams differ in their membership, purpose, scope of influence, and means of designating the leader.

Membership of a functional operating team is relatively stable because the team is formed to deal with operational matters that are usually continuous. Also, the members come from the same organizational subunit. Management often appoints the team leader. The leader has considerable authority over internal operations and in representing the team to other subunits of the organization (Yukl, 2002). The tasks of the appointed leader of a functional operating team include the following:

- Motivating the members to work toward shared goals, that is, sell the vision
- Communicating the message that team effort can result in greater accomplishments than solitary efforts

- Building members' confidence in the possibilities of the team effort
- Selecting members with relevant essential skills
- Assisting members to develop their team skills and an understanding of their role on the team
- Securing the resources necessary for the team to operate
- Representing the team positively to others

Functional operating teams are commonly formed to coordinate the delivery of services to various categories of patients. Management may assign the group leader. In health care, an example of a functional operating team is a departmental team made up of individuals whose jobs are specialized by license yet organizationally similar, that is, physical therapists, physical therapist assistants, and occupational therapists.

The second type of team is cross-functional. Its purpose is to improve coordination between distinct but interdependent organizational subunits and external stakeholders. The possible inclusion of members from outside of the organization is one of its differences from a functional operating team. Other distinctions include these: The team is formed for a limited duration. It has a high level of autonomy over its work procedures. The members have diverse backgrounds, experience, and expertise. The membership may change with the nature of the teams' work (Yukl, 2002). The group leader may be assigned by management, recommended by the group for approval by management, chosen by the group, or alternated, depending on the work of the team. A team made up of a home health physical therapist, an occupational therapist, a nurse, a social worker, a case manager, a durable medical goods vendor, and a Meals on Wheels representative is an example of a health care cross-functional team. A cross-functional team has a membership that is more heterogeneous than a functional operating team. This adds some challenges for the cross-functional team leader that a functional operating team leader does not have. For example, the leader may have more difficulty in scheduling meetings and reaching members; meetings may take longer because of communication lapses; technical jargon varies by discipline; and health care professionals may have greater loyalty to their functional unit than to the team. To counter the personal agenda issue, the designated leader needs recognized organizational power, support, and excellent human relations skills (Yukl, 2002). The success of the leader of a cross-functional team can be further bolstered by these abilities:

- To communicate about technical matters in ways all team members understand
- To plan; for example, assign work and schedule appropriately
- To articulate strategies that support an expressed vision
- To resolve disputes, that is, help the group formulate win-win decisions

A third type of team is the self-managed work team. It may be made up of any mix of individuals, but the members are typically from the same organizational subunit and have similar jobs. Examples of self-managed team responsibilities are making hiring decisions, determining work schedules, and setting productivity goals. What makes a self-managed work team unique is that many of the responsibilities and the authority of one or more managers are, to varying degrees, turned over to the team. Langfred and Shanley (2001) characterize self-managing work teams thus:

- They control their work.
- They manage themselves within the context of the team and their usual work, that is, take responsibility for their work outcomes.
- They distribute the work within the group.
- They make operations-related decisions.
- They actively seek help and resources from the organization.
- They use their discretion to take initiative when problems arise.
- They monitor their own performance and seek candid feedback.

Self-managing teams are autonomous or semiautonomous in terms of direction and oversight. The members usually have similar backgrounds, are assigned to the team for extended periods, and deal with operational issues. These are also characteristics of a functional team. However, the common operational and professional backgrounds of the members and the ability of the team members to elect the leader, or to rotate the leadership role as circumstances change, gives a self-managing team much flexibility. The shared responsibility for the team's performance lessens the need for centralizing power in the position of team leader. To prepare team members to be contributors and leaders requires cross-training. Cross-training for these roles can enhance the skills of each member and enhance the team's performance. To help self-managing team members develop requisite knowledge and skills there is often a manager available to coach, consult, and teach the team members (Yukl, 2002). Yukl (2002) recommends that management fulfill the following conditions as a foundation for successful self-managing teams:

- Clear organizational objectives
- Demonstrable management support
- Meaningful, challenging tasks
- Significant authority
- Significant discretion within defined areas
- Access to necessary information
- Appropriate interpersonal skills
- Competent and committed coaching by managers

A challenge posed by shared leadership is the struggle to find a balance between individual and team leadership. Reports of how to achieve a balance have been contradictory. Successful self-managing teams have been found to have democratic leadership and active leader involvement in facilitating group participation (Stewart and Manz, 1995). However, others have found that leaders of self-managed teams more often than not controlled the decisions (Levi and Slem, 1995).

Student Notes

The first opportunity to develop managerial skills is often by volunteering to take on extra responsibilities. Volunteering to serve on a team at school, at work, or at your local American Physical Therapy Association affiliate provides a means of gaining skill in organization, decision making, budgeting, and other areas. Coaching can be expected. Becoming a valued contributing member of a successful team advances the department, the organization, and in time, the team members. Use team membership to grow in the area of leadership concurrent with improved clinical efficiency and effectiveness. Recognition as a valuable team member and a capable therapist are worthwhile goals.

Summary

The issues that each level of management typically deals with are generally the same. What differs is the magnitude or scope of the actions taken by different levels of managers. Setting the future course for the organization, implementing a new service or product line, and hiring a physical therapist assistant differ in the magnitude of their potential effect on the overall welfare of the enterprise. All managers supervise the work of others. That is what distinguishes managers from staff. The list of attributes and skills of managers is long; however, no single attribute or skill makes a good manager. Managers direct the work of others, teach others, develop others, plan for the success of the organization, make decisions, and inspire others to do more and do it better than they thought they could. Managers thus supervise and lead. Leadership in organizations can be formally recognized, as with the head of a department, or not, as with the new graduate who is instrumental in the development of a niche practice within a department. The commonalities ascribed to formal and informal leaders include a clear vision understandably expressed and the ability to inspire others to take desirable actions beyond those they would usually carry out. Under guidance, participation in work teams provides opportunities to learn management, supervisory, and leadership skills. The development of these skills in employees requires encouragement and support from management. Among the rewards for fostering leadership within an organ-

INDIVIDUAL CASE STUDY

You graduated on Sunday, started work on Monday at a facility where you had an internship, and by Friday were assigned to a five-member functional operating team. The team leader is your former clinical supervisor. You would classify your student–clinical supervisor relationship with the team leader as having been interpersonally lukewarm. You know several of the other members slightly. Those that you know have 5 to 10 years of clinical experience.

The issue for the team is to develop productivity standards for staff physical therapists and physical therapist assistants. Based on what you know about functional operating teams and your assessment of your leadership knowledge and skills, what would you like to happen at the first team meeting you attend? What will you do to help make this happen?

GROUP CASE STUDY

Think about the managerial, supervisory, and leadership implications of the following three statements:

1. Lead, follow, or get out of the way.
2. Great leaders are born, not made.
3. It's them (management) hindering us (the staff).

After formulating your individual thoughts, gather a small group of peers and discuss the accuracy, logic, originality, and usefulness of your individual responses and points of view. By consensus, form a single set of best responses. Present your responses to another group, listen to theirs, and meld the best of the responses, again to form a single set of responses.

ization is a unified view of the organization's purpose and aspirations. Organization-wide guidance information comes from the highest level of management. This guiding information includes what the organization values, what it wishes to become, what it does best, and who it serves. This information is often presented in three types of statements called the organizational values or philosophical statement, the vision statement, and the mission statement. These important fundamental documents are the topic of the next chapter.

REFERENCES

Bandura A. Self-efficacy: The exercise of control. New York: WH Freeman. 1997.

Bennis W. On becoming a leader. Cambridge, MA: Perseus. 1994.

Bennis WG, Nanus B. Leaders: The strategies for taking charge. New York: Harper & Row. 1985.

Caroselli M. Leadership skills for managers. New York: McGraw-Hill. 2000.

Charan R, Drotter S, Noel J. The leadership pipeline: How to build the leadership-powered company. San Francisco: Jossey-Bass. 2001.

Clarkson KW, Miller RL, Jentz GA, Cross FB. West's business law: Text, cases, legal, ethical, regulatory, and international environment, 6th ed. St. Paul: West. 1995.

Cohen SG, Bailey DE. What makes teams work: Group effectiveness research from the shop floor to the executive suite. Journal of Management. 1997;23:239–290.

Dunn RT. Haimann's supervisory management for health care organizations, 6th ed. Boston: McGraw-Hill. 1998.

Fayol H. General and industrial management. Translated by C Stores. London: Pitman & Sons. 1949.

Hiebert M, Klatt B. The encyclopedia of leadership: A practical guide to popular leadership theories and techniques. New York: McGraw-Hill. 2001.

Kirkpatrick SA, Locke EA. Leadership: Do traits matter? Academy of Management Executive. 1991;5:48–60.

Langfred CW, Shanley MT. Small group research. Autonomous teams and progress on issues of context and levels of analysis. In Golembiewski RT, ed. Handbook of organizational behavior, 2nd ed. New York: Marcel Dekker. 2001:81–111.

Levi D, Slem C. Team work in research-and-development organizations: The characteristics of successful teams. International Journal of Industrial Ergonomics. 1995;16:29–42.

Locke EA. Motivation by goal setting. In Golembiewski RT, ed. Handbook of organizational behavior, 2nd ed. New York: Marcel Dekker. 2001:43–56.

Longest BB Jr., Rakich JS, Darr K. Managing health services organizations and systems, 4th ed. Baltimore: Health Professions. 2000.

McConnell CR. The effective health care supervisor. Gaithersburg, MD: Aspen. 2002.

Mintzberg H. The nature of managerial work. New York: Harper & Row. 1973.

Mintzberg H. The manager's job: Folklore and fact. Harvard Business Review. 1975; July-August: 49–61.

Mintzberg H, Quinn JB, Voyer J. The strategy process, Collegiate ed. Englewood Cliffs, NJ: Prentice-Hall. 1995.

Nosse LJ, Friberg DG. Management principles for physical therapists. Baltimore: Williams & Wilkins. 1992.

Nosse LJ, Friberg DG, Kovacek PR. Managerial and supervisory principles for physical therapists. Baltimore: Williams & Wilkins. 1999.

Peterson MF, Smith PB. Sources of meaning, organizations and culture. In Askanasy NM, Wildcromm CPM, Peterson MF, eds. Handbook of organizational culture & climate. Thousand Oaks, CA: Sage. 2000.

Rahim MA. Managing organizational conflict. Challenges for organization development and change. In Golembiewski RT, ed. Handbook of organizational behavior, 2nd ed. New York: Marcel Dekker. 2001:365–387.

Rainey HG. Work motivation. In Golembiewski RT, ed. Handbook of organizational behavior, 2nd ed. New York: Marcel Dekker. 2001:19–42.

Section on Administration. LAMP Leadership, Administration, and Management Preparation. Available from: http://www.aptasoa.org. Accessed 1/20/03.

Stewart GL, Manz CC. Leadership for self-managing work teams: A typology and integrative model. Human Relations. 1995;48:747–770.

Stogdill RM. Handbook of leadership: A survey of the literature. New York: Free Press. 1974.

Umiker W. Management skills for the new health care supervisor, 3rd ed. Gaithersburg, VA: Aspen. 1998.

Wexley KM, Latham GD. Developing and training human resources in organizations, 2nd ed. New York: HarperCollins. 1991.

Yukl G. Leadership in organizations, 3rd ed. Englewood Cliffs, NJ: Prentice Hall. 1994.

Yukl G. Leadership in organizations, 5th ed. Upper Saddle River, NJ: Prentice Hall. 2002.

MORE INFORMATION RELATED TO THIS CHAPTER

A classic article on leadership styles for managers is Tannenbaum R, Schmidt WH. How to choose a leadership pattern. Harvard Business Review. 1973;May-June:163–180.

Quick leadership self-assessment instruments can be found in Beck JDW, Yeager NM. The leader's window: Mastering the four styles of leadership to build high-performing teams. New York: John Wiley & Sons. 1994.

Clawson presents leadership in the context of affecting human activity. Human activity is described in three levels, that is, behaviors, conscious thoughts, and values and assumptions (Clawson JG. Level three leadership: Getting below the surface. Upper Saddle River, NJ: Prentice Hall. 1999).

Cohen uses military examples and analogies to explore leadership principles. Eight universal principles of leadership are offered (Cohen WA. The new art of the leader: Leading with integrity and honor. Paramus, NJ: Prentice Hall. 2000).

Drath presents strong arguments to foster leadership throughout an organization along with means of doing so by following three leadership principles (Drath W. The deep blue sea: Rethinking the source of leadership. San Francisco: Jossey-Bass. 2001).

An interesting perspective on cross-cultural teams is offered by Gibson, Conger, and Cooper. They use the concept of perceptual distance, that is, variance in perception to the same social stimuli, in their discussion of leadership of teams (Gibson CB, Conger J, Cooper C. Perceptual distance: The impact of differences in team leader and member perceptions across cultures. In Mobley WH, McCall MW, Jr., eds. Advances in global leadership. New York: JAI. 2001;245–276).

An excellent discussion of the culture and leadership of transactional (focus on managing and outcomes) and transformational (focus on concepts and communication) organizations can be found in Bass BM. Transformational leadership: Industry, military, and educational impact. Mahwah, NJ: Lawrence Erlbaum. 1998.

Organizational Culture and Fundamental Guiding Documents

Learning Objectives

1. Identify the components of high-performing organizational culture and analyze the intended effect of each component on workplace behavior.
2. Compare and contrast the content and intended purposes of the fundamental guiding documents of an organization, that is, define philosophical or values statement, vision statement, and mission statement.
3. Analyze the congruency of the fundamental documents of several health care organizations in terms of behavioral expectations.
4. Evaluate the implications for your behavior as a member of each of these organizations.

Key Words

Assumption, belief, core values, culture, fundamental guiding document, goal, high-performance organization, high-performance organizational culture, mission statement, organizational culture, philosophical statement, values, values statement, vision statement, visionary

Introduction

In the process of forming a formal business entity, owners often seek advice about the amount of legal oversight, taxes, and liability associated with each of the alternative forms the entity might take (Chapters 4, 5, 7, and 33). State and federal laws regarding businesses are important external factors that guide how businesses must operate in a variety of areas (Chapters 3 and 4). Upper managers of businesses of all types also formulate other guidelines for behavior, attitudes, and values. These guidelines are internal, that is, formed inside the business, and they are intended to shape the behaviors of the employees according to a specific point of view that is unique to the organization.

Organizations strive to distinguish themselves from their competitors in terms of their quality and integrity. Organizations also develop assumptions about their external environment, their place in their particular business arena, and the nature of human behavior and values. These assumptions are the elements of **organizational culture** (Schein, 1992). Organizational culture affects the social and behavioral life of organizational members (Pettigrew, 1979).

Organizational cultural assumptions are passed on to the organization's members in formal and informal ways. The formal way is through written documents that are distributed within and outside of the organization. The less formal way of acquiring knowledge about the organizational culture is by learning about it on the job and through spontaneous social interactions with coworkers. Since social interactions are variable, opportunities for employees to learn the informal assumptions are uneven. Another possible source of variation is between the informal cultural assumptions and the official assumptions.

The formal guiding assumptions are often expressed in documents commonly called statements. Three documents express the official fundamental assumptions that are to guide the organization's members. These **fundamental guiding documents** are individually known as the organization's philosophical or values statement, vision statement, and mission statement. The combined purpose of these statements is to provide a cohesive framework to guide every member of the organization to make culturally acceptable decisions.

Each fundamental document gives direction to somewhat different areas of human action. A **philosophical statement** expresses the organization's philosophy, that is, its principles and values. Some organizations identify their values in a separate statement. Other organizations highlight their core values by listing, defining, and disseminating them. A narrative values document and a list of core values are known as a **values statement** and **core values**, respectively. Values statements both deal with issues encountered in human interactions. They set down guiding principles directed at how members of the organization are expected to treat one another and how they are to treat other stakeholders (Darr, 1997). A second guiding document describes the ideal future position of the organization as envisioned by the organization's leadership. This document lays out the long-term aspirations for the organization. Its intent is to inspire people to work diligently to achieve the desired future. This future is expressed in a **vision statement**. The third guiding document is a statement that describes the purpose or purposes of the organization. Such a statement usually includes what the organization does well, defines its customers, and states how, when, and where services are provided. This document is called a **mission statement**. The relationships between the values, vision, and mission statements are summarized in Figure 9.1.

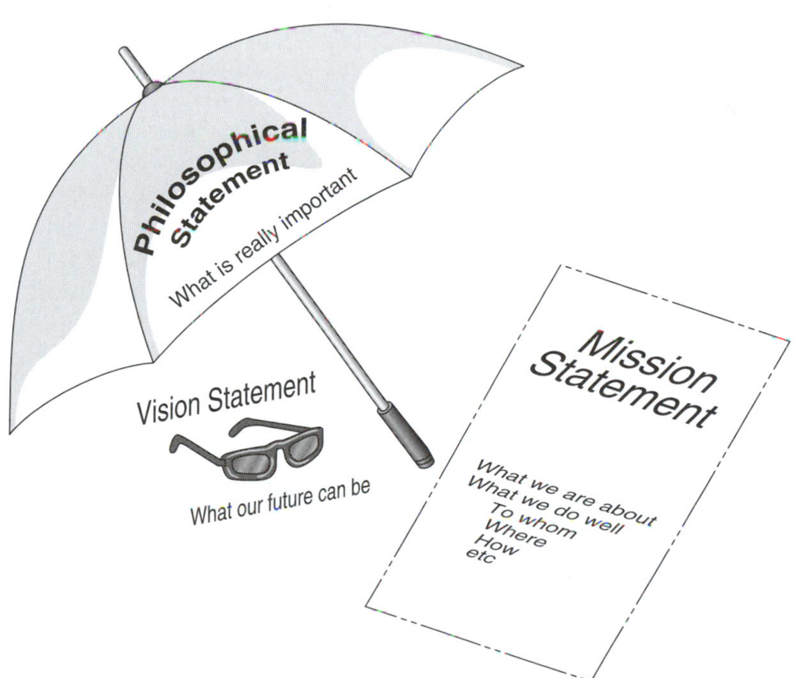

Figure 9.1. Relationship of a philosophical, vision, and mission statement.

Actual statements vary from this idealized depiction (Fig. 9.1). The formation of formal written fundamental documents takes time. Not all organizations have had the time to formalize their beliefs to the point of being able to share them with all members of the organization and other stakeholders in writing. Some organizations choose to express their philosophy within their mission statement rather than in a values statement. Some organizations extract the core values from their philosophical statements as a means of highlighting what they prize.

The discussion that follows presents information on organizational culture and the fundamental documents. A process for formulating fundamental documents is provided. The process incorporates concepts introduced in Chapters 6 and 8. Health care and physical therapy examples are used to demonstrate how staff and managers may use fundamental documents to guide their behavior.

Organizational Culture

Organizational culture consists of values, assumptions, and beliefs. "Top-performing organizations start with a values-driven culture" (Sherman, 1999, p. 339). **Values** represent goals that are sufficiently desirable to stimulate taking actions likely leading to goal fulfillment (Chapter 6). For example, an organization that prizes financial growth over staff development may encourage therapists to increase the number of patients they see each hour and eliminate the continuing education budget. **Assumptions** about job-related behaviors also affect organizational culture. Assumptions are things that people take for granted. Some—but not all—of an organization's assumptions are written down. Written or not, job-related assumptions must be understood by all members of the organization for work to proceed smoothly. Workplace assumptions may be seen in two general forms: (1) the official expression of what is important and how things should be done and (2) the unofficial expression that says what is really important and how the work actually gets done. In the organization's culture, the official version of the assumptions places the focus on assumptions related to values, attitudes, and behaviors. The official culture addresses how members ought to behave in a number of circumstances. In contrast, in an unofficial version of an organization's culture, assumptions focus on actual day-to-day behaviors. The unofficial culture is about how members behave to get along and get the job done.

Everyone in an organization makes decisions. When there are many decision makers at various levels of the organization, something must guide decisions so that important common goals can be achieved. The members need guidance regarding appropriate behavior, direction of work efforts, and clarity in determining what the business is about. When everyone in the organization understands what is important, what they are working toward, what the core service or product is, and who the customers are, everyone is more likely to work toward the same overall goal or goals. In the ideal case, official and unofficial assumptions are congruent and complementary.

Beliefs are also important aspects of culture. Beliefs differ from assumptions in that they are presumed to derive from experiences and be somewhat situational (Hannagan, 2002). This distinction is made in the following example. Your assumption is that your immediate supervisor should deal with a scheduling problem. However, because of the way your supervisor has handled similar matters in the past, you do not believe that she will make the effort to resolve the issue. To get an answer quickly, you follow an unofficial assumption of your peer group. You seek advice elsewhere.

The combined values, assumptions, and beliefs of organizational leaders, along with every other employee, make up an organization's culture. However, it is the responsibility of the formally appointed leaders to set and share the official assumptions with the organization's members and external parties (Chapters 7, 8, and 10). Organizations whose cultures motivate their members "to act in ways that are consistent with customers' expectations and the core values that drive the organization" (Beck and Yeager, 1994, p. 18) enhance the chances for a successful future for the organization. Schein (1992) has identified mechanisms that managers commonly use to foster and reinforce the kind of organizational culture they want:

1. *Attention*: What is important to a manager is what the manager focuses on when interacting with others, for example, paying attention when the manager brings up values, asking questions, making specific requests, giving criticism, choosing measuring tools, or expressing concern.
2. *Criteria*: The criteria the manager focuses on for in recruiting, selecting, promoting, and terminating members, for example, acquiring more expertise, adding a generation X perspective, reducing labor cost.
3. *Reactions*: The intensity and duration of emotional reactions associated with crises, for example, raising one's voice, flushing, haranguing.
4. *Rewards*: What managers give recognition for, for example, verbal praise for a new insight, a raise for achieving high customer satisfaction ratings, a new company car for home health visits.
5. *Role modeling*: Matching words and actions, for example, improving community relations and sponsoring and coaching a Special Olympics soccer team.
6. *Statements*: Formal public statements, verbal and written, about the assumptions and beliefs of the organization, for example, "We believe everyone deserves our best effort from admission through discharge 24/7/365. Come and experience quality care as it should be."

This list makes clear that organizational culture is expressed informally and formally and directly as well as through inference. The central practical purpose of organizational culture is to get everyone focused on working toward the same goals. New employees are exposed to the culture through socialization and the organization's fundamental guiding documents. This combination of influences transmits and perpetuates an organization's culture (Major, 2000).

High-Performance Organization

There is a general feeling among many managers that the only thing that can be counted on as a sure thing is unpredictability (Haeckel, 1999). Examples of unpredictability in today's health care environment include uncertainty of receiving payment (Chapters 26–28), increasing competition for market share (Chapters 21–25), and continual improvements and innovations in technologies. Situations are ever changing and doing so at increasingly fast rates (Chapter 10). In response to these conditions some organizations have become more flexible and innovative. They have reconfigured to have fewer management levels (Chapter 10). They have altered arrangements with their workforce by using pools, part-time workers, and contractors to meet some service needs. Decision making and planning roles have been distributed rather than centralized so that many decisions relevant to meeting customers' expectations can be made more immediately. These examples are among the attributes of a **high-performance organization.** Mische (2001) summarized the characteristics of an exemplary high-performance organization thus:

1. Sets and maintains the industry performance standard for its services or products
2. Creates and sustains a competitive advantage over an extended time
3. Has a financial performance record that is out of the ordinary for a long time
4. Has stakeholders who continually value its services or products

Besides designing its strategy (Chapter 11) to be the best gauged by key business measurement tools, an organization that aspires to be a successful high-performance organization has to develop a culture to support the aspiration.

High-Performance Organizational Culture

A culture is necessary to influence how people orient to each other in the workplace. A culture to achieve high-performance organizational goals is naturally known as a **high-**

performance organizational culture. Several authors have set forth a set of characteristics that typifies a high-performance organizational culture (Hall and Mirvis, 1996; Mirvis and Hall, 1996; Major, 2000). These desirable expectations and understandings are to be shared with new employees in a high-performance organizational culture:

- Being adaptable, that is, being receptive to new ideas, relationships, and techniques, and the ability to develop new skills quickly are essential for success.
- Actively supporting coworkers, anticipating problems, and taking preventive actions.
- Understanding that the nature of the work changes as the organization's goals change.
- Continual learning is necessary to do the job tomorrow.
- Doing more than is asked and doing it well.
- Realizing that everyone's job may be temporary.
- Being flexible, that is, able to change quickly and efficiently, is essential for success.
- Reflecting, that is, mentally gathering, processing, interpreting, and assessing the worth of an experience, is the key to learning from experience.
- Self-assessment is necessary for learning from experience and eventually for growth.
- Self-development is a personal and organizational responsibility.
- Skill in communication with a variety of individuals is necessary.

The transmission of the information in this list is the responsibility of core employees (Major, 2000). Core employees are those who are most important to getting the organization's work done. They are usually full-time members who have shown themselves to be flexible and adaptable. They have been and continue to be involved in substantive decision making. The core employees are instrumental in the acculturation of new employees and students. They know the culture, and they are adept in communicating it to others. In a physical therapy environment, examples of core employees are supervisors, senior staff members, and coordinators of clinical education.

Fundamental Guiding Documents

The pursuit of worthwhile ends has to have some directional guidance and behavioral expectations. This is so members know what they are working toward and what is considered right and wrong. Guidance is commonly found in three organizational documents. These written documents identify what is important to the formal leadership of the organization, what the business of the organization is, and where the organization is ultimately headed. The remainder of this discussion concentrates on the guiding fundamental documents that explicitly or implicitly express the official values, assumptions, beliefs, and future expectations of health care and other types of organizations.

Philosophical or Value Statement

The term *values* means different things to different people. Here values are defined as expressions of need, that is, what is important to us. Our needs are hierarchical. This means that our values are hierarchical. Values differ in the relative degrees of importance we ascribe to them and the amount of effort we are willing to exert to fulfill the valued goal. In this perspective of values, the action that is most likely to fulfill the most important (most valued) need or goal is the one to take. Philosophical principles can be applied to help weight desirable values and the actions that further them. Deciding which principles to follow entails setting a high priority on the values that are maximized by each of the principles (Chapter 6). Given this interdependence, it is understandable that some organizations call their fundamental guiding document a philosophical statement, while others call it a values statement. Values are associated with actions. This means that if priority values are made clear to all members of the organization, there is a common directive to influence and guide actions taken by all members. The priority values of an organiza-

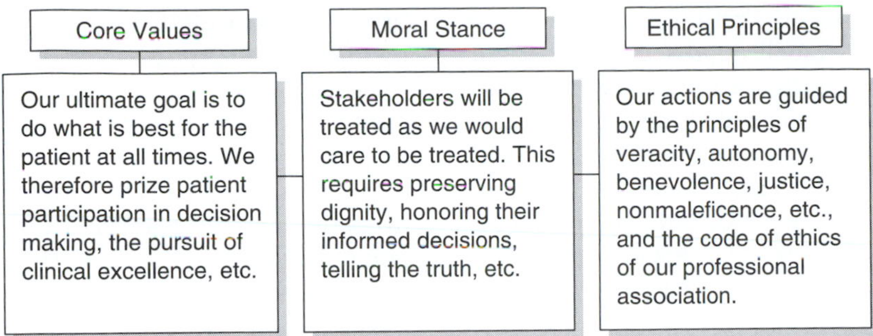

Figure 9.2. Categories of information in a philosophical statement.

tion are those chosen by upper management (see Chapters 8 and 10). Organizations that are values driven are consistent in their behaviors and decisions when everyone in the organization understands what is valued (Sherman, 1999).

An organization's values are expressed in a statement that defines what is important, that is, what is valued in the course of interpersonal behaviors by members. This statement contains values and the philosophical principles that guide behavior (Darr, 1997; Longest, Rakich, Darr, 2000). Ideally, a philosophical statement is formulated before any other fundamental documents. This helps ensure that other guiding documents fit within the philosophical context (Darr, 1997). The practical use of the philosophical statement is to remind everyone associated with the organization of what is held in highest esteem in human interactions. The philosophical statement can also help workers make decisions that are consistent in underlying purposes and effects on stakeholders, because it clearly identifies important values. This foundational consistency counters alternative perspectives that stem from competing values. A philosophical statement generally focuses on three areas: values, moral matters, and ethical principles (Fig. 9.2).

The initial category, values, is noted first because values reflect the needs that must be fulfilled before others. Identification of important values is a product of reflection (Chapter 6). In reality, the values that are seen as most important are those identified by the organization's top management. Table 9.1 lists categories of values relevant to health care providers. Chapter 6 elaborates on the examples in the table.

Moral matters relate to societal guidelines. Specifically, these are behaviors that society values most highly because they are necessary for productive social interactions (Purtilo, 1993). Moral issues arise from human interactions. The moral domain encompasses obligations and judgments about justice, rights, and welfare (Chapter 6). Moral obligations are universal as well as noncontingent, that is, absolute: there are no exceptions to moral obligations (Berkowitz, 1995). The moral stance is explicit about how people ought to relate to one another. The stance is about what is right and acceptable and directly or by inference, what is wrong and unacceptable (Laupa and Turiel, 1995). It also provides the context from which other fundamental documents are developed (Darr, 1997). The last component of the philosophical statement, ethical principles, lists principles that allow

Table 9.1 Example Categories of Value Goals Appropriate for Health Care Providers

Values that reflect:

Acceptance and respect for the customs and ideas of various cultures or religions, e.g., respect for traditions

Appreciation, tolerance, understanding and concern for the welfare of all things, e.g., equality

Competence-based success, e.g., capability

Desire for harmony and safety for self and in relationships with others, e.g., security

Enhancement and preservation of the welfare of others, e.g., loyalty

choosing actions compatible with the values and the moral stance. As discussed in Chapter 6, obligations that are reasoned to by applying ethical decision-making principles are ideals or rules that are applicable in individual situations. This narrow scope of influence is different from universal absolute moral obligations (Barker, 1992). Ethical principles such as those discussed in Chapter 6 provide ways to compare moral options stemming from different perspectives on the relative importance of values (Hall, 1996).

The intent of a philosophical statement is to guide behaviors in certain ways. This function underscores why it is important to think about the consequences to others of proposed actions. Ideally, a written philosophical statement is prepared to guide behaviors throughout the organization. The reality is that new or small organizations may be so busy establishing themselves that there is little time to prepare a formal philosophical statement. This means that the beliefs about human interactions, that is, those learned on the job, become the de facto guide to behavior. Variation in what people say and do make it likely that subsequently developed directive statements will be inconsistent with or different from the ways people actually behave. Without a clear statement of what is right and what is wrong, behavior can be driven by the desire to fulfill self-interests rather than organizational or group interests.

Two additional statements ideally are developed to guide an organization or department. These are the mission and vision statements.

Mission Statement

A mission statement expresses why an organization exists and sets out its aims. Almost all hospitals have mission statements (Gibson, Newton, Cochran, 1990). The mission is the organization's purpose (Ginter, Swayne, Duncan, 1998). It makes clear what the business is. It is written for dissemination to members of the organization and to external stakeholders. For members of the organization, the mission statement expresses the distinctive qualities of the organization and its broad **goals** (outcomes). The mission statement helps anchor plans made to achieve organizational goals (Chapter 11). Of the three guiding documents, the mission statement is most operations oriented and therefore is the most concrete. It gives direction to the actions that expend resources and produce revenue (Chapter 27). Health care mission statements are broad statements of purpose. Purposes are enduring in their essence. They focus on the unique aspects of the organization and present a clear expression of the scope of services and target market (Ginter et al., 1998).

Table 9.2 contains the common parts of health care mission statements. Anyone who reads a mission statement should be able to understand what the organization does, who it serves, where services are provided, how they are provided, and the expectations that are to be fulfilled. The specific items that are included reflect the philosophical statement and the central purpose of the organization. The following list includes items that are often found in a mission statement:

- What the organization does well, such as treating adults who have functional limitations following strokes.
- Characteristics of the target customers you wish to treat or attract in large numbers, such as private pay or those with multiple physical problems in addition to stroke.
- Where services are offered, such as at a privately owned outpatient clinic and in the patient's home.
- Characteristics of the clinical staff members, such as adjunct faculty of a local physical therapy program, board-certified clinical specialist, 10 years of experience, doctorate in physical therapy.
- Geographical site or sites, such as multiple locations on the East Coast, 25 sites in North Carolina, 5 locations in Raleigh.
- Organizational culture, such as commitment to excellence, patients first, history of promotion from within, dedicated to equality in the workplace.
- Third-party payers, physicians, and others you might wish to influence to increase pa-

Table 9.2 Example Mission Statement Elements (Ginter et al., 1998)

Target customers and markets

Kinds of customers, e.g., adult outpatients with cardiovascular and orthopedic diagnoses, managed-care organizations, family practice, cardiology, and orthopedic physicians

Customers who reside or work on the north side of Milwaukee bounded by highways 43 and 45, North Avenue, and Capitol Drive

Core services

Cardiac rehabilitation, manual therapy, work hardening, stress management, and fitness

Self-image

We are experts, e.g., board-certified cardiopulmonary specialist staff, members certified by the American College of Sports Medicine, and members with certificates in manual therapy

Desirable public image

To be recognized as community oriented by regularly volunteering to meet local needs, providing pro bono care, and offering community screenings and educational programs

Elements of philosophy

In the absence of a separate written philosophical statement, prized values and beliefs may be included in the mission statement, e,g., treat all with dignity; join with stakeholders to form win-win solutions; provide liberal terms of payment for those without health insurance

tient volume, such as a managed-care organization, largest family practice group in target area, local industry leaders.

Mission statements are unique to organizations. This makes sense because each organization seeks to distinguish itself from competitors (Chapters 21–25). The items addressed in the mission statement must be congruent with and supportive of the philosophical statement. This means that actions are carried out in ways that are acceptable and supported throughout the organization.

The mission statement is close to the work. The mission gives direction to the planning of everyday work. Goals are set, plans are made, and actions appropriate to fulfilling the purpose of the organization are carried out and evaluated. The work goals are often short-term, perhaps a quarter or a year. Another fundamental guiding document deals with the longer-term future of the organization. This is the vision statement.

Vision Statement

Managers of new and small organizations often must respond to unanticipated problems. There is little time to look or think ahead. In such circumstances management may have verbalized in vague or general terms the hopes for the organization's future. These hopes are refined over time, and eventually everyone in the organization has heard one or more versions of the organization's desired future. Building a vision for an organization has been called pathfinding (Morris, 1988). Upper management defines the path that leads to the desired future. At some point in the pathfinding the path to the future becomes refined enough to formulate in a written document. This document is called the vision statement. A vision statement identifies a highly desirable future state of the organization. It expresses a long-term goal that drives current efforts expected to make measurable progress toward the ultimate goal expressed in the vision. Progress toward the vision is made in steps over time. The vision is something to aspire to; therefore, the vision must serve as an inspirational and motivational communication tool to guide efforts over time (Hoyle, 1995). Because the end expressed in a vision statement does not exist, the vision must give this end a reality through words. A vision should be:

- Stated in terms that help the reader or listener form a clear and vivid image of what the organization can become (Clawson, 1999)
- Expressed in terms that are powerful reminders of what the future may hold and in terms that stimulate diligence in working toward this desired future (Ginter et al., 1998; Darr, 1997)
- Concise enough to be remembered by members at all levels of the organization
- Consistent with and an extension of the other fundamental documents (Darr, 1997)
- Attainable and realistic given the organization's strengths and weaknesses (Ginter et al., 1998)
- Repeated at every opportunity (Ginter et al., 1998)

A vision encourages changes in behavior. It encourages striving, that is, doing more, better, creatively, taking some risks, to complete tasks that are expected to help achieve the imagined possibilities. When people do more than they have in the past or exceed their own expectations, they have been motivated. A viable vision statement motivates. When people direct their personal attributes for extended periods toward overcoming novel problems, they are inspired. A viable vision statement inspires. When people consistently give their full effort to achieve something that is out of reach at the moment, they are aspiring to achieve an ideal. A viable vision statement is an ideal that fosters aspirations. Those who are able to form and communicate a vision that others grasp, voluntarily accept, and are moved to act upon are not just leaders; they are **visionaries**. Visionary managers are able to create and market an idealistic image of a unique future (Kouzes and Posner, 1996) that others bring to life through their best work. More discussion of managers who define the path for others can be found in Chapters 8, 10, 11, and 17.

Student Notes

Take note of the fundamental documents of the institutions with which you are affiliated. Do you see congruence between what is done and what is said? Were you oriented to the culture? Did you discover that there are unwritten expectations? Practice exploring the relationship between what an organization or department says is important in human relations, what is proclaimed as strong points, and where they say they are headed. Compare it with what you see. If there are matches, the organization is probably on track toward realizing its vision. If there are inconsistencies, what problems arise?

By attending to how an organization is doing in relationship to its purpose, priorities, and long-term goals, you can gauge the effectiveness of management. A well-managed organization or department provides direction, support, expectations, and opportunities to use your talents to meet the organization's valued priorities. If there are no formal fundamental documents, it may be either because management has not been in place long enough or because business is brisk and there is no time to work on the documents. The content of the documents is in someone's mind. This can cause difficulties for new employees if there is insufficient time to share the important thoughts on values, beliefs, and assumptions.

Summary

Three fundamental guiding documents represent managers' thinking on values, beliefs, and assumptions about what is important, the core business of the organization, and the future of the organization. When formally written, these documents are called a philosophical or values statement, a mission statement, and a vision statement, respectively. Together these statements provide a cohesive set of

INDIVIDUAL CASE STUDY

So had any visions lately? Given no restraints:

1. What is your vision for yourself within 5 years?
2. What is your vision for your department within 5 years?
3. What is your organization's vision?

Your answers should paint your picture of your idealized professional future.

GROUP CASE STUDY

Form a group of three. Each of you take on a topic: values, vision, or mission. Consult your university's bulletin or Web site or your employer's sources of information and find the philosophical or values, vision, and mission statements. If your department has fundamental guiding documents, review them. Come together as a group and identify one issue that shows continuity among the three guiding documents and *personal experiences* you have had. Now, find one issue that shows discontinuity between the documents and discrepancies with your own experiences. Form a list of suggestions to rectify the discrepancies. Discuss your findings and experiences with others in the class. Determine whether there is a recognizable pattern in the findings and experiences or inconsistencies. If the latter case holds, what does it mean?

guidelines for each member of the organization. The philosophical statement speaks to moral matters, that is, what is acceptable and not acceptable when interacting with others within and external to the organization. The philosophical statement sets the moral foundation under which the other fundamental documents must operate. The vision statement speaks to the ideal future status of the organization, that which can be achieved if everyone does his or her best. The mission statement clearly summarizes what the business does best and whom it serves, where, and how. The mission statement is oriented to operations. It sets performance goals and broadly lays out how to fulfill goals that will in time lead to the realization of the vision. These three documents provide guidance for interpersonal interactions, define the business, and provide inspiration to work hard to achieve something uniquely meaningful.

One influence of guiding documents has not been discussed yet. This is how the organization is structured to work toward its vision and how authority is dispersed within the organization. The next chapter uses your understanding of the fundamental documents to see how they enter into the discussion of the way an organization is structured, that is, levels of authority, and how the structure affects decisions.

REFERENCES

Barker SF. What is a profession? Professional ethics. 1992;1:73–99.

Beck JDW, Yeager NM. The leader's window. Mastering the four styles of leadership to build high-performing teams. New York: John Wiley & Sons. 1994.

Berkowitz MW. The education of the complete moral person. Aberdeen: Gordon Cook Foundation. 1995.

Clawson JG. Level three leadership: Getting below the surface. Upper Saddle River, NJ: Prentice Hall. 1999.

Darr K. Ethics in health services management, 3rd ed. Baltimore: Health Professions. 1997.

Gibson CK, Newton DJ, Cochran DS. An empirical investigation of the nature of hospital mission statements. Healthcare Management Review. 1990;15:35–46.

Ginter PM, Swayne LM, Duncan WJ. Strategic management of health care organizations, 3rd ed. Malden, MA: Blackwell. 1998.

Haeckel SH. Adaptive enterprise. Creating and leading sense-and-response organizations. Boston: Harvard Business School. 1999.

Hall DT, Mirvis PH. The new protean career: Psychological success and the path with a heart. In Hall DT and Associates. The career is dead—long live the career: A relational approach to careers. San Francisco: Jossey-Bass. 1996:15–45.

Hall JK. Nursing ethics and law. Philadelphia, PA: WB Saunders. 1996.

Hannagan T. Mastering strategic management. New York: Palgrave. 2002.

Hoyle JR. Leadership and futuring: Making visions happen. Thousand Oaks, CA: Corwin. 1995.

Kouzes JM, Posner BZ. Envisioning your future: Imagining ideal scenarios. The Futurist. 1996;30:14–19.

Laupa M, Turiel E. Social domain theory. In Kurtines WM, Gewirtz JL, eds. Moral development: An introduction. Boston: Allyn & Bacon. 1995:455–473.

Longest BB Jr., Rakich JS, Darr K. Managing health services organizations and systems, 4th ed. Baltimore: Health Professions. 2000.

Major DA. Effective newcomer socialization into high performance organizational cultures. In Ashkanasy NM, Wildercom CPM, Peterson MF, eds. Handbook of organizational culture and climate. Thousand Oaks, CA: Sage. 2000:355–368.

Mirvis PH, Hall DT. New organizational forms and the new career. In Hall DT and Associates. The career is dead—long live the career: A relational approach to careers. San Francisco: Jossey-Bass. 1996:72–101.

Mische MA. Strategic renewal. Becoming a high-performance organization. Upper Saddle River, NJ: Prentice Hall. 2001.

Morris GB. The executive: A pathfinder. Organizational Dynamics. 1988;16:62–77.

Pettigrew AM. On studying organizational cultures. Administrative Science Quarterly. 1979;24: 570–581.

Purtilo R. Ethical dimensions in the health professions, 2nd ed. Philadelphia: Saunders. 1993.

Schein EH. Organizational culture and leadership. 2nd ed. San Francisco: Jossey-Bass. 1992.

Sherman SG. Total customer satisfaction: A comprehensive approach for health care providers. San Francisco, CA: Jossey-Bass. 1999.

MORE INFORMATION RELATED TO THIS CHAPTER

These texts are compilations of hundreds of mission and corporate guiding documents for a variety of businesses including health care entities:

Graham JW, Havlick WC. Mission statements: A guide to the corporate and nonprofit sectors. New York: Garland. 1994.

Haschak PG. Corporate statements: The official missions, goals, principles, and philosophies of over 900 companies. Jefferson, NC: McFarland. 1998.

Examples of online information on developing fundamental guiding documents:

http://www.allianceonline.org/faqs/spfaq7.html for help on a vision statement.

http://www.allianceonline.org/faqs/spfaq6.html for help on a mission statement.

Fundamental guiding documents of selected health care organizations are available from these Web sites:

http://cms.hhs.gov/about/mission.asp
http://www.hopkinscme.org/cme/CMEmission statement1.pdf
http://www.mayoclinic.com/invoke.cfm?objectid=C6D70201-14A9-4FF8-9EA1B053265DC2F5
http://www.rehabchicago.org/about/history.php
http://www.wakemedfoundation.org/

Chapter 10

Organizational and Operational Structures

Learning Objectives

1. Summarize the concept of organizational structure and include it in your summary of practical examples relevant to management of physical therapy services.
2. Evaluate the main internal factors considered when choosing an organizational structure.
3. Evaluate the main external factors considered when choosing an organizational structure.
4. Contrast methods of coordinating work in a health care organization.
5. Integrate the concepts of organizational structure, stages of organizational development, and coordination of work.
6. Differentiate the influence of different operational structural models on managers and staff.
7. Given any organizational chart, analyze the supervisory relationships, official communication patterns, and ability to quickly respond to changing needs.

Key Words

Age, bureaucratic stage, centralized, complexity, craft stage, culture, divisional stage, entrepreneurial stage, external factor, government ownership, horizontal integration, hostile environment, market diversity, mass production, matrix model, mutual accommodation, operating core, operating structure, operational structure, organization, organizational chart, organizational design, organizational structure, organizing, private ownership, process production, product line model, public ownership, reorganization, simplicity, size, skill standardization, stability, structural configuration, structure, supervision, support services, unit production, vertical integration, work design, work standardization

Introduction

Whenever two or more individuals work together to accomplish a single task, there is a need to coordinate their efforts. Coordination creates a common understanding of the work to be done and how individuals will work together. Coordination is needed to develop a shared understanding of the goal, define performance expectations, establish a work plan, assign responsibility, and coordinate assignments between individuals. As the numbers of employees increase, the need for coordination will increase (Nosse and Friberg, 1992). By definition, an **organization** is an administrative or functional structure, and **organizing** is the act of applying systematic planning and a unifying effort toward the arrangement of independent elements into an interdependent whole (Merriam Webster, 2003).

In this chapter the focus is upon the topics of internal organizational structure and work design. The terms **organizational design** (Champoux, 2000), **organizational structure**, (Longest, Rakich, Darr, 2000), **structural configuration**, and **structure** (Nosse and Friberg, 1992) are used to describe how management structures the organization to fulfill its mission. The structure is the way authority and decision-making relationships are organized. A diagram of the structure is called the **organizational chart**. Assigning content to jobs—the duties, responsibilities, interactions, training, and work process—is an inherent element of organizational structure. Defining jobs this way is known as **work design** (Mintzberg, Quinn, Voyer, 1995). Decisions about organizational structure and work design are dynamic. The same factors that influence management to adopt any specific organizational structure will subsequently be influenced and possibly changed by the adopted structure. The selection of organizational structure and work design are a management responsibility. To manage these dynamic processes, managers must be familiar with the many factors that may or should influence their decisions about structure and design. At the same time, the manager must understand how the organizational structure and work methods affect the organization's ability to perform in various circumstances.

Knowledge of organizational structure and work design is particularly important to health care managers. The rapid rate of change in the external environment of health care organizations can be readily observed. Management efforts to accommodate external change have left many health care organizations in a state of continual organizational restructuring. Increased market and competitive pressures in health care have led to increased organizational complexity. Each time the organizational structure and/or work methods change, the division of work and methods of coordination of work may also change. While management and employees learn new jobs and develop new relationships, work coordination and productivity can decrease. At the same time, growing organizational complexity increases the need for effective work coordination. In these circumstances, organizational performances depend increasingly on management's ability to understand, support, and assist the change process (Schneller, 1997).

Finally, business success depends on management's ability to maintain a workforce that is prepared to work effectively under a continually changing set of performance expectations. Therefore, this chapter reviews human resource management practices and skills related to work design, setting performance standards, performance appraisal, and performance management.

Operating Structure

There are many ways to approach a discussion of organizational structure. Chapter 7 discusses the concepts of legal forms of businesses and the implications of tax status. The additional component of organizational structure is its **operating structure**. Operating structure provides insight into the organization's response to all of the internal and external factors that influence its success. Mintzberg (1979) and associates (Mintzberg et al., 1995) described the organization of human activity as the act of balancing two opposing requirements: The first is the division of work between employees. The second is the coordination of the work of two or more employees to achieve a common goal. An organization's operating structure provides the framework for both division and coordination of work. There are numerous ways to divide the work of the organization. Mintzberg (1979) suggests three methods to coordinate work between individuals:

1. Work standardization
2. Supervision
3. Mutual accommodation

Health care organizations use all three methods. Management's decisions about operating structure are influenced by factors both internal and external to the organization. Table 10.1 shows these factors. There is a dispute over the relative importance and the interrelationship of any of these factors in determining a specific organization's structure (Brown and McCool, 1986; Liedtka, 1992; MacMillan

Table 10.1 Factors Influencing Operating Structure

Internal	*External*
Ownership	Industry trends
Mission	Performance benchmarks
Purpose	Environmental stability
Values and philosophy	Environmental complexity
Production technology	Market stability
Strategic direction	Market competition
Competitive strategies	Environmental predictability
Age	Legal climate
Size	Legislative climate
History	

and Jones, 1984; Mintzberg, 1979; Schneller, 1997). Knowledge of work coordination methods and an understanding of the potential effects of these factors will help managers determine the operating structure that best fits their situation.

Work Standardization

Work standardization can be approached from three points (Mintzberg, 1979). Standardization reduces the need for direct supervision and mutual accommodation because it reduces the variation between the performance of employees. Work processes and tasks can be standardized through the use of such things as policies, procedures, work (treatment) protocols, or standardized work (treatment) plans. The use of output (outcome) standardization is on the rise in health care. An example of outcome standardization is a treatment protocol for care of the patient with a joint replacement that uses mobility status and range of motion to guide care and determine discharge. **Skill standardization** through education, training, and licensure are fundamental elements of work coordination for health care organizations. The requirement that employees meet job qualifications such as physical therapy licensure, experience, and/or postgraduate education are all examples of skill standardization methods. Application of on-the-job competency testing is another example of skill standardization.

Supervision refers to the control and direction of the work of one or more employees by another employee (Chapter 8). Supervision can be used to coordinate the work of the organization. When this occurs, the supervisor must have direct knowledge of the work of a group of employees. The supervisor directs the employees to perform their work in a manner and time frame that complements the work of others in the work group. The supervisor is responsible for coordinating the work of the group.

Mutual accommodation is the simplest method of work coordination. Mutual accommodation results from the ongoing interaction between individuals. This interaction results in continual adjustment between individuals toward the achievement of their shared goals. This method of work coordination is common in simple organizations. It may also be the most effective method of work coordination for the most complex situations. Management should consider the alternative methods of work coordination whenever organizational structure may be changed or performance fails to meet expectations. Organizational structure must be supported by the way work is divided and the method for coordination of those divided efforts. Table 10.2 provides an overview of the work coordination methods used in therapy practice. If it does not implement work coordination, the business will not perform to its maximum capabilities, and its strategic goals may not be met.

Internal Factors Influencing Operating Structure

Internal factors are those under the control of management. The major internal factors affecting operating structure are ownership, production technology, culture, size, and age.

Ownership

The three basic types of ownership are private, public, and governmental. All three types are used in the health care industry (Chapters 2 and 7). **Private ownership** is ownership solely by an individual, a group of individuals, or another privately owned business. **Public ownership** comes about through trading shares on a stock exchange. A

Table 10.2 Production Technology and Work Coordination in Therapy Practice

Production Technology	*Work Standards*	*Supervision*	*Mutual Accommodation*
Professional education	X		
Advanced certification	X		
Assessment practices	X		
Treatment algorithms	X		
Clinical resource staff		X	X
Advanced training	X		
Patient care conferences		X	X
Treatment teams			X
Flexible schedules			X
Licensure requirements	X	X	
Policies and procedures	X		
Treatment protocols	X		
Standardized care plans	X		
Job descriptions	X		
Performance standards	X	X	
Staff schedules	X	X	
Practice guidelines	X		

publicly traded business is owned by a group of diverse individuals who have elected to invest in the business through the purchase of stock. They are the stockholders. Under **government ownership**, a health care organization is owned directly by a local, state, or federal government body and indirectly by the citizens of that government's jurisdiction.

As long as a business functions within the requirements of the law, it is accountable only to its owners. Adherence to ethical guidelines is a different matter, focusing on doing the right thing for the right reasons for all stakeholders (Chapter 6).

Production Technology

Businesses can be differentiated by the type of work and the technology they use to produce their product. Three types of production technology systems can define a business: unit, mass, and process production systems (Woodward, 1965). **Unit production** describes a production system that is based on customer-specific requirements. This includes the production of prototypes or a customer-specific product. Health care is provided on a patient-specific basis. **Mass production** describes a business that produces a large volume of a product. Producers of health care products, such as walkers and wheelchairs, are a good example of a mass production health care business. The description of mass production can also apply to some health services. Laboratory tests, radiology examinations, even certain elements of therapy service are mass produced. **Process production** describes the production technology of large quantities of liquid, gas, or other continuous-flow products, such as electricity. Process production is not typical of health care delivery.

Production technology influences the type and division of the work to be performed. How work is divided determines the need for work coordination. Table 10.2 provides examples of standardization and customized work coordination methods associated with unit and mass production that are common to therapy practice.

Culture

Culture is the term used to describe the patterns of social interaction that define the norm within the organization (Goffee and Gareth, 1996). Culture is learned and shared with others (Chapters 9 and 11). Goffee and Gareth (1996) describe two types of human relations: sociability and solidarity. Sociability measures the true friendliness between employees. Solidarity measures the organization's ability to pursue shared objectives quickly and effectively. The way things are done on the job is learned through formal and informal interactions among organizational members. The aspects of the job that are not formally described in the organization's guiding documents are transmitted to new employees by those who have experience and wish to share it. Solidarity reflects the ability of management to form a vision and communicate it to those who provide the services (Chapter 9).

Size and Age

Mintzberg (1979) summarized several hypotheses regarding the relationship between the **size** and **age** of an organization. His observations indicate that as organizations age, size increases, and so does the division of labor, leading to a larger, more complex management structure, differentiation of organizational subunits, and a more dominant organizational culture.

External Factors Influencing Operating Structure

External factors are things that originate or act from outside the organization (Chapter 11). Numerous external factors (Chapter 11) affect the operating structure of health care organizations:

- Customers
- Competitors
- Demographic shifts
- Economic climate
    - Governmental regulation
    - Technological innovation

The extent of the effects can be understood by assessing the condition of the health care environment for stability, complexity, market diversity, and hostility (Schneller, 1997). The **stability** of the external environment is related to the rate and predictability of environmental change. The faster the rate of change and the less predictable the changes, the more unstable the environment is. Businesses have difficulty adopting a strategic direction in this type of environment. **Complexity** is best explained by comparison to its opposite, simplicity. **Simplicity** refers to an external environment in which customers, products, regulations, and competitors are easily understood because there is little diversity among them. A complex external environment is one in which a high level of technical expertise and in-depth knowledge of all environmental factors are needed for success. Given the diversity of customers, products, and services, the highly technical nature of health care, and the required levels and varied types of expertise needed to deliver care, the current health care environment is an example of a highly complex environment. It is again helpful to talk of opposites to explain **market diversity**. An integrated market is one with few products, services, and customers. The greater the numbers of these factors, the greater the diversity in the organization's market. This requires more diversity in the organization's activities. The more diverse the activities, the greater the need for work coordination. Some health care organizations operate in diverse markets (Chapters 21–24). The last aspect of environment is the degree of unpredictability in the external environment. A **hostile environment** can arise when an organization faces unpredictable demands from multiple sources, for example, its labor force, the government, the community, or its competitors. The health care environment has and continues to face rapidly changing environmental demands. The health care environment is hostile (Nosse, Friberg, Kovacek, 1999).

Common Organizational Structures

Depending on the size of the organization, owners and employees may function within one or more of the organization's parts. Every organization has three basic parts:

Supervision (management): the first division of labor in developing organizations (Chapter 8). With the addition of supervision, those who do the work are separated from those who supervise the work. Supervision brings the first division of the organization into distinct parts (Mintzberg, 1979). As an organization continues to grow, the reliance on support services increases.

Operating core: the part of the organization that actually does the work. As the size of the organization increases, the division of labor increases.

Support services: two groups, technical and general. Technical support consists of experts who direct their efforts toward the development of work standards and responding to environmental complexity. A clinical lead or senior therapist might fill this role in a physical therapy practice. The purpose of the technical expert is to enhance the performance of the operating core. The second group of support personnel are those whose work is not directly related to the operating core. Marketing, the business office, the mailroom, and cafeteria workers are examples of general support functions.

The organizational structure defines the relationships among and between the parts of the organization. The right structure will support the functions of the organization, facilitate performance, accommodate internal factors, and position the organization to respond to external threats and opportunities. In the same way, the wrong structure will impede the performance and success of the organization. When you are considering the structure of a specific organization, it is appropriate to ask whether form fits function.

The Organizational Chart

The organizational chart is a graphic representation of structure. Using boxes and lines, an organizational chart presents graphically the relationships between the owners, management, support functions, and operating core departments. Solid lines represent direct reporting relationships. Reporting relationships indicate both communication and top-down control. Dotted lines represent communications and/or indirect control (MacStravic, 1986). An organizational chart can be used to depict a simple or complex organization and can depict all or part of an organization's structure.

Organizational structures are typically pyramidal, representing the hierarchy of the management structure. Depending on the part or parts of the organization depicted, the most senior management position goes at the top of the chart. Subordinate positions and departments follow in order of organizational position from high to low. Traditionally, the organizational chart describes the authority and responsibilities of positions within the organization. Occasionally, an organization will develop a structure that eliminates the typical management hierarchy. An organizational chart may be used to depict such a structure, but it may have little meaning outside of the organization. Also, the organizational chart should represent the actual structure, not a desired culture or set of relationships. Figure 10.1 depicts the organizational structure of the sole proprietorship therapy practice (Chapter 7).

Operating Structure at Progressive Stages of Organizational Development

As an organization grows and develops, the need to divide and coordinate the work of its employees will grow. As this happens, organizations will pass through classic stages of development. Mintzberg (1979) and associates (1995) have described five stages of organizational development:

1. Craft stage
2. Entrepreneurial stage
3. Bureaucratic stage
4. Divisional stage
5. Adhocracy (matrix stage)

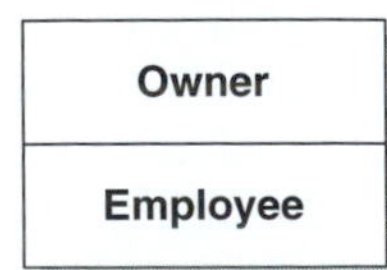

Figure 10.1. Sole proprietorship.

The Craft Stage

The first stage of organizational development is the **craft stage**. At this stage, the organization is small, and there is little or no division of labor. The term craft is not intended to describe the work of the organization but rather to describe an organization in which all of the members can effectively perform all of the tasks necessary to achieve the organization's common goal with little direct supervision. The work of the craft organization can be coordinated through mutual adjustment, standardization, and/or supervision. If there is supervision, the role is likely to be defined as a working supervisor: that person commonly performs all of the work of the organization alongside other organization members. The use of standardization as a method of coordination largely depends on the work of the craft organization. Mutual adjustment is more common than supervision at this stage. Figure 10.2 represents the organizational structure of the craft stage of development.

The description of a craft organization fits many small private therapy practices in which the organization consists of one or more therapists who share responsibility for the work. Work standardization is a key method of coordination. Standardization occurs as a result of such things as professional education, licensure, standards of practice, policies, procedures, and protocols. Mutual accommodation is sufficient to coordinate the work shared by the therapists.

With luck, the therapists in this example have the choice to maintain their practice at its current size or take advantage of growth opportunities. If they choose expansion, they will need additional partners and/or employees. Eventually they will have to expand both the supervisory and support functions of the organization. When that occurs, the organization will move into the entrepreneurial stage of development.

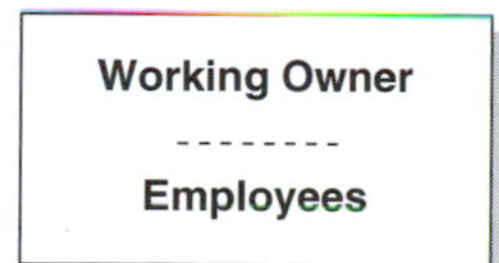

Figure 10.2. The craft stage.

The Entrepreneurial Stage

The second stage of organizational development is represented in Figure 10.3. At the **entrepreneurial stage**, standardization supported by mutual accommodation can no longer be relied upon to coordinate the work of the organization. Additional supervision and support are required. Further division of labor provides the opportunity to improve performance through increased efficiency. Alternatively, it may place the organization at a disadvantage. Additional management layers lead to greater separation between senior management, employees, and customers. More management can translate into slower decision making. Increased reliance on standardization can decrease flexibility. A longer decision-making cycle, coupled with decreased flexibility, has the potential to make an entrepreneurial organization less responsive in a rapidly changing environment than a craft stage organization.

The Bureaucratic Stage

As the organization continues to grow, the demand for continued division of labor and a more complex work coordination system increases. At this point, the organization begins to move into the **bureaucratic stage**. Figure 10.4, *A* to *C*, illustrates various forms of the bureaucratic organizational structure. A bureaucracy is characterized thus:

- A large, complex management structure
- Highly specialized employees
- Distinct functional operating segments (departments) structured along lines of specialization
- Large technical and general support service functions
- Much standardization

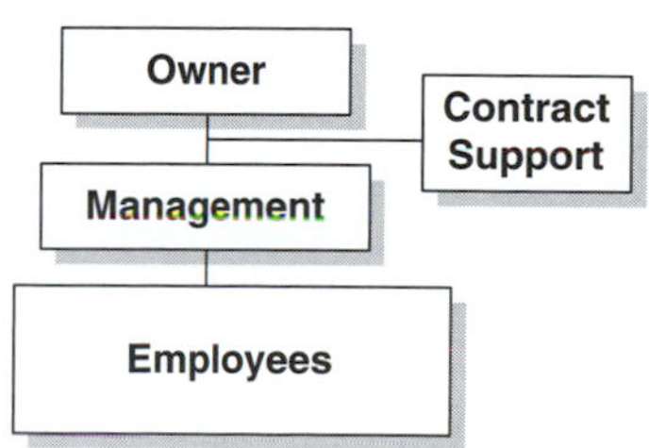

Figure 10.3. The entrepreneurial stage.

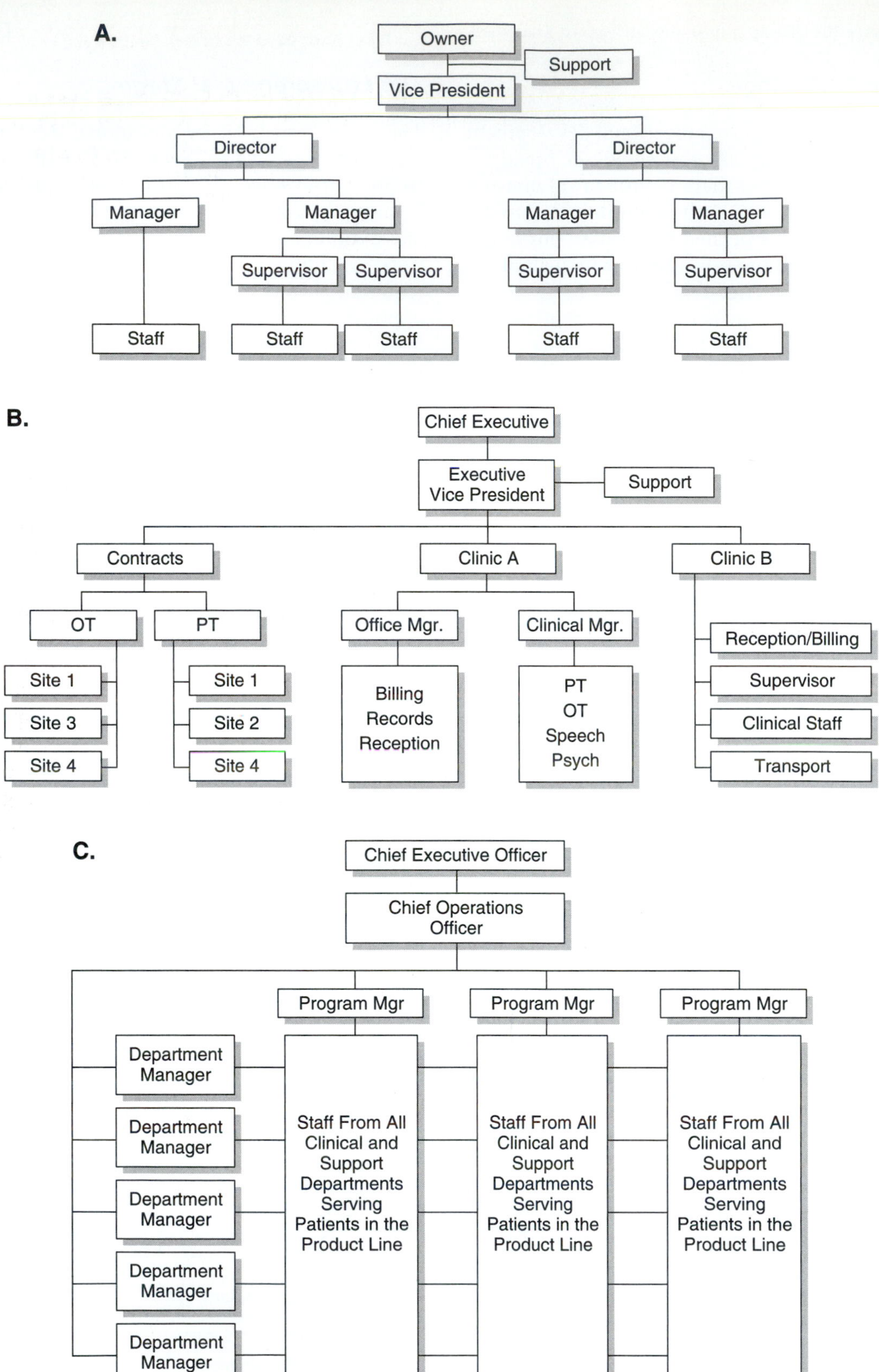

Figure 10.4. A. The bureaucratic stage. B. The divisional stage. C. The matrix model.

Bureaucratic organizations, made efficient through high standardization and specialization, can be very successful when the external environment is stable. However, where the entrepreneurial organization is at risk from decreased flexibility, the bureaucratic organization requires even more effort to respond to environmental changes. Without special mechanisms in place, the lack of ability to respond to change, foster new ideas, and stay in touch with customers and employees can significantly interfere with the survival of a bureaucratic organization that finds itself in an unstable, hostile, and/or competitive market.

Recent and rapid changes in the health care industry have left many large health care organizations in exactly this situation. Having found success in a relatively unchanging but growing market, bureaucratic health care organizations face continual challenges in adapting to the new health care environment (MacStravic, 1986).

Only organizations that can adapt to meet this challenge will be successful. Evidence of this threat can be found in the experiences of health care businesses in areas hardest hit by managed care initiatives. Minneapolis–St. Paul is one of those areas. Between 1981 and 1992, the number of hospitals in the Twin Cities declined from 24 to 19. The number of hospitals not affiliated with a larger health care system declined from 13 to 5. Roughly 62% of the independent hospitals have joined a larger system (AHA, 1992). These figures are representative of a continuing national trend toward health care business failures and consolidations. Increased employee participation in organizational problem solving and the use of work teams are two examples of work design approaches used by bureaucratic organizations to address these weaknesses (Chapter 17).

An organization that continues to expand through product diversification and/or market expansion may move into the **divisional stage** of development as in Figure 10.4, *B*. This type of business expansion can be achieved through vertical or horizontal integration of the existing business with new or acquired businesses. Or a company may adopt a divisional structure as it ventures into a new line of business. The remaining comments will be focused on the first two options for growth into a divisional structure.

Horizontal and Vertical Integration

Expansion of an organization's current business into new markets is called **horizontal integration**. A physical therapy practice that acquires or develops additional physical therapy practices to cover a larger geographical region expands by providing the same service to more customers. The addition of these similar business units is an example of horizontal expansion. Growth in this manner moves the organization into a divisional structure.

Business expansion through product diversification, whether by broadening services to the same customer base or by adding a new customer base, is called **vertical integration**. A hospital that expands through the acquisition of a primary care physician practice, a long-term care facility, and a home care agency is expanding through vertical integration (Brown and McCool, 1986). Organizations may have concurrent strategies for growth through both horizontal and vertical integration.

Centralization Versus Decentralization

A key organizational question for the divisional organization relates to the centralization of senior management and support functions. If decision making rests largely with management at the corporate (central) office, the organization is **centralized**. Similarly, if support services are part of the corporate office and have authority over activities of other divisions, they are described as centralized. To the extent that decision making and support functions are left to the divisions, the organization is decentralized. Full centralization or decentralization should be viewed as a continuum, with most organizations resting somewhere between the extremes.

A centralized organization relies on supervision and standardization to coordinate the work between its divisions. Centralized standardization works well for divisional organizations whose success is tied to product consistency, such as a nationally known fast food chain. The same concept is equally applicable to a national therapy contract service. If, however, individual divisions must respond to local market demands or provide different products or services, centralization may decrease a division's flexibility and ability to respond to local market conditions. Performance may be hampered.

Additional Operational Structural Models

The **product line model**, unlike the bureaucratic structure, is an operational structure that shuns work-specific operating units, such as a physical therapy department. In place of individual units there is a preference for product-based operating units, such as a pain management program. Multiple approaches have been taken to product line structuring. In one case, only a portion of the organization, such as the marketing department, will be organized along product lines. In another case, the entire organization may be aligned with specific products.

A hospital that maintains distinct centralized physical and occupational therapy departments and has managers for both departments with all therapists serving all patient types is a work-specific department model. If the same hospital were to reorganize; assign physical and occupational therapy staff to distinct orthopedic, neurologic, and geriatric treatment teams; and eliminate the department management positions in favor of team supervisors, it would move toward a product line structure. A product line structure is more likely to use mutual adjustment than supervision to coordinate work. Standardization is still used to coordinate work. Instead of department-based standards, however, you might see team care plans or other forms of product-specific standards of care.

The product line structure focuses the organization's attention out toward the customer rather than in toward specialized departments. Products are defined by customer needs. Reasons that an organization might move to a product line model include several different customer markets or a large enough demand for a single product to commit dedicated resources. The use of a product line approach may attract customers in need of a specific service or set of services (Fottler and Repasky, 1988; MacStravic, 1986).

Another operational structure is called an adhocracy, or a **matrix model** (Figure 10.4, *C*). This model provides an alternative to the traditional bureaucratic structure. A matrix-structured organization is a hybrid between the traditional bureaucratic and the product line structure. A matrix organization maintains a department structure but overlays a product line structure onto the department structure. The product line unit is organizationally equal to the functional departments. The matrix model allows an organization to respond to external factors while maintaining a high degree of internal efficiency. The work of a matrix health care organization is most efficient when coordinated through standardization and mutual accommodation with relatively little reliance on supervision. The matrix model does create a dual system of responsibility and accountability. Staff working in a matrix structure are accountable for meeting the expectations of both department and program management. This can become difficult should there be an adversarial relationship between the product manager and the functional manager. Unproductive conflict can be a difficult problem (Timm and Wanetik, 1983).

Organizational Structure and Product Strategy Decisions

The method of work coordination should not be confused with the strategic decision-making process of the organization covered in Chapters 15 and 11, respectively. At the craft stage of development, the approach to product or service strategy decisions depends on the ownership structure and values. If the company is jointly owned by the employees, a collaborative approach is likely. If it is solely owned, decision making may be an autocratic process. In a traditional bureaucratic organization, product strategy and alignment of strategy with functional department performance requirements happen at the senior management level. Under the product line model, product strategy development happens at the product unit level. Because there are no functional departments, the product manager is also responsible for direction and coordination of the functional resources that support the strategy. In a matrix organization, the product manager is responsible for product strategy development. The functional department manager participates in product planning and is responsible for determining the resource needs required to achieve the performance objectives. In both the product line and matrix models, decision making is pushed down to middle management, resulting in decisions made by people who are closer to the customers and the employees. This enhances the organization's ability to respond to change (Timm and Wanetik, 1983).

Reasons to Change Organizational Structure

In response to significant environmental pressures, health care organizations have undergone partial or total **reorganization** to improve the potential for continued success (Fottler and Repasky, 1988; Timm and Wanetik, 1983). Reorganization may be considered when an organization is not meeting quality, productivity, and/or financial expectations. A fundamental change in an organization's purpose, vision, and/or strategic direction is another reason for reorganization. Such a change often occurs when an organization is sold, changes its chief executive, or merges with another organization. Sometimes organizations change structure simply because reorganizing is popular. Reorganization usually produces profound change. A true reorganization entails an assessment (Chapter 11) and possibly redesign of many organizational functions, such as these:

- Division of work
- Employee relationships
- Employee skill needs
- Methods of work coordination
- Number and type of people employed
- Work group composition
- Work processes
- Work standards (policies, procedures, and protocols)

The planning required to implement a successful reorganization is significant. As a result, a poorly planned or implemented reorganization can hurt rather than help the organization (Roach, 1996). For this reason, reorganization should be undertaken only after comprehensive planning.

Reorganization: Part of the Strategic Planning Process

Reorganization should be undertaken to improve some aspect of performance. However, performance problems that are significant enough to risk the disruption of reorganization are unlikely to be corrected by simply rearranging the structural elements of the organization. Reorganization should be one possible outcome of strategic planning (Chapter 11). It is not a goal to be achieved. Rather, it is but one way to achieve a strategic objective.

For reorganization purposes, strategic planning should start with the reaffirmation or revision of the purpose and vision of the organization. Successful strategic planning requires a clear direction for the future. An organization's vision is the target upon which the energies of the organization should be focused (Chapters 9 and 11).

The first step in an organizational assessment is an internal and external assessment (Liedtka, 1992). The internal assessment is used to identify both strengths and weaknesses. The internal assessment should provide a clear understanding of how the organization accomplishes its work (Chapter 11). Answers to several questions help guide this assessment:

- What type of work is done?
- How is work divided and coordinated between individuals, departments, divisions?
- What operates smoothly?
- Where are the barriers and bottlenecks in work flow?
- Does the organization meet its performance expectations?

An external assessment should be used to determine the current and projected state of the organization's environment (Chapter 11). Guiding questions for an external assessment:

- What threats does the organization face now?
- What opportunities are there for the organization now?
- What about future threats?
- What about future opportunities?

All internal and external factors that influence structure should be addressed during the assessment. Information obtained during the assessment can be used to set strategic directions and performance expectations. Gaps between current performance and performance expectations should define what must be done (Chapter 11). The work to be done can be expressed as short- and long-term goals and objectives. Once management has defined the work to be done, it must ask two questions: (1) Do I have the resources to get the job done? (2) Will the organization's infrastructure support the work that must be done? If the resources are inadequate, management must obtain additional resources or redefine the strategy. If the infrastructure is inadequate, reorganization should be considered (Bhide, 1996). Again, reorganization means significant change. All aspects of the infrastructure will undergo some degree of change in making a reorganization work.

The relationship between strategic planning and reorganization can be illustrated by example. Our theoretical therapy practice, Do It All Therapy, Inc., is privately owned and has a vision of the future that includes continued growth and expansion. Unfortunately, the company has been losing business for the past 6 months. Assessment has shown that the volume decline is due to an increase in the number of people enrolled in managed care insurance plans, as local managed care plans have been directing patients to use other therapy providers. Further investigation has shown that Do It All will have to provide broader geographical coverage and offer large price discounts to win managed care business from its competitors. To compete for

INDIVIDUAL CASE STUDY

You are the manager of a department that has grown from 5 to 30 employees over the past 5 years. In addition to your position, your department now has 17 therapists, 5 therapist assistants, 5 therapy aides, 2 office workers and 1 receptionist-secretary.

Until 2 weeks ago, all of the staff reported directly to you. The staff really liked that, but you found it overwhelming. You devised a reorganization plan that includes two supervisors. Under your plan everyone reports to one of the two supervisors. Only the supervisors report to you. You are excited about reorganizing, but your staff are openly against it. It has caused hard feelings between the therapists who were promoted and the others who applied for the positions. Many of the staff members are upset because they always dealt with you directly. Since the change 2 weeks ago, no one has talked with you. Is that good? What does the organizational chart look like now? What else might you anticipate that the reorganization will change?

GROUP CASE STUDY

Form a group of five members. Each member represents a different discipline: nursing, occupational therapy, physical therapy, recreational therapy, and speech therapy. Figure 10.5 is the organizational chart for the organization. It is an inpatient rehabilitation hospital that provides care to the patients with the most complex problems.

Situation

Recently the coordination of work and general performance of the interdisciplinary care teams has been on the decline. Professional staff are frustrated by some team members' unwillingness to compromise and cooperate. Patients and families are complaining because they are receiving conflicting information, are double-booked for appointments, and have competing therapy goals when treated by different therapists.

Task

How might the staff be reorganized to address some of these problems? Why would your reorganization suggestions help? Formulate your solutions; then join with another group and compare and contrast your reorganization suggestions and make one reorganization plan you can all live with.

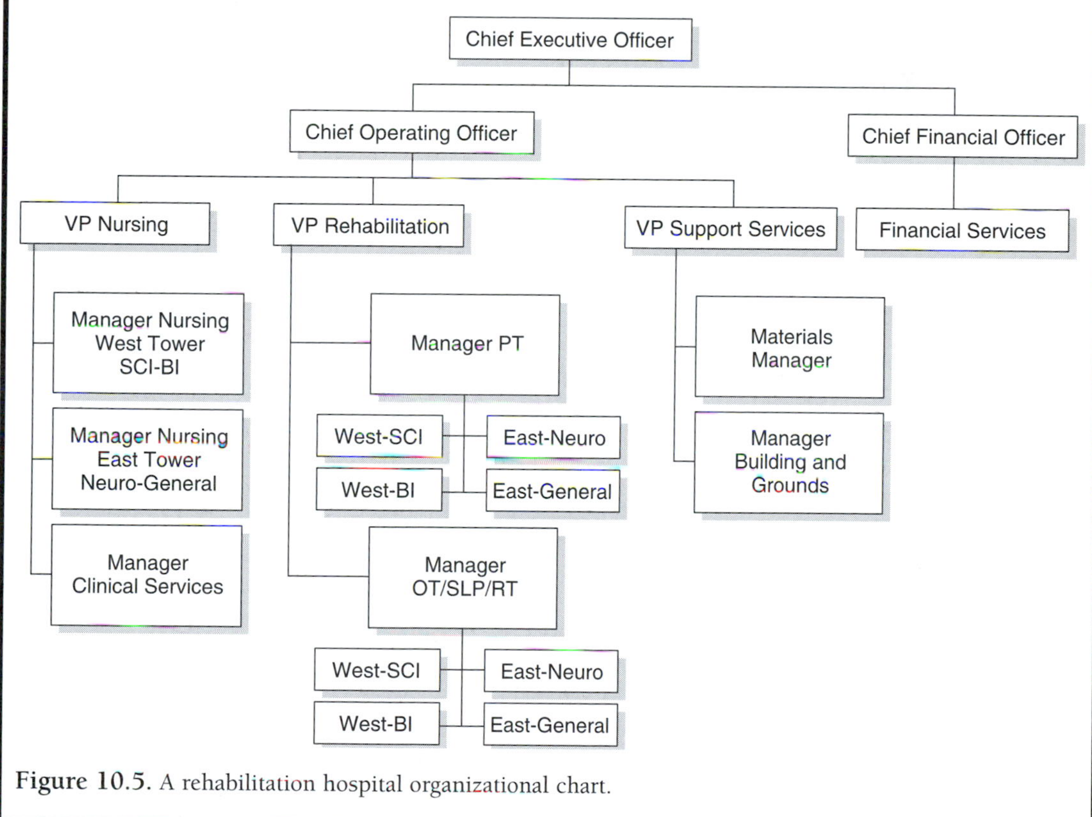

Figure 10.5. A rehabilitation hospital organizational chart.

managed care business, Do It All will have to open at least two additional clinics. Clinic expansion will require external funding, such as a loan. The added costs of expansion combined with price discounts will cause a decline in profitability. To remain profitable, Do It All must reduce its expenses. The owner has decided to decrease the number of clerical staff, use more physical therapist assistants, and increase the hours of operation.

These changes will affect the division of work, number and type of people employed, work group composition, employee relationships, methods of work coordination, and work processes. These changes will occur because the company's structure will change.

Student Notes

The organizational structure, specifically the operational structure, directly affects you as a staff member. Think about your place in an organization with the following legal forms and organizational configurations:

- The employer is a for-profit private physical therapy partnership in which you are the newest of three staff. The owners manage the business more than they treat patients. The clinic is the only one for a radius of 20 miles. There is little managed care in the area. Think entrepreneurial model in a stable, simple, integrated, nonhostile external environment.
- The employer is a not-for-profit neurologic rehabilitation center with a staff of 35 licensed therapists of all types. The center is one of three in the state owned by an order of nuns. Several hospitals nearby also have inpatient rehabilitation units. You are a member of the brain injury team. Think matrix model in an unstable, complex, diverse, hostile external environment.

Compare and contrast the two examples and consider what you think it would be like to work in each type.

Summary

Management has the responsibility for maximizing the performance of the organization. Business structures have legal, tax and, operating structures that define an organization's form and function. Performance is influenced greatly by the structure of the organization. The structure of a specific organization is influenced by diverse internal and external factors. Examples of all common business forms and operational structures may be found in the health care industry. Through careful planning, management should look within and outside the organization at the environmental factors that will influence its success. Organizational structure and work design should be dynamic and should change as an organization matures or changes its focus to meet internally and externally driven performance demands. Structure should be linked with and support the organization's product or service strategy. How to examine the external environment and develop responsive strategies for an organization is addressed in Chapter 11. The internal and external environmental factors discussed in this chapter are an essential component in planning strategies for success.

REFERENCES

AHA Guide to the Healthcare Field, 1979–1992. Chicago: American Hospital Association. 1992.

Bhide A. The questions every entrepreneur must answer. Harvard Business Review. 1996;Nov-Dec:120–130.

Brown M, McCool BP. Vertical integration: Exploration of a popular concept. Healthcare Management Review. 1986;11:7–19.

Champoux JE. Organizational behavior. Essential tenets for a new millennium. Cincinnati: South-Western College. 2000.

Fottler MD, Repasky LJ. Attitudes of hospital executives toward product line management: A pilot survey. Healthcare Management Review. 1988;13: 15–22.

Goffee R, Gareth J. What holds the modern company together? Harvard Business Review. 1996; Nov-Dec:134–149.

Liedtka JM. Formulating hospital strategy: Moving beyond a market mentality. Healthcare Management Review. 1992;17:21–26.

Longest BB, Jr., Rakich JS, Darr K. Managing health services organizations and systems. 4th ed. Baltimore: Health Professions. 2000.

MacMillan IC, Jones PE. Designing organizations to compete. Journal of Business Strategy. 1984;4:11–26.

MacStravic RS. Product-line administration in hospitals. Healthcare Management Review. 1986; 11:35–43.

Merriam Webster's Collegiate Dictionary. 11th ed. Springfield, MA: Merriam-Webster. 2003.

Mintzberg H. The structuring of organizations. Englewood Cliffs, NJ: Prentice Hall. 1979.

Mintzberg H, Quinn JB, Voyer J. The strategy process, Collegiate ed. Englewood Cliffs, NJ: Prentice Hall. 1995.

Nosse LJ, Friberg DG. Management principles for physical therapists. Baltimore: Williams & Wilkins. 1992.

Nosse LJ, Friberg DG, Kovacek PR. Managerial and supervisory principles for physical therapists. Baltimore: Lippincott, Williams & Wilkins. 1999.

Roach SS. The hollow ring of the productivity revival. Harvard Business Review. 1996; Nov-Dec:81–89.

Schneller ES. Accountability for health care: A white paper on leadership and management for the U.S. health care system. Healthcare Management Review. 1997; 22:38–48.

Timm MM, Wanetik MG. Matrix organization: Design and development for a hospital organization. Hospital Health Service Administration. 1983; Nov/Dec:46–58.

Woodward J. Industrial organization. Theory and practice. Oxford, UK: Oxford. 1965.

More Information Related to this Chapter

Three books that expand the discussion on organizational structure and add some interesting perspectives are:

Aldrich HE. Organizations evolving. Thousand Oaks, CA: Sage. 1999. The author provides an analysis of the key variables that affect contemporary organizations which include new knowledge and entrepreneurship.

Robbins SP, Coulter M. Management. Upper Saddle River, NJ: Prentice Hall. 2002. Chapter 10 is titled organizational structure and design. The information deepens the discussion and is complementary to the introduction presented in this chapter.

Stroh LK, Northcraft GB, Neale MA. Organizational behavior: A management challenge. Mahwah, NJ. Lawrence Erlbaum. 2002. The authors nicely discuss managing individuals and groups, performance management, managing change and of course, organizational structure and design.

On the topic of reorganization of organizations, Andersen challenges the adage of a connection between function and form (Andersen JA. Organizational design: Two lessons to learn before reorganizing. International Journal of Organization Theory and Behavior. 2002;5:343–358. The concept of the evolution of organizations is the focus of the article by Djiksterhuis et al. (Dijesterhuis MS, Van den Bosch FAJ, Volberda HW. Where do organizational forms come from? Management logics as a source of coevolution. Organizational Science. 1999;10:569-582.)

Chapter 11

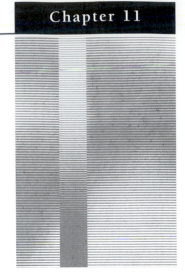

STRATEGIC MANAGEMENT AND STRATEGIC PLANNING

Learning Objectives

1. Compare and contrast the terms strategic management, strategic intent, strategic thinking, and strategic planning: definitions, purpose, key elements, and interrelationships.
2. Correctly differentiate the components of an internal and an external environment and how they relate to an overall environmental scan.
3. Analyze the strengths, weaknesses, opportunities, threats (SWOT analysis) of a hypothetical health care organization in a defined market.
4. Synthesize the information from a SWOT analysis and develop strategic plans to accomplish desirable organizational ends.
5. Evaluate (by gap analyses) the performance of a strategic planning process and improve it.
6. Comprehend the purpose of various types of strategies to meet organizational ends.

Key Words

Adaptive strategy, competitive advantage, directional strategy, environmental scanning, external environment, gap analysis, goal, internal environment, market entry strategy, objective, operational strategy, plan, policy, positioning strategy, procedure, sector environment, strategic action plan, strategic intent, strategic management, strategic planning, strategic thinking, strategy, strength, weakness, opportunity, threat (SWOT) analysis

Introduction

Generals want to win wars. Coaches want to win games. Health care managers want their organization to succeed in the marketplace. The commonality between generals, coaches, and health care managers noted here is the desire to defeat enemies, opponents, and competitors, respectively. To help ensure their future, successful members of the three groups lead efforts to formulate plans, **strategies** as they are called in military circles, for dealing with their opposites prior to encountering them.

Thinking in terms of strategies is a hallmark of a management philosophy known as **strategic management** (Ginter, Swayne, Duncan, 1998). This chapter covers the major components of strategic management and its associated process for formulating, implementing, and evaluating strategies called **strategic planning**. Under the leadership of top-level organizational and departmental managers, the result of strategic planning is strategy aligned with the organization's fundamental guiding documents (Macmillan and Tampoe, 2000). Through planning the ideal organizational outcomes are identified and guidelines developed for making decisions about actions intended to better the organization's future (Ginter et al., 1998). Strategy formation entails gathering and analyzing multiple sources of information. Information the organization has about itself and what it can find out about outside factors that affect its viability is considered.

A more complete discussion of the essential elements of strategic management and strategic planning follows. To aid in understanding how the concepts apply to health care and clinical practice, health care and physical therapy examples are used.

The Start: Strategic Intent, Management, and Thinking

Strategic management begins with the intent to have the organization succeed now and in the future. The basic question regarding intent is where we want to go. An established organization's intent is officially expressed several ways. For example, it may be called aspirations, goals, motives, or purpose. However, the richest sources of intent are found in the organization's fundamental guiding documents: philosophy, values, vision, and mission statements, presented in depth in Chapter 9. In strategic management terms intent is logically called **strategic intent**.

Strategic management is described earlier as an integrated way of thinking about how to achieve a desired future position for an organization. **Strategic thinking** involves complex mental processing to select and synthesize large amounts of data relevant to the organization (Koch, 2000). To think in terms of strategies requires the ability to assess and learn from experience, have intimate knowledge and understanding of the present, and use these resources to envision a desirable future state of the organization (Ginter et al., 1998). Strategic thinking initially comes from top-level managers (Chapter 8) who lead the effort to orient others to make the connection between their actions and desired outcomes. To embark on vision quests involving an entire organization requires organizational guidance and directional clarity at the top (Chapter 9). Strategic thinkers need to be influential within their organization (Chapter 10) for their thoughts to reach all organizational members and for the thoughts to be translated into actions. While top-level management may initiate strategy formation throughout the organization, operational managers are involved as strategies evolve (Rouse, 2001). Operational managers, that is middle and lower-level managers, are closer to the point of delivery of services and products, and they have unique knowledge and insights to contribute.

Strategic Planning

Figure 11.1 summarizes a strategic planning process. It shows that everything associated with strategic management flows from the fundamental guiding documents (Chapter 9) and coalesces under the term **strategic intent**. Once strategic intent is identified, it is necessary to gather and analyze data, interpret the results, and make decisions. Interpretation of the analyses is enriched and modulated by the experience, intuition, and creative thinking of those involved in the formation of strategies (Helms, 2000). To do this in a systematic way requires a process. The fact gathering, analysis, option formation, option selection, and strategy formation process associated with strategic management is called strategic planning. Key questions that facilitate strategic planning are noted in Table 11.1.

The parts of the process (Fig. 11.1) and their interrelationships from the analysis component on are discussed next.

Sources of Data for Strategic Analysis

Strategic decisions are made on the basis of organizational intent, management's experience, and internal and external influences that have, do, and may affect the success of the organization. In short, strategy decisions are informed decisions based on the analysis of current, accurate, and well-digested data and interpreted by judgment supported by intuition, insight, gut feelings (Helms, 2000), and personal values (Mintzberg, Quinn, Voyer, 1995). The data of interest come from

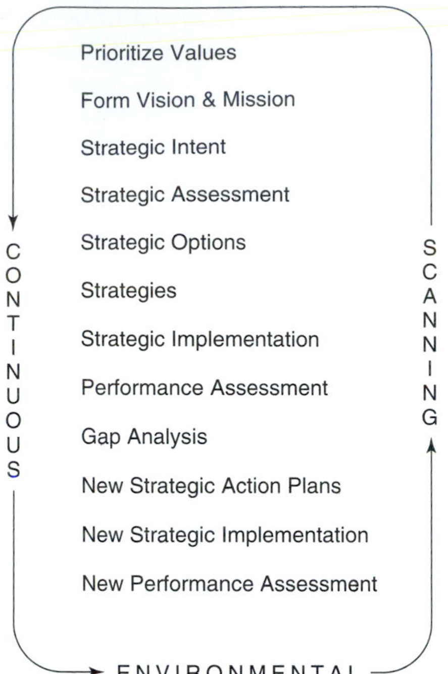

Figure 11.1. A general strategic management model based on Ginter et al., 1998; Macmillan and Tampoe, 2000; Nosse and Friberg, 1992.

the business's setting, surroundings, conditions, and outside influences. All together, these factors make up the business's environment. Gathering environmental data from the perspective of how it has, does, and may affect the viability of the organization is called **environmental scanning**. The food for thought comes from data that can be sorted into two sources: (1) the organization itself, that is, information about its **internal environment** and (2) data from the world beyond the organization, that is, information about its **external environment**.

The internal environmental analysis provides a candid view of the organization's resources, that is, its capabilities, competence, and strengths. The information is often readily available because it has been compiled for a variety of other uses. Because the information is at hand, its accuracy can be checked if necessary. Examples of important internal sources of data for analysis:

Consultant reports
Financial reports
Human resources reports
Information technology reports
Marketing reports
Treatment outcomes reports

An external environmental analysis depends on sources of information that may be difficult to obtain because they come from outside of the organization. Most businesses do what they can to limit access to sensitive information, such as costs, litigation, and plans. Information that is circulated, like annual reports, announcements in trade journals, presentations by top managers, and government reports are common external sources of data.

An external environmental assessment has two components, the general external environment and the **sector environment** (Hannagan, 2002). The general external environment includes everything that affects health care businesses, such as federal and state leg-

Table 11.1 Questions to Help Drive Strategic Planning

Key Questions	*Sources of Answers or Actions to Get Answers*
What is important?	Core values and motives, philosophical and mission statements
What is the ideal goal?	Vision statement
What is the real world like?	Environmental assessment to inform and validate vision and mission statements
Are adjustments needed?	Update vision and mission statements
What direction(s) to pursue?	SWOT analysis; match goals and resources
What must be done?	Formulate strategies
How do we get it done?	Implement strategies
How do we know how we are doing?	Monitor, do gap analyses, interpret
How do we improve?	Determine what has and has not worked; improve strategies; improve strategic planning process
What's next?	Do it all again, because environments are dynamic

islation, the state of the economy, and threats of terrorism. The sector component of the external environment refers to the specific environment of a particular industry. In the health care industry, this includes availability of a trained workforce, Medicare payment rates, technology, and accreditation bodies. Not-for-profit, for-profit, and governmental health care organizations and durable medical equipment vendors, while all part of the health care industry, are affected by some common general factors and some unique sector factors.

A rule of thumb regarding the scope of an environmental assessment is to investigate areas known or anticipated to have an effect on the ability to carry out the strategic intent (Dunn, 1998) and actualize the vision. Hannagan (2002) suggests using the word *spectacles* to categorize the main external environments that affect businesses. These are groups of external factors in the spectacles categories:

Social (for example, population demographics)
Political (for example, health and safety regulations)
Economic (for example, interest rates)
Cultural (the organization's way of doing things)
Technological (for example, computer networks)
Aesthetic (for example, organizational and facility images)
Consumer (those with needs for the organization's services)
Legal (for example, possible risks)
Environmental (impact on nature)
Sector (for example, accreditation)

Strategic Options and Strategy Decisions

So far, the picture of strategic management and strategic planning has been by three brushes: (1) organizational intent, (2) analysis of the internal environment, and (3) analysis of the external environment. Analysis is only as good as the available data. Good information is objective, accurate, up-to-date, and reasonably complete. A common way to examine information gathered in environmental scanning is to subject it to a **strengths, weaknesses, opportunities, threats (SWOT) analysis** (McConkey, 1976). Figure 11.2 presents a template for a basic SWOT analysis.

The assessment of strengths and weaknesses focuses on the internal environment of the organization. The opportunities and threats are individuals, groups, or circumstances outside of the control of the organization, that is, the external environment. Strengths and weaknesses (S and W) clarify an organization's capabilities or resources and deficits or limitations. Together S and W candidly identify the extent of the organization's assets and its areas of limited capacity, respectively. Opportunities and threats (O and T) expose areas where the organization may use its limited resources advantageously and where others have an advantage, respectively. O and T help identify possibilities, that is, what might be done with the available resources. The SWOT analysis provides a way to identify both matches between capabilities or resources and external voids or opportunities that the organization may take advantage of to achieve its strategic intentions (Mintzberg et al., 1995).

INTERNAL FACTORS			EXTERNAL FACTORS	
PRODUCT	STRENGTH	WEAKNESS	OPPORTUNITY	THREAT

Figure 11.2. Template for SWOT analysis.

Kinds of Strategies

Large health care corporations have overall corporate strategies, strategies for the corporation's different businesses, and departmental or unit strategies. Strategic management starts at the top and flows downward. This means that operational managers, such as managers of rehabilitation services or physical therapy departments, are involved in strategic management and the development of strategic plans for their unit or organization.

The foundational documents expressing the organization's intent, that is, motive, values (Chapter 6), philosophy, vision, and mission, are discussed in Chapter 9. These three directive statements provide the basis for **directional strategies** (Ginter et al., 1998) (Chapter 8). In Figure 11.1 these documents are listed at the top, indicating their wide breadth of influence on direction. Several other kinds of strategies may also be organization-wide or specific to an organizational unit.

Adaptive strategies relate to what the organization will do to continue on its vision quest. The options include expansion, retraction, and maintenance (Chapters 23 and 24). A health care organization may merge with a similar organization. A national corporation with outpatient clinics may withdraw from a state or region. Partners of a private practice may opt to stay in their current facility. When an adaptive strategy includes expansion, **market entry strategies** must be considered (Chapters 23 and 24). Market entry strategies include acquiring other businesses and seeking additional investors to provide capital. **Positioning strategies** are ways to differentiate the organization's services from those offered by competitors. For example, an organization may reduce its prices, offer a new service, or expand a service line (Chapters 22–24). For strategies to be carried out, means of implementing them have to be formulated. Implementation strategies are known as **operational strategies** (Chapters 16, 18, and 23). Operational strategies are developed where they will be carried out, that is, within the functional units that will put them into action. These strategies take into consideration the horizontal and vertical linkages (Chapter 8) necessary for implementation, such as budget for marketing, human resources, and information systems (Ginter et al., 1998).

Strategic Implementation

Strategies have to be enacted. These are the four general terms that are used to link operational strategies and actions:

1. Goals
2. Objectives
3. Policies
4. Procedures

Goals are statements of desired ends that specify actions, means of discerning accomplishment, and time lines (Helms, 2000). A guide for formulating goals is represented by the word *smart* (Hannagan, 2002).

*S*pecific
*M*easurable
*A*cceptable
*R*ealistic
*T*imed

To be *smart* a goal should be specific enough for those who are working toward it to understand it. To gauge whether there is progress, a goal has to be reliably measurable. The goal should also be acceptable to the individuals who are charged with reaching it. Finally, a goal has to have a completion time or date to allow planning for its fulfillment.

The ultimate overall goal of an organization is to realize its strategic intent (Macmillan and Tampoe, 2000). The ultimate goal for health care organizations is to meet the real needs of consumers. Up to seven goals has been suggested as a reasonable range (Helms, 2000). Goals are both tangible and quantifiable, but they are seldom inspirational. That is why a vision statement is needed to give added impetus for goal achievement.

Objectives are short-term goals that are connected to accomplishing longer-term goals. Objectives are formed for all levels of the organization. For example, an organizational goal may be that when people think about the finest five hospitals in the state, they will include this one in their thinking, that within the next year this hospital will be among the top 100 in the United States in *U.S. News* rankings, and that within 2 years it will be among the top 50. Associated objectives affect all functional units, including accounting, marketing, nursing, and rehabilitation services. Rehabilitation services may undertake a number of objectives to contribute to the overall goal. The unit head may facilitate publication of community interest articles on former patients who live in the state. Staff members may go to state and national meetings to give presentations on programs the hospital offers. Human resources and marketing departments may send articles for publication in trade journals and newsletters noting accomplishments of staff members, such as attendance at continuing education programs, completion of certification requirements, or completion of a residency program.

Policies and procedures are an organization's officially expressed means to guide managers' and staff members' behavior, decision making, and mode of thinking (Longest, Rakich, Darr, 2000). Policies establish parameters within which managers may direct, reward, and reprimand those who report to them. Policies are statements of what an organization or part of an organization will do in a given situation and who will be responsible for the action and its results (Nosse and Friberg, 1992). In this way policies help carry out strategies to meet the organization's goals. Policies are formulated to be consistent with the guiding documents of the organization, and as such, they support the strategic intent. Policies are intended to ensure fair and equitable management of all organizational members. The amount of latitude allowed the manager by policies varies by topic and by organization. For example, an organization with a rigid salary administration policy may give the manager little leeway in adjusting salaries for recruitment and retention. The same organization may provide managers with significant freedom in the design of the department's organizational structure, career ladder, and job descriptions. ***Procedures*** are how policies are put into action. Without a procedure for implementation, a policy cannot be consistently followed; in fact, the policy may not be followed at all. Procedures are detailed statements of when, where, and how an activity should be done. They spell out, step by step, how to do a task. Example procedures in physical therapy are how to obtain informed consent and what to do in an emergency. More will be said in Chapters 16 to 20 regarding specific ways of managing people so they contribute in ways that support the organization's intent.

Performance Assessment

No plan is perfect. There is always a difference between what is and what should be. This is called a gap. In Figure 11.1 the placement of the **gap analysis** denotes that following implementation of strategic **action plans**, an assessment is carried out to determine how well or how poorly the strategy worked. A gap analysis is determination of the difference between the expected condition, such as an increase in patient volume or decrease in per diem help, and what actually occurred.

Gap = expectation − actual

The continuous environmental scanning loop shown in Figure 11.1 represents a continuously occurring event. When a gap analysis has identified a variance from expectation, newly gathered gap-relevant data can be accessed and analyzed, and one or more new strategic action plans may be formed and implemented. The last item in Figure 11.1 shows that the strategic planning process allows for change in the light of new data.

Strategic Issues

Any force, internal or external to the organization, that is perceived as having a detrimental effect on the organization's ability to develop and sustain a **competitive advantage** is a strategic issue (Clawson, 1999). A competitive advantage is a result of strategic thinking that facilitated a strategy or set of strategies that led to the organization's success. Success often means that the organization has earned more on its investment than did its competitors and has done so for a long enough time to raise its standing among its competitors (Hannagan, 2002). The important part of the definition of a competitive advantage is sustainability. The strategic issues related to having a sustainable competitive advantage center on questions of cost, replication, and flexibility (Clawson, 1999). To sustain its competitive advantage, a service should be:

- Difficult for others to duplicate, imitate, or develop substitutes for
- Flexible, so it can be quickly and continually improved
- Perceived as an excellent value by consumers

Reality

No matter how diligently one works to gather appropriate information from within and outside of the organization, there will always be more data to collect. No one has all of the information on everything they would like to know about. The first reality rule is that decisions are made on incomplete data. Analytical procedures are useful, but less so if they are based on incomplete and possibly outdated information. The second reality rule is that management has little time for strategic planning. Most product industry managers are occupied with operational matters most of the time. They have few uninterrupted periods for contemplative, long-range thinking (Mintzberg et al., 1995). Finally, although plans are imperfect, not to plan is actually planning to fail (Olsen, 1999).

Student Notes

You may think the concept of strategic management and strategic planning are out of context for an individual professional at the onset of a clinical career. The following dialog may bring the material in this chapter into focus for you.

You probably have engaged in strategic management to get where you are, but you probably managed things without the formal structure presented in this chapter. As an example to support this statement, let's see how a person may become a physical therapist. The following scenario matches a general progression of becoming a physical therapist, with italicized strategic management and planning terms woven in:

- What you knew and liked about physical therapy seemed in line with your *priority personal values*.
- Your *vision* was to become a physical therapist by getting admitted to an accredited educational program, meet the program's *objectives*, and graduate at a certain time.
- As you progressed in your educational preparation, you gained knowledge, preferences, understanding of your strengths and weaknesses (*SWOT*), and clinical experience (*internal and external environmental scanning*), and your *mission* (what you are good at) became clearer.
- Everything was interesting at first, but eventually a special interest may have emerged. To nurture this interest required *selecting and implementing strategies*, that is, informational interviewing, lobbying for certain clinical sites, seeking a faculty member or clinician to be your mentor, Internet searches, and so on.
- Time is always limited. What you still need to fulfill your mission (*gap analysis*) and which strategies are likely to work (*assessment*) to meet those needs requires *new action plans*.
- While on affiliations, new information and experiences (*environmental scanning is continuous*) helped focus your interest (*assessment* again).
- You *rerun the process* that worked for you minus what you know did not work to come closer to reaching your sharpened *vision*.

While this scenario is generic, everyone has used some aspect of strategic management and planning in personal life. If you have a model like the one presented in Figure 11.1 in mind, you can see where you are in the process, anticipate your next actions, and see what you have to improve for future use.

Summary

This chapter covers the major components of strategic management and its associated process for formulating, implementing, and evaluating strategies called strategic planning. Under the leadership of top managers, strategies are formed to achieve an organization's goals. The goals of an organization are best identified in its foundational documents, that is, philosophy, vision, and mission statements. Together these documents describe the organization's intent—its ultimate goal. Thinking in terms of strategies and managing according to strategies is called strategic management. This way of managing links strategies with actions to achieve the organization's intent. Strategies can be developed through a 10-step progression called strategic planning. Strategic planning requires accurate and current information. Information gathering is a full-time endeavor called environmental scanning. Two sources of relevant information are the organization itself, that is, its internal environment, and information about the outside forces that affect the organization, that is, its external environment. Environmental information is analyzed quantitatively and interpreted within the context of management's experience, values, intuition, and creativity. Strategies that affect the entire organization are corporate strategies. Strategies that affect a segment of the organization are divisional or departmental strategies. Following the implementation of strategies, periodic checks are made to reveal any gaps between what has occurred and what was intended. This gap analysis identifies variances. When variances occur, the strategic planning is repeated, new strategies formulated, and associated actions implemented. This makes planning somewhat self-adapting.

Operational managers such as physical therapy department managers often participate in formulating strategic plans for their unit. To guide the implementation of strategies, goals (ends), objectives (means), policies (who does what), and procedures (how they do it) are formulated. At all levels of an organization strategic planning is a useful way to formulate strategies, evaluate outcomes, and improve efforts to fulfill the departmental and organizational intents. This last activity, continually improving the planning system and bettering outcomes, is a special topic of great importance for managers. Improvement means progress toward goal achievement. This improvement is known as quality control, continuous quality improvement, or other similarly descriptive term. The core philosophy of quality improvement may be summed up thus: we may be happy with how we are doing, but we are not yet satisfied. This concept will be developed and expanded in the next chapter.

INDIVIDUAL CASE STUDY

The time to see what you have learned is right now. Do a self-check. In your own words compare and contrast strategic management and strategic planning. First, do it without going back through the chapter. Then go back and compare what you said and what was written. Are there any gaps? What strategy will you formulate to meet the intent of complete accuracy? Are you getting the picture? Strategic planning can be used to guide actions toward any goal.

GROUP CASE STUDY

Divide the class into four groups. Each group will have one problem to work on. You can apply a part of the strategic planning process in this exercise. These assumptions are safe:

1. Environmental scanning was done.
2. Directional strategies were in place; that is, values were established, and vision and mission statements were recently revised.
4. The strategic intent has been identified and shared with all employees.
5. Operational managers were included in the strategic analysis.
6. Numerous strategic options were presented, discussed, and weighed.

Situation

These strategies are ready to be implemented:

- An adaptive strategy to leave the home health market (expected savings of $850,000 this year)
- A positioning strategy calling for recognized clinical expertise, such as hiring only experienced clinical staff, preferably those who are board certified and/or have special credentials (expect an increase in outpatient market share from 15% to 30% within a year)
- A market entry strategy to acquire the three private physical therapy practices within a 5-mile radius of the organization's primary location (expect an increase in outpatient market share from 15% to 75% within a year; combined with first strategy, it would be possible to acquire up to 90% of targeted outpatient market share)
- An operational strategy that calls for paperless record keeping and new software to ensure HIPAA compliance (see Chapter 4) (expect 100% compliance within 3 months)

Task

The task for each group is to take any one of these strategies and continue strategic planning. It will be helpful to review Figure 11.1. Complete the next four steps: strategic implementation, performance assessment, gap analysis, and new strategic action plan. For the gap analysis assume that expectations were not met. Variations can include making up data from environmental scanning to support the new strategy. When the strategy is complete, meet as a class and discuss your experiences. How can you improve the process for future use?

REFERENCES

Clawson JG. Level three leadership. Getting below the surface. Upper Saddle River, NJ: Prentice Hall. 1999.

Dunn RT. Haimann's supervisory management for health care organizations, 6th ed. Boston: McGraw-Hill. 1998.

Ginter PM, Swayne LM, Duncan WJ. Strategic management of health care organizations, 3rd ed. Malden, MA: Blackwell. 1998.

Hannagan T. Mastering strategic management. New York: Palgrave. 2002.

Helms MM, ed. Encyclopedia of management, 4th ed. Detroit: Gale Group. 2000.

Koch R. The Financial Times guide to strategy: How to create and deliver a useful strategy, 2nd ed. London: Financial Times–Prentice Hall. 2000.

Longest BB Jr., Rakich JS, Darr K. Managing health services organizations and systems. Baltimore: Health Professions. 2000.

Macmillan H, Tampoe M. Strategic management. New York: Oxford University. 2000.

McConkey DD. How to manage by results. New York: AMACOM. 1976.

Mintzberg H, Quinn JB, Voyer J. The strategy process, collegiate ed. Englewood Cliffs, NJ: Prentice Hall. 1995.

Nosse LJ, Friberg DG. Management principles for physical therapists. Baltimore: Williams & Wilkins. 1992.

Olsen D. Entrepreneurship: Ownership and private practice physical therapy. In Nosse LJ, Friberg DG, Kovack PR. Managerial and supervisory principles for physical therapists. Baltimore: Williams & Wilkins. 1999:278–298.

Rouse WB. Essential challenges of strategic management. New York: John Wiley & Sons. 2001.

MORE INFORMATION RELATED TO THIS CHAPTER

Original papers on strategic management or strategic planning:

Eisenhardt JM. Strategy as strategic decision-making. Sloan Management Review. 1999; Spring:65–72.

Korsgaard MA, Schweiger DM, Sapienze HJ. Building commitment, attachment, and trust in strategic decision making: The role of procedural justice. Academy of Management Journal. 1995;38:60–84.

Miller CC, Cardinal LB. Strategic planning and firm performance: A synthesis of more than two decades of research. Academy of Management Journal. 1994;37:1649–1665.

Mintzberg H, Lampel J. Reflecting on the strategy process. Sloan Management Review. 1999; Spring:21–30.

Porter ME. What is strategy? Harvard Business Review. 1996;74:61–78.

Elaborate models of strategic planning specifically for health care organizations are offered by Longest et al., pp. 364, 365 and Ginter et al., p. 22 (see references). There are many contributors to the concept of strategic management. An informative summary of the contributions of 39 noted individuals from around the world can be found in Chapter 3 in Koch (see references).

Chapter 12

QUALITY ASSESSMENT AND IMPROVEMENT

Learning Objectives

1. Relate quality assessment and improvement to a health care professional, a physical therapy department, and a physical therapy organization.
2. List and then apply the steps of a quality improvement process to minimize variation in outcomes in a hypothetical physical therapy situation.
3. Interpret a quality improvement diagram or chart.
4. Suggest what specific quality improvement tool might be used by summarizing the indications and anticipated information to be gained by a physical therapy manager.
5. Evaluate and compare the methods associated with quality improvement and the methods associated with benchmarking.
6. Summarize and contrast the main elements of quality improvement from the perspective of a health care accreditation agency and from a health care provider's point of view.

Key Words

Benchmarking, best practices, cause and effect diagram, common cause variation, continuous quality improvement (CQI), control chart, decision matrix, exemplar, fishbone diagram, Joint Commission on Accreditation of Health care Organizations (JCAHO), ORYX, Pareto chart, process chart, quality, quality improvement (QI), scatter diagram, special cause variation, spider diagram, time plot, total quality management (TQM), variation, work flow

Introduction

The focus of health care is on patients. This means that quality of health care service to patients is the responsibility of each and every health care provider. This chapter examines the concept of quality improvement in health care organizations. As will be discussed shortly, quality means different things to different individuals and organizations. Quality therefore is addressed from several viewpoints. The perspectives include those of an accreditation agency, consumers, and health care organizations. The general process of improving quality is continual, because factors that affect quality are changeable. Some organizations in every kind of business are the recognized leaders. These organizations are distinct from their peers in their ability to maintain a high level of performance in activities considered markers of success. To be competitive, peer organizations have an incentive to learn from the most successful organizations. Through a process called benchmarking, organizations identify what the exemplary organizations are doing that they themselves are not. This information is used to form and implement plans to improve the organization's performance in a competitive marketplace. This process is repeated periodically, which means that benchmarking and quality improvement are interrelated. These two concepts are explored next within the context of improving health care organizations in several areas, including the delivery of physical therapy services.

Quality Improvement

According to the **Joint Commission on Accreditation of Healthcare Organizations (JCAHO)**, (Chapter 32) an organization's performance of important functions significantly affects its patient outcomes, the cost to achieve these outcomes, and the perception of its patients and their families about the quality and value of its services (JCAHO, 1996; 2003a–c). This linking of processes and outcomes is the hallmark of what is known as **quality improvement (QI)**, **continuous quality improvement (CQI)**, or **total quality management (TQM)**. The goal of improving organizational performance is ultimately constant improvement in patients' health outcomes. A key to strong outcomes is process improvement through continual quality improvement. This sentiment is mirrored throughout health care as evidenced by the large number of health care organizations engaged in CQI initiatives. Because of the emphasis on CQI and its purported impact on outcomes, this section reviews the movement toward QI in health care, key concepts of QI, and applications of QI for the physical therapist.

The process of improving an organization's processes consists of several specific activities. Measurement of **quality** can be difficult, in part because its definition is contextual. Nonetheless, a two-part definition, one for services and one for processes, can be useful in defining health care quality. Quality in health care is a result of what is done to a consumer, that is, input, that is converted into output through work processes (Tweet and Gavin-Marciano, 1998). For services, quality output is output with the characteristics it is supposed to have. It is what the consumer expects it to be. However, health care organizations have many types of consumers, with each type having different expectations (Chapters 20–24). Quality comes from processes that do what they were intended to do, that is, result in quality outputs, for example, consumer satisfaction, profit, or improved public image.

Improving quality within an organization, even a simple organization, is complex and involves extensive examination of inputs, processes, and outputs. CQI consists of first defining and doing the right thing, and then doing the right thing well. To be successful and achieve the desirable performance outcomes, the organization must provide appropriate care. That care must also be well done to be successful. Although this concept sounds simple, it is the basis for efforts to improve performance. Two simple questions arise from this position: (1) What is the right thing to do? (2) What is the best way to do it? CQI strives to answer each of these questions by developing a body of knowledge and procedures to help the clinician and manager examine internal procedures and daily activities in standardized ways so that performance can be improved efficiently.

W. Edwards Deming

Much of the body of knowledge collectively known as CQI was pioneered by W. Edwards Deming. Deming (1986) developed his philosophies in work in Japan after World War II. At that time the Japanese manufacturing industry had a reputation for producing poor-quality products. To reverse this situation according to Deming's concepts entailed determining what customers wanted and studying and improving product design and production to a point of excellence. The processes and procedures Deming put in place in Japan were later distilled into what are frequently referred to as Deming's 14 principles of quality leadership (Table 12.1).

These principles provide a blueprint for successful organizational improvement through CQI. In Deming's opinion, these principles are the cornerstone of creating an organization that is adaptive and constantly

Table 12.1 Deming's 14 Principles for Continuous Improvement

1. Create constancy of purpose for service improvement.
2. Adopt the new philosophy.
3. Cease dependence on inspection to achieve quality.
4. End the practice of awarding business on price alone; make partners of vendors.
5. Constantly improve every process for planning, production, and service.
6. Institute training and retraining on the job.
7. Institute leadership for system improvement.
8. Drive out fear.
9. Break down barriers between staff areas.
10. Eliminate slogans, exhortations, and targets for the work force.
11. Eliminate numeric quotas for the work force and numeric goals for the management.
12. Remove barriers to pride of workmanship.
13. Institute a vigorous program of education and self-improvement for everyone.
14. Put everyone to work on the transformation.

Modified from Deming WE. Out of Crisis. Cambridge: Massachusetts Institute of Technology. 1986:23–24.

improving. Constant improvement, rather than accepting the status quo, became Deming's goal. Sayings like "If the thing ain't broke, don't fix it" were replaced with "If the thing ain't broke, make it work better." Deming believed that his constant pattern of evaluating processes and gradually gaining improvement would strengthen the organization's position and create growth and profit.

Deming also described what he called a chain reaction in improvement (Deming, 1986). The chain includes both internal and external variables. Each link in the chain encourages and catalyzes the next. In the list below internal variables are indicated by (I). External variables are indicated by (E).

- Decrease costs (I & E)
- Decrease price (I)
- Improve productivity (I)
- Improve quality (I)
- Increase market share (E)
- Increase return on investment and profit margin (I & E)
- Provide jobs and add more jobs (I & E)
- Stay in business (I & E)

Clearly, each of these steps is desirable and should be pursued, for they can lead to a competitive advantage (Chapter 11). Today, quality improvement should be a basic aspect of all physical therapy missions, that is, to be better therapists, to be a more successful organization, and so on.

Specific tools and techniques are required to improve quality. CQI is a discipline. As such, it should be studied, practiced, and perfected. CQI seeks to identify problems at their root and then to develop solutions to eliminate the problems. To identify problems in organizations, it is necessary to examine what causes process problems and to recognize them when they arise. Excessive complexity of the process is often the cause of problems. So are mistakes and defects, breakdowns and delays, inefficiencies, and process variation. An understanding of the variation in terms of CQI is important to outcomes management.

Variation

Once asked what he considered his greatest contribution to CQI, Deming (1986) indicated that he had worked to eliminate variation. **Variation** is a key focus of many CQI projects in health care because it is something different from what was expected (Chapter 10). Variations can be positive or negative. A positive variation may be an unanticipated increase in percentage of bills paid. A negative variation may be a decrease in number of physical therapy visits. In the health care industry events that are two standard deviations either side of the mean often trigger efforts to find the root cause of the variation (Longest, Rakich, Darr, 2000). Even though statistical quality control was developed to study variation in manufacturing process, it is applicable to health care services. The basic assumption is that variation in input (service) leads to inconsistency in output or outcome.

There are two forms of variation. These are **common cause variation** and **special cause variation**. It is important to recognize the difference between them before taking action to correct variation problems, because solutions are very different for each type. Common cause variations are typically due to the cumulative effect of a large number of small sources of variation. The variation is within two standard deviations (depending on the limits the organization sets). Common cause variation, which typically is outside the control of the individual doing the work, is considered a part of the process itself and is generally thought of as a normal byproduct of the work process. It is noise in the system. In physical therapy this could be discharge of patients before a final assessment is complete. This results in incomplete and inaccurate records and hinders determining whether care pathways were adequate.

Special cause variations are outcomes that are greater than two standard deviations from the mean. They are not considered to be process related because most of the outcomes are within acceptable levels of quality. Special cause variation is due to something out of the ordinary that is having an impact, good or bad, on the work process. A physical therapy example might be an organizational mandate that no external contractors can be used to cover weekend and holiday service needs. This might result in unacceptable delays in treating scheduled patients, a waiting list for new patients, and poor customer satisfaction ratings.

Working to reduce variation in outcome is integral to the CQI concept. The specific actions that are effective in resolving common cause and special cause variation are different. To improve performance in common cause variation, it is necessary to redesign the process. Special cause variations are often resolved by identifying the condition outside of the process that must be addressed. This may include operator training or replacement of faulty equipment.

Tools of Continuous Quality Improvement

The tools of CQI are the steps of process improvement. CQI tools are primarily designed to help identify the root cause of the quality problem so that an appropriate and effective resolution can be planned. The most common quality control tools are shown and discussed next.

Control Chart

Among the basic tools is a **control chart.** A generic control chart is shown in Figure 12.1. A control chart is used to determine whether a system is in control, that is, whether outputs are within a predetermined spread (standard deviation value). Data are gathered over a specified time. The outcomes of interest, such as financial health and absenteeism, are measured. Comparisons are then made between the data plotted and some standard that is indicated on the chart, in this case as dotted lines. The standard may be based on the organization's experience or it may be an industry standard. Figure 12.2 is a control chart showing a year of hypothetical data on absenteeism due to injuries and the acceptable range for days lost. The upper and lower control levels bound the range of acceptable variation. It is assumed that variations plotted between these boundaries are primarily due to common cause variation and deviations outside of these boundaries are due to special cause variation. These assumptions require additional sources of information for confirmation.

Work Flow or Process Charts

Work flow or **process charts** detail the stages of a process. In the case of a work flow chart, it may also include the physical movement through space of the work or workers. Figure 12.3 depicts the flow or progression of steps in a quality improvement process. Such a chart is helpful for communication, directing actions, tracking progress, identifying where errors are likely, planning future activities,

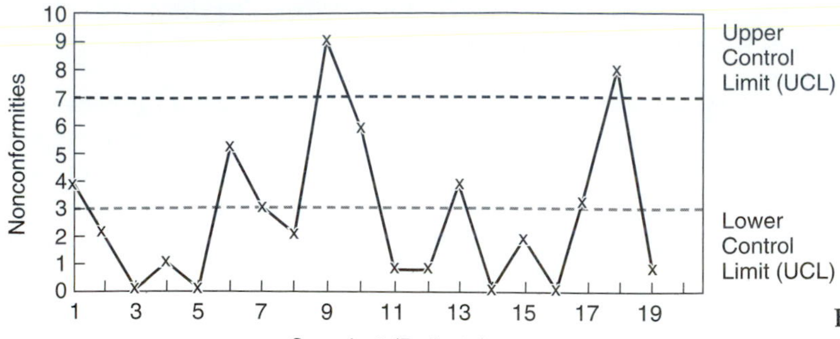

Figure 12.1. Generic example of a control chart.

and estimating completion time. The flow of activities in Figure 12.3 shows a final step that includes refinement of the process so its next iteration will lead to a higher-quality outcome.

Cause-and-Effect Diagram

Cause-and-effect diagrams allow the listing of factors thought to affect a problem or desired outcome. Also known as **fishbone diagrams** or Ishikawa diagrams, such diagrams can help focus attention on a desired result or problem. Given an outcome, the diagram is constructed to identify and organize the assumed causes of the outcome. Figure 12.4 is a fishbone chart that illustrates the many factors reported to be associated with the development of quality leadership (Chapter 8). The head end of the central arrow represents the core area of interest, while the skeleton represents the supporting elements or groups of elements. In the case of a variance problem, the head end of the diagram represents the central problem or the variation to be controlled. The skeleton represents the various contributing causes. Cause-and-effect diagrams can become more elaborate as minor branches are added to the skeleton. These additions represent contributory but subtler effects on outcome of interest.

Pareto Chart

Pareto charts are useful for identifying which of many contributing factors have the most effect on a process. This allows the focus to be placed on the most influential contributing factors. A Pareto chart is a horizontal or vertical bar graph with bars whose heights or lengths reflect the frequency or impact of problems or conditions. Figure 12.5 is a Pareto chart that illustrates the use of wound care supplies in a physical therapy department. The data plotted are frequency counts. From the chart it is easy to see that 45% of the supplies are not available for patient or staff use because of loss, theft, and waste and for

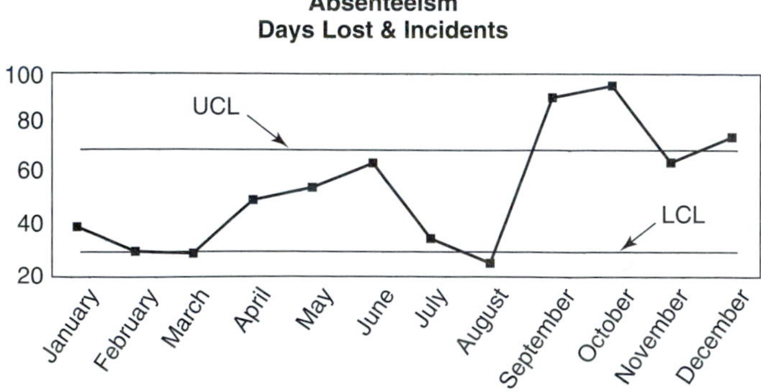

Figure 12.2. Sample control chart: absenteeism.

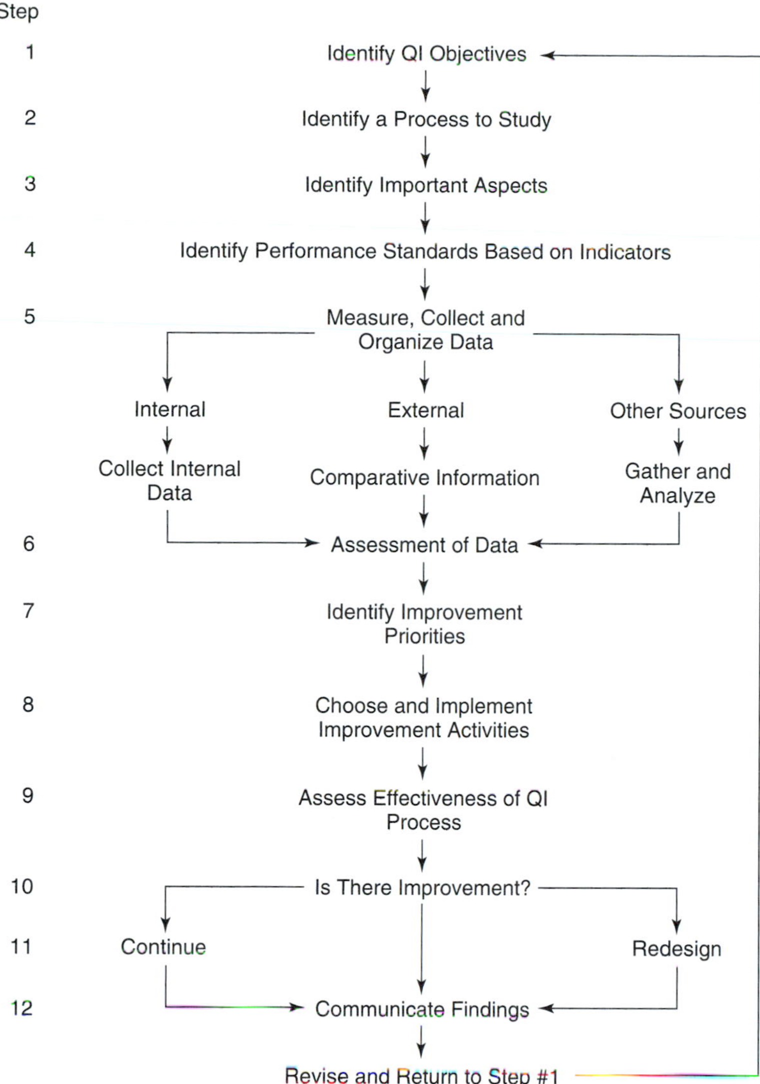

Figure 12.3. Sample work flow chart based on the JCAHO (1996) accreditation grid.

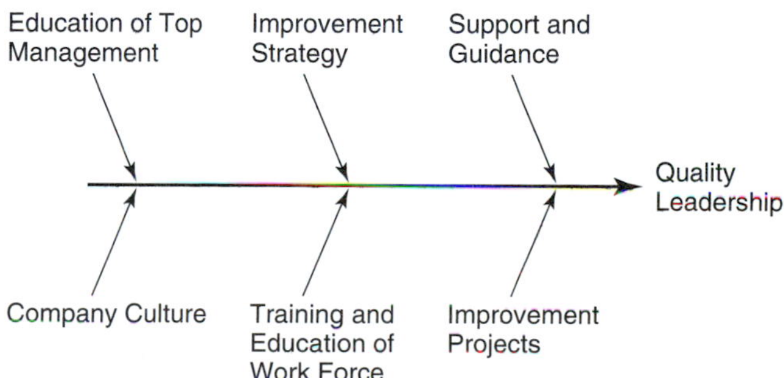

Figure 12.4. Sample fishbone chart: components of quality leadership.

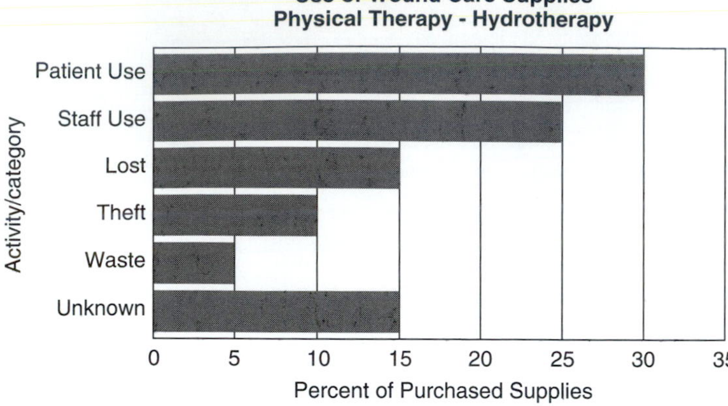

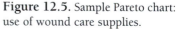

Figure 12.5. Sample Pareto chart: use of wound care supplies.

unknown reasons. The priority for follow-up action would be to deal with the two main causes of unavailability of supplies.

Scatter Diagram

A **scatter diagram** is a graphic tool that depicts the influence of one variable on another. The values of each variable are plotted on a separate axis. Once the variables are plotted, the relationship between them can be seen. Figure 12.6 is a scatter diagram showing the relationship between the number of physical therapy visits and the percent of patient improvement on a standardized measure of function in one clinic. From this figure it is easy to see there is a general relationship between number of visits and percent of improvement. A statistical procedure known as regression analysis may be calculated to determine the line of best fit for the data to provide a more accurate estimate of the relationship.

Spider Diagram

Spider diagrams indicate multiple characteristics in a graphic form. By plotting the scores for various indicators on a single graph, the observer can recognize certain patterns or combinations in multiple axes or indicators. Figure 12.7 is a spider diagram that illustrates the average scores for a group of patients with anterior cruciate ligament repairs on seven function-related characteristics. The center of the web represents poor, or the lowest level of function. The more peripheral rings represent increasing degrees of function. The example shows the pattern for the seven functions for people who have been discharged. Plotting the same data for individual patients will produce patterns more or less like the discharge

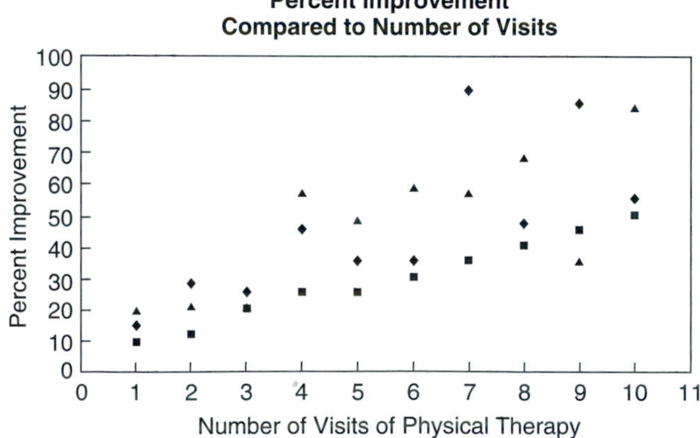

Figure 12.6. Sample scatter diagram: percent improvement compared to number of visits for patients with three different diagnoses.

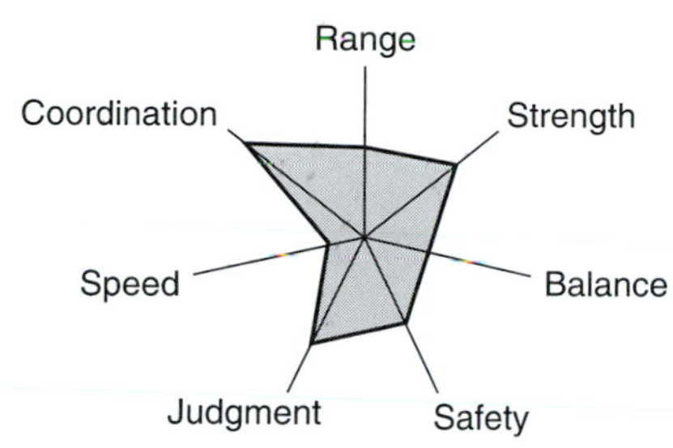

Figure 12.7. Sample spider diagram: average discharge ability for patients following anterior cruciate ligament repairs.

group's pattern. These differences can be used to depict current status, that is, highlight the deficits to be remedied before discharge and the results of individual aspects and overall outcome of current treatment.

Decision Matrix

A **decision matrix** in its simplest form is a four-compartment box that organizes two categories of choices and two categories of outcomes for comparison. A matrix can handle an unlimited number of choice and outcomes categories. Figure 12.8 is a decision matrix that examines the cost, ease of implementation, and return on investment (Chapter 27) factors and four options: expanding the existing clinic, developing a new clinic in the same town, developing a new clinic in a new town, and doing nothing. The utility of a decision matrix depends on the worth of the discussion and background information gathered to develop the assessments of the various factors (Chapter 11). The completeness, timeliness, and accuracy of the information all affect the quality of the decision.

Time Plot

Time plots can look like control charts without the upper and lower limits shown on the figure. They both follow events over time. Figure 12.9 is a time plot. It shows the relationship between days of work lost to work-related incidents within monthly periods. The time frame is relative, that is, specific months as well as over a year. Time frames can also be absolute, such as the status on January 1, 2006. Time plots are an excellent way to study the flow of information across time to identify delays or lags. Time plots are also excellent for describing specific projects that are unique or not typical. Time plots for projects can be thought of as time budgets for project completion. Since time is a critical and scarce resource within any organization, the use of time plots to budget time is appropriate (Chapter 27). Time plots can also be used to measure events within specific time frames to identify patterns or relationships.

Tools Are Just Tools

These tools of CQI are just that—tools. They should be used to study and learn about the practice of physical therapy within an

Problem: Outgrowing Existing Facility

	Cost	Implementation	ROI
Expand	4	2	1
New - Same Town	2	3	3
New - New Town	3	4	2
Do Nothing	1	1	4

Score: 1 = Best; 4 = Worst

Figure 12.8. Sample decision matrix: outgrowing existing facility.

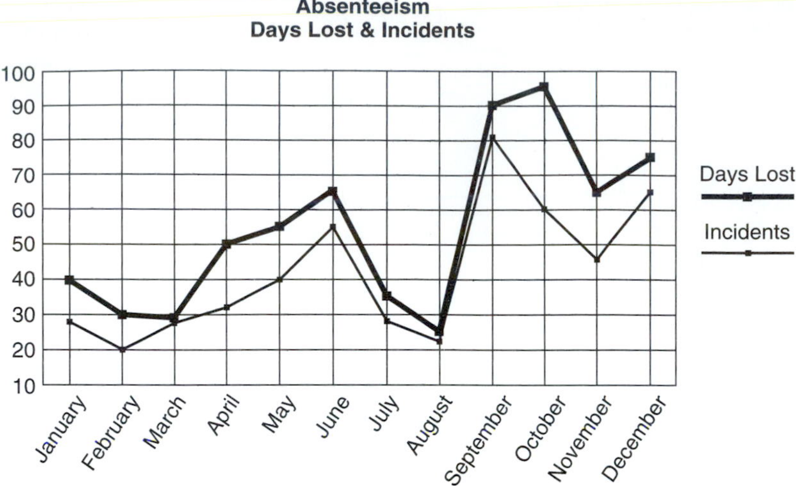

Figure 12.9. Sample time plot: absenteeism.

organization. Neither individually nor collectively can they replace good managerial judgment or rational analysis of practice (Chapter 11). They will, however, aid management in making effective and accurate problem analyses that support making good decisions.

Other CQI-Based Perspectives on Health Care Quality

The quality of health care can be bettered though evidence-based decision making, benchmarking, and CQI. With notable voids in the physical therapy literature on leadership, administration, management, and related processes, business-related evidence-based decision making for physical therapy managers is a vision to aspire to (Wiersma, 2002a,b). There is a developing literature on benchmarking in health care. Benchmarking also incorporates CQI concepts, yet it differs by focusing on a specific part of the external environment, the exemplary organizations. CQI principles are also clearly the basis for the JCAHO accreditation process (Chapter 32) (Fig. 12.3). This organization has recently embellished its accreditation process with a more refined application of CQI principles in a project called ORYX. Benchmarking and ORYX merit discussion because both will influence the delivery of physical therapy and other services in many settings.

Benchmarking: CQI Plus

Benchmarking is a process similar to CQI in that it is a management tool; it is a phased process for identifying and assessing information and making decisions intended to improve organizational outcomes (Tweet and Gavin-Marciano, 1998). It differs from CQI because it is more oriented toward using the external environment (Chapter 11). Benchmarking is a means of getting insights provided by other organizations for the purpose of improving performance. Uniting these concepts results in benchmarking being defined as "the process for identifying, understanding, and adapting outstanding practices from organizations from anywhere in the world to help your organization improve its performance" (Benchmarking Exchange, 2003). All businesses have enabling processes, such as marketing and accounting, to support the delivery of their services and products. These common processes make it worthwhile to benchmark the functions of any successful business to find out what it is doing that your business is not. These are examples of common functions that are applicable to health care businesses:

- Employee evaluation
- Employee training
- Knowledge management
- Mentoring
- Quality improvement
- Self-directed teams

Figure 12.10 presents benchmarking in a flow chart. The figure is based on the model offered by Tweet and Gavin-Marciano (1998). The flow chart is organized into four primary phases, with each phase having a variable number of steps. The planning phase starts with key questions. These are some of the questions:

- What do we want to benchmark and why? Clinical outcomes? Financial outcomes?
- What measures of quality are we going to use? Adherence to processes? Output quality?
- Who are the **exemplars** (the best)? Who are the best practitioners? Whom do we admire?
- How will we gather detailed information about and from the exemplars? Written questionnaire? Interview?

The collection and analysis phase begins with collecting detailed information from willing exemplars and other sources. Responses are categorized according to the key question they answer. The categorized responses are examined to determine practices of the benchmarked exemplars. The practices

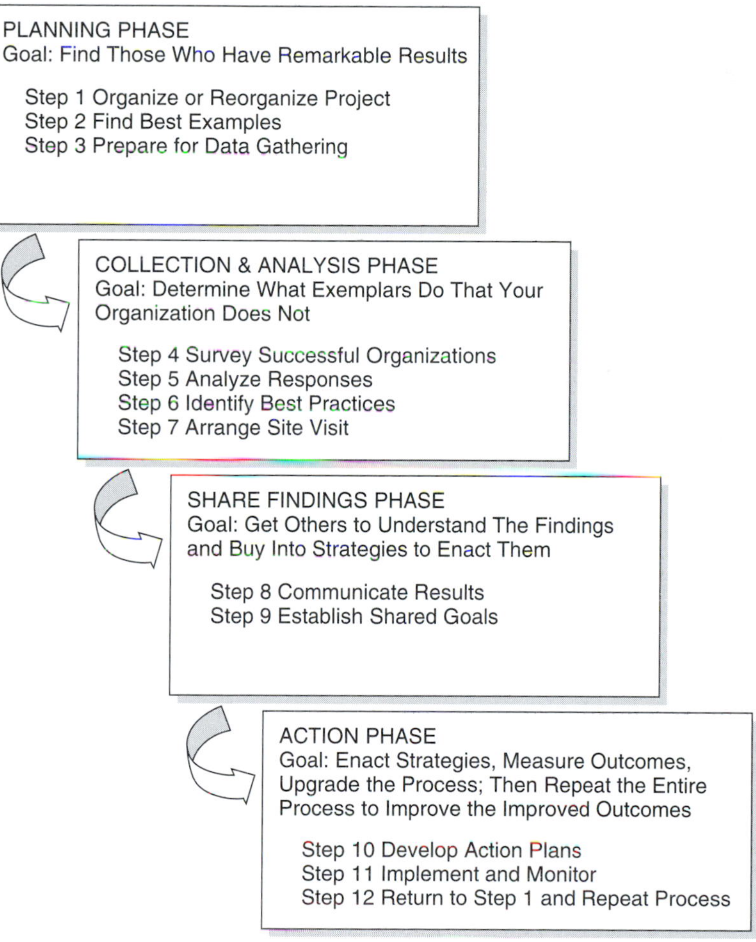

PLANNING PHASE
Goal: Find Those Who Have Remarkable Results
Step 1 Organize or Reorganize Project
Step 2 Find Best Examples
Step 3 Prepare for Data Gathering
COLLECTION & ANALYSIS PHASE
Goal: Determine What Exemplars Do That Your Organization Does Not
Step 4 Survey Successful Organizations
Step 5 Analyze Responses
Step 6 Identify Best Practices
Step 7 Arrange Site Visit
SHARE FINDINGS PHASE
Goal: Get Others to Understand The Findings and Buy Into Strategies to Enact Them
Step 8 Communicate Results
Step 9 Establish Shared Goals
ACTION PHASE
Goal: Enact Strategies, Measure Outcomes, Upgrade the Process; Then Repeat the Entire Process to Improve the Improved Outcomes
Step 10 Develop Action Plans
Step 11 Implement and Monitor
Step 12 Return to Step 1 and Repeat Process

Figure 12.10. A benchmarking model. (Derived from ideas presented by Tweet and Gavin-Marciano 1998.)

that enable the exemplars to achieve superior results are called **best practices** (Tweet and Gavin-Marciano, 1998). What the exemplars are doing is compared to what your organization or department is doing and differences identified (gap analysis). A SWOT analysis (Chapter 11) can be done to identify which of the best practices would most help the organization improve its relative position. Plans to implement changes are formulated.

Communication is the focus of the share findings phase. It requires getting others to understand the assumptions, the methods, and the recommended plans. Communication goes two ways: expressing and listening (Chapter 16). The ideal outcome is that plans are refined and all participants willingly share ownership.

Outcomes of the action phase include goals for action plans, timetables, resource allocation, implementation, and as always, CQI. Through the monitoring of outcomes, the source or sources of unexpected results can be traced and adjustments made in the benchmarking process (Fig. 12.10) so outcomes are closer to expectations.

ORYX: A New JCAHO Version of CQI

In 1997 the JCAHO took CQI in another direction by adopting the ORYX initiative (JCAHO, 2003a). ORYX is a union of patient outcomes data, other performance measures, and statistical analysis bundled together within the JCAHO accreditation process (JCAHO, 2003a–c). The JCAHO's goal is to use ORYX to "create a more continuous, data-driven, comprehensive and valuable accreditation process—one that not only evaluates a health care organization's methods of standards compliance, but the outcomes of these methods as well" (JCAHO, 2003c). These are some of the unique features of the ORYX initiative:

- *It starts with the known.* ORYX uses existing JCAHO standards to assess organizations seeking accreditation.
- *CQI is practiced.* JCAHO develops and field-tests new standards for each type of health care organization it accredits.
- *Customers can see into the process.* The JCAHO Web site presents a staged implementation of new standards and a degree of transparency in the development process.
- *It is flexible.* JCAHO-accredited organizations may choose which of 197 performance measurement systems is or are most appropriate to their operation.
- *It provides customized input and feedback.* Accredited health care organizations continually contribute data that is assessed in terms of its past performance and in comparison to like organizations.
- *It provides comparability and reporting based on statistically acceptable analyses.* That is, it uses quantitative measures to evaluate and improve patient outcomes or organizational function processes.
- *It is government friendly.* That is, it uses core measure sets that are compatible with the requirements of the Center for Medicare and Medicaid Services.
- *It is linked to on-site survey.* It is the intent that future on-site survey teams will plan their evaluation activities in part according to the core measure data submitted by the health care organization.

At present there are four core measurement areas for hospitals. These are acute myocardial infarction, heart failure, community-acquired pneumonia, and pregnancy and related conditions. More will eventually be developed for hospitals and other health care settings that JCAHO accredits (Chapter 32). For updates on ORYX see Web sites listed under More Information Related to This Chapter.

Student Notes

In case you have questions about how benchmarking and CQI are relevant to the new clinician, here are some answers. The assumptions are that many of you will soon be entering the physical therapy workforce, that your experience is limited to supervised internships, and that you have a strong desire to improve in many areas.

People get skillful at what they do by doing it. Efficiency and economy of effort are hallmarks of skill. New graduates generally have sufficient initial knowledge supported by limited skills. New graduates usually benefit from more repetitions to improve their physical performance, integrate knowledge and circumstances, and set realistic future goals for patients. Sometimes these areas are improved through trial and error. Sometimes one or more experienced physical therapists are available to help.

The realization that something is needed to provide better care leads to reflection about specific personal needs and thoughts about seeking a willing and exemplary clinician to help one to improve. These actions are all steps in the first phase of benchmarking (Fig. 12.10). Making contact with an exemplary therapist and expressing the desire to learn are steps in phase two. Convincing the exemplar to share wisdom and time with you to meet specific purposes are components of phase three. When the experienced therapist agrees to work with you and you both decide how you can find the time and what the possible outcomes will be, you are ready to move on to phase four. This final phase involves making specific plans, carrying them out, assessing the results, and making changes as new circumstances arise. Together both parties can determine where they can sharpen the process for future use. Benchmarking and CQI can result in win-win situations for all stakeholders: patients, new graduates, experienced therapists, the department, and the organization.

Summary

High quality is exemplary performance based on specific measures. In health care, quality performance is ultimately superior outcomes as judged by consumers, accreditation bodies, professional associations, and other stakeholders as well as by organizational standards. To produce high-quality outcomes also requires organizational processes for managing and carrying out multiple activities from accounting to measuring consumer satisfaction. Measurement of quality can be difficult, partly because its definition is contextual. Nonetheless, for health care services, a quality outcome has the characteristics it was supposed to have, that is, the outcome that the consumer expected. For organizational processes, quality outcomes result from processes that do what they were intended to do, such as produce satisfied consumers, improved income, or increased percentage of patients covered under Medicare. A key to strong outcomes is process improvement through CQI. CQI entails first defining and doing the right thing; second, doing the right thing well; and then continuing to seek better ways of doing both in the future. CQI has tools to look for variation between what should be occurring and what actually is occurring. This information is used to make changes to reduce variation as well as to improve the process. The ORYX project of the JCAHO is a recent innovation in CQI that is intended to provide JCAHO accreditation customers statistically derived feedback on a regular basis and use of the information for on-site accreditation visits.

Another way to improve organizational and clinical performance is benchmarking, a process similar to CQI. Benchmarking is a management tool that has a phased process for identifying and assessing information that leads to decisions and actions intended to improve organizational outcomes. Benchmarking differs from CQI because it is more oriented toward the external environment. The information used for improvement is derived from other organizations that have achieved superior outcomes. The insights gained from such organizations lead to changes to improve organizational performance in ways that are expected to give it a competitive advantage.

The concept of a competitive advantage is also discussed in Chapter 13, which deals with information management. In an age when rapid access to information is considered a competitive advantage, information management is essential to the success of an organization. Clinical documents are also discussed, because the recent implementation of the Health Insurance Portability and Accountability Act (Chapter 4) has special issues for patient care records, privacy, and security of clinical documents.

INDIVIDUAL CASE STUDY

Quality is in the eye of the beholder. Respond to these questions to get a glimpse of how you see quality:

What does quality care mean to you?
How do you define quality care?
Do you have personal clinical standards?
If you use external standards, what are they?

GROUP CASE STUDY

Situation

Divide the class into groups of 10. One person in each group is a supervisor. Everyone else is a staff physical therapist or a physical therapist assistant.

Situation

A new pay raise system has been implemented throughout your organization for nonunionized staff and managers. The system is based on merit. For professional staff this means no more automatic pay raises. It has been left to department managers to allocate merit increases in salary from funds allocated for that purpose. This means that various staff members may get different levels of increased pay.

The annual performance review date has been set to correspond to the organization's budget year. This means all reviews will take place 3 months from now. Your department manager has asked that the staff and supervisors divide into small groups to develop criteria for each of six categories of merit. Everyone was encouraged to be fair but to set the bar high, because organizational and departmental visions are to become the health care facility and department of choice in the city. These are the six institution-wide merit categories:

1. Meets expectations less than half of the time
2. Meets expectations more than half but less than 75% of the time
3. Meets expectations up to 90% of the time
4. Meets expectations all of the time
5. Meets expectations all of the time and occasionally exceeds them
6. Meets expectations all of the time and regularly exceeds them

There is a quality improvement progression here. Consider what one will have to do to earn a merit increase at the next review time and thereafter.

Task

- Choose one clinical skill, such as conducts functional assessments, or one supervisory skill, such as instructs nonprofessional staff in departmental procedures.
- Develop a strategy to benchmark the chosen skill (Fig. 12.10).
- Discuss your strategy with other groups.
- Reconvene and assess your outcomes.
- Improve your strategy and benchmarking process according to your experience with this case.

ticated information systems should be the ability to improve, refine, or enhance services offered to patients and other consumers. Information systems with more options are not necessarily more beneficial to patients.

Meeting the training needs of staff is essential to the successful and efficient use of information systems. Staff must be adequately trained and allowed adequate time to become comfortable with any system if the system is to contribute to better care of patients. Patience is necessary. Each person has his or her own learning rate for new technology. It takes time to get accustomed to new systems, and there are inevitably unanticipated transitional difficulties no matter how judicious the planning may have been (Garson, 2001). Adopting the principle of beneficence suggests overestimating the time it will take for users to become efficient with new or updated systems rather than pushing quick deadlines. Finally, the time for selection and installation of a new system and user training can be considerable. A system considered good at selection time may be less good when it is put into operation.

he Information Crunch

e amount of information that crosses the ical health care manager or clinician's desk omputer screen is increasing. Increasingly isticated automated systems present the rtunity to record, monitor, and analyze more things than was possible in the Although attempting to manage a dent, practice, or clinic without adequate ation is difficult and risky, the opposite true: managing with too much foris also difficult and risky. Finding a is a challenge to the manager. As d more information becomes availprudent manager must ask what in- is most important, given deadlines eed to spend time on a variety of

tomated information systems are purchase and operate. Necessary clude capable IT personnel and e and software to develop and red databases and time-sensitive reports. Also, the human resources of time and energy to collect data, review and interpret the information, and develop and implement actions based on the information are also critical.

Physical therapy managers and clinicians spend much time dealing with information sources that could be spent on activities to improve the lives of patients. There is a constant competition for the attention and focus of managers and clinicians at work. Clearly, automation and information systems have great potential to improve efficiency. But efficiency alone is not enough. How managers and clinicians choose to spend their time and energy will determine how effective they are. Even with many opportunities for distraction, the continued focus on the efficient performance of clinical tasks will increase the emphasis on effectiveness.

The Management and Flow of Information in an Organization

In most if not all organizations, control of and access to data and information is a source of power. It is often also a source of competition within an organization (Major, 2000). How internal information is accessed and by whom is very important to any organization.

Historically, organizations have much protected their information. Frequently, it was available only as needed. Access to information was granted only to those who could demonstrate a need to know. This sort of approach leads to a hierarchy of information access. Those with access to the information (and consequent power) are the haves, and the rest are the information have-nots.

The flow of information in organizations has changed over time. Historically, information was collected both centrally and locally. Locally gathered information was dispersed to a central depository of data. There it was aggregated and finally shared with a limited number of selected individuals by overt action of leaders who saw their role as including protection of the corporate data.

More recently, information continued to be collected locally, but began to be aggregated

References

The Benchmarking Exchange. What is benchmarking? Available from http://www.benchnet.com/.wib.htm. Accessed 5/28/03.

Deming WE. Out of crisis. Cambridge, MA: Massachusetts Institute of Technology. 1986.

Joint Commission on the Accreditation of Healthcare Organizations. 1996 comprehensive accreditation manual for hospitals. Oak Terrace, IL: Joint Commission on the Accreditation of Health care Organizations. 1996.

Joint Commission on the Accreditation of Healthcare Organizations. Facts about ORYX: The next evolution in accreditation. Available from http://www.jcaho.org/accredited+organizations/home+care/oryx/the++next+evolution.htm. Accessed 5/24/03a.

Joint Commission on the Accreditation of Healthcare Organizations. Weaving the fabric: Strategies for improving our nation's health care. Available from http://www.jcaho.org/about+us/weaving+the+fabric.pdf. Accessed 5/24/03b.

Joint Commission on the Accreditation of Healthcare Organizations. Facts about the review of performance measurement systems. Available from http://www.jcaho.org/accredited+organizations/home+care/oryx/review+of+systems.htm. Accessed 5/24/03c.

Longest BB Jr., Rakich JS, Darr K. Managing health services organizations and systems. 4th ed. Baltimore: Health Profession. 2000.

Tweet AG, Gavin-Marciano K. The guide to benchmarking in health care: Practical lessons from the field. New York: Quality Resources. 1998.

Wiersma B. Every morning. The Resource. 2002a;2:20.

Wiersma B. So, how you a-doin? The Resource. 2002b;3:13–15.

More Information Related to This Chapter

Information about ORYX for preferred provider organizations:
http://www.jcaho.org/accredited+organizations/health+care+network/oryx/oryx_ppo.htm.

For managed care networks and ORYX access:
http://www.jcaho.org/accredited+organizations/health+care+network/oryx/oryx+for+networks.htm.
http://www.jcaho.org/accredited+organizations/health+care+network/oryx/requirements/index.htm.

Ambulatory care information and ORYX:
http://www.jcaho.org/accredited+organizations/ambulatory+care/advisor/2003issue1/jcr.htm.

To check on facilities accredited by JCAHO:
http://www.jcaho.org/qualitycheck/directory/directory.asp.

Deming electronic Web site:
http://deming.eng.clemson.edu/pub/den/deming_map.htm#files

A tutorial on CQI tools:
http://deming.eng.clemson.edu/pub/tutorials/qctools/stdntndx.htm.
http://deming.eng.clemson.edu/pub/tutorials/qctools/ccmain1.htm.
http://deming.eng.clemson.edu/pub/tutorials/qctools/qct.htm.

Continuous quality improvement home page:
http://deming.eng.clemson.edu/

Additional types of QI diagrams and examples of their use:
http://www.goalqpc.com/whatweteach/RESEARCH/7mp.html.

Benchmarking:
http://www.benchnet.com/.

Information about an ongoing physical therapy benchmarking project:
bob@thenedgroup.com.

Information Management and Documentation

Learning Objectives

1. Construct a list of the important kinds of information needed by each level of management in a health care organization, analyze it, and determine who should have access to which kinds of information.
2. Construct a list of the important kinds of information needed by physical therapist managers and staff who are primarily engaged in treating patients.
3. Evaluate the concept of having access to information on a need-to-know basis.
4. Contrast the information needs of a manager in a medium-sized hospital and a medium-sized privately owned physical therapy practice.
5. Evaluate common technologies for clinical documentation.
6. Analyze the internal and external environment variables that affect the choice of information technology systems.

Key Words

Aggregated, clinical documentation, data, database, hardware, health information system (HIS), information technology (IT), local area network (LAN), management information system (MIS), mainframe computer, node, software, wide area network (WAN)

Introduction

This chapter discusses the critical role of the management of information and automated systems in the everyday operation of a typical health care organization, physical therapy department, and private physical therapy practice. This chapter reviews the most typical types of **data** (graphic, numeric, or written information) that have to be collected and organized, discusses appropriate and inappropriate uses of these data in everyday or internal operations, investigates the options available for automation, and addresses differences in these systems between departments that are part of an integrated health care system and private clinics. Additionally, this chapter examines **clinical documentation** (therapist notes) in an information technology system.

Information Knowledge and Strategy

The U.S. health care system is undergoing an historic shift from a conceptual view concentrating on individual care to one focusing on the health of populations and the care of individuals across a health care continuum. To understand and eventually manage the health of a population requires managing massive amounts of integrated data. For upper man-

agement the breadth and volume of information that has to be filtered, screened, digested, and acted upon is daunting. Knowledge is essential to develop or maintain a competitive advantage (Chapter 11). To help do this, **databases**, which are **aggregated** sources of information, are developed. Managers at the upper levels need databases to plan strategies so the organization prospers (Chapter 11). To support strategy development an information system must be capable of accessing, organizing, and helping to analyze information gained through the external environmental scanning process (Chapter 11).

The need to manage external and internal sources of information (Chapter 11) has added stress to many existing information processing systems. Some systems are outdated or inadequate to meet increasingly vigorous data processing requirements.

The demand for new information will become more evident as we shift toward outcomes analysis and management, that is, ORYX (Chapter 11); the development of automated documentation, scheduling ,and billing systems; and integrated, automated **management information systems** (**MIS**) and **health information systems** (**HIS**). The design and implementation of MIS and HIS will have a significant impact on the completion of work within organizations. This will be true especially for large organizations with a large central computer, called a **mainframe computer**, that requires **information technology** (**IT**) specialists to maintain function. Because of the complexity of large organizations, systems that are intended to bring order and efficiency to daily processes can, if poorly designed, actually interfere with the performance of meaningful work and deter real progress. Among the problems is that the product life cycle (Chapter 23) of computer **hardware** (internal components) and **software** (programs that make the internal components work) is extremely short. By the time new mainframe-based systems are bug free, better products are usually available.

Nonetheless, strategic, clinical, marketing, and financial decisions should be based on information and assumptions that are timely, accurate, and understandable. These trends encourage managers and staff to manage information in a way that will optimize its usage and usefulness.

Although there have been and will continue to be tremendous advances in the management of information within health care organizations, it is imperative to remember that information systems are merely tools. They are used as an adjunct to the primary work that managers and therapists perform, which ultimately is to provide effective and compassionate therapeutic care to patients. To this end the tools of information management should be used as efficiently as possible to help manage organization-wide and specific clinical processes that foster the delivery of quality care for patients (Chapter 11).

Patient Information, Ethics, and Federal Law

In accord with the ethical principle c dentiality, as progress is made toward ingly fast and easy ways of accessing tion and data, the informatio collected, accessed, and managed stricted to those who are privil such information. The patient's privacy does not change in an e ronment. It simply becomes r accomplish. A simple rule is t tion only with those who care of the patient or auth tient to have such inform 2003, requirements fc providers regarding th security of patient inf eral law under the He ity and Accountabilit 4). Additionally, the obligates health ca that the data coll able. The princir data be used or benefits a mu principle of lo information the organiza the patient driving fo

and interpreted locally before it was sent to a central repository. There it was reaggregated and dispersed in aggregate by actions of leaders who continued to control access.

Today information is often collected and aggregated locally. It is then available to be retrieved from a local depository by a central communication center where local users as well as organizational leaders can retrieve it on demand.

In the near future, organizational data will be collected locally and dispersed to the entire organizational community. Data will be aggregated according to needs and retrieved on demand by the entire community as needed. In this way all members of the organization can contribute to and access relevant data to enhance the overall knowledge housed in the organization's information system (Macmillan and Tampoe, 2000). This is a dramatic change in the manner in which data are accessed and controlled, a democratization of data and information within organizations. Decentralization of information systems also carries with it some increased expenses and challenges. Among these are the demands for protection of the organization's data from corruption, destruction, theft, and misuse.

Confidentiality also is much more difficult when a larger population has access to the data. However, there is new software to combat inappropriate release of organizational data or patient data to parties who might use the data against the organization.

Finally, in a disseminated information system, there will be increased time and expense for education and training of many more members of the organization than in systems in which only a few highly skilled personnel interact with a central system.

Traditional Areas of Information Management

Table 13.1 lists typical categories of internal data that health care organizations collect and manage in the course of clinical and managerial operations. Several additional types of information must be considered. This information comes from the external environment (Chapter 11). Ginter, Swayne, and Duncan (1998) have identified five categories of external environmental data that a health care organization's information system should be able to deal with (Table 13.2).

Table 13.1 Types of Information an Organization Collects About Its Internal Operations

Accounts receivable data
Confidential records
Patients' clinical data
Patients' financial data
Scheduling information
Staff clinical efficiency data
Staff benefit, demographic, disciplinary, employment, performance, and payroll data

Typical Information Needs of Organization-Based Clinical Services and Private Practice

Large and small organizations have many similarities of information management along with the differences. These differences are often related to the size of the physical spaces and the complexity of the organizations. This section describes the typical information systems from the perspective of the department manager in a medium-sized hospital, ABC Community Hospital (ABC), and in a medium-sized private practice, Super Rehabilitation Agency, Inc. (Super, Inc). We do not intend to describe the most or least advanced information systems but rather to present a comparative picture of how information

Table 13.2 Five Categories of External Environment Information to Track

1. Competitor data, such as market share
2. Consumer data, such as characteristics of past and present users
3. Economic data, such as information on the economy that will impact on health care
4. Regulatory data, such as HIPAA regulations
5. Target market information, such as rate of growth

systems may be organized to handle internal environment information in two different health care environments. Table 13.1 lists the common areas so they can be compared.

Information Systems at a Community Hospital: ABC Hospital Scenario

ABC is a 350-bed acute-care hospital in a medium-sized city. Approximately 2,000 employees work there, 50 in therapy. Therapy services are provided to patients who are acutely ill, including those in the emergency department and intensive care unit. Services are also provided to patients in the 15-bed inpatient medical rehabilitation unit and in the 35-bed skilled nursing facility on ABC's campus. Outpatients are also treated at ABC; however, these services are housed in a separate building from the main hospital. The therapy staff also serves home care patients. The main hospital uses a mainframe computer. The inpatient medical rehabilitation unit and the skilled nursing facility are not physically connected to the mainframe. They are, however, connected to each other through a local server and multiple computers throughout the unit and facility; this is known as a **wide area network** (WAN).

Therapy Department at ABC

A single therapy manager supervises physical therapy, occupational therapy, speech and language pathology, rehabilitation nursing, rehabilitation psychology, and therapeutic recreation in all locations. The therapy manager reports to the vice president of patient care services, who reports to the president of the hospital.

Information Systems at ABC

The information systems at ABC are typical of smaller hospitals. *Patient demographic data* are collected in the admitting and registration department. The data are entered into the hospital-wide admitting, discharge, and transfer system (ADT). When any patient care department needs demographic data on any patient, that department uses data terminals in the local department to access this data. Many but not all departments can alter demographic data on patients. Access to the system is by password and user identification code. The records are stored in a mainframe computer that keeps a record of who accessed the system and what activities they performed.

Patient clinical data are collected on paper in each individual clinical area and compiled into a central medical record. Each patient has only one medical record, but components of that record may be kept in many locations. For patients who receive outpatient therapy, a unique therapy chart is kept for each episode of care that the patient receives. For inpatient care, the therapists keep the therapy record for each patient in the nursing station or at bedside. It is difficult to coordinate multiple disciplinary charts such as those from radiology and therapy.

Patient financial data are coordinated in a central database in the finance department. This information is based on a unique patient identification number that is given at the time of admission. This information is also coordinated with credit checks and insurance verifications performed to determine the patient's ability to pay. It is also used to identify the viability of health insurance coverage and past financial performance for returning patients. Included in the financial system is a method to track the patient's insurance company and to indicate whether it requires payment approval prior to treatment. Except for the data on prior approval of care, the therapy manager does not routinely access this data.

Billing data are closely coordinated with the other financial data. All departments, including therapy, enter daily billing data into the same terminals that are used for the ADT system. This information is aggregated into a bill that is mailed to the patient or to the patient's insurance company. The therapy manager routinely reviews reports showing the amount of billing in his area of responsibility.

Accounts receivable data indicate unpaid bills that the hospital has issued to patients and insurance companies (Chapter 28). Such data are closely coordinated with the billing data. The therapy manager does not routinely access this report.

Scheduling data are not centralized at ABC. However, in many hospitals, scheduling is centralized. The times patients are to receive care and when additional patients can be scheduled are recorded separately in each department. Conflicts between staff for access to patients are common. The only exception to lack of centralization of scheduling is on the medical rehabilitation unit, where all services and care are scheduled on a board that is coordinated by the nursing staff.

For outpatients receiving therapy, the schedule is kept in a departmental personal computer, which is one of several in the department linked by a multihub server. This system is called a **local area network** (LAN). Clerical personnel are active in trying to match staff availability with patient appointment preference. All staff within the department can access the scheduling data. In addition to clerical personnel, therapists and therapist assistants can change patient times and days from any of the seven **nodes** (computers connected to the network) on the LAN in the outpatient department.

The therapy manager reviews the scheduling data daily, often runs reports on the staff's productivity, and frequently uses this system to accommodate high-priority patients who need therapy immediately. Reports from this system are also sent to the vice president of patient care services and the president of the hospital. Additional information available to the therapy manager is the frequency with which referrers sent patients to the center and attendance history of individual patients.

Human Resource Information at ABC

Staff demographic data and *performance*, *disciplinary*, *employment*, *payroll*, and *benefits* records are centralized in the human resource department of the hospital. This information is closely held in confidence and requires password and identification codes for access. Much of this information is automated, but some of it exists only on paper. Performance and disciplinary records are initiated at the department level and stored as redundant systems in the individual department and the human resources department. The therapy manager regularly receives and reviews reports from human resources. These written reports are then filed in the department records. Payroll data for the therapy department is routinely reviewed and approved by the therapy manager.

Staff medical records, including employment physical examination data, are maintained in the employee health department of the hospital. Access to these records is restricted. Both the entire employee health department and the file area are kept under lock and key. There is very little automation in the employee health department.

Staff clinical efficacy data, including individual and collective productivity and clinical outcomes, are collected and maintained in the departmental personal computer that is part of a LAN. Clerical personnel enter the data once the supervisor or clinician supplies it. All supervisory staff within the department can access the productivity and outcome data.

The therapy manager reviews this information on a regular basis, often runs reports, and frequently uses this system in performance appraisals. Reports from this system are also sent to the vice president of patient care services and the president of the hospital.

Organizational Information at ABC

Accounts payable data are maintained in the purchasing and finance departments. This information is part of the same automated financial system that includes patient finance and billing. Individual departments can use this system from the terminals in all departments. The therapy staff uses this system to place orders for supplies and equipment. The therapy manager routinely reviews reports on the expenses associated with these purchases.

Corporate confidential records are key documents such as real estate records; trade secrets; internal communication records, such as meeting minutes and memos; contracts; records and information required by external agencies, such as accreditation, governance, and legislative bodies; some endowments; physician credentials; quality improvement activities, and other records needed to establish and maintain the organization. With the exception of medical staff credentials, most of these documents are filed as paper copies rather than being electronically stored. This information is kept in the administrative department and in the legal department. The therapy manager rarely if ever accesses these records.

Performance data of the entire organization are also maintained in the administrative and financial departments. These data are part of the financial information system and are the source of reports on the performance of the entire organization and the individual departments within. The therapy manager receives regular performance reports on the therapy department and can review some of this information on the terminals in the therapy department.

Typically, personnel in the department in which the system is housed maintain each of the various information systems. These departments are thought of as users of the system rather than its owners. There is a substantial IT department to assist department personnel in the selection, use, and maintenance of these systems.

Information Systems at a Private Therapy Practice: Super, Inc.

For comparative purposes, similar categories of information that were provided for the hospital are presented for a hypothetical private physical therapy practice. Super, Inc. is a single-site private rehabilitation agency in the same medium-sized city as ABC Hospital. Super, Inc. has approximately 20 full-time employees. The practice owner, a physical therapist, is the manager of the clinic. As the only shareholder in the corporation, the owner is also the board of directors (Chapter 7). Of the employees, 15 work directly with patients, and 5 are employed in the billing and collections department. Only outpatient physical therapy and social services are provided.

Information Systems at Super, Inc.

Demographic data are collected and entered into an automated practice management program by the receptionist, who also schedules the appointments. This information is available, via password and identification code access, at all five nodes of the LAN that runs throughout the clinic. An external consultant (Chapter 34) administers the system in case of trouble or problems with the software.

The *patient's clinical data* are collected on paper in a folder that comprises the patient's medical record. Each patient has only one medical record, which includes all of the information for each episode of care. Open records (for patients receiving care) are stored in a file in the business office. Closed records (for patients who have completed therapy) are stored in a file in a locked area in the basement.

The receptionist enters the *patient's financial data* into the practice management program at the time of the patient's first appointment. The finance staff coordinates this database. This information is organized around a unique patient identification number that is given at the time of admission.

The patient's financial information is coordinated with credit checks and insurance verification by the finance staff to determine the patient's ability to pay for therapy. Historical financial information for patients who have been cared for at ABC Hospital in the past is also part of this system. Included in the financial system is a method to track the patient's insurance company and to indicate whether it requires approval of payment prior to treatment. The owner reviews this data on a regular basis.

Billing data are closely coordinated with the other financial data. The clerical staff enters daily billing data into the same practice management program that is used for financial data. Clinical staff provide billing data to the clerical staff at the end of each treatment day. This information is aggregated into a bill that is reviewed by the owner and sent to the patient or insurance company. The owner reviews individual bills daily and aggregate reports for monthly and quarterly summaries.

Accounts receivable data are unpaid bills that the practice has issued to patients and insurance companies. These data are coordinated with the billing data. Because the speed with which a bill is paid is closely related to cash flow, hence the ability of the practice to pay its bills, the owner closely monitors accounts receivable data. Much like the hospital's outpatient area, scheduling data at Super, Inc. is kept in a personal computer that is part of the LAN. Clerical personnel work hard to match staff availability with patients' appointment preferences. All staff in the department can access the scheduling data. In addition to clerical personnel, therapists and therapist assistants can change appointments from any of the five nodes on the clinic's LAN.

The owner of the practice reviews the scheduling data at least daily, often runs reports on the staff's productivity levels, and frequently uses this system to fit in high-priority patients who need therapy immediately. Additional information available to the owner is the frequency with which referrers send patients to the clinic and the attendance history of individual patients. The owner also previews the patient load over the next few days and weeks to determine whether staffing changes are needed.

Human Resource Information at Super, Inc.

Staff demographic data and *performance*, *disciplinary*, and *employment records* are maintained in the owner's office. This information is maintained as a collection of forms and files kept in locked cabinets. Only the owner has access to these files. None of this information is automated; it exists only on paper. Performance and disciplinary records are also kept in the personnel records in the owner's office. The owner reviews these files before performance reviews and when a problem with an employee's performance arises. *Payroll* is outsourced to a local payroll service company. The payroll company performs all payroll functions for a percentage of the total payroll expense.

Staff medical records, including employment physical examination data, are maintained by an external company that provides employee health services to small businesses. These data are stored offsite and therefore are not available to any staff in the clinic, including the owner.

Staff clinical efficacy data, including individual and collective productivity and clinical outcomes, are collected and maintained in a personal computer that is part of a LAN. Clerical personnel enter this information once the owner or clinician supplies it to them. Only the owner has access to this information. The owner reviews it on a regular basis, often runs reports, and frequently uses this system in marketing activities and in the performance appraisal of staff.

Access to the many types of data that are stored offsite or locked in the owner's office is sometimes difficult or cumbersome for staff who need to use these records.

Organizational Information at Super, Inc.

A local certified public accountant provides consultation to the practice on *financial* and *tax related-matters*. The finance staff maintains accounts payable data. This information is part of the same practice management system that includes patient finance and billing. Staff can use this system from any of the five computers connected to the LAN, but password and identification codes are required. The owner, clerical staff, and finance staff use this system to order supplies and equipment. The owner routinely reviews reports on these purchases when the practice pays its bills. The owner personally signs all checks written by the clinic. Finance staff, in cooperation with the owner, monitor all of the practice's bank accounts to ensure that funds are adequate to cover payroll and other expenses.

Corporate confidential records, such as real estate records, trade secrets, internal communication minutes and memos, contracts, records and information required by external agencies, and other records needed to establish and maintain the organization are filed as paper copies in the owner's office or in the office of the clinic's corporate legal counsel. Legal counsel is provided by a local attorney who is experienced in health care and small business matters (Chapter 34). The owner and corporate legal counsel frequently review these records.

Performance data of the clinic are also maintained in the owner's office. These data are part of the financial information system. The owner reviews the clinic's financial performance reports regularly. Typically, the owner maintains all of the information systems with the assistance of the IT systems consultant.

Comparison of Information Systems in Large and Small Organizations

As the various systems in ABC Hospital and Super, Inc. show, there are many differences and many similarities in the ways information is managed. Although the same basic information systems must be addressed in each setting, the manner in which the organization structures itself to address these systems is dramatically different. Each structure presents certain advantages and specific challenges.

In the larger setting of the hospital, many specialized departments have developed to assist and support the therapy manager in the daily operations of the department. These support departments, such as finance, admissions, and information systems, act as internal consultants to the patient care areas. Allowing these support departments to monitor and handle some of the functions of the business lets the department manager focus attention more closely on the aspects of the business that are unique to therapy, especially clinical care and referral development. However, the therapy manager may become too focused on the clinical aspects of the department, hence isolated from many of the critical functions outside of his or her typical areas of focus. The therapy manager in the larger organization must be willing to make the extra effort to establish strong relationships with the support departments to ensure that he or she is aware of any potential problems as early as possible. Additional concerns for larger, more bureaucratic organizations are the potential for systems and communication to require substantial resources to support the corporate overhead of the system itself, and the potential for the decision-making time to become excessively long because of the large number of individuals to be consulted about the decision.

In the smaller setting of the private practice, it is often not possible to employ a staff of professionals to function as internal consultants in finance, accounting, legal affairs, and so on. This expertise is no less important in a small organization than in a large one. To provide this expertise, the owner must either develop those skills internally or contract with external professionals to provide the services as needed. An advantage of the contracting arrangement is that the owner continues to be involved in all aspects of the business. However, the potential for the owner to be distracted from the clinical development of the practice by the business and finance activities is substantial. The owner of a small practice must learn to balance the finance and clinical leadership of management.

An advantage of a smaller, more compact information system is quicker decision time and less bureaucracy. However, quicker decisions are not always better ones, and the quality of the information provided to support the decision is critical to optimal decision making.

Use of Data

Collection of data for their own sake has minimal value. How the data are used in the daily operations of the organization is much more important. There are appropriate and inappropriate uses for all data. Some individuals should have access to each of the data types listed earlier, and some should not. Employees need access to patients' medical records to give effective treatment. However, if a staff physical therapist is also the neighbor of a person who is admitted as a patient, there may be some concerns when discussing what information the therapist–neighbor really needs. For example, to treat an orthopedic problem, does the therapist need to know that the patient had a hysterectomy 5 years ago?

Every organization should have clearly defined rules of access to any data. These rules should define who has access to what data and clearly state what they may do with the information (Chapter 11). The standard rule is that caregivers have the minimum necessary information to treat the patient. Rules should be universally applied across the organization and should be routinely monitored, reviewed, and updated as needed.

The ability to use an organization's data should be based on real working requirements. For example, clinical department requirements typically consist of access to past clinical information on a patient. Most but not all of the patient's medical history should be made available to those who treat the patient. Particularly difficult questions arise when the patient has requested that specific information be withheld from the caregivers, especially when the patient has an exceptionally communicable disease that may endanger the clinicians. The requests of the patient must be weighed against the safety of the care team. Risk management team members should be brought into the picture to help protect the care team members and the organization (Chapter 33). Any regulations on this topic must be followed.

Information management requirements are also often conflicting. One example is when an employee is injured at work. The employee has specific rights and privileges for workers' compensation health care and indemnity benefits. The employee's records should be given the same level of confidentiality as those of any other person in need of health care. However, because of the preexisting relationship, there may be a role conflict, that is, between roles of employer to employee and caregiver to patient and friend. Organizational policies and procedures should be followed (Chapter 11). If these are insufficient to deal with the situation, consultation with the institutional ethics committee may be helpful (Chapter 6).

Documenting Patient Status: Some Thoughts

Clinical notes make up a large portion of the data entered into health care information systems. There are several options for recording, sharing, and storage of notes. The manner in which the staff record clinically relevant information is clinical documentation. Documentation systems may be automated or manual. The style and format of documentation unfortunately varies throughout the country and sometimes even within a single clinic. This variation may have many reasons, including requirements of third-party payers, peculiarities of specific legal and legislative jurisdictions, varying requirements for staff communication, and the clinician's experience, skill, and preference.

Clinical documentation is an important function of all professional members of a therapy department. Decisions on the structure of documentation and processes of producing it influence reimbursement, legal liability, productivity, teamwork, and to a significant extent, the structure of clinical care. Because of its importance to the department, special care should be taken in considering alternative methods of producing and managing documentation.

Practical Considerations For Clinical Documentation

Clinical documentation has four primary purposes:

1. To communicate what treatments we give, how we give them, and why. We may have to communicate in a timely and effective manner to others such as payers, referrers, clinical team members, and other clinicians with whom we coordinate care. We also frequently communicate to ourselves with our documentation by using it as a reminder of the details of clinical findings and actions or of the clinical options we considered and rationale for our chosen interventions.
2. To provide optimal protection against undue litigation and other external liabilities (Chapter 33).
3. To ensure adequate and acceptable reimbursement for therapy from third-party payment systems (Chapter 29).

4. To document our actions so that it is possible to perform an effective, ongoing practice analysis and improvement program. This may be done either in a formal research mode or more informally as part of clinical or administrative outcomes analyses (Chapter 12).

The Process of Clinical Documentation

The actual process of creating the permanent record that is the medical record can vary tremendously. A wide variety of possibilities exists for formats and technologies used to create those formats. Several considerations should be kept in mind:

- Have realistic expectations. Documentation is frequently a major source of complaints by staff. Even in the most efficient documentation systems, it is unlikely that staff will derive much satisfaction from this aspect of the job. Making sure that the staff view documentation systems as what Herzberg (1968) calls hygiene factors (Chapter 14) is important to developing realistic expectations about the system. Clearly, documentation system management is not likely to be a motivator. Furthermore, streamlining is not likely to mean elimination of documentation activities by clinical staff. Since documentation is often the only tangible source of credibility to many external agencies, therapy services will continue to emphasize the importance of these systems as a means to differentiate a clinic in what is likely to be a crowded market.
- Few other areas of documentation seem to create so much discussion in rehabilitation as what system to use. Possibly this is related to the observation about motivation. Clearly, there is no single best system for every situation. Many factors determine what is a preferred system versus one that clearly will not work in a given setting. We identify features of selected technologies and systems so that appropriate discussions can compare specific products within each category and across categories. Because of the rapid rate of innovation in this industry, we will not discuss specific products within any category.

Technology

A wide variety of technologies should be considered in this discussion. Although it is not exhaustive, we offer our view of the relative advantages and disadvantages of nine ways of recording clinical data. Table 13.3 identifies these technologies and a comparative summary based on our experiences.

As always when a change in any system is under consideration, it is necessary to examine the effects of change from a variety of perspectives. In the case of documentation technology, the perspectives to be considered are personnel, reaction to standardization, differences in computer skills and experience, location of terminals, the organization's resources, and productivity. In each of these discussions, we consider a variety of issues. Our discourse is not meant to be exhaustive but rather to illustrate key factors to be considered during analysis of technology alternatives.

Personnel

Any discussion of technology that does not consider the individuals who will be using it is doomed to fail. Technology for its own sake has no value. The value of technology is applied by the individual who uses it. Therefore, it is absolutely critical to fully consider the abilities and barriers of the individual members of your staff in conjunction with any given technology. Garson (2001) has reviewed the literature on human factors in information systems and has identified several user arguments against computerization. These are among the deterrents to accepting computerization on the job from a user's perspective:

- Cynicism: "To err is human, but to really foul things up takes a computer" (Garson, 2001, p. 287).
- Concern about dehumanization: "The machines are taking over my job and making me one of them in the process."

Table 13.3 Variables for Evaluation of a Computer Documentation System

Factor	*Importance Rank*	*Comments*
Ease of use		
Ease of learning		
Start-up time		
Start-up costs		
Maintenance costs		
Ongoing costs		
Staff efficiency		
Access to data		
Flexibility of system		
Level of standardization		
Maturity of the technology		
Ease of maintenance		
Quality of reports		
Stability of system		
Integration into existing systems		

- Fear of deskilling: "The machine does it all; I do not have to think anymore."
- Increased frustration: "I can do it faster by hand."

There is some truth behind cynicism regarding computers. However, it is people who put together computers, design the software, and enter the data. It is a human error matter in design or use that is the problem. Dehumanization has been a concern since computers came into existence. It is an argument based on people being separated from one another by an electronic device. Some people see time in front of a monitor and keyboard as time taken from face-to-face interactions. Deskilling refers to a reduction in the need to be cognitively engaged. An example is that computer templates require the entry of specific information, generally in a specified order. The fear is that over time skill in composing a unique document customized for the reader will be diminished. Frustration may be caused by time taken from direct patient care duties to learn to use the hardware and software components of a clinical documentation system.

There are also practical implications of these general affective responses. Specific areas to keep in mind when considering a change in the form or method of clinical documentation also should be addressed.

Willingness to Standardize

Staff willingness to standardize the collection and organization of data in the form of a medical record is often the largest single block to successful adoption of technology. Staff may have myriad reasons to resist adopting a single structure or format for notes, including personal preference, educational preparation, what worked in a prior job, and so on.

Perceived Basic Computer Skill

In some cases, resistance to change related to technology may be generational or age related. A person's comfort level with technology is usually related to experience and past successes (Garson, 2001). Younger staff members who have passed through an educational system laden with requirements for technological competence may be more comfortable with change and new technologies. Older staff members who do not own a personal computer or have someone who is knowledgeable and skilled in computer use to mentor them may be reluctant to embrace new technology. Some staff members lack specific skills, such as keyboard skills and use of a multibutton mouse. When this is the case, a manager may facilitate specific training courses to staff to develop these skills.

Geographic Dispersion of Personnel

Another consideration when deciding on technology options will be the relative geographic dispersion of the personnel who will be using the technology. When staff members are concentrated in a relatively small geographic area, it may be easier to supervise, train, and support them as they develop the skills necessary to succeed with the new technology.

Organizational Ability to Support Automation

A final critical consideration is the ability of the organization to support automation of its documentation systems. Because documentation systems are mission critical, you must be able to recover from any technology errors quickly and efficiently. Any long period without access to documentation systems results in inaccurate and possibly absent documentation. If support resources are inadequate or cannot be made available on a timely basis, it is likely that the ultimate transition to technology based documentation will be incomplete, inadequate, and frustrating.

Productive Documentation

Although at present there is no single ideal documentation solution for every situation, it is reasonable to apply a productivity standard in the analysis of documentation options. The following activities should be considered as ideals to be pursued by any documentation system if at all possible:

1. *Standardization across staff and sites.* When patient care in the organization crosses the continuum of health care settings, it is necessary to analyze documentation alternatives from the perspective of following the patient across that continuum. For example, a documentation system that is unique to inpatient care but ineffective in an outpatient setting would be less attractive to an integrated delivery system than to a practice that treats only hospitalized patients. Although it is likely to require a more complex and possibly cumbersome documentation system, big gains in efficiency may be realized when the information can be transferred from one setting to the next without duplication or redundancy. At a minimum, evaluation tools, documentation forms, and documentation philosophies should be consistent across all settings and between all staff members. There is little justification for a wide variety, for example, of back evaluation forms simply because the various staff members were trained with different forms. It is the responsibility of each and every practice to establish a consistent standard of practice for all employees and all clinicians within that practice.
2. *Maximum value with minimal staff effort.* One of the overall goals of a documentation system should be to provide maximal flexibility and quality of documentation with minimal effort from and frustration to the staff. A corollary is that time spent on documentation is time not spent treating patients.
3. *Collection of data elements*, not narrative, to allow coordination with outcomes. There is tremendous advantage in the collection of elements of data as opposed to narrative information. The primary advantage is in the analysis and reporting of the data in summary fashion. When an organization collects data rather than narrative information, analysis of outcomes in the aggregate is simple and efficient. Because of the potential costs of outcomes analysis and the relatively low-cost analyzing and reporting of already collected data, there is a financial imperative whenever possible to docu-

ment data elements rather than narrative information about patients.

3. *Timely, attractive, meaningful notes.* Documentation must not only be accurate and timely, it must also be attractive to those who will read it. This means that reports and communications derived from the documentation should be legible and understandable to both the medical professional and the lesser trained reviewer, that is, third-party payer staff. Documentation is often the only source of credibility to many external agencies. Because of that, it must be attractive and reader friendly. That is not always consistent with being the easiest to produce.
4. *Standard formats for payer source.* Documentation is often a major source of complaints by staff. Even in the best of situations, this may continue to be true, even after significant improvements in the systems themselves. The real source of complaint may come from the frustration of staff trying to comply with the many regulatory and reimbursement requirements imposed by those who oversee care. User-friendly and receiver-friendly forms can streamline documentation.
5. *Avoidance of duplication.* A reasonable goal of any documentation system is to avoid duplication and waste. Duplication of activities across the staff and waste of time and energy of staff and patients for inefficient collection and recording of the same data more than once is often a major cause of inefficiency and frustration for both patients and staff.

Best Documentation Systems

So what is the best documentation system? That depends. In your setting, your staff will have to analyze many factors to determine what is best for your practice. There are, however, some general considerations to include as you move forward with your analysis.

A computer-automated system has many advantages. It is more standardized, makes data easier to store and retrieve, and is accessible from many locations at once. But can it work in your setting, and if so, at what price? What happens if the system goes down? Table 13.4 is a list of factors to consider when considering computer documentation.

Voice recognition is on the horizon. It can be standardized, uses an intuitive interface, and does not have the costs or delays of using a transcriptionist. But can it work for you? It improves from month to month. We used voice recognition technology to write much of this chapter, and it improved dramatically from the time we bought the software to the completion of this chapter. We are still not convinced that voice recognition technology is mature enough for everyday patient care documentation, but it is worth watching.

The best choice among all the imperfect options seems to be to standardize documentation in hard copy before moving to automation. This allows easier editing, is usually less threatening to clinical and clerical staff, and still allows some level of integration with outcomes. Since significant learning time and mistakes are likely as you develop your documentation system, it seems prudent to err at the less expensive hard copy rates than at the much more expensive computer programmer rates of automation.

Although there are many options for methods and mechanisms to clearly and efficiently document clinical care, there is no single best or preferred method for every setting.

Student Notes

There is a spectrum of hardware, software, peripheral equipment, and differences in knowledge about these items and skill in using them. In health care, like other industries, individual circumstances influence what equipment is bought, what programs are developed, and what training users receive. As technology changes, systems will change. Be prepared. Be flexible and adaptable. Be able to use technology efficiently, so more of your time can be spent in direct care activities.

The success of an organization is linked to its knowledge about itself and the world. Knowledge is the only thing that is unique to an organization. Others can duplicate services,

Table 13.4 Technologies for Note Taking

Method	***Description***	***Advantages***	***Disadvantages***
Handwritten narrative	Paper and pen	Readily available Inexpensive Relatively easy to teach Easy to customize Reliable	Difficult to standardize Data collection challenging Storage expensive and cumber-some Completeness not guaranteed Time consuming
Hand-written on forms	Paper and pen on a printed form	Standardized Relatively easy to customize Date collection less cumbersome than narrative Reliable	Storage expensive and cumber-some Data collection still quite cumber-some Completeness not guaranteed
Logs and flow sheets	Typically daily exercise logs and records only	Quickly completed Standardized if done correctly Easy to customize Reliable	Most focus on objective information only Not effective for assessments or evaluations
Dictation and transcription	Electronic voice recording of narrative typed into written format	Eliminates poor handwriting Produces attractive, professional format Equipment relatively inexpensive Relatively easy to teach Easy to customize Relatively reliable	Difficult to standardize Data collection challenging Storage expensive and cumber-some Transcription expensive Time delay for completed note Proofreading notes may be inaccurate
Automated entry	Therapy-specific documentation program or ser-vice	Standardized data collection Remote access possible Efficient storage Allows electronic submission May integrate with other computer systems such as billing and out-comes	Difficult to customize May not integrate with other computer systems Hardware and software may be expensive May require technical sophistica-tion for customization and up-keep Reliability not established Staff may lack data entry skills
Template word processor	Standardized formatted templates	Standardized data collection Less expensive than dictation Many advantages of automated entry Expensive hardware and software not usually required	Relatively cumbersome to cus-tomize Data analysis difficult and cum-bersome Proofreading by clinician required
Scanned	Hardcopy forms scanned into electronic data bases	Familiarity of forms in hard copy Relatively easy to customize Data analysis easier than in narrative Efficient storage and retrieval	Hardware can be difficult May require technical sophistica-tion for setup, customization, upkeep
Voice recognition	Dictate to com-puter; translates to electronic document	Familiar interface Becoming much less expensive Minimal new hardware required	Voice recognition improving but not perfect Background noise can affect transcription Proofreading can be challenging
Database	Collection of data elements on components of intervention, assessment, evaluation	Standardized data collection Efficient analysis Efficient storage and retrieval Data can be manipulated for reports or narratives	Difficult to customize Expertise on data collection and forms design needed Technical sophistication required Hardware and software can be costly

INDIVIDUAL CASE STUDY

Look at the templates for documentation in the guide (APTA, 2001b). Choose one. Scan and save it as a .jpg file. Import it to an MS Word document. Make up data and fill out the template. Copy the template from the guide. Fill it out by hand using the same data you made up for the computer template. Assess the pros and cons of each documentation method based on your experience with this exercise. Include preferences, skill, knowledge, and efficiency.

but they will never know everything that competitor organizations know. This applies to individual therapists also. The information technology system ought to have the capability to continually update your managerial and clinical knowledge and in some areas, your skills. This should be an incentive for developing a high level of competency in the use of the organization's information technology system. A high level of competency may be a competitive

GROUP CASE STUDY

Your Background

Assume this is you. In school you took two computer courses, one on Web site development and one on computer networking. You enjoy computer and related technologies and you are very comfortable with using all forms, such as digital recording, photography, and some games. You deal with your bank and pay your bills electronically. You have a slick cell phone with visual capability. You use a personal data manager that links with your laptop. Your Internet service provides you with broadband service plus up to three Web sites. You use them all. You have subscriptions to two popular PC magazines, you regularly participate in an online chat group dedicated to the future of technology, and you occasionally go to computer swap meets looking for inexpensive upgrades.

The Situation

You have recently been employed as a part-time aide in a physical therapy department (you have to pay your Internet provider and your credit card bill). Your employer is a private practice owner with two locations, both of which she services herself. You travel with her and provide support services at both locations. Business is booming. Your employer comments that she is seeing so many patients that keeping up with the paperwork is becoming impossible. She also notices that you do some of your schoolwork in the car as you travel between sites and that you programmed the day's schedule on your personal data manager. She asks what you think it would take for her to learn to use a laptop from her car, set up schedules with a personal data manager, and perhaps have her clinical documentation at hand no matter where she is.

What Are Your Responses?

Formulate your answers. Be specific in terms of time, equipment, estimated cost, training, learning curve, HIPAA regulations (see Chapter 4 if you need a review), and probable effect on productivity compared to writing notes by hand. If you form groups to work on this case, be sure that at least one member is computer savvy. Compare group responses when you

advantage when desirable opportunities materialize.

Finally, regarding clinical documentation, you have most likely been oriented to documentation guidelines as developed by the APTA (2001a). The information categories and templates (APTA, 2001b) are ideal for part of an automated clinical documentation system. However, third-party payers often require some unique information and prefer that their own forms be used. Again, be flexible. Change is one of the few things you can count on.

Summary

Information management is necessary for effective health care management. This chapter examines some of the critical criteria for determining the type of information management system that will meet a health care organization's needs for data management.

As the health care system continues to shift toward management of the health of populations, additional emphasis on information management will be needed. Physical therapists need the skill, hardware, and software to enter and access the kinds of data that can continually improve the quality and management of physical therapy services.

The needs for information technology among organizations differ. Variables include the size of the organization, the types and complexity of the databases needed, and the distance between users and computers. A number of alternative clinical documentation technologies are compared on the basis of advantages and disadvantages. Attention is also given to human factors related to computer use. Users need to be brought into the picture during selection of a technology for clinical documentation. Training to use information technology to improve clinical care is a key element for providing information that enhances the organization's knowledge about itself and the external variables that can affect the success of the organization.

Chapter 14 is the first in a new topic, managing human resources, specifically, selecting, developing, and keeping productive staff.

REFERENCES

American Physical Therapy Association. Guidelines for physical therapy documentation.
Physical Therapy. 2001a;81:703–705.

American Physical Therapy Association. Documentation template. Physical therapy. 2001b;81:707–719.

Garson GD. Human factors in information systems. In Golembiewski RT, ed. Handbook of organizational behavior, 2nd ed. New York: Marcel Dekker. 2001:287–326.

Ginter PM, Swayne LM, Duncan WJ. Strategic management of health care organizations, 3rd ed. Malden, MA: Blackwell. 1998.

Herzberg F. One more time: How do you motivate employees? Harvard Business Review. 1968;Jan-Feb:53–62.

Macmillan H, Tampoe M. Strategic management: Process, content, and implementation. New York: Oxford. 2000.

Major DA. Effective newcomer socialization into high-performance organizational culture. In Askanasy NM, Wilderom CPM, Peterson MF. Handbook of organizational culture and climate. Thousand Oaks, CA: Sage. 2000:355–368.

MORE INFORMATION RELATED TO THIS CHAPTER

The APTA's Section on Health Policy and Administration has a special interest group (SIG) on technology. The SIG is an invaluable source of practical information on technology in physical therapy practice and educational environments. This group sponsors educational presentations at national meetings and solicits articles on technology for each edition of the section's newsletter, HPA Resource. Contact http://www.aptahpa.org for more information about this organization.

A recent book on the relationship between health care organizational strategy and information technology is Glaser JP. The strategic application of information technology in health care organizations. San Francisco: Jossey-Bass. 2002.

Lengnick-Hall recently published a book dealing with the importance of knowledge to an organization and the relationship between information technology and human resources: Lengnick-Hall, ML, Lengnick-Hall CA. Human resource management in the knowledge economy: New challenges, new roles, new capabilities. San Francisco: Berrett-Koehler. 2003.

The concept of a learning organization and the role of information technology is addressed in Pedler M, Burgoyne J, Boydell T. The learning company: A strategy for sustainable development. New York: McGraw-Hill. 1997.

Part III

Managing Human Resources

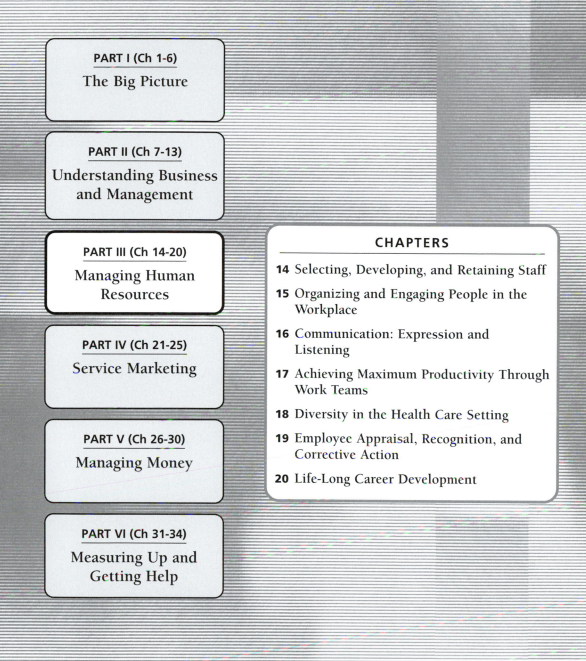

PART I (Ch 1-6)
The Big Picture

PART II (Ch 7-13)
Understanding Business and Management

PART III (Ch 14-20)
Managing Human Resources

PART IV (Ch 21-25)
Service Marketing

PART V (Ch 26-30)
Managing Money

PART VI (Ch 31-34)
Measuring Up and Getting Help

CHAPTERS

Chapter 14

Selecting, Developing, and Retaining Staff

Learning Objectives

1. Analyze the roles of the human resource professional, physical therapy manager, and physical therapy staff in employee recruitment, development, and retention.
2. Evaluate the elements of a successful recruitment process.
3. Compare and contrast possible approaches to employee development.
4. Contrast the ways management may standardize the work of employees.
5. Analyze traditional management theories in the context of job satisfaction.
6. Evaluate why people leave a job and actions management may take to minimize such actions.

Key Words

Behavior formalization, compensation, contingencies, employee turnover, employment benefits, horizontal specialization, job competencies, job description, job specialization, management, professional, professional training, qualified candidate, recruiter, selection criteria, support, vertical specialization, work design

Introduction

Managers are responsible for attracting and retaining people who are capable of maximum performance (Schemerhorn, 1987). Managers can meet this responsibility only if they have an effective employee recruitment, selection, and development process. Several benefits come from an effective staff recruitment and development program. First, the organization will have the right number of qualified employees to get the work done. Staff vacancies hinder existing employees. Employees who work in the conditions created by long-term staffing shortages may become less satisfied and less productive and ultimately leave the organization. Thus, employee recruitment is also critical to employee retention. Second, managers with full knowledge of employees' qualifications, experience, and past performance make better situational assessments and decisions. Employees are assigned to tasks that best fit their capabilities and/or their development goals. Finally, employees are more likely to meet performance expectations and have higher job satisfaction. Each of these benefits is essential if an organization is to reach high performance goals. This chapter is about high performance and how to achieve it.

Recruiting the Right People

In today's environment of cost containment, staffing levels are lean. Most physical therapy departments hire just enough staff to get the work done. For a department to operate effectively in this environment, every employee must be working at maximum effectiveness and productivity. In other words, everyone must get his or her work done right, in the least amount of time, and step in when others need help. Ultimately, recruiting the right people is the first and most important step toward delivery of quality services.

A typical physical therapy department has at least three categories of employee:

1. **Management:** any director, manager, and sometimes supervisor (Chapter 8).
2. **Professional:** physical therapists and physical therapist assistants. Supervisors are sometimes placed in this category. In very large departments and private practices, this category might include other professional staff, such as accountants and systems analysts.
3. **Support:** clerical, office, housekeeping, and clinical support positions.

The recruitment process may vary somewhat by category of employee, job requirements, and the size of the labor pool. Regardless, hire decisions are the most important decisions a manager will ever make.

Recruiting a new employee is a multistep process. It starts when management determines that new or replacement personnel are needed. The process ends when the selected candidate is settled into the new position. Usually, there is a specified probationary period. When an organization is sufficiently large to employ human resource professionals, employee recruitment is accomplished through a collaborative effort between human resources and department management.

To get the recruitment process started, management must define the job opportunity. Several decisions must be made along the way. The first is how to define the work. Next, management must decide on the minimum requirements for education, knowledge, skills, and experience. The final decision is how to define the position in relation to other individuals and parts of the organization. These three decisions are necessary to ensure that when interviews begin, the candidates will have a complete understanding of the organization's needs, performance requirements of the job, and what it will take to be successful. Management has several options to consider during this work design process.

Work design encompasses everything an organization does to structure and regulate the work of its employees. Each employee's work must define all of the following elements:

1. Specific job duties
2. Personal and/or physical requirements
3. Minimum education, skills, and experience
4. Work standards, such as policies, procedures, and protocols
5. Performance expectations
6. Standards by which the employee's work will be evaluated
7. Relationship to management, other employees, and/or work groups
8. Work group affiliations and assignments
9. Methods by which the employee's work will be coordinated with the work of others

The three parameters of work design are job specialization, behavior formalization, and professional training (Mintzberg, 1979; Mintzberg, Quinn, Voyer, 1995).

Specialization in designing work is described in two-dimensional terms. The first dimension of specialization focuses on the content of the job, its breadth or scope. It is called **horizontal specialization**. A position that is highly specialized will include only a few narrowly defined tasks. A position with a high degree of horizontal specialization has few tasks and thus a narrow scope of responsibility. The more limited the scope, the greater the degree of horizontal specialization. A physical therapist's job that is limited to the treatment of adult patients following joint replacement is an example of high horizontal specialization.

The second dimension of specialization relates to the employee's degree of control or autonomy over the tasks to be performed. It is called **vertical specialization**, or the depth of the job. The more vertically specialized the job, the less control the employee has over the work performed.

The division of work through horizontal specialization is intended to increase employee and consequently organizational efficiency and performance. The division of work through vertical specialization (supervision) is intended to direct and coordinate the work of employees so productivity is acceptable.

Figure 14.1 demonstrates how the concept of job specialization typically applies to physical therapy practice. Too often job specialization is based on the need for control, assumptions about employees' capabilities, or employees' lack of skills to perform the work without a clear division of tasks. Unfortunately, this approach may lead to unnecessary specialization. See Chapter 17 for additional discussion about engaging people for maximum performance. Unnecessary vertical specialization is a barrier to maximum contribution by employees because it limits professional autonomy. High horizontal and vertical specialization can lead to boredom, doing the job automatically, and dissatisfaction. Work design should start with a clear understanding of what the organization requires from its employees. Whenever possible, employees should be allowed maximum latitude and autonomy to get their work done in the most efficient way possible.

Traditionally, health care has been dominated by highly specialized jobs with limited autonomy. This has limited employees to a relatively small number of job tasks to achieve a high degree of performance reliability, that is, care pathways, or standard operating procedures. A highly specialized job can also limit the ability of an employee to use skills or develop new ones. Over time, this can decrease the range of an employee's abilities and the willingness to be flexible when there is a need to change. This can lead to tremendous upheaval when change is needed. It also decreases the ability of the business to respond quickly and efficiently to environmental

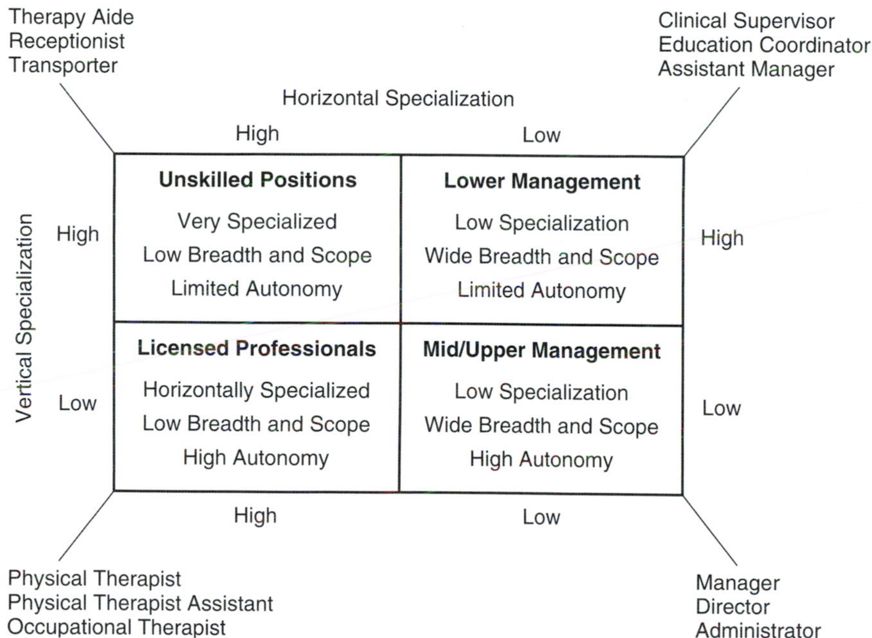

Figure 14.1. Job specialization in physical therapy practice. (Modified from Nosse LJ, Friberg DG. Management principles for physical therapists. Baltimore: Williams & Wilkins. 1992:64.)

opportunities or threats. In today's environment, health care businesses are wise to foster the development of flexibility and limit specialization (as defined in this section) whenever possible.

Behavior formalization describes the ways a business can standardize the work of its employees (Mintzberg, 1979; Mintzberg et al., 1995). The health care industry relies heavily on standardization. Standardization can increase efficiency, but more important in health care, it results in consistency of work performance. An error in the delivery of health care services can have serious and costly consequences (Chapters 5 and 33). The potential for errors is decreased when performance consistency is high. As a result, health care businesses rely heavily on behavior formalization. There are three methods of formalizing behavior: (1) by position, (2) by workflow, and (3) by rules. Job descriptions, standard care plans, treatment referrals, policies, procedures, operating manuals, and licensure requirements are means used for behavior formalization (Chapters 9 and 11). These means of facilitating behavior formalization should be addressed in the work design. All are part of the infrastructure that supports the work of the health care business.

Professional training is the process by which job skills are taught (Chapter 20). Complex and nonroutine tasks require the greatest amount of training to standardize job performance. Training can occur inside or outside of the organization. The more training takes place outside of the business, the less control the business has over the work methods taught (Mintzberg, 1979). When basic work methods are learned outside the business, it is incumbent on the business to validate and where necessary enhance and standardize work methods used by its employees. Therapists learn basic skills during their professional training. Each time they take a new job, they can expect to receive an orientation to the way their employer wants therapy services to be provided. Written guidelines such as policies and procedures (Chapter 11), training, mentoring, job competencies, performance standards (Chapter 12), and supervision are all commonly used professional training approaches.

Writing a Job Description

The **job description** documents the decisions made during work design. If management has done its work right, the job description should be a road map to the employee's success. A well-written job description will contain the following elements:

1. The organizational relationships of the position. The employee's job title, work group, supervisor, subordinates, and relationship to other employees should be defined.
2. A list of duties with enough detail to delineate the tasks to be performed and with enough latitude to allow for flexibility in responsibilities.
3. A description of the decision-making authority (autonomy) of the position. If variable, the degree of autonomy for specific duties should be clear or the mechanism for determining degree of autonomy by task should be clear.
4. Applicable work standards, such as policies and professional standards.
5. A description of the minimum job requirements, including formal education, knowledge, skill, work experience, licensure or certifications, physical abilities, and personal characteristics. All of the minimum requirements should be clearly related to the demands of the job.
6. Any responsibility for the work of others.
7. Methods by which the work will be coordinated with the work of others.

When available, human resource professionals may be able to assist with work design and preparing a job description. They generally take the lead when it comes to setting compensation and benefits eligibility for a specific position.

Compensation, Benefits, and Other Important Things

A well-written job description announces that management knows what it needs. But that's only half of the story. A job candidate also wants to know what to expect in return for the work. In preparing to answer that question, **compensation** is the obvious place to start. In case there is any doubt, let us say it for the record: *compensation is very important*. In addition to wages, compensation may include bonuses, an expense allowance, relocation allowance, shift premium, on-call pay, tuition repayment, and other forms of payment. Most organizations have an established schedule of pay ranges, that is, a minimum and maximum allowable pay rate for a given job. Typically, when a position is approved for hire, its pay range is based on job duties, minimum requirements, going market rates, and equity in relation to other positions within the organization. Using a pay range allows employers to raise employees' pay over time, base pay on experience, and limit the maximum pay for a particular position. Ranges also allow for flexibility when hiring into a position. For example, a newly graduated physical therapist may be hired at the minimum of the range, while an experienced therapist is hired at the midpoint of the range. Department management and human resources together usually determine the rate of pay offered to a candidate. Another aspect of compensation is the classification of the position under federal wage and hour rules. In the simplest terms, positions can be salaried or hourly. While this may vary somewhat, salaried employees are typically in professional or managerial positions. They are paid for a 40-hour work week and are expected to complete their assigned work within that time frame. However, if they work additional weekday, weekend, or holiday hours, they receive no additional compensation. Hourly employees are generally in support positions. Therapy aides, office clerks, receptionists, and housekeepers are examples of hourly employees. Hourly employees typically earn less per hour but are paid for every hour they work. Depending on their standard work schedule, they may be eligible for time and a half (overtime pay) for extra hours worked in a day or a week. To obtain additional information about federal wage and hour guidelines, see the suggested resources at the end of this chapter.

In addition to compensation, most employers offer **employment benefits**. Common benefits include the following:

- Health, dental, disability, and life insurance
- Paid time off for vacation, holiday, illness, or bereavement
- Health club fees (on site or community based)
- Subsidized child care
- Paid or subsidized education
- Travel subsidy or car allowance
- Paid parking
- Tax-deferred savings plans; may include contributions by the employer
- Retirement benefits
- And more...

The benefits available vary by employer, job, and the number of hours an employee is hired to work. Before interviews begin, benefit eligibility should be determined.

Other important things candidates might consider in accepting a position include geographic location; type of work to be done; educational or skill development opportunities; advancement opportunities; reputation, size, and resources of the employer; opportunity to work with experienced peers; and comfort level with the department manager and staff (Chapters 20 and 25).

Set Selection Criteria

The next step is to set **selection criteria**. Selection criteria can be thought of as a characterization of the perfect candidate. For example, the ideal candidate for a physical therapist position may possess more than 5 years of specialty experience working with brain-injured adults in an outpatient setting. The goal of any recruitment effort is to identify a large number of **qualified candidates**. A qualified candidate is one who meets all of the minimum requirements of the position. It is not practical to interview every qualified candidate. Selection criteria are used to narrow the field to a few top candidates. Setting selection criteria before interviews start ensures that all interviewers evaluate candidates against the same benchmarks. Typical means of ranking candidates include assigning candidates a point ranking for each selection criterion and comparing their point totals and ranking candidates high to low for each criterion. The latter approach is more beneficial when all of the candidates are similarly qualified and differentiation is difficult.

Get the Word Out

Okay, the stage is set, and its time to get the word out about the job opportunity. Once again, human resources will likely play a major role in identifying candidates. Internal job postings will reach current employees who may be qualified candidates. External candidates can be reached by word of mouth, advertising, direct mail, or direct solicitation (Chapters 21–23). Frequently used advertising media include newspapers, magazines, recruitment publications, Internet job boards, and radio.

A professional recruiter may be needed for positions that are difficult to fill. A professional **recruiter** is a type of human resource consultant (Chapter 34). Recruiters are used to locate key and/or hard-to-find employees. This service has been used extensively by health care organizations to fill physical therapist positions. Typically, a professional recruiter will search for qualified applicants to interview for employment. Should the recruiter's candidate be hired, the employer pays the recruiter a percentage of the first year's wages. This percentage varies but can be as high as 30 to 40%. This is far less than the cost of not meeting patient care needs because of staff shortages. Part of the recruitment fee may be refundable if the employee does not complete the probationary employment period or a full year of employment. Some recruiters insist on an arrangement under which they receive their fee even if a candidate they did not recruit fills the position. Arrangements with professional recruiters do vary and should be negotiated case by case.

Candidate Interview and Selection

Job interviews offer both employer and candidate the opportunity to learn more about each other. The employer is looking to validate what has been presented in the written job application or resume. He or she may also want to get a sense of how a candidate will fit into the culture of the organization. For hard-to-fill positions the interview may also be a time for an employer to sell the candidate on the position. Generally, the more important the position, the longer the interview process and the more people involved. An employer can do some things to make the interview process more effective:

- *Define the role of each interviewer.* Each interviewer should have a clear understanding of why he or she was selected to participate. For example, human resources may be involved to share information about compensation and benefits and to evaluate the character and fit of the candidates.
- *Prepare interviewers in advance.* Interviewers should be provided with information about each candidate and the selection criteria. They should also understand the type of feedback they will be expected to provide on each candidate.
- *Interviewers should prepare and use standard questions.* This will allow for a fair and accurate comparison of candidates.
- *Interviewers should prepare informational materials in advance.* If part of an interviewer's role is to provide candidates with specific information, materials should be prepared and information shared in a consistent manner.

A well-planned interview will make candidate selection much easier. Candidates will have received the same information and responded to the same questions. When evaluated against the agreed-upon selection criteria, differences between the candidates should be fairly clear. Management should be well prepared to select the top one or two candidates.

On the other side of the table, job candidates want to impress interviewers with their qualifications, but they also want to learn more about the organization, the job, and the people they would work with. It is a two-way conversation. To be successful, candidates must also prepare for the interview. Before the interview, candidates should find out as much as possible about the position and the organization from sources such as annual reports, marketing materials, and interviews with former employees. Business dress is the right choice for any interview. Candidates should arrive at the interview with prepared questions and be ready to discuss their knowledge and experience as it relates to the job opportunity. For first-time job seekers, general abilities such as willingness to learn, flexibility, and enthusiasm are worth pointing out. Another good idea is to be prepared to provide an explanation for any gaps in education or employment history or any positions that were held for less than 2 years. After the interview, it is wise to follow up with a note thanking the interviewers for their time and interest.

Once the top candidate has been selected, it's time to make a job offer. Human resources in collaboration with department management should define the offer in terms of compensation, benefits, and contingencies. **Contingencies** might include such things as a response within a specified time, ability to start on a specified date, clean arrest record, negative drug test results, acceptable references from a current employer. Once the contingencies are defined, it is time to make the offer. Now it is the candidate's turn to respond by accepting the offer, countering with a request for modification of the offer or contingencies, or declining the offer. Until the offer is accepted and the contingencies are clear, it is advisable to keep the door open with the other top candidates. Once the position has been filled, all qualified candidates or at a minimum those who were interviewed should be notified that the search is closed. This courtesy will be rewarded in the long run when another job opening occurs. Figure 14.2 summarizes the multistep recruitment process.

Employee Development

Employees cannot be productive if they do not have the knowledge and skills to do the job. Recruiting the best employees is not enough. Great employees have to be developed to work at their maximum effectiveness and highest level of productivity (Chapter 20). Development of new employees should start as soon as they do and *never stop*. Effective employee development does not happen by chance. It takes planning, management effort, and money to pay for employees' time and for educational resources. An employee development plan starts with management's knowledge of the work to be done. Job duties will determine the knowledge and skills needed now and in the future. An employee development plan should be designed to train employees so they can do the following:

- Adapt to changes in job duties and/or performance expectations
- Do their job well today
- Do their job better tomorrow
- Do a different job in the future
- Keep pace with new technology
- Fulfill their professional goals
- Meet continuing education needs for maintaining licensure

In health care, required knowledge and skills are called **job competencies**. Job competencies are clearly defined and measurable tasks that an employee is required to perform to meet performance expectations and accreditation requirements (Chapter 20). For example, the ability to deliver ultrasound treatment is a job competency for a physical therapist assistant. The procedure for giving an ultrasound treatment is defined in the department procedure manual. The employee's knowledge and performance of the procedure can be evaluated by direct observation. Less technical but equally important, age-related competencies measure knowledge of age-related differences and an employee's ability to apply that knowledge in caring for patients.

Training programs can be provided on the job or through external sources (Chapter 20). Common external sources of employee training programs include self-study materials, Internet courses, continuing professional education programs, and educational institutions. Rotating employees to a variety of work settings can also develop employees. This method provides opportunities to gain advanced

STEP 1

Define the Work to Be Done.

STEP 2

Determine Minimum Requirements for Any Employee Assigned the Position.
- What physical abilities are required?
- What education is required and/or preferred?
- What knowledge and job skills does an entry-level employee require?
- What type of previous experience will an entry-level candidate require?
- What and how much previous experience will an entry-level candidate require?

STEP 3

Determine Where the Position Fits in the Organizational Structure.
- Who will supervise the employee?
- Whom will the employee supervise?
- With which work teams will the employee work?

STEP 4

If This Is a New Position:
- Prepare a job description that reflects work to be done, minimum requirements, and organizational relationships. Include specific job competencies used to evaluate an employee's performance.
- Coordinate with human resources staff to get approval of the position description, determine the exemption status, assign a job code, set the compensation range, determine eligibility for other elements of the compensation and benefits plan, and obtain any needed approvals.

STEP 5

The Department and Human Resources Will Collaborate to Plan for Candidate Identification and the Interview Process. There Are Questions to Be Answered and Responsibilities to Be Assigned to Ensure That this Part of the Process Goes Smoothly.
- How will qualified candidates be informed of the job opportunity?
- How will interested parties be instructed to respond?
- How and by whom will responses be screened?
- What criteria will be used to select candidates for interview?
- What interview expenses will be paid and out of what budget?
- Who will act as the point of communication with the interviewees?
- Who will schedule and coordinate the interview appointments?
- Who will participate in the interviews?
- What specific information will be shared with the interviewees and by whom?
- How will input be gathered and a candidate selected?
- Who will determine the specifics of the job offer?
- Who will make the job offer and negotiate with the selected candidate?
- Who will follow up with interested parties and interviewees when the interview process is completed?

STEP 6

Get New Employees off to a Good Start.
- Develop a structured orientation plan.
- Prepare a work area with needed equipment, supplies, and reference materials.
- Assign a buddy to help them through the first weeks of the new job.
- Keep the management door open so they can ask questions and get help.

Figure 14.2. The six steps for recruitment and hiring.

expertise and to deal with stretch goals, that is, goals that challenge an employee to do new things that apply skills in different ways. Mentoring programs that pair an experienced employee with less-experienced employees to pass on expertise, act as a resource, and provide ongoing constructive feedback are other ways to develop employees.

Internal and external consultants are frequently used to support staff training and development (Chapter 34). Consultation may be provided in a variety of ways including lectures, the provision of training materials, off-site training, and teleconferences. Reliance on other employees to provide in-service education is a form of internal consulting. Diversity training is one type of employee training and development that is often done by external consultants (see Chapter 18).

How to Keep Good Employees

Organizations invest substantial resources in recruiting, training, and developing people so they are prepared to do their work. As an organization's investment in developing employees goes up, so does the value of the employee as an asset of the organization. It is a real loss when a valued employee leaves the organization. The loss of an experienced employee can impair organizations in several ways:

- Decreased productivity
- Lost business opportunities
- Lost revenue
- Decreased customer satisfaction
- Decreased employee satisfaction for those remaining

Employee turnover is the term used when an employee leaves an organization. Turnover is often expressed as the percentage of employees who have terminated their employment during a specified period. For example, if 2 of 10 physical therapists working in a department terminated their employment during the past year, the department's annual turnover was 20%. Turnover rate may be used as a performance outcome measure.

Employees leave organizations for a variety of personal and professional reasons. One study on turnover of physical therapists found that 26% of therapists who had been in the field less than 2 years had had 2 to 5 jobs, and 75% of physical therapists who had been in the field more than 5 years had had 2 to 5 jobs (Harkson, Unterreiner, Shepard, 1982).

In our experience employees may leave an organization for reasons unrelated to the work setting. Some turnover can be influenced by management action and some cannot. Family responsibilities, spouse relocation, return to school, or a change in career are all reasons to leave an organization. Managers have little ability to affect turnover that is driven by such personal values. Controllable turnover is driven by individual, organizational, and environmental factors (Abelson, 1986; Smith, 1988). Herman (1999) identified five common reasons employees leave their jobs:

1. Corporate culture
2. Perceived lack of appreciation
3. Insufficient resources in the workplace
4. Lack of advancement opportunities
5. Inadequate compensation

Managers should concentrate their efforts on the turnover factors they can influence.

The effects of turnover and costs of recruitment go up when positions remain vacant for extended periods. Given the potential negative impacts, it is in an organization's best interest to retain employees whose performance meets expectations. Management is responsible for providing a work environment that motivates employees to remain with the organization. A supportive environment starts with the basics (Mintzberg, 1979):

1. Employee compensation, including wages and benefits, should be competitive for the market area and type of position.
2. Strategic and financial management practices should be sound, resulting in reasonable job security.
3. Management style should reflect the situation and needs of the employees.
4. Positive relations among employees and between management and employees should be fostered.
5. Management should provide clear goals, objectives, and performance expectations.
6. Employees should be provided with the right tools, equipment, and facilities.
7. Employees should be free from unnecessary organizational barriers.
8. Employees should be provided with opportunities for achievement and advancement.
9. Management should be generous with its recognition and rewards.

Herzberg (1966) and associates (1959) identified factors that lead to job satisfaction (Table 14.1)

Similarly, Maslow (1943, 1968) identified a hierarchy of needs that must be fulfilled in a logical order. Comparative lists of Herzberg's

Table 14.1 Herzberg (1966) Two-Factor Theory of Job Satisfaction

Factors Leading to Job Dissatisfaction and Satisfaction

Dissatisfiers	*Satisfiers*
Administration	Achievement
Benefits	Advancement
Interpersonal relations	Growth potential
Job security	Interpersonal relations
Organizational policy	Power
Salary	Recognition
Supervision	Responsibility
	Salary
	Status

and Maslow's human needs concepts are presented in Table 14.2.

Herzberg (1966) suggests that job satisfaction and worker motivation are enhanced by the presence of reasonable working conditions, equitable treatment, and fair pay. However, these so-called satisfier items are insufficient to inspire optimal worker performance. The absence of benefits, supervision, job security, and other factors called dissatisfiers can result in disenchantment with a job even if the satisfiers are present (Chapter 15). Maslow (1943, 1968) suggests that performance is driven by the desire to fulfill unmet human needs. He has argued that people have a number of wants and needs arranged in an ascending hierarchy from the most basic physiological needs to the fulfillment of personal objectives. He suggests that the lowest level in the hierarchy must be fulfilled before the next higher level can be approached.

Table 14.2 Comparison of Human Needs Theories

Herzberg's Factors	*Maslow's Needs Hierarchy*
Achievement Advancement Growth potential	Self-Actualizing Needs
Power Recognition Responsibility Status	Esteem needs
Administration Interpersonal relationships Supervision	Love needs
Benefits Job security Organizational policy	Safety needs
Salary Working conditions	Physiological needs

Table 14.3 was formulated by using the concepts of Herzberg (1966) and Maslow (1968) in combination with our experience regarding job dissatisfaction and management's means of dealing with such matters.

A manager may use the factors in the table to estimate the level of staff job satisfaction. The table also offers suggestions for action to deal with job satisfaction issues. For job seekers, the list may be used to formulate questions to ask of those who are working or have worked at places of interest. For employees, the list may help identify issues that can be brought up to management and jointly addressed. The list offers practical options for resolving employees' concerns.

Student Notes

Understanding what makes a good working environment for recruitment and retention should help as you complete your education and take on the role of job candidate. Look for employers who are well organized and thoughtful about recruitment. It is a good indicator of how they run the rest of the business. For your part, make sure you get the information necessary to do a thorough assessment of the position, the department, the organization, and the individual to whom you will be responsible. Ask to speak with someone who is relatively new to the organization and would be your peer. Be prepared to ask questions about what the environment is like now and what it may be like in the near future.

Summary

Management has the responsibility for maximizing the performance of the organization. An organization can be successful only if it is able to recruit and retain good people. It is up to management to design the work to be

Table 14.3 Turnover Factors And Management Actions Encouraging Employee Retention

Turnover Factors		*Management Actions Encouraging Retention*
Poorly defined responsibilities	➡	Clearly define performance expectations.
High-stress position	➡	Remove obstacles that interfere with job performance and provide needed resources.
Work that does not use employee's skills	➡	Define job prior to employment. Match employee's skills with job.
Unreasonable performance expectations	➡	Involve employees in setting performance expectations.
Limited growth opportunities	➡	Create opportunities for growth and development. Involve employees in the work design process.
Lack of recognition for accomplishment	➡	Recognize good performance. Provide opportunity for peer recognition.
Lack of opportunity to express concerns and dissatisfaction	➡	Provide formal mechanisms and encourage employees to express work-related concerns.
Inflexible work conditions	➡	Make flexible work arrangements whenever possible.
Pay inequities	➡	Use market information to determine wage and benefits programs.
Limited autonomy	➡	Encourage employee participation and a level of autonomy based on ability.
Open job market	➡	Develop jobs with competitive compensation and challenging content.
Undesirable work conditions	➡	Correct dissatisfying conditions where possible. Put in place offsetting conditions that decrease the impact of undesirable conditions.

Modified with permission from Nosse LJ, Friberg DG. Management principles for physical therapists. Baltimore: Williams & Wilkins. 1992:90.

done. Work design can be viewed as a fleshing out of the organization's structural skeleton. It is the process of deciding who will do what in relation to all of the other activities of the organization. The larger and more complex the organization, the more challenging work design becomes. The challenge is to balance job specialization with the organization's ability to coordinate the work of many into unified health care delivery. Work design is the prelude; hiring and keeping good employees is the key to success. Management can do that by creating an environment that supports employee needs and is rewarding experientially and in terms of compensation. Once employees are hired and provided with necessary resources, their work efforts have to be coordinated so that it is efficiently and effectively carried out. The next chapter deals with managing staff so that their work is

INDIVIDUAL CASE STUDY

No matter how well managed the recruitment process, it sometimes fails to find the right candidate. Consider this situation: For 6 months your department has been looking for a new physical therapist assistant. You are the interim person responsible for contributing to the hire decision. You are uncomfortable with this role. One internal candidate meets some of the agreed-upon selection criteria. Human resources wants to know whether they should search for more candidates or offer the position to the internal candidate. What factors do you consider in making your decision?

GROUP CASE STUDY

Form groups of 5 to 10 members. Each member is to assume the role of department manager. Consider the following situation and as a group formulate answers to the questions that follow the scenario.

Situation

The City Hospital is recruiting a senior physical therapist for a new outpatient clinic. A well-liked staff therapist has applied for the position. This therapist does not meet the criterion of previous supervisory experience.

Through the grapevine you have heard that most of the department therapists think this employee has done a nice job, has been an informal leader (see Chapter 8), and deserves this opportunity. In fact, two of four staff therapists scheduled to work at the new clinic have told you that they will consider leaving if an external candidate is hired to supervise them. They do not understand why you, the manager, have decided to open the position to external candidates. Even after you explain that the human resources department requires all new positions to be advertised, these therapists are peeved.

You have high regard for the internal candidate's clinical expertise, but as an informal leader, this person has caused you some difficulty. Consider the following:

- How should you respond to the two therapists who are thinking about leaving?
- Does informal leadership count as experience?
- What will the recruitment plan be?
- Should you include the unhappy therapists in the interviews, as you had planned?
- What should you tell the external candidates about this internal dynamic?
- If you have difficulty with any of the preceding items, how will you deal with them?

Task

Resolve these issues in your group. Then join another group to compare and discuss your answers.

highly productive. Methods of work coordination, management theory, and management styles are discussed in depth.

References

Abelson MA. Strategic management of turnover: A model for the health service administrator. Health Care Management Review. 1986;11:61–71.

Harkson DG, Unterreiner AS, Shepard KF. Factors related to job turnover in physical therapy. Physical Therapy. 1982;62:1465–1470.

Herman R. Keeping good people: Strategies for solving the #1 problem facing business today. Winchester, VA: Oakhill Press. 1999.

Herzberg F, Mausner B, Snyderman B. The motivation to work, 2nd ed. New York: Wiley. 1959.

Herzberg F. Work and the nature of man. Cleveland: World. 1966.

Maslow A. A theory of motivation. Psychology Review. 1943;50:370–396.

Maslow A. Towards a psychology of being. Princeton: VanNostrand. 1968.

Mintzberg H. The structuring of organizations. Englewood Cliffs, NJ: Prentice-Hall. 1979.

Mintzberg H, Quinn JB, Voyer J. The strategy process, Collegiate ed. Englewood Cliffs, NJ: Prentice Hall. 1995.

Nosse LJ, Friberg DG. Management principles for physical therapists. Baltimore: Williams & Wilkins. 1992:64, 90.

Schemerhorn JR. Improving health care productivity through high-performance managerial development. Health Care Management Review. 1987; 12:49–55.

Smith HL, Discenza R. Developing a framework for retaining health care employees: A challenge to traditional thinking. Health Care Supervisor. 1988;7:17–28.

More Information Related to This Chapter

The U.S. Department of Labor Internet site, http://www.dol.gov, offers employment outlook, employment statistics, wage reports, consumer price index and other information useful for long-range planning.

A compendium on organizational culture that includes most of the topics dealt with in this chapter is Ashkanasy NM, Wilderom CPM, Peterson MF, ed. Handbook of organizational culture and climate. Thousand Oaks, CA: Sage. 2000.

Motivation in organizations is addressed in: Golembiewski RT, ed. Handbook of organizational behavior, 2nd ed. New York: Marcel Dekker. 2001:7–43.

For an industrial psychology perspective on personnel selection, including legal issues, see Schmitt N, Borman WC and associates. Personnel selection in organizations. San Francisco: Jossey-Bass. 1993.

Practical employee development methods from a human resource viewpoint is available in Wexley KM, Latham GP. Developing and training human resources in organizations, 2nd ed. HarperCollins. 1991.

For information about mentoring in physical therapy, access http://www.apta.org/Career_center/Career_management.

Chapter 15

Organizing and Engaging People in the Workplace

Learning Objectives

1. Explain productivity from the perspectives of a manager and a staff member.
2. Analyze the common methods of coordinating work presented in this chapter and give examples of these methods in a physical therapy context.
3. Synthesize selected theories of management using Miles' classification, that is, traditional model, human relations model, human resource model, and contingency model.
4. Evaluate the major forces on a manager that influence choice of management style and provide examples from your experience as part of your evaluation.
5. Apply management principles explored in this chapter to suggest means of motivating individuals to be productive in the workplace.

Key Words

Contingency model, contextual element, continuum of management styles, cost containment, employee/group maturity, human relations model, human resource model, Hawthorne effect, life cycle theory, mutual accommodation, organization, productivity, standardization, supervision, traditional model

Introduction

The U.S. health care industry is under continuous pressure to change the way health care is delivered. Our customers, those who pay for health care, including government, businesses, taxpayers and patients, are the source of this pressure. What our customers want is quality health care at a price they can afford. So in order to control health care costs (**cost containment**), our customers have adopted their own cost containment strategies. These strategies have been effective in significantly decreasing the reimbursement for health care services (Kiesler and Morton, 1988). An important outcome of cost containment pressure is a need for health care providers to find new and better ways to maximize employee productivity (Chapters 17, 28, and 29). Personnel costs are the major portion of costs associated with physical therapy and other health care services. Therefore, to increase productivity, we have to continually find improved ways of organizing and engaging people in the work of the organization.

The why and how of organizing and managing people has been and continues to be a focus of concern for organizations. Managers have been presented with theory after theory in an ongoing effort to discover the secret to maximizing the potential contribution of employees to the success of the organization. Management theories and practices evolve as assumptions about human behavior and the potential contributions of employees change over time. Over the past 50 years, assumptions about human behavior have shifted dramatically. At the start of this period, management based its practice on the assumption that employee contribution was a reflection of how well management could standardize and control their work. Current theory tells us that employees' contributions reflect management's ability to provide required education, tools, autonomy, and support so the employee can determine the best way to get the job done. The implications for management are obviously on the other end of the spectrum compared to earlier decades. This chapter will explore both contemporary theory and management practices for organizing and engaging people in an effort to maximize their contributions to the fulfillment of departmental and organizational immediate and long-term goals.

Achieving the Organizational Vision Through People

An **organization** is "a system of two or more persons, engaged in cooperative action, trying to reach some purpose" (Bernard, 1938, p. 73). People are the fundamental element of every organization. People determine the purpose of an organization. Their values shape an organization (Chapter 2). They create the vision (Chapter 9) of what their organization can and should strive to accomplish. People are responsible for organizational action or inaction. The key to any organization's success lies with its members.

The Concept of Productivity

The employee's contribution to organizational goals sought by management can be summarized into one word, **productivity**. Productivity in accrual accounting (Chapter 27) terms is determined by relating the cost of resources used (INPUT × EXPENSE) to the value of the outcome produced (OUTPUT × PRICE). If an organization spends more to produce a product or service (INPUT × EXPENSE) than the customer is willing to pay (OUTPUT × PRICE), it will lose money.

The concept of productivity can be applied to all of an organization's resources: humans, equipment, buildings—everything. Health care is a human resource–intensive industry. That means that a high percentage of health care cost is associated with employing people. This is certainly true for physical therapy. Salaries, benefits, recruitment, training, retention, employee health, and workers' compensation insurance are all examples of employee expenses (Chapter 27). With payment declining and costs increasing, health care providers must control the cost of human resources to stay in business and fulfill organizational goals. The total cost of human resources can be reduced if employee productivity is increased (Porter, 1966). The options for increasing productivity are (1) to increase output without increasing cost and (2) to decrease cost without decreasing output.

For example, assume it takes 2 hours to complete a physical therapy home visit. If a home care agency pays a physical therapist $30 per hour, the labor cost of a home therapy visit is $60. If the agency is paid $55 per visit, the agency is losing $5 per visit. If it continues to lose money, it will cease to exist. But if the time to complete a physical therapy visit can be reduced to 90 minutes, the labor cost is reduced to $45 per visit. Increased productivity could make the agency $10 per visit. Productivity depends on having the right people (recruitment and retention), dividing the work between them (organizational structure [Chapter 10]), and coordinating their work into a productive whole (Chapters 12, 17, and 18).

The Coordination of Work

Mintzberg (1979, 1983) and associates (1995) describe the organization of human activity as the act of balancing two opposing requirements. The first is division of work between employees. The second is coordination of the work of two or more employees to achieve a common goal. Three methods can be used to coordinate work between individuals. All three are used by health care organizations to coordinate the efforts of employees:

1. Standardization
2. Supervision
3. Mutual accommodation

Standardization can occur through work processes and tasks, work output, and/or worker skills (Mintzberg, 1983). Standardization reduces the need for direct supervision and mutual accommodation because it reduces the variation in the performance of employees (Chapter 10). Performance consistency also reduces the need for direct or frequent communication between workers.

Work processes and tasks can be standardized through the use of such things as policies, procedures, work (treatment) protocols, and standardized work (treatment) plans. For example, a physical therapist's work may be standardized through the use of written guidelines for the delivery of a treatment procedure such as ultrasound. Other examples are the use of a treatment protocol to guide the course of care for a patient following joint replacement and the use of a care plan for a patient following a stroke.

The use of output (outcome) standardization is on the rise in health care. A treatment protocol for care of the joint replacement patient that uses mobility status and range of motion to guide care and determine discharge is an example of outcome standardization.

Skill standardization through education, training, and licensure are fundamental to work coordination for health care organizations (Chapter 10). Standardization reduces the need for supervision or mutual accommodation (Mintzberg et al., 1995). Jobs that require professional and educational credentials such as physical therapy licensure, completion of postgraduate educational programs, and/or specific types of experience are examples of skill standardization. Application of on-the-job competency testing is another example.

Supervision refers to the control and direction of the work of one or more employees by another employee. Supervision can be used to coordinate the work of the organization. When this occurs, the manager must have direct knowledge of the work of a group of employees. The manager directs the employees to perform their work in a manner and time frame that complements the work of others in the group. The manager is responsible for coordination of the work of the group. For supervision to be effective, the manager must do the following:

- Be recognized as a formal or informal leader (Chapter 8)
- Have expertise in the work to be performed
- Be available to the employees under his or her direction
- Be consistent in directions over time and between employees
- Be able to address and resolve conflict situations
- Be credible in the eyes of those supervised
- Inspire employees to follow his or her direction (Chapter 8)

In physical therapy practice, supervision commonly occurs between (1) management and staff, (2) senior (more experienced) professional staff and junior (less experienced) professional staff, (3) professional staff and students, and (4) professional and support staff (Chapter 10). Management titles roles vary greatly between organizations (Chapter 8). Supervision may be performed by individuals with titles such as director, manager, supervisor, clinical specialist, or clinical lead.

Mutual accommodation, the simplest method of work coordination, results from ongoing interaction between individuals (Chapter 10). This interaction results in continuous adjustment between individuals to the achievement of their shared goals. This method of work coordination is common in simple organizations and within long-term work groups. It may also be the most effective method of work coordination for the most complex situations.

The movement toward less supervision has resulted in greater reliance on standardization and mutual accommodation for work coordination. Standardization has increased in such things as care plans. The use of mutual accommodation is supported by the use of human resource–focused management methods, work teams (Chapter 17), and continuous quality improvement methods (Chapter 12). However, both supervision and mutual accommodation depend on the communication skills of the employees. The effectiveness of both methods can be impaired when members of a work group have inadequate communication skills (Chapter 16) or are in conflict. Table 15.1 summarizes the uses of the three methods of work coordination.

Theories About Managing People: Past to Present

Assumptions about human attitudes, aptitudes, and behaviors are the foundation upon which personnel management theories and related management practices are built. As research and experience contribute to our knowledge of human behavior, approaches to achieving maximum employee contribution change. Miles (1975) provides a conceptual model for understanding the evolution of management theory. He recognizes three basic models of management theory and suggests that most, if not all management theories fall in line with one of these models. His models of management theory are the traditional model, the human relations model, and the human resource model. These models reflect knowledge and experience gained over the past 50 years (Champoux, 2000). Because our experience suggests that practices reflecting all three models are seen in today's organizations, an overview of the underlying assumptions, characteristics, and representative theories of all three models are relevant to today's managers.

The Traditional Model

Miles (1975) applies the theories of Darwin to describe assumptions underlying the **traditional model** of managing people. People of superior ability should lead and direct others of lesser ability. Max Weber promoted the concept of work standardization and job specialization at all levels of the organization (Gerth and Mills, 1958). The assumption was that peak performance was achieved when each employee was required to perform a minimum number of standardized tasks on a repeated basis. Organizational performance

Table 15.1 Production and Mass Technology Concepts and Examples of Work Coordination in Physical Therapy Practice

Production Technology	*Work Standards*	*Supervision*	*Mutual Adjustment*
Unit production			
Professional education	X		
Advanced certification	X		
Assessment practices	X		
Treatment algorithms	X		
Clinical resource staff		X	X
Advanced training	X		
Patient care conferences		X	X
Treatment teams			X
Flexible schedules			X
Mass production			
Licensure requirements	X	X	
Policies and procedures	X		
Treatment protocols	X		
Standardized care plans	X		
Job descriptions	X		
Performance standards	X	X	
Staff schedules	X	X	
Practice guidelines	X		

results from management's ability to provide a decent physical environment, design efficient tasks, and provide close supervision.

An example of the traditional model can be found in the writing of Taylor (1967). Based on his observations and analyses of work activities in an industrial setting, he postulated that even skilled workers required the guidance of managers to achieve optimal performance of standardized tasks. Workers were thought to be incapable of independently designing or carrying out their work.

In the traditional model, the management style is authoritarian and directive. Employees are discouraged from giving input and decision making on any level. Work consists of standardized tasks performed under the watchful eye of the manager.

The Human Relations Model

Miles's (1975) **human relations model** reflects management theories that identify the importance of dealing with needs of individual workers. The human relations model evolved from experiments conducted at the Western Electric Company of Hawthorne, Illinois, by Mayo (1933). Mayo's' intent was to determine the effect of the work environment (that is, work hours, temperature, light, humidity) on productivity. During the course of the experiment, the work environment of the subject group was manipulated to make it more or less comfortable. He found that the workers performed at continuously improved levels of productivity even when the work environment was manipulated to make working conditions difficult. Surprised by these findings, Mayo ultimately concluded that the high levels of productivity he had observed in the subject group were due to the attention paid to the workers by the researchers. This relationship between attention and productivity became known as the **Hawthorne effect**. Miles's human relations model promotes the demonstration of concern and consideration for employees' feelings and personal needs. Employees are kept informed and allowed to give input on routine matters. Management is encouraged to use nonmonetary rewards, such as recognition. Management's intent is to make employees feel good. This model falls short of substantial inclusion of the employee in decision making.

The Human Resource Model

The **human resource model** also recognizes the importance of meeting workers' needs for recognition, inclusion, attention, and contribution. But the model goes further. It recognizes that workers want the opportunity to develop and use all of their skills. Miles' (1975) human resource model contends that employee satisfaction comes not from external reward but from a personal sense of accomplishment. In this model, organizations receive greatest benefit when they encourage full participation of all employees. An organization's leadership is challenged to provide an environment that supports and facilitates maximum involvement to produce maximum contribution and productivity.

Herzberg's two-factor theory (Herzberg, 1966; Herzberg, Mausner, Snyderman, 1959) is an example of the human resource model (Chapter 14). Herzberg and associates theorized that two categories of job attitude factors influence performance. He labeled these categories dissatisfiers and satisfiers. Organizational and job factors that led to dissatisfaction were called hygiene factors. When deficient, dissatisfaction prevailed. But when present, hygiene factors did not improve employee motivation to work harder. Alternatively, when present, job satisfiers act as employee motivators. Herzberg (1959) postulated that the higher the level of employee satisfaction, the greater the level of cooperation and productivity. Table 15.2 lists the job factors Herzberg defined as dissatisfiers and satisfiers.

A Continuum of Management Styles: Push, Pull, or Lead

Miles's (1975) three models represent a **continuum of management styles** in which the manager's role moves from one of total control, the dictator, to one of total collaboration with employees at all levels of the organiza-

Table 15.2 Herzberg's (1966) Job Dissatisfiers and Satisfiers

Dissatisfiers	*Satisfiers*
Administration	Achievement
Benefits	Advancement
Interpersonal relations	Growth potential
Job security	Interpersonal relations
Organizational policy	Power
Salary	Recognition
Supervision	Responsibility
	Salary
	Status

tion, the democrat. This continuum of management styles is represented in Figure 15.1. As indicated in the figure, as the management style moves toward the democratic or human resource end of the continuum, the influence of employees over their work increases.

As noted at the outset of this discussion, we have observed that the full continuum of management styles is evident in today's health care organizations. In fact, the same manager may be observed using different styles at different times or different styles with the same individual in different circumstances. Management theories that promote and defend the use of varying management styles are said to fall under the **contingency model** (Miles, 1975).

The Contingency Model

It takes little interaction with today's managers to realize that the search for the one best approach that will always work for everyone to motivate all workers to maximum productivity is ongoing. This has led to the development of theories proposing that the right management approach is contingent on situational factors.

The work of Tannenbaum and Schmidt (1973) suggests that management style may be influenced by three **contextual elements**:

1. The situation
2. The employee
3. The manager

Table 15.3 lists some of the contextual forces that may influence management style. Con-

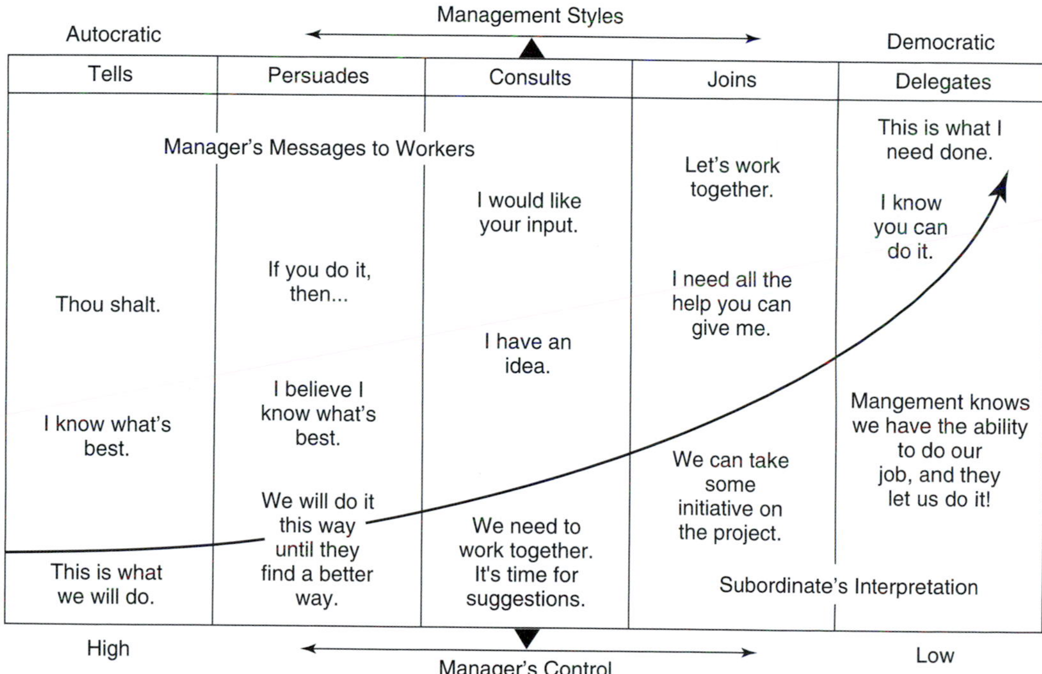

Figure 15.1. A continuum of management styles. (Based on Tannenbaum and Schmidt [1973:165] and modified from Nosse and Friberg [1992:48].)

Table 15.3 Contextual Factors Influencing Management Style

Manager	*Employee/Work Group*	*Situation*
Competencies	**Acceptance of responsibility**	**Organization**
Confidence in employees	Availability	Available resources
Experience	Competencies	Culture
Leadership	Education	Environment
Tendencies	Experience	History
Perceived risk	Level of satisfaction	Ownership
Performance history	Level of interest in job	Practices
Sense of security	Manager's expectations	Purpose
Situational comfort	Skills	Strategies
Skills	Values	Vision
Values		Values
		Job characteristics
		Importance
		Scope
		Urgency

textual forces may work in concert, moving the manager's style toward the same end of the style continuum. Or the forces may conflict, which makes it difficult to choose between approaches. Pressures that result from multiple contextual forces can be complex, challenging the abilities of even the most skilled organizational leaders. Figure 15.2 depicts the **life cycle theory** of Hersey and Blanchard (1982). The life cycle theory suggests that management style should be primarily determined by employee maturity. Assessment of employee maturity is based on achievement motivation, task-relevant education, ability to do the work required, and willingness to take responsibility.

Figure 15.2 suggests that when average group maturity is low, management should adopt a highly directive style (box D). This may be an appropriate tack to take with newly graduated therapists. It includes specific instructions and close supervision. As the group maturity increases, a highly directive management style should be incorporated with the highly supportive approach (box B). In this way management continues

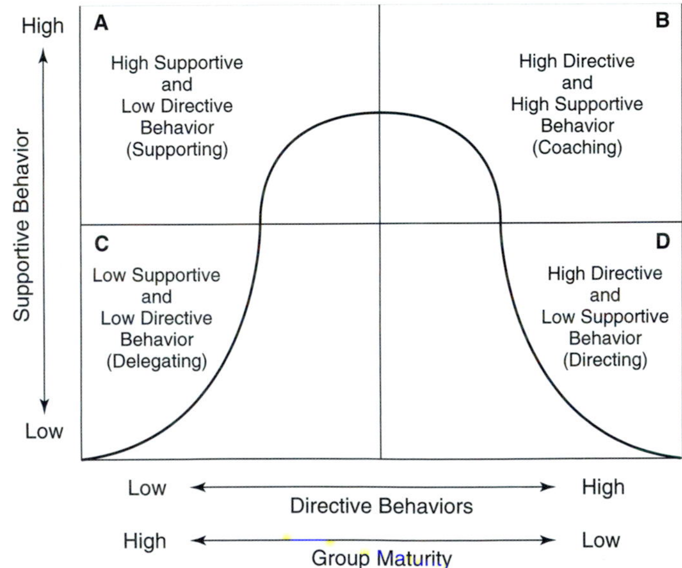

Figure 15.2. Leadership styles based on the job-related maturity of the work group. (Modified with permission from Nosse, Friberg, Kovacek [1999:68].)

to ensure the performance of the work group while beginning the transition to a more autonomous style. This may be an appropriate technique to use with experienced therapists new to the department. The approach is to explain and clarify as needed rather than issue directives. As the group maturity continues to increase, management's directive behaviors should decline (box A). This approach is appropriate for therapists who have some history of efficiency and effectiveness in a variety of patient care and management areas. The transition continues until at full maturity management style is minimally supportive and directive (box C). Groups with a track record of success are given responsibility for choosing and carrying out a variety of actions. This cycle may repeat itself as group composition and membership, the task, and the organization change over time.

The implication of the life cycle theory (Hersey and Blanchard, 1982) is that employee and/or work group factors may influence management style more than manager or situational factors. As we continue this discussion, the reasons for this should become more evident.

Contingency models do not provide all of the answers on how best to manage people for maximum performance. They do suggest that managers can and should modify their approach to leadership according to the situation. Even if current theory does not leave struggling managers with the one best way, it does provide some guidelines for action.

Managers seek information about managing people for one reason, to assist them in their continuous efforts to maximize employee productivity. If you accept the idea that situational factors should and often do determine the best management approach, managing the variables of the situation seems to be an obvious place for the manager to focus effort. That is not to say that all variables can or should be controlled. The intent is to identify key variables that can be controlled so that in complex situations the manager is most likely to adopt the best approach. The fewer variables, the more likely that is. So what can a manager do to control situational factors?

A review of Table 15.3 indicates that some situational factors and pressures can be minimized through management action. Organizations spend a lot of time talking about motivating employees to achieve higher levels of productivity. The manager who is successful at controlling situational variables, particularly employee or work group factors, may still use the continuum of management styles but has already taken a step toward motivating employees to high performance. The opportunities for action are expanded later in this chapter, in the discussion of practice implications for health care managers.

Practical Applications: Motivating Employees Toward High Productivity

Management's goal is to ensure the success of the organization. Management cannot accomplish that goal without the support and effort of each employee. But how does a manager promote a high level of organizational support from employees? While motivation is not a one-size-fits-all concept, some common themes apply to most situations (Qubein, 2001):

1. *Know the work.* Motivation has to start with the knowledge and skill to get the job done. To hire the right employees, you have to understand the specifics of their work.
2. *Set clear performance expectations.* Some employees will respond to the vision and intuitively know and do what has to be done. Others will need a clearly defined route and end point. Match the approach to the person, but channel effort in the required direction. Do not be afraid to set specific goals, objectives, and productivity standards. Employees will respond to what they think they hear, so be very clear.
3. *Help employees understand what's in it for them if they meet expectations.* Understand what your employees want and try to deliver it in response to good performance. Employees may be rewarded by any of a

number of things, including but not limited to compensation, recognition, flexibility, time off, education, a new job assignment, more responsibility, a promotion, a good reference, freedom to pursue a pet project, and more. The possibilities are almost limitless.
4. *If you want your employees to pay attention to you, pay attention to them.* Get to know your employees as individuals. Listen and respond when they need your attention. Leave your door open literally and figuratively. More often than not, your employees will return the favor.
5. *Let personal pride and a sense of purpose work for you.* Health care organizations are well positioned to build on the pride and sense of purpose that comes from helping those in need. Even if a job doesn't directly involve the hands-on delivery of care, make sure all of the employees know that their role is essential. Patients benefit when employees are effective and productive.
6. *You usually get what you expect and reinforce.* Once performance expectations are set, watch carefully. When you see the right behaviors, recognize and reinforce them as often as possible. Immediately point out undesirable behaviors and clarify expectations. Nothing reinforces poor performance more than a manager who looks the other way. Not only will offending employees learn to repeat the error, but others may follow their example.
7. *Focus on behaviors.* Accept that you cannot change employees' beliefs, attitudes, or values. What you can change is specific behaviors that are exhibited in the work setting. Focus on that.

Student Notes

While much of the work of organizing and engaging employees falls to management, very often employees have input into some aspects of the process. This is true particularly with the increased use of work teams and today's focus on employee empowerment. Entry-level therapists can apply many of the principles presented in this chapter as they manage the performance of support employees. It is helpful for new employees to realize that managers use various leadership and management styles in accord with the circumstances. The contextual forces (situation, employee, manager) combine to influence a manager's reactions to direct reports. Also, the life cycle theory draws attention to the fact that differences in the job experience of the employee call for different management strategies. A new employee with little experience can expect to be treated differently later on as the contexts change and as his or her competencies broaden.

Summary

Few would disagree that the greatest challenge of today's leaders is engaging and directing the commitment and energy of people. Leaders who are recognized as exemplary are those who recognized that success is about managing human interactions (Zuckerman, 1989). For this reason, the leaders of successful organizations commit both attention and resources to organizing and fully engaging its members in the purpose, values, vision, and activities of the organization.

One of the critical factors affecting organizational success is productivity. The key to productivity in labor-intensive health care organizations is worker commitment and effort. Managers fulfill this responsibility by adopting a management style and organizational structure that facilitate employee engagement and productivity. There is a continuum of management styles. From autocratic to democratic, a leader may use a single approach or modify style and actions to fit the situation. Organizational structure should support workers' efforts and where feasible encourage performance so that the potential productivity of individual workers can be maximized. The concepts presented in this chapter are enacted through communication with others. The next chapter focuses on communication. A two-sided communication paradigm will be

INDIVIDUAL CASE STUDY

Customer satisfaction surveys have made it clear that my hospital's outpatient physical therapy department should offer Saturday morning appointments. Eight therapists are employed by the department. Five are assigned to the inpatient department and three to the outpatient department. Two of the employees work half time and receive limited employment benefits. Management has determined that everyone will have to be on the Saturday rotation schedule to provide the needed coverage. No one is going to be happy, especially not the inpatient therapists. What advice can you give the manager who has to motivate the therapists to pick up this additional work? How should staff be scheduled to cover the additional hours? What about the part-time staff?

GROUP CASE STUDY

Form a group of five managers. You all have the same task in the same organization, but you are members of different departments.

Think back to the discussion of productivity. An assumption in the example was that 2 hours was necessary to complete a home visit. If the agency pays a physical therapist $30 per hour, the labor cost of a home therapy visit is $60. If the agency is paid $55 per visit, the agency is losing $5 per visit. If it continues to lose money, it will cease to exist. But if the time to complete a physical therapy visit can be reduced to 90 minutes, the labor cost is reduced to $45 per visit. If productivity increases, the agency stands to make $10 per visit.

Task

Your group should describe at least four ways to improve productivity to reduce labor costs per home care visit and turn a per-visit loss into a profit. (Most of the staff members in this scenario are experienced and work less than 30 hours per week—job sharing.) Discuss your ideas and decide which one would be the best. Finally, decide which leadership pattern (Fig. 15.1) would be best to use given the staff you have. What is your rationale? Once you have your thoughts together, join with group to discuss your suggestions. Critically assess both groups' suggestions and by consensus formulate a single final suggestion.

used to discuss written and verbal expression and the concept of active listening.

References

Bernard CI. The functions of the executive. Cambridge, MA: Harvard University. 1938.

Champoux JE. Organizational behavior: Essential tenets for a new millennium. Cincinnati: South-Western College. 2000.

Gerth HH, Mills CW. From Max Weber: Essays in sociology. New York: Oxford. 1958.

Hersey P, Blanchard KH. Management of organizational behavior: Utilizing human resources. Englewood Cliffs, NJ: Prentice Hall. 1982.

Herzberg F. Work and the nature of man. Cleveland: World. 1966.

Herzberg F, Mausner B, Snyderman B. The motivation to work. 2nd ed. New York: Wiley. 1959.

Kiesler CA, Morton TL. Psychology and public policy in the "health care revolution." American Psychologist. 1988;43:993–1003.

Mayo E. The human problems of an industrial civilization. New York: Macmillan. 1933.

Miles RE. Theories of management: Implications for

organizational behavior and development. New York: McGraw-Hill. 1975.

Mintzberg H. The structuring of organizations. Englewood Cliffs, NJ: Prentice Hall. 1979.

Mintzberg H. Structure in fives: Designing effective organizations. Englewood Cliffs, NJ: Prentice-Hall. 1983.

Mintzberg H, Quinn JB, Voyer J. The strategy process, Collegiate edition. Englewood Cliffs, NJ: Prentice Hall. 1995.

Nosse LJ, Friberg DG. Management principles for physical therapists. Baltimore: Williams & Wilkins. 1992.

Nosse LJ, Friberg DG, Kovacek PR. Managerial and supervisory principles for physical therapists. Baltimore: Lippincott Williams & Wilkins. 1999.

Porter ME. Operational effectiveness is not strategy. Harvard Business Review. 1966; November-December:61–77.

Qubein N. 10 principles of motivation. Financial Executive. 2001;Jul-Aug:37–38.

Tannenbaum R, Schmidt WH. How to choose a leadership pattern. Harvard Business Review. 1973;May-June:162–180.

Taylor F. The principles of scientific management. New York: Norton. 1967.

Zuckerman HS. Redefining the role of the CEO: Challenges and conflicts. Hospitals and Health Services Administration. 1989;34:26–38.

More Information Related to This Chapter

A classical article on leadership style is by Tannenbaum and Schmidt (1973). Another classical article is by French and Raven. They note that while power comes with the title manager, it is not the only source of social power in an organization. French and Raven describe a spectrum of sources of interpersonal power applicable to workplace interactions (French JRP, Raven BH. The basis of social power. In Cartwright D, ed. Studies of social power. Ann Arbor, MI: Institute for Social Research. 1959;150–167). With increasing diversity in the workplace, information on leading cross-cultural teams is an area managers may need more information. See Gibson, Conger, and Cooper regarding the concept of perceptual distance, that is, cultural variance in perception to the same social stimuli (Gibson CB, Conger J, Cooper C. Perceptual distance: The impact of differences in team leader and member perceptions across cultures. In Mobley WH, McCall MW, Jr., eds. Advances in global leadership. New York: JAI. 2001;245–276).

Chapter 16

Communication: Expression and Listening

Learning Objectives

1. Summarize principles of workplace nonverbal communication.
2. Summarize principles of workplace oral communication.
3. Analyze the four purposes of oral communication as presented in this chapter.
4. Explain the four types of formal presentations and the common process suggested for their development.
5. Describe the concept of active listening.
6. Analyze the cognitive stances that hinder communication.
7. Generate recommendations for effective communication between physical therapist managers and their direct reports.

Key Words

Communication, communication goal, complex audience, debate, deliberation, dialog, discussion, executive, expert, explanatory, feedback, instructional, introduction, lay person, mixed audience, nonverbal communication, oral communication, oral report, persuasive, receiver, sender, user

Introduction

Communication includes a message being sent and received along with confirmation that the message sent was the message received. The process can be derailed at any point along the way. Besides describing the communication process, this chapter serves several functions. The first is to guide thinking about the interpersonal process of communication in the context of work. The second is to classify types of interpersonal communication so the component parts can be explored. The third is to provide practical suggestions for effective interpersonal communication at work so that work is carried out efficiently and effectively. A manager needs effective verbal, nonverbal, and written communication and listening skills to plan, organize, staff, direct, and control.

Communication Basics

Communication is a process by which information is exchanged between individuals through a common system of symbols, signs, or behaviors (Merriam-Webster, 2003). The communication process is circular (Fig. 16.1). It starts when a message is sent. When the message is received, the **receiver** closes the loop by sending confirmation (**feedback**) to the **sender**.

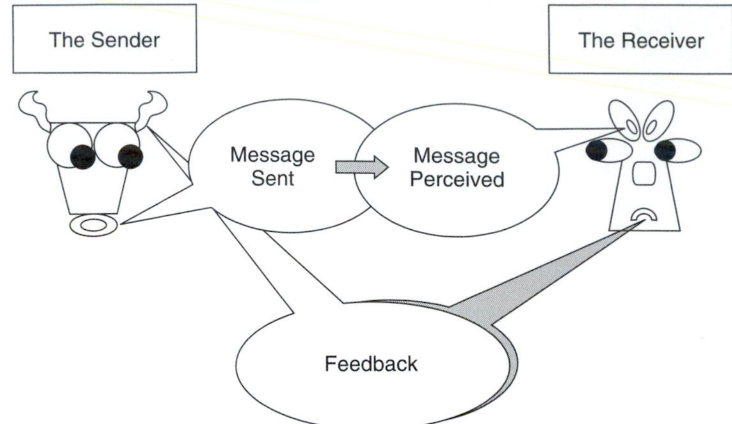

Figure 16.1. The communication process.

To be maximally effective, communication has to have the full participation of everyone concerned. Communication starts with a sender who has a **communication goal**, a message to send, and one or more identified receivers. To achieve the desired goal, the sender must design the message so the receiver can understand it and is open to receive it. The receiver must be open to receive the message, pay attention to the message, and then send verification that he or she received the message as intended. Between the sender initiating the process and the receiver completing it there are many opportunities for the communication to break down.

Business communication occurs when a sender wants to achieve one or more of the following goals (Simmons, 2002):

1. Gain the receiver's understanding.
2. Gain the receiver's response.
3. Establish a favorable relationship.
4. Establish goodwill.

Nonverbal Communication

Communication may be nonverbal, oral, or written. A **nonverbal communication** is the most dependent on context and most open to interpretation. Nonverbal messages may be intended, such as a pat on the back, or unintended, such as a small hesitation when a disliked colleague enters the room.

Consider a simple hand wave. It may mean hello, come here, good-bye, or stay away. The receiver's interpretation of a hand wave depends on knowledge of the sender and the context in which the message is sent. If the receiver's understanding of the situation is different from that of the sender, a nonverbal message may be easily misunderstood. Anderson (2001) advises that during a conversation the ability to interpret a person's nonverbal communication may be as important as the ability to understand the words. However, interpretation of nonverbal messages should be approached with a degree of caution. A person's interpretation of nonverbal behaviors is based at least in part on culture and life experience. Take for example a manager who is redirecting a new employee's nonproductive behaviors. The employee avoids making eye contact throughout the conversation. The manager's own background and communication style lead him to interpret the employee's avoidance behavior as an indication of guilt or lack of interest in the message. However, the manager does not realize that in the employee's culture, making eye contact with an authority figure is a sign of disrespect. See Chapter 18 for more information about the effects of diversity on the delivery of health care.

Anderson (2001) offers some suggestions on using nonverbal messages to assist communicating effectively:

1. *Motion enhances communication.* Movement can increase the receiver's attention to and retention of information. Shaking hands, walking, and conversing over a meal are all ways to bring motion into the message.

Shared motion brings the participants into alignment and increases the likelihood that they will get along.
2. *Press a point when the receiver is most at ease.* Good timing, especially if the receiver may be resistant, will increase receptivity.
3. *Receptivity will be higher if listeners have invested time, money, or other resources into their relationship with the sender.* This occurs because there is a better understanding of the needs of each person and the possibilities of fulfilling those needs, and by nature people hate to lose the value of the time and effort already invested.
4. *People get along better when they stand or sit side by side than face to face.*
5. *Loud, patterned clothing, tie, or jewelry will distract the listener and interfere with message reception.*

Oral Communication

Oral communication occurs along a continuum from informal and formal conversation to a formal presentation. According to Yankelovich (1999), conversation can be debate, discussion, deliberation, and dialog. In **debate** the goal is to have your opinion prevail over that of your opponent. It is about winning through defending one's viewpoint against the viewpoint of another. Participants in a debate actively look for weaknesses in their opponents' position that they can attack. In debate there is no give and take, compromise, or acknowledgment that any opinion other than one's own has merit. Debate is adversarial by design. The only goal for communication based on debate is to gain the receiver's response in the form of agreement regarding the sender's position on the topic under debate. In essence, the person taking the lead in a debate becomes a listener only when he or she stops to take a breath. However, sometimes debate serves the valuable purpose of clarifying the pros and cons of a speaker's position on an issue. Debate is appropriate in these circumstances:

1. Parties on both sides of an issue know to expect a debate.
2. Guidelines have been established to direct the behaviors of the debaters.
3. A third party is present to facilitate the debate.

Discussion is a formal treatment of a topic in speech or writing (Merriam-Webster, 2003). In our experience, discussion is the most common form of communication inside and outside the business setting. A discussion can occur spontaneously or be orchestrated by an individual. A departmental staff meeting is a form of organized discussion. Discussion may occur between two individuals or in a large group. It can be used to achieve any of the common communication goals. As long as an interaction occurs for the purpose of exchanging information, ideas, and/or opinions that are generally held to gain shared understanding of a topic, the communication is a discussion.

Deliberation is a discussion and consideration by a group of persons of the reasons for and against a measure (Merriam-Webster, 2003). As a form of discussion, deliberation can be an element in any type of conversation other than debate. Deliberation may follow debate in a conversation and set the stage for decision making.

Defined as an exchange of ideas and opinions, **dialog** is another form of discussion (Merriam-Webster, 2003). Dialog has three specific characteristics that differentiate it from other forms of conversation or discussion (Yankelovich, 1999).

1. *All participants in a dialog must be considered equals.* This does not imply that a dialog cannot occur between supervisor and subordinates, therapist and therapist assistant, or for that matter, therapist and patient. It does imply that for the period of the dialog, the authority positions (Yankelovich, 1999) of participants must be put aside so that they do not influence or act as a barrier to the contributions of any other participant. While this may sound simple, in many relationships and settings, the authority and subordinate roles (Chapter 10) may be so well established that they cannot be breached.
2. *Participants must be empathetic to the opinions of other participants.* Dialog requires

that participants be willing and able to put themselves in the other person's place. Divergent or even disagreeable ideas must be met with acceptance.

3. *Assumptions must be revealed.* All of us bring our beliefs and assumptions with us when we enter into discussions. Our assumptions can act as barriers to understanding. By revealing our assumptions, we give others an opportunity to respond. Once revealed, barriers may be minimized and/or the sender will have a better understanding of how to modify the message to get the point across.

This last characteristic may be best illustrated by an example. Recently, one of us attended a management meeting scheduled to discuss work distribution between managers assigned to a new project team. At one point in the meeting, the newest manager, Steven, volunteered to take on a specific task that no one seemed to want to do. Immediately the project leader volunteered to assist him. Surprisingly, Steven's reaction to the project leader's offer was silence for the remainder of the meeting. He assumed that the project leader had volunteered to assist him because he didn't believe Steven could do the work on his own. On the other side of the table, the project leader was confused by Steven's response. His intent was to demonstrate support and to recognize Steven for stepping forward when others who could have more easily completed the work held back. The tension was obvious, and the meeting broke up early. If the project leader had understood Steven's assumption, the discussion would have gone much better for everyone. Yankelovich (1999) is a proponent of dialog as the most effective method of oral communication for business success. Maurer (2001) also considers dialog one of the most powerful tools available to shift an individual's thinking. He attributes this to the fact that dialog, if done correctly, creates a safe environment that nurtures mutual trust and openness to the ideas of others.

Oral communication is always more likely to achieve the intended goals if the sender has prepared the message. Preparation is important.

Formal Presentation

At the other end of the oral communication continuum is the formal presentation. There are four types of formal presentations: persuasive, explanatory, instructional, and oral report (Morrisey and Sechrest, 1987).

1. The first job of the **persuasive** presenter is to persuade the audience that the presenter is credible. Beyond that, this presentation might be designed to lead employees, managers, and/or customers to take a desired course of action. For example, it might be used to encourage investment in an automated documentation system.

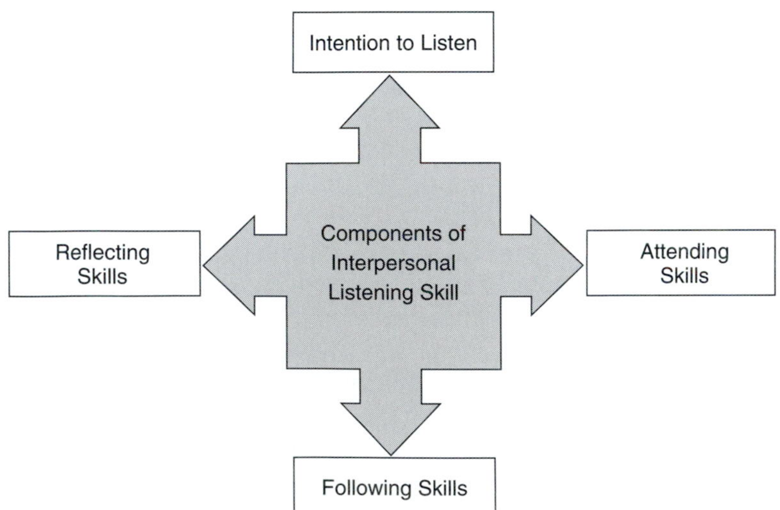

Figure 16.2. Four component skills of interpersonal listening.

2. An **explanatory** presentation can be used to familiarize the audience with new information or provide an update on a given topic. A management review of department policies is an example of an explanatory presentation.
3. An **instructional** presentation teaches the audience something, such as a continuing education session on a new therapeutic technique. This type of presentation is likely to involve audience participation to reinforce learning. The shared information may be very detailed.
4. A common type of presentation in business settings, the **oral report** is used to bring the audience up-to-date on a topic of interest. A quality improvement team progress report is one example. Monthly management reports are another. Discharge meetings also include oral reports.

A formal presentation also has four parts, the introduction, body, conclusion, and questions (Morrisey and Sechrest, 1987; Simmons, 2002).

1. The **introduction** should be used to tell the audience what the presentation is about.
2. The **body** contains the main ideas and any supporting information.
3. The **conclusion** should be used to restate the main points and if appropriate, restate the objective of the presentation.
4. Following the conclusion, the presenter may take audience **questions**.

There are many things to consider in preparation to give a formal presentation. These are the key steps to preparing a quality presentation, according to Morrisey and Sechrest (1987):

1. *Set clear objectives.* What will happen if the presentation is effective? The communication goal for the presentation should be clearly understood by the presenter and the audience. (Refer to the types of presentations). The objectives should be achievable within the time allotted.
2. *Know your audience.* To be effective, a presentation must be geared to the specific characteristics of the audience. Demographic and cultural characteristics, level of knowledge, and predisposition to the topic must all be taken into consideration in designing a presentation.
3. *Plan your presentation.* Planning is required to prepare an effective oral presentation. What are the main points of emphasis? What is the format? In what order will information be presented?
4. *Identify resource material to support the presentation.* What supporting information will you need? All types of presentations may benefit from facts to support the speaker's main points.
5. *Practice and reorganize when necessary to maximize effectiveness.* Practice delivery of the presentation as many times as it takes to feel comfortable with the flow of information, the transition points, and the timing of the whole presentation.

Several things can reduce the effectiveness of a presentation (Simmons, 2002). Word choice should be geared to the audience. Words that are too simple, difficult, or technical or that have multiple meanings may interfere with message reception. Poor word choice may also cause the audience's attention to drift. The pace of delivery should reflect the complexity of the information and the sophistication of the audience. Information should be presented fast enough to keep the attention of the audience while allowing them sufficient time to understand and absorb the message.

Logistics must also be considered when planning a presentation. Logistics includes such things as audience notification, room size, room setup, seating arrangement, presentation equipment, and amenities such as food, beverages, and breaks (Morrisey and Sechrest, 1987). Audience notification may happen in many ways, such as a printed brochure, memorandum, letter, e-mail, and/or oral message. Whatever the method, notification should provide complete and accurate information about the presenter, topic, objective, time, place, required audience preparation, and target audience. Room size, setup, temperature, and seating arrangement should be comfortable and distraction free.

The goal is to enhance the audience's ability to focus on the presenter and the message. PowerPoint has templates to aid this. Templates include selling your idea, communicating bad news, and motivating a team.

Presentation equipment may include audiovisual aids, poster displays, flip charts, models, exhibits, handouts, samples, specimens, and computer-generated materials. Presentation aids, especially computers, data projectors, and microphones, should be checked in advance to make sure the equipment works so that the presentation will start on time and flow smoothly. When using audiovisual equipment, *always* assume that the equipment will fail and have a backup plan, that is, have transparencies and an overhead projector in case of computer problems. Visual aids should be used only when they add to the clarity of the oral presentation. Depending on the type of presentation, the audience may have specific expectations regarding amenities. Amenities that fall short of the audience's expectations can cause dissatisfaction and distraction. Breaks should be provided at reasonable intervals.

Effective oral communication starts with a well-designed message that is understandable to the intended audience. However, it is up to the audience to actively listen to the message and confirm understanding through feedback to the sender. Oral messages to the speaker are clearer than nonverbal messages, especially for inexperienced speakers.

Active Listening

Active listening is an acquired skill that creates a connection between the sender and the receiver. This means the receiver hears what the speaker is saying, understands how the message applies to him or her, and will likely remember it for future use. Several skills are involved in active listening (Fig. 16.2).

Active listening starts with a positive commitment to receive the message. Controlling distracting thoughts, having goals for the interaction, and having an open mind are basic features of a positive intention. An intention to listen is necessary preparation to use the other component skills. Attending involves keeping focus on the message, maintaining interest, and using nonverbal signs of being alert, such as making eye contact with the message sender. Following skills include the ability to make connections between recently presented points, identify the logic of arguments, grasp progressions, and anticipate what should come next. Following helps the receiver to understand the sender's broad concepts as well as the component parts of the concepts. Reflection entails critical evaluation and assessment of the message. Silent reflection allows time to search for and review the other person's key points. Table 16.1 includes a reflective progression.

Chisolm (1997) recommends additional suggestions for effective communication:

- Avoid tuning out subject matter because of poor delivery.
- Be open to new ideas and possibilities.
- Do not interrupt until the whole message has been presented.
- Identify an area of interest to counter tuning out on dry subjects.
- Ignore any potential distractions.
- Listen for themes not just the facts.
- Pay attention and actively engage in listening.

Table 16.1 A General Reflection Process

Mentally review these items:

Core message from presenter's comments, handouts, notes, and so on.
Based on your understanding, state the presenter's frame of reference.
Acknowledge presenter's and your own emotions.
Paraphrase the message.
Formulate statements for verification.
Formulate statements for clarification.

Feedback to message sender:

Present your understanding of the points made. Confirm understanding with open-ended questions to probe, such as "It sounds like...," "Are you saying...?" Ask close-ended questions to assess, such as "Is it correct to say...?" "Do you agree...?" "Is it important to...?"
Reply to sender's responses and questions.
Summarize to confirm new understanding.

After the message is received, the listener should check his or her perceptions by providing the speaker with feedback. Feedback can be given by summarizing the message, paraphrasing what was heard, and/or asking questions (Table 16.1). However, in providing feedback, the listener should avoid behaviors that can interfere with communication (Johnson, 1999). According to Johnson, these behaviors can block communication:

1. *Advising.* A listener who is in a hurry to provide advice fails to listen to the whole message.
2. *Being right.* The listener is so concerned with being right that he or she cannot listen to differing opinions.
3. *Derailing.* The listener changes the subject before the message is complete.
4. *Judging.* A listener who has already decided the speaker's credibility is poor is not likely to pay attention to the message.
5. *Placating.* The listener may state false agreement to make the sender feel good.
6. *Rehearsing.* The listener is so engaged in thinking about how to respond to the speaker's comments as to be unable to receive the message.
7. *Sparring.* The listener immediately engages in debate, so that the speaker is never able to send the message.

Any of these behaviors on the part of the listener will decrease the effectiveness of the communication.

Managing Conflict Through Effective Communication

Because no two people are alike (Chapter 18), valued goals differ (Chapter 6). This leads to conflicts. Conflict is not necessarily bad for a department or organization. Discussion that results from conflicting viewpoints may increase creativity and innovation. Conflict counters accepting an idea without sufficient analysis. What is damaging to an organization is unresolved conflict. Unresolved conflict can hamper an organization in several ways. First, unresolved conflicts tend to grow in magnitude over time. The bigger the magnitude of the conflict, the more difficult it will be to resolve. Growing conflict also tends to spread to include people who were not involved in the original conflict but are sympathetic to one party or the other. When conflict is present, communication and cooperation are reduced. Work effectiveness is impeded by the lack of coordination, and employee productivity declines (Knippen and Green, 1999). For obvious reasons, managers must be able to recognize unresolved conflict and work to resolve the core issues they have the authority to resolve.

To minimize the negative consequences, conflict should be resolved as quickly as possible. However, two conditions should be met before the conflict is addressed (Knippen and Green, 1999). The involved individuals must be in an acceptable emotional state to be able to engage in dialog and have sufficient uninterrupted time to reflect and work through the conflict. With those conditions met, the principles of dialog can be applied. When the involved parties have insufficient knowledge and skill in the use of dialog, a manager may have to fill the function of facilitator.

Written Communication

Written communication follows many of the same principles as oral communication. As with oral communication, written communication can be persuasive, explanatory, instructional, or a report. Effective written communication is designed to send a message that is meaningful and understandable to the receiver. The starting point in designing effective written communication is to know the audience. Fitzgerald (1998) identifies several categories of audiences. A **lay person**, someone who has little or no knowledge and possibly little natural interest in the topic of the message is one type of audience. A staff presentation on HIPAA (Chapter 3) may have little appeal to a physical therapy aide. In contrast, an **expert** is someone who has a natural interest in the message and desires a significant amount of detailed information. Physical therapists and medical records office staff are likely to be very interested in HIPAA. The

executive is someone who wants the highlights and the bottom line, but spare the details. Managers of some nonclinical departments fall into this category regarding HIPAA. The **user** needs the information to determine how to act. The **complex audience** is one with mixed users such as the lay user. The **mixed audience** includes representatives of all audience types. The written message must be designed to meet the needs of the target audience. In this way, the sender (writer) has the best chance of holding the receiver's (reader's) attention. Writing starts with a plan or outline that organizes the written message in a meaningful way. The writer should lay out elements of the message in a way that will catch and hold the attention of the reader. Using the outline, the details of the message should be added. Ultimately, the amount of detail in the finished communication should be determined by what the audience needs. At this stage in the process, the writer should include as much information as desired. The message can be revised and refined through editing.

Revision should start at the highest level and work down into the detail (Fitzgerald, 1998). The first step is to verify that the message meets the overall communication goal in a way that is meaningful to the target audience. The next level of edit should be focused on the organization and structure of the material. Is the material presented in a way that is easy to follow and holds the attention of the reader? After that the accuracy should be checked at the paragraph and sentence level. Finally, the grammar and spelling should be checked. It is often helpful to enlist the help of others during the edit. Someone reading the material for the first time may spot problems the author would overlook.

We offer the following tips:

- Written messages should be as simple and direct as possible.
- Few things distract the reader more and reflect more poorly on the writer than poor grammar and misspelled words.
- The reading skill of the target audience should determine the grade level of the writing.
- Never write and send anything in anger.
- *NEVER* write in all capitals; it is equivalent to *SHOUTing* at the reader.
- Always reference the sources of information in a written report.
- Include the date the message was written.
- If written communication has to be translated into another language, a professional translator should be consulted.

Student Notes

As a physical therapist, you will be called upon to communicate with people in some difficult circumstances. In both oral and written communications you will need to be well organized and brief but specific enough for others to gain quick understanding of any situation. Communication with professional colleagues will generally be constrained by time. Often your patients will be in pain or under the emotional stress that accompanies disability. Families of the disabled are often tired and fearful of the future. Yet in all of these situations you will have to send and receive messages accurately to achieve the best outcomes for your patients. It should be no surprise that effective dialog will be an essential treatment skill.

Summary

This chapter reviews the principles of nonverbal, oral, and written communication and listening. Nonverbal communication, the most difficult form of communication to interpret, is totally dependent on context and the perceptions of the receiver. The application of oral communication skills in conversation and formal presentations in the work setting is discussed along with the importance of dialog for encouraging participatory discussion, effective decision making, and conflict resolution. Finally, the role of active listening to complete the communication loop and the barriers to active listening are reviewed. Keep in mind the communication and listening principles presented in this chapter as you go through the next chapter, which deals with the principles of employee productivity. Employee productivity depends on the coordination of work between individuals. Coordination in turn depends on effective communications; it is an essential component of achieving maximum employee effectiveness. Another work-related context in which communication and listening are critical will be presented in the next chapter, which addresses employee appraisal. Performance feedback is a common topic of discussion in any work environment. Managers often have concerns about how consistent they are in judging the performance of their staff members. Staff members are typically anxious about being appraised because they are often unsure how the appraisal criteria will be applied in their evaluation. The rules for effective communication suggest that observed behaviors should be the focus of the evaluative discourse. This principle will be reinforced in Chapter 17. The essential information about conducting employee appraisals, development of standards and criteria, and helpful ways to improve performance are discussed.

INDIVIDUAL CASE STUDY

Suppose a 15-year-old girl has been referred for treatment of a newly diagnosed spinal curvature. During your initial conversation, the patient declines to sit, stands with one hand on her hip, responds to most questions with single words, and frequently sighs deeply. It is time to move on to the physical examination. You find yourself getting annoyed with this patient's behavior. What do you do? Apply the principles discussed in this chapter to formulate your answer.

GROUP CASE STUDY

You need a group of three for this scenario. Each of you take one of the roles: a male physical therapist, a female physical therapist, and a supervising physical therapist.

Situation

One of the other therapists in your department has been driving you to distraction. This person is constantly talking about how his patients really benefit from his advanced training and skills. Yet he doesn't seem too eager to pick up new referrals. In fact, as far as you are concerned, he does not do much other than talk about himself. You have one last nerve intact and this guy is standing on it.

A few days ago you e-mailed a friend in the department, venting your frustrations about this guy. But guess what? She forwarded your e-mail to a friend, who forwarded it to—you know it—the guy who's driving you crazy. You noticed earlier how quiet he was today. Now you know why.

Task

Your supervising therapist has asked to meet with you and the guy today at 4:00. What do you do now (see libel in Chapter 5)? How do you think he will react? What do you think your supervising therapist will do? As a group, apply the principles discussed in this chapter and develop the scenario further. When you have your plan together, act out your scenario for another group who will focus on how well they think you applied principles of communication and listening.

REFERENCES

Anderson K. What you can say without speaking. Journal of Property Management. 2001;66:12–14.

Chisolm A. Effective listening skills. Medford, MA: Tufts Leadership Institute. Available from http://www.tufts.edu/as/stu act/leadership/listening.html. Accessed 6/01/97.

Fitzgerald SS. Schaum's quick guide to great business writing. New York: McGraw-Hill. 1998.

Johnson KR. Effective listening skills. Itm WEB Site, Ken Johnson. 1999:12.

Knippen JT, Green TB. Handling conflicts. Journal of Workplace Learning. 1999;11:27–32.

Maurer R. How to use dialogue. Journal for Quality and Participation. 2001;24 (Summer): 64–66.

Merriam-Webster's collegiate dictionary, 11th ed. Springfield, MA: Merriam-Webster. 2003.

Morrisey GL, Sechrest TL. Effective business and technical presentations. Reading, MA: Addison-Wesley. 1987.

Simmons J. Business communication and presentation skills. Available from http://134.48.50.238/classwork/Simm ons/EMBA/EXBU%20presentation%20skills.ppt. Accessed 10/19/02.

Yankelovich D. The magic of dialogue. New York: Simon & Schuster. 1999.

MORE INFORMATION RELATED TO THIS CHAPTER

Additional models of the communication process in health care settings that include communication throughout an organization can be found in Longest BB Jr., Rakich JS, Darr K. Managing health services organizations and systems. 4th ed. Baltimore: Health Professionals. 2000.

Practical information on written and oral communication, including e-mail and phone calls, can be found in two chapters in Umiker W. Management skills for the new health care supervisor. 3rd ed. Gaithersburg, MD: Aspen. 1998.

Introductory information on the legal aspects of communication, that is, libel, slander, informed consent, and others are available in Scott RW. Health care malpractice: A primer on legal issues for professionals. 2nd ed. New York: McGraw-Hill. 1999.

A unique discussion of the roles people play in communication, including 20 noncontributory roles employees can take and 20 excuses they commonly use when confronted for unacceptable actions, are found in Lombardi DN. Handbook for the new health care manager: Practical strategies for the real world. 2nd ed. San Francisco: Jossey-Bass. 2001:88–107.

Chapter 17

Achieving Maximum Productivity Through Work Teams

Learning Objectives

1. Define *work team* and differentiate the types of work teams common in health care environments.
2. Discuss the variables to consider when contemplating the formation of a work team.
3. Evaluate common benefits expected from successful work teams and constraints a manager may face when forming and developing work teams.
4. Explain the management processes associated with work team formation, development, and information exchange.
5. Summarize a common way work groups organize and function in health care settings.

Key Words

Facilitator, interdepartmental, interdisciplinary, intradepartmental, quality circle, team leader, work group, work group process, work rules, work team

Introduction

At a time when the health care industry has been struggling to meet growing customer expectations with shrinking resources, there has been an increasing awareness of and interest in the success of Japanese organizations in motivation of employees to achieve high levels of productivity (Mintzberg, Quinn, Voyer, 1995). Ouchi (1981) observed Japanese organizations and reported that their success was due to their collaborative management style. They placed great value on their employees. Employees were consulted on issues that affected them and their work. Employee participation was achieved through the use of a group process. A common **work group process** was that work groups would meet regularly to review operations, identify opportunities for improvement, and make changes necessary to improve quality and productivity. These work groups were referred to as **quality circles**.

The concept of quality and productivity improvement through employee empowerment and the use of work groups caught on quickly. Following the lead of other U.S. organizations, the health care industry began to turn its attention away from the individual employee and toward the work group and eventually into teamwork as the unit from which major productivity improvements could be derived.

Work Group Formation

A **work group** consists of individuals who are organized in a set of processes to perform a set of assigned tasks. Work groups have a general level of cohesion, a general central purpose, and communication provided by the processes that support them. The characteristics of work groups vary with the purpose for which they are formed. Work groups may be together on a permanent basis or assemble to tackle a specific time-limited task. Work groups have many names. Intact team, department, committee, council, task force, treatment team, project team, process improvement team, hot team, steering committee, integration team, and management group are just a few of the names organizations use to describe work groups (Clemmer, 1992). Project team, performance improvement team, and integration team are names that imply a time-limited, task-focused work group. Work groups that focus on core production tasks, such as treatment teams, are generally together for a longer term.

Within work groups, individuals may be performing the same task or components of a larger task. Here are some examples:

- Physical therapy department X has organized its employees into two work groups. Members of work group A, the transport aides, transport patients to and from a care setting, while work group B, the therapists, prepare patients to receive care, perform the care, and prepare patients to return to their room. Members of group A perform a single task. Group B members perform a process made up of several tasks.
- Physical therapy department Y has also organized its employees into two work groups. Members of work group A, a transport aide and therapist team, are assigned to the second floor. Together they divide the work of transporting and preparing patients and delivering care. Members of work group B, a second transport aide and therapist team, is assigned to the third floor. They also divide the work. Members of both group A and group B perform the same process made up of several tasks.

In both of these examples, the same work gets done. The work group membership, task structure, and scope of work differ. Work groups may perform one function, such as the work of the physical therapy department. A group consisting of members from a single department is **intradepartmental**. A group may be cross-functional, including members from many departments. Such a work group is **interdepartmental** or **interdisciplinary**. An example of an interdisciplinary team is a rehabilitation treatment team consisting of the patient, physician, nurse, physical therapist, occupational therapist, speech and language pathologist, and others. Organizing people into a work group is the starting point, but it takes more than structure to turn a group of employees into a functioning work team.

Transformation: Work Group to Work Team

Similar to a work group, a **work team** consists of individuals brought together for a specific function; however, they usually have a more specific common purpose and more cohesion than a work group. Work teams typically have more specific constraints, such as targets, outcomes, and available resources (Macmillan and Tampoe, 2000).

For a work group to become a highly productive work team takes commitment and a lot of hard work. Management can take these six steps to increase the chances of a successful transformation from an individual to a team focus:

1. Establish open and honest communication between team members and between the team and management.
2. Set clear performance expectations.
3. Make members aware of the barriers and constraints they face.
4. Have the team adopt work rules to accomplish the task.
5. Structure and position the team within the organization to achieve expected performance.
6. Make sure members have the needed skills, knowledge, and experience to perform the tasks.

Performance Expectations

The first thing a team needs is specific performance expectations defined in terms of quantifiable outcomes. Performance expectations may originate with management or with the team. Expectations should be consistent with the basic purpose and vision of the organization (Chapters 9 and 11). The scope of a work team's performance expectations may be broad in that it affects the entire organization (for example, board of trustees) or narrow, affecting a small part of the organization (for example, project team assigned to open a new outpatient physical therapy clinic). Whatever the source or scope, performance expectations must be clear and concise. There should be no room for differing interpretations of the expected outcomes. Performance expectations are best when they are quantifiable and can be used to objectively evaluate the work group's performance (Chapters 19 and 31).

Open Communication

An open line of communication between the work team and management is necessary for several reasons:

- Setting performance expectations
- Ongoing performance evaluation
- Understanding and addressing work barriers
- Obtaining the resources necessary to meet performance expectations

Open lines of communication between team members are necessary for the team to maximize productivity and performance. Team communication allows members to:

- Contribute ideas
- Express opinions
- Share knowledge
- Coordinate work assignments
- Accommodate change

Performance Constraints

The team members should be aware of any constraints that they must accommodate to meet their performance expectations. Constraints should be identified and defined. These are common constraints faced by work teams in health care organizations:

- Lack of information
- Limited money, equipment, space, or information
- Lack of qualified members
- Time restrictions
- Competing organizational interests
- External restrictions

External restrictions are generally the most difficult barriers to overcome because they are outside the control of the organization. Restrictions affecting health care organizations come in many forms, such as licensure laws (Chapters 3 and 5), wage and salary guidelines, service certification requirements, accreditation requirements (Chapter 32), customer needs (Chapters 21–25), and building codes. In addition, some limitations may be based on professional organization positions, such as the American Physical Therapy Association's (APTA) stance on cross-training and disclaimers when giving continuing education for non–physical therapists or physical therapist assistants (APTA, 2002).

Work Rules

The next step is for the team to agree upon a common set of work rules. **Work rules** are tools that group members can use to anticipate the actions of other members. They provide structure for group interactions and group tasks. Clinical care protocols, policies, procedures (Chapter 10), and defined decision-making processes, such as standard assessment tools, are all forms of work rules. Agreed-upon procedures for member interactions, organizing and holding meetings, and conflict management are also important rules for any team. Rules do not necessarily limit group creativity, flexibility, or responsiveness to change. In fact, rules about how the group will respond to new ideas may increase members' comfort with sharing ideas. Work rules may limit the individuality of group members. However, group performance should be enhanced even in times of change and uncertainty. This happens because members can count on the support, stability, and predictability of the group. Finally, work rules should not be etched in stone. To the contrary, rules should be flexible, changing as the needs of the group, organization, and its customers change. In fact, changing the work rules of the health care delivery process is exactly what some of our customers are expecting providers to do.

Team Structure

Significant attention should be paid to the structure of the group. Group structure includes such things as member roles, membership characteristics, and group size. The group structure should reflect performance expectations and constraints. The objective is to assemble the right people in the right way to get the job done.

Member Roles

Work groups mirror larger organizations in that their members are assigned to perform specific roles. Group roles include a leader, members, and often support staff and a facilitator. An individual team member may perform one or more roles. Assignment and definition of group roles will help members understand their contributions to the group process.

The **team leader** is responsible for getting the work done. The team leader should also be an active member in the group process. In a true group decision-making process, team leaders have no more authority than any other member regardless of management authority. See the Chapter 16 discussion of dialog. Leaders can be appointed by the organization or selected by the group. Generally, the team leader's areas of responsibility are significantly affected by the kind of work the group is doing. A team leader's role changes with the activity of the group. Moving along a continuum from total control of the group process to total collaboration with employees, managers must match their role to the needs of the group (Chapters 8 and 15). The **facilitator** is responsible for managing group dynamics and the group process and for reinforcing group work rules. The facilitator often is required to break down barriers that limit the group process and progress. Frequently encountered barriers include: varied statuses of members, poor communication, conflicting goals, member characteristics, lack of information, lack of group process skills, and failure to follow established work rules. The team leader or a team member may function as the facilitator. Or the facilitator may be a neutral outside party who is not considered a team member. Long-term work groups with well-established relationships and work rules often use the team leader to facilitate their work. In contrast, work groups with less-cohesive members, conflicting agendas, or minimal shared work rules are likely to be more productive with a neutral facilitator.

Member Selection

Members contribute their energy, ideas, talents, and skills to meeting the team performance expectations. Considerations for member selection should start with the team's performance expectations. The work to be done, people affected, organizational priority, time available, and the individual's ability to contribute to a successful outcome are some of the considerations related to performance expectations. Constraints may also play into the choice of members. Members who have the potential to limit or remove constraints are highly valued. The constraint may be limited availability of desirable members. Team member balance, fit, and diversity (Chapter 18) should also be considered. Considerations of team fit may begin during employee recruitment and selection. Table 17.1 provides a list of factors that may influence the choice of members.

Team Size

There is no magic formula for determining the best group size. The most productive groups are no larger than they have to be to get the job done. Each member should add value, that is, bring something useful to each meeting. Group size should not be used to limit participation of any individual or other work group whose interests are influenced by the decisions of the work team.

Information

The value of information has long been recognized (Chapter 14). Information is an organizational asset (Rouse, 2001). Organiza-

Table 17.1 Work Team Member Selection

Factors For Consideration		
Performance Expectations	***Known and Potential Constraints***	***Group Balance, Fit, and Diversity***
Define work to be done	Define constraints to be accommodated	Group dynamics and process
Scope of impact	Organizational values, vision, culture	Group process skills
Priority	Divergence from norms	Leadership skills
Time available	Resources	Worker representation
Potential contribution	Member availability	Diversity of group member work styles
People affected	Information access	Education
Functions affected	Potential for internal resistance	Skills
Roles within the group	External factors	Experience
		Organizational position
		Knowledge of the organization

tions that have and know how to use information about customers, the environment, and self-understanding have a competitive advantage in the marketplace (Chapters 11 and 21).

Drucker (1954) tells us that information is the key to improving employee performance. Access to the right information at the right time affects the performance of a work team the same way it does an individual. It defines performance expectations and constraints in objective terms. It can be used to educate and align team members. Information is needed for the team to assess its performance. It is the foundation for setting direction and decision making. Information gives a team the power to maximize its performance.

Information is a source of power (Case, 1994). It positions an organization to be more influential in its environment and marketplace (Chapter 13). It offers the potential to limit the success of competitors (Chapter 11). Information is also a source of internal organizational power. Unfortunately, this can create the potential for individuals who control the flow of information to acquire influence and personal success. A powerful incentive may exist to keep information from others (Case, 1994). Information can be withheld by restricting access, delaying access, or failing to educate others so they have the skill to understand and use information to improve performance. The practice of withholding information to control and limit the activities of others is a common criticism directed at today's organizations (Chapter 13). And it limits the productivity of an organization.

Stages of Team Development

When all of the right elements are in place, everyone is communicating, and group members understand what they are to do, the barriers they face, resources available, how the group will be structured and whom they will work with, the group is well positioned to become a high-performance work team. Weber (1982) provides us with the forming, storming, norming, performing model, which describes how groups pass through stages as they develop into highly productive work teams. LaPenta and Jacobs (1996) expand on the model by providing insight into leadership issues, group and task issues, interpersonal issues, and group behavioral patterns that correspond to each developmental stage. Table 17.2, modeled on the work of LaPenta and Jacobs (1996) provides an overview of developmental stages and related issues.

A Performing Work Team: Would You Know It If You Saw It?

Performing work teams share certain characteristics that differentiate them from work groups. When a work team is at a high performance level, members demonstrate an

Table 17.2 Team Development: Stages, Issues, and Behavior Patterns

Stages				
Issues/Behaviors	***Forming***	***Storming***	***Norming***	***Performing***
Leadership issues Group tasks	Dependence Membership Roles Similarities Differences	Independence Decision making Power Influence	Interdependence Build relationships	Interdependence Productivity
Interpersonal Group behaviors	Inclusion Seek similarities Anger Frustration Politeness Vagueness Confusion	Control Set work rules Create order Attack leader Negative about task demands	Affection Cohesion Negotiation	Affection Growth Understanding Teamwork

obvious commitment to their shared purpose. Open communication and a collaborative working style between members are the norm. When members disagree, the group employs a comfortable, well-established approach to conflict resolution. The team also uses an established decision-making process. Once decisions are made, the group demonstrates a common level of support and dedication to action. Morale is high. Often, the team shares a sense of excitement. Most important, assignments are completed efficiently, effectively, and result in realistic solutions. The team exhibits a high level of productivity (Chapters 8 and 17).

Work Teams and Productivity

Enhanced productivity can be attributed to the work team structure that gives individuals the opportunity to develop a broader focus of their roles, responsibilities, and contributions to the organization. Because performing work teams have an established process for information sharing and broad organizational networks, team members have more and better information upon which to base decisions. Inclusion in the decision-making process enhances member buy-in to group commitments and change initiatives. As a result, members are likely to work harder to engage others in the group's efforts. Team pressure and support help team members to maintain their level of commitment and follow-through over time. All of these factors contribute to productivity. These characteristics of a high-performing group cannot be duplicated with the focus on individual performance.

Self-Directed Work Teams

Self-directed work teams are different from other work teams in that they lack the formal role of team leader. In the absence of a team leader, team members share responsibility for most or all aspects of the team process. Also referred to as work cells, self-directed work teams are organized around a specific work process (Clemmer, 1992). More prominent in manufacturing, the use of self-directed work teams is growing within the health care industry (Clemmer, 1992). Use of self-directed work teams is often viewed as an opportunity to reduce the number of employees, often at the lower levels of management, without reducing productive capabilities.

Self-directed teams operate with a higher degree of autonomy and less supervisor influence than other types of work teams. Increased member collaboration and the resulting reduction in conflicting influences that may occur within self-directed work teams have the potential to provide many organizational benefits. However, for the same reason, the performance of self-directed work teams is more sensitive to relational conflicts arising from personal differences between members of the work team. Without a leader to focus the team on its common goals, relational conflict can divert energy and undermine the work team's effectiveness. Solutions to such conflicts are offered in Chapter 16.

When Are Work Teams the Wrong Choice?

Scarnati (2001) identifies several factors to consider when determining whether work teams are the right choice for an organization or a specific task. Factors to be considered include the flexibility of employee recognition programs, communication systems, ability to provide needed resources, and urgency.

1. *Employee recognition*: By design, work teams deemphasize the importance of individual performance in deference to work team performance. This implies that team members are recognized as part of the team rather than as individuals. Most traditional employee performance evaluation, recognition, and compensation programs have been based on individual achievements. An organization must be willing to change these programs to fully support the work team concept.
2. *Communication systems*: To be effective, work teams need access to the right information in a timely manner. Either unwillingness to share needed information or inability to provide it may make the work team structure impractical.
3. *Ability to provide resources*: A work team should never be formed unless the organization has the resources to support its work.
4. *Urgency*: By their nature, work teams make decisions more slowly than an individual. This occurs because it takes more time to obtain and assimilate the input and get buy-in on a decision from a group than from an individual. Some decisions must be made quickly. According to Scarnati, "teams best function on long-term issues that are important but not urgent" (2001, p. 9). He suggests that time-critical decisions be deferred to management. In our experience it takes 2 to 3 months for a team to form and organize their efforts sufficiently to address even the simplest issue.

Student Notes

The new graduate is typically the newest hire with the least experience in patient care and in organizational and departmental functioning. Among the methods managers use to develop new staff members is to assign them to work groups. There is a learning process whenever a new member is added to a group. From the new member's perspective, being part of a work group is an early opportunity to learn how coworkers think, how they act under pressure, what they become emotional about, what they will work hard to attain, and so on. The other members also learn these things about the new member.

Work group membership is one of the workplace contexts in which one can earn respect. Ideally, a new graduate begins to be recognized as a contributing group member by offering fresh insights that are expressed tactfully and clearly. Contributions to the discussion that move the group toward their common goal are valuable.

The value of becoming a team is that the individual strengths of each team member are applied to solving the issue at hand. This collaboration can produce a composite outcome that is superior to what any one team member might arrive at as an individual.

A facilitator can bring together the thoughts of many to accomplish a group goal. However, regardless of the skill of the facilitator, a group becomes a team only if each group member is willing to listen, willing to offer constructive insights, positive and optimistic, and committed to working as part of a unit rather than as an individual. This takes time, and the process can be bumpy (Table 17.2).

INDIVIDUAL CASE STUDY

Your employer is considering deployment of an automated, fully integrated, interactive medical information management solution. This will be the biggest information technology (IT) project the organization has ever undertaken. The project has an estimated cost of $10 million. According to the management advisory, an interdisciplinary project team is being formed. Team members will work full time on the project for at least 2 years. No other information is available. You have expressed an interest in joining the project team and have a 30-minute interview with the chief information officer tomorrow during which she will spell out the task. You have time to ask five questions that will both impress her with your qualifications and get you enough information to know what you would be getting yourself into. What five questions do you ask?

Summary

Work teams, when structured and used appropriately, can enhance worker satisfaction and improve organizational productivity. Work teams can be formed for short-term focused projects or can be a permanent part of the organization's structure. To be maximally effective, work teams require management support, resources, clear performance expectations, the right team members, and a shared plan for how the work of the group will be performed. With all of the required elements in place, the performing work team can be expected to exceed the combined productivity of its individual members many times over.

Issues that impede a group from becoming a team have been discussed generally. An-

GROUP CASE STUDY

Earlier in the chapter is an example describing two physical therapy departments that perform similar work, hire the same types of employees, but organize those employees into different types of work groups as follows:

- Physical therapy department X has organized its employees into two work groups. Members of work group A, the transport aides, transport patients to and from a care setting while work group B, the therapists, prepare patients to receive care, perform the care, and prepare patients to return to their inpatient rooms. Members of group A perform a single task. Group B members perform a process made up of several tasks.
- Physical therapy department Y also has organized its employees into two work groups. Members of work group A, a physical therapist assistant and physical therapist team, are assigned to the second floor. Together they divide the work of transporting and preparing patients and delivery of care. Members of work group B, a second transport assistant and therapist team, are assigned to the third floor. They also divide the same work. Members of both group A and group B follow the same process made up of several tasks.

Your task is to consider and discuss the pros and cons of each approach. Your discussion should include a variety of factors such as job satisfaction, workload balance, productivity, customer service, and flexibility to adapt to staff absences or vacancies.

other perspective on understanding how to manage people should be discussed. Human differences can lead to wonderful insights, and they can lead to problems due to goal incongruity or differences in self-interests. The importance of understanding human differences and the development of skill in managing conflict are essential team and personal skills. A topic that needs to be addressed to complement what has already been said in the preceding chapters is diversity. The opportunities and challenges of managing diversity in the health care setting are covered in Chapter 18.

REFERENCES

American Physical Therapy Association. Section I: Professional and societal standards, policies, positions. Available from http://www.apta.org/pdfs/governance/hodpolicies.pdf. Accessed 8/19/02.

Case J. Open-book management. New York: HarperCollins. 1994.

Clemmer J. Firing on all cylinders. Burr Ridge, IL: Irwin. 1992.

Drucker P. The practice of management. New York: Harper & Row. 1954.

LaPenta C, Jacobs GM. Application of group process model to performance appraisal development in a CQI environment. Health Care Management Review. 1996;21:45–60.

Macmillan H, Tampoe M. Strategic management. Process, content, and implementation. New York: Oxford University. 2000.

Mintzberg H, Quinn JB, Voyer J. The strategy process, collegiate edition. Englewood Cliffs, NJ: Prentice Hall. 1995.

Ouchi W. Theory Z: How American business can meet the Japanese challenge. Reading, PA: Addison-Wesley. 1981.

Rouse WB. Essential challenges of strategic management. New York: Wiley. 2001.

Scarnati JT. On becoming a team player. Team performance management. Bradford. 2001:5–10.

Weber RC. The group: A cycle from birth to death. In Porter L, Mohr B, eds. NLT reading book for human relations training, 7th ed. Alexandria, VA: NTL Institute. 1982.

MORE INFORMATION RELATED TO THIS CHAPTER

A classic article on leadership patterns is Tannenbaum R, Schmidt WH. How to choose a leadership pattern. Harvard Business Review. 1973;51:162–180.

A short but informative discussion on the development of the Japanese style of management from post World War II to the present is in Brannen MY, Kleinberg J. Images of Japanese management and the development of organizational culture theory. In Ashkanasy NM, Wilderom CPM, Peterson MF, eds. Handbook of organizational culture & climate. Thousand Oaks, CA: Sage. 2000:387–400.

Leadership techniques, intuition, and personal attributes as they relate to leadership are discussed in Nahavandi A. The art and science of leadership. Upper Saddle River, NJ: Prentice-Hall. 1997.

A short, current and well-referenced review of research on small groups can be found in Langfred CW, Shanley MT. Small group research: Autonomous teams and progress on issues of context and levels of analysis. In Golembiewski RT, ed. Handbook of organizational behavior, 2nd ed. New York: Marcel Dekker. 2001;81–112.

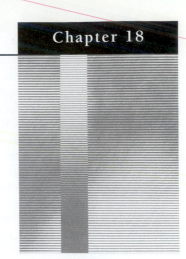

Chapter 18

Diversity in the Health Care Setting

Learning Objectives

1. Evaluate the framework for discussing diversity presented in this chapter, that is, 6 primary and 10 external dimensions.
2. Contrast the concepts of assimilation and accommodation as they relate to the philosophy of an organization formulating diversity management strategies.
3. Analyze diversity from a health care business perspective, that is, a diverse workforce and a diverse customer base.
4. Compare the models an organization with a goal of fostering a diverse workforce might use to achieve this goal.
5. Summarize the principal elements of a diversity program that a health care manager should be familiar with.

Key Words

Accommodation, assimilation, baby boomer, culture, demography, diversity, ethnicity, Gen Xer, Hispanic, minority, natural population growth, stereotype

Introduction

We use the word **diversity** to denote the differences between people that influence how they view the world and how others view them. **Ethnicity**, an individual's relation to a specific cultural or national group, is only one characteristic that can differentiate people from one another. Race, gender, class, religion, sexual orientation, physical ability, and age are all attributes that make people unique individuals. The impact of diversity on health care delivery has not gone unnoticed. The rapidly growing population of diverse ethnicity has increased the awareness of and attention paid to the influences of all types of diversity. The health care industry as a whole is scrambling to accommodate the growing diversity of its customers and its workforce. Health care providers are being called upon to understand the characteristics that contribute to diversity, learn new interactive skills, provide care in different ways, and commit significant resources to accommodate an increasingly diverse customer base and workforce. Along the way, everyone is learning that diversity can bring opportunity along with challenges.

Demographic Trends

Demography is the statistical study of population trends, especially with reference to age, gender, and geographic location, along with social characteristics, for example, employment, education, and ethnicity (Kovner and Jonas, 1999). Changes in the ethnic makeup of the U.S. population through immigration is one of the demographic shifts that will have a significant impact in the 21st century (Shi and Singh, 2001). Most Americans can trace their ancestry to another continent. In the early 1900s, drawn by economic opportunity, a large number of Europeans immigrated to the United States. By 1940, 70% of U.S. immigrants came from Europe (Roosevelt, 1993). In the last decades of the 20th century, America has seen another significant wave of immigration. Driven by world events and the hope of a better life, people of widely varied cultures, languages, and experiences have immigrated from Asia, Latin America, and many other parts of the world. These new immigrants have changed the face of America. According to the 2000 U.S. Census results, ancestries logged by recent immigrants from Asia and Spanish-speaking countries increased 28% to 91.6 million (El Nasser and Overberg, 2002). Salimbene and Graczykowski reported, "Latinos and Asians will account for more than half the growth in the U.S. population every year for the next half century and beyond" (1995, p. 1).

The United States has one of the highest population growth rates of the industrialized nations, adding about 2.5 million people annually. Immigration accounts for a third of that growth, with **natural population growth**, defined as births minus deaths, accounting for the remainder (Bottomley and Lewis, 2003). In the early 1990s, approximately 45% of net additions to the labor force were nonwhite (Cox, 1995). Projections from the 2000 Census estimate that 30% of the U.S. population is nonwhite (U.S. Census Bureau, 2003a). Projections estimate that within 50 years the percentage of minorities will grow to nearly half the total population (U.S. Census Bureau, 2003b). Growth of the **Hispanic** population, individuals of any Latin American nationality, including Mexican, Puerto Rican, and Cuban, will increase to about 24% of the total U.S. population (U.S. Census Bureau, 2003c). Thus, by the middle of the century, the label of **minority** defined as a part of a population differing from the majority in some way and often subjected to differential treatment (Merriam-Webster, 2003) may be difficult to apply based on color. Another aspect of America's changing demographic profile is regional differences. The effects of changing ethnic composition are not evenly spread throughout the country. While all communities will be affected to some extent, the type, rate, and degree of change will vary widely. For more detail consult http//www.census.gov.

The aging of the population is another significant demographic change on our horizon. Over the next 30 years, the over-65 population is projected to increase more than 70% while without a change in the law governing the age of retirement, the taxpaying population will rise less than 4% (Congressional Budget Office, 1997). This trend is in part due to affluence and advances in medical technology. However, this shift in age demographics will increase the demand for resources to provide for the economic, social, and physical well-being of the elderly. At the same time, we will be facing a shortage of workers and a declining tax base (Burman, Penner, Steuerle et al., 1998). It is ironic that affluence and access to medical care are both the causes and potentially the casualties of shifting demographics.

The important thing to health care providers is the day-to-day effects of demographic trends on their ability to deliver quality services. Shifting ethnic composition will be reflected in changing customer needs and the makeup of our health care workforce. Both population growth and aging will increase the need for most health care services. The aging of the population can be expected to result in an increased demand for adult primary care, cardiac care, orthopedic care, inpatient hospitalization, long-term care, and physical therapy. The aging of the population will also make it increasingly difficult to find the resources, money, and skilled staff to deliver the level of medical care that has allowed the current generation to live longer, more active lives than prior generations. These challenges also exist within the field of physical therapy. In 2002, more than 90% of the membership of the American Physical Therapy Association (APTA) was white. Fewer than 2% of the members identified themselves as Hispanic or Latino (APTA, 2002a). As will be discussed next, these percentages are not representative of the diversity among the patient populations of many health care settings.

Defining Diversity

Diversity can be defined by words such as variety, assortment, and array. For our purposes, diversity refers to the characteristics that make people different from one another. Differences, obvious or hidden, can and do influence our beliefs, attitudes, expectations, and assumptions about one another (Gardenswartz and Rowe, 1998). Loden and Rosener (1991) offer us a framework for looking at the differences that contribute to diversity. They describe 6 primary and 10 external dimensions.

The six primary dimensions:

1. Age
2. Ethnicity
3. Gender
4. Physical ability
5. Race
6. Sexual orientation

The 10 external dimensions:

1. Appearance
2. Education
3. Geographic location
4. Income
5. Marital status
6. Parental status
7. Personal habits
8. Recreational habits
9. Religion
10. Work experience

Primary dimensions are for the most part out of the control of the individual and have the potential for a great impact on health care delivery. These external dimensions are the result of circumstances, opportunities, individual choice, and directed effort.

Age

Age makes a difference in how we are seen and how we see others. Our attitudes about age are shaped by our culture, experience, and age. For example, all it takes is a quick look at our advertisements to conclude that Americans value youth. Advancing age is often thought to be a negative characteristic symbolized by the color black. Signs of aging are hidden by cosmetic coverups, such as makeup and Botox injections or cosmetic surgery. Age is often associated with frailty and forgetfulness. In the workplace, age may be associated with outdated skills, low productivity, and resistance to change. In contrast, Asian cultures place great value on age. Their elderly are recognized for their wisdom and contributions to society. Age is not a characteristic to hide or fear.

Age will also influence a person's values and expectations (Chapter 6). Much has been written about the differences between members of different generations. Their Depression era parents influenced **baby boomers**, born between 1946 and 1964. Boomers entered the workforce with an attitude saying "*thank you for the job; I will try to exceed your expectations*" (Bova and Kroth, 2001, p. 57). In contrast, **Gen Xers**, those born between 1965 and 1981, grew up in relative affluence but underwent corporate downsizing, which led to layoffs and the disillusionment with corporate loyalty. Xers entered the workforce thinking, "*I'll stay as long as it serves my purposes, my needs for continuing skill development are met, and I can maintain a balanced life.*" You can imagine what each might think when a boomer and a Gen Xer work in a peer or a supervisor–subordinate relationship. According to recent surveys of APTA members, approximately 44% and 45% of the physical therapists would be classified as baby boomers or Gen Xers, respectively. For physical therapist assistants the rates were approximately 30% and 54%, respectively, indicating a younger sample (APTA, 2002b).

Ethnicity

Ethnicity refers to a person's national and cultural background as well as native language. Many authors have documented the myriad of differences among the **cultures** of the world. The purpose here is not to repeat all of those differences. However, it will be helpful to understand how cultures differ. To bring together multiple cultural differences in an understandable format, Carr-Ruffino (1996) suggests examining nine major areas. These areas of cultural distinctiveness should be considered when attempting to understand the values, norms, and behaviors of any given cultural group. They should not be used to stereotype individuals but rather to assist in understanding individual differences. Each of the nine defining areas listed in Table 18.1 should be used to understand cultural distinctiveness and how these differences can benefit the organization.

Native language is also an aspect of ethnicity and an important factor influencing the interactions between diverse groups (Gardenswartz and Rowe, 1998). Consider the importance of language in the effective delivery of a physical therapy evaluation or treatment. In the absence of a qualified interpreter, a therapist and patient who do not share a common language cannot communicate effectively. The therapist must guess about the patient's condition and treatment needs. The patient is uncertain about the therapist's plan of care and cannot provide informed consent for treatment. Words or phrases that sound familiar may be totally misinterpreted. Both parties are likely to be frustrated, and the risks of providing inappropriate care are high. The value of a qualified interpreter in such situations is obvious. A qualified interpreter is someone who has an expertise in the native languages of everyone in the conversation and a working knowledge of health care and medical terminology. A volunteer interpreter or family member, for example, a child, who lacks these skills, should not interpret for the purposes of patient assessment, care planning, or obtaining informed consent for treatment. When no qualified interpreter is available, an option is to subscribe to an interpreter phone service.

Table 18.1 Nine Areas of Cultural Distinctiveness

Areas of Cultural Distinctiveness
Locus of control. What is the focal point of authority?
Individualism versus collectivism. What has higher value, individual rights or the good of the group?
Achievement versus affiliation. Are individuals valued for individual success or contribution to and support of the group?
Equality versus hierarchy. Are decisions made by a few leaders or through group majority?
Risk-taking versus security seeking. What lifestyle is idealized? Adventurer, thrill seeker, entrepreneur versus employed manager, salaried staff member, government employee.
Single-task time use versus multiple-task time use. Do things get done in good time or at double time?
Personal distance and space. What are the rules regarding personal space?
Direct versus indirect communication. Are difficult or sensitive subjects addressed directly or through indirect reference?
Industrial versus agricultural versus postindustrial economic system. How does the economic system affect cultural values?

Developed from Carr-Rufine (1996:41).

Food preference is also an element of ethnicity that comes into play for health care providers. Good nutrition is important to health and wellness. Recovery from injury or illness may be slow if proper nutrition is not provided. Inpatient settings are finding it increasingly important to offer patients food choices that are ethnically familiar to stimulate appetite and improve customer satisfaction.

Cultural values (Chapter 6) are a part of ethnicity that manifests in a person's behaviors. For example, if deferential treatment of authority figures is a person's normal behavior, a patient may find it difficult to disagree with a physician's recommendations. Cultural norms may also affect the behaviors of a patient's family. While one family may come to visit a patient every evening, another family may be present in large numbers and want to stay with the patient at all times. Culture also influences a person's view of illness, health care beliefs, and treatment preferences (Gardenswartz and Rowe, 1998).

Gender

Gender has long been recognized as a factor influencing such things as family responsibilities, education, employment, and the delivery of health care. In the United States, in terms of social and organizational power, men have historically been the dominant gender. This dominance has lead to differential treatment in such areas as hiring and compensation. A 1990 study by the American College of Health Care Executives and the University of Iowa compared men and women who entered the same field at the same time and who achieved similar education levels. It showed that women did not achieve parity with men in salary, position level, or job satisfaction. In a 1996 follow-up to the 1990 study (Weil, 1996), the following findings were reported:

- Women with comparable education and experience continued to earn less than men.
- Men advanced further in their organizations than women.
- Men and women are perceived to have different management skills.
- Women have more home and family obligations than their male counterparts.
- While gender continued to affect workplace recognition and compensation, some improvements were noted, with men and women now reporting similar job satisfaction rates.

While this example is from a health care setting, the same gender differences can be found in many employment settings. In the United States, physical therapy has always been a female majority profession. There are approximately twice as many female as male members of the APTA (APTA, 2002c). Even in a female majority profession there has been longstanding concern about pay inequity (APTA, 2002d). Successive studies of APTA members in 1992, 1995, and 1998 showed that full-time salaried female therapists earned 77.6 to 86.7% as much as their salaried male counterparts. For full-time self-employed individuals, females reported earnings that were 59.2 to 80.2% of what the average male private practitioner earned per year.

Gender may also affect employee performance. In many cultures the female is expected to be the primary caregiver for children and later for infirm parents. The role of family caregiver may reduce a female employee's productivity as a result of such factors as fatigue, distractions related to family responsibilities, and absenteeism. In our experience, a mother is much more likely than a father to be late or absent because of a child's illness. However, it has also been our experience that women who are important contributors to household income are more likely to share caregiver responsibilities with others.

Gender differences are also influenced by age and cultural norms. Some examples:

- An elderly woman is overwhelmed by the role changes required when her husband has a stroke. She does not drive, knows nothing about the family finances, does not have a checking account or credit history, and has never had to make any significant decisions about her life or lifestyle. Lacking other family support, she wants to defer critical decisions to the physicians, nurses, and therapists caring for her husband.
- A young Hispanic woman has just been told she could benefit from immediate care for a herniated vertebral disc. Despite significant pain, she declines to stay for treatment, indicating that she needs to return home in time to make dinner for her husband. When she has a break from her family responsibilities, she will attend to her own health care needs.
- Female physical therapists at a local hospital complain because a foreign-trained physician, the department's largest source of patient referrals, does not return their phone calls but does return calls from the only male therapist in the department. He often asks their male peer to relay information. This same physician requests that only female therapists be assigned to his female patients, which makes it hard to balance the department's workload. The female therapists feel overworked and devalued.
- An elderly Asian patient has a serious illness. She and her family have requested that all members of her health care team communicate with the eldest son before any information is shared with the patient. The son decides what the patient is to be told and what care is to be delivered or declined. Information about the extent and prognosis for the patient's illness has not

been shared with the patient. The treatment team is uncomfortable with this arrangement.

In each of these examples, gender roles, influenced by age and/or cultural values, have the potential to affect the way patient, family, and caregivers interact and ultimately the outcome of the care delivered.

Last, gender may affect the quality of health care an individual receives for several reasons:

1. Health care delivery may be influenced by the gender biases of the provider. For example, a male patient might be expected to tolerate more pain and as a result be given less pain medication. Increased pain could unnecessarily limit tolerance for physical activity and progress in therapy.
2. A patient may be uncomfortable with an opposite-gender health care provider and not share complete information about medical history and physical condition.
3. In cultures whose men are authority figures, a female patient may hesitate to express a conflicting opinion to a male health care provider concerning her plan of care.
4. Historically, much health care research has used healthy male research subjects. As a result, medications and other types of treatment may be less effective in treating female than male patients. Similarly, clinical trials have usually included few nonwhite subjects.

Physical Ability

Differentiation based on physical ability is something that physical therapists are uniquely qualified to understand. Differing physical abilities may be obvious or hidden from the uninformed observer. For example, the altered physical abilities of a person following a complete thoracic spinal cord injury are obvious, whereas the effects of mental illness or learning disability may be hidden. Altered physical abilities can evoke a variety of interpersonal reactions based on the beliefs, expectations, or ignorance of others:

- A client is uncomfortable and unsure how to interact with an attorney who is quadriplegic.
- A sales clerk talks slowly and in short sentences, assuming a young man with cerebral palsy and impaired speech has diminished intelligence.
- An elderly woman hesitates, then changes direction to avoid walking down the hallway with a woman who walks with an ataxic gait due to multiple sclerosis.
- An employee is resentful when a coworker is given a new ergonomic desk chair. The employee has no idea that the new chair is an accommodation to minimize back pain and may view it as favoritism on the part of the manager, who is the same race as the coworker.
- Despite his above-average intellect, his peers label a child with a learning disability as slow.

Race

The 2000 Census (U.S. Census Bureau, 2002) identified white, black, American Indian, Asian, Pacific Islander, and Hispanic as the primary races that make up the American population. A recent Census Bureau questionnaire lists 15 options to classify race plus three other categories (U.S. Census Bureau, 2003d). Race is an observable dimension of diversity. Often race is associated with a stereotyped set of expectations about an individual. A **stereotype** is "a standardized mental picture that is held in common by members of a group and that represents an oversimplified opinion, prejudiced attitude, or uncritical judgment" (Merriam-Webster, 2003). Frequently, the influence of stereotypes on our opinions or actions is overlooked. When we do think about stereotyping, it can be negative thinking. For example, "upper-class white people are materialistic and arrogant." But stereotypes are not always negative. Stereotyping can also be positive. For example, Asian students are diligent and good at math and science. Regardless, negative or positive stereotypes are broad-based assumptions that affect the quality and effectiveness of human interactions when applied to any individual person. Stereotypes can:

- Affect your judgment of individuals
- Affect how communications are interpreted
- Affect how behaviors are interpreted
- Lead to deferential or discriminatory treatment of individuals
- Lead to personal dissatisfaction

In the health care setting, stereotypes can reduce the quality of care. Stereotype-based assumptions made by a patient about a health care provider or conversely by a provider about a patient act as a barrier to communication. They can lead either party to filter out valuable information or make assumptions about the other party's intent. The result may be an incorrect assessment of a patient's health care needs and ineffective treatment. For example, if a physical therapist assumes that most black males are drug seeking, the therapist may not pay attention to a black male who complains of severe pain during a postoperative therapy session.

Sexual Orientation

In any setting you may find people with heterosexual, bisexual, or homosexual orientation. People with a heterosexual orientation are generally open about it. For heterosexual individuals, sharing information about their family orientation, dating partners, spouses, and children is a widely accepted, perhaps expected, behavior. The same cannot be said for people who are bisexual or homosexual. Attitudes about sexual orientation differ widely because of cultural norms, religion, age, and personal experience. Consider for a moment your own attitudes about sexual orientation. Are they the same as your parents'? Have your religious beliefs, personal experiences, or friends influenced your attitudes?

Some organizational environments are open to the variety of sexual orientations and offer such accommodation as employee benefits for same-sex partners. Other environments are closed or even hostile to anyone who is not heterosexual. This may force concealment of one's orientation or risk ridicule and/or discrimination.

Challenges and Opportunities Related to Diversity in the Health Care Setting

There are three main challenges and seven main opportunities for organizations as they manage a diverse workforce.

Challenges and Opportunities

Managing the effects of diversity in a health care setting challenges managers and staff. First is the challenge of awareness. Health care providers have to recognize the effects of a diverse workforce and patient population on their ability to deliver quality health care. Individuals tend to perceive a situation from their own perspective or world view. Ideally we put ourselves in someone else's shoes. But what if you do not know their shoes are different from yours? Even if you recognize the differences, you may not know what their shoes look or feel like. This may be true especially for therapists and other professionals who are well educated and white, because diversity is more prevalent in lower-paying or entry-level positions in health care environments, that is, custodial staff, housekeeping, and nursing and therapy aides. Therapists may not know what it is to be a member of a minority or hold these types of jobs. As will be discussed, the workplace can offer opportunities to experience being in the minority, to develop empathy, and widen one's world view.

The second challenge is desire. Once the effects of diversity are recognized, there has to be a desire to accommodate rather than assimilate diverse individuals. **Assimilation** implies that differences are minimized in favor of a common set of values and behavioral norms. Assimilation implies that diversity is unwelcome. **Accommodation** of diversity implies that differences are embraced. Diversity is encouraged as beneficial. Accommodation requires providing training and guided interactive opportunities. It must be fostered. This leads to the third challenge, resources. Awareness and desire are not enough to manage diversity. To accommodate diversity and turn challenge into opportunity takes a commitment of personal and organizational resources. Individuals must take advantage of opportunities and commit time and effort to learn about the dimensions of diversity with enough specificity to understand and accommodate individual differences. Organizations must invest in such things as:

- Surveys to determine the types and extent of an organization's customer and workforce diversity
- Planning for diversity management
- Management and employee training
- Process improvement to make employment and/or services friendly for diverse groups
- Conflict management
- Materials and qualified interpreters to accommodate for diverse languages
- Menus with ethnic specialties

Benefits of Diversity

Several researchers have proclaimed that diversity is good for business. These benefits occur at the personal, interpersonal, and organizational levels. According to Carr-Ruffino (1996), Cox (1995), and Roosevelt (1991), there are at least seven benefits of a diversity management strategy include the following:

1. *Ability to attract and retain the most creative and talented employees.* Employers who limit their pool of potential job candidates to members of a homogenous group severely limit the talent pool from which they recruit. Overall, they recruit a less talented workforce.
2. *Improved innovation by enlarging the base for new ideas.* A diverse group of individuals will view any situation from a wider range of perspectives, generating a greater number of unique ideas that may benefit an organization.
3. *More effective problem solving.* Acceptance of diversity will lead to broader participation in addressing problems and greater openness to new ideas. Here again a broader range of backgrounds and perspectives will improve problem solving.
4. *Reduced costs through improved productivity.* Accommodation of diversity will encourage employees to contribute fully to the benefit of the organization.
5. *Increased market size as a result of an enlarged market base.* An organization that actively promotes itself to diverse individuals will have a greater market base from which to draw its customers. The diversity of the market area will determine how important this is for an organization to be competitive.
6. *Improved employee and customer satisfaction.* An organization that invests in accommodations will make diverse customers and employees more comfortable and ultimately more satisfied.
7. *A higher quality of customer service.* Improved communication, recognition of unique needs, and accommodation for special requirements of customers improves quality. In health care this means better outcomes for the patients.

Diversity as an Organizational Goal

Despite the challenges, many organizations have recognized that if they embrace diversity they may avoid any negative consequences while enjoying the potential benefits. These organizations have taken strategic steps (Chapters 9 and 11) to promote awareness, understanding, and appreciation of their diverse customers and workforce. The goal of a strategic organizational diversity program should be to create an environment in which each individual can develop and realize his or her maximum potential to contribute to the organization. A diversity management program consists of systems, processes, and practices put in place to manage people so that the potential advantages of diversity are maximized within the organization while the potential disadvantages are minimized (Weltman, 1997). An organization's approach to diversity management typically follows one of the models discussed next.

The Quality and Fairness Model

The goal of this model is to seek quality and fairness in the workforce. In this approach, members of minority groups are encouraged and expected to blend in with the majority group. This model is based on the assimilation of diverse individuals. The assumption is that the primary value of diverse groups in the workplace is understanding and knowledge of people with characteristics similar to their own. Obviously, this assumption is limited and in the long run can be inconsistent with the overall goal of maximizing opportunities that may come from diversity. In this model, leaders have two major focuses. First is to right wrongs that have been propagated upon the minority groups. In that case a major focus of the organization's diversity efforts will be compliance with equal employment opportunity requirements. In 1964, Title VII of the Civil Rights Act established the Equal Employment Opportunity Commission (EEOC) to define and enforce acceptable employment policies and practices as they affect minorities and women (Chapter 3). This was an important step forward for people of color and women. It allowed people who felt they were discriminated against to bring complaints to their employers based on EEOC guidelines. Second is to establish mentoring and career development programs for specific members of previously underrepresented groups.

According to Roosevelt (1991), under this model the staff becomes more diversified but the work itself does not. This is because the quality and fairness paradigm insists that everyone is the same. With its emphasis on equal treatment, it puts pressure on employees to make sure that significant differences between them do not count. By limiting the ability of employees to acknowledge openly their work-related cultural differences, the paradigm actually undermines the organization's capacity to learn how to improve its strategies, processes, and practices (Roosevelt, 1991).

The Access and Legitimacy Model

The access and legitimacy model recognizes that the value of diversity comes from the varying perspectives and approaches to work diverse individuals bring to the workplace (Roosevelt, 1991). This model focuses on accommodation of individual diversity. Organizations who use this paradigm identify a need for a diverse workforce. A diverse workforce will understand and serve culturally diverse markets better. In this model, diversity is not a question of fairness; it is a requirement for improved business performance, relationships, and practices.

The Learning and Effectiveness Model

The learning and effectiveness model incorporates aspects of the first two models but goes beyond to analyze the benefits of diversity from the perspective of diverse approaches to the work itself (Roosevelt, 1991). A major advantage of the learning and effectiveness model is the recognition that members throughout the workforce frequently make decisions and choices based on their cultural background. Organizations that use this paradigm develop systems that incorporate employee perspectives in the primary work of the organization. This means that these companies adopt a diverse perspective of their primary tasks, market definition, strategies, products, mission, long-term vision, business practices, and organizational culture. We believe that the learning and effectiveness model is most appropriate for long-term success of health care organizations for the values it reflects and for the reality of the demographic changes noted earlier. To implement a program based on learning and effectiveness requires that eight conditions be met. Table 18.2, following Roosevelt (1991), lists conditions necessary for making the shift to a learning and effectiveness paradigm for any organization.

Elements of a Diversity Program

A diversity program has several key components. Among the components identified by Thomas and Ely (1996) are the following:

1. Fostering awareness and acceptance of individual differences
2. Fostering greater understanding of the nature and dynamics of individual differences
3. Helping members of the workforce understand their own feelings and attitudes about people who are different
4. Exploring how differences among members of the workforce can be developed into opportunities and assets for the organization

Table 18.2 Organizational Conditions Needed for a Learning and Effectiveness Diversity Model

1. The organization must understand that a diverse workforce will result in multiple perspectives and approaches to work. The organization must value this variety of opinion and insight.
2. The organization must recognize that different perspectives will present organizational learning opportunities and challenges.
3. High standards of performance must be expected from everyone within the organization (Chapter 11).
4. Personal development must be stimulated by the organizational culture (Chapters 14 and 20).
5. The organization must value openness, debate, and constructive conflict.
6. All workers must feel valued (Chapter 6).
7. There must be a well-defined and well-understood organizational mission statement (Chapter 9).
8. The organization must support decentralized decision making in a nonbureaucratic structure (Chapter 10).

Developed from Roosevelt (1991:16–33).

5. Enhancing relations between members all through the workforce who are different from each other

These examples are just a few of things an individual or organization can do to accommodate and benefit from increased diversity. External consultants often do diversity training (Chapter 34), which may touch on any or all of these key components. Health care organizations and individual providers, including physical therapists, must recognize the value of diversity training from both a management and patient care perspective. For example, physical therapists should be as well aware of cultural differences concerning touching and other intimate contact between patient and clinician as they are of the need to detect changes in the integument of patients who are persons of color (Arriaga, 1994).

However, when establishing a diversity program, management should proceed with thoughtful caution. Some attempts to address diversity in the workplace have backfired, resulting in increased tension between employees and interference with organizational success. Differences in backgrounds, as noted earlier, can lead to viewing issues and problems differently (Chapter 16). Misinterpretations can arise from differences in nonverbal communication, language (Champoux, 2000), and even inflections. On the positive side, different points of view add new thoughts to discussions. Staff members of minority groups can enhance customer satisfaction among members of their group and this can increase the volume of clientele.

Student Notes

It is no longer enough to have the knowledge and technical skills of a physical therapist. Effective delivery of physical therapy services depends on the therapist's knowledge and accommodation of the diverse characteristics that define each individual patient. Each patient assessment and plan of care must be performed and carried out with consideration for the uniqueness of the person who is being cared for. Stereotypes must be recognized for what they are, tossed aside, and the individual patient's cultural needs met while effective treatment is delivered. In the case of new graduates, age-related stereotypes are among the first that should be recognized and countered by the positive attributes gained through longevity.

Summary

The rapidly changing ethnic diversity of the U.S. population has increased our awareness of the effects of all dimensions of diversity on all aspects of life. Race, gender, religion, sexual orientation, physical ability, and age all play a role in defining who we are and how we perceive the world. Awareness of diversity is the first step toward responding to or managing the effects of diversity. Both desire to address diversity and resources to accommodate diverse needs of employees and customers must also be present. Once diversity management becomes an organizational goal, one of several approaches may be taken. Some approaches focus on assimilation of diverse people. Other approaches focus on the accommodation of diversity so that the organization

INDIVIDUAL CASE STUDY

Review the list of primary and external dimensions of diversity in the section on defining diversity. Identify one person you know who differs from you in at least three of the dimensions. Privately, write down any assumptions you have about this person. Use a work group that you both belong to as your frame of reference. Be honest with yourself. To guide your efforts consider the following questions:

1. How do you differ from each other?
2. How might those differences affect your interactions with each other in the workplace?

Are any of your assumptions based on stereotypical beliefs? Are any based on actual experience? How do you feel about working with this person? Now consider the following questions:

1. How have your assumptions influenced your views about the person?
2. How have your assumptions influenced the way you treat this person?

GROUP CASE STUDY

This is a pairs exercise intended to engage you in a deeper level of thought about diversity than the above activity. Pair up with someone who is different from you in at least two ways, for example, gender and age or race and country of birth.

Task

The task has three phases: (1) self-assessment, (2) peer assessment, and (3) group discussion. For the self-assessment, take the information in Table 18.1 and describe yourself in each of the nine categories. Then find out which of your peers you are most distinct from based on your respective self-assessments. Compare and contrast each other's responses. Determine a hierarchy of importance for your pair. Share your reasoning as to why the more important items are important to each of you. Now, as a group, summarize: discuss your reactions, emotions, things you learned, and so on and how this exercise might be modified to better meet the needs of the group.

can maximize the potential benefits that diversity may offer. The points made about cultural differences in response to authority figures, gender, and other variables should be kept in mind when issues related to job performance are raised. Keep in mind the principles introduced in this chapter as you consider the next chapter, since it will deal with employee appraisal, rewards, and corrective actions. Assessment of job performance is addressed next, along with means of rewarding job performance and corrective measures aimed at improving job performance.

REFERENCES

American Physical Therapy Association. Race/ethnic origin of members (n = 43,304). Available from http://www.apta.org/research/survey_stat/pt_demo/pt_race. Accessed 9/18/02a.

American Physical Therapy Association. Age. Available from http://www.apta.org/research/survey_stat. Accessed 9/18/02b.

American Physical Therapy Association. Women's issues in physical therapy. Available from http://www.apta.org/advocacy/womansinitiatives/womansissuesinpt. Accessed 9/18/02c.

American Physical Therapy Association. Sex of members. Available from http://www.apta.org/research/survey_stat/pt_demo/pt_sex. Accessed 9/18/02d.

Arriaga RL. Cross cultural considerations. Rehab Management. 1994;9(5):99–101.

Bottomley JM, Lewis CB. Understanding the demographics of an aging population. Geriatric rehabilitation: A clinical approach. Upper Saddle River, NJ: Prentice Hall. 2003.

Bova B, Kroth M. Workplace learning and generation X. Journal of Workplace Learning. 2001:13:57–65.

Burman L, Penner R, Steuerle G, Toder E, Moon M, Thompson L, Weisner M, Carasso A. Policy challenges posed by the aging of American. Urban Institute. May 1998.

Carr-Ruffino N. Managing diversity: People skills for a multicultural workplace. San Francisco: Thompson Executive. 1996:21–46.

Champoux JE. Organizational behavior. Essential tenets for a new millennium. Cincinnati: South-Western College. 2000.

Congressional Budget Office. Long-term budgetary pressures and policy options. Washington: U.S. Government Printing Office. March 1997.

Cox T, Jr. Diversity in organizations: Theory, research & practice. San Francisco: Berrett-Koehler. 1995.

El Nasser H, Overberg P. More people identify themselves as just "American." USA Today. June 5, 2002:A01.

Gardenswartz L, Rowe A. Managing diversity in health care. San Francisco: Jossey-Bass. 1998.

Haub C. Global and U.S. national population trends. Consequences. 1995;2.

Kovner AR, Jonas S, eds. Jonas and Kovner's health care delivery in the United States, 6th ed. New York: Springer. 1999.

Loden M, Rosener J. Workforce America! Burr Ridge, IL: Irwin. 1991.

Merriam-Webster's Collegiate Dictionary, 11th ed. Springfield, MA: Merriam-Webster, 2003.

Roosevelt TR. Beyond the race and gender: Unleashing the power of your total workforce by managing diversity. New York: American Management Association. 1991.

Roosevelt TR. The New Face of America. Time. Fall 1993 (Special Issue):14–15.

Salimbene S, Graczykowski JW. When two cultures meet: American medicine and the cultures of diverse patient populations. Hawthorne, CA: Inter-Face International. 1995.

Shi L, Singh DA. Delivering health care in America: A systems approach, 2nd ed. Gaithersburg, MD: Aspen. 2001.

Thomas DA, Ely RJ. Making differences matter: A new paradigm for managing diversity. Harvard Business Review. 1996;74:79–90.

U.S. Census Bureau. 2000 Census Data. Available from http://www.census.gov. Accessed 8/14/02.

U.S. Census Bureau. Population projections. Available from http://census.gov/population/projections/national/summary/np-15-b.txt. Accessed 10/30/03a.

U.S. Census Bureau. Population projections. Available from http://census.gov/population/projections/national/summary/np-15-g.pdf. Accessed 10/30/03b.

U.S. Census Bureau. Population projections. Available from http://census.gov/prod/1/pop/p25-1130/p251130a.pdf. Accessed 10/30/03c.

U.S. Census Bureau. The American community survey. Available from http://www.census.gov/acs/www/Downloads/SQuest.pdf. Accessed 10/05/03d.

Weil PW. Exploring of the gender gap and health care management. Health care Executive. 1996; Nov/Dec:18–21.

Weltman B. The big idea book for new business owners. New York: Macmillan Spectrum. 1997.

More Information Related to This Chapter

See the APTA Web site. In particular, see the House of Delegates policies regarding minority affairs including affirmative action, cultural competence, and nondiscrimination (http://www.apta.org/pdfs/governance/hod/policies.pdf).

A discussion of 29 contemporary issues related to advancing the status of women in physical therapy is available from http:www.apta.org/About/special_interests. Minority issues are also addressed at this site.

For a practical guide to managing diversity in the workplace, consult Arrendondo P. Successful diversity management initiatives: A blueprint for planning and implementation. Thousand Oaks, CA: Sage. 1996.

For a summary of research on self-directed work groups, see Langfred CW, Shanley MT. Small group research: Autonomous teams and progress on issues of context and levels of analysis. In Golembiewski RT, ed. Handbook of organizational behavior 2nd ed. New York: Marcel Dekker. 2001:81–111.

Chapter 19

Employee Appraisal, Recognition, and Corrective Action

Learning Objectives

1. Compare the perspectives of a health care manager and a direct report regarding performance appraisal and feedback.
2. Analyze alternative methods of conducting performance appraisals.
3. Explain the relationship between performance appraisal and employee recognition.
4. Discuss the relationship of performance expectations, performance standards, and competencies.
5. Summarize the purposes and indications for coaching, mentoring, and other managerial options to improve work behaviors.

Key Words

360-degree feedback, coaching, compensation, corrective action, job competencies, job description, mentoring, performance appraisal, performance discrepancy, performance expectations, performance goals, performance standards, recognition

Introduction

Few of us enjoy evaluating the performance of other people. Even fewer enjoy being evaluated. Unfortunately, as uncomfortable as it may be, performance appraisal is essential to maximize the performance of an individual employee (Chapter 15). Here is the good news: the discomfort of performance appraisal can be minimized if management prepares well and embraces appraisal as an ongoing activity rather than an annual event. Organizations invest time and resources in the orientation, training, and development of employees. This investment can be maximized if employees know what is expected of them and receive objective ongoing feedback about their performance (Chapter 15).

Performance Appraisal

Annual employee performance appraisal is without a doubt one of management's most important and least favorite activities (Anonymous, 2001). It is often time consuming, anxiety producing, and questionably effective in improving employee performance. **Performance appraisal** is the act of comparing an employee's performance to management expectations for their job. Because employee capabilities vary, so does their ability to perform a specific job. For this reason, managers often deal with an assessment tool that gauges performance on a continuum of exceptional to unacceptable with an identified minimum acceptable level of performance. This rating continuum allows for the identification of performance deficits, opportunities for performance improvement, and recognition of exceptional performance. Both the employer and the employee benefit from the insight that this approach can provide (Lachman, 1984). There is no one best performance appraisal system that works in every situation. Regardless of the system used, an appraisal system should have the following characteristics:

- A common set of expectations shared by employee and employer
- Employee perception of an accurate and equitable way to measure performance
- The information required to manage and improve employee performance

The negative aspects of performance appraisal can be minimized for managers and staff and the positive aspects can be maximized through effective planning. Performance appraisal should not be a random act of feedback from manager to employee that occurs once a year. Rather, it should be an ongoing process that involves the manager, employee, peers, and even customers. The appraisal should be founded on specific, clearly understood performance expectations. Tools such as performance standards should be developed to measure performance in an objective and consistent manner. Feedback should be dynamic, occurring regularly or at least at regular intervals. Potential rewards and consequences should also be agreed upon in advance. In this way the annual performance appraisal is the culmination of a process, a time to summarize the past and plan for the future.

Setting Performance Expectations

Setting **performance expectations** starts with a well-written **job description** (Chapter 14). The job description should define the following:

- Applicable work standards
- Decision-making authority
- Job duties
- Methods by which work will be coordinated
- Minimum job requirements
- Organizational relationships
- Responsibility for the work of others

Elements of the job description should be defined with enough specificity to delineate the tasks to be performed. **Performance standards** expand upon the information in the job description by defining how the organization expects the duties to be performed and how performance will be measured. Figure 19.1 shows how a specific job duty, such as patient evaluation, can be further defined using a range of performance descriptions. In this example, the performance descriptions have been rated on a five-point scale. Level 3, "meets expectations," represents the minimum acceptable level of performance. It may be acceptable for employees who are new to a job to perform below the minimum for some specified period. When an employee continues to perform below the minimum, management intervention is required.

Job competencies are a form of performance standard. Competencies typically incorporate knowledge, skill, and professional behaviors (Salvatori, Baptiste, Ward, 2000). For example, knowledge of age-related characteristics that affect patient behavior and communication is essential for effective delivery of physical therapy. A therapist may be evaluated on his or her knowledge of age-related competencies as well as the ability to apply this knowledge in the care of the patient. Staff competencies are also important for institutional accreditation (Chapter 32).

Performance goals are another factor considered in employee appraisal. Performance goals measure outcomes and are often specific to an employee or a work group rather than a job class. For example, a physical therapist may have a performance goal to complete all patient discharge summaries within 2 days of the discharge date. Another example is a project team (Chapter 17) whose shared performance goal is to open a new rehabilitation clinic on schedule and within budget. Performance goals often change as they are achieved or the needs of the organization change.

Comparing actual performance against performance standards (including competencies) and goals lets employees' appraisal reflect their competency to do the work, the way they get the work done, and the outcomes they achieve. Scott and Einstein (2001) stress that the importance of this broad approach becomes even more important when work teams are used to achieve

I. Basic Duties:

A. Evaluation and Treatment:

2. Performs comprehensive physical therapy evaluations.

Performance Rating and Description:

Level 5 Exceptional Performance

Independently and appropriately selects, performs advanced physical therapy evaluation procedures or recommends medical evaluation procedures.

Level 4 Exceeds Expectations

Recognizes the need to perform advanced physical therapy evaluation procedures. Seeks input from others on the appropriate implementation of unfamiliar procedures, such as pediatric evaluation, quality of movement evaluation, and advanced orthopedic evaluation.

Level 3 Meets Expectations

Completes all basic physical therapy evaluations independently and in a timely manner. Refer to department policies for a description of basic evaluation procedures.

Level 2 Meets Some Expectations

Occasionally requires assistance to select appropriate basic evaluation procedures. Sometimes requires assistance with the performance of basic evaluation procedures.

Level 1 Unsatisfactory Performance

Consistently requires assistance to select appropriate basic evaluation procedures and assistance with the performance of these procedures.

Figure 19.1. Example of performance rating scale with performance standard descriptions. (Modified from Nosse and Friberg, 1992:85.)

organizational goals. Take for example an employee who is highly competent and produces great work but who cannot complete the work on time. Because the employee is part of a project team, his or her poor performance has the potential to reduce the entire team's effectiveness. If the appraisal only considers competency and quality of the work, this important performance issue may be overlooked. Many managers struggle with how to incorporate work team performance into an individual employee's appraisal. While it seems easy enough, organizational structures do not always support this approach. One of the biggest concerns is the close relationship between rewards and group performance. The American culture places a high value on individualism (see Chapter 1). It is hard for both managers and employees to view individual performance as subordinate to group performance. This is true particularly when (1) the individual is perceived to be performing better than the group as a whole and (2) performance appraisal is tied to employee recognition.

The adoption of performance standards and competencies for a specific position is often a collaborative effort. Administration, human resources, occupational health and safety, and department management may all contribute to the list. Potential participants who may be overlooked are the employees themselves. In our experience, involvement of the employee in the determination of performance standards and the method of measuring performance has the potential to improve performance. First, the employee will most likely have a better understanding of what is expected than otherwise. Second, the employee is much more likely to believe that the system is an accurate and equitable way to assess, measure, and evaluate performance.

Performance standards and competencies can be assessed in a variety of ways:

- Customer feedback
- Documentation review
- Observation
- Peer review
- Subordinate review
- Self-report
- Written test

Regardless of the assessment method, performance standards and competencies are the benchmarks against which an employee's performance can be compared. When the same standards and competencies are used to assess all employees in a job class, such as all physical therapists in staff positions, the performances can be compared. Management can use the outcomes as a standardized rating system to identify areas of overall performance deficiency for the job class. Consider a rating system in which level 3 is the minimum acceptable level of performance. If the average rating of all physical therapists for any performance standard is below level 3, management knows that some intervention is needed. This knowledge can be invaluable for selecting continuing education and training (Chapter 20).

360-Degree Feedback

Introduced in the 1990s, **360-degree feedback** refers to several evaluators using feedback tools to evaluate employee performance. These tools integrate management, peer, subordinate, and self-report feedback into a composite assessment for evaluation. The 360-degree feedback data collection tool is a standardized list of knowledge, skills, and professional behaviors. Typically, several individuals, including the employee's manager, subordinates, peers, and sometimes customers rate an employee. The employee also completes a self-rating using the same tool. The ratings are consolidated into a single report that allows the evaluator (manager) to compare the employee's perceptions to those of the other evaluators. The manager and the employee self-report can be identified. The ranking of other contributors is anonymous. This information may be incorporated into the performance appraisal.

There is much debate over the use of the 360-degree feedback in the formal assessment process. Peiperl (2001) has identified four paradoxes that may affect the value of the 360-degree feedback tool in employee appraisal:

1. *Roles*. Peers who complete 360-degree feedback struggle with the balance between their role of colleague and judge.
2. *Group performance*. As organizations become more focused on the use of work teams, 360-degree feedback remains focused on the performance of the individual.
3. *Measurement*. The 360-degree feedback tools are standardized, yet we believe individualized feedback has the greatest potential to affect performance.
4. *Rewards*. During the formal evaluation most employees are focused less on the feedback than on the rewards. Thus, the value of the 360-degree feedback may be missed.

Scott and Einstein (2001) suggest that 360-degree feedback is best if administered on a regular basis, used for employee development and setting performance goals. In all types of appraisal situations keep in mind the communication suggestions offered in Chapter 16 and understand how diversity may influence performance and its appraisal (Chapter18).

No Surprises

No discussion of performance appraisal would be complete without talking about the *zero surprise imperative*. Formal performance appraisals are typically done at the end of a hire probationary period, at the conclusion of a major project, or annually. At the time of a formal performance appraisal, no employee should be surprised by management's appraisal of his or her performance. As mentioned earlier, employee appraisal should be a dynamic process, with performance expectations, potential rewards, and consequences agreed upon after preparatory work is done. Now the actual employee appraisal begins. Management feedback to employees should occur regularly, or at least at regular intervals. Feedback can be formal or occur during the course of day. Feedback should be timely, given as close to the time of performance as possible. This is important when performance is not meeting expectations so that adjustments can be made immediately. It is also important when performance is exceeding expectations so that desirable behaviors can be reinforced. In this way the annual performance appraisal is the culmination of a process, a summary of past feedback. There should be no surprises. There should be a common understanding on the standards of performance (for example, Fig. 19.1). The standards should be shared with all who are to be appraised, clarified as needed, reviewed periodically, and applied fairly.

The Link Between Performance and Recognition

Employee appraisal is often used as a basis for employee recognition and reward. **Recognition** may take many forms. The most common is the link between performance ratings and **compensation** adjustments. These are terms used by organizations that formalize the relationship between individual employee performance ratings and annual pay adjustments:

- *Performance bonus.* A one-time payment awarded for achieving a specific performance objective. Performance bonuses may be awarded on an individual basis, to a work group, or to all employees. A therapist's end-of-year bonus for exceeding productivity targets is an example of a performance bonus.
- *Merit pay or pay for performance.* Annual pay increases determined at least in part by the employee's annual performance rating.

Table 19.1 Merit Pay Grid

Performance Rating	*Merit Increase (%)*
0.00–0.99	0
1.00–1.99	0
2.00–2.99	1.0–2.0
3.00–3.99	2.1–3.0
4.00–4.50	3.1–4.5
4.51–5.00	4.6–5.5

Table 19.1 is an example of a merit pay scale. The assumption underlying pay linked to performance is reasonable: employees will work harder and perform better if they can see a direct relationship between their effort and their reward (Chapter 15). We generally agree, with a few caveats:

1. Employees must understand what is expected in advance.
2. Employees must believe that the system is an accurate and equitable way to measure their performance.
3. Tools such as a job description, performance standards, and goals must be used as benchmarks against which performance is measured.
4. Management must appraise all employees in the same way and award pay increases according to a preestablished formula (Table 19.1) without exceptions.

In addition to compensation many types of recognition can be tied to the appraisal. These alternative methods are increasingly important as health care organizations face diminishing amounts of reimbursement and find it more difficult to pay market-competitive salaries or award pay increase (Chapters 27 and 28). Recognition (internal or external), increased responsibility, promotion, prestigious job assignments, learning opportunities, mentoring opportunities, flexible schedules, new equipment or facilities, and time off are some of the common forms of rewards that are used to motivate high-performing employees. Having a variety of recognition methods increases the likelihood of having something that is valued by most employees.

Performance Management

Managing employee performance is a key role for the health care manager (Waldroop and Butler, 1996). A **performance discrepancy** occurs any time an employee is doing something that is different from the expected performance. If an employee is performing better than expected, the discrepancy is positive and the employee should be supported and encouraged toward continued development (Chapter 20). Most often managers are called upon to support an employee so that good performance can become exceptional. Occasionally, managers must address situations involving negative performance discrepancies.

Assuming that the identification of a negative performance discrepancy is based on an objective performance appraisal, the manager must correct the discrepancy (**corrective action**) or replace the employee. The first step toward resolution is to determine the cause of unacceptable performance. Common causes of unacceptable performance generally fit into one of three categories: (1) employee ability, (2) inadequate support, or (3) inadequate effort (Lachman, 1984). Resolution of performance discrepancies is best carried out as a collaborative process between the manager and the employee. Figure 19.2 presents a performance discrepancy analysis and remediation process for consideration. Using this figure, the manager and employee are guided to move through a series of remediation steps until the discrepancy is resolved, the employee is transferred to another job within the organization, or employment is terminated.

When organizational obstacles and ability have been eliminated as the cause for poor performance, the manager may wish to coach the employee toward improved performance. **Coaching** is an interactive process used to analyze and improve performance. Coaching should be undertaken with the intent of making the most of a valuable resource, the employee (Chapter 20). Coaching takes time, and there is no guarantee of a successful outcome (Waldroop and Butler, 1996). These seven steps enhance the probability of success:

1. The manager must accurately identify the discrepancy between performance and expectations.
2. The manager must help the employee understand why the discrepancy is important.
3. The employee must agree that a discrepancy exists.
4. The manager and employee must work collaboratively to develop shared strategies for performance improvement. The employee must commit to an improvement plan.
5. The manager and employee must agree on deadlines for improvement. The manager must follow up on a predetermined schedule.
6. Clear and meaningful consequences for lack of improvement must be established.
7. The manager must recognize improvement as it occurs.

When an employee demonstrates exceptional performance, a manager has a unique opportunity to contribute to the future of both the organization and the employee through encouragement, support, and the opportunity for development. This type of supportive interaction is **mentoring.** Mentoring can be defined as the personal and professional development of the protégé under the guidance and experience of a more clinically mature, knowledgeable individual in that profession (Gandy, 1993). Mentoring has both costs and benefits.

These are costs of mentoring:

- Balance of time spent developing protégé versus continued personal development (mentor)
- Risk of backlash from protégé's mistakes (mentor)
- Risk of the protégé leaving company before completion of commitment to mentor
- Time commitment and availability (both)

These are benefits of mentoring:

- Access to network and specialized experience (protégé)
- Affirmation of skills (protégé)

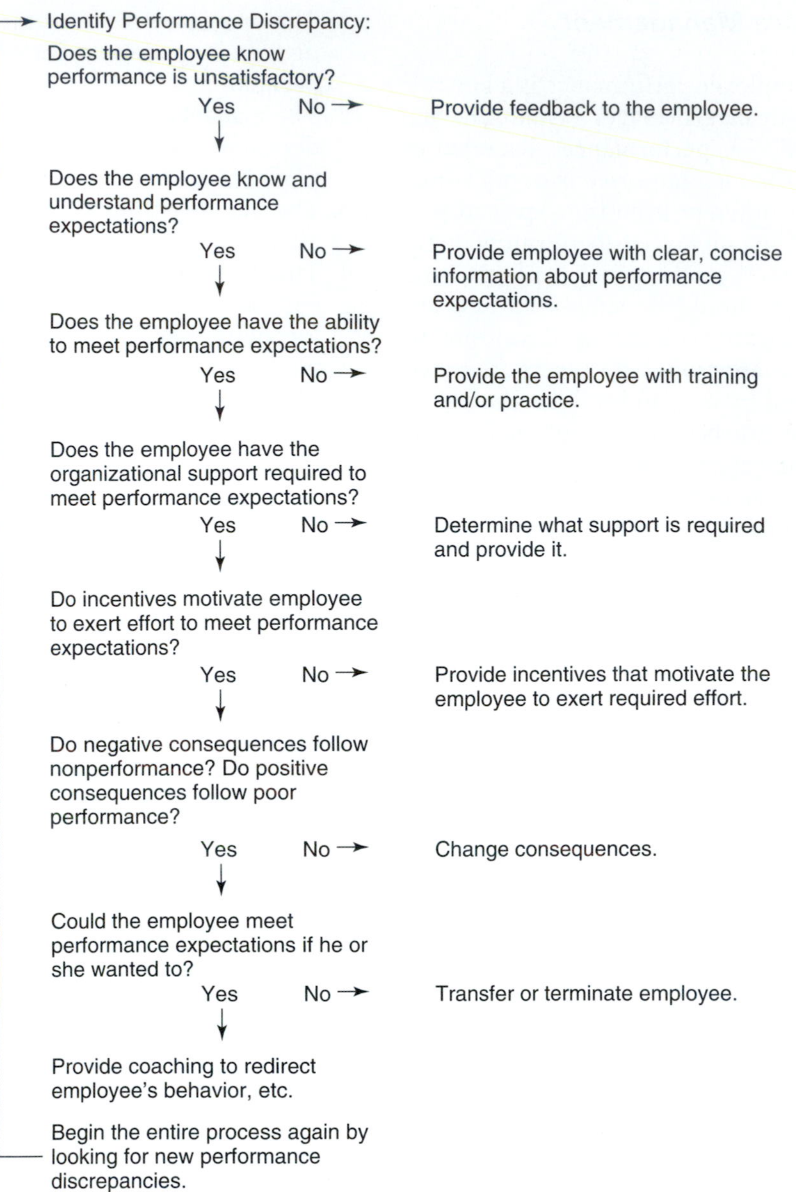

Figure 19.2. Performance discrepancy analysis. (Modified with permission from Lachman VD, [1984:11] and Nosse and Friberg, [1992:87].)

- Decreased job turnover (protégé)
- Growth, development, and excellence maintained in the profession as a whole (mentor)
- Opportunity to debate and discuss specific professional issues (both)
- Professional and leadership development (both)
- And many others...

Both coaching and mentoring can contribute to the success of an organization because both result in more productive employees. Exceptional managers may coach and mentor to some degree with all of their employees. It can also be rewarding to help another person (Waldroop and Butler, 1996). Organizations invest time and resources in the orientation, training, and development of employees. This investment increases an employee's value to the organization. Given the costs, it is in the employer's best interest to retain employees whose performance meets, or with the support of management, exceeds expectations.

Student Notes

While management typically carries out performance appraisal, staff often participate in the appraisal of students, subordinates, and support staff. At times, staff members are also asked to provide input for appraisal of their managers and peers (360-degree feedback). Feedback should be thoughtful and based only on direct observation of work. The concepts discussed in this chapter should provide guidance to anyone engaged in self-appraisal or the appraisal of others in the workplace. The topics should help students understand both sides of the issues when their own performance is appraised.

Summary

In this chapter we discuss the responsibilities of a health care manager related to appraisal of employee performance. Methods of performance appraisal include 360-degree feedback. The relationship between employee rewards and appraisal are discussed with special note that recognition goes beyond compensation. You should clearly understand the importance of ongoing communication as a key to reinforcing desired behaviors. When performance gaps do exist, they should be addressed through analysis of observable behaviors and management intervention aimed at advancing performance to an acceptable level. Mentoring, coaching, and corrective action may be required.

In this chapter the discussion on training and development opportunities are delimited by the needs of the employer. The training and development provided by or paid for by an organization to enhance employee performance is done to meet departmental and organizational needs. Ideally, what the employer and employee need coincide.

For various reasons, it is unusual to work for one employer throughout one's clinical career. Over time, physical therapists accumulate new knowledge and skills that are learned and mastered in their various workplaces. It is wise to manage one's own career development because of employment uncertainties in health care associated with mergers, restructuring, and other factors. From a professional perspective, career development is a personal responsibility. Career development throughout one's working life is the focus of the next chapter. Much of what has been discussed in Chapters 14 to 19 are applied on an individual level. Business principles are used to create a desired professional future.

INDIVIDUAL CASE STUDY

Do It All Physical Therapy, Inc., has just adopted a 360-degree feedback tool to obtain a well-balanced appraisal of its employees. You have been given six copies of the tool to distribute to peers, subordinates, and/or customers so they can complete an assessment of your performance. Assume that there are several individuals in each category from whom to choose. Their feedback will remain anonymous to you and your manager. What will you consider when you select your six evaluators?

GROUP CASE STUDY

Groups of six members are needed for this case. Each member should take the role of a manager of a department of physical therapy. From this management perspective, consider the following scenario and respond to the questions at the end.

Situation

By measuring actual performance against performance standards (including competencies) and goals, an employee appraisal reflects competency to do the work, the way the work gets done, and the outcomes. Scott and Einstein stress that the importance of this broad approach becomes even more important when work teams are used to achieve organizational goals. Recall the example of the employee who is highly competent and produces excellent clinical outcomes but is unable to complete the work on time. Assume that this employee's performance has hampered his or her work team's performance. The team has not met its performance goals.

Task

Put yourself in management's shoes. Should a high-performing employee be downgraded because the assigned work team failed to meet performance goals? In other words, to what extent would you use work team performance in the appraisal of this employee? Even more complicated is the question, to what extent would you use work team performance in appraising all of the members of the team?

REFERENCES

Anonymous. Conducting effective performance appraisals. Clinical Leadership & Management Review. 2001;15:348–352.

Gandy J. Mentoring. Orthopedic Practice. 1993;5:6–9.

Lachman VD. Increasing productivity through performance evaluation. Journal of Nursing Administration. 1984;14:7–14.

Nosse LJ, Friberg DG. Management principles for physical therapists. Baltimore: Williams & Wilkins. 1992.

Peiperl MA. Getting 360 degrees feedback right. Harvard Business Review. 2001;79:142–147, 177.

Salvatori P, Baptiste S, Ward M. Development of a tool to measure clinical competence in occupational therapy: A pilot study? Canadian Journal of Occupational Therapy. 2000; 67: 51–60.

Scott SG, Einstein WO. Strategic performance appraisal in team-based organizations: One size does not fit all. Academy of Management Executives. 2001;15:107–116.

Waldroop J, Butler T. The executive as coach. Harvard Business Review. 1996; Nov-Dec: 111–117.

MORE INFORMATION RELATED TO THIS CHAPTER

Assistance in analyzing job tasks for job descriptions or identifying components of tasks that might need improvement, including mentoring and coaching, can be drawn from Fine SA, Getkate M. Benchmark tasks for job analysis. A guide for functional job analysis (FJA) scales. Mahwah, NJ: Lawrence Erlbaum. 1995.

An interesting perspective on management of human resources in health care settings under various environmental conditions can be found in Ginter PM, Swayne LM, Duncan WJ. Strategic management of health care organizations, 3rd ed. Malden, MA: Blackwell. 1998:341–366.

Employee appraisal in nonprofit organizations is addressed in Koteen J. Strategic management in public and nonprofit organizations. Managing public concerns in an era of limits, 2nd ed. Westport, CN: Praeger. 1997:314–338.

A wider perspective of human resource management that includes labor laws can be found in Longest BB, Jr., Rakich JS, Darr K. Managing health services organizations and systems, 4th ed. Baltimore: Health Professions Press. 2000:531–588.

McConnell's fifth edition contains a chapter on employee appraisals: McConnell CR. The effective health care supervisor, 5th ed. Gaithersburg, VA: Aspen. 2002:174–195.

The APTA's mentoring link is a helpful source for basic information on the mentor–protégé concept, and it is a starting point for finding or becoming a mentor (http:www.apta.org/advocacy/womaninitiatives/membersmentor).

Career Development Is a Life-Long Process

Learning Objectives

1. Discuss the four components of organizational career development presented in this chapter from the perspectives of a manager and a staff member.
2. Evaluate career development as it relates to high-performance health care organizations, first- and middle-level managers, staff professionals, and nonprofessional staff members.
3. Compare on-site and off-site career development options a manager may consider for his or her own career development and for the development of direct reports.
4. Use a SWOT analysis and the futuring model presented in this chapter to develop a long-term management-related career development plan to increase career relevant knowledge, enhance work-related motivation, improve ability to self-assess, and improve job skills.
5. Use a SWOT analysis and the futuring model presented in this chapter to develop a long-term career development plan for staff personnel.

Key Words

Career, career development, development, direct report, futuring, high-performance organization, knowledge, motivation, self-awareness, skill, SWOT, training

Introduction

In the broadest sense a **career** can be described as a cumulative series of work and non–work-related experiences that continually modify one's knowledge, skills, and perspectives (Hall and Associates, 1996). Under this broad view this chapter might have been titled Life and Career Development. To take this perspective would require that all experiences, that is, work, family, recreational, social, and so on, be considered. Space being limited, and the emphasis of this book being management and business matters, the discussion of career will be limited to choices and behaviors that have a direct connection to work and the workplace.

In this chapter, the word **development** generally refers to a person's work-related choices and behaviors over time (Issacson and Brown, 1993). **Career development** means the organizational and personal management of a cumulative series of work experiences that add to one's knowledge, motivation, perspectives, skills, and job performance. Development in these areas can benefit health care customers because they are likely to be best cared for by service providers who are motivated to practice with current knowledge and improved skill. For a manager, improvement in these areas can enhance the performance of those they supervise, that is, their **direct reports**. Organizations that support career development throughout their workforce benefit by being able to shape the workforce to meet future demands. Because an organization and its individual employees are all stakeholders when it comes to career development, the following discussion integrates concepts from organizational development and personal career development literature. This chapter addresses career development options for managers as well as what managers can do to develop their direct reports.

Rationale for Career Development

Today's business environment is dynamic and unpredictable, and it continually generates new information (Mohrman and Cohen, 1998). The word chaos has been applied to many aspects of the health care industry (Kongstvedt, 2002). In a turbulent environment laws, revenue, competitors, technology, communication systems, research evidence, and other areas change constantly (Chapters 10, 11, and 31). This means there is a continual need to modify knowledge, skills, and perspectives (Hall and Associates, 1996) to compete, maintain a competitive advantage, or just survive as an organization or as a manager. Change is constant, so there is a continual need for the acquisition of new knowledge, skills, and other career-advancing assets. This cycling of knowledge and skill that become outdated and are replaced by new knowledge and skill is very much like what is described by the product life cycle model (Chapter 23). In this cycle a product declines in sales volume over time in stages: introductory, growth, maturation, and decline. For illustration, a product life cycle and a career life cycle are compared in Figure 20.1.

Number 1 in the upper figure marks the introduction of a new service or product and the introduction of new knowledge and skill in the lower figure. Numbers 2-3 in the upper figure reflect sales growth, and possibly profit, and the achievement of a plateau in these areas. Similarly, 2-3 in the lower figure depicts progressive increases in the frequency of use of new knowledge and skill and a point of peak usage. Numbers 4-5 in the upper figure represent a progressive decline in sales volume, and possibly profit. In the lower fig-

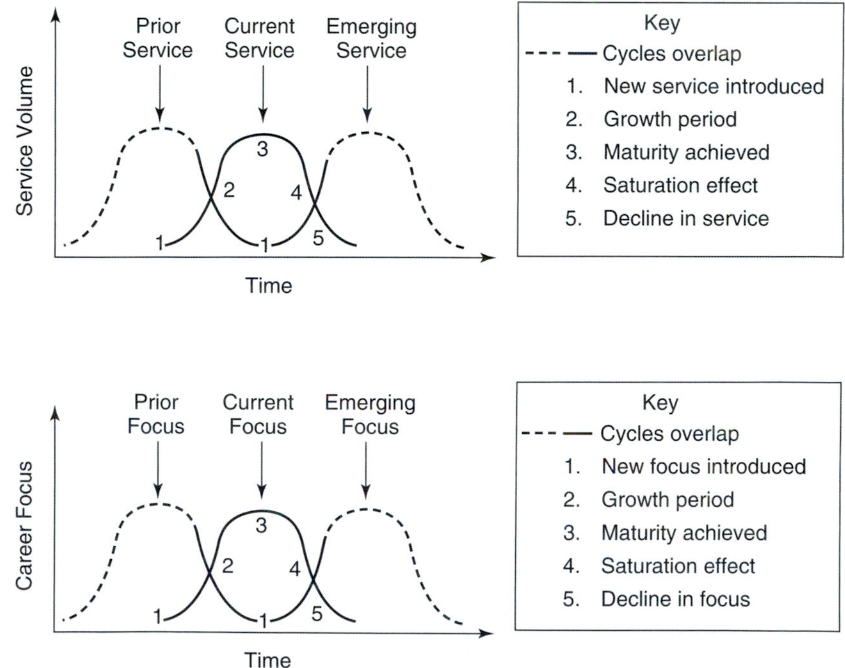

Figure 20.1. Similarities between successive service/product life cycle curves (top) and changes in career focus/emphasis over time.

ure 4-5 indicate less frequent use of what was new knowledge and skill. The intersection of the curves indicates that old and new products, and old and new knowledge and skill, are equal in volume or use, respectively. After this point, the old service, product, knowledge and skills is replaced by the new. Thus, old is cyclically replaced by new.

From an organizational perspective it is crucial to recruit, develop, and retain managers (Chapter 14) who are adaptable, flexible, and willing and able to acquire new knowledge and improve their skills (Major, 2000) throughout their tenure. These are the desirable attributes of employees sought by **high-performance organizations** (Chapter 18). The culture of a high-performance organization is typified by encouraging speedy reactions to opportunities and threats (Chapter 11), flexibility, allocation of discretionary power to act, and decentralization (Major, 2000). High-performance organizations can respond quickly when change is called for. In such organizations the status quo is not an option. High-performance organizations therefore foster development in their workforce so they can meet performance expectations in an information-packed environment (Major, 2000). They make meaningful efforts (incentives) to retain high-performing management and staff personnel.

Not all health care organizations are high performance oriented. Some health care organizations maintain bureaucratic or line and box characteristics. These characteristics include centralization of power, tiers of management, and relatively long reaction and response times (Chapter 10). In traditional organizational structures and cultures, individual managers have little discretionary leeway. Nonetheless, speedy processing, flexibility, and a desire to learn are desirable characteristics of personnel in any work setting.

Career Development From an Organizational Perspective

From an organizational standpoint the primary purpose of training and development of human resources is to improve job performance in terms of productivity and quality. Organizational career development activities should focus on these four areas:

1. **Knowledge**: Information necessary to carry out usual work activities (Wexley and Latham, 1991).
2. **Motivation**: The degree to which a person is driven to work hard and well (Rainey, 2001) to achieve a valued goal (Locke, 2001). (Chapters 6 and 26).
3. **Self-awareness**: Understanding of work responsibilities, the relationship between what management says and what management does, how personal actions affect others, and others' view of you (Wexley and Latham, 1991).
4. **Skill**: The psychomotor ability to apply knowledge to carry out job tasks safely, efficiently, and effectively (Wexley and Latham, 1991).

Management efforts to bring about desirable changes in the four areas can take place at more than one level of the organization. **Training** programs directed at all organizational members cover diversity, introduction of new services, new emergency procedures, sexual harassment, and use of new software. These types of programs are usually conducted to meet organizational needs associated with accreditation, governmental requirements, risk management, and other needs of the whole organization. Human resource personnel are among those who handle general training. To varying degrees, human resource departments also participate in development efforts. Technically, training and development differ. Training is the organization, delivery, and evaluation of instructional programs. Development refers to growth in one or more of the four core areas, that is, knowledge, motivation, self-awareness, or skill (Wexley and Latham, 1991) that facilitate improvement in job performance.

Participation in development activities can occur at the workplace (on site), away from the workplace (off site), or both. One can pursue for personal enhancement career development activities not related to current job needs. The lists that follow contain numerous career development strategies for managers (personal career development) and staff alike.

On-Site Career Development Opportunities

On-site programs are provided at the workplace. On-site programs are usually less costly than off-site programs. Less time is taken from direct care, attendance is usually high, and the content and quality of programs can be monitored. Copies of presentation materials are reusable and available for review. New skills are learned in the environment where they will be applied. This may enhance carry-over and shorten the time it takes to integrate the new information into daily work efforts.

A manager should be aware of several criticisms of on-site programs. A common criticism is unevenness in instructional quality when staff members teach. When clinical staff members are called upon to share their knowledge and skills with others, a range of teaching abilities become evident. Some do well. Some do not. Management can provide teaching tips in a variety of ways to help bring about a consistent level of performance. There is often some anxiety associated with teaching peers. Some staff members may be highly motivated to share knowledge, while others refuse to go in front of a group. Management can counsel anxious staff members, bolster a staff member's self-confidence through positive feedback, or mentor the individual. Peers sometimes do not respect the knowledge and skills of their colleagues, and they show their disinterest or boredom through body language and sometimes verbally. A manager can make clear that the intent of sharing new information is to stimulate discussion and alter practice to better meet the needs of consumers and the organization. Disagreement is a healthy way to deepen thought and sharpen responses. It is as much the listener's as the presenter's responsibility to make a session interactive and intellectually stimulating. Finally, some competent and experienced staff members perceive their job as treating patients and nothing more. A manager can provide stimulus for staff members with a limited perspective of professional behavior by discussing criteria for promotion, professional obligations, and the need to bring all staff members up to the level this person has attained. On-site training can be used many other ways besides peer education to increase knowledge, job skills, motivation, and self-awareness.

Additional on-site development opportunities in health care settings are:

- **Career ladder**: Opportunities for advancement within an organization based on criteria such as specific skills, knowledge, experience, and personal attributes. Advancement may include a new title, new responsibilities, new lines of communication, and increased compensation.
- **Case presentation or case report**: A management issue, such as how to schedule existing staff to cover patient care services 7 days a week, or a direct care matter, such as sharing something unique about a patient's response to treatment over time (Dahl, 2001). Recommendations can be supported by an evidence-based data search (Riolo, 2002).
- **Coaching**: One-to-one interactions between a manager and a direct report intended to improve understanding and performance, for example, clarify performance expectations, shape attitudes, foster growth in knowledge, and advance skills (see Chapter 19).
- **Cotreatment or patient exchange**: A supervising therapist and a less experienced therapist treat the same patient with the intent of jointly determining how to improve the care of the patient.
- **Computer-based instruction**: Educational software that provides information, tests the student, grades the degree to which the information has been learned, and provides feedback regarding answers.
- **Distance learning**: Computer or real-time video communication between a learner and an instructor (e.g., via e-mail, streaming video, instruction). One site is http://www.hippo-therapy@wmich.edu.
- **E-group or chat group**: Membership in an on-line group for the purpose of reading communications on a variety of topics with options to participate in dialog and solicit response. One site is http://www.aptasoa.org.
- **Full text documents on-line**: Access complete journal articles from a variety of

sources (some require paid subscriptions, e.g., http://www.ptjournal.org).

- **Consultant**: Contract with someone deemed capable of fulfilling a specific need or set of needs that cannot be met by organizational members, for example, http://www.PTManager.com.
- **Continuing education programs**: Arrange for educational programming on site for organization members or on a fee basis to the public, with a reduced or waived fee for organization members.
- **In-service programs**: Presentations to organization members, usually during the workday, by staff members or invited speakers with special knowledge, skill, or experience.
- **Programs by experts in the organization**: Programs formulated by the human resources department to meet the needs of the organization or a segment of the organization using the expertise of organization members.
- **Instruction in observation coupled with observation of exemplars**: Identification of ideal behaviors and opportunities to observe the behaviors being demonstrated (behavior modeling).
- **Invited presenters**: Guest speakers (paid or voluntary) sharing knowledge, skills, or experiences considered useful to help advance departmental or organizational plans.
- **Job rotation and job enrichment**: Opportunities for a series of assignments in various parts of departmental or organizational operations for specific durations to take advantage of knowledge and skills or to expand them, such as for cross-training, changing team membership, adding new responsibilities.
- **Journal or book club**: Regular group meetings for critically analyzing, interpreting, and discussing specific articles, chapters, or books read by members with the intent of determining the applicability of the information at work.
- **Interdisciplinary or interdepartmental meetings**: Formal and informal interactions between functionally related group members for improving performance in areas of mutual interest.
- **Mentors**: A mentor is commonly a person with long experience in a department who has management responsibility and who accepts the responsibility to nurture a younger, less experienced member of the organization, known as a protégé (Chapter 19). The arrangement may be formal, that is, assigned by someone with authority to make such assignments, or informal, that is, a relationship arrived at through the initiative of either party.
- **Mental practice**: Cognitively reiterating sequences, for example, how to proceed in a gross screening examination or the sensations associated with a "good" performance; can lead to improved efficiency when the behavior is actually carried out.
- **Networking**: Contact to share knowledge, perspectives, and understanding; to attain increased recognition or exposure; and to make socially and professionally beneficial contacts.
- **On-line databases**. Health care databases available to the public, including government (e.g.,http://www.hhs.gov) and private sites (e.g., http://www.mayoclinic.org). Some sites require subscriptions for key information (e.g., http://www.aha.org).
- **On-the-job training**: Assign a new employee to observe and work with an experienced employee or manager to learn the other person's job.
- **Opportunities to become a protégé in a mentoring relationship**: A protégé is someone who is nurtured, advised, supported, taught, shown the ropes, introduced to helpful others, and socialized to the organizational culture by a willing, usually older experienced member of the organization, that is, a mentor. Consult http://www.apta.org/advocacy/womaninitiatives/membersmentor.
- **Peer assessment**: Purposeful observation and discussion (formal or informal) of one colleague by another to evaluate knowledge, skill, and other variables related to job performance (Chapter 19).
- **Periodic performance appraisal**: Formal evaluative exchange between manager and staff regarding the level of job performance demonstrated according to previously identified objective criteria (Chapter 19).

- **Programmed learning materials**: Hard-copy materials that provide information and examples. They pose questions based on the material for the reader to answer, identify the correct response and its rationale, and analyze the shortcomings of each of the incorrect options (Stahl and Hennes, 1980).
- **Research**: Any planned observation of the natural state or the effects of manipulation of conditions done with the intent of developing new understanding or knowledge (Levine, 1975).
- **Rounds**: Formal multidisciplinary review and discussion of patients in their presence.
- **Self-assessment inventories**: Questionnaires whose responses can be measured and scaled in terms of the level of importance, degree of agreement or disagreement, capability, and so on or that define beliefs, (Longest, Rakich, Darr, 2000).
- **Video conference**: Two-way real-time visual and audio contact via computer between individuals or groups within the facility with others at different locations.
- **Video and audio tapes**: Instructional video or audio tapes purchased or made in house to increase knowledge, skills, or motivation or shape other behaviors (http://www.cms.gov/OASIS/hhtrain.asp, http://www.apta.org/Products services/Online shopping).

Some on-site activities can be arranged in collaboration with the human resources department, for example, presentations by internal experts, payment for distance learning coursework, and video conferencing. Some activities, such as coaching, job rotation, and interdepartmental meetings, may be departmental management prerogatives. Some on-site activities can be self-initiated, such as entering into a protégé–mentor arrangement, mental practice, and watching or listening to video or audio tapes, respectively, when there is time. The list of potential on-site career development activities is extensive. Even so, few organizations can provide for all of the career development needs of their employees on site.

Off-Site Career Development Opportunities

Career development off-site includes activities that a manager and other personnel engage in to increase their capacity to meet departmental or organizational needs. An advantage of off-site group activities is the opportunity to network, that is, interact with and learn from others with similar interests but different perspectives from your own. Generally an atmosphere of excitement and expectation among attendees flows from the opportunity to learn something useful. There are also off-site activities for individuals.

Sending an employee off-site has costs. When an employee is absent from work for any reason, the workload for his or her colleagues is likely to increase. This may affect productivity. There are also financial costs for the employer (employee educational benefit, possibly hiring a temporary replacement) and possibly for the employee (costs exceeding educational benefit amount). The employer may continue paying salary while the employee is off site. When this is the case, it is usually expected that the employee will return to work for the organization for a time after completing employer-paid training. Costs may also be shared. Tuition, travel, board, and other costs may be split between employer and employee. While the employee is off site, regular pay may be continued unchanged, or it may be reduced. Accrued vacation or compensation time (time off earned by working extra hours without additional pay) may be used in some cases to avoid a loss of pay.

The following list of off-site strategies contains some development means also identified as on-site activities, for example, mentoring and research, because these opportunities may take place anywhere. These are common off-site development resources:

- **Assessment centers**: Specialized centers for assessment of capabilities on a specific set of job constructs and tasks (Schmitt and Borman, 1993).
- **Career counseling**: Interaction with career development center personnel at an academic institution or commercial agency to

explore career options and strategies and develop skills to advance in a chosen career path.

- **Continuing education**: Educational sessions, usually short, offered by a variety of volunteers and vendors to increase participants' knowledge, skills, motivation, and attitudes. Evidence supporting claims made by the instructor is essential to give credence to the information (Rothstein, 2001).
- **Exchange programs**: A temporary arrangement in which individuals from one organization go to another organization to share and learn.
- **External mentor arrangements**: As defined earlier but with a mentor outside of the employment setting (http://www.apta.org/Advocacy/2oman/initiatives/membermentor/onlinemembersmentoring).
- **Home study courses**: Hardcopy instructional material and assessments to enhance knowledge in a variety of areas with a means of recognizing completion of the course (http://www.apta.org/Bulletin/Course_Listings).
- **Informational interviews**: Prearranged or spontaneous face-to-face interactive video, phone, or e-mail contact between a person seeking information and another person who has the information or knows how to find it.
- **Local, national and international meetings**: For examples go to http://www.apta.org/Education/ed_resources.
- **On-campus education**: See current trade publications, for example, *Physical Therapy*, *PTMagazine*, *Advance for Physical Therapists*, and *PT Assistants*.
- **Special interest groups**: For example, http://www.aptasoa.org/sig.html or the Arthritis Foundation.
- **Part-time clinical work at another location**: Pursue local opportunities by checking newspapers, trade publications, network, attend local professional meetings, make cold calls, and so on.
- **Part-time teaching for a physical therapist assistant or physical therapist program**: Pursue options noted earlier. School listings can be found at http://apta.org/Education/Schoollistings.
- **Pro bono service**: Providing free service to those who need it but cannot pay. See principle 10 of the American Physical Therapy Association (APTA) Guide for Professional Conduct at http://apta.org/pt_practice/ethics_pt/pro_conduct.
- **Pursuit of an additional credential**: Fulfillment of the knowledge and skill criteria of a recognized educational organization to be granted its credential, for example, http://www.support@icatric.org.
- **Residency program**: Intensive long-duration guided study and practice in an accredited program that focuses on a specific clinical area, for example, http://apta.org/Education/clinical.
- **Study at special institutes**: Intensive guided study and practice in an educational setting that focuses on a specific clinical methodology, for example, http://www.lymphedemaservices.com.
- **Workshops**: Practical instruction with practice, usually in clinical methods in which the presenter is most knowledgeable.

Reality

The expectation of long-term employment in an organization that will lead to increased responsibility, income, influence, and status in exchange for competence, loyalty, and honest effort is not consistent with recent observations (Hall and Associates, 1996) in health care or other fields (Mohrman and Cohen, 1998). It is unwise to depend solely on an employer for career development. There are at least four central reasons for an individual manager or any other employee to manage their own career development opportunities:

1. Preparation for advancement within an organization beyond what is available through the organization.
2. Employability in a larger market.
3. Autonomy: An individual with the skills, knowledge, and attributes necessary to do a job may choose to use those attributes when and where he or she chooses.
4. Fulfillment of professional association membership obligations (American Physical Therapy Association, 2001)

The first reason to continue to grow in multiple areas is to move up the career ladder where you work. Pertinent to fulfilling this aspiration is knowledge of advancement criteria and preparation to meet them. This can be done through organizational offerings and relevant growth experiences outside of the organization. The latter action may be considered a competitive advantage (Chapter 11) over candidates who have only had internal development. A broad range of development programs for managers is likely to be limited to large health care organizations. Organizations develop people for the organization's purposes. Some of what is learned may have limited applicability outside of the organization.

The second reason to manage your own career development is for continued employability. This relates to job security within an organization as well as being able to interest other employers in hiring you. Even if an employee has competently meet departmental, organizational, and patient-care needs, no one in an organization can ensure the continued existence of the organization or promise long-term employment to anyone. A background that includes continual growth in knowledge, skills, and responsibility—a history of continuous quality improvement (Chapter 12)—that is applicable to other settings is likely to be attractive to other employers.

A third reason for taking care of one's own developmental needs is professional autonomy, that is, the right to make personal career development choices. Opportunities in the workplace may or may not be compatible with career aspirations. In some settings desirable experiences may be available on a competitive basis. Personal and organizational goals differ in scope. The scope of the individual includes pursuit of a wide variety of personal goals, while an organization pursues a relatively narrow scope of specific and short-term organizational goals related to quality, productivity, revenue generation, and customer satisfaction (Chapters 9, 11, and 12). Organizations allocate resources according to priority needs based on environmental assessment (Chapter 11). Resources are finite. This means there is not enough money available to facilitate every employee's career objectives that are related to the work of the organization, much less to pay for things that less tangibly support the organization's priorities. When the pursuit of career development interests within an employment setting is not available or is limited or uncertain (Chapter 26), it may be time to shop around for an employer who offers more attractive opportunities.

The final reason for managing one's own career development is to fulfill a professional obligation. Principle 5 of the APTA Guide for Professional Conduct says that members shall assess their competencies and enhance their knowledge and skill throughout their career (APTA, 2002). Similarly, dialog associated with the APTA Vision Statement urges members to pursue life-long learning (APTA, 2001). In sum, career development can be good for all parties: health care employers, the professional service provider, and ultimately the customers. Ideally, career development is a personal quest (Hall and Associates, 1996) carried out in concert with one's employer but not dependent on an employer. The bottom line is that the responsibility for long-term career development for most employees is in their own hands. It is your career, so you should be more interested in its development than anyone else.

Self-Managed Career Development

If you accept the idea of personal ownership of your career, you can more easily see career development as a personal quest (Hall and Associates, 1996). Management of your career is similar to management of a sole proprietorship (Chapters 7 and 25). Just as an onboard navigation system in a car can keep a driver on course, having an idea about what you want to do with your career helps set a course for decisions. A way to give direction to efforts to develop your career is to make informed estimates of probable and improbable future trends (Macmillan and Tampoe, 2000). This process is known as **futuring** (Nosse, Friberg, Kovacek, 1999). The process incorporates the strengths, weaknesses, opportunities, and threats (**SWOT**) method (Learned, Christensen, Andrews, Guth, 1969). SWOT analysis (Chapters 11 and 21) is a way to identify your capability to deal with forces that have the potential to impede your career. The method requires reflection about personal aspirations, values, national and industry trends, personal attributes and deficits, and the assets and deficits of competitors. These tasks may sound familiar, because they were discussed in connection with philosophical, vision, and mission statements; environmental assessment; and SWOT analysis (Chapter 11). Figure 20.2 depicts the main elements of the futuring model to guide you toward the development of a desirable career; that is, it depicts a process for developing a plan of action focused on achieving specified goals. The strategic plans are linked to your vision and mission and are consonant with your most important personal values (Chapters 6 and 11). Assessments of exemplary individuals, that is, those who are respected for their accomplishments, are carried out along with assessment of yourself. Personal strengths and weaknesses can be weighed on a comparative basis. This helps to clarify which career development components—knowledge, skills, motivation, and/or self-assessment—you may have to improve. Then you make a strategic plan to bring about growth in the chosen area. The process also incorporates a feedback mechanism to use outcomes to improve the process.

Table 20.1 supplements the explanation of the futuring strategy shown in Figure 20.2. The first two steps in the process suggest asking yourself what you are willing to do to accomplish what is important to you. This is an assessment of value priorities (Chapters 6 and 25). Values propel behaviors that are likely to lead to desired goals. Once you know what you are willing to work to achieve, seek relevant information from a wide range of resources. University career centers can provide assistance in clarifying values and other aspects of career development. Services are usually available to alumni and students. Private career counseling services offer much the same services and often also have current knowledge of the specific job market you are interested in. From exemplars, those whose achievements you admire, learn the lay of the land. What have they done to get where they are? Where have they succeeded? What obstacles did they encounter? Weigh this information against your understanding of your own knowledge, skills, motivation, and ability to self-assess. Choose the area or areas you should improve on to reach the level of those you consider exemplars. From the on-site and

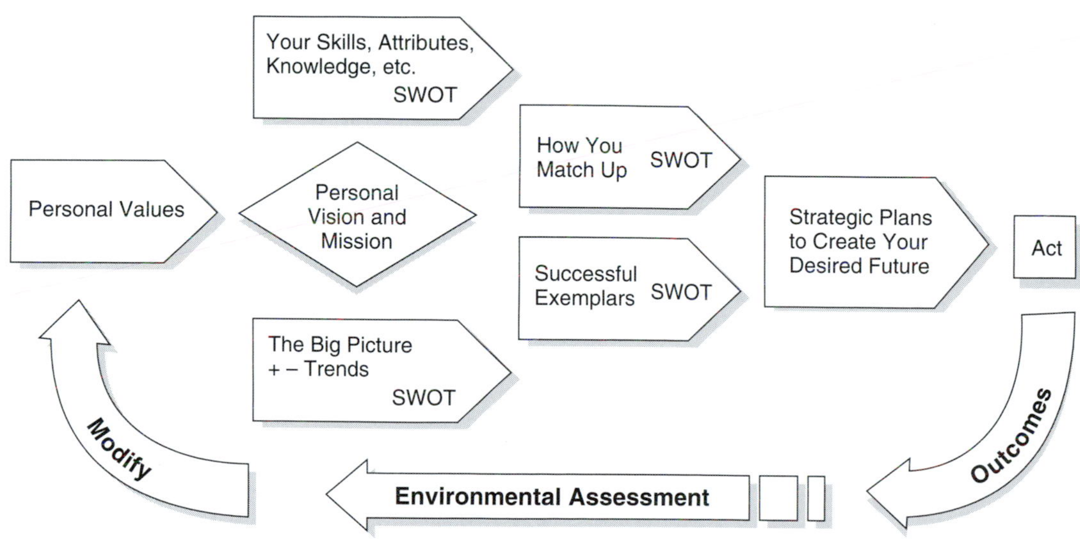

Figure 20.2. A strategic planning–based process for career development.

Table 20.1 A Process for Career Self-Management

1. Do your homework. Know yourself and your customers and potential customers (e.g., employers, direct reports, referral sources).
2. Know what you really want; prioritize your values.
3. Prepare your approach: gather information from pertinent sources, including those who are not physical therapists.
4. Make strategic plans for knowledge enhancement, skill improvement, and effective self-assessment. If motivation is an issue, reassess career goals and other employment opportunities or seek career counseling.
5. Regularly reassess your growth progress and needs.
6. Periodically assess each step of this process.
7. Adjust the process as needed.

off-site strategies for development listed earlier, select the options you believe will meet your needs. Seek involvement in the selected developmental strategies that will meet your needs; for example, form a development plan with your manager, talk with human resource personnel, approach a potential mentor, attend a national meeting, enroll in a course. Once you have completed the developmental activity, assess your progress toward your goal. The last step in the process is revision. Adjust your goals to fit your new understanding. The areas you wish to grow in may have changed. The exemplar may be a different person. You may have to put more effort into assessing strategy options. As with all skills, the more you use the process, the better you can use it to manage your career.

Student Notes

You are in the introductory part of your career development cycle, the first curve depicted in Figure 20.1. Many more curves will come and go as you learn more, improve your skills, get other points of view, and so on. Table 20.2 has a sort of menu of what is available to you after graduation.

You are in the mode of studying. Stick with it. Take advantage of every opportunity to learn. Remember that the useful life of much of the material you have been studying for the past few years may already be over (Anonymous, 1997).

Summary

Work and other experiences can contribute to growth in some desirable capacities. In this

Table 20.2 Some Career Development Opportunities for Physical Therapists

Degree		*Nondegree*	
Academic[a]	***Professional***[b]	***For Credit and NonCredit Education and Training***	***Workplace Opportunities***
EdD	DC	Board-certified specialist	CCCE
DSc	DDS	Clinical fellowship	Committee member
Fellowship	DO	Clinical residency	Consultant (internal)
MA	DPM	Continuing education credits	Manager
MAPT	DPT (entry to field)	Home study	Mentor/protégé
MEd	DScPT (advanced)	Other certifications	Mid-, upper-level management
MS	MBA	Professional assoc. committee	Networking
MSPT	MD		Partner/associate
PhD	MPT (entry to field)		Private practice owner
	Nurse practitioner	Can include targeted formal coursework and distance learning	Rotate services/departments
	t-DPT (transitional)		Special clinical focus

[a]Traditionally admitted to an academic program through the graduate school.
[b]Traditionally admitted to a professional program by the programs' admission committee.

INDIVIDUAL CASE STUDY

Think about the following questions in the context of your own career development. Would you rather have an extra $1000 in salary or an education benefit of $1000? What is the rationale for your choice?

chapter we call this series of experiences career development. The general areas of career development are knowledge, skill, motivation, and self-awareness. Opportunities to grow in desirable ways in these four areas exist within and outside of the workplace. It is beneficial for organizations in rapidly and unpredictably changing environments to foster career development so that the organization's managerial and core workforce can keep pace with the market. We name nearly 50 specific opportunities for career development that managers may use themselves and employ to develop direct reports. Many career development opportunities can be implemented within the workplace, and some can be realized only outside of the workplace. The benefits and limitations of these opportunities are discussed with an eye to choosing the right methods to meet specific needs. Finally, career development is ultimately a personal obligation. To facilitate self-management, we offer a process for planning for one's career development based on strategic planning and futuring concepts. To bring about personally desirable ends often entails dealing with the perceptions of others. In business influencing perceptions is one aspect of marketing. The next part of the book deals with this topic. The information in the next several chapters complements several of the concepts in this and the preceding chapters. Among the concepts to come are essential marketing principles (Chapter 21) and organizational strategic planning (Chapter 22). Chapter 25 applies marketing principles to the individual. This chapter builds nicely upon the idea of taking charge of your own career development because it adds depth to the strategic planning process.

GROUP CASE STUDY

Depending on your entry-level educational program, some options in Table 20.2 will be more relevant than others. First, take a few minutes and do a self-assessment of knowledge, motivation, self-awareness, and skill. Once everyone has done this, as a class, think out loud about the four areas of career development and your general strengths and weaknesses in the areas you examined in your self-assessment.

Task

As a class, develop a generic career plan based on your common education and clinical education. Use Table 20.2 as a menu and Figure 20.2 as a process guide. You may want to divide into smaller work groups and integrate your thoughts later.

REFERENCES

American Physical Therapy Association. APTA vision statement. Annual Report 2001. Supplement to PT Magazine. Alexandria, VA: American Physical Therapy Association. 2001.

American Physical Therapy Association. APTA guide for professional conduct. Available from http://www.apta.org/pt_practice/ethics_pt/pro_conduct. Accessed 8/02/02.

Anonymous. How to self-manage your professional development. PT Magazine. 1997;5:43.

Dahl CS. Physical therapist management of tuberculosis arthritis of the elbow. Physical Therapy. 2001;81:1253–1259.

Hall DT, Associates. The career is dead—Long live the career. San Francisco: Jossey-Bass. 1996.

Isaacson LE, Brown D. Career information, career counseling & career development, 5th ed. Boston: Allyn & Bacon. 1993.

Kongstvedt PR. Managed care: What it is and how it works, 2nd ed. Gaithersburg, MD: Aspen. 2002.

Learned EP, Christensen CR, Andrews KR, Guth WD. Business policy text and cases, revised ed. Homewood, IL: Richard D. Irwin. 1969.

Levine RJ. The boundaries between biomedical or behavioral research and the accepted and routine practice of medicine. In The National Commission for the Protection of Human Subjects of Biomedical and Behavioral Research. The Belmont report: Ethical principles and guidelines for the protection of human subjects of research. Appendix Volume I. Washington: U.S. Government Printing Office. 1975. DHEW Publication OS 78-0013.

Locke EA. Motivation by goal setting. In Golembiewski RT, ed. Handbook of organizational behavior, 2nd ed. New York: Marcel Dekker. 2001:43–56.

Longest BB, Jr., Rakich JS, Darr K. Managing health services organizations and systems, 4th ed. Baltimore: Health Professions. 2000.

Macmillan H, Tampoe M. Strategic management process, content, and implementation. New York: Oxford University. 2000.

Major DA. Effective newcomer socialization into high-performance organizational cultures. In Ashkanasy NM, Wilderom CPM, Peterson MF. Handbook of organizational culture & climate. Thousand Oaks, CA: Sage. 2000:358–368.

Mohrman SA, Cohen SG. When people get out of the box: New relationships, new systems. In Murray B. Notion of a life long career is now a thing of the past. APA Monitor Online. 1998;5:29. Available from http://www.apa.org/monitor/may98/career.html. Accessed 10/31/02.

Nosse LJ, Friberg DG, Kovacek PR. Managerial and supervisory principles for physical therapists. Baltimore: Lippincott, Williams & Wilkins. 1999.

Rainey HG. Work motivation. In Golembiewski RT, ed. Handbook of organizational behavior, 2nd ed. New York: Marcel Dekker. 2001:19–42.

Riolo L. Evidence in practice. Clinical question: Does the presence of ideomotor apraxia affect the prognosis of functional recovery in a woman who has had a stroke? Physical Therapy. 2002;82:912–922.

Rothstein JM. Are you financing a sham? Physical Therapy. 2001;81:1500–1501.

Schmitt N, Borman WC. Personnel selection in organizations. San Francisco: Jossey-Bass. 1993.

Stahl SM, Hennes JD. Reading and understanding applied statistics: A self-learning approach, 2nd ed. St. Louis: Mosby. 1980.

Wexley KN, Latham GD. Developing and training human resources in organizations, 2nd ed. New York: Harper-Collins. 1991.

MORE INFORMATION RELATED TO THIS CHAPTER

A book that focuses on career in the broad context of life is Super DE, Sverko B, Super CM, eds. Life roles, values, and careers: International findings of the Work Importance Study. San Francisco, CA: Jossey-Bass. 1995.

The APTA Web site address for career management information is http://www.apta.org/Career_center/Career_management.

Two short articles about career development from a physical therapy perspective are Wynn KE. Charting a course: Profiles in self-managed careers. PT-Magazine. 1997;5:40–42, 44–46, and Rone-Adams S. The changing culture of rehab. Rehab Management. 2002;15:16, 18, 70.

For mentoring information see Ries E. Members mentoring members. PTMagazine. 2001;9:82–83.

An interesting discussion of the characteristics of high-performance organizations in which data from a 1991 survey of U.S. businesses were used to analyze the outcomes of training, compensation, and other variables in a high performance culture can be found in Marsden PV, Kalleberg AL, Knoke D. Surveying organizational structures and human resource practices: The National Organizations Study. In Golembiewski RT, ed. Handbook of organizational behavior, 2nd ed. New York: Marcel Dekker. 2001:175–201.

Part IV

Service Marketing

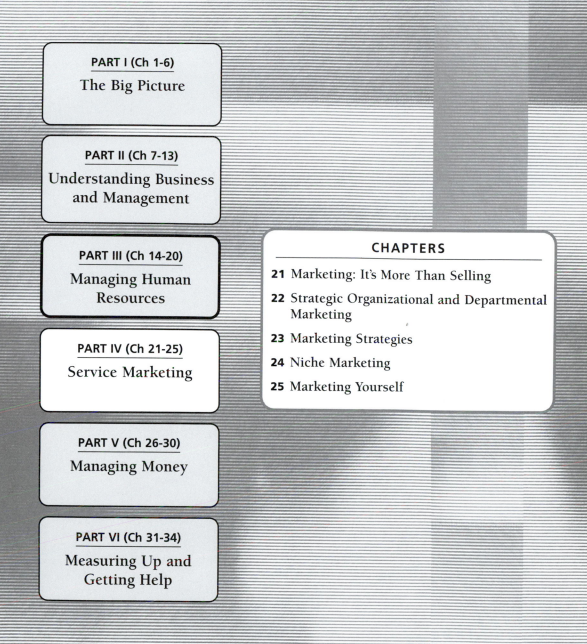

PART I (Ch 1-6)
The Big Picture

PART II (Ch 7-13)
Understanding Business and Management

PART III (Ch 14-20)
Managing Human Resources

PART IV (Ch 21-25)
Service Marketing

PART V (Ch 26-30)
Managing Money

PART VI (Ch 31-34)
Measuring Up and Getting Help

CHAPTERS

Chapter 21

Marketing: It's More than Selling

Learning Objectives

1. Contrast the general concepts of marketing and selling.
2. Contrast the key elements of a marketing program for a health care product and a health care service.
3. Analyze the components of the marketing mix or communications mix.
4. Provide examples of a physical therapy target market, market segment, and niche market.
5. Apply the marketing principles in this chapter by preparing an outline of a marketing plan to enter a new physical therapy market of your choice.

Key Words

Communication mix, customer, forecasting, managed care organization, market, market diversification, market orientation, market penetration, market segmentation, market share, marketing, marketing mix, niche market, opportunity cost, principles, product, product line, promotion, promotional mix, selling, service, service line, strategic marketing campaign, target market, third-party payment system

Introduction

Attracting customers—individuals or groups who directly or indirectly may need or want to use a product or service—is the basis for marketing. **Customers**, clients, buyers, markets, and patients are all words that marketers of physical therapy services use to describe individuals who may want or need our services. In this chapter we use these terms somewhat interchangeably to refer to the generic purchasers of our services. We use a specific term, such as patient, when it is necessary to be more specific about the type of purchaser. This is not meant to confuse you but rather to help you understand the various customers and complexity of the audiences we serve.

Marketing, according to the American Marketing Association, "is the process of planning and executing the conception, pricing, promotion, and distribution of ideas, services and goods, to create exchanges that satisfy individual and organizational objectives" (AMA Board Approves, 1985, p. 1). From this definition it is clear that marketing is much more than just face-to-face selling. This chapter examines marketing. As physical therapists, we constantly must market our services and products. Marketing decisions are often related to basic business decisions. For example, we have to decide about the services to offer, how much to charge for the services, and where to locate clinics. Throughout this chapter, we explore principles of marketing and how they interface with physical therapy practices. In Chapters 22 and 23 we examine additional aspects of physical therapy marketing. While we highlight the differences between marketing services and marketing products, in many ways marketing services is similar to marketing goods or products. Our emphasis here is on the marketing of physical therapy services along with a significant presentation of marketing topics that are applicable to any health care business. Among the covered key components of marketing physical therapy services and products are the core elements of the **marketing mix** or **communication mix**, the combination of means used to communicate with customers about services and products, and the development of a physical therapy–specific marketing and communication plan.

Marketing Is More Than Selling

Marketing includes planning, design, and development of services and products. It also includes pricing, promotion, and distribution of services and products to the customer (Herzlinger, 1997). **Selling** is the specific process of arranging the exchange and negotiating the details of that exchange. Selling focuses on encouraging the potential buyer to purchase a specific product. The needs of the customer are considered only in the context of what the seller has to offer. Marketing entails more than selling. It requires the manager to identify, anticipate, and satisfy customers' requirements efficiently and profitably (Cooper and Arcyris, 1998). Individual services and products are developed to meet the customers' requirements.

Financial Success in Marketing

Like any other aspect of business management, successful marketing management requires simultaneous attention to various details (Figure 21.1).

Quality

Quality is the cornerstone of any successful service, product, or company. Although quality is difficult to define (Chapters 12 and 31), it must be clear to customers that the quality is outstanding if you expect your customers to continue to allow you the privilege of caring for them. Processes to ensure quality include ongoing system and staff development (Chapter 14), quality assessment and improvement programs, outcomes analysis, and patient satisfaction programs (Chapter 31). Ask these key questions as you think about marketing plans:

- Will this service or product contribute to the overall perception of high quality for our clinic?

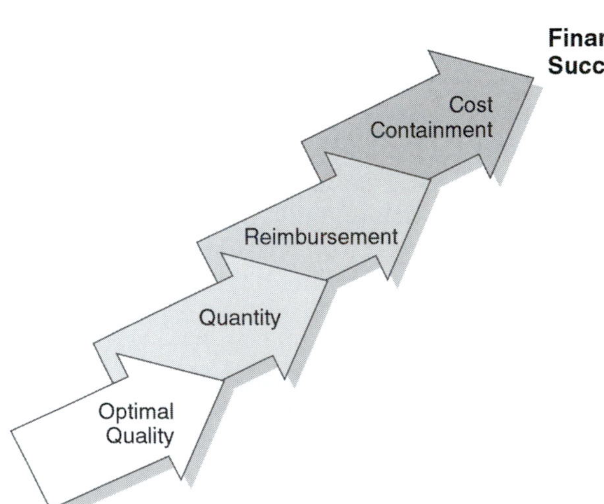

Figure 21.1. The wide scope of considerations underlying marketing management.

- Will this service or product be perceived as important for our markets?
- Will this service or product be perceived to be consistent with the other services and activities for which we are known?

Quantity

Once you have developed systems and staff to provide a high-quality product, an adequate amount or quantity of work must be done. This is simply an economic reality. To succeed financially, you must provide not only a high quality of care but also enough of it to survive financially. This is also a key benefit of a good marketing program. This means the program will identify areas where there is adequate need for services and help attract a enough customers for the business to succeed.

Reimbursement

While high quality and an adequate volume of care delivery are essential, it is also necessary to get paid for the services. Reimbursement, addressed elsewhere in this text, is always a consideration in the development of marketing new services and programs. Developing marketing plans with reimbursement realities in mind allows development of more realistic financial plans, pro forma, and budgets.

Cost Containment

Any activity of a business and the business itself overall must over time generate more revenue than expenses. Marketing programs and activities can be a significant expense. It is important to examine the potential return on these expenses, since even if the plan is successful, expenses for marketing activities always fall due before the revenues that they generate.

Marketing Functions

Marketing starts with identification of customers and their needs. This means providing an appropriate quality of care at a time, place, and cost that meets clients' wants and needs. Additionally, in order to choose your services, your potential clients must be aware of your practice's existence, what services are available (the scope of services), and the potential benefits of the services available (Nosse, Friberg, Kovacek, 1999). A manager is always marketing service to potential customers, who include peer managers, physicians, and family members of current clients. The marketing functions of a manager can include planning, organizing, implementing, and controlling activities to facilitate and expedite exchanges effectively and efficiently (Cooper and Arcyris, 1998).

Principles of Marketing

Principles are rules or methods that are essential to produce a specific effect. The marketing principles that follow are focused on the delivery of service to specified groups of potential health care consumers.

Definition of a Market

The many possible definitions of a **market** include the following:

- Any network involving dealings between buyers and sellers of a particular service or product
- A public gathering held for buying and selling services or merchandise
- A place where goods and services are offered for sale
- A store or shop that sells a particular type of service or merchandise (Boon and Kurtz, 1986)

Each of these definitions may at one time or another apply to a physical therapy practice. The primary activity of most physical therapy clinics is to provide a **service**. This is an exchange in which ownership does not change. Physical therapists also often sell **products**. In this situation the exchange involves a transfer of ownership (Hannagan, 2002). Some examples are the sale of exercise equipment and durable medical equipment. Therefore, physical therapists should fully understand all aspects of marketing services and products.

Market Share

Market share is the percentage of the entire market that is served by a given organization (Cooper and Arcyris, 1998). Market size and market share are shown in Figure 21.2.

If the entire pie is the universe of customers who use physical therapy services and products in a particular geographic area, the various slices represent the relative size of each competitor's business. The business with the smallest percentage of customers is Our PT Company, which holds a 21% market share according to the chart. The biggest competitors to Our PT Company are Competitor A (43% of the business), followed by Competitor C (29% of the business).

Growth Through Market Penetration

Growth of Our PT Company (Fig. 21.2) in the geographic area it draws patients from can come only from increasing the relative market share (grabbing a larger slice) or increasing the overall size of the market (creating a bigger pie). In a static-sized universe, growth of Our PT Company can come only from a decrease in market share of one or more of the competitors. This is done through strategies to increase **market penetration**, which is the intent to increase market share. Market penetration strategies typically promote to consumers the benefits of one specific physical therapy practice over the other choices available in the market.

Growth Through Market Expansion

The differences between the circles in Figure 21.2 show the hypothetical result of an overall market expansion strategy. A **strategy** is the conceptualization of the desired future and the actions to secure it (Macmillan and Tampoe, 2000) (Chapter 11). An alternative growth strategy is to work to increase the size of the overall market for physical therapy services in this market. In effect, this creates a bigger pie. Typically this is done through **promotion** of the *concept* of physical therapy as opposed to promotion of a specific practice or business. Promotional materials such as a flyer, billboard, radio advertisement, or per-

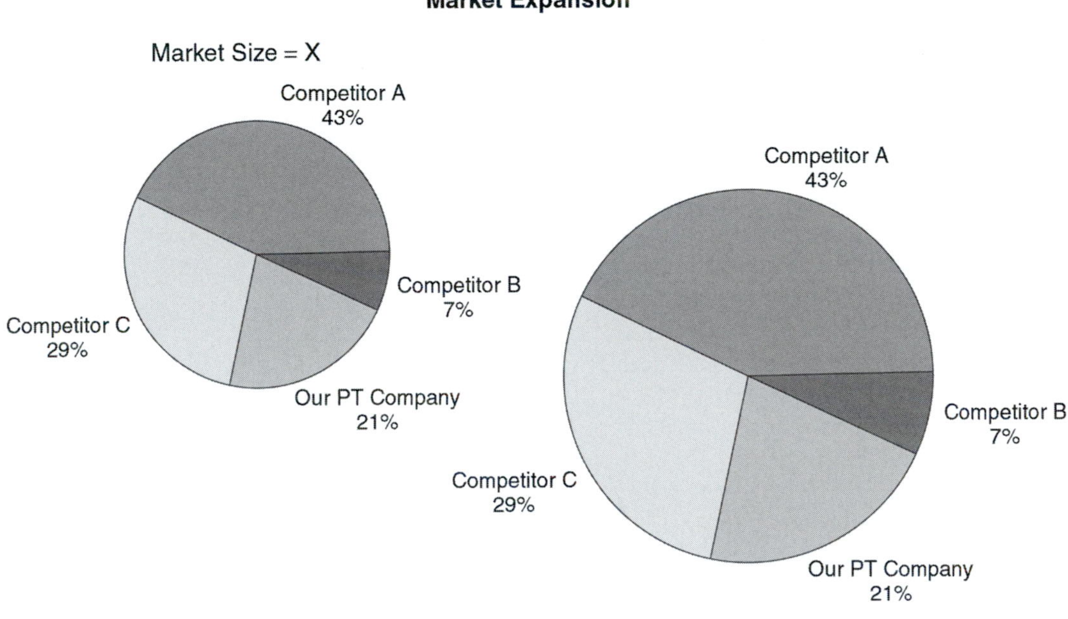

Figure 21.2. A physical therapy market expansion example focusing on market share.

sonalized letter could be used to encourage potential patients to choose physical therapy instead of chiropractic service for spinal dysfunction, for example.

Typically, marketing campaigns are designed to address market share, market penetration, and overall market growth.

Target Market

A **target market** is a selected group, or submarket, in which members share specific characteristics that may affect their interest in a specific product or service. Demographics is often used to identify submarkets in a general population; for example, senior citizens have significantly different physical therapy needs from those of children. Obviously, physical therapy programs must be customized for each of these groups.

There are many possible ways to differentiate one selected target market or audience from others. Discriminators that can be used to identify a specific target market are listed in Table 21.1.

Market Segmentation

An alternative way of considering target markets is illustrated in Table 21.2. The table shows that markets can be divided into a more specific but numerically smaller group. This is known as **market segmentation**. Market segmentation is splitting the known market for a service or product into separate parts. Consumers within segments may be categorized in a variety of ways, for instance by age, social class, lifestyle, setting, geography, avocation, or purchasing habits. These subcategories are the target markets (Kotler, Ferrell, Lamb, 1983).

Market segmentation is the development and delivery of services designed for specific groups of potential buyers. Rather than trying to satisfy the needs and wants of everyone, the astute physical therapy marketer directs the organization's efforts toward the unique needs and characteristics of particular groups. Organizations that use market segmentation strive to serve market targets that they are able to satisfy rather than just any large group of buyers. They market to *segments* (groups of customers), not the entire population in an area.

In physical therapy, consumers may be segmented in various ways: by client, referral source, payer, or employer. Clients may be subdivided into more discrete segments based on how they use physical therapy services. For example, clients may use aquatic therapy, sports injury care, incontinence therapy, wound care, spine care, occupational services, pediatric therapy, intensive care therapy, or pain management (Schaefer, 1991).

The advantages of segmentation are substantial. Segmentation results in the creation of a specific marketing mix for each subgroup of potential buyers that the company intends to satisfy (Kotler et al., 1983). This is true as much for a small physical therapy practice as

Table 21.1 Examples of Market Segmentation and Target Markets

Market Segment	*Differentiating Factor*	*Example Service*
Parents of children with developmental disabilities	Significant familial stress due to the demands of caring for an ill or handicapped child	Pediatric therapy in day rehabilitation with significant parental respite components
Adult children whose elderly parents live independently but who are beginning to have difficulty with independent mobility or self-care	Many middle-aged children of elderly parents in period of highest discretionary income Considering assistance for a parent stressful	Fall prevention programs for independent senior citizens, especially those with balance or orthopedic problems
Clients under age 45 who have had a CVA	Most CVA clients older; younger clients post stroke may feel isolated	Young adult stroke survivor support group

Reprinted from Nosse LN, Friberg DG, Kovacek PR. Management and supervisory principles for physical therapists. Baltimore: Williams and Wilkins. 1999:50.

Table 21.2 Example Factors for Market Segmentation in Physical Therapy

Age	*Nature of problem*
Affiliation with community group	Previous experience with physical therapy
Avocation	Projected volume of patients
Behavioral factors	Relationship with referrers
Childbearing status	Risk of health problems
Employment status	Shared vision, beliefs
Gender	Socioeconomic factors
Geographic location	Transportation
Hours available for appointments	Type of therapy

Modified from Nosse et al., 1999:50.

for a physical therapy department in a large health care system. The goal is to produce goods and services t hat furnish substantial value to selected groups of potential buyers as efficiently as possible.

Segmentation can lead to high customer loyalty. Competitors hoping to increase their market share will have difficulty winning away the patronage of loyal customers.

Like any other strategy, market segmentation has its drawbacks. It can lead to focusing on one portion of the population to the neglect of the rest. The management of a physical therapy clinic is not likely to succeed by marketing its post partum services in a senior citizen center (except perhaps on a gift certificate basis); however, it may be very successful marketing urinary incontinence or fall prevention services to that same market. A second disadvantage of market segmentation is that it may lead to redundancy and thereby increase costs. A clinic that pursues two or more market segments normally has to develop and offer two or more different sets of marketing materials. If the company appeals to two different segments, it may have to design two individual sets of services or products, physical distribution systems, price structures, advertising programs, personal selling programs, and sales promotion programs. This may or may not be duplicative and inefficient, depending on the circumstances.

Market Diversification

In addition to target marketing and market penetration activities, **market diversification**, or expansion of the scope of a product, service, or organization, can also be an effective strategy for increasing business. A key question when considering diversification is who besides current customers could benefit from services such as ours? Diversification should always be viewed in much the same way as a new service or product line or entry into a new market (Hiam and Schewe, 1992). It is important to undertake a systematic examination of the potential benefits and risks for each product or market decision (see Chapter 11).

Consumers of Services or Products

So who are our customers? Patients are the focus of most health care organizations. In health care, however, because of the third-party payment systems and the typical need for patients to be referred by a physician, it is important to include all three of these groups (patients, payers, and referrers) in any discussion of marketing.

As always, profitably satisfying consumer needs is at the heart of successful marketing. Understanding why each of these key consumer groups is interested in our services instead of those offered at other clinics or other providers of similar services—such as athletic trainers, chiropractors, exercise physiologists, kinesiotherapists, myomassologists, and occupational therapists—is key to the development of successful marketing programs. Why each of these consumer groups favors certain services or providers and avoids others and how they make decisions is a vital interest to physical therapy managers. All consumers are people, acting as individuals or in small groups, who buy goods and services for personal purposes, in contrast to commercial buyers, who buy and use items for commercial purposes. However, commercial purchasers who represent managed care and other insurance companies also act as individuals to some degree. Understanding their personal needs as health care consumers is important to physical therapy managers who wish to do business with them (Mullin, Hardy, Sutton, 1993).

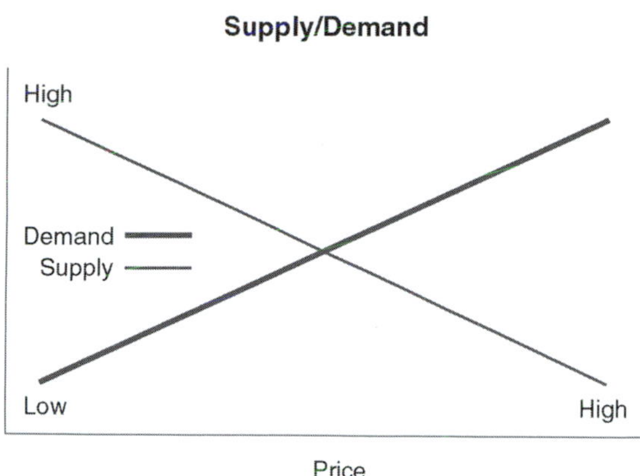

Figure 21.3. A supply and demand relationship.

Supply and Demand

A principle of economics states that there is an inverse relationship between availability of a product or service and the market demand for it (Cooper and Arcyris, 1998) (Chapter 26). Figure 21.3 shows such a relationship. Many exceptions exist, but in an open market, as the price of a service or product rises, the demand typically falls. Price elasticity, or price sensitivity, relates to the relative responsiveness of a market to a price change for a given service or product (Kotler, 1982). Physical therapy managers should question whether supply and demand as a concept applies to physical therapy and health care in general. Evidence suggests that the law of supply and demand does not always apply to health care. For example, health care costs are often highest in regions with a very high concentration of health care providers. Extrapolation of supply and demand theory (Chapter 26) suggests that as more services become available in a given market, the demand for those services (and thus the market price) should go down. One plausible explanation for this phenomenon is that health care is different from typical businesses that offer consumer services and goods. Health care is a heavily regulated industry.

There is a unique relationship between the providers and consumers because of the **third-party payment system**. Figure 21.4 shows that in this system the patient (first party) deals with the provider (second party), but in most cases the payer of the service is a third party chosen by an employer to arrange for health care for his or her employees and their families. The third-party payer system is more fully explained in Part V. Also, patients are often at a distinct disadvantage in making health care decisions because of the emotional and sometimes life-threatening nature of their health status (Herzlinger, 1997; Hiam and Schewe, 1992; Kotler, 1982; Kotler et al., 1983). Recently there has been more of a tendency for the law of supply and demand to hold true in health care. Third-party payers have evolved (some would say devolved) into what are known as **managed care organizations**, organizations that consolidate purchasing and financing of health care services (Chapter 22). For managed care organizations to make a profit, price often becomes the single most important factor in their thinking about which providers they will and will not deal with. Although it is not universally true, many markets have a large number of physical therapy providers. In these cases, managed care organizations have been able to negotiate much lower prices for their services because of the intense price competition between the providers in that market (Kotler, 1983; Levinson, 1993; Schaefer, 1991). When physical therapy and health care services do not follow the law of supply and demand, it is generally because government regulations have established price controls or at least price consistency in the market. This is contrary to the principles of free-market eco-

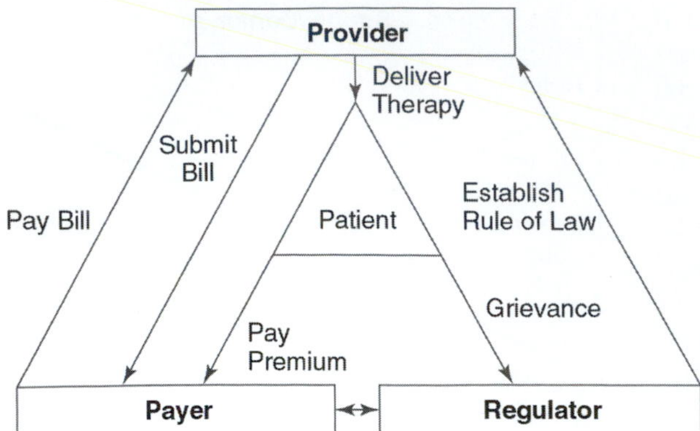

Figure 21.4. Third-party payer system. (Reprinted with permission from Nosse et al., 1999:48.)

nomic theory, which posit that open markets are needed for supply and demand forces to dominate (Chapter 26).

Introduction to Niche Marketing

A niche is a specific market that can be identified for a specific product, service, or intervention. Niche marketing is mentioned here because of the importance of a company having a strong niche to reach its profit goals. If a physical therapy practice hopes to establish a strong niche in the market, it must effectively differentiate its offering from those of competitors (MacStravic, 1977). Chapter 24 examines niche marketing in more detail.

Service Versus Product Marketing

There are differences between marketing services and products. As previously mentioned, physical therapy clinics are primarily in the service business. However, products are also frequently offered for sale to supplement the direct physical therapy services provided. Sometimes, physical therapy businesses offer products for sale to the general community, not just patients. One significant issue in marketing services is the need to make tangible to the consumer something that is inherently intangible; that is, the consumer does not keep the service as he or she keeps a cane. Later in this chapter we examine the implications of this intangibility on the components of the product marketing mix compared to a service marketing mix.

Marketing Planning Overview

One of the most important ways managers plan is by deciding what new products, services, and interventions should be made available (MacStravic, 1977). Consumers' needs and desires change continually. This change creates a need for new products and services. In addition, there is always demand for new offerings that fulfill needs and desires more effectively than do existing services and products. For example, consumers want automobiles that are increasingly more fuel efficient, computers that are faster and easier to use but that have more functions and lower costs, and topical analgesics that do not smell or irritate the skin.

Marketing Mix

The components of the marketing mix, or communication mix as it is also called (Lewis, 1999), are the controllable variables that an organization can actively manage to satisfy the needs of target markets (Fig 21.5). The term marketing mix refers to the tool kit or recipe that organizations use to match services and products with consumer needs. It is a combination of thoughts, analysis, and actions to deal with the critical factors that must be considered in determining a marketing strategy.

The marketing mix concept in Figure 21.5 depicts the combination of factors that are used to market any service or product. The five key factors in the mix are:

Figure 21.5. Basic market mix. (Reprinted with permission from Nosse, Friberg, Kovacek. Management and supervisory principles for physical therapist. Baltimore: Williams & Wilkins. 1999:51.)

1. **Product**: the characteristics of the product or service itself
2. **Promotion**: the methods of communication used to inform the public and sell the product or service
3. **Price**: the amount charged and the mechanisms used to justify the amount
4. **Place**: the location or locations chosen to deliver the service or product to its consumers
5. **Packaging**: the manner in which the service or product is presented, that is, its special features.

These five key factors are often known as the five Ps of marketing. In the service sector, three additional factors can be identified (Fig. 22.5):

6. **Physical evidence** of quality or effectiveness
7. **Personnel** providing the service and the way they are selected and trained
8. **Processes** offered by the service and the extent to which they instill a sense of confidence in the client, referrer or payer

With these additional factors the service marketing mix consists of **eight P's** (Fig. 21.6). We will examine more completely each of the eight components of a typical service marketing mix.

Product

A product can be an idea, service, good, or combination of these that is offered to a market. Although clearly there are differences between marketing products and marketing services, for this discussion we consider the term *product* to include services. Product management has three steps:

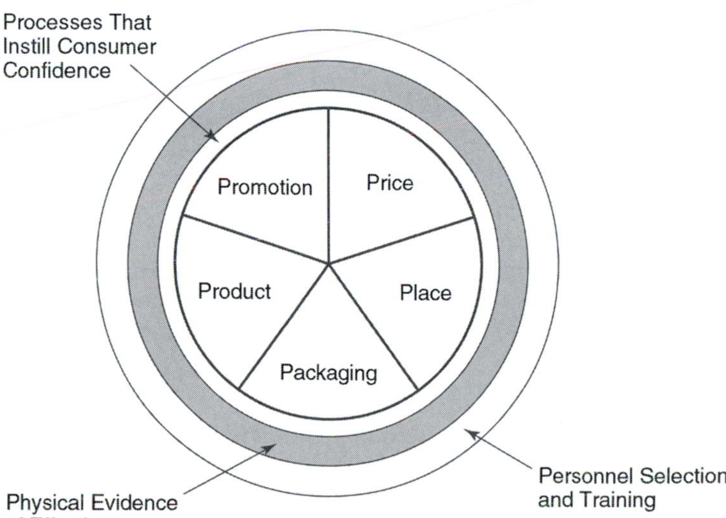

Figure 21.6. The eight P's of the service marketing mix.

1. Monitor existing product performance.
2. Change strategy when performance is unfavorable.
3. Decide when to introduce new products.

People seeking relief from back pain will consider physical therapy if they think it is more likely to promote that relief than competing services and products, such as chiropractic, a special mattress, or faith healing. Managers therefore must view the concept of a service or product from the perspective of the ability to fulfill the potential consumers' perceived needs.

The consumer of physical therapy services can be a variety of individuals or organizations such as the patient, the referring physician, a case manager representing an insurance company, a family member of a potential patient, or an employer of an injured worker. Each of these parties may have quite different perceived needs for the physical therapy organization to satisfy.

Promotion

Many organizations engage in promotion, including large and small businesses, political candidates, not-for-profit organizations, and health care organizations. Physical therapy companies often allocate substantial resources to **promotion**, which includes a spectrum of means of communicating with potential buyers about a service or product to stimulate sales. According to Hannagan (2002), a successful promotional program has six steps. Potential customers

1. Become aware of the service
2. Add to their knowledge of the service
3. Increase their understanding of differences and similarities
4. Draw comparisons and weigh options
5. Form a preference based on steps 1 to 4
6. Act on this preference by purchasing the preferred service

The **promotional mix** has four components:

1. Advertising
2. Personal selling
3. Sales promotion
4. Public relations

All promotional activities have the same general objective—to turn customers into actual or repeat buyers of a particular service, product, or idea. In its simplest form, promotion of a service or product can simply be telling people about its existence. One example is the signs that one sees along highways that call out "food ahead" or "last gas station for 99 miles." More often, however, promotional activities extend far beyond this by involving persuasion, that is, attempting to convince people that the sponsor's service, product, or idea is better than others. For instance, through promotion, managers, supervisors, and staff can persuade some customers to believe that one clinic is preferred over others.

Promotional campaigns help to develop and maintain such preferences. TV ads, contests, and sweepstakes are among the many promotional techniques that can help to position a product or service and develop its link with needs and social acceptance. This does not mean that false promises lead to lasting relationships. Lasting relationships depend on delivering services and products that actually satisfy needs. But promotion efforts can help to bring this about. Specific components of typical promotional campaigns may or may not be deemed appropriate for a physical therapy or other health care practice.

An effective and cost-efficient method of promotion is word of mouth endorsements from customers who have had a positive experience with your clinic (Stone, 2001; Thompson, 2002). The positive experience can come from any of various factors, including the price, the place, or the packaging.

Pricing

Pricing is one of the most important marketing decisions that management makes. It is usually related to a strategy the organization has adopted (Chapter 11). In health care generally and physical therapy specifically, pricing decisions can be very complex and at times may seem daunting to even the most experienced manager. There is no doubt that the third-party payment system and intense government regulation and oversight (Chapters 1 and 2) have had a profound effect on pricing of health care and physical therapy. The stakes are high for pricing decisions. Too high a price means that the service or product will not sell, while too low a price dictates low profits or even losses. For the time being suffice it to say that there are three major times to make pricing decisions:

1. When new services and products are introduced
2. In reaction to competitor-initiated price changes
3. When the firm itself initiates the price changes

More on costs and pricing is presented in Part V.

Place

Few decisions have greater impact on the ultimate success or failure of a physical therapy practice than location. As in real estate, for many practices the three most important practice decisions are location, location, and location. As trite as this may seem, it is often true.

Although picking the right location will not ensure success, it is a great first step. Picking the wrong location can ensure that the practice fails.

Components to be considered in decisions about the physical plant and location of your clinic include place, packaging, and a host of others. Here are some considerations for choosing a location for your clinic:

- Will you need to be near referral sources?
- Will you be on a medical campus or hospital site?
- What is the referrer density?
- What is the population density?
- Do many people who may need your services work in the area?
- What are the demographics of the people who drive or live near the location?
- What are the traffic patterns and volumes in the area?
- Is your site visible from the street?
- Does the population consider this a "good" neighborhood?
- Can you place visible signs outside to attract business?
- Is parking accessible?
- Is the facility friendly to persons with mobility limitations or concerns?

Packaging

Packaging services and products well may be as important as developing good products or services. Developing a good product or service is necessary to generate a strong product or service mix but does not constitute the whole of product or service decision making. Managers must also pay close attention to packaging. Packaging applies as much to services as it does to products. The manner in which services are packaged, however, is not so easily described or understood as it is for products. The promotional materials, the physical setting, and the attitude of the staff are all packaging items for services.

Physical Evidence of Quality or Effectiveness

A physical therapy practice demonstrates physical evidence of quality or clinical effectiveness in many ways. Posting of licenses, certifications, and certificates in a public area shows the customers that certain minimal requirements for operating a physical therapy business have been met. Letters of commendation and statements of gratitude from past patients or referral sources also add an air of credibility to the practice, and these can be available in a binder or display case in a public waiting area. It may be appropriate to post philosophical, mission, and vision statements in common areas for review to inform visitors of organizational ideas and goals that they may share (Chapter 11). All of these practices help the recipient of intangible physical therapy services feel more comfortable in assessing the quality of those services prior to consenting to be treated.

Personnel Providing the Service and the Way They Are Selected and Trained

In a service industry, front desk staff and staff that provide the service have tremendous impact on the perception of quality of the business by the consumer. The manner in which all the staff members interact, hold themselves out to the public, and even their appearance and dress are critical factors to the image of the company. Therefore, it is important for all staff members to act in a professional manner and provide services that consistently meet or exceed customer expectations. This mandate applies not only to the professional clinical staff but also to other staff members who encounter the public in person, by phone, or via mail, including e-mail (Chapter 33). *Image matters*. Staff should be dressed appropriately for clinical health care. Personal hygiene should be beyond reproach. Typical patient interactions such as initial phone contact, scheduling, insurance verification, and explanation of benefits should be scripted, and staff should be well trained in customer relations. This should include conflict resolution and handling patients' complaints. The aspect of management that has arguably the greatest effect on customer relations is staff selection. Staff who are initially prone to strong customer relations and good interpersonal skills are most likely to develop strong patient relations and promote a strong positive image for the practice.

Processes Offered by the Service and the Extent to Which They Instill a Sense of Confidence in the Customer

Much of the therapeutic aspect of a physical therapy business is difficult for the typical patient to evaluate. They may not be familiar with what is reasonable to expect in physical therapy or may not be cognitively or emotionally able to logically assess the physical therapy process because of injury or illness. What most patients can assess is whether they are treated with respect, dignity, and common courtesy. They are also adept at judging cleanliness and cosmetics of the facility. All aspects of the clinic should be professionally designed and neat. This includes not only the physical facility and staff but also all of the written materials distributed to patients and their families, third-party payers, and referrers. Poorly designed materials, hard-to-read forms, typographical errors, or poorly reproduced copies promote an amateurish image and diminish the customers' confidence in the facility. Consultants can help (Chapter 34).

Student Notes

It is important to understand the marketing principles encompassed in the five traditional P's of marketing and the additional three P's that apply to service providers. Together, the eight P's are useful to enhance communication at all levels from one-on-one discussions with potential and actual customers to groups outside of the health care environment. The insight to be gained from the idealized six-step progression of marketing communication, from awareness through making a sale, lies in knowing where the potential customer is in the progression and then selecting the appropriate promotional medium to move through the progression to the sale. The marketing foundation set in this chapter will be used in the next four chapters. The eight P's will be reiterated in a wide array of clinical circumstances. Thus, this introduction to marketing principles is critical to advancing your knowledge and understanding of service marketing. Remember, students in the clinic carry the same marketing responsibilities as all other members of the organization.

Summary

Physical therapy services and products are used or have potential use by a wide spectrum of people. In aggregate, these people are customers. A population of potential customers can be subdivided on the basis of any demographic or health status characteristics. A specific segment of the chosen population is the target market. A number of marketing concepts have evolved for influencing customers' purchasing behavior. Marketing is the process of anticipating, identifying, and satisfactorily dealing with customer needs in a profitable way. A number of marketing principles help move a potential customer from

INDIVIDUAL CASE STUDY

Assume you know nothing about physical therapy. You do not know whether there are any physical therapy practices in your area. You are at the awareness step. If a friend, spouse, or close family member had a condition or illness that required physical therapy intervention, how would you inform yourself so you could help your friend or others decide which clinic was the right one? Consider the following questions as you make your decision:

- How would you find out about physical therapy?
- How would you identify which clinics are possible choices for you?
- Where would you look to find a clinic?
- To whom would you speak about the various choices?
- What marketing elements might you be exposed to?
- What criteria would you set for making a decision about the clinic?
- If you personally toured a clinic, what would you look for as you visited the facility and the staff?
- What marketing elements would you expect to observe at the clinic?

GROUP CASE STUDY

Two-person groups are appropriate for this case.

Situation

Two staff physical therapists were daydreaming about the possibility of doing something to increase their number of patients with neck and shoulder pain. The orthopedic physicians who account for most referrals for physical therapy typically send people with lower back and lower extremity problems. The occupational therapy staff has shown more interest in patients with neurological and cognitive deficits than upper limb orthopedic problems. One teacher who is also a certified athletic trainer at the high school sees most of the athletes in the school's training room. To the best of your knowledge, most of the people with neck and upper extremity problems who live in your area drive 25 miles to a sports injury clinic.

Task

Your task is to flesh out your ideas and formulate a marketing plan for your target market. Use this list to get started:

- What other information do you need?
- Where will you get it?
- If you get stuck, be creative and make up the information to meet your needs.
- In the broad sense, who are the potential customers?
- Select the target groups you consider most important so as to focus your efforts.
- Identify the marketing mix (the eight P's) you would consider for each of the targeted customer groups.
- Do they differ?
- If so, how and why?
- Assess your performance.
- What needs do you still have?
- What will you do to meet them?

Armed with your marketing plan, meet with another pair and compare and contrast your plans. Form one plan that incorporates the best marketing mix for the target customers.

unawareness of a service or product to actually making a purchase. Collectively these principles are known as the marketing or communication mix. The basic mix is product (or service), promotion, price, place, and packaging, known collectively as the five P's. For service providers there are three additional P's: physical evidence of quality or effectiveness, personnel selection and training, and processes to instill confidence. Together the eight P's can be used to plan and conduct marketing activities specific for targeted customers. The specificity comes from selecting the appropriate mix of the eight P's for the targeted group.

In Chapter 22, we apply a 10-step strategic planning process to organize the formation of a marketing strategy in a health care context.

REFERENCES

AMA Board Approves New Marketing Definition. Marketing News. 1985; March 1:1.

Boone LE, Kurtz DL. Contemporary marketing, 5th ed. New York: Dryden Press. 1986.

Cooper CL, Arcyris C. The concise Blackwell encyclopedia of management. Malden, MA: Blackwell. 1998.

Hannagan T. Mastering strategic planning. New York: Palgrave. 2002.

Herzlinger R. Market driven health care. Reading, MA: Addison Wesley. 1997.

Hiam A, Schewe CD. The portable MBA in marketing. New York: Wiley. 1992.

Kotler P. Marketing for nonprofit organizations. Englewood Cliffs, NJ: Prentice-Hall. 1982.

Kotler P, Ferrell OC, Lamb C. Cases and readings for marketing for nonprofit organizations. Englewood Cliffs, NJ: Prentice-Hall. 1983.

Levinson JC. Guerrilla marketing: Secrets for making big profits from your small business. Boston: Houghton Mifflin. 1993.

Lewis B. Communication mix. In Lewis BR, Littler D, eds. The Blackwell encyclopedic dictionary of marketing. Malden, MA: Blackwell Business. 1999.

Macmillan H, Tampoe M. Strategic management process, content, and implementation. New York: Oxford University. 2000.

MacStravic RE. Marketing health care. Germantown, MD: Aspen. 1977.

Mullin BJ, Hardy S, Sutton WA. Sport marketing. Champaign, IL: Human Kinetics. 1993.

Nosse LJ, Friberg DG, Kovacek PR. Managerial and supervisory principles for physical therapists. Baltimore: Lippincott, Williams & Wilkins. 1999.

Schaefer K. Marketing techniques for physical therapists. Gaithersburg, MD: Aspen. 1991.

Stone CE. Effective marketing of CAM services. In Faass N, ed. Integrating complementary medicine into health systems. Gaithersburg, MD: Aspen. 2001:135–140.

Thompson G. A niche master. Physical Therapy Products—The Magazine for Physical Therapy Professionals. 2002:July/August:14.

MORE INFORMATION RELATED TO THIS CHAPTER

A home study course on marketing is available for purchase from www.apta.org.

Rehab Management is a free publication with interdisciplinary interest that regularly has articles on marketing. Go to http://www.rehabpub.com.

The concept of market justice and market forces is addressed in Shi L, Singh DA. Delivering health care in America: A systems approach, 2nd ed. Gaithersburg, MD: Aspen. 2001.

Service marketing is the focus of Chapter 1 in Ashkanasy NM, Wilderom CPM, Peterson MF, eds. Handbook of organizational culture and climate. Thousand Oaks, CA: Sage. 2000.

The latter part of Chapter 25 contains a discussion of health care consumers, their characteristics, and health care preferences in Kongstveldt PR, ed. Essentials of managed health care, 4th ed. Gaithersburg, MD: Aspen. 2001.

Chapter 22

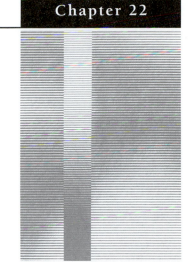

Strategic Organizational and Departmental Marketing

Learning Objectives

1. Define the concept of strategic planning and provide examples using health care businesses in general and physical therapy departments and clinics specifically.
2. Analyze the 10-step strategic planning process discussed in this chapter.
3. Apply market analysis tools, for example, strengths, weaknesses, opportunities, threats (SWOT) analysis and growth rate matrix, to specific physical therapy information.
4. Determine what types of information are usually gathered in an environmental assessment (scan) for health care marketing and where such information is likely to be found.
5. Discuss the concept of differential marketing and contrast the common ways to differentiate health care services from one another.
6. Evaluate four marketing orientations and compare them on the basis of the marketing strategies they adopt.
7. Evaluate the concepts of physical therapy service as a commodity and branding.

Key Words

Aim, branding, commodity, differential marketing advantage, environmental analysis, environmental scanning, ethics in marketing, goals, market attractiveness, market demand, market expansion, marketing plan, market retraction, mission statement, objective, orientation, philosophical statement, service or product revision, stakeholders, strategic marketing, strategic planning, strategy, SWOT analysis, vision statement

Introduction

A **strategy** consists of ideas and actions that focus on securing a desired future for an organization (Macmillan and Tampoe, 2000), group or individual. For an organization, a strategy is the plan that infuses the vision and mission into actions that are taken to assure a prosperous future for the organization (Mintzberg, Quinn, Voyer, 1995). Strategic planning links an organization's aspirations and purpose with its operations. It involves a candid assessment of the organization's strengths and weaknesses in relation to the threats and opportunities posed by factors external to the organization (Koteen, 1997; Mintzberg et al., 1995). This chapter builds on the basic information presented in Chapter 11 on strategic management and planning. It readdresses the basic steps of strategic planning in a focused application to marketing. The result of strategic planning is a **strategic marketing** plan. After identifying and discussing a 10-step strategic planning model, we examine special situations and considerations for physical therapy marketing and business development.

Ten-Step Strategic Planning Model

Strategic planning is "the continuous process of making entrepreneurial (risk-taking) decisions systematically and with the greatest knowledge of their futurity; organizing systematically the efforts needed to carry out these decisions; and measuring the results of these decisions against the expectations through organized, systematic feedback" (Drucker, 1993, p. 125). Figure 22.1 depicts a strategic planning model of 10 steps. The relative importance given to each step may vary with the nature of the organization and its planning needs. We describe each of the 10 steps in depth.

Step One: Define the Organization's Beliefs, Aspirations, and Purpose

The initiation of the strategic planning process as introduced in Chapter 11 is formulating three fundamental documents to guide the organization. Through introspection and discussion some, but not all, organizational leaders define what behaviors are valued and considered right and form a **philosophical statement** or values statement (Darr, 1997). Concurrently, the leaders outline what they believe the organization can become and describe the future in a **vision statement**. At the same time they state the more tangible mission of the organization. The **mission statement** typically contains the purpose of the organization, what it does well, for whom, where, and how. When there is no formal philosophical or values statement, mission statements often contain mission values, such as care for individuals with low income, patient advocacy, and teamwork (Pugno, 2001). Of all of the fundamental documents, health care workers are most intimately and consistently aware of the mission statement. The mission statement typically answers most of the following eight questions:

1. What are our central values? (if there is no separate philosophical statement)
2. What do we believe in?
3. What are we committed to?

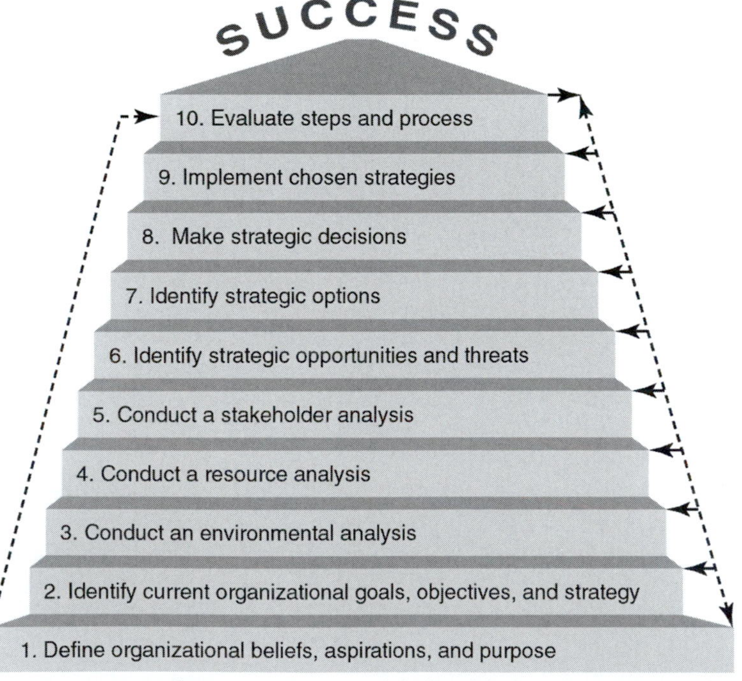

Figure 22.1. A 10-step strategic planning process model. (Modified with permission from Nosse, Friberg, 1992:147.)

4. What is our philosophy or ideology (if there is no separate philosophical statement)?
5. Who are we?
6. What needs do we intend to meet?
7. Whose needs? Who are our consumers?
8. What do we intend to do to satisfy the consumer's needs, that is, what services do we do well and intend to provide?

Mission statements can be as short as a sentence or a paragraph. They are useful as an agreed-upon statement of what the organization is about.

In a new project or service it is important to identify what is intended to happen. In an existing project or service it is important to identify what is actually happening. Whether what is happening should continue is a question throughout the strategic planning process, especially in steps 7 and 8 (Fig. 22.1). This must all be considered in the context of the vision of the organization (Chapters 11, 20 and 25).

Step Two: Identify the Organization's Aims or Goals, Objectives, and Strategy

To **aim** is to take sight of a target and direct efforts to hit it (Webster's II, 1984). Similarly, a **goal** is a statement of what is to be accomplished, such as increase the number of physical therapy referrals by 5% during the next fiscal year. Aims and goals are often used interchangeably. However, goal may be the preferred term because there are specific criteria for stating goals that allow their outcomes to be measured. One set of criteria for stating goals says they should be *s*pecific, *m*easurable, *a*greeable (to those responsible for carrying them out), *r*ealistic, and *t*ime bound (SMART) (Hannagan, 2002). Organizational goals therefore are the major targets at which management aims. A goal could be for a physical therapy manager to increase outpatient volume 5% within the next quarter. **Objectives** are necessary for goals to be realized. "An objective is a statement that complements the goal by stating how the goal is to be achieved" (Nosse and Friberg, 1992, p. 148). To bring about the goal of increased patient volume, an objective might be for the department manager to take the leadership in developing contracts with five local industries to provide physical therapy services at their work sites. The strategy used to meet the goal may be to differentiate the physical therapy organization from competitors by providing a new service that local competitors have not offered.

Step Three: Conduct an Environmental Analysis

The purpose of an **environmental analysis** is to identify the ways changes in the environment can indirectly influence the organization (Chapter 11). The environment has two perspectives: (1) the internal environment, or the organization itself, and (2) the external environment, or forces outside of the organization that can affect its success. The internal environment includes the organization's resources, competencies, structure, personnel and current, past, and future consumers. The external influences include changes in the economy and health care industry and competition in the marketplace (Macmillan and Tampoe, 2000). Some writers see the external environment as the focus of the assessment, that is, to identify opportunities that will benefit the organization and any threats to its welfare (Mintzberg et al., 1995). The focus of the internal environment assessment is on the organization's strengths and weaknesses (perceived as the opportunities and threats in the external environmental assessment of a competitor organization). Together analysis of *s*trength, *w*eaknesses, *o*pportunities, and *t*hreats are known as a **SWOT analysis** (McConkey, 1976).

Step Four: Conduct a Resource Analysis

This analysis includes a summary of all available resources for the development of the organization. The determination of available resources comes from the internal analysis. Resource analysis is therefore likely to be considered in the analysis of the organization's strengths and weaknesses. Organizations can often successfully build on their strengths and develop strategies to minimize their weaknesses.

Step Five: Conduct a Stakeholder Analysis

Stakeholders are defined as individuals or groups who are interested in an organization's products, services, or operations (internal and external environmental factors) (Longest, Rakich, Darr, 2000) (see Chapter 6). Stakeholders differ from stockholders, who are individuals and groups that buy shares of stock in a business with the intent of financial gain. It is important for an organization to know:

- Who their stakeholders are
- What their specific needs and wants are
- What their expectations of services and outcomes are
- What it will take to satisfy them and have them as future consumers

Key stakeholders include funding bodies, current and future consumers, staff, third-party payers, managers, volunteers, and suppliers. These people have a variety of views, values, and needs that influence the plans that are developed.

Step Six: Identify Strategic Opportunities and Threats

Opportunities and threats arise from sources outside the organization. This part of a SWOT analysis is often one of the initial analyses used to contribute to the strategic planning. In this case it provides a format and process for the identification, assessment, and evaluation of possibilities for and risks to the organization (Hannagan, 2002).

Step Seven: Identify Strategic Options

After the environment has been analyzed and the SWOT results have been reviewed, the outcomes of the existing strategy are clearer. The organization's management can then identify strategic options, for example, whether or not to modify the existing strategy or develop new strategies. There can be many specific strategic options to choose from (Ansoff, 1965; Mintzberg, et al.,1995; Porter, 1980), but most can be categorized as serving one of three goals (Hannagan, 2002):

1. Increase market share
2. Hold market share in an existing market
3. Withdraw from market

Market share is increased by **market expansion**. This can be done in the same market, in new markets, or in a new business. This is an aggressive approach that requires significant investment of resources to acquire, develop, and market expanded or new services or products. Purchasing a competitor is an example of market expansion. Holding market share can be accomplished by **service or product revision**, that is, some kind of modification. This can be considered a form of consolidation. This could be accomplished by reducing price. Doing so is likely to mean a reduction in income, because the strategy may not increase volume. Leaving the market is also called **market retraction**. It may be getting out of a market by terminating a service or selling a business. This strategy may stop financial loss and allow the remaining resources to be invested in expanding markets. In physical therapy this may be elimination of the sale of durable medical goods, that is, canes, wheelchairs, raised toilet seats, and so on. The storage space for such goods might be turned into a treatment area.

Step Eight: Make Strategic Decisions

A variety of decision models are available to help make a choice from among competing options. Some models, such as a simple vote for or against, are quite simple and expeditious, and some, for example, Delphi technique, focus groups, and multiple weighting, are fairly complex and time consuming. Figure 22.2 presents one of the decision-making processes that supports the 10-step strategic planning model. The figure reflects the incorporation of the organization's fundamental documents (Chapter 9) and SWOT analyses of all options to narrow the number down to those that best meet the organization's needs.

The large rings in Figure 22.2 represent steps 1 to 8 in the strategic planning model (Fig. 22.1). The gray areas and the connecting small circles reflect the results of steps 6 and 7, the identification of opportunities and threats and strategic options, respectively. The small centered circle represents the few viable options that meet organizational and stakeholder needs. These are the options considered in step 8. Typically, strategic marketing decisions mean choosing which services in a service line to expand, promote, rehabilitate, or discontinue. This is often a difficult choice. To help make these decisions we present additional information later, in the section on market attractiveness.

Step Nine: Implement the Chosen Strategy

Once the appropriate strategy has been chosen, it is implemented. A specific plan that includes assigned responsibilities, allocation of resources, time frame for start and finish, and measurable outcomes for goal achievement is formed. Goals should be SMART, and objectives leading to their completion should be complementary to the goals.

Step Ten: Evaluate Steps and Process

Evaluation of the level of success derived from the implemented strategy grades the strategic planning process. This means that the steps of the process should be evaluated individually and in aggregate. In Figure 22.1 the arrow with connections to each step in the process represents this evaluation. A minimal evaluative criteria set for any project, especially something as important to an organization as strategic planning, should include completion of the objectives in a timely manner in compliance with the established budget. Many other evaluative criteria are possible, depending on the nature of the plan. Any information gleaned from the evaluation should be used to improve the next cycle of strategic marketing and planning. In this way, the process is continually improved (Chapter 31).

Special Considerations in Strategic Marketing of Health Care Services and Products

Health care is a service industry, as are food services, travel services, realty services, and retail and wholesale clothing sales. Other than many health care service organizations having not-for-profit status, there are no

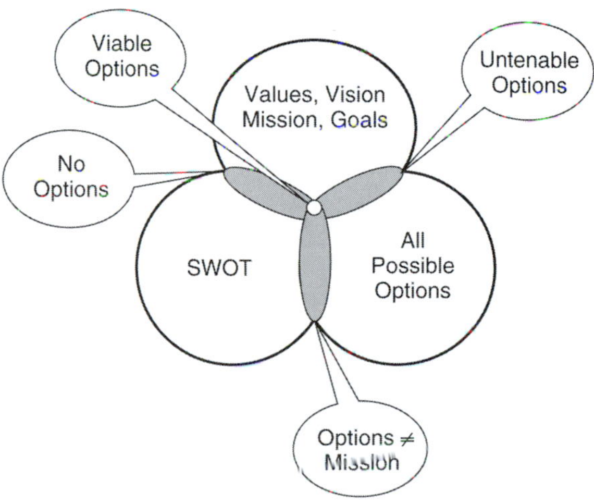

Figure 22.2. The interaction of the fundamental guiding documents of an organization and internal and external environmental analyses as means of reducing the number of options to those that are best for the organization.

major differences in the business sense between health care and other service businesses. The commonality among service industries is that their success ultimately depends on satisfying consumer needs. This commonality leads to the assumption that general service marketing principles are applicable to the marketing of health care services.

Financial Viability of a Market

Market demand is the desire of a group of potential consumers for a particular service or product. The individuals who are members of the targeted market may or may not recognize this need. Unrecognized demand for services can be overcome through education. It is critical to realize that there may be a huge difference between the need for a service or product and a market's ability to support the service or product. For example, many busy people might benefit from owning their own personal jet airplane, but few can afford it. In health care, the difference between market demand and financial viability is often not so clear. This is partly due to the third-party payment system, which has somewhat isolated patients from the financial implications of their health care services. While the need for physical therapy is not likely to recede with the graying of the baby boomers, the ability to pay the ever-increasing costs of health care services, including physical therapy, is limited. In fact, reimbursement for all health care services, especially in the Medicare population, has changed dramatically in all venues. These pending and probable changes in the physical therapy environments must be considered in any marketing activities for marketers and managers of physical therapy services.

Service Economy Issues

The demand for services and goods can be greatly affected by general economic conditions (Chapter 26). For example, fluctuating prices for home fuel have altered the market for products such as home insulation, storm windows, solar water heaters, and solar space heaters. Physical therapists practicing in 1997 will not forget the effect of the Balanced Budget Act of 1997 (Chapters 1 and 2) on reimbursement, employment, and health care organizations' viability. Astute managers carefully follow economic trends and shape their decisions accordingly. For example, casual dress at the workplace has led producers of clothing to shift much production from formal to informal attire. Changes in food preferences have led fast food operators to offer more chicken and fish in addition to the typical high-fat entrees. An example of international events affecting health care is mad cow disease. During the mad cow disease scare in Europe animal products were in limited supply. Drug manufacturers were limited in their ability to produce drugs such as glucocorticoids. One of these, dexamethasone sodium phosphate, is used in iontophoresis treatments. The scare caused a temporary shortage of the product and in some cases unavailability of some physical therapy.

Significant differences may exist within many regions, states, and cities of the United States. Managers must take these differences into account when assessing opportunities. Economic fluctuations are also important to decision making. Changing economic patterns affect future demand. U.S. economic expansion has been running 3 to 6% per year. All managers should be aware of the relationships between the growth rate of the nation or a particular region and trends within their own business. Also significant are the differential rates of growth of a particular segment of a population and how that may affect your target market. Knowledge of the relationship between economic fluctuations and demand for health care and physical therapy can help physical therapy and other health care managers plan marketing actions. Even otherwise sound strategies can fail if an organization launches them at the wrong time.

Market Attractiveness

Figure 22.1 shows the **market attractiveness** matrix (Henderson, 1984). Its purpose is to examine each service or product and market together. Four market growth acronyms represent different degrees of market growth and relative market share. This figure provides general criteria to evaluate each couplet, that is, a service or product in relation to its market growth rate and market share, both of which relate to profitability. There are four categories of couplets, that is, items assessed on the basis of market growth rate and relative market share. A manager can plug in his or her individual services or products to make comparisons. Couplets with low market growth and market share have low profitability. The market is flat and the organization has a relatively small portion of it, that is, they are dogs. Services in this quadrant may be terminated or reorganized depending on the growth possibilities if the service is reconfigured. Couplets with high market growth but low market share and low profitability are problem children. Services in this quadrant may require increased investment in marketing to increase market share. Couplets with low market growth but a high percentage of the market are profitable. They are known as cash cows. Cash cows may be services at the end of their life cycle (Chapters 20 and 23). Managers must decide about terminating, expending resources, or accepting the current level of performance. Finally, the most desirable couplet is the one with a high market growth rate and a high percentage of the market, which in combination produce high profits. These are stars. Stars represent the best changes for long-term growth and profitability and typically receive resources to improve, diversify, and capture greater market share (Ginter et al., 1998).

Management strategies for dealing with less attractive services and products may be quite different depending on the relative attractiveness of the various couplets. Clearly stars are more desirable than dogs or problem children. Each service and product in each market should be analyzed periodically according to this market attractiveness matrix.

Orientations Toward Marketing

Over the long run, success requires that a company find and maintain some type of **differential marketing advantage.** The task is to communicate to consumers the superiority of the organization's services and products over those offered by its competitors. Lazer and Culley (1983) suggest four managerial orientations or business philosophies that managers can take to develop a differential marketing advantage:

- Production orientation
- Sales orientation
- Marketing orientation
- Societal orientation

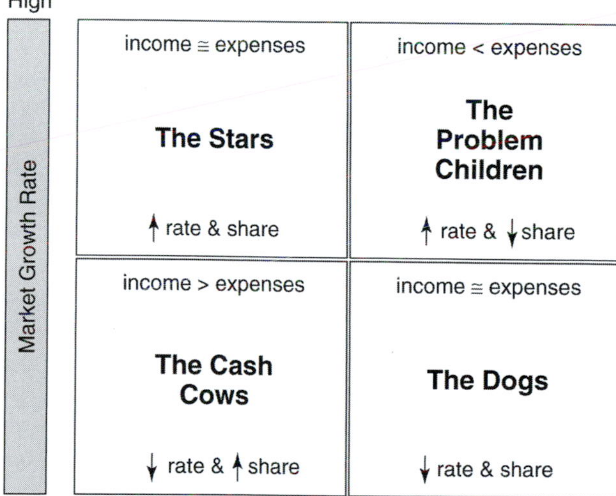

Figure 22.3. Growth rate–market share matrix. (Based on Henderson [1984] and Ginter et al. [1998:222].)

In this context the **orientation** refers to the primary activities and operations of the business. Is the major objective to produce, to sell, to market services and goods, or to maintain the physical environment? A company's orientation can be discovered by asking management, why are you in business? Quite different answers will come from different companies, revealing major disparities in business philosophy. A for-profit physical therapy organization may answer the question by saying it is in business to serve stakeholders and shareholders. A not-for-profit physical therapy organization may limit the answer to stakeholders (Chapter 7).

Production Orientation

An organization with a production orientation holds that the key to business success lies in solving technological problems. Managers may insist on service or product quality, but they do so from a technical perspective, seeking services and products that program developers and others view as useful or important. They seek standardization and place less emphasis on designing the right service or product to meet unique consumer needs. They also downplay the importance of promoting the service or product, securing the right distribution, and other marketing activities. Essentially, the business philosophy underlying a production orientation assumes that good services, products, and ideas will sell themselves. Some of the U.S. auto manufacturers held this philosophy up to the 1970s. They were generally engineering oriented. But major inroads by foreign competition forced a change in management and the adoption of a marketing orientation. A physical therapy example of the assumption that good things sell themselves would be to build a therapeutic pool that is attractive, safe, and spacious and expect patients to automatically come for aquatic therapy.

Managers with a production orientation may overengineer or overdesign a service or product. This means creating an offering that has more features and that costs more than consumers, particularly managed care organizations, want to pay. It is possible to create a health care facility that is so expensive that few consumers will be able to afford the care offered there. An example is an architecturally beautiful women's health facility attached to a hospital. The women's facility could have an atrium with a garden, rooms with fireplaces, marble bathrooms, multiple-head showers, and gourmet low-calorie meals. However, the cost to patients after their insurance paid its share of the bill would probably be more than most are willing to pay. What it comes down to is that most buyers look for value, that is, the best service at the lowest cost.

Sales Orientation

An organization with a sales orientation acts as if the key to business success lies in better selling systems, structures, and personnel. Some managers insist on intensive selling activities. This at times seems to reflect minimal interest in service quality. A sales-oriented manager downplays listening to the market during the service or product development stages and focuses on pushing product on a waiting market. Managers and employees are promoted or rewarded based on their relative ability to get product out the door or on the volume of treatments given each day. The risk to the sales-oriented organization or manager is that they will create a group of dissatisfied consumers who may be wary of doing business with them again. Physical therapy clinics with a very high patient to therapist ratio coupled with minimal contact with therapists face this risk.

Marketing Orientation

Central to any organization's business success is the adoption of a strong marketing orientation. A marketing orientation increases the likelihood of success. It is necessary to identify the company's market alternatives and then try the most promising of these. This requires a thorough understanding of the basic marketing concepts. The physical therapy manager should pursue the organization's overall objectives and goals. This is accomplished by identifying and satisfying the needs of target consumers.

Societal Orientation

An organization with a societal orientation acts as if it exists primarily to serve the community at large. Services and products that promote the general good and welfare of the immediate or expanded community are deemed desirable. Managers insist on developing services and products that will be for the greater good, sometimes to the detriment of the organization itself. Managers and employees are rewarded and promoted for their community service rather than for generating revenue. The risk to the organization is that without a strong philanthropy program or ability to garner consumer support for even weak services and products, the very existence of the organization is at risk.

Generally organizations develop an orientation that is a combination of these choices.

Strategic Aspects of the Marketing Plan

A **marketing plan** is a basic component of every good business plan. A strong marketing plan offers a wealth of information that if applied correctly can enhance the chances of success. Therefore, it is important to develop a comprehensive, effective marketing plan. A well-written, comprehensive business plan with a well-defined marketing plan is one of the focal points of all business ventures. This is because the marketing plan describes how you plan to attract and retain consumers. This is the most crucial aspect of a business. This section focuses on the marketing plan.

Tools of Marketing Analysis

The main purpose of marketing tools and analyses is to clarify the future for the organization so that it is possible to develop an effective strategy that will provide real solutions to patient, client, and consumer problems. The most frequently used tool is the SWOT analysis (McConkey, 1976) (Table 22.1). The SWOT analysis allows the organization to identify the building blocks upon which to develop further programs and services (strengths), the areas for improvement (weaknesses), the external situations that could become advantages (opportunities), and external situations that could hinder the future development of the organization (*t*hreats) (Chapter 11).

Sources of data outside the organization can include government information, trade associations, and private companies that spe-

Table 22.1 SWOT Analysis Template

Service/Product ____________________	*Completion Date* _____
Internal Factors	
Strengths	Comments
1.	
2.	
etc.	
Weaknesses	Comments
1.	
2.	
etc.	
External Factors:	
Opportunities	Comments
1.	
2.	
etc.	
Threats	Comments
1.	
2.	
etc.	
Analysis conducted by____________________	From _______ to_______

cialize in providing information. While external information may be expensive, it can be worth the expense to remove some of the uncertainty of the proposed venture. Despite having the best information, no business can predict everything; there are always surprises in store. The question is where to get strategically useful external information. The next section describes environmental scanning, one of the ways to acquire external information (Chapter 11).

Environmental Scanning

Another tool for market analysis is **environmental scanning**. This is systematic surveillance and interpretation designed to identify events, elements, and conditions of the environment with the potential to affect the organization. This process monitors ongoing changes that may affect the business (Hiam and Schewe, 1992; Tull and Hawkins, 1987).

Marketing managers do not make their decisions in a vacuum. Rather, they consider what is happening in society. Societal considerations are those imposed by groups, among the most important of which are cultures and subcultures. An important environmental input to marketing strategy originates from the culture in which the company operates, that is, core values and philosophy of the organization that reflect the beliefs of those at the highest managerial level (Chapter 9).

Managers who are aware of and understand trends and developments in their markets or potential markets are in a position to develop new strategies through better satisfaction of existing markets and penetration of new markets.

Cultural Issues in Strategic Marketing

Special attention should be given to the culture of the identified markets. Culture is the combination of values and norms that governs behavior in a large group and is passed on from generation to generation (Chapters 11 and 18). It includes moral philosophy, customs, taboos, laws, beliefs, and knowledge. Members of a culture receive rewards, in the form of economic benefits and the approval of others, when they adhere to values of that culture. Deviation from these values is often followed by various forms of punishment, including subtle consequences, such as the loss of esteem in important groups. Hence, there is considerable incentive to conform. It is important that physical therapy managers formulate strategies that are in accordance with the value priorities of the society in which they practice (Chapter 6). The culture is an important determinant of consumer behavior, law, ethics, and the conduct of intermediaries, suppliers, employees, and other groups. It is especially important in the design and delivery of health care services such as physical therapy. Marketing strategies that are not in agreement with important cultural values often fail. It is in the self-interest of managers to become students of the culture in which they operate.

Governmental Issues

Clearly, government actions can have an impact on the marketing activities of all companies. One of the most important of the political variables is government's overall attitude toward business. If government and society are reasonably satisfied with the performance of the business sector, the political climate tends to offer a large number of marketing opportunities. On the other hand, if there is public displeasure, businesses face the threat of punitive or restrictive legislation and regulation.

Government's attitude toward business is generally positive in the United States today. However, this is not true for health care. There is a trend toward more control of health care business practices (Chapters 1–4 and 10). Anticipating changes in government regulation enables an organization to set in motion the processes to change the procedures and the practices necessary to address the change.

Ethics in Marketing

Ethical issues often arise in marketing. Ethics relates to philosophical rules for acceptable actions that one employs as a guide for day-to-day behavior (Chapter 6). In marketing, ethical conduct is related to interactions with other parties. Such interactions are ideally guided by an organization's philosophical statement and by the application of principles of ethics, professional codes, and interpretive guides, such as the American Physical Therapy Association's Code of Ethics and Guide for Professional Conduct (www.apta.org/About.core_documents). An example is a private practice owner whose respect for the principle of justice leads him to provide pro bono services one afternoon a week in economically depressed areas. A different example is a hospital's orthopedic and sports injury outpatient site that does not put up pictures or posters of very thin women because this may encourage young girls to engage in unhealthy nutritional practices.

Marketing ethics is a cloudy issue because different individuals value philosophical principles differently. Ethical questions are answered through guided reasoning. They do not have fixed answers. Managers must select a standard of conduct that fits both their personal beliefs and their environment. To some degree, managers learn ethical principles from their culture. They also learn these values from the specific company for which they work. Each health care organization has a culture including a set of ethical beliefs that may or may not be formally stated (Chapter 9). Most new employees quickly learn these beliefs, or they have difficulty fitting in. Professional associations also have established ethical standards to guide their members. It is important that all personnel for an organization familiarize themselves with the guiding principles of their profession and those of their employer.

Health Care and Commodity Selling

A **commodity** is a service or product that is not differentiated from competitive offerings by any characteristic other than price. Typically products are more likely to be thought of as commodities than are services, although services can be considered commodities.

Some of the best examples of commodities are agricultural products such as grains and meat products. In a typical market, there is little to differentiate one source of wheat, corn, or unprocessed meat from another. Companies that sell commodities must stand out in the market because of either lower prices or other value-added characteristics such as prompt delivery or special guarantees. An additional example of commodity marketing is seen in the office supply industry. All of the competitors in this market carry more or less the same products and offer essentially the same services. They compete on price, satisfaction guarantees, and location.

How does the concept of commodities relate to physical therapy? Well, third-party payers and government are applying pressure to standardize physical therapy services. In some ways this may be good for the profession, especially as we consider outcomes (Chapter 31). However, it also moves physical therapy closer to being a commodity, that is, business transacted primarily on the basis of price. The potential sequela of standardization (when taken to a not-too-distant extreme) can be that physical therapy services will be considered a commodity for which the major points of competition are on price rather than quality or differentiation of services. The commodity trend should be resisted, as it may limit professional autonomy, and from a marketing perspective, differentiation of services to consumers.

When we contemplate physical therapy as a commodity, it is helpful to examine other industries that have gone through this process (office supplies, optical services, and grocery stores) and determine strategies to maintain high quality and affordable prices.

Few if any industries want to provide services or products as commodities. Physical therapists should be no different.

Marketing the Concept of Physical Therapy

In addition to promoting our physical therapy organization, it is important to recognize that each promotional message also has influences the recognition and understanding of physical therapy as a general concept. Many individuals in the general population are not familiar with physical therapy. Our promotional efforts may be their only exposure.

There is a saying in the fast food business: McDonald's advertising sells a lot of Burger King Whoppers. Although McDonald's advertising encourages consumers to buy at the Golden Arches, it also promotes the general concept of fast food and burgers, and all of the competitors in the fast food business benefit.

So it is with physical therapy marketing. Much of the advertising of the larger corporate physical therapy companies has also promoted the concept of physical therapy to the general public. This may have indirectly helped other physical therapy practices. The American Physical Therapy Association has undertaken to market the concept of physical therapy through ads in women's magazines, production and dissemination of a variety of posters, and the release of 30-second videos for public service announcements.

Branding

Branding is the positioning of services or products as high quality to influence the consumer to choose that service or product even at a premium price (Hannagan, 2002). Nike does it. So does McDonald's. So does Mercedes Benz (now part of Daimler Chrysler). In the service industry, few do it as well as Disney. In health care, Columbia HCA has worked to establish brand recognition. In rehabilitation, branding has been a major strategy for Health South.

Successful branding allows the company to develop consumer loyalty and possibly charge a higher price. At the minimum, consumers may develop a greater trust for branded services and products. For example, many people buy Craftsman tools from Sears, not because they are necessarily better tools, but because of the lifetime guarantee. Other people frequent McDonald's, not because the quality of food is so high, but because they feel safe assuming the rest rooms will be clean. A physical therapist who worked in professional athletics was one of the first to fill a medically oriented fitness niche. He promoted education, experience, energy, environment, and equipment (Thompson, 2002) as his name became synonymous with this niche. In the 1980s and early 1990s his centers were high profile. He capitalized on his brand name by eventually selling his business for a reported $40 million (Thompson, 2002). There are also branding examples in continuing education for physical therapists. These include the Upledger Institute (craniosacral therapy), Barnes' myofascial release (treatment of fascial tissue restrictions), and the Leduc method (lymphedema management).

An interesting question is what we can do to establish physical therapy as a brand. At this point, reputation does not matter much because of limited public recognition of the concept of physical therapy as being different from other services such as chiropractic, athletic training, and massage therapy. Only time and a strong commitment to evidence-based practice complemented by a distinguished clinical success record can a supportable and favorable concept of physical therapy be communicated to the general population. Consumer satisfaction and marketing are critical to this effort.

It is often difficult—but not impossible—to develop brand recognition for small or single-site businesses or clinics. Exceptions to this statement are frequent. For example, many cities have favorite restaurants that frequent travelers go out of their way to visit. Some have almost developed cult followings that give evidence to very strong customer loyalty. Some continuing education providers of courses for physical therapists, particularly those dealing with manual therapy in its various forms, have this kind of consumer loyalty. The LAMP Summits developed originally by the Section on Administration for managers have had success in attracting many repeat attendees as well as faculty. Perhaps continued individual successes can act in synergy with profession-wide efforts to bring about a wider recognition of the concept of physical therapy.

Student Notes

This chapter discusses a process and guidelines for formulating and measuring strategic plans specifically for marketing physical therapy services. The difference in responsibility and organizational influence between those who make organization-wide strategic plans and the responsibilities and influence of a new graduate employee may make this information seem unimportant to staff therapists.

In the real world strategic planning of some type is done in all organizations. For those who are affected by strategic plans it is important to understand the process and how strategic plans affect the everyday work of the organization. If you know the process, you have a chance to influence those who make the decisions. Furthermore, knowing the process allows you to use it to your advantage, be it to get a hearing on a clinical program or to get responsibility to develop new programs. Employing some form of strategic planning is a way to become a balanced physical therapist, one who can do a credible job with management tasks *and* direct care tasks.

Summary

A strategy is a set of ideas and actions directed toward securing a desired future. An organization-wide set of strategies is developed by upper-level managers through strategic planning. This chapter introduces a 10-step strategic planning model and applies the steps to developing a strategic marketing plan. Each step of the model is discussed in terms of generic service and product businesses and then applied to physical therapy issues. The key concept is that the process links an organization's aspirations and purpose with its operations through identification of its strengths, weaknesses, and the opportunities and threats posed by various external forces. The application of the SWOT analysis coupled with an external environmental assessment uncovers options that the organization may use to fulfill its mission and vision under the umbrella of its philosophy. The pros and cons of common strategies for dealing with stakeholder needs with the available resources are considered. The latter part of the chapter introduces ethical aspects of marketing, the idea of marketing the concept of physical therapy (as opposed to a single organization), and branding.

The general concepts of strategic planning are covered in Chapter 11. This chapter applies them specifically to the development of a strategic marketing plan for several aspects of physical therapy. The next chapter builds on this familiarity with strategic planning and adds more depth to selected concepts that have already been introduced, for example, the eight P's. New concepts include the life cycle of services and products and the communications mix acronym AIDA (*a*ttention, *i*nterest, *d*esire, and *a*ction).

INDIVIDUAL CASE STUDY

You have been in enough clinical situations as a volunteer, observer, consumer, intern, or employee to recognize differences and similarities between the services and products offered by different organizations or by various departments within an organization. Think about and answer the following questions:

1. What was distinguishable, notable, got your attention, rang your bell about each clinical situation?
2. From the perspective of a consumer, what were the distinctive characteristics of each facility?
3. Was anything associated with these facilities that you consider brandable?

If nothing stood out as unique in any of your clinical education experience, identify something that had the potential to advance the concept of physical therapy.

GROUP CASE STUDY

Form small groups of class members who have been to one or more of the same clinical experience sites.

Tasks

Answer the questions in the individual case study. Come to agreement on which site had the greatest differential marketing and branding potential. Either develop a marketing plan to communicate the potential differential marketing advantage to consumers or develop a strategic plan focused on branding whatever the unique service or product the facility had.

REFERENCES

Ansoff HI. Corporate strategy: An analytic approach to business policy for growth and expansion. New York: McGraw-Hill. 1965.

Darr K. Ethics in health services management, 3rd ed. Baltimore: Health Professions. 1997.

Drucker PF. Management: Tasks, responsibilities, practices. New York: Harper and Row, 1974. Reprinted by Harper Business. 1993.

Ginter PM, Swayne LM, Duncan WJ. Strategic management of health care organizations, 3rd ed. Malden, MA: Blackwell. 1998.

Hannagan T. Mastering strategic management. New York; Palgrave. 2002.

Hiam A, Schewe CD. The portable MBA in marketing. New York: Wiley. 1992.

Henderson B. The logic of business strategy. New York: Ballinger, 1984.

Koteen J. Strategic management in public and nonprofit organizations, 2nd ed. Westport, CT: Praeger. 1997.

Lazer W, Culley JD. Marketing management foundations and practices. Boston: Houghton Mifflin. 1983.

Longest BB, Jr., Rakich JS, Darr K. Managing health services organizations and systems, 4th ed. Baltimore: Health Professions. 2000.

Macmillan H, Tampoe M. Strategic management process, content, and implementation. New York: Oxford University. 2000.

McConkey DD. How to manage by results, 3rd ed. New York: AMACOM. 1976.

Mintzberg H, Quinn JB, Voyer J. The strategy process, Collegiate edition. Englewood Cliffs, NJ: Prentice Hall. 1995.

Nosse LJ, Friberg DG. Management principles for physical therapists. Baltimore: Williams & Wilkins. 1992.

Porter ME. Competitive strategy: Techniques for analyzing industries and competitors. New York: Free Press. 1980.

Pugno PA. A mortgage on the house of God. In Loewy EH and Springer Loewy R, eds. Changing health care systems from ethical, economic, and cross cultural perspectives. New York: Kluwer Academic/Plenum. 2001:63–69.

Thompson G. A niche master. Physical Therapy Products. 2002;July/August:14.

Tull DS, Hawkins DI. Marketing research measurement and method, 4th ed. New York: Macmillan. 1987.

Webster's II New Riverside University Dictionary. Boston: Houghton Mifflin. 1984.

MORE INFORMATION RELATED TO THIS CHAPTER

More on making strategic choices and marketing can be found in Chapter 11 of Macmillan and Tampoe (2000).

Health care strategic marketing is the focus of Chapter 8 in Ginter et al. (1998).

Strategic tools and techniques are the focus of Part 4 in Koch R. The Financial Times guide to strategy: How to create and deliver a useful strategy, 2nd ed. New York: Prentice Hall-Financial Times. 2000. The section includes substantial information on the market growth-market share matrix and branding.

A unique perspective on marketing, competitive advantage, and a concept called market space can be found in Chapter 1 in Mische MA. Strategic renewal: Becoming a high-performance organization. Upper Saddle River, NJ: Prentice Hall. 2001.

Chapter 23

MARKETING STRATEGIES

Learning Objectives

1. Analyze the five P's of product marketing and the three P's of service marketing in the context of physical therapy services.
2. Contrast the major approaches to maximize profit: increase market share, expand the market, enter a new market, and retrench.
3. Compare the major pricing strategies presented in this chapter.
4. Compare the major approaches to position a product: leadership, innovation, and customer orientation.
5. Discuss the concept of the product life cycle and analyze the marketing strategies applicable at each part of the cycle.
6. Examine the concepts known as product mix, promotional mix, and communication mix.
7. Explore the AIDA model in relation to potential consumers' reactions to advertisement.

Key Words

AIDA model, communication mix, competition-based pricing, copy, cost-based pricing, cost plus pricing, diversification, format, high-profile marketing, low-profile marketing, market expansion, market position, market share, marketing, marketing mix, markup pricing, opportunity costs, preemptive penetration, prestige pricing, pricing, product life cycle, product mix, product portfolio analysis, product position, profit maximization, promotional mix, public relations, selective penetration, theme

Introduction

This chapter builds upon the marketing principles and strategies introduced in Chapters 21 and 22, respectively. The focus of this chapter is on the application of the marketing principles to circumstances frequently encountered in building a physical therapy practice in any environment. Each component of the marketing mix, that is, the five plus three P's, are examined in the specific context of physical therapy, and examples of successful marketing decisions are discussed. Strategies for differentiating services and products are blended into the discussion.

Much more research has gone into the marketing of products than services. One reason is that marketing can make up as much as 50% of the cost of a product (Schoch and Yap, 1998). For service industries like health care, the largest proportion of the cost of service is labor (Chapter 28). Whether the offering is a service, a product, or both, potential consumers need to be informed of its availability and unique characteristics. Communicating these facts through the 5 + 3 P's is service **marketing**. Marketing is important to influence potential consumers to act on the com-

...nications conveyed so they ultimately purchase the service or product.

Marketing Principles

The marketing principles to be discussed are linked, more or less, to making a profit on the services or products. While several new principles are presented in this chapter, most of the material adds depth and refines the principles introduced in Chapters 21 and 22. The key business principles associated with marketing are discussed first.

Profit Maximization Strategies

Profit maximization requires that a high price be received while the costs associated with the delivery of a service or product are minimized (Chapter 29). In the case of products, it is necessary to minimize production and delivery costs. Because most physical therapy businesses strive for profit, let us examine the strategies that are available to increase profits in the delivery of services. Recognize that these same strategies are available to minimize or reverse a deficit.

The price that a given service will bring is based on many things. We discuss these briefly here and in progressively more detail throughout this chapter. Although the third-party payment system has substantial effects on the delivery of all health care services, variation in pricing to at least some degree is possible and desirable in physical therapy.

Several key factors are involved in the successful pricing of physical therapy services. Among these are competition and price elasticity, reputation, branding, and organizational objectives.

Market Share Maximization

Market share is the proportion of members of a defined market that have the potential to patronize a particular business entity (Sherman, 1999). Regarding market share, a business can do three things: (1) increase market share by expanding efforts in the existing market, (2) enter a new market, or (3) drop out of a market. Therefore, the three major strategies that a practice or department may select to increase their market share are (1) market expansion, (2) market entry, and (3) retrenchment. All three of these strategies are widely used in business, and each has its particular strengths and weaknesses.

Market expansion is generally the safest and most conservative of the strategies. It is based upon trying to improve organizational performance by more fully satisfying an existing market target as opposed to selecting new or additional ones. Many physical therapy practices are attracted to this strategy, as it keeps them in their current market. Since expansion is doing more of what has been done, it is familiar and comfortable, both to managers and to employees. Both groups are likely to feel that straying into new fields is risky. Risk is closely associated with the degree to which the company extends its efforts into new areas.

Market Entry

Market entry refers to offering a service or product to a new market. Environmental assessment may point out an opportunity for a new service or product to be offered. To bring this service or product to a new market at a price that consumers will pay requires having the following information:

- How well competitors are doing in this market: if they are doing well, that is good for new entrants.
- How large the target market is: large is good for new entrants.
- How many competitors there are: a large number is not good for new entrants.
- How much rivalry there is among competitors: strong rivalries, brand recognition, and others with large marketing budgets make entry difficult.
- How many other potential new entrants there are: a large number of new entrants increases competition, which is not good for most of them.
- How quickly competitors will respond: slow is good for new entrants.
- How sustainable the service or product is: the longer the better for new entrants.

Obviously, some of this information is difficult to obtain. Some of it does not yet exist. And predicting what others will and will not do is speculation. For all of these reasons gaining a share of the market through the market entry strategy can be challenging.

Retrenchment

When an existing service or product has a small share of the market and the market is not growing, there are two main options. The first is to do nothing, that is, accept the status quo. This is done when the offering is profitable. It allows a presence in the market. This may help sales of other of the company's services and products. The second option is to drop out of the market. Doing so frees resources to be invested in the company's more profitable services and products to increase market share.

Product Quality Leadership

Another pricing strategy is the pursuit of leadership in perceived quality. Simply put, this strategy is to create the perception that you are better than your competitors. In product marketing it is often possible to arrange objective, reproducible tests to compare. This is more difficult in the service industry, but there are some common mechanisms of comparison in health care. Most of these are related to hospitality services or clinical outcome. Examples of indicators of quality in the hospitality arena are waiting times for services, facility cleanliness, and customer-perceived quality of food services. Outcome indicators of quality, addressed more thoroughly later in this course, include mortality, morbidity, discharge to unsupervised environments, functional outcomes, and level of impairment following intervention. Many of these indicators are difficult for even a knowledgeable and experienced physical therapist to interpret. Because of the difficulty in interpretation, the general public is often poorly prepared to compare quality of health care in any manner other than their personal perception of overall satisfaction.

The complexity of measuring quality in health care creates great difficulty establishing a credible claim of superior quality for one health care provider over the competition. However, when one provider in a market has either the general perception of higher quality or objective credible evidence of superior quality, that provider should make every effort to capitalize on it.

Pricing

Of the five P's, pricing may be the most difficult for marketing managers to deal with (Schoch and Yap, 1998). **Pricing**, or attaching a dollar value to a service or product, is one of the most important marketing decisions that management makes. In health care generally and physical therapy specifically, pricing decisions can be complex and at times may seem daunting to even the most experienced manager. There is no doubt that the third-party payment system and intense government regulation and oversight have had a profound effect on health care and physical therapy pricing (Chapters 2, 3, and 28).

We examine the nuances of reimbursement and finance in much greater detail later in Part V of this text. For now, attention will be limited to the examination of the role of pricing as part of the total marketing mix.

The stakes are high when making pricing decisions. Too high a price means that the product will not sell, while too low a price dictates low profits or even losses. Basically, there are three major instances when management makes pricing decisions:

- When offering new services and products
- In response to competitor-initiated price changes
- When the organization itself initiates the price changes

Before setting a price, management must decide what it wishes to accomplish with the particular product. If the target market and market position have been selected carefully, the marketing mix strategy, including price, will be relatively straightforward. For example, auto detailers have targeted themselves at the customized, top-quality end of the car cleaning market. Accordingly, they must charge a high price to reflect their time and costs and to portray a prestige image. If the company portrays itself as a low-price contender, actual prices should reflect this objective. Advertisements may carry the message that the firm offers low prices, but if consumers who consider the product find that the prices are not especially competitive, the promotion will fail. In fact, considerable consumer hostility can result when actual prices do not live up to the status promised in the advertisements.

Pricing Strategies

The law prohibits price discrimination, that is, selling the same item to competitive buyers at different prices. However, if there is a difference in costs based on, say, volume, that is, fixed costs per item are less for sale of a large amount, different prices can be offered (Clarkson, Miller, Jentz, Cross, 1995). Other than this limitation, pricing is mostly a managerial decision. What strategies should management consider when setting prices? There are several approaches to pricing:

- Cost-based pricing
- Competition-based pricing
- Demand-based pricing

Cost-Based Pricing Strategies

Cost-based pricing strategies are cost driven (Schoch and Yap, 1998). Prices are set relative to costs, that is, relatively little emphasis is placed on demand and competition. In physical therapy, determining the actual costs of the provision of services is difficult because clinical managers often do not have full access to such information or the information is gathered for purposes other than what the clinical manager needs. These are the four major **cost-based strategies**:

- Markup pricing
- Cost plus pricing
- Target return pricing
- Payback period pricing

Markup pricing is widely used in health care and physical therapy. Companies mark up services and products by a fixed percentage over costs. This is a common pricing method for middlemen in many industries. For instance, clothing retailers may apply a markup of 40%, while confectionery wholesalers may use a 10% margin. At one time many trade associations issued books or lists of suggested markups for members of the industry. Items with elastic demand generally had smaller percentage markups than did those with inelastic demand (Chapter 26). Markup pricing is often used in the marketing of durable medical equipment.

Many service managers also use markup pricing. To illustrate, accounting, consulting, and law firms often bill clients at a percentage over labor costs. Some organizations that market many different items find standard markups to be the only feasible way to set prices. Many contract physical therapy companies use markup pricing to provide an understandable mechanism to determine fees for services provided to hospitals and skilled nursing facilities.

Large retail organizations sell thousands of different products. In this scenario, complicated pricing methods are impractical, despite other virtues that they might have, after multiplying the difficulty of using such methods for a single service or product by the many items that a firm might handle. More complicated pricing methods make estimates of demand, cost, and competition and combine these estimates to produce sophisticated pricing models. Cost reimbursement for physical therapy services (Chapter 28) is a method of markup pricing.

Cost Plus Pricing

Cost plus pricing entails summing the costs to develop, produce, market, and sell services and products and adding an arbitrary margin of profit. Cost plus pricing disregards competitors' prices and what potential consumers are willing to pay. It may be difficult to determine the costs because of accounting procedures, especially for costs of transferring services or goods between units within the same organization. Discounts, bad debts, and new technology are other costs that at best can only be estimated. Difficulty in determining costs is a common problem for the following cost-focused pricing methods as well.

Target Return Pricing

Target return pricing computes the price starting with a desired percentage of return on the investment. With this set, the other costs are computed and summed. The target return percentage is calculated and added to the sum of the costs to get the final price. As with the other cost-based pricing methods, customers and competitors are not given direct consideration.

Payback Period Pricing

Payback period pricing looks forward to a time at which the return on investment will be at a desirable level. This means basing the profit level on expected sales volume by a specific time before the service or product is launched. Pricing this way helps to ensure acceptable cash flow (Wilson, 1999) (Chapter 27). Organizations that use this method of pricing do not look beyond their own profit needs when considering how to price their offerings.

The next types of pricing differ from cost-based pricing because they have an external focus. They take into consideration what potential consumers are willing to pay and their competitors' prices.

Competitor Pricing

Competitor pricing plays a dominant role in influencing the practices of some organizations. Generally, the less differentiated services or items are within a market, the greater is the need to determine prices in relation to those of competitors. At an extreme, the lack of differentiation forces organizations to adopt prevailing market prices. In health care this occurs when insurance companies agree to pay providers usual and customary prices for a given service or set of services. This method determines the typical price for services in a specific market and prices new providers or services according to existing practice.

Probably no industry completely satisfies the conditions of perfect competition, but some commodity markets closely approximate this condition. Consider the wheat industry. Wheat is clearly a commodity. With some minor exceptions and assuming it is the same type, the wheat produced by one farmer is essentially the same as that produced by another (Chapter 22). The product is undifferentiated. No farm would raise its price above the market level, because no one would buy the wheat. And there is no incentive to sell below the market level, because that would only lower profits. But often there are some differentiation possibilities, such as through delivery schedules, location, or some other variation in the marketing mix (Mintzberg, Quinn, Voyer, 1995). The greater the differentiation, the more a firm can price independently from competitors and possibly improve profits. If a physical therapy practice wants to differentiate its offering, there are ways to change the situation. One way is to appeal to what consumers value.

Prestige Pricing

Prestige pricing is a form of demand-oriented pricing (Koschnick, 1995). Prestige pricing is charging a premium price for a service or product. It is a strategy designed to capitalize on the perception that cost and quality are linked. Some consumers have a strong conviction that you get what you pay for. These consumers perceive quality and prestige to be proportional to an item's price, and they will pay more in the expectation of getting the best available. Whether this is true for health care is unclear. Prestige pricing applies to fee-for-service but not managed care (Chapters 2 and 28). Traditional economic theory of supply and demand predicted that as companies lowered their prices, they should sell more (Chapter 26). That idea holds true for many goods and services. Prestige items bring about the opposite behavior, however. Health care managers seeking to penetrate high-prestige or high-quality market segments should be aware that many buyers expect relatively high prices. This does not mean that other elements of the marketing mix are unimportant. An item's actual quality, even when quality is difficult to measure as in physical therapy, must at least meet the buyer's expectations. Similarly, other marketing mix elements, such as promotion, should be blended with the price mix to augment a high-quality or prestige element. These might include distinctive packaging. Personal mannerisms of clinical and office staff assist in conveying a quality image.

Most services and products, even a product as commonplace and plain as bottled water, has prestige, high-quality market segments made up of buyers who expect to pay more for the best. When consumers have difficulty in objectively assessing a service or product's quality (such as is the case with physical therapy services), some may use high price as a signal of quality and prestige.

From the perspective of costs, creating an image worthy of prestige pricing usually has increased expenses. The resulting lower profit margin may make prestige pricing cost prohibitive. These competing factors must be analyzed as various strategies are considered.

Place

The place where services are provided should match the tastes of the targeted consumer groups as well as the mission of the service organization. Place has a relationship to prestige pricing. A location in a desirable, convenient, safe area that is attractive, tastefully decorated, and well maintained is in line with the perception that quality and high price are related.

Some key considerations for choosing a location for a clinic are accessibility, convenience for targeted consumers, cost, distance from competitors, space, and pricing strategy. The appropriate place to provide services is in line with consumers' tastes, preferences, the sources of payment for services, competitors' locations, and the organization's goals.

Packaging

Packaging is closely related to place; however, packaging is a broader concept. Packaging is the process of bringing together all of the features of the organization, department, practice, services, and products so they can be appreciated by consumers. Packaging includes promotional materials, the physical setting, the attitude of the staff, and the ambiance. These are things that are manageable. Packaging can perform a number of functions. For services and products, packaging is more than just the container. It is the part of the marketing mix in which the service or product is the focal point. In other words, a package can help demonstrate value to buyers. Cost considerations are important in packaging decisions. Generally, the more functions the organization attempts to provide, the larger the total packaging costs. More detail on packaging follows in Chapter 24.

Product Positioning

Positioning a service or product is establishing a unique image in the minds of target customers. This image can be for a specific or general service or product, in other words, for your specific physical therapy practice or for physical therapy in general. Management may position services and products according to target customers, product characteristics, or product benefits. In all of these cases, they attempt to create an image of value among target customers.

Market Positioning

A physical therapy organization can pursue many possible philosophical positions. Each of these necessitates decisions concerning how the organization wishes to be perceived by its communities of interest. These are three typical philosophical positions for achieving a **market position**:

1. Leader (instead of follower) reputation allows the organization to be perceived as a resource for the most advanced and effective treatment techniques. Quality and price orientations are not necessarily mutually exclusive, although the target audiences may perceive them as such. Health care organizations have typically pursued a

quality reputation because of the emotional intensity and importance of health care to the patients served.
2. Innovator (instead of adapter) orientation allows the physical therapy practice to develop a reputation for both quality and leadership.
3. Customer orientation (instead of a sales or product orientation) shows the physical therapy practice as humanistic and caring rather than self-serving and arrogant.

Product Life Cycle and Marketing

The sales and profitability of services and products typically change over time in a predictable manner, the **product life cycle** (Figure 23.1). The time it takes to complete a life cycle differs from one product or service to another. Fads such as clothing styles typically have very short life cycles, perhaps only months or weeks. At the other extreme, products like sheet steel and gasoline may have cycles spanning decades. A physical therapy example is a set of therapeutic exercise techniques known as proprioceptive neuromuscular facilitation (PNF) (Knott and Voss, 1968). These techniques were introduced in the 1950s, build up to maturity in the 1970s, and have been in decline since. In the late 1980s and mid 1990s PNF was combined with other therapeutic techniques and became a new and viable continuing education product.

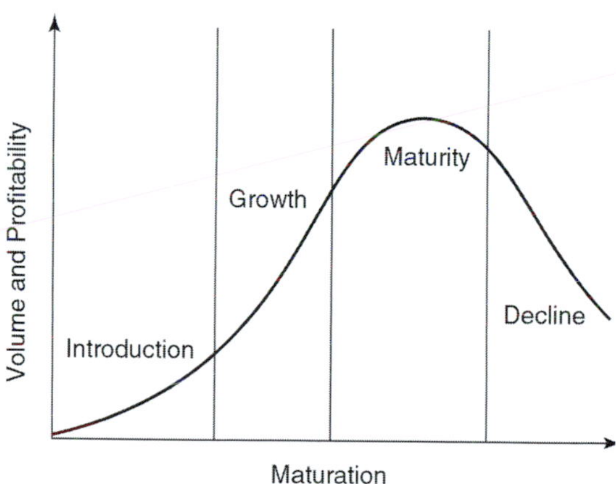

Figure 23.1. Product life cycle.

The product or service life cycle illustrates the typical growth path of a product or service from introduction to decline. The product life cycle helps to anticipate the revenue and market potential of a service, product, or a combination of both.

Although Figure 23.1 depicts the typical growth path, it is not the only possible path. Some services, such as preventive services, take a significant amount of time for consumers to understand their purpose, effectiveness, or usage. Other services, such as emergency care, may be obvious and immediately understood by consumers. Easily understood services are more likely to progress rapidly into the growth and maturity stages.

The average product life cycle is shortening over time. In health care, there are often many new and exciting approaches to care. Some suffer from unproven scientific merit. This means that it is not always easy to distinguish between fads and true industry trends. Trends are more lasting and have greater marketing planning implications than fads.

In the general services and goods markets, experts differ on what factors determine whether a service or product is a fad or a genuine new fashion. Most agree that fads do not satisfy basic needs. Rather, they provide amusement, novelty, a topic of conversation, a means of being different from others, and other relatively insignificant rewards, as compared to longer-lived services and products that satisfy more important needs, such as health and safety. Still, even the experts have trouble predicting how long a product life cycle will last. Hopefully, the general public, our referrers, governmental agencies, and third-party payers will not conclude that physical therapy services are faddish or fail to satisfy important health care needs.

The stages of the product life cycle have names. Following Digman (1990) the cycle's parts are as follows:

- Introduction or embryonic
- Growth
- Maturation
- Decline or aging

We examine each stage in turn as we more fully review the product life cycle and its implications for physical therapy practices.

An organization may have several service lines at various stages along the product life cycle. Because each stage of the product life cycle brings with it different opportunities, challenges, and rewards, it is necessary to develop a well-balanced portfolio of services from each of the stages of a product's life cycle.

Introduction Stage

In the introduction stage a company introduces a new service or product. This period is usually marked by low sales and financial losses. The introduction stage is expensive. Introduction usually requires a heavy financial investment in marketing to create product awareness and investments in other areas, such as production, research, and development. During this period much time, energy, and expense are devoted to informing potential customers of the service or product benefits. Some potential markets accept new services and products very slowly, while some services and products virtually bypass this stage.

During the introduction stage of the product life cycle, the company can use several strategies to speed introduction:

- High-profile marketing
- Preemptive penetration
- Selective penetration
- Low-profile marketing

A **high-profile marketing** strategy introduces a product with substantial promotion expenditures and at a high price. The purpose is to recover as much cost and generate as much profit as possible in a short period. This strategy is most effective when a large portion of the market is unaware of the item, price is relatively unimportant to the target market, and the organization wants to develop high preference for its brand because extensive competition is expected. There are some good reasons for pursuing a high-profile policy. Heavy promotion levels can inform target customers of an item's existence. A high price can both help to build an item's prestige and generate funds for the extensive promotion effort. A physical therapy example is a luxury women's health pavilion attached to a community hospital that offers everything from skin care and stress reduction through exercise and nutrition programs.

A **preemptive penetration** strategy requires a heavy promotional expenditure accompanied by a low price. Managers adopting this strategy believe that target customers are largely unaware of their product's existence, price is relatively important to them, a large potential market exists with economies of scale possible from large sales volumes, and substantial competition is expected. Low margins and high costs tend to discourage competitors from entering a market, while scale economies are expected to help profitability. This is rarely if ever a viable strategy for a small, private physical therapy practice. Networks of clinics or large integrated delivery systems may use this strategy effectively.

Selective penetration consists of pricing a product relatively high while keeping promotional expenditures at a moderate level. Organizations typically introduce prestige items like furs and high-fashion attire in this way. Selective penetration can be a good decision when numerous target customers are aware of an item, customers are willing to pay a high price, the potential market is relatively small (substantial economies of scale are unlikely), and little competition is expected. In-home personal physical therapy services, including fee-for-service aquatic therapy in an area where home pools are common, is an example of selective penetration.

A **low-profile marketing** strategy combines a small promotional budget with a low price. Managers introduce many industrial goods, such as lubricants and cleaning and office supplies, through this strategy. It is most effective when many target customers are aware of a product, the market is large and price sensitive, and a significant level of competition is expected. This strategy may be very effective for a late entry into a crowded physical therapy market. However, this is a weak competitive position (Macmillan and Tampoe, 2000).

Growth Stage

The second stage of the product life cycle is growth. During this stage profits and sales increase. Because rapid growth in sales and increasing profits signal opportunity to other organizations, increasing competition in the same generic class often evolves as the growth stage progresses. Rapidly expanding demand may be sufficient to enable several competitors to maintain prices and profits. In the growth stage there are two fundamental and opposing strategic options. First, management may opt to earn as much short-term profit as possible by holding prices up and spending only moderate sums on marketing effort.

As an alternative, other organizations reinvest profits in substantial marketing efforts to build a strong market position for future profitability. Organizations electing to pursue this strategy emphasize some combination of tactics, including large-capacity production facilities to bring about greater scale economies, changes in quality, adding more intermediaries, and heavy promotion efforts to build brand preference and customer loyalty.

Maturation Stage

During maturation, high volume and profit occur with little additional investment in promotion. As the service or product reaches its peak of popularity and market penetration, typically additional services or products are developed by competing organizations in an attempt to garner some of the market acceptance that the original service or product has earned. Some of these products may closely mimic the original. This can in turn lead to market saturation of the service or product (Hannagan, 2002). To deal with saturation, competitors may promote themselves as better or less expensive substitutes for the original service or product.

Decline Stage

The final stage of the life cycle is decline. During this time, the popularity and market share of the original service or product decrease. The service or product is old. It is no longer unique or offered more or less exclusively by a few organizations. Typically, unless there was no real utility in the original service or product (as is the case with fads), the benefits that the market once sought in the original product are perceived by that same market as being better satisfied by substitutes or replacement. These new services or products may be less costly or more effective.

For a service or product in true decline, no amount of additional promotion or consumer education will revive the once healthy demands. Sometimes it is possible to find alternative uses for a product that can allow it to run through the entire life cycle again. Often these alternatives are created by repackaging the original. An excellent example of this in consumer products is seen in baking soda. Baking soda was originally promoted as an ingredient in food preparation and baking. Most baking soda sales since the 1990s are for nonfood uses such as fabric cleaning, dental hygiene, and odor absorption. In health care, a similar repackaging and recycling through the product life cycle is seen in the pharmaceutical uses of common aspirin. Aspirin was first used as an analgesic, then as an anticoagulant. Aspirin is also promoted for its purported primary and secondary atherosclerosis prevention benefits. In physical therapy, pool therapy and hydrotherapy in a Hubbard tank of the 1940s and 1950s were reconfigured as aquatic therapy in the 1990s.

Implications of Product Life Cycle for Physical Therapy Services and Products

In physical therapy it is necessary to examine individual components or interventions rather than the field as a whole in the context of the product life cycle. This is because the field is in constant flux, hopefully because of evolution rather than fad. The influence of evidence-based decision making on physical therapists, ongoing research, and technological advancements on the duration and progression of a product life cycle cannot be overlooked. Reimbursement policy has also had a significant impact on the movement of various interventions through the product life cycle. Medicare payment for wound care is a stellar example of the connection between reimbursement and new services and products.

Product Mix

A **product mix** can be thought of as all of the services and products an organization offers that contribute to the specific goals of the organization. Specific services and products are offered for specific purposes, such as increased community visibility, to replace a little-used offering, and of course to make a profit. Many organizations that offer a variety of services and/or goods use a technique called **product portfolio analysis** to integrate goal achievement strategies for their entire product mix (Mintzberg et al., 1995). A portfolio analysis (Fig. 23.1) is possible only if the service and/or product line of the organization is diversified.

Diversification is based upon the principle that if management considers all product strategies in conjunction with one another, the company is more likely to benefit than if individual product decisions are made independently. This approach is analogous to the investment portfolio strategies (mixing growth and value stocks, bonds, and equities) used by various individual investors and companies.

Managers of physical therapy practices can use the same principles in producing a desirable and diversified portfolio of services and products. In so doing, they can set up a product mix that allows them to best reach their objectives. For example, a physical therapy clinic may choose to add home care or self-care products and educational courses to its existing outpatient orthopedic and sports therapy services.

It is also necessary to consider the effect of new ventures and programs on existing programs. Typically, new programs that are synergistic with existing programs are found to be more attractive. Here is an example. In a major city with a dominant health care organization there was a premier cardiac care program. The organization built a cardiac rehabilitation building and upgraded its cardiac care facilities at another of its hospitals less than 5 miles from the premier facility. Significant promotional funds were spent first to bring customers to the new facility and soon after to also promote the premier facility. Better cardiac care was the common message. An additional advantage of diversification for physical therapy clinics is that a wide variety of services and products can establish the image of the clinic as a resource to the community for a wide variety of services and products instead of simply as a place to go for therapy.

Diversification can, however, also confuse a market if the range of services and products is not well coordinated. Conflicting programs can confuse a market and actually interfere with the future success of existing successful programs. For example, some physical therapists who have diversified into nontraditional services, such as massage therapy, have noticed that patients (consumers) have difficulty differentiating between the physical therapist and massage therapist.

Diversification can also be expensive. As always, the costs and anticipated benefits must be carefully examined. The costs are not all directly financial. It is important to consider the costs in time, energy, and attention. **Opportunity costs** are opportunities that must be bypassed to pursue one strategy rather than another (Nosse, Friberg, Kovacek, 1999). For example, a practice may not have the resources (either financial or human) to pursue two new projects. To pursue one project, the second project may have to be delayed or not pursued at all. The benefit of the project not pursued is the opportunity cost.

Marketing Communications

To promote an image, that is, a conception of a service or product, communication with potential and current customers has to take place. Promotion requires communication

(Lewis, 1999). Marketing communicates an image of an offering through what is called the **promotional mix**:

- Advertising
- Personal selling
- Public relations and publicity
- Sales promotion

These components were discussed generally in Chapter 21. Here the discussion will focus on physical therapy. Physical therapy companies frequently allocate substantial resources to promotion, which is communicating with potential buyers about a service or product to stimulate sales.

All promotional activities have the same general objective: changing customers' behavior to turn them into actual buyers of a particular service, product, or idea. Promotional campaigns help to develop and maintain preferences. TV ads, contests, and sweepstakes are among the many promotional techniques that can help to position a service or product and develop its link with needs and social acceptance. This does not mean that false promises lead to lasting relationships. Lasting relationships depend on delivering services and products that actually satisfy needs. But promotion can help to bring this about. Specific components of typical promotional campaigns may or may not be deemed appropriate for a physical therapy or other health care practice. Ethics is a priority concern in most health care environments. This extends to advertising, as exemplified in the American Hospital Association's literature:

> Advertising may be used to advance the health care organization's goals and objectives and should, in all cases, support the mission of the health care organization. Advertising may be used to educate the public, to report to the community, to increase awareness of available services, to increase support for the organization, and to recruit employees. Health care advertising should be truthful, fair, accurate, complete, and sensitive to the health care needs of the public. False or misleading statements, or statements that might lead the uninformed to draw false conclusions about the health care facility, its competitors, or other health care providers are unacceptable and unethical. (American Hospital Association, 2003)

Once overall marketing objectives are set, it is time to design a promotional program. When designing the program, keep the findings of communication researchers in mind. Effective promotion begins by learning as much as possible (focused listening) about the consumer. Even though the most effective and cost-efficient method of promotion is positive word of mouth or endorsements from consumers who have had a positive personal experience with your health care organization, other promotional actions are needed.

The promotional mix is directed at potential consumers. This group is usually composed of a target market. This is not always the case, however. Sometimes the groups differ. For example, Saturday morning commercials for expensive toys have an intended receiver group made up of children, while the actual target market consists of parents and grandparents. In health care, research on decision making related to health care purchases has shown that within the typical family, it is most often the mother who makes the health care decisions for each member of the family, including the adult males.

Table 23.1 presents a comparison of the components of the promotional mix in terms of their relative cost, advantages, and disadvantages.

Advertising

Advertising is an important promotion medium. Health care advertising, once considered unprofessional, is now a big and rapidly growing business in this country. In general, though, physical therapy companies allocate a modest fraction of their total marketing costs to advertising. Advertising is by no means a marketing tool only for large companies. To the contrary, organizations of virtually every size use it in some way.

Managers should set specific goals for advertising. These serve as focal points to structure budgets and provide a means of evaluating performance.

To develop realistic advertising goals, managers must critically examine these factors:

Table 23.1 Comparative Value of Various Promotional Components

Promotion	*Type*	*Relative Cost*	*Advantages*	*Disadvantages*
Advertising	Impersonal	Depending on the medium, very expensive or relatively inexpensive.	Communicates to largest audience with relatively little individual effort. Allows control over the message.	Many in audience may not be potential customers. Difficult to measure results.
Personal selling	Personal	Most expensive per individual contact.	Helps develop a relationship. Allows flexible presentation to meet target needs and preferences.	Expensive! Highly trained and qualified sales personnel can be difficult to attract and manage.
Sales promotion	Impersonal	From inexpensive to very expensive, depending on format and scope.	Event marketing can gain immediate attention of potential customers. Can build relationship with customers.	Easily imitated. Can be difficult to find a creative approach that will attract customer attention.
Public relations	Impersonal	Relatively inexpensive. Publicity is free.	Credible to customers because it is not paid advertising.	Can present an organization in a positive or negative light. Difficult to control, time, or measure results.

Reprinted from Nosse, Friberg, Kovacek, 1999:59.

- What they know and do not know about their intended customers
- How well past advertising efforts worked so that needed corrections can be made
- The types of messages needed

Experienced managers try to design advertising goals so that they augment and complement personal communication promotion, especially personal selling. Developing a message is a crucial part of advertising.

Most important is that the message coincide with the needs of the audience. Message development involves making decisions about an ad's three basic components: **theme**, **copy**, and **format**.

1. **Theme** (the overall information to be conveyed): Themes are essentially appeals to potential buyers. For instance, a physical therapy practice may want to emphasize "the best tune-up my body ever had" or "becoming pain free and sleeping well.."
2. **Copy** (an ad's pictures, words, and symbols used to present the theme): For example, a physical therapy advertisement featured an intelligent elderly woman at her daughter's house, concerned about not being able to pick up her new grandchild because of her "bad back."
3. **Format** (the layout, including specific colors, the length of a TV or radio commercial, the space for print, type sizes, and so on): Creative copy and presentation are essential to effectiveness in advertising. Managers of physical therapy practices usually rely on specialists, designers and illustrators formally trained to develop the ads. Nevertheless, managers should be familiar with guidelines for generating favorable audience response so that they can evaluate the messages suggested by such experts.

Media Decisions

The media to be used in advertisements should be considered so that the messages fit the characteristics of the media. Billboards, for instance, require relatively simple messages.

Types of media:

- Billboards
- Broadcast media (radio, television)
- Internet
- Personal selling
- Phone solicitation
- Print media (direct mail, magazines, newspapers)

AIDA Model

The acronym AIDA stands for *a*ttention, *i*nterest, *d*esire, and *a*ction (Figure 23.2). The **AIDA model** is widely used by managers in developing communications for marketing purposes. It explains how prospective consumers are likely to progress in their thinking in response to advertising or sales approaches (Koschnick, 1995).

The four terms in the AIDA model suggest that a potential consumer reacts to sales or advertisement messages thus:

- **Attention**: Focusing on the media, service or product name recognition and features
- **Interest**: Becoming willing to hear more about the advantages of the service or product
- **Desire**: Responding with an urge to purchase because of the perceived benefits of the service or product
- **Action**: Committing to act in accord with the intent of the message.

To be effective, advertising must get and hold the audience's attention. Color, loud or unusual voices, humorous lines, or something to grab the audience may be necessary. Using celebrities is another technique to catch an audience's attention. Sometimes the president of the company, such as the late Dave Thomas of Wendy's, is sufficiently well known for this purpose. In health care, physicians are often used as trusted spokespersons. In most cases however, popular sports, motion picture, and television stars are used. Effective advertisements must stimulate interest in both the ad and the service or product. Some ads stimulate interest but not in the service or product. Picturing an attractive man or woman, for example, may generate interest in the ad, but it may be ineffective unless it also develops interest in the service or product. It is also possible to generate a negative image if the advertisement is poorly done or excessively controversial, for example, showing thong bikinis on preteens.

Suggesting that a service or product may assist customers in satisfying their needs can generate interest in the service or product, as is seen in advertisements that promise improved health and fitness without diet, exercise, or almost anything other than the customers' credit card numbers.

Advertisements should stimulate the audience to try the service or product. This can be difficult, because it requires knowledge of the audience's motivation and needs. Desire can be built by showing how your physical therapy services and products can satisfy these needs. Sometimes advertisements that favorably compare your clinic with competitors are useful in building desire for your services over the competition. This is relatively rare in health care, but accreditation agencies and others are producing provider report cards to the general public (Chapters 31 and 32).

The ultimate test of a message's effectiveness is whether it brings about the desired action. Offering a need-related incentive for buying may best stimulate business. A toothpaste company offers the possibility of reducing tooth decay while improving bad breath. An oil filter ad shows a mechanic working on an engine, stating either pay me now (for a

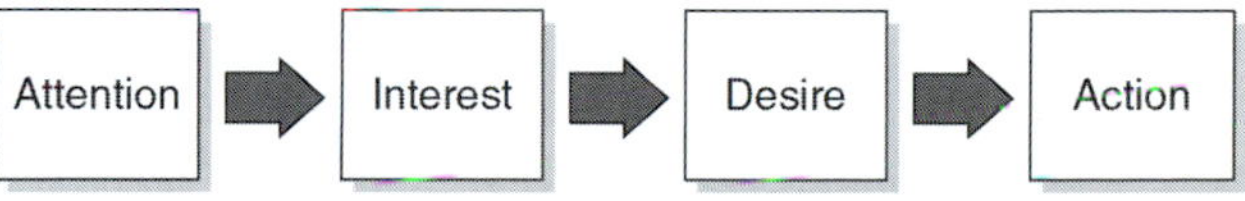

Figure 23.2. AIDA model of marketing communication.

filter) or pay me later (for a major engine repair). The incentives in these examples are clear. A physical therapy ad has to communicate the benefits of services just as clearly. Some relevant examples are "run, don't walk" for a sports injury clinic and "aging is a women's issue" for a women's health care center.

The AIDA model does not imply that silly or cute advertisements are necessarily effective. Messages should state something desirable about a service or product in terms of needs, something unique or exclusive about the services and products offered compared with close substitutes. The statements must be believable. This is true especially for physical therapists, since the public frequently misunderstands our role in the health care system and has difficulty in distinguishing physical therapy services from those offered by other types of therapists. In time, the evidence-based research efforts of the American Physical Therapy Association, the Foundation for Physical Therapy, the LAMP project of the Section on Health Policy and Administration, and individual researchers will provide evidence that differentiates the benefits of physical therapy services from those of similar health care providers.

Communication Mix

A mix of channels to communicate promotional messages is used to achieve synergy. Each type of promotion should complement the others. Management makes two fundamental types of decisions when designing a **communication mix**: how to integrate each of the promotions (the campaign), and the relative emphasis on each medium (the mix) (Chapter 22).

Single-event (rather than campaign) marketing is generally effective. This is true especially in health care. A promotional program is integrated through a campaign—a unified, well-organized series of promotional messages with one theme or central idea. A campaign may include advertising, service or package design, point-of-purchase displays, and customer incentives around the central theme to gain a cumulative impact.

Coordination is very important in a promotional campaign. Some of these marketing activities are concurrent, while others flow in sequence. It is important that all marketing messages tell the same story and carry the same theme. The appropriate duration of a campaign depends on its success and whether its theme goes stale. An excessively long-running campaign loses its impact. A new campaign may be needed to restimulate interest and excitement in an existing service or product among customers, referrers, payers, and staff.

Public Relations

Perhaps the first step in developing an effective advertising and public relations strategy is to understand the difference between advertising and public relations. Many people think that advertising and public relations are the same; however, there is a difference. While both advertising and public relations use a variety of media formats (print, radio and television) as a way of conveying a message, public relations promotion encompasses much more.

Public relations promotion entails more than just selecting the media format to market a service or product. It can and often does encompass community involvement. Public relations is defined as the deliberate, planned, and sustained effort to establish and maintain mutual understanding between an organization and its public (Hannagan, 2002). While advertising is a way of keeping your business in the public's eye, public relations is a way of signaling that you are concerned and committed to the welfare of the community and its residents. This commitment may be one of the most effective techniques for building trust and customer loyalty. People tend to support businesses and organizations that give something to the community rather than those that just take from the community. Especially for an independent practice, public relations is an important way to demonstrate commitment to the community at large.

An excellent way to foster this type of involvement is to meet with community leaders to find out how you can help and what forthcoming events you can support. Interaction with business and community leaders can be an excellent networking opportunity, especially if your involvement in and commitment to improving the community are genuine.

This involvement can range from sponsoring a local baseball or softball team to hosting a charity ball for senior citizens or allowing not-for-profit organizations to use your facilities. This type of approach to promotion should encompass more than creating awareness of the service or product. It should represent a sincere commitment to community involvement—the desire to give something back to the community and its residents. Something of community interest should be of interest to local media and result in free publicity regarding the event. Additional examples of community programs that may be considered:

- Sponsor a Little League team
- Sponsor the cleanup of a local park or roadway
- Sponsor an underprivileged child in day camp
- Sponsor cooperative education for high school and/or college students
- Volunteer as a tutor for at-risk (those likely to drop out or fail in school) students
- Sponsor a fundraiser for the homeless or day care tuition assistance for children of single-parent households
- Offer summer employment to local high school, middle school, and college students
- Become active in the local chapter of the Big Brothers or Big Sisters
- Volunteer in a local literacy program

Other inexpensive and indirect ways of promotion that do not require physical community involvement:

- Employee tee shirts, hats, aprons, or jackets with the name of your clinic and logo
- Ballpoint pens with the name, telephone number, and logo of your clinic
- Balloons with the name, telephone number, and logo of your business
- Free samples of your services or products, such as a screening event at a mall

While it is impossible for anyone to participate in every event or program in the community, selective involvement in a few activities or events, even if it's only on a part-time basis, can help meet promotional goals.

Sales Promotion

Sales promotion is a marketing activity intended to stimulate consumer purchasing and seller effectiveness. Sales promotion includes displays at trade shows and expositions, demonstrations, and other single-event selling efforts. In health care, the most common sales promotions are health fairs, community outreach programs, and special promotional activities, such as sponsorship of a disabled athlete in a competition. A physical therapy sales promotion could include the sponsorship, physical training, and injury prevention and care of a wheelchair basketball team.

Student Notes

It is common for students to have had experience with fundraising, recruitment of volunteers; group promotion of a service, product, or idea; sales; service learning; and volunteering. Thinking retrospectively about the efforts that were made to market the various causes, services, or ideas you have been involved with, you are likely to remember what worked and what did not work. Armed with the information in this chapter, you should be able to identify the specific promotional strengths and weaknesses of the programs you participated in. The eight P's provide a framework for analyzing the marketing mix. The merits of the message and how it was promoted can be examined by considering the utility of the offering for the targeted group, the appropriateness of the promotional mix, and the uniqueness of the message and promotional approaches relative to the messages and methods used by competitors. With this additional background in marketing principles, keeping in mind guidelines

INDIVIDUAL CASE STUDY

Although some of the concepts of marketing are different for services from those for products, examine several commercials on network and local television or ads in the newspaper. Ideally, you will be able to find information related to health care services or products. Answer the following questions about each commercial or ad you review.

- What service or product is being sold?
- How did the commercial or ad attempt to get your attention? Did it work?
- What is the benefit of the service or product to you as the potential consumer?
- Is the advertisement selling a specific service or product or the concept of the service or product?
- Is it clear why you should take action right now to acquire the service or product?
- Are there any disadvantages of not getting the service or product?
- What commercials or ads competed for your attention?
- Do you consider the commercials or ads you focused on successful in meeting basic promotional goals?

for choosing particular forms of promoting services or products and the need for a cohesive approach to guide marketing, your next marketing experience is likely to be successful. Knowing what you now know, you can objectively analyze a wide variety of marketing efforts. The importance of marketing skills is made personal in Chapter 25, which asks you to apply them to advance your professional career.

GROUP CASE STUDY

This task is well suited for work in small groups. There are six roles. One member should take on the part of a director of rehabilitation services to guide the process. The group's task is to formulate a marketing plan based on the principles presented in this chapter.

Situation

You are a (*choose your position*: new staff member, staff member, senior staff member, director of rehabilitation services, marketing staff member, physician) at Midtown Memorial, the largest hospital in the region. Recently the state governor signed into law a revised physical therapy practice act that allows patients to access physical therapists directly for evaluation and treatment. The director of rehabilitation services sees this change as an opportunity to increase the number of physical therapy patients who come to the main campus of the hospital and its five satellite locations. The director has called a meeting to discuss this idea with the staff. You are present. Everyone is expected to contribute to the development of the marketing plan. Before beginning, take a few minutes to review this chapter, clarify who is playing what role, and how much time you have to work on this case study. What will the focus of the message be? How will the message be promoted and to whom, and so on?

Summary

This chapter examines a wide variety of concepts in the development of a marketing program, with special emphasis on physical therapy. The eight P's provide the framework for building a marketing program for a targeted audience. Pricing strategies are given extensive coverage because cost is important to most customers. The product life cycle is introduced as a consideration for appropriately selecting marketing strategies at each of the four stages. The promotional mix is identified as advertising, personal selling, sales promotion, and public relations. The indications for each are presented along with pertinent physical therapy examples. Three considerations to give when forming the message to communicate in an advertising campaign are the theme, copy (the words), and format (the visuals). The acronym AIDA is used to place the focus on what an advertisement should accomplish, that is, get the *attention* of the targeted audience, stimulate *interest* in the service or product, create a *desire* to have the service or product, and ultimately take *action*, that is, buy the service or product. Criteria for identifying a cohesive and successful promotional campaign are also presented and discussed.

We have not yet completed the discussion of marketing. We have not yet addressed principles of niche marketing of physical therapy practices. Chapter 24 defines and examines niche marketing in detail.

References

American Hospital Association. Ethical conduct for health care institution. Available from http://www.hospitalconnect.com/aha/resource_center/resource/resource_ethics.html. Accessed 6/24/03.

Clarkson KW, Miller RL, Jentz GA, Cross FB. West's business law: Text cases legal, ethical, regulatory, and international environment, 6th ed. Minneapolis/St. Paul: West. 1995.

Digman LA. Strategic management: Concepts, decisions, and cases, 2nd ed. Homewood, IL: BPI/Irwin. 1990.

Hannagan T. Mastering strategic management. New York: Palgrave. 2002.

Knott M, Voss DE. Proprioceptive neuromuscular facilitation, 2nd ed. San Francisco: Harper & Row. 1968.

Koschnick WJ. Dictionary of marketing. Brookfield, CN: Grower. 1995.

Lewis B. Communication mix. In Lewis BR, Littler D, eds. The Blackwell encyclopedic dictionary of marketing. Malden, MA: Blackwell Business. 1999.

Macmillan H, Tampoe M. Strategic management process, content, and implementation. New York: Oxford University. 2000:106.

Mintzberg H, Quinn JB, Voyer J. The strategy process, collegiate edition. Englewood Cliffs, NJ: Prentice Hall. 1995.

Nosse LJ, Friberg DF, Kovacek PR. Management and supervisory principles for physical therapists. Baltimore: Lippincott, Williams & Wilkins. 1999.

Schoch HP, Yap TH. Cost-pricing relationship. In Abdel-Khalik AR, ed. The Blackwell encyclopedic dictionary of accounting. Malden, MA: Blackwell. 1998:109–112.

Sherman SG. Total customer satisfaction: A comprehensive approach for health care providers. San Francisco: Jossey-Bass, 1999.

Wilson D. Pricing objectives. In Lewis BR, Littler D. The Blackwell encyclopedic dictionary of marketing. Malden, MA: Blackwell. 1999:160–162.

More Information Related to This Chapter

Managers as well as staff need preparation for organizational change such as market expansion and new services or products. For concise chapters on dealing with stress and organizational change consult Champoux JE. Organizational behavior. Essential tenets for a new millennium. Cincinnati, OH: South-Western College. 2000: Chapters 16, 18.

An alternative to our conceptualization of the product life cycle is presented in Rouse WB. Essential challenges of strategic management. New York: Wiley. 2001:32.

Sources for comparison of hospitals available to the general public include US News 100 best hospitals list www.usnews.com; AARP 50 best hospitals published in Modern Maturity Magazine, May/June, 2002.

For outpatient facility ratings consult the National Committee on Quality Assurance www.ncqa.org.

Niche Marketing

Learning Objectives

1. Explain the relationship between a target market and a niche market.
2. Discuss the main considerations for determining what market segment is best for your circumstances.
3. Relate the four C's (consumer, convenience, choice, cost) to marketing physical therapy.
4. Evaluate use of the 5 + 3 P's (product, promotion, packaging, price, place and physical evidence, personnel selection/training, and process) of service marketing in niche marketing.
5. Use the principles of marketing to develop a hypothetical physical therapy niche practice.

Key Words

Four C's, eight P's, differentiated, emerging market, niche, niche marketing, niche physical therapy market, niche practice

Introduction

A **niche** (nĭtch) is a specific identifiable market for a particular service, product, or intervention. Niche marketing is the targeting of a specific group (subset) of consumers with a service or product (Nosse, Friberg, Kovacek, 1999) (Fig. 24.1). In recent years a number of specialty practices in physical therapy have developed. These practices generally specialize in a particular type of therapy. As perceived needs of consumers for various types of therapy change, new niches to satisfy these needs become available. The alert provider who anticipates this change early on is poised to develop strategies and mobilize resources to capture a percentage of this niche market.

The provider of niche services has **differentiated** his or her services from those offered by others by concentrating on satisfying the consumers of a small market segment, that is, a niche market. The principles of marketing (see Chapter 21) and the processes associated with strategic marketing (see Chapters 22 and 23) in this chapter are applied to niche practices.

Niche Markets and Marketing

A wide variety of niche markets are available, so many that *PT–Magazine of Physical Therapy* ran a series of articles on emerging and **niche physical therapy markets** (for example, Davolt, 1997; Fosnaught, 1995; Johnson, Ries, Reynolds, 2001; Mangano, Heisel and Dawson, 1999; Monahan, 1995; Reynolds, 1995; Ries, 2001; Rollins, 1999; Wilson, 2001; Woods, 1998a,b, 1999, 2002).

The value of niche programs and niche markets (targeted customers) is the sharply focused ability to pair up a key market segment with a specific program, service, or product. It lets you speak clearly and concisely in a spe-

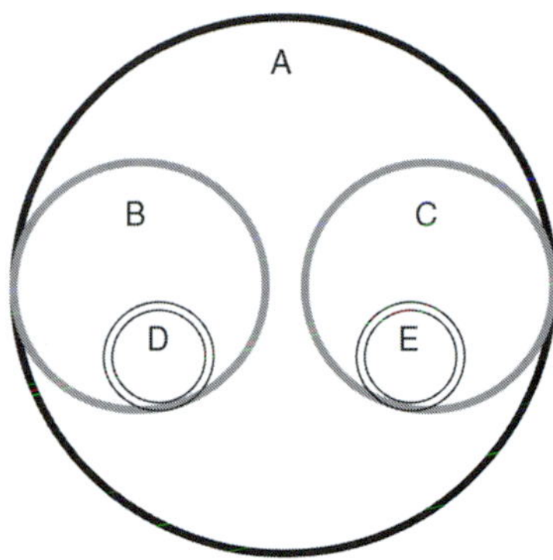

Figure 24.1. Relative size of physical therapy markets. *A*, All potential physical therapy markets. *B* and *C*, Different targeted market segments. *D* and *E*, Different niche market segments.

cific vocabulary to a clearly identifiable audience. It allows your organization to focus its resources. It prevents wasting time, energy, and money on communication programs to the wrong people about the wrong subject or at the wrong time. It allows you to focus your clinical development and create a high level of staff or program expertise.

This chapter reviews two niches to demonstrate some of the issues that a niche program must address and to expand the basic marketing and business development principles discussed in Chapters 21 to 23.

Why a Niche?

There are many possible motivations for entering into a niche market. Some clinicians have narrowly focused interests in specific markets. Also, the market may not be able to support yet another general physical therapy practice and a niche practice may be the only option available. Or the niche program may be the first of many programs that a practice may offer as it grows and develops.

Are there indications that a niche market is beginning to develop? Sometimes the answer is an obvious yes; sometimes that yes is not nearly so obvious. In some situations, the practitioner may have to stimulate the market for the niche to develop.

Niches are sometimes thought of as exclusively **emerging markets**, but this is not always the case. When a new market (possibly a niche) does not produce a sustainable demand over time, it may be best to consider that new market not as an emerging trend but rather as a fad or temporary phenomenon. It is incumbent on every practice decision maker to determine what is likely to be an emerging (niche) market as opposed to a fad. If pursued, fads are likely to cause allocation of excessive resources without adequate return of revenue on that investment (Chapter 29).

Niches as Strongholds for Your Organization

A niche can also be thought of as a stronghold for your company. Without a strong niche or stronghold, it may be difficult for a company to reach its revenue goals. If a physical therapy practice hopes to establish a strong niche in the market, it must effectively differentiate its offering from those of competitors.

Niche marketing requires targeting a specific subset of consumers—a niche market—for a specialty service or product.

Niches have been developed in a wide variety of business areas, both service and product.

Many marketers believe that 20% of buyers consume 80% of product volume (the Pareto rule [Koch, 2000]). If you could identify that key 20% and find others like them, you could be much more efficient in your marketing with much less effort. Niche marketing today involves targeting, communicating with, selling, and obtaining feedback on the heaviest users of your business's services or products.

Picking the right segment of the market is important to achieving sufficiently large volumes of patients and profitability to prosper as an organization. These are characteristics of the right market segment:

- Measurable in quantitative terms
- Substantial enough to generate planned volume
- Accessible to your company's operational methods
- Sensitive to planned and affordable marketing spending events

It is also important to examine other factors that can affect your company's success:

- Strength of competitors to attract your niche buyers away from your offerings
- Consumers' perception of similarity of competitors' offerings
- Tolerance of the consumer audience to more and different options in health care
- Ease of entry
- Difficulty of duplication for competitors

Perhaps the driving force behind niche marketing, or segmentation, is the need to satisfy and keep consumers who really appreciate your services or products. Consumers, especially in health care, continue to become increasingly sophisticated and demanding. And service and product choices continue to expand with prosperity and world market competition.

It is also important to identify and estimate the size of a target market, particularly if the offering is new. It is very important to determine whether the customer base is large enough to support the new offering. It is not enough that people like a concept. There must be enough customers who will buy often enough to sustain the company's sales, spending, and profits from year to year. Table 24.1 presents 33 possible niches for physical therapy practices.

Target Consumers: four C's

Throughout these discussions of marketing, the consumer has always been the focus of attention: the individual to whom the marketing communication is directed, who must be satisfied, who has needs, perspective, and so on. A way to keep the needs of targeted consumers in mind is to think about the following **four C's**:

Consumer: Understand the target group's desires and level of understanding of current offerings, whether they are new or recurrent consumers, and most of all, their needs as they perceive or express them.

Convenience: How easy it is to schedule, get to, receive, and pay for the services. The less time the consumer spends in noncare activities, the more convenient it is.

Choice: Know the consumer's other options. Are your customers in immediate need of services? Is a competitor closer, better known, less expensive, or actively promoting its services?

Cost: A consideration in any transaction. Costs in time and resources are always in the minds of consumers. Therefore, you need to know the consumer's idea of a good value.

These four C's are useful in developing a marketing strategy based on specific consumer groups' perceptions, interests, tastes, and desires (Hannagan, 2002). They are complementary to the eight P's of service marketing, which emphasize the organization's perspective and how to influence the consumer's behavior (Chapter 21). Because niche practices are developed to serve a specific and finite

Table 24.1 Examples of Niches for Physical Therapists

Aquatics	Ergonomics	Physical therapy for persons with dementia
Back care	Fall prevention, balance, vestibular rehabilitation	Postpolio therapy
Bariatric patient care	Fitness and health promotion	Rodeo participant care
Cardiopulmonary care	Golf rehabilitation	School-based therapy
Case management	Home care	Sports physical therapy
Community-based therapy, not homebound	Industrial rehabilitation	Skilled nursing facility program
Complementary (holistic) health care	Lymphedema treatment	Urinary incontinence treatment
Consulting	Manual therapy	Wellness for the worried elderly (functioning but concerned)
Electrotherapy	Mobile unit services	Women's health
Emergency department	Osteoporosis program	Wound care
End of life care, hospice	Pediatrics	
	Physical therapy in health clubs	

target market, the four C's are particularly important to successful marketing. Keep them in mind as the niche marketing plan develops.

Examining a Niche Practice

Any of the niches listed in Table 24.1 and many more could be examined and developed in more detail. However, for illustration purposes, we will examine aquatics and physical therapy for persons with dementia.

Issues to address in each example include defining the eight P's (Chapters 21–23) for the niche, that is, *p*roduct, *p*romotion, *p*ackaging, *p*ricing, *p*lace, plus *p*hysical evidence, *p*ersonnel selection and training, and *p*rocess. The four C's are given consideration within the context of the P's to which they relate.

Aquatics

Aquatic physical therapy involves land- and water-based therapeutic exercises using a variety of positions and equipment. The purpose is to assist individuals of all levels of functional ability to improve their physical and functional levels (Institute for Rehabilitation and Research, 2003). The American Medical Association and many third-party payers recognize aquatic physical therapy in Current Procedure Terminology (CPT) code 97113, that is, aquatic therapy with therapeutic exercises (American Medical Association, 2002) (Chapter 30). The various patient populations that may be served by an aquatics program include those who are likely to benefit from the unique aspects of water-based therapy as detailed later. An additional population may include those who merely prefer to receive therapeutic exercise in a water environment.

What Is the Benefit to the Market of Your Niche Service?

Depending on the specific target group, aquatic therapy may have various benefits. These may include (among many others) ability to bear more weight in water than on land, increased ease of general or local movement as a result of buoyancy, enhanced resistance of water against movement, relaxation, pain relief, increased lean mass, strength gain, endurance gained through resistive exercise in water, and socialization with a group of peers in a pool. Another component of aquatics that must be considered is that for some consumers, it is simply more enjoyable, interesting, or fun than land-based exercise.

Define the Overall Niche Market

Your niche aquatic population may or may not be age or geographically specific. Certainly both children with developmental delays and tone problems and older persons with arthritis or joint disorders are likely candidates for aquatic therapy programs. These populations may be geographically concentrated but often are not.

Depending on the analysis of the general market, several subsegments may benefit from aquatics. It may be desirable to offer a menu of aquatic programs to attract a wider range of patients at a variety of times and possibly a variety of locations throughout the community.

What Characteristics Differentiate This Niche Market From the Larger General Population?

The primary characteristics (among many others) of this niche market are the desire to exercise in a less stressful or painful environment, the specific benefits of water related to buoyancy, resistance, and pain reduction, and the social aspects of pool therapy.

Who Are the Key Decision Makers for This Niche Market?

As is the case with many types of therapy, the referring physician is a key decision maker for aquatics. Additional input is likely to be from family members of elderly or juvenile patients, case workers of third-party payers, and previous users of aquatic services, either at your facility or at other aquatic programs.

The simplest and often most expeditious way to determine the key decision makers is through direct contact with the potential influencers of decisions. Focus groups, experience in the field, and networking with key groups are often beneficial for determining this sort of information. Less typical for smaller practices but sometimes useful are surveys and formal market research studies.

Promotion: How Will You Communicate in a Focused Manner With This Niche Market?

All of the guidelines for developing and implementing a communication plan that were discussed in Chapter 16 are helpful in most niche markets. A possible key advantage is the ability to identify previous users of aquatics or similar services and communicate directly with them. Also, groups of individuals with characteristics similar to those of previous program users can be identified. For example, persons in self-help groups for osteoporosis or post knee surgery are more likely to find aquatic programs attractive than are persons in the general population. For the sake of efficiency and economy of marketing expenditures, these are the individuals to whom you will want to target your communications.

Resources for finding this information are available through community health directories and medical staff and specialty directories of the local medical society or hospital. The Yellow Pages may also list many of these groups or referral sources. Pediatric and geriatric networking groups are often excellent sources of contacts and referrals. Many of these groups have as their mission the identification and promotion of health resources such as your aquatic program.

Packaging: What Specific Way You Deliver This Service Will Appeal to the Niche Market?

Several aspects of packaging are universal. These include attractive, clean, and pleasant facilities that are easy to find and use. Staff should always be clean, appropriately dressed, polite, cheerful, and well informed about your programs, operations, and services. Written materials should always present a professional and informative tone that is welcoming and appropriate for the audience. Signage and logos should be easily read even by individuals with vision impairments and should illustrate your purpose and philosophy of service.

Pricing: What Pricing Strategy Will Appeal to the Market Most Effectively?

There are many sources of information on pricing. Usual and customary charges for similar services in your area should be a starting point. The scope of additional services that each program offers can significantly affect the cost of delivering the service and therefore may dramatically affect the overall pricing strategy. For example, many aquatic programs are simply exercise programs at a local pool. Other programs may be more spa-like, offering a soothing music, aromatherapy, availability of massage, and health food and beverages. Pricing is likely to be dramatically different for these two very different programs.

Place: Where Should This Service Be Offered, and Why?

We have discussed some of the considerations for location. For convenience, some programs are offered in clients' own backyard pools. The choice of location will be individualized by program. It may be necessary to begin an aquatic program in leased or rented space in a community pool and once success has been demonstrated, build your own pool. Construction adds to the cost of the service but may lead to a facility more convenient to the target market than are competitors' facilities.

How Will You Give Physical Evidence of Quality or Effectiveness for Your Service?

Certainly safety issues must be considered in any setting (Chapter 33). Because of the unique aspects of water therapy, you must explicitly explain all safety procedures and practices to all potential consumers.

Any special architectural components of your facility also should be highlighted to demonstrate your competence and effectiveness. For example, special nonslip flooring, air filtration, and water treatment demonstrate thought and consideration for providing clients with the safest and most pleasant and effective experience possible (Chapter 34).

Any special certifications or accreditations should also be prominently displayed in your facility. Articles that you wrote or were mentioned in should be available for review in your waiting areas. Pictures of past successful participants in the program make for excellent decorations throughout the facility and reassure new participants as they enter your programs that a successful outcome is possible.

How Will Your Selection and Training of Personnel Differ From Competitors'? How Will the Public Know?

You must have a detailed plan for both clinical and customer relations training of *all* staff members. This plan should detail the expectations for performance of all staff members in all aspects of their job. Training should be included in the performance reviews of all staff members (Chapter 19). Although there is some controversy on the inclusion of incentive programs to enhance staff performance, we believe that when possible there is much to be gained from considering performance incentives for all staff members.

How Will You Instill Confidence in Your Abilities and Services?

An obvious area to consider here is dress. Look like what a consumer expects a professional health care provider to look like, bearing in mind that different types of consumers have different expectations. There are many options. For a general practice, business casual may be appropriate. In a practice near physician referral sources, dress as they do, for example, in white coats or dress suits. Quality of care is very important, but much of the therapeutic aspect of a physical therapy service business is difficult for the typical patient to evaluate. Your customers may not be familiar with what is reasonable to expect in physical therapy or may not be cognitively or emotionally able to logically assess the physical therapy process because of injury or illness. What most patients can assess is how well they are treated with regard to respect, dignity, and common courtesy. They are also adept at judging facility cleanliness and cosmetics. All aspects of the clinic should be professionally designed and neat in appearance. This includes not only the physical facility and staff but also all of the written materials distributed to patients and their families, third-party payers, and referrers. Poorly designed materials, hard-to-read forms, typographical errors, and poorly reproduced copies all promote an amateurish image and diminish the confidence. A tangible indicator of quality is outcomes data. If such information is available and it places the practice in a good light, it will enhance the consumer's confidence in the practice.

Physical Therapy for Persons With Dementia

The population with dementia has been growing in recent years. In addition to the classic memory loss and forgetfulness, these individuals often have trouble solving problems of everyday life, including basic and instrumental activities of daily living and motor planning. Also, many persons with dementia also have coexisting orthopedic, neurologic, or musculoskeletal problems, just like the general elderly population that does not have dementia. Physical therapists certainly have a role in helping this population. The need for physical therapy services for this population has always existed, but until recently therapy claims were automatically denied if an individual had been diagnosed with dementia. The federal government has recently clarified its policy regarding Medicare's coverage of some services for people affected by dementia. This policy change permits greater access to speech, occupational, and rehabilitation therapies. The policy change signaled a greater opportunity for seniors and caregivers of individuals with Alzheimer's disease to appeal unfair denials and work with doctors to provide therapy services. According to the internal memorandum that mandated the policy change, Medicare may now consider on a case-by-case basis paying for evaluation and management visits to a doctor and physical therapy for an individual with dementia (Centers for Medicare and Medicaid Services, 2001).

Product: How Does Your Niche Service Benefit the Market?

Like many physical therapy interventions, physical therapy services for persons with dementia do not directly affect the underlying pathology. The goal of therapy is to facilitate adaptation or compensation for the functional deficits and impairments that the dementia causes. The eventual benefit to the patient is a more functional, enjoyable, and independent life. Additional benefits are often realized by families and loved ones of the person with dementia, as they can feel more confident and comfortable in the patient's safety and well-being.

Define the Overall Niche Market

Dementia is primarily an affliction of adults of at least middle age with increasing incidence in advancing years. This market consists of persons with dementia, especially those in its early stages; decision makers, such as spouses, adult children, and those with power of attorney; and decision influencers, such as physicians, community health professionals, leaders of support groups, and others with frequent contact with the patients' caregivers. A study of 2313 persons aged 65 years and older who were initially free of Alzheimer's disease estimated the annual incidence of Alzheimer's disease in the population was 0.6% for persons aged 65 to 69 years, 1.0% for persons aged 70 to 74 years, 2.0% for persons aged 75 to 79 years, 3.3% for persons aged 80 to 84 years, and 8.4% for persons aged 85 years and older (Hebert, Scherr, Beckett et al., 1995). Table 24.2 summarizes the estimated incidence and prevalence of the major causes of brain impairment in adulthood in the United States (Family Caregiver Alliance, 2003). Data were compiled from multiple sources, allowing for both high and low population estimates.

The potential market for physical therapy services for persons with dementia is not limited to those with the condition and their family members. Many health care professionals in the social or medical environment of persons with dementia are also potential targets for our marketing efforts of these programs. Convenience and choice may be important factors for these potential referral sources.

What Characteristics Differentiate This Niche Market From the Larger General Population?

The needs and wants of this submarket are different from those of the general population in many ways. This is not yet a population that thinks first of physical therapy as a

Table 24.2 Estimated Prevalence of the Major Causes of Adult-Onset Brain Impairment in the U.S. Population

Cause	*Prevalence: Low Estimate*	*Prevalence: High Estimate*
Alzheimer's disease	4,000,000	4,000,000
Amyotrophic lateral sclerosis	30,000	30,000
Epilepsy	1,750,000	1,750,000
HIV	60,500	157,300
Huntington's disease	30,000	30,000
Multiple sclerosis	250,000	350,000
Parkinson's disease	1,500,000	1,500,000
Stroke	3,000,000	4,000,000
Traumatic brain injury	2,500,000	3,700,000
Totals	13,120,500	15,517,300

Modified with permission from the Family Caregiver Alliance (2003).

potential source of assistance. Many of the caregivers for persons with dementia are concerned about safety, and many are in need of physical therapy intervention or assistance themselves, as the workload of caregiving is substantial and rarely the only activity in their life. Often the role of primary caregiver falls to adult children of the person with dementia. This generation is often referred to as the sandwich generation because they are sandwiched between caregiver responsibilities for their own children and for their aging parents. Readily available therapeutic services that give them a break yet contribute beneficially to the person with dementia is a helpful feature for a niche practice for people with dementia.

An additional characteristic of some members of this target audience is a significant amount of discretionary income that they may willingly use to supplement inadequate insurance coverage for physical therapy services. This presents an opportunity for development of cash-based rather than insurer-based reimbursement, certainly a consideration when developing pricing policies in the marketing plan. Offering a choice of services at home or at an outpatient site on an individual or group basis provides additional features to the niche service that can help distinguish it from competitors.

Who are the Key Decision Makers for This Niche Market?

Both the person with dementia and the myriad individuals who influence them can be key decision makers or influencers. Additionally, staff at assisted living centers, skilled nursing facilities, community-based senior activity centers and geriatric outreach programs, in addition to primary care physicians and geriatric specialists are often key decision influencers for physical therapy programs for persons with dementia.

Promotion: How Will You Communicate in a Focused Manner With This Niche Market?

A reasonable communication plan includes a three-phase approach that includes the person with dementia, their medical and social service community resources, and their caregivers and/or family. A recent *Wall Street Journal* article on assisted living centers recognized the importance of this group. It reported that competition for consumers has increased among assisted living centers nationwide. Owners and operators of these types of facilities have begun targeting adults with aging parents who help both financially and with decision making when it comes to moving parents to assisted-living facilities (Smith, 2002).

Packaging: What Specific Characteristics of Your Service Delivery Will Appeal to the Niche Market?

Packaging is the process that puts together all of the features of the service organization so they can be appreciated by potential and actual consumers (Chapter 23). The primary packaging element for this niche market is safety and peace of mind. Recent media reports about health care practitioners who have preyed on persons with dementia, poor judgment, or decreased ability to make decisions have increased the general population's level of skepticism about all senior services. Even more important in a typical physical therapy program will be factors of the program that relate to client respect, dignity, and safety. These should be significant components of any communication plan associated with a physical therapy program for persons with dementia.

An example of focused packaging was done at Oatfield Estates, an assisted living center in Milwaukie, Oregon. This facility uses surveillance and monitoring gear to help care for its 35 residents. Oatfield's ambiance is homelike, with plants, pets, and live-in caregivers, yet it is also high tech. Small sensors dot the walls to track residents' movements, and security cameras are mounted near the campus boundaries. The residents all wear transponders around their necks. These transponders serve multiple functions: an alarm, a room key, and a location monitor. Residents' beds also have sensors that monitor their weight and movements (Shellenbarger, 2002).

Pricing: What Pricing Strategy Will Appeal to the Market Msost Effectively?

General pricing considerations are discussed in Chapter 23. These apply to non-Medicare third-party payers. The prevalence of dementia increases with age; therefore, many of the interventions associated with services to this niche market are potentially covered under the Medicare program. Since many persons with dementia are also Medicare beneficiaries, refer to the pricing structure of the Medicare program (Chapters 27–30). Cost is clearly a concern for Medicare beneficiaries, who have to pay deductibles or copayments (Chapter 2). Additional information, including access to a free Medicare rehabilitation fee schedule calculator, is available online at http://www.PTManager.com.

In the event that services are offered fee-for-service or out-of-pocket, a clearly defined fee structure for all services will be necessary. It is critical that all fees be disclosed before initiation of services to avoid problems in collection or disagreements on fees due. Many successful programs that focus on out-of-pocket payment for services have developed a menu of services to be provided and often have patients sign a contract before services begin so that there are no questions about the responsibilities of the parties to deliver services, participate in the program, and pay fees (Chapters 28 and 29).

An additional aspect of out-of-pocket programs that many physical therapists find helpful is the option of payment by credit card. This allows easy collection of fees, and the ability to receive payment often offsets the additional costs associated with processing credit card payments. The decision to offer credit card payments may not be cost effective for very small programs or programs in which many small fees are processed throughout the day. The practice considering the use of credit cards should carefully investigate the costs and advantages before proceeding.

Place: Where Should This Service Be Offered, and Why?

Because of the changes in mental status inherent in dementia, physical therapy services for persons with dementia are often provided at the person's place of residence or at a specialized center. Such centers are designed to address the unique needs of individuals with poor memory, poor judgment, decreased functional skills, and problem-solving skills. Any facility in which consumers with known judgment problems are treated will be held to a higher standard of safety precautions, so care must be taken in the design and development of any such center. From a marketing perspective, this is also a packaging issue, as many potential consumers are likely to tour the facility prior to making a purchase decision.

How Will You Give Physical Evidence of Quality or Effectiveness for Your Service?

Decision making for persons with dementia, whether by the patient or caregiver, is often fraught with emotional issues. Common questions and thoughts include the following: Is this the right thing to do for mother? Can I be sure that I am thinking straight today? How do I know I can trust these physical therapists with my hard-earned (and rapidly dwindling) savings? As mentioned in the section on niche marketing of the aquatics program, any special certifications or accreditations should be prominently displayed in your facility. Articles that you wrote or were mentioned in should be available for ready review by individuals in your waiting areas. Pictures of past successful participants in the program make for excellent decorations throughout the facility and reassure new participants as they enter your programs that a successful outcome is possible. Few things if any are so valuable and reassuring to future clients than the opportunity to interact with current or even past clients. There may also be some hesitancy among potential consumers based on the fear of physical injury from other program participants, who may be less rational than they are. Meeting current program participants and seeing what safeguards are in place will help to overcome these concerns.

How Will Your Selection and Training of Personnel Differ From Competitors'? How Will the Public Know?

There must be a detailed plan for both clinical and customer relations training of *all* staff members. This plan should include competencies specific to the geriatric population and to persons with problem-solving, memory, and judgment problems. This plan should detail the expectations for performance of all staff members in all aspects of their job. As with the aquatics program, training of staff members to treat persons with dementia should be included in the performance review process of all staff members.

What Will You Do to Instill Confidence in Your Abilities and Service?

It will be necessary to communicate the complexity of the services you provide regardless of what type of niche program you offer. Because by their very nature these specialized programs may not be well recognized or understood by the general consumer market, you will often have to educate potential customers on the need for the type of services you offer and then convince them that you are the provider of choice for those services. Even in a general physical therapy program, it is often necessary to sell the general concept of physical therapy and then sell the benefits of your particular service (Chapter 23).

Student Notes

Niche practices can be very beneficial to the community. They can also be successful businesses for the organization or individual physical therapist. Be careful to apply the general concepts of marketing to the development of niche practices and to understand some of the unique aspects of the niche practice compared to a more general physical therapy practice. A niche is a unique offering for very specific consumers. There are fewer consumers to target for a specialty practice than for a general practice. Be careful in determining the viability of a niche practice in terms of need, volume, payment, competition, and human and other resources needed to provide quality care. Expertise in a niche is likely to be developed through a combination of continuing education and mentoring. However, opportunities to develop new niches may precede the availability of organized education or people who have experience with the niche service. Such cases provide an opportunity to lead rather than follow for those who are willing to take risks.

Summary

A niche is a specific identifiable market for a specific service, product, or intervention. The marketing of niche services follows the eight P's of service marketing: price, place, packaging, product, promotion, personnel selection and training, physical evidence of effectiveness, and processes that instill consumer confidence. Integrated with the eight P's is a parallel set of considerations that focus on the consumer's interests, that is, convenience, choice, and cost (four C's). Together, the marketing strategy and planning take place with a balanced consideration of the needs of the physical therapy organization and the consumer.

Table 24.1 lists 33 examples of physical therapy niche opportunities. Two of them, aquatic therapy and therapy for persons with dementia, are presented to exemplify how the eight P's and four C's can be used to guide niche practice development. Specific questions are asked about each of the eight P's to individualize the issues. The strengths and weaknesses of such practices in various geographic markets are discussed along with suggestions for answering the many questions used to guide the development of these niche programs.

The next chapter is the last one to deal specifically with service marketing. It inte-

INDIVIDUAL CASE STUDY

The following information about a possible physical therapy niche is factual. As you read, take note of which of the eight P's have been addressed.

Between 1991 and 1998 the prevalence of obesity in the U.S. population increased nearly 5% to 17.9% (Daus, 2001). Many hospitalized patients who weigh 300 pounds or more have diabetes. Some of these patients are blind. Some have had one or more limbs amputated. Some have pressure ulcers. Most of these patients are unable to transfer without maximal assistance. Providing care for very large dependent patients poses a risk of back injury for staff and family members. Several people may be needed to move these patients. Heavy lifting equipment may be needed. Extra wide beds and wheelchairs are often necessary. Given the recent trend, the percentage of obese individuals in the community living and institutionalized populations is expected to continue to increase.

Task

Answer the following questions:

Which of the eight P's do you have information about?

What information do you still need?

If you were going to explore this niche further, who would your target market be?

grates much of the material from the preceding chapters, particularly those with marketing content. Marketing principles, strategic planning, marketing strategies, and niche marketing concepts are applied to a business of one, that is, an individual physical therapist. The uniqueness of Chapter 25 is its focus. The business principles are applied to the marketing of an individual physical therapist as if the therapist were a niche business. An individual therapist will be considered the owner of the knowledge, skills, and attributes necessary to deliver physical therapy services. Thinking of oneself as the sole proprietor of these core elements facilitates thinking of oneself as a business and conceiving of those who need or may need your services as your consumers. The next chapter forges the connections between business, service marketing principles, and self-marketing.

GROUP CASE STUDY

Divide the class into four groups. In each group, designate one person to be the recorder and reporter.

Task

Each group is to contemplate the formation of a niche. Come to agreement on the kind of setting (e.g., physical therapy clinic, part of a large health care organization, sole proprietorship) for which you will be developing a niche practice. The niche may be part of an existing organization or a new business. Use Table 25.1 to give you ideas about potential niches for physical therapy services. Choose one that interests most of the group members. List and discuss 10 things you will do to develop a niche practice in your chosen environment. When everyone is finished, the four group reporters should present their respective groups' lists. Discuss the similarities, differences, and voids (review the four C's and eight P's).

References

American Medical Association. Physician's current procedural terminology, 4th ed. Chicago: American Medical Association. 2002.

Centers for Medicare and Medicaid Services. Program Memorandum AB-01-135. Available from http://www.hcfa.gov/pubforms/transmit/AB01135.pdf. Accessed 9/25/01.

Daus C. Rehab and the bariatric patient. Rehab Management. 2001;14(9):42,44,45.

Davolt S. Walking in their footsteps. PT–Magazine of Physical Therapy. 1997;5 (11):40–43.

Family Caregiver Alliance. Incidence and prevalence of the major causes of adult-onset brain impairments in the U.S.. Available from http://www.caregiver.org/factsheets/brain_impairment.htm. Accessed 6/27/03.

Fosnaught M. From "a duty to die" to successful aging. PT–Magazine of Physical Therapy. 1995 (5):42–47, 97.

Hannagan T. Mastering strategic planning. New York: Palgrave. 2002.

Hebert LE, Scherr PA, Beckett LA et al. Age-specific incidence of Alzheimer's disease in a community population. Journal of the American Medical Association. 1995;273:1354–1359.

Institute for Rehabilitation and Research. Rehabilitation. Available from http://www.tirr.org/rehab/?page=47. Accessed 6/25/03.

Johnson LH, Ries E, Wilson M. Setting the scenes. PT–Magazine of Physical Therapy. 2001;9(7): 34–42.

Koch R. The Financial Times guide to strategy: How to create and deliver a useful strategy, 2nd ed. New York: Prentice Hall. 2000.

Mangano Heisel J, Dawson T. Under one roof. PT–Magazine of Physical Therapy. 1999;7(12): 28–33.

Monahan B. How the West is won: A day in the life of a rural PT. PT–Magazine of Physical Therapy. 1995;3(1):32–37.

Nosse LJ, Friberg DG, Kovacek PR. Managerial and supervisory principles for physical therapists. Baltimore: Lippincott, Williams & Wilkins. 1999.

Reynolds JP. Working around dementia. PT–Magazine of Physical Therapy. 1995;3(5):64–69,78,79.

Ries E. Passions for the profession. PT–Magazine of Physical Therapy. 2001;9(6):34–36.

Rollins G. The new era of home care. PT–Magazine of Physical Therapy. 1999;7(4):26–32.

Shellenbarger S. Do high-tech facilities promise brave new world of eldercare? Wall Street Journal. July 18, 2002.

Smith RA. Assisted-living centers court adult children to fill spaces. Wall Street Journal. July 3, 2002.

Wilson M. Computerized prosthetics. PT–Magazine of Physical Therapy. 2001;9(12):34–38.

Woods E. Quality of life: Physical therapy in hospice. PT–Magazine of Physical Therapy. 1998a;6(1): 39–45.

Woods E. Innovative ideas in private practice: The sports rehabilitation center at Georgia Tech. PT–Magazine of Physical Therapy. 1998b;6(2): 50–57.

Woods E. PTs in health clubs. PT–Magazine of Physical Therapy. 1999;7 (12):22–27.

Woods E. The emergency department: A new opportunity for physical therapy. PT–Magazine of Physical Therapy. 2002;10(9):42–47.

More Information Related to This Chapter

Many relevant resources are available and readily accessible through the use of online databases, such as Medline/PubMed, which is available at the Web site of the National Library of Medicine at http://www.ncbi.nlm.nih.gov/entrez/query.fcgi.

To review the contents of PT–Magazine of Physical Therapy from1995 on go to http://www.apta.org/publications. Also check this site for emerging practices, among which is complementary care.

An excellent resource on complementary care as a niche is Faass N. Integrating complementary medicine into health systems. Gaithersburg, MD: Aspen, 2001.

For more information on starting a specialty business, go to http://www.sba.gov. See starting your business, online library, and financing your business.

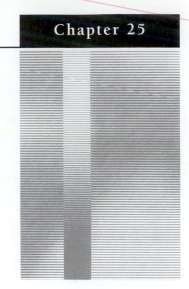

Chapter 25

Marketing Yourself

Learning Objectives

1. Examine yourself in the context of being a service business of one person.
2. Apply a strategic management approach to develop a personalized marketing strategy.
3. Formalize personal guidance statements, that is, philosophical, vision, and mission statements to give direction to an environmental assessment.
4. Conduct a SWOT personal environmental assessment from the perspective of being a service business of one person.
5. Draft a personalized service-marketing strategy and plan based on general and niche marketing principles.

Key Words

Business of one, competitor, consumer, differentiation, eight P's, four C's, fundamental guiding documents, goals, marketing, marketing process, niche practitioner, niche practice, objective, self-marketing, self-marketing plan, sole proprietor, strategic planning, strategic process, strategy

Introduction

Much of the marketing information presented in Chapters 21 to 24 is quickly summarized in the following discussion. What is new is the frame of reference: that you are the manager or owner of your own one-person physical therapy business. In this frame of reference you are a **business of one**.

Quick Review of Marketing Principles for a Business of One

A general definition of marketing is that **marketing** includes all communications between the owner of a service or product business and targeted consumers. The purpose of the communications are to inform these targeted consumers about the service or product so they buy what is being offered. In this chapter the marketing discussion focuses on the application of marketing concepts to market a specific individual. For example, a soon-to-graduate student physical therapist will be marketing to potential employers. A licensed physical therapist may be interested in applying for a first-level management position in his or her organization. This application of principles of service and product marketing to yourself is **self-marketing**. Self-marketing incorporates general business (Chapters 21–23) and niche service marketing principles (Chapter 24).

The goal of self-marketing is to move toward the fulfillment of the envisioned future. This goal supports physical therapists becoming autonomous in their career development (Chapter 20) and becoming autonomous practitioners as described in the vision statement of the American Physical Therapy Association (2002).

How Do Business Marketing Concepts Relate to a Business of One?

To question the relevance of using business concepts to advance an individual physical therapist toward the fulfillment of career goals is logical. A reasoned transition from marketing a health care business to marketing an individual health care provider requires discussing four business concepts: individual ownership, consumer, differentiation, and competitors.

1. **Individual Ownership**: Even with treatment protocols, availability of evidence-based Internet sites, standard procedures, care pathways, and common educational backgrounds, no two physical therapists regularly treat their patients exactly the same way. This is because each licensed physical therapist has unique knowledge, skills, experience, and psychosocial dispositions that he or she applies to physical therapy services. In this sense each individual can be considered as a **niche practitioner**. Each therapist possesses, or in business terms, owns, the core labor resources for providing physical therapy services to a variety of markets. Physical therapists are like one-person businesses: they are both the owner of the labor resources and the provider of services. Again, using business terms, an individual who has the core resources to provide a needed service to a target or niche market fits the description of a **sole proprietor** (Chapter 7). Owners have the right to use profits as they see fit. Even though most physical therapists are not formally business owners, there is an analogy. Employees exchange their knowledge, skills, and efforts with an employer for an hourly rate, salary, or other incentives. This is a business transaction in which compensation is paid for providing services.
2. **Consumers**: Anyone in need or potentially in need of the services of a physical therapist may be considered a **consumer** (Chapter 21). This broad conceptualization of a consumer includes actual and potential patients, family and friends of patients, referral sources, fellow employees, friends, friends of friends, managers, and of course, employers. Marketing is consumer focused (Chapter 22). A spectrum of consumers calls for a spectrum of marketing communications to achieve desired goals. Having a marketing strategy and a strategic marketing plan is one way to manage the marketing messages for various types of actual and future consumers (Chapter 11).
3. **Differentiation**: Having something a consumer wants that other providers have less of, do not have, or charge more for (Mintzberg, Quinn, Voyer, 1995). As discussed in previous chapters, differentiation is a market positioning strategy (Chapters 22 and 24). For self-marketing purposes, communicating to consumers your unique set of attributes gives them the information they need to differentiate your services from others'. Understanding what options consumers have helps guide the differentiation communication effort. Thinking about the **four C's** (consumers, convenience, choice, cost) (Chapter 24) is helpful when developing differentiation-based marketing communications.
4. **Competitors**: Numerous individuals have the potential to meet almost any consumers' need for some aspect of physical therapy service. **Competitors** who offer consumers some aspects of physical therapy service include athletic trainers, chiropractors, massage therapists, occupational therapists, and personal trainers (Chapter 21). Physical therapists also compete with each other for jobs, promotions, contracts, continuing education funds, and other developmental opportunities.

Competitors compete for consumers' attention as they try to communicate the positive attributes of their service offerings. When competition is plentiful, a marketing plan built upon the **eight P's** (product or service, price, place, promotion, packaging, processes, physical evidence, personnel) is likely

.o be more effective in communicating the desired message to targeted consumers (Chapters 21–24) than an informal or self-constructed marketing approach.

Marketing and Strategy for a Business of One

Marketing is a generic component of a business of any size. The **marketing process** (Chapter 21) involves all activities that help inform potential consumers so they can distinguish one organization's services and products from others (McConnell, 2002). To meet this goal a marketing **strategy** is chosen and a **strategic planning** process is enacted to develop marketing objectives and plans (Chapters 22 and 23). A **strategy** is the conceptualization of a desired future along with the actions to secure it (Macmillan and Tampoe, 2000).

Strategy development and planning take place within the boundaries set by the organization's fundamental documents. The traditional **fundamental documents** (Chapter 9) are value or philosophical, vision (the future aspired to), and mission statements (e.g., what the business does, its consumers). In large health care organizations it is the responsibility of executive management to develop the fundamental documents and the marketing strategy and marketing plans (Chapters 8 and 11). An individual service business owner is the top-level manager of the business. The responsibility for formulating the personal fundamental documents to guide the strategic planning process lies with the owner.

A personal strategic planning process is summarized in Table 25.1. The important strategic questions are shown in the right side of the table. The benefits of going through this or any other planning process are to avoid overlooking critical items and to assess the process once it has been applied. The items in the left-hand column of Table 25.1 are discussed next within the framework of a sole proprietor of a service business.

Personal Value Priorities, Core Values and Motives, Philosophical Statement

To have a career direction you need to know what is important to you, that is, what your career must provide for your psychological satisfaction. Achieving satisfaction is the ultimate purpose for developing any plan. When you know what is most important to you (what you value) and have reflected upon it (understand the motive or goal of the prized value), you have a reasoned basis for making informed choices that are likely to lead to self-fulfillment. Some ways self-fulfillment can occur through work include helping others, acquiring wealth, and feeling needed.

Values may be thought of as windows to motives and precursors to conscious actions

Table 25.1 Strategic Planning for a Marketing Plan for an Individual Service Business Owner

Process	*Key Questions*
Identify personal value priorities, core values, motives	What is important?
Formulate personal philosophical statement	How will I treat others?
Formulate initial personal vision and mission statements	What is the ideal goal? What are my attributes and focus as a service business owner?
Conduct a personal environmental assessment to inform vision and mission statements	What is the real world like? What direction to take? What opportunities are there? What threats are there?
Refine vision and mission statements	Does the assessment call for adjustments?
Formulate personal marketing strategy	How to match goals, objectives, resources to meet consumers' needs (eight P's, four C's)?
Develop a personal marketing mix to meet targeted consumers' needs	How to communicate to prospective consumers about service offerings?
Monitor, evaluate, and improve process to be more efficient and effective next time	How have things gone at each step? What can be improved, and how?

(Sagiv and Schwartz, 1995; Schwartz, Verkasalo, Antonovsky, Sagiv, 1997). Thus, it is from values that planned actions spring. Just as for a business, the formation of a values or philosophical statement is the initial step in strategic planning (see Chapters 9 and 11).

Identify Personal Values

A quick, simple and private way to identify personal value priorities is to ask and candidly answer the question, "if I get X (name anything you consider important, for example, accomplishment, position, recognition), what will that do for me?" Answer your own question and ask again, "What will that do for me?" After a few rounds of self-questioning and answering, the probable underlying motive will emerge because you run out of answers to your question. The final answer reflects the personal motivation underlying what was said to be valued. The progressive questioning stimulates thought and sheds some light on one's values and motives.

Figure 25.1 summarizes a second way to identify important values. This is a card sort method. Start by writing on individual note cards every single value term that you think is important to you, that is, the things you would work hard to achieve or acquire. Security, substantive social interaction, desire to help others are example value terms (see Table 6.1 for a list of personal value terms). Place cards with terms that you feel are related in columns so you can read all of them. Related cards might be associated with gaining social power, sustaining culture, religion, or family. Make as many columns as you need to organize individual value terms.

Go to the first column and find the most personally important item. Move this card to the top of the column. Next, find the least personally important item in the column. Move this card to the bottom of the column. Place the remaining cards in descending order between the most important and the least important value terms. When you finish, the cards in the column will represent the relative degree of importance you assigned to your personal values in that column. Repeat the process for the remaining columns. When you finish sorting, the top row of cards will contain your most important personal value terms, the bottom row of cards will contain the least important value terms, and the intermediate value cards will be ordered in terms of their personal importance.

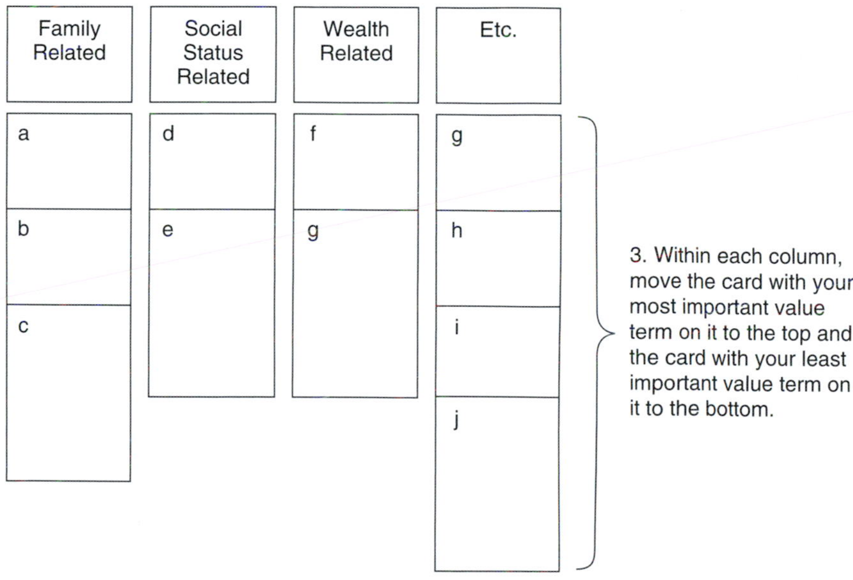

Figure 25.1. Card sort method of identifying and prioritizing personal values.

The prioritized value terms should be incorporated into a personal philosophical statement, for they represent what is important to you, that is, what you will work to accomplish and what gives you psychological satisfaction. Your prioritized values form a part of the next guiding fundamental document, your personal philosophical statement.

Develop a Personal Philosophical Statement

A philosophical statement contains prioritized values and the philosophical principles that guide behavior (Darr, 1997; Longest, Rakich, Darr, 2000). Ideally, a philosophical statement is formulated before other fundamental documents, that is, vision and mission statements. This preparation order helps ensure that the latter documents fit within the philosophical context (Darr, 1997). The practical use of a personal philosophical statement is as a of what the person holds important in human interactions and for self-fulfillment. The content of a personal philosophical statement includes the following:

- Core values
- Moral stance
- Ethical principles

Draft Personal Vision and Mission Statements

A vision of a desirable future expresses a highly valued goal that serves to inspire efforts to reach an eventual goal (Chapter 9). A vision is a wish list or a stretch goal. It is something that is out of reach, but with effort and commitment, it would be possible to achieve. Progress toward a vision occurs in irregular amounts.

Employers are often interested in an applicant's aspirations. A common interview question is where you see yourself in 3 to 5 years. A well-thought-out vision statement answers this question and helps both parties gauge the match between the organization, the job, and the applicant's long-range goals. A vision can be tied to a time frame. Examples of short- to long-term vision statements are stated in Table 25.2. The example in this table is a hypothetical recent physical therapy graduate.

A mission statement is another directive document (Chapters 9 and 11). A personal mission statement includes what you do well, your target market or market segment (Chapter 24), where and when you do what you do, and how well you do it. A personal mission statement should inform potential consumers and others about your abilities and intentions and the mission should keep your actions focused on your intentions.

An individual physical therapist preparing to develop a plan to market his or her knowledge, skills, and psychosocial dispositions as a service is responsible for developing vision and mission statements. These tasks can be difficult when clinical experience is limited. Nonetheless, with general knowledge and relevant examples, these documents can be created. The following list includes items that can be included in a personal mission statement:

- Job title you are qualified for (what you do well)
- Type of experience you seek (target consumers, e.g., orthopedic, intensive care, management)

Table 25.2 Sample Progressive Personal Vision Statement for an Entry Level Physical Therapist

Short-range personal vision: Be employed full time as a staff physical therapist in a clinical environment noted for its excellence in caring for members from diverse segments of society who have orthopedic problems and for the quality of the clinical education opportunities available to staff, that is, paths leading to fulfillment of requirements to sit for the orthopedic specialization examination and to clinical residency.

Intermediate-range personal vision: Within 3 to 4 years pass the orthopedic specialization examination and become a board-certified orthopedic specialist. Within 5 years complete a clinical residency program to receive credential as a physical therapist in orthopedics.

Long-range personal vision: In 5 years be a respected partner in a private physical therapy practice in an urban area in a direct-access western state where all partners are doctors of physical therapy and/or board-certified orthopedic or sports specialists who value providing physical therapy services pro bono to individuals unable to pay.

- Characteristics of the clients you wish to treat or attract in larger numbers (target consumers, e.g., private pay, multiple co-morbidities, women, middle management, the owner)
- Type of organization you prefer (target consumers, e.g., hospital, national corporation, sectarian skilled nursing facility)
- Individuals you want to work with (target consumers, e.g., a clinical coordinator of clinical education, a board-certified clinical specialist, an experienced therapist with doctor of physical therapy (DPT) degree, a respected department manager)
- Geographic location (target location, e.g., east coast; North Carolina; Raleigh, North Carolina)
- Organizational culture (target values, e.g., commitment to excellence, patients first, history of promotion from within)
- Third-party payers, physicians, and others with whom you may wish to develop professional relationships to increase patient volume (target consumers, e.g., a managed care organization, largest family practice group in target area, local industry leaders)
- Physical therapists you may want as mentors or business associates (target consumers, e.g., experienced colleague, president of the Section on Health Policy and Administration, a private practice physical therapist with a master's of business administration (MBA) and board-certified specialization).

The actual items in a personal mission statement depend on your vision, self-assessment, and target consumers. Table 25.3 contains a personal mission statement for a new graduate based on selected items from this list. This mission statement is compatible with the vision presented in Table 25.2. For a physical therapist the vision example changes to reflect the vision quest. This might be a long-range aspiration to own a multidisciplinary pediatric clinic, an intermediate vision of completing an MBA on line, and a short-term vision of being promoted to manager of a new children's outpatient clinic.

Table 25.3 has vision statements for different time frames. These statements exemplify a progression in aspirations and focuses as clinical experience is gained, skills mastered, and new interests and opportunities emerge (service/product life cycle, Chapter 20). This progression serves as a reminder that a vision is pursued and not necessarily reached. The road to a personal vision is always under construction. Therefore, when it becomes likely that a vision is on its way toward fulfillment, the next edition of the future should be determined and a revised vision formulated. An experienced physical therapist has developed many skills and preferences through clinical experience. This rich background allows such therapists to state with confidence what they do well, whom they treat excellently, where they do it, how they do it, and when they do it.

These three fundamental guiding documents are obviously connected. They are as important in giving direction to an individual service business owner as they are for members of a large health care organization. This unity was expressed well by Koteen (1997), who wrote, "Visions weave together the essence of the mission and values to be accomplished and the fundamental directions for change to take. The constant components of vision are mission, goals, and values that can serve as the adhesive to bring everybody together" (p.59).

Table 25.3 Personal Mission Statement for an Entry-Level Physical Therapist

Personal mission: Secure a full-time staff physical therapist position in an organization in a western state where culturally and diagnostically diverse clientele with orthopedic problems are treated. Treatment of this diagnostic category is my strength because of my clinical experience, extra coursework, and continuing education. The ideal organization is one that has a credentialed clinical residency program in orthopedics for physical therapists that incorporates fulfillment of board-certified specialist certification requirements and is available to its staff members. The primary instructors to be experienced faculty, including physical therapists who have board specialization in orthopedic or sports physical therapy. The faculty to be nationally recognized for its teaching, diagnostic, and manual therapy knowledge and skills and for its desire to mentor staff.

Assess Relevant Environments

A personal environmental assessment (Chapter 11) for a business of one includes self-assessment (internal environment) along with an assessment of variables not under personal control (external environment). The content of the assessment is determined by the person's view of the future as expressed in the vision and mission statements. These fundamental documents facilitate asking pertinent questions and aid the interpretation of the answers.

Students and recent graduates often have loosely envisioned and incomplete expressions of their vision and mission. Practicing physical therapists may be going about their work with a vague idea of what they want to do next. Hazy guiding documents can result in gathering inappropriate as well as insufficient information. Imprecision limits the degree of confidence in decisions based on the data collected. A rule of thumb regarding the scope of a personal environmental assessment is to investigate areas known or anticipated to affect the ability to carry out the mission and actualize the vision (Dunn, 1998). Not having plans has been phrased positively as having a plan to fail (Olsen, 1999).

A strengths, weaknesses, opportunities, threats (SWOT) analysis (McConkey, 1976) is a commonly used means to assess oneself and external variables. Table 25.4 contains a SWOT-based personal environmental assessment for a student physical therapist. The example vision and mission statements in Tables 25.2 and 25.3 guided this SWOT analysis. The initial goal of the hypothetical student is within 6 months to secure a full-time staff physical therapist position in an orthopedic care setting in a western state. The initial target consumers are human resource and physical therapy department representatives of organizations with credentialed orthopedic residency programs. For a physical therapist aspiring to a management position the process of forming values, vision, and mission statements and conducting SWOT analyses is the same as for a student. What differs most is the external environment of interest, that is, the influences related to attaining an initial job compared with seeking a promotion or a management position.

Self-Marketing Strategy and Objectives

Objectives are lesser goals that contribute to fulfilling a complex and broad-scoped goal (Chapter 22). The objectives listed next are intended to gather hard data about potential consumers to identify those who are compatible with the philosophy, vision, and mission. These consumers become the target market for the job seeker. These are the objectives of the data-gathering effort:

- Identify the institutions that meet fundamental criteria
- Identify specific individuals and find out how to contact them
- Identify students and graduates of target institutions and find out their contact information
- Make initial contact with identified institutional, student, and graduate representatives
- Organize the information
- Produce templates for future communications
- Follow up with respondents as needed
- Thank respondents
- Assess information using SWOT format and concepts
- Weigh information within the context of personal fundamental documents
- Rank target consumers according to the degree to which they meet criteria stated in your fundamental documents
- Make initial and follow-up contacts with top-ranked target consumers regarding openings

Personal Marketing Mix for a Business of One

Once target consumers have been identified, you, the service business owner, need to inform them of the advantages of your service. This requires a **self-marketing plan** based on the variables that you can control. These are the eight P's (Chapters 21–24). Your task

Table 25.4 SWOT Analysis of a Final Year Student Physical Therapist

Internal Factors	*External*
Strengths	**Opportunities**
Doctor of physical therapy (DPT) degree	Number of job openings promising
40 weeks of clinical experience in a variety of settings	Some private practitioners perceive having staff with DPT advantageous for gaining market share
High satisfaction ratings among outpatients of all ages who had orthopedic diagnoses; functional outcomes for orthopedic outpatients with total knee replacements above department norm	Increasing numbers of physically active baby boomers maturing as potential consumers
Carried a full load final 2 months of internship	APTA's vision statement identifies the DPT as the degree of choice
Experienced screening patients for medical conditions in a direct-access state	Only a small percentage of practicing physical therapists have DPT degree
Strong differential diagnosis coursework from a nationally known professor	Salaries continuing to rise
Experience working with a diverse client population of various ethnic groups, all ages, with neuromusculoskeletal problems	Several accredited orthopedic clinical residency programs in western states
Available immediately	**Threats**
Physically strong, well conditioned, even keeled, friendly, respectful, team player; extremely motivated to develop manual therapy skills and pursue board certification in orthopedics	Increasing numbers of programs offering clinical doctorate
Spanish as a second language	Demand specifically for DPT graduates spotty
Advanced computer skills including experience upgrading PCs, setting up local networks, home page development, experience with most PC database programs	Starting salaries for entry-level physical therapists likely to be unrelated to degree
Weaknesses	Employers giving preference to experienced physical therapists over new graduates
Educational program new	Where supply of physical therapists is greater than demand, trend is toward hiring part-time workers and having them compete for full-time openings as available
Average length of clinical experience	Programs that offer orthopedic specialization and orthopedic residency are popular, making admissions very competitive
All but final 8 weeks of clinical experience was two students to one supervisor	Increasing popularity of complementary therapies means greater competition from non–physical therapists for the same patients
Few DPT graduates in practice at this time	Political strength of local and national bodies representing chiropractic interests that run counter to interests of physical therapists, e.g., limitations on doing joint manipulation; not all western states allow direct access to physical therapists, which limits locations for fulfilling long-term vision
Little experience with workers' compensation	Rising standards for becoming a certified athletic trainer
No experience working with board certified orthopedic specialists, experienced DPT practitioners; little interaction with physical therapist assistants; minimal experience as a member of an interdisciplinary team	National Athletic Trainers Association's efforts to promote its members as the providers of choice for the physically active
Interest limited to patients with neuromusculoskeletal problems	Successful efforts of American College of Sports Medicine to be agency for certification of exercise specialists of various types
Geographic and facility limitations (organization must have or be near an approved clinical residency program in orthopedics)	Possible unfavorable bias against DPT graduates by physical therapists with other degree designations
Need relatively high initial salary because of student debt in excess of $50K	
No contacts at any institution in the western states that offer a residency program	
No experience negotiating wages	

requires choosing the appropriate combination of the eight P's to get the attention of each potential consumer. This combination of marketing efforts, known as the marketing mix or communication mix (Lewis, 1999), may be different for each consumer, especially the promotional component. For example, some consumers may be near enough for in-person contacts, while others will have to be contacted by e-mail or fax. Some of the information for the marketing mix comes from the personal guiding documents, that is, what the service is, where services will be delivered, the packaging, personnel training, and physical evidence. The price is determined by local rates, supply and demand, urgency or lack of urgency to hire, other recent hires, and negotiation. The promotional mix options available to an individual to disseminate the information include the following:

- **Advertising**: send hard copy and electronic résumés, cover letters; develop a personal Web site; send message and link to target consumers
- **Direct marketing**: interviews, face to face communications, word of mouth, professional socialization, networks, references
- **Personal selling**: employ a career consultant to market your services; go from employer to employer in person to drop off your résumé and cover letter and meet anyone who will talk with you; follow up the visits in a variety of ways to show your sincere interest
- **Offer a premium**: Offer to work under supervision without compensation for a week to show your core abilities
- **Public relations**: volunteer for potential employers; participate in community events sponsored by potential employers or the employees of the potential employers
- **Publicity**: get involved in activities of human interest in the employer's community; provide the media with information about you; volunteer for interviews, teaching; spend time on activities likely to be covered by the media
- **Telemarketing**: make phone calls to human resource departments and others to inquire about current and future openings; call about ads in the newspapers, trade journals, posted at professional meetings, posted on line

To aid making marketing mix decisions that are appropriate to potential target consumers, it is helpful to consider their views, interests, and needs. Generally consumers' interests fall into one or more of four general areas that all begin with the letter C (Hannagan, 2002). The **four C's** that are complementary to the eight P's:

1. The *consumer*
2. *Convenience*
3. *Choices*
4. *Costs*

The four C's are summarized in Table 25.5. Use the table to gain insight into the concerns of the consumer, for example, a physical therapy or human resource manager who might hire you. Some applications of the four C's for an experienced physical therapist seeking a management position are:

- Treat peers and other managers as *customers*
- A positive history with an employer and immediate availability when an opening arises provide incentives to save recruitment *costs* and promote from within the organization

Table 25.5 A Potential Employer's Thinking About a New Graduate Based on the Four C's

C's	*Employer's Analysis*
Consumers' characteristics	New graduate, service relatively untried (patients, staff, physicians); limited scope of experience, initially limited to locations with supervision and a specific type of patient load
Cost	Relatively low initial wage, no real pay history, limited negotiation experience, likely to take first offer, some training necessary; will the applicant stay at least a year?
Convenience	How much time to learn about this applicant? How quickly does the applicant respond? Does the applicant seem to know what he or she wants? Do I know anyone who knows the applicant?
Choice	How quickly must the job be filled? Is the applicant pool large or small? What is the quality of the applicant pool? Do the better applicants have other offers? Can I live with per diem rather than another full-time employee?

- Being known to those who recommend hiring, readily available to interview, and able to respond quickly to questions make it *convenient* for an employer to deal with you
- The *choice* to promote an internal applicant or to solicit external applicants is influenced by the immediacy of the need, the perceived qualifications of applicants, and most important, organizational goals

Feedback Loop: Monitor, Evaluate, and Improve

It is important to compare the results of each part of the strategic marketing process against the intended results. This means comparing related goals, objectives, plans, and outcomes at each step of the process (Chapter 22). Monitoring and evaluating the results of the planning process and the action plans helps to identify the imperfections and where improvements can be made. A self-marketing planning process edified by actual experience is invaluable. A good process is improved with use. It is important to have a good personal marketing process and use it, because in today's health care environment it is likely that your consumers, particularly employers, will change periodically. The self-marketing concepts described in this chapter can keep you moving toward your personal vision.

Student Notes

There are costs associated with completing a step-by-step strategic personal self-marketing process like the one presented in this chapter. The process is thought provoking, which is good. But it is also time consuming, which is not good when there are time constraints. We offer a suggestion for developing and completing a self-marketing project within one or two semesters.

The following schedule can be completed as part of a management course or for personal interest with the help of friends, and if available, career development center staff. The schedule allows for progressive refinements and increased specificity as more is learned and more clinical experience is gained. An example week-by-week schedule for developing a self-marketing plan:

Weeks 1 and 2: Draft fundamental documents: personal philosophy, vision, and mission statements.

Weeks 3 and 4: Refine the statements, especially the mission; have the statements critiqued; start writing résumé; set up templates for cover letter, thank you notes, and information tracking.

Weeks 5 and 6: Finish résumé with a hypothetical target consumer in mind; have résumé, mock cover letter, and thank you note critiqued for format and content; make clear work-related competencies, that is, knowledge, skills, dispositions.

Weeks 7 to 9: Use feedback to revise these items; gather information about target consumers.

Weeks 10 and 11: Reduce target consumer list to the best matches with your mission; refine résumé (consider eight P's, four C's) to match your assets with target consumers' needs; identify the marketing mix for each consumer, that is, truthfully work your résumé and cover letter to match target consumer's needs.

Weeks 12 and 13: Seek information on interviewing (career development center, online, videos); review selling concepts; role-play in groups or in pairs, alternating acting as interviewee and interviewer. Get feedback. Send thank you note to interviewer.

Week 14: If possible, arrange for an informational interview with a local potential consumer; bring résumé (in case the interviewer asks for it); ask for feedback; reflect on the experience; review which questions you asked and how, and improve the responses you gave if needed; send a thank you note.

Weeks 15 and 16: Final examination time; put materials away where you can find them.

Clinical Affiliations: Continue refinement efforts; take advantage of interview opportunities; continue narrowing list of target consumers; continue updating experience section of your résumé as each clinical experience is completed. Determine which of your clinical supervisors will provide references for you.

Summary

The self-marketing thrust of this chapter is based on conceptualizing an individual as a business of one. The individual is viewed as the sole proprietor (the owner) of the necessary knowledge, skills, and dispositions to provide a physical therapy service. For services to be used requires consumers. Envisioning all others you are in contact with as potential consumers of your service completes the linkage between them and you, the individual physical therapist with strategic marketing processes and principles.

Consumers of a physical therapist's service include employers and others besides patients who may need physical therapy services now or in the future. To maintain or gain consumers, service businesses organize marketing efforts to communicate with past, present, and future consumers. Strategic marketing processes and service-marketing concepts are reviewed and adapted for application to a hypothetical new graduate service business owner. The strategic self-marketing planning began with the development of personal guidance documents called the philosophical, vision, and mission statements. These statements are used to give direction to information seeking and assessment, an environmental assessment to determine the strengths and weaknesses of the service owner, and the opportunities and threats posed by external variables.

Cost, supply and demand, price, and salary are mentioned in this chapter. Up to this point discussion of economic and financial matters has been rather general and superficial. The next part of the book deals in depth with both health care economics and financial information. Economics is the theory of business, and accounting is its language. Starting with economics, the next chapters provide substantive information on these topics. Organizational and departmental finances are discussed. The saying "no money, no mission" is used as a catchall concept to make

INDIVIDUAL CASE STUDY

This case requires you to think about your strengths and weaknesses as regards securing employment. Your competitors are others who have applied for the same jobs as you. Assume you are in an interview. These questions are similar to those you might expect in a job interview:

Task

Reflect and formulate the responses you would give to these statements. Choose the questions that are most relevant to your educational and clinical experience.

- Tell me what you think are some advantages and disadvantages of hiring you, a new graduate. (SWOT)
- Tell me about your relationships working with physical therapist assistants. (values)
- You have worked with some good physical therapists. Tell me what you think makes a good physical therapist. (vision, values, mission)
- In your education you had some exposure to making physical therapy diagnoses. Tell me what diagnostic skills you have. (SWOT)
- You have learned a bit about us. Now tell me why do you think you are a good fit for us. (SWOT)
- Where do you see yourself a year from now? (vision)

GROUP CASE STUDY

This case is for groups of three. All group members should first scan the following three ads for physical therapists. These ads were published in newspapers and trade journals.

1. Enthusiastic, hard-working, outgoing physical therapist licensed in (your favorite state) or license pending, needed immediately full-time in a busy multidisciplinary clinic in (your favorite city). Facilities are new and spacious. Large, well-established patient population. Treatment emphasis is on functional rehabilitation, including stabilization protocols, and other treatments for spinal complaints. Competitive wage and compensation package. Please send résumé to PO Box ___________.
2. Rapidly growing national outpatient rehabilitation organization with special emphasis on pediatric patients seeks new graduate and experienced physical therapists full time for our (your favorite city) facility. Hours 7:30 A.M. to 4:30 P.M.. We offer an attractive salary, bonus incentives, and full benefits. Please submit résumé and salary history via e-mail to ___________. Several new locations opening soon. Opportunities to move between facilities and for promotion.
3. Outpatient orthopedic setting with offices in (three cities near one another that you know). Two positions available. Settings offer a large degree of autonomy; 40 hr/wk. Hourly rate commensurate with experience. New grads encouraged to apply. Contact ________ at 555-555-5555.
4. Physical therapist III (clinical supervisor) for a large medical center. Candidates should have a minimum of 10 years of experience, be licensed in _______, and have an area of clinical expertise. Responsibilities include management of student clinical education programs (12 affiliating schools), on-site educational programs, and consultation with staff members and other departments. One quarter of the workday is spent in direct patient care in area of expertise. This position is available (date). Qualified individuals are invited to submit their résumé at http://www.superplace.org. We are an EEO organization.

Task

Each group member should identify the key criteria for employment stated in each ad and pick the job that best matches his or her mission statement. Discuss your criteria for making a match. What additional information would each member like to have? Discuss where you would get the information. What changes would you make in your résumé to suit the ad (in accord with your mission of course)? Discuss your changes. Assuming that you would pursue this job, what would you do next? Discuss your plans.

the point that physical therapist employees are part of an organization that requires more income than it spends to carry out its mission over the long term. Basic economic theory, accounting conventions, and financial and other reports relevant to health care service providers are presented and analyzed. Methods of payment for services, more on productivity, patient mix, cost behavior, and cost control are among the important topics addressed in the next five chapters.

REFERENCES

American Physical Therapy Association. APTA house of delegates endorses a vision for the future. Available from http://www.apta.org/news_releases/news_archives/visionstatementrelease. Accessed 7/01/02.

Darr K. Ethics in health services management, 3rd ed. Baltimore: Health Professions. 1997.

Dunn RT. Haimann's supervisory management for health care organizations, 6th ed. Boston: McGraw-Hill. 1998.

Hannagan T. Mastering strategic management. New York; Palgrave. 2002.

Koteen J. Strategic management in public and nonprofit organizations: Managing public concerns in an era of limits, 2nd ed. Westport, CN: Praeger. 1997.

Lewis B. Communication mix. In Lewis BR, Littler D, eds. The Blackwell encyclopedic dictionary of marketing. Malden, MA: Blackwell. 1999:120, 121.

Longest BB Jr., Rakich JS, Darr K. Managing health services organizations and systems, 4th ed. Baltimore: Health Professions. 2000.

Macmillan H, Tampoe M. Strategic management process, content, and implementation. New York: Oxford University. 2000.

McConkey DD. How to manage by results, 3rd ed. New York: AMACOM. 1976.

McConnell CR. The effective health care supervisor, 5th ed. Gaithersburg, MD: Aspen. 2002.

Mintzberg H, Quinn JB, Voyer, J. The strategy process, Collegiate ed. Englewood Cliffs, NJ: Prentice Hall. 1995.

Olsen D. Entrepreneurship: Ownership and private practice physical therapy. In Nosse LJ, Friberg DG, Kovacek PR. Managerial and supervisory principles for physical therapists. Baltimore: Williams & Wilkins. 1999:278–298.

Sagiv L, Schwartz SH. Value priorities and readiness for out-group social contact. Journal of Personality and Social Psychology. 1995;69:437–448.

Schwartz SH, Verkasalo M, Antonovsky A, Sagiv L. Value priorities and social desirability: Much substance, some style. British Journal of Social Psychology. 1997;36:3–18.

MORE INFORMATION RELATED TO THIS CHAPTER

For information on strategic planning, see suggested reading in Chapter 11. For more on career development, see suggested reading in Chapter 20.

An interesting perspective on self-assessment relative to self-management skills, including activities for identifying personal values can be found in Weis DH. The self-management workshop: Helping people take control of their lives and their work. New York: AMACOM. 1999:29–75.

Lewis introduced the term *service product* to discuss marketing much as self-marketing is presented in this chapter: Lewis B. Service product. In Lewis BR, Littler D, eds. The Blackwell encyclopedic dictionary of marketing. Malden, MA: Blackwell. 1999:213, 214.

Finally, for practical and helpful information about formulating résumés for electronic transmission consult Smith, R. Electronic résumés and online networking, ed. Franklin Lakes, NJ: Career Press. 2000.

Part V

Managing Money

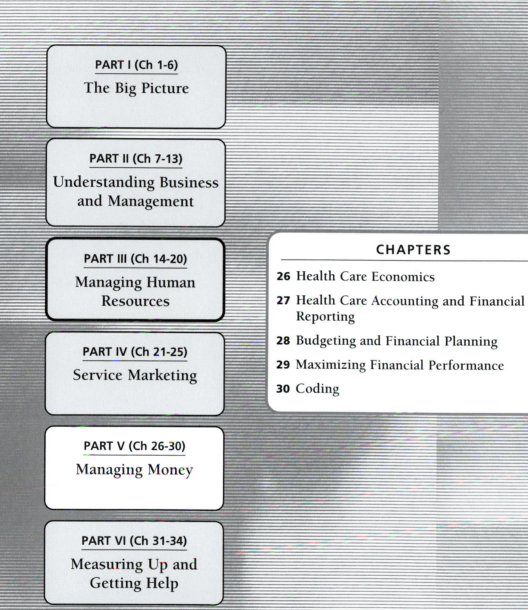

PART I (Ch 1-6)
The Big Picture

PART II (Ch 7-13)
Understanding Business and Management

PART III (Ch 14-20)
Managing Human Resources

PART IV (Ch 21-25)
Service Marketing

PART V (Ch 26-30)
Managing Money

PART VI (Ch 31-34)
Measuring Up and Getting Help

CHAPTERS

Chapter 26

Health Care Economics

Learning Objectives

1. Understand the basic economic concepts presented in this chapter, for example, market economy, markets, demand and supply, opportunity cost, price elasticity, economy of scale, and cost behaviors.
2. Summarize the principles of a market economy in relation to the health care industry, that is, consumers and service providers, income and price, consumer demand, and competitive market.
3. Correctly use economic terms in discussing the business aspects of the health care industry in general and physical therapy in particular, for example, supply curve, input (resources) versus output (units of service), direct and indirect expenses, margin, and fixed and variable costs.

Key Words

Break-even point, capital equipment, command economy, community, competitive market, consumer, consumer demand, consumer goods, cost per unit, cost–volume–profit analysis, demand curve, demand growth, demand shift, direct expense, economic concept, economic stability, economic system, economics, economy of scale, expense, fixed cost, for profit, growth, income, indirect expense, inelastic, initiation cost, input, intangible value, labor, labor market, land, loss, macroeconomic model, margin, marginal analysis, marginal value, market, market economy, microeconomic model, mission, money market, monopoly, net income, not-for-profit, opportunity cost, output, price, price elasticity, producer, production, production goods, profit, resource distribution, resource productivity, retail, revenue, scarcity, semivariable cost, substitution, supply, supply curve, supply shift, tangible value, total cost, transaction, value, variable cost, wholesale

Introduction

Thus far this textbook has dealt with management and leadership. In this part we add two new dimensions of business, economics and accounting. Our selection of topics is based on the following perspective:

- Management is the science of business
- Leadership is the art of business
- Economics is the theory of business
- Accounting is the language of business

Why is economics the theory of business? The following definition and discussion will answer this question. **Economics** is the study of the arrangements that societies make for the use and development of their scarce resources (Burningham, 1992). Because economics cannot be researched through controlled laboratory studies, economists use models to explain and predict the workings of an economy. Use of economic models can help organizations and communities understand relationships between the demand for, supply of, and price of services and goods. The impacts of resource distribution and inflation can be managed. Modeling can also help us understand the consequences when society interferes with natural economic forces, such as with price fixing. **Macroeconomic models** look at an economy as a whole, while **microeconomic models** focus on factors such as the supply, demand, and price of goods and services (Wessels, 1997). Most of the following discussion deals with microeconomic matters related to health care. Economic principles have been derived mostly for products. Given this history, the term product will be used more than the term service.

Burningham (1992) suggests that there are three concerns associated with economics:

1. **Economic stability**: Economic instability can result in price inflation, resource scarcity, or inefficient product surpluses. For example, if a major employer moves its operations to another state, the health care facilities in the previous location may have an excess of beds and staff. Among the hospital management's options are reducing services, mothballing a portion of the facility, and laying off staff.
2. **Demand growth**: As the population shifts and grows, can the supply of goods and services meet changing market demand? If a large number of our example company's employees are offered jobs at the new location or people move to the new area to work for the company, the local health care facilities may have to build more capacity.
3. **Resource distribution**: Resources may be unequally distributed between communities and between individuals. At times, a community may determine that equalization of resource distribution is desirable. This is often the case with health care resources. The move of the example company likely hurt the financial position of many people in the area the company left, while it likely enhanced the financial position of many people in the new location.

Economic Concepts

While a comprehensive review of **economic concepts** is beyond the scope of this book, an understanding of selected economic concepts will help you explain and in some circumstances predict the financial performance of a health care organization and/or the health care industry.

Market Economy

Understanding **economic systems** starts with the premise that the services and/or products that a **consumer** or **community** wants inevitably exceeds available resources. That leads to the concept of **scarcity**. In the face of scarcity, societies must make decisions about how resources will be used. Burningham (1992) identifies three questions that face every society:

1. What services and goods will be produced?
2. How to produce the desired services and goods?
3. Who will have access to the services and goods produced?

When a central authority, such as a government, answers these questions according to a master plan, it is a **command economy**. A modification of the command economy is one in which the consumer has some limited choices. In a **market economy** consumers and producers interact to determine what, how, and for whom goods will be produced, with some restrictions related to the public good. For example, law enforcement, the military, and health care are essential for the common good and can be provided better by a central authority than individual consumers. The forum for consumer and producer interaction (**transactions**) is a **market** (Chapter 21). There are markets for **consumer goods** (**retail**), **production goods** (**wholesale**), **labor market** (human resources) and **money market** (financial instruments) (Burningham, 1992).

The right to own property and consumers' and producers' freedom of choice characterize a market economy. Consumers have the freedom to spend their resources as they see fit. Producers (providers) are free to allocate their resources to produce the type and amount of services and products they desire. The role of government in a market economy:

- Establish restrictions to the free market that are in the interest of the public good or health
- Provide goods or services that would not otherwise be produced such as public safety
- Accommodate for weaknesses in the market economy that may result in an unacceptable distribution of specific resources, such as health care.

The rest of this chapter will be applicable to a market economy.

Opportunity Cost

The concept of **opportunity cost** is related to scarcity of resources. Consumers have finite resources. When expending limited resources, consumers strive to gain maximum value. They cannot afford all of the goods and services they might desire. As a result, they must choose between all of the possible goods and services available to them. The goal is to make the choice that results in the greatest added **value**. To do this, the consumer must compare the relative value of alternative purchases under consideration. The opportunity cost of an acquisition is the value of the alternative opportunity that was forgone (Finkler and Ward, 1999).

Value

Value may be **tangible value** (quantifiable), **intangible value** (not quantifiable), or both. Consider deciding on a spring vacation. Assume the alternatives have been narrowed down to a ski trip or a tropical cruise. If the ski trip and cruise are the same price, both trips will result in the same decline in the vacationer's resources. The final choice will be based on the vacationer's assessment of intangible value. Intangible value might be a measure of expected enjoyment, prestige, social contribution, or anticipated future good will. If the cruise is twice as expensive as the ski trip, the vacationer has both tangible and intangible value to consider. Intangible value may weight a decision in favor of the more costly alternative. The concept of intangible and tangible value applies to organizational decisions as well. When an organization has the opportunity to invest in one of two alternative business ventures, management uses financial information to identify the resource requirements (cost) and projected value to the organization. Often managers want to determine which venture will yield the greatest projected financial return (Chapters 28 and 29). However, in some circumstances the venture with the lower financial return may be selected because of its intangible value. For example, a community hospital may select among ventures the one that does most to further its mission of community service or has the lowest short-term return but positions it for high return over the long term.

Marginal Value

Marginal analysis is used to solve economic problems by looking to the **marginal value**, the value of the last increment of service or product sold or purchased. Marginal value is not static. Rather, the marginal value and the demand for a specific service or product may decline as consumption increases. For example, the value a consumer places on the first two scoops of ice cream may be significantly higher than the value of the third scoop. As the value declines, the consumer becomes less willing to spend limited resources to purchase an additional scoop of ice cream. In other words, the marginal value of a scoop of ice cream is declining. The ice cream seller must either sell the third scoop at a lower price or see a decline in sales. If the seller lowers the price, the marginal value to the seller also declines.

Demand and Supply

Burningham (1992) tells us that a market provides a forum for transactions between buyers and sellers. The amount and type of goods a buyer will purchase depend on a variety of factors such as **income** (available re-

Table 26.1 Demand Data

Price per Unit	*Demand 1*	*Demand 2*
32	1	2
16	2	4
8	4	8
4	8	16
2	16	32

sources) and **price**. The relationship between **consumer demand** and price can be demonstrated by the data in Table 26.1 and the related graph in Figure 26.1. Assuming all other factors remain the same, as the price of a product or service increases, demand is likely to decrease and vice versa.

The sensitivity of demand to changing price is called **price elasticity**. Price elasticity is calculated by dividing the percent change in quantity demanded by the percent change in price.

$$\text{Price elasticity} = \frac{\text{percent change in quantity}}{\text{percent change in price}}$$

The price elasticity of a product or service dictates the shape of the demand curve for any specific product or service.

When a price change has minimal impact on the quantity demanded, demand is described as **inelastic** (Burningham, 1992). Demand may be inelastic or insensitive to price changes when the service or product is essential to the consumer. For example, the demand for survival levels of water, food, and shelter are relatively insensitive to price increases. Demand may be also be inelastic because consumers have sufficient resources (income) to buy when there is a substantial price change. We see this when the cost of luxury products, such as designer clothing, increases but demand stays high. When the quantity demanded changes significantly in response to a price increase, demand is said to be highly elastic. In conditions of high elasticity, price increases may result in an overall decrease in demand, or in a **competitive market**, the consumer may switch to a comparable producer or product. Switching to an alternative source or product is called **substitution**. The more alike the original and alternative products are, the more likely the consumer is to substitute when prices increase.

Income may also affect **demand** by causing a **shift** in the **demand curve**. Figure 26.2 demonstrates movement in the demand curve to the right. This can happen if income growth provides consumers with more disposable income to spend on desirable services or products. For example, as disposable income rises, the overall demand for high-end day spa services might increase. Conversely, if disposable income declines, the demand for high-end day spa services may decline while the demand for less expensive personal care services may increase. These kinds of changes result in an overall shift in the demand curve shown in Figure 26.2.

The influence of price and income on demand is of great interest to **producers**. Producers desire to maximize their **income**. Their goal is to charge the price that gives the greatest net income.

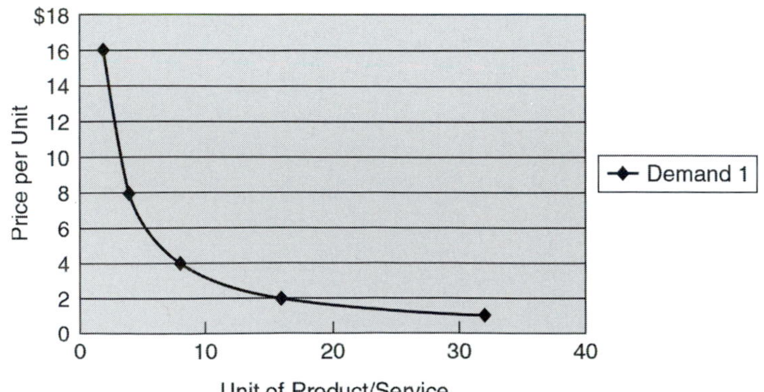

Figure 26.1. Demand curve.

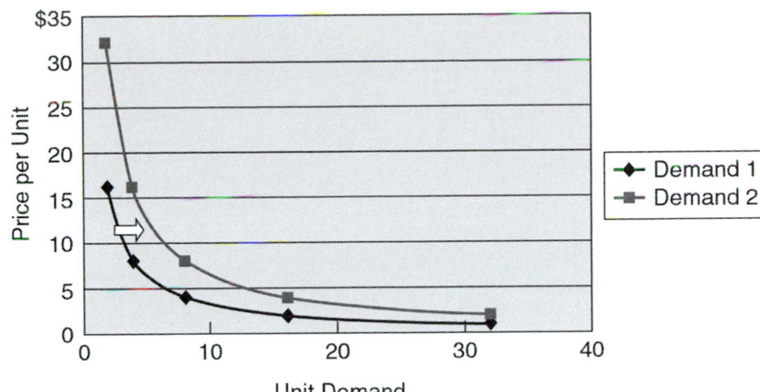

Figure 26.2. Demand shift.

Total revenue =
price per unit × quantity of units sold

Total expense =
cost per unit × quantity of units produced

Net income (profit) =
total revenue – total expense

Simplistically, producers will maximize **net income** (profit) by

1. Charging the highest price that does not reduce demand to the extent that it offsets the price increase
2. Producing goods or services at the lowest per unit cost
3. Selling everything they produce

Figure 26.3 depicts a typical **supply curve**. As price rises, producers are motivated to increase the amount of product they provide. However, price elasticity may diminish demand as prices rise. Figure 26.4 demonstrates the relationships between price, demand and **revenue** when demand is price elastic.

As price increases, demand will decrease. At some point, total revenue (units of product multiplied by price) will reach a maximum and then began to decline. Producers must determine how much of which products to produce based on their available resources and price.

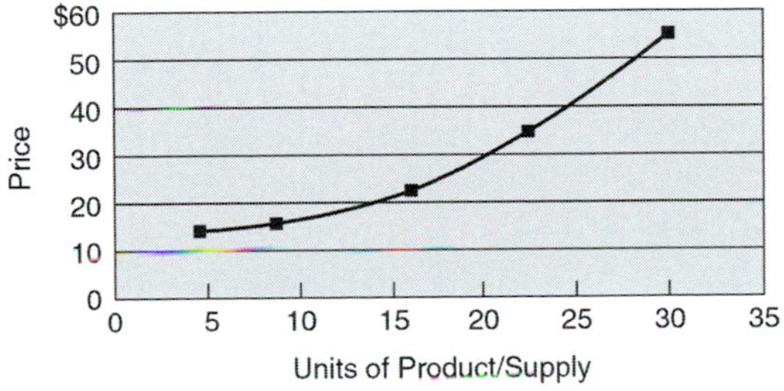

Figure 26.3. Supply curve.

In a perfectly balanced market economy, demand for a product equals supply. The interactions among price, supply, and demand work in concert to maintain a balance. For example, holding supply constant, when demand increases, some consumers will pay more, driving the price upward. As price increases, demand will decrease, coming back in line with the supply. The increase in price will also act as an incentive for producers to increase the supply. As long as they can increase total revenue and net income, producers are motivated to increase the supply.

Producers may also change their willingness to supply a product or service if their cost of production changes. Recall that income is equal to revenue less expenses (Chapter 27). Holding price stable, if the cost of producing a unit of service or product declines, the revenue per unit will rise. When this occurs, a producer is likely to produce more units at the current price. This will cause the **supply** curve to **shift** to the right as in Figure 26.5. If the cost per unit rises, the producer's income at each quantity level will decline, shifting the supply curve to the left.

Role of Competition

A **competitive market** is characterized by multiple producers, each having a minority share of the market. In a competitive market

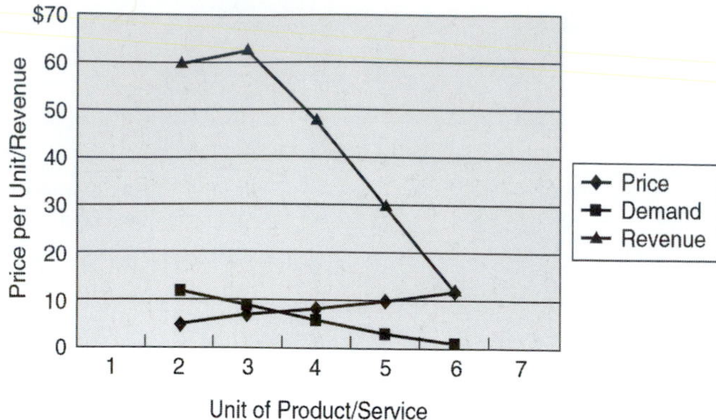

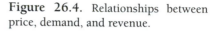

Figure 26.4. Relationships between price, demand, and revenue.

consumers have a choice of products and producers or services and providers. If one producer raises the price or decreases production, the consumer can substitute another producer or similar product. The result is that price increases are constrained. When one producer dominates a market, it is called a **monopoly**. In a monopoly market, the consumer cannot substitute products or producers. As a result, demand is price inelastic. The monopoly producer is able to raise prices to the point where remaining demand for units multiplied by price maximizes revenue.

At times, a free market economy may find a monopoly desirable because of the high **initiation costs** of producing essential services or products. Initiation costs are the costs of entering the market. For example, a community may have only one source for utilities, land phone, cable TV, cable Internet, or hospital care because the cost of supporting multiple service providers of the same product or service is prohibitive. When a monopoly for essential services occurs, government may respond with regulation to control price and ensure equitable distribution.

A practical example of economic modeling applied to physical therapist data was the Vector report (Vector, 1997; Anonymous, 1997), which the American Physical Therapy Association (APTA) commissioned. The issues of supply, demand, and competition were addressed along with the potential effects on employment, salaries, and use of substitutes. Among the predictions from the economic models were an increasing oversupply of physical therapists and physical therapist assistants starting in 1998, leveling off of salaries, and an assessment of the potential substitutes for physical therapists. The report also implied that enrollment in physical therapy and physical therapist assistant educational programs would likely decline (Nosse, Friberg, Kovacek, 1999). While seven subsequent employment surveys conducted between 1998 and 2001 by the APTA Department of Research (APTA, 2001a) had some potential to verify a number of the Vector predictions, verification was complicated by the implementation of the Balanced Budget Act of 1997 (Chapter 4).

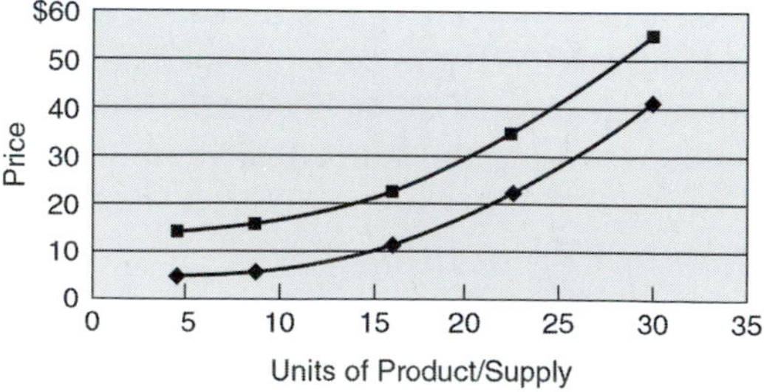

Figure 26.5. Supply shift.

Productivity and Costs

Burningham (1992) defines **production** as the process of transforming **inputs** into **output** (see Chapter 18). Inputs include such things as **labor**, **supply**, **capital equipment**, and **land**. Each of the inputs has a cost. Total cost of inputs divided by total units of output equals the cost per unit of product or service.

$$\text{Cost per unit} = \frac{\text{total cost of inputs}}{\text{total units of output}}$$

A producer wants to minimize the input cost per unit to maximize income. The lower the amount of a resource used to produce a unit of product or service, the higher the **resource productivity**. Effective management of cost requires knowledge of the types of costs and how different types of costs behave in relation to volume of units produced.

Direct and Indirect Expenses

Direct expenses can be directly associated with the production of goods and services. **Indirect expenses** are costs incurred by the organization that cannot be directly associated with the production of any specific service or good. Direct expenses are generally easy to identify. Indirect expenses are sometimes less clear.

For a therapy department or clinic that is part of a larger organization, salaries, benefits, supplies, depreciation of equipment, and staff education are examples of direct expenses. Indirect expenses include administrative salaries, financial services, information services, grounds and building maintenance, and the cafeteria.

In larger organizations, indirect expenses are generally not listed as department expenses but are allocated to all departments as shared overhead. Indirect expense allocation is determined by use of a relevant basis such as square footage, revenues, expenses, number of employees, volume of service. A department is allocated a percentage of overhead expense equal to its percentage of the basis. For example, a department that occupies 15% of floor space is allocated 15% of the expense of building services. Managers can control the direct expenses related to their area of responsibility. The same managers may have some influence but will have no direct control over indirect expenses. In the case of a small independent therapy practice, all of the expenses can be directly associated with the production of services. All of the expenses are under the control of the manager–owner.

Expense Classification

Every manager with responsibility for cost control needs to understand how expenses change in response to changes in production or service volume. Technically, the definition of a cost and an expense are different. Cost is the amount paid to obtain a resource. When the resource is used, it is an expired cost known as an expense (Finkler and Ward, 1999). **Expenses** are classified by their relation to volume: (1) fixed costs, (2) variable costs, and (3) semivariable costs (see Chapter 27).

Fixed cost remains unchanged despite changes in service volume. For example, assume the property and casualty insurance paid by a small independent therapy practice, Do It All Therapy, Inc., is $1500. Insurance is paid in advance for the upcoming year. If there are no coverage changes during the year, insurance is fixed at $1500 for that period. It will stay at $1500 whether the company treats no patients or 1000 patients. Fixed costs may be committed for several years or discretionary on an annual basis. Figure 26.6 provides a graphic representation of fixed cost in relation to volume changes. The flat line indicates that the total fixed cost remains unchanged even though the volume of sales increases.

Of key importance is what happens to the cost per unit of service (UOS) or product. Because the total fixed cost remains unchanged by volume, the fixed cost per UOS decreases as volume increases. This is **economy of scale**, the reduction in the cost of providing services or goods in relation to increases in volume because the fixed cost is divided among more units of the service or product (Finkler and Ward, 1999). A practical example of this concept is evident in Do It All Therapy. Referring to the formula for per unit cost and Do It All Therapy's property and casualty insurance cost of $1500, if Do It All Therapy serves just one patient for one UOS, the insurance cost per UOS is $1500. In contrast, if Do It All Therapy serves 1000 patients for one UOS each, the insurance cost per UOS drops to $1.50 ($1500 ÷ 1000).

Variable cost increases or decreases in direct proportion to the quantity of units. For

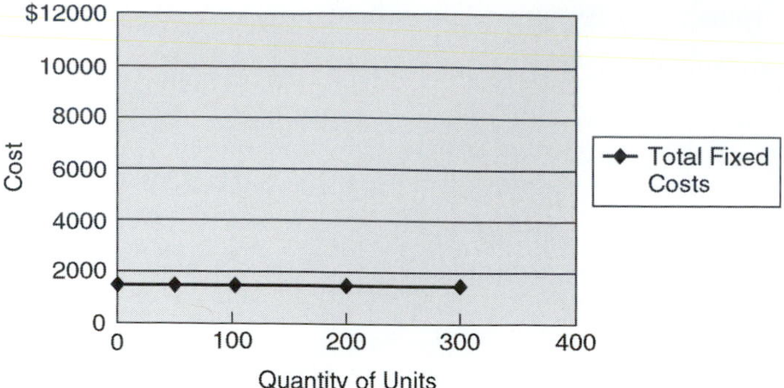

Figure 26.6. Fixed costs.

example, the cost of direct physical therapy treatment salaries, linen, and medical supplies are variable. Consumption of these resources will increase and decrease as volume of UOS change. If the average cost of linen is $0.42 per UOS, the total cost of linen will be $420 at 1000 UOS and $1000 at 2,381 UOS. Variable costs per unit stay the same, but total costs increase or decrease as sales volume (UOS) change. Figure 26.7 shows the relationship between variable cost and volume.

Semivariable costs have both fixed and variable elements. These costs must be evaluated so that the fixed and variable components can be addressed separately. Otherwise, total and per UOS cost projections will be inaccurate. Business telephone service is an example of a semivariable cost. The equipment and basic service are a fixed cost. Once the service is available, the business is charged an additional fee for each call. This usage fee is variable because use increases as the volume of service increases. When a cost is semivariable, the fixed portion remains constant, and the fixed cost per UOS decreases as volume increases and increases as volume decreases. The variable portion will increase or decrease in proportion to the change in sales volume.

Total cost is the sum of fixed costs, variable costs, and semivariable costs. Figure 26.8 shows fixed, variable, and semivariable costs combined to equal total cost. The graph demonstrates how total cost changes in relation to volume.

Cost–Volume–Profit Analysis

The key to successfully managing financial performance is a working knowledge of the mathematical relationship between:

- Fixed, variable, and semivariable costs
- Cost per UOS
- Sales volume
- Profit (loss)

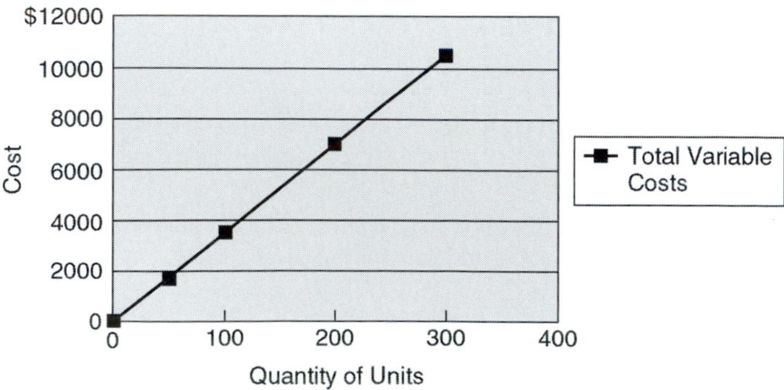

Figure 26.7. Variable costs.

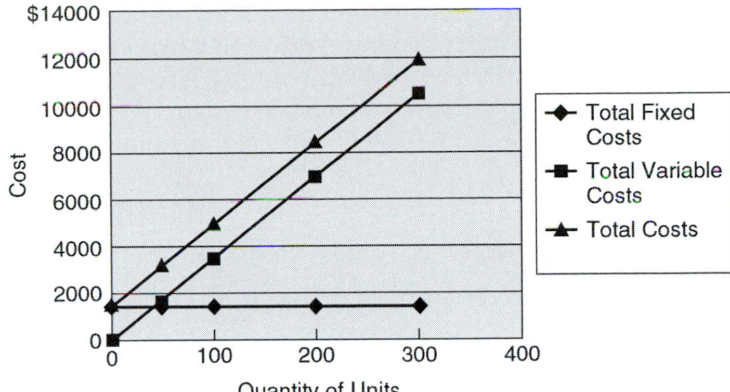

Figure 26.8. Relationships between fixed, variable, and total costs.

Use of **cost–volume–profit analysis** allows managers to predict the overall financial impact of cost or volume changes. The goal is to minimize total expense by matching capacity for production to the demand for production. The cost–volume–profit analysis relates cost to revenue. In doing this matching, cost–volume–profit analysis can be used to determine revenue and expenses at any sales volume. This can be useful for assessment of past performance, current position, and future performance. It can also be used to model the effects of proposed expenditures with or without volume change. Figure 26.9 shows this cost–volume–profit relationship. It depicts total costs and total revenue from sales.

At zero volume (no units), total cost equals fixed costs. As sales volume increases, total revenue increases at a rate equal to price per UOS times the quantity of UOS sold. At point A, total revenue equals total cost. This is the **break-even point**, where net income equals zero. Until the break-even point, the company is operating at a loss. After the break-even point, the company is operating at a profit. If a company understands its current position, proposed changes in volume, charges, or costs can be inserted into the model to determine the impact on total revenue. The break-even point can be calculated with the following formula:

X = quantity of units
P = price
FC = fixed costs
VC = variable costs per unit:

$$\text{Total revenue} = \text{total cost}$$
$$P\,(X) = FC + VC\,(X)$$

Rearranging:

$$X = FC \div (P - VC)$$

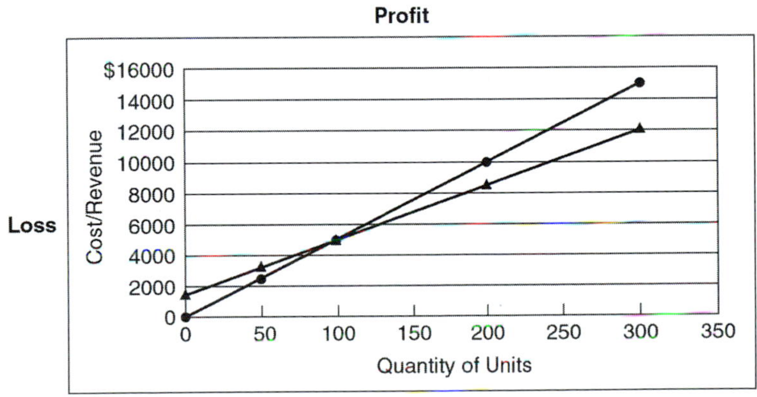

Figure 26.9. Cost–volume–profit analysis.

This formula lets you calculate the revenue impact of changes in price, volume, or cost. The cost–volume–profit analysis is the foundation for financial planning and modeling. These concepts will be discussed further in Chapters 28 and 29.

The Reality of Health Care Economics: No Margin, No Mission

Mission is the purpose of an organization (see Chapter 9). **Margin** is the difference between total revenue and total expenses. A positive margin, revenue greater than expense, is a **profit**. A negative margin, expense exceeding revenue, is a **loss** (Chapter 27). To fulfill its mission over time, an organization must have a positive margin. When an organization operates at a loss, there are no new resources flowing into the organization. Existing resources are consumed to fund operations (provide services, make products). A business operating at a net loss may be able to continue operations for a short period. How long will depend on the financial resources the organization has in reserve and how well the organization can control its costs. Eventually the organization's resources will be depleted and the organization will shut down. Operating at breakeven, where revenue equals expense, may sustain an organization for a short period. Unfortunately, a business must have some level of profit even to maintain its current financial position over time. Additional resources will be required for nonroutine expenses, such as equipment replacement. Over time, reserves will be depleted and the break-even company will be unable to sustain operations. The bottom line: to continue into the future, an organization must bring in more money than it spends.

Should Businesses Profit From Health Care Delivery?

During our many years in health care management we have observed that some people are bothered by the thought of making a profit from delivering health care services or products. This concern is not limited to customers but is shared by many practitioners as well. We have heard many such concerns expressed by practicing physical therapists. Some examples of staff therapists disassociating clinical care from the costs of delivering care are evident in the following statements:

"Why do they charge so much for my services?"
"I did not charge the patient because it only took a few minutes for me to review the exercises."
"I know the patient does not have insurance to pay the bill, but I treated him anyhow."

These are statements heard time and again. They may represent advocacy for patients and criticism of the system. Most therapists have the good sense to address their concerns by working through the system. When it comes to health care, the normal business practice of making a profit is sometimes viewed as negative. This sentiment indicates general lack of appreciation for the fact that every health care business, large or small, **not-for-profit** or **for-profit**, must make more money today than it spends if it is to provide health care in the future (Chapter 2).

We contend that when any other alternative is available, it is unethical to operate a health care business in a manner that does not have the potential to result in a profit (Chapter 6). This holds true for both not-for-profit and for-profit businesses alike. Not-for-profit health care providers benefit from the use of community services, money from deferred taxes, and the personal contributions of community members. These resources are provided by a community with the expectation that the organization will contribute to the current and future well-being of its members. The community has a reasonable expectation that health care services will be available as needed. The owners and operators of not-for-profit health care businesses are the stewards of community resources. It is their responsibility to manage these resources in a way that causes the business to grow and prosper. For-profit health care organizations provide a return to the community by paying taxes.

The ability to meet financial obligations is another reason health care organizations need to be profitable. Many have financial obligations, such as debt owed to other community businesses and/or governing bodies. Poor profitability can result in inability to meet financial obligations. That would harm other businesses. It is not within the standards of acceptable business behavior to act in a manner that will result in an inability to meet business obligations. Knowing that a health care business needs to make a profit to survive supports the conclusion that the health care manager who deliberately continues to operate without producing a profit is acting in an unethical manner (Cava, West, Berman, 1995).

Student Notes

To help you see a closer link between economic concepts and physical therapy, consider the following comments. Physical therapy, in economic terms, is a resource that is allocated among various health care markets. On the supply side, an estimated 90,000 physical therapists are employed or seeking employment. In this decade the unemployment rate for physical therapists seeking work has been between 1.1% and 3.2% (APTA, 2001a). When adjusted for inflation, salaries in 2001 were estimated to be up 0.6%. This was the first increase since 1996 (APTA, 2001b). Among the demand side components are the aging of the baby boomers (those born between 1946 and 1964); increasing life expectancy, especially for women; and increasing niche markets for physical therapy services. Physical therapists with clinical doctoral degrees and a recognized area of specialization, such as board-certified specialist, completion of a residency program, or another professional degree or certification, are likely to have a competitive advantage over most substitutes. The pursuit of postgraduate education on a full-time basis does have opportunity costs, that is, cost of tuition, loss of income, and possibly loss of direct clinical experience. Finally, in the workplace the concept of economy of scale may be recognized in the form of productivity expectations. If salaries are considered a fixed cost, increasing the volume of work carried out by existing staff distributes the fixed cost over a larger number of UOS and thus reduces labor cost per unit.

Summary

You should now be able to demonstrate an understanding of fundamental economic concepts at work in a market economy. Economics is the study and modeling of the arrangements that societies make for the use and development of scarce resources. In a market economy consumers and producers interact to determine what, how, and for whom services and goods will be produced, with some restrictions related to the public good. Such choices introduce the concept of opportunity cost. Consumers have finite resources. When expending limited resources, consumers strive to gain maximum value. To do this, the consumer must compare the relative value of alternative purchases. The opportunity cost of an acquisition is the value of the alternative opportunity that was forgone. Value has an economic and a psychological meaning. The economic meaning may be quantifiable, that is, tangible. The psychological meaning may not be quantifiable, that is, may be intangible. Alternatively both may be quantified. Value is often associated with price. The concept of price elasticity is important. It is calculated by dividing the percent change in quantity demanded by the percent change in price. As the value of a good or service declines, the consumer is less likely to expend the same amount of resources to obtain more of that item. Supply of a resource affects both demand and price. Assuming all other factors are constant, as the price of a product or service increases, demand is likely to decrease and vice versa. Less expensive substitutes become more attractive to buyers. The closer the alternative service or product to the original, the more likely the consumer is to substitute when the price of the original choice increases. Alternative providers of services and products compete for market share. A competitive market is characterized by multi-

INDIVIDUAL CASE STUDY

Review the sections on value and marginal value. Concentrate on the information on the concepts of tangible (economic) value and intangible (psychological) value as well as marginal value. Take the perspective of a consumer of physical therapy services and form three possible tangible and possible intangible values of physical therapy services. Next, consider the marginal value aspect as it might relate to subsequent physical therapy treatments. Be prepared to participate in a class discussion.

ple producers each having a minority share of the market. In a competitive market consumers have a choice of products and producers from which to choose. If one producer raises the price or decreases production, the consumer can substitute another producer or similar product. This constrains the result of the price increase. Cost of providing services and products includes fixed costs, which are expended but unrelated to volume. A related economic concept is called economy of scale. In essence, the economy of scale is the extent of a cost reduction as the volume increases because more units of the service or product share the fixed cost. Mathematical formulas for cost–volume–profit analysis are presented to clarify the relationships of a variety of costs and as a means of making financial decisions.

GROUP CASE STUDY

Form a group of four members. Each of you review this chapter for information on the situation described next. Meet to discuss a group response to the situation.

Situation

Table 26.2 contains comparative data on the number of U.S. educational programs listed in physical therapy in selected years. Educational programs are the source of new entrants to the physical therapy workforce. They can add to the supply. Consider the change in the total number of accredited programs and comment on the economic possibilities related to this change. To guide your thinking, consider the following economic concepts:

- Supply
- Demand
- Substitutes
- Price (salary)

Task

Formulate a group answer and meet with another group to compare and discuss your thoughts.

Table 26.2 Number of Accredited Entry-Level Physical Therapist and Physical Therapist Assistant Educational Programs

Year	*Physical Therapist*[a]	*Physical Therapist Assistant*[b]	*Total*
1997	173 (10 international)	211	384
2002	196 (3 international)	236	432

[a]APTA, 1997a; 2002a
[b]APTA, 1997b; 2002b

Many of the terms introduced in this chapter are discussed in more depth in Chapter 27. While economics is the theory of business, accounting, the next topic, is its language. Basic accounting concepts relevant to health care managers and their staff make up the core content of Chapter 27. Organizational and departmental information is no longer limited to management. Those who provide direct care need to know how they are doing, how the department is doing, and how the organization is doing financially. Reports from accounting services are the essential sources of such information.

REFERENCES

American Physical Therapy Association. Educational programs leading to qualifications as a physical therapist. Physical Therapy. 1997a;12:1766–1777.

American Physical Therapy Association. Educational programs leading to qualifications as a physical therapist assistant. Physical Therapy. 1997b;12: 1778–1789.

American Physical Therapy Association. APTA employment survey, November 2001. Alexandria, VA: Department of Research Services. 2001a.

American Physical Therapy Association. Practice profile survey, 2001. Alexandria, VA: Department of Research Services. 2001b.

American Physical Therapy Association. Accredited physical therapist education programs in the United States and its territories. Physical Therapy. 2002a;12:1240–1244.

American Physical Therapy Association. Educational programs leading to qualifications as a physical therapist assistant. Physical Therapy. 2002b;12: 1246–1251.

Anonymous. APTA workforce study looks at supply and demand of PTs. PT Bulletin. 1997;12(20):1, 10.

Burningham D. Economics. Lincolnwood, IL.: NTC. 1992.

Finkler SA, Ward DM. Essentials of cost accounting for health care organizations, 2nd ed. Gaithersburg, MD: Aspen. 1999.

Cava A, West J, Berman E. Ethical decision making in business and government: An analysis of formal and informal strategies. Spectrum: The Journal of State Government. 1995;Spring:28–36.

Nosse LJ, Friberg DG, Kovacek PR. Managerial and supervisory principles for physical therapists. Baltimore: Lippincott, Williams & Wilkins. 1999.

Vector. Physical therapy workforce study executive summary. Ann Arbor, MI: Vector Research. 1997.

Wessels WJ. Microeconomics the easy way. Hauppauge, NY: Barron's Educational Series. 1997.

MORE INFORMATION RELATED TO THIS CHAPTER

A thought-provoking book that intertwines the ethical and economic aspects of health care is Loewy and Loewy (2001). Two particularly thoughtful chapters are Kluge EHW. Health care as a right. In Loewy EH, Loewy RS, eds. Changing health care systems from ethical, economic, and cross-cultural perspectives. New York: Klüver. 2001:29–48; and Rich B. The old ethics and the new economics of health care: Are they compatible? (pp.113–126).

Health policy is inseparable from health care economics according to a health economics researcher. An in-depth look at the linkage between these topics is offered in Fuchs VR. The future of health policy. Cambridge, MA: Harvard. 1993. Chapter 1 focuses on basic concepts associated with health related economics.

A clear presentation of costs and break-even analysis with hospital-relevant examples can be found in Chapter 11 of Cleverly WO, Cameron AE. Essentials of health care finance, 5th ed. Gaithersburg, MD: Aspen. 2002:227–254.

Data entered in Excel can be analyzed through the chart wizard, which will plot data to compare pairs of values (choose scatter), trend lines (choose add trend line), regression line (six options) and other modes of describing data. These analyses help determine relationships among cost, volume, and profit.

The APTA Web site, http://www.apta.org, regularly offers readers information of economic importance.

Chapter 27

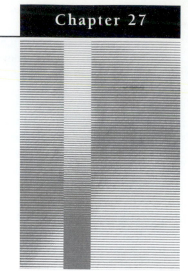

Health Care Accounting and Financial Reporting

Learning Objectives

1. Discuss the role of the financial services professional, for example, financial manager, CPT.
2. Understand standard accounting practices reporting, for example, entity, transaction, cost valuation, double entry, accrual method, cash basis, and matching.
3. Understand standard accounting conventions, for example, relevance, reliability, materiality, comparability, and conservatism.
4. Interpret common financial statements, for example, balance sheet, income statement, cash flow statement, comparative report, and ratio report.
5. Examine the concept of variance based on the content of common financial statements.
6. Examine performance indicators relevant to physical therapy practice, for example, volume, revenue, costs, and efficiency.

Key Words

Account, accounting, accounting concept, accounting convention, accounts payable, accounts receivable, accrual, accrual basis, accrued expense, acid test ratio, activity ratio, allowance for contractual deductions, asset, balance sheet, budgeting, capital asset, capital ratio, cash basis, cash flow statement, certified public accountant (CPA), chart of accounts, common-size statement, comparability, comparative analysis, comparative statement, conservatism, cost valuation, costs and benefits, current ratio, days cash on hand ratio, days in net accounts receivable ratio, debt service ratio, double entry, earnings statement, entity, expense, financial management, financial planning, financial ratio, financial report, financial reporting, financial statement, fiscal year (FY), fixed asset, fund accounting, funded depreciation, income statement, intangible, inventory, liability, line of credit, liquid asset, liquidity ratio, loan agreement, long-term debt to equity ratio, long-term debt to fixed assets ratio, matching, materiality, net income, net loss, net worth, neutrality, note payable, operating margin, owner's equity, performance indicator, prepaid expense, profit (loss) center, profit (loss) statement, ratio analysis, relevance, reliability, return on assets, revenue, revenue and expense statement, statement of operations, transaction, variance analysis

Introduction

Financial management refers broadly to the actions taken by an organization to obtain and maximize the use of monetary resources. The most obvious aspect of financial management is the gathering and use of financial information. Berman, Kukla, and Weeks (1994) identified three key uses of financial information. It can be used (1) to support planning, (2) to assess the relative impact of investment options, and (3) to assess and improve performance. **Financial reports** are statements of performance and position that can be used to compare actual performance to projected performance. Financial reports can also be used to compare past to current performance, revealing trends that can be used to predict future performance.

Projected financial performance is reflected in financial plans or budgets. An annual financial business plan or budget represents management's best estimate of what will happen in the future. It is the internal benchmark against which day-to-day performance can be assessed. Cost information can be used to manage expenditures and to set prices. This last use is critically important for managed care contracting.

Historically, access to and use of financial information has been limited to management. Financial information was often available only on a need-to-know basis. The recent trend toward the use of work teams for problem solving and performance improvement has altered this practice (see Chapter 17). Many businesses now distribute financial information to employees at all levels of the organization. In theory, employees who understand the company's financial position are better able and willing to contribute to performance improvement (Case, 1995). Employees involved in performance improvement, gain sharing, or performance-based compensation programs are more likely to be interested in the success of the organization. They will be prepared to make a greater contribution if they have access to financial performance information.

People outside of the organization also use financial information to evaluate the performance and financial viability of a business. These are outside parties who use financial information:

- Creditors
- Industry analysts
- Government agencies
- Philanthropists
- Potential investors
- Stockholders

Any one of these outside parties has the potential to affect the success of a health care business (Nosse and Friberg, 1992). This chapter lays the foundation for understanding the in-depth discussion of third-party payment, presented in Chapter 30.

Financial Management Services

Financial management is the "art of both obtaining the funds that the enterprise needs in the most economic manner and of making optimal use of those funds once obtained" (Berman et al., 1994, p. 156). It is a decision-making process that relies on the information provided by the company's accountant to operate effectively. The services of a financial professional are essential to the development of an effective financial management system. Financial management is a recognized profession, just as physical therapy is a profession. Academic preparation for a career in financial management can be through a baccalaureate and/or graduate degree in business administration, accounting, or economics. Advanced certification can be achieved through successful completion of a standardized examination prepared by the American Institute of Certified Public Accounts. Designation as a **Certified public accountant** (CPA) can be equated to a board-certified specialist designation for a physical therapy professional. The CPA designation offers assurance of advanced knowledge of accounting and financial management. The CPA designation is often listed as a minimum requirement for financial management positions.

A business can obtain the services of a financial professional by hiring or by contracting services from a public accounting firm (Chapter 34). Employment versus contracting decisions should reflect the needs of the organization. It is common for large organizations to have in-house financial management. A smaller business may find it more economical to purchase services as needed from an individual practitioner or a larger firm.

Financial Reporting

The Financial Accounting Standards Board (FASB) sets the standards for accounting and **financial reporting**. The FASB defines the objectives of financial reporting in its Statements of Financial Accounting Concepts No. 1. FASB-defined objectives for financial reporting include the provision of information:

1. That is useful to present and potential investors, creditors, and other users in making rational investment, credit, and similar decisions.
2. About the economic resources of an enterprise, the claims to those resources, and the effects of transactions, events, and circumstances that change resources.
3. About an enterprise's financial performance during a stated period.
4. About how an enterprise obtains and expends cash, about its borrowing and repaying of borrowed funds, about its capital transactions, and about other factors that my affect its liquidity or solvency.
5. About how management of an enterprise has discharged its stewardship responsibility for the use of enterprise resources.
6. That is useful to managers and directors in making decisions in the interest of owners.

Financial Accounting Principles

Accounting is the process of "collecting, summarizing, analyzing, reporting and interpreting, in monetary terms, information about the enterprise" (Berman et al., 1994, p.7). Accounting principles guide the way financial accounts are kept. Because these principles are followed by all businesses, similar reporting transactions yield similar results. This uniformity in record keeping means that financial accounting records are understandable to all internal and external parties who use them (Berman et al., 1994).

Berman and associates (1994) identify several basic **accounting concepts** with which managers should be familiar to understand financial data and reports. Their list of concepts includes the following:

1. **Entity**: For the purpose of financial reporting, a business is considered to be an entity capable of economic action. It is assumed that the entity will be ongoing, so financial reporting reflects the assumption of continuity over time.
2. **Transactions**: A transaction is a product or service provided for compensation. For the financial information of an entity to be accurate, all transactions affecting the entity must be recorded. Transactions may be summarized to a manageable level of detail as long as the financial condition and performance of the entity are accurately reflected.
3. **Cost valuation**: The value of transactions must be recorded in a consistent way. There are several options, such as the price at sale, replacement cost, or purchase price. Accountants we have consulted indicated that price paid for an asset is often the most useful basis for valuation of that asset.
4. **Double entry**: Each transaction has two aspects, the change in the entity's assets and the change in the source of financing. Both aspects of a transaction should be recorded. For example, the purchase of a piece of equipment is reflected as an increase in the value of equipment owned and a decrease in cash holdings and/or increase in debt.
5. **Accrual**: The concept of accrual refers to the practice of recording financial transactions within an appropriate period. For example, a company using accrual accounting records the cost of the vacation pay earned by employees as a liability in the period it is earned. This liability is carried until the employee takes vacation time. When the vacation is used, the liability is reduced. In this way, the expense of the vacation is recorded in the period it is earned, not when it is paid out. If it were not recorded (accrued) in this manner, the

expenses for the period when vacation is earned would be understated, the expenses for the period when vacation time is used would be overstated, and the company's real liabilities would be understated by the total amount of vacation pay owed to employees. For one employee paid $20 per hour, a bank of 20 vacation days (160 hours) constitutes a liability of $3200. Consistent recording procedures prevent the manipulation of financial performance for an entity during any specific period. The rules for transaction recording are as follows: (1) Revenue and expenses should be recorded when services and/or products are sold or costs are incurred. (2) Expenses should be recorded during the period in which the item purchased is used in the production of the entity's goods or services.

6. **Matching**: To evaluate the actual performance of an entity, income from an activity must be matched with expenses of the same activity so that performance can be assessed. Matching is the only way an organization can determine whether a specific product contributes to the organization's performance. Comparing the price of a treatment to the cost of delivering the treatment is an example of matching.

Accrual Method of Accounting

The concept of matching is consistent with use of an **accrual basis** for accounting. The accrual basis requires that revenue be recorded within the period it is earned. Likewise, expenses must be recorded in the period when the resources are consumed for the production of related revenue. For example, payment is received in advance for services to be delivered in 3 months. Employee salary expense for the delivery of service is incurred during the month of delivery. The revenue should be credited in the same month the services were provided and the expense incurred. Otherwise, a business may think it is performing well in the month cash was received and substantially worse when it pays the related bills (Weltman, 1997).

Cash Method of Accounting

The **cash basis** is used as an alternative to the accrual method of accounting. Under the cash basis for accounting, revenue is recorded when cash is received, and expenses are recorded when bills are paid. This approach fails to match revenue and expenses. It will not support management efforts to determine the costs of individual products and services. It is used on a limited basis in health care, most commonly in small private practices and partnerships (Weltman, 1997).

Accounting Conventions

In practice accounting concepts are modified by **accounting conventions**. Both general and industry-specific accounting conventions guide the design of financial management systems (Berman et al., 1994). General accounting conventions include these factors:

- **Relevance**: Information is relevant if it helps users assess past and future efforts.
- **Reliability**: Information is reliable if it can be verified.
- **Neutrality**: Information is neutral when relevance and reliability determine its use rather than a need to demonstrate any particular result.
- **Materiality**: The detail reflected in financial information should be kept to a level that is useful to management's decision making.
- **Comparability**: To be useful, financial reports should be comparable between organizations and over time.
- **Conservatism**: When in doubt, financial reporting should err in the direction of underestimating benefits and overestimating the potential costs.
- **Costs and benefits**: When determining the amount and specificity of information collected, the cost of obtaining and recording information should be weighed against the potential value of the information obtained.

The accounting conventions particular to health care should also be understood. Conventions significant to health care businesses are allowances for contractual deductions, fund accounting, and funded depreciation.

- **Allowances for contractual deductions**: A convention common to health care accounting that addresses the difference between the price charged for a service and the price paid by third-party payers. This approach is taken because the third-party payment system for health care services causes prices to be set much higher than the average payment. The amount of payment varies significantly between payers and is seldom under the control of the health care provider. To account for the difference between the amount charged and the amount paid, an account called allowances for contractual deductions is used.
- **Fund accounting**: Often found in hospitals and larger health care businesses because a health care business may need to separate the financial information of one or more sections from that of the total entity. For example, if a health care organization received a philanthropic gift to be used only for the support of a special program or building project, a separate fund would be set up to account for this donor-restricted gift. This separation prevents the commingling of restricted with general funds. Types of accounting funds that may be seen in health care are endowment funds, specific purpose funds, plant funds, and construction funds. The need for and use of fund accounting should reflect the individual needs of the entity (Berman et al., 1994). Individual fund accounts are part of a larger financial entity; therefore, the performance and condition of the fund accounts are included in the financial reports of the total entity.
- **Funded depreciation**: A method that can be used to set aside money for the addition and/or replacement of buildings and equipment. Funded depreciation occurs when management determines that a certain amount of cash will be set apart from general operating funds to ensure the future availability of building and equipment. This money is usually invested to earn interest to counter the effects of inflation. Although not required, the use of funded depreciation can be a welcome safety net in a rapidly changing environment.

Financial Statements

Information collected through the financial management system is used to support management and others in evaluating and directing the activities of the business. This information is presented in financial statements and reports. **Financial statements** contain information collected over a specific period and/or reported as of a specific date. The specific date is the last date for which information was included. The time frame varies with the needs of the organization. Common time frames are yearly, quarterly, monthly, and semiweekly. Detailed activity tracking reports may be produced weekly or even daily. Occasionally the time frame for a report will roll forward. In this case, there is a designated time range, such as the most recent 6 months. The time range is consistent from report to report, but the months covered change over time. Each time the report is prepared, the earliest month is dropped and the most recent one is added. This approach can help managers identify subtle performance trends.

Financial reporting does not follow the chronological year. It follows a **fiscal year (FY)**. A FY may follow the calendar year but can be any 12-month cycle. Once a business has established its FY, it continues to operate and report performance on that FY cycle. The FYs of related businesses are often the same. This allows for the comparison and cumulative reporting of financial results among related entities.

Several financial statements are common to all businesses. These include the balance sheet, income statement, and cash flow statement.

Balance Sheet

The **balance sheet** is a statement of financial condition. It provides information about a company's assets, liabilities, and owner's equity as of a specific date. That date is commonly the end of a usual reporting period, such as a quarter or year. A balance sheet gives a picture of a business's pluses and minuses at a glance. Figure 27.1 depicts a balance sheet for Do It All Therapy, Inc., as of September 30, 2007. The FY for Do It All Therapy runs from October 1 to September 30. This balance sheet represents status at the end of the year and includes all activity of the business prior to that date. The format of the balance sheet is represented by this equation:

Total assets = total liabilities + owner's equity

Assets

According to Weltman (1997), **assets** are economic resources that are owned by a business and are expected to benefit future operations. Assets include such things as

- Cash
- Investments
- Prepaid expenses
- Inventories
- Accounts receivable
- Capital assets
- Intangibles

Prepaid expenses include such things as salary advanced or insurance payments made for a future period. **Inventories** represent the value of supplies or products that will be used or sold during future periods. **Accounts receivable** represent money that is owed to the business for already delivered products and services. **Capital assets** include land, buildings, and equipment. Sometimes assets are called **intangible**, meaning the asset has no physical substance. Patents, trademarks, copyrights, and goodwill are examples of intangible assets (Weltman, 1997).

Assets are important in determining the financial health of the organization. For purposes of reporting, the value of an asset is its current value to the business. A business views its assets as resources available to continue operation. Potential creditors view a business's assets as resources available to cover debt, including the creditor's investment. For the creditor, more assets mean a better chance of repayment if operation of the business does not produce enough income to cover expenses. Creditors value assets for their worth and the speed with which the asset can be converted to cash. Cash and assets that can be readily converted to cash are

Do It All Therapy, Incorporated
Balance Sheet
September 30, 2008

ASSETS		**LIABILITIES AND OWNER'S EQUITY**	
Cash	$45,000	Liabilities:	
Investments	60,000		
Prepaid Expenses	2,000	Accounts Payable	$50,000
Inventories	10,000	Accrued Expenses	5,000
Accounts Receivable	60,000	Notes Payable	225,000
		Total Liabilities	$280,000
Land	40,000		
Buildings	90,000		
Equipment	200,000	Owner's Equity	$227,000
TOTAL	$507,000	Total Liabilities and Owner's Equity	$507,000

Figure 27.1. Balance sheet.

liquid assets. Assets that require a long conversion period are **fixed assets**.

The true value of an asset to the business can change over time and with circumstances. A company might find it has assets on its books that are no longer expected to benefit the business. For example, some accounts receivable may go unpaid so long it is unlikely the debt will ever be paid. These items should be removed from the books. This reduces total assets and total owner's equity (Weltman, 1997).

Liabilities

Liabilities are debts of the business. Total liabilities can be thought of as the amount of assets that are owned by its creditors. Liabilities that are repayable within a year are considered to be short term. Liabilities not due or payable for longer than a year are considered to be long-term liabilities.

Accounts payable are debts payable to individuals who have provided products or services to the business on credit. Outstanding bills for supplies, professional services, and cleaning services are examples of debts that fall under accounts payable.

Accrued expenses are the value of debts held for payment (Berman et al., 1994). The time or need for payment may not be known. As discussed previously, vacation is a good example of an accrued expense. The business owes its employees the value of their accrued time off. Often, employees are able to bank or use accrued time off at their discretion. Should they terminate employment, they may or may not be able to claim the value of their banked time. If accrued vacation is paid at prevailing wages instead of the wage at the time of accrual, the value to the employee and size of this accrued debt can grow over time. As long as the employer has the potential to pay for this accrued debt, it is listed as a liability.

Notes payable are loans evidenced by **loan agreements** indicating the loan amount and interest due. Amounts owed for **lines of credit**, start-up capital, and mortgages are notes payable.

Owner's Equity

Owner's equity or **net worth** is the difference between total assets and liabilities. Owner's equity can be a positive or negative value. It is the portion of the assets that belong to the owners. The net worth of the owners can increase in two ways. First, owners can invest additional resources in the business. Second, net worth can increase as a result of profitable operations.

Income Statement

The **income statement** is a report on the performance of a business over a specific period. It provides a comparison of money earned (revenues) to money spent (expenses). The difference between revenues and expenses is the **net income** or net loss from operations during the reporting period. A net income indicates that revenues exceeded expenses. The business made a profit. Net worth was increased. A **net loss** indicates that expenses exceeded revenues. The business lost money. Net worth was reduced. The income statement is represented by this equation:

Revenue – expenses = net income (net loss)

Figure 27.2*A* provides the income statement for Do It All Therapy, Inc., for the FY ending September 30, 2007. Figure 27.2*A* is an annual income statement. Income statements can be prepared to cover any increment of time but should be prepared at least once per year. A more frequent time interval should reflect management's need for performance information. The income statement is also called an **earnings statement**, **statement of operation**, **profit (loss) statement**, and **revenue and expense statement**.

The income statement can reflect the past or the future. The scope of the income statement as discussed is the whole organization. However, the income statement format is also used to reflect the profit (loss) of discrete parts of larger organization. **Financial planning**, often called **budgeting**, uses the income statement format to reflect the anticipated performance of each discrete depart-

Do It All Therapy, Incorporated Income Statement Year Ending September 30, 2008		
REVENUE:		
Gross Revenue		
Services	$832,818	
Equipment	60,000	
Total Operating Revenue		$892,818
Less:		
Allowance for Deductions		203,563
Gross Revenue Net Deductions		689,255
Non–Operating Revenue		23,000
Total Revenue		$712,255
EXPENSES:		
Salaries	$361,421	
Benefits	65,056	
FICA	28,191	
Education	6,300	
Recruitment	5,000	
Professional Services	11,000	
Purchased Services	600	
Supplies	51,095	
Travel	4,000	
Dues	2,000	
Equipment	1,200	
Rent/Lease	20,000	
Utilities	9,000	
Communication	3,375	
Environmental Services	5,300	
Accrued Expenses	40,083	
Insurance	6,100	
Total Expenses		$619,721
Net Income (Loss)		92,534
Taxes		30,536
Net Income After Taxes		$61,998

A

Figure 27.2. A. Income statement. B. Detailed version of the income statement.

ment or function. These discrete departments are usually referred to as cost centers or **profit (loss) centers**. A true cost center will have an expenses budget but no directly related revenue. A profit (loss) center will have both an expense and revenue budget. Physical therapy departments are profit (loss) centers. Departmental budgets are combined to form the budget for the whole organization. The income statement is also a key part of any business plan. See Chapters 7 to 11 for additional information on business planning.

Revenue

Revenue is income. A health care business has several potential sources of revenue:

- Sale of service
- Sale of products
- Grant funds
- Governmental funding
- Seminar income
- Income from investments
- Philanthropic gifts
- Assumption of risk for services

Do It All Therapy, Incorporated
Income Statement
Year Ending September 30, 2008

REVENUE:			
Gross Revenue			
Services		$832,818	
Equipment Sales		40,000	
Equipment Rental		20,000	
Total Operating Revenue			$892,818
Allowance for Deductions			
Medicare		$88,389	
Medicaid		35,713	
Managed Care		40,177	
Commercial		8,928	
Charity Care		8,928	
Self Pay		21,428	
Total Deductions			203,563
Gross Revenue Net Deductions			$689,255
Non–Operating Revenue			
Interest Income		3,000	
Education Offerings		20,000	
Total Non–Operating Revenue			23,000
Total Revenue:			$712,255
EXPENSES:			
Salaries			
Management	$70,096		
Professional	145,725		
Technical	33,280		
Support	49,920		
Clerical	62,400		
Total Salaries		$361,421	
Benefits		65,056	
FICA		28,191	
Education		6,300	
Recruitment		5,000	
Professional Services			
Legal	$2,000		
Accounting	3,000		
Marketing	6,000		
Total Professional Service		$11,000	
Purchased Services			
Storage	$600		
Total Purchase Service		$600	
Supplies			
Supplies, General	$4,595		
Supplies, Medical	10,500		
Supplies Sold	36,000		
Total Supplies		$51,095	
Travel		$4,000	
Dues		$2,000	
Equipment			
Small Tools	$500		
Repair	200		
Replace	500		
Total Equipment		$1,200	
Rent/Lease			
Equipment	$4,000		
Facilities	16,000		
Total Rent Lease		$20,000	
Utilities			
Gas	$4,200		
Electric	4,800		
Total Utilities		$9,000	
Communication			
Telephone	$3,000		
Pagers/Cellular Phone	375		
Total Communication		$3,375	
Environmental Services			
Maintenance	$500		
Grounds	1,200		
Cleaning Service	2,600		
Linen Service	1,000		
Total Environmental Service		$5,300	
Accrued Expenses			
Depreciation	$26,624		
Interest	13,459		
Total Accrued Expense		$40,083	
Insurance			
Malpractice	$1,200		
Property/Casualty	1,500		
Auto	800		
Personal Liability	200		
Workers Compensation	2,400		
Total Insurance		$6,100	
Total Expenses			$619,721
Net Income (Loss)			92,534
Taxes			30,536
Net Income After Taxes			$61,998

B

In accrual accounting, revenue is recorded in the period it is earned. In cash accounting, revenue is recorded when the money is received. Revenue from the sale of services or products is calculated by multiplying the price of the service or product by the number sold. The revenue recorded for items sold at discounted or government-established price is adjusted by recording a deduction to revenue. For example, a $150 evaluation provided under a contract requiring a 10% discount is recorded with two entries. The first entry records revenue of $150. A second entry records a $15 deduction from revenue. The revenue net deductions equal the $135 discounted price. Revenue is also classified by its origin. Revenue for the sale of services or products provided by the company is revenue from operations or simply operating revenue. Revenue from all other sources is non–operating revenue.

Income in return for the assumption of risk, relatively new to health care providers, is a characteristic of a capitated payment arrangement. Under capitation, the health care provider receives a set payment per period, such as a payment per covered person per month. In return for the payment, the provider agrees to provide all agreed-upon services to each covered person for the period. The payment amount remains unchanged no matter how much service is delivered. If the provider's expenses exceed the payment, the result is a loss. If no service is delivered, the provider still receives the set payment for the assumption of the risk of providing care.

Expenses

An **expense** is money spent to produce or purchase the services and products sold. In accrual accounting, expense is recorded in the period the service or item is produced. In cash basis, expense is recorded when the bill is paid. Figure 27.2*A* clearly shows that there are many more ways to spend money than to make money.

The amount of detail in a given version of an income statement depends on the needs of the user. Generally, the more day-to-day accountability for revenue and expense managers have, the more detail they require. Figure 27.2*B* is a more detailed version of the income statement presented in Figure 27.2*A*. Managers with direct responsibility for revenue and expenses typically require the level of detail presented in Figure 27.2*B*. Information related to the development of the expense section of an income statement and the types and management of expenses is provided later in this chapter.

Cash Flow Statement

The availability of cash to cover short-term liabilities is critically important to any business. The last choice management wants to make is between defaulting on short-term liabilities and liquidation of needed assets. Cash flow management helps a business avoid this situation. A **cash flow statement** is used to track the sources, use, and availability of cash. This financial statement shows how a company's cash position changes over time. Figure 27.3 is the cash flow statement for Do It All Therapy, Inc., for October 1, 2007, through September 30, 2008. Typically a business has limited sources of cash but many uses for it. Cash flow statements can be prepared for past, present, and future periods. Cash flow statements that look to the future, called pro forma statements, can help management identify potential problems before they happen.

Financial Analysis

Information in the balance sheet and income statement can be subjected to a variety of analytic techniques to assess a company's performance, financial position, and relative financial viability. These techniques include **comparative** and **ratio analysis** (Berman et al., 1994).

Comparative and Common-Size Financial Statements

More often than not, financial statements are used for comparative analysis. Comparison

Cash Flow Statement Do It All Therapy, Incorporated Year Ending September, 2008			
Cash Balance, October 1, 2007			
Cash in Bank		$39,517	
Petty Cash		500	
Cash Balance			$40,017
Sources of Cash			
Cash from Operations	$51,613		
Accounts Receivable	751,910		
Owner Investment	-		
Total Sources of Cash		$803,523	
Uses of Cash			
Accounts Payable	$213,110		
Payroll	495,568		
Owner Withdrawal	25,000		
Capital Purchase	4,862		
Land and Building	60,000		
Total Uses of Cash		$798,540	
Increase (Decrease) in Cash			$4,983
Cash Balance, September 30, 2008			$45,000

Figure 27.3. Cash flow statement.

can be made between elements of the financial statement, among time periods, or between planned (budgeted) and actual performance. To aid in the comparison of financial statement entries, entries may be expressed in dollar amounts and as a percentage of a total category. For example, salary expense for FY 2007 can be expressed as an amount, $361,421, or a percentage of total expenses, 58.3%. Comparative percentages used to further define elements of a financial statement are a **common-size statement** (Dillon and LaMont, 1983). Information on a financial statement can also be expressed for more than one date or period. Financial statements that provide information for more than one date or period are called **comparative statements**. Figure 27.4 shows both a common-size and a comparative financial statement.

Comparative analysis allows for the identification of trends and financial patterns. It is up to management to determine the meaning of information relative to the performance of the business. In the case of the example in Figure 27.4, the statement shows an improved financial performance over time. Use of the common-size presentation demonstrates that the expense associated with some resources has declined as volume increased. This important phenomenon is addressed in more detail under the topic of cost–volume–profit analysis.

Variance Analysis

A key to effective financial management is the ability to compare projected to actual performance. This is **variance analysis**. Management time is limited. If financial information is difficult to obtain or presented in a format that requires extensive rework, management is not likely to identify performance variances. Variance analysis can also be complicated by lack of detail in the information. Financial information systems should be flexible enough to provide more or less detail depending on the needs of management.

Do It All Therapy, Incorporated
Compararative-Size Income Statement
Year Ending September 30, 2008 and September 30, 2007

			Common-Size Percentages	
	FY 2008	**FY 2007**	**FY 2008**	**FY 2007**
REVENUE:				
Gross Revenue				
Services	$832,818	$666,254	93.3%	93.3%
Equipment	60,000	48,000	6.7%	6.7%
Total Operating Revenue	892,818	714,254	100.0%	100.0%
Less:				
Allowance for Deductions	203,563	162,850	22.8%	22.8%
Gross Revenue Net Deductions	689,255	551,404	96.8%	96.8%
Non-operating Revenue	23,000	18,400	3.2%	3.2%
Total Revenue	$712,255	$569,804	100.0%	100.0%
EXPENSES:				
Gross Revenue	$361,421	$335,124	58.3%	54.8%
Gross Revenue	65,056	60,322	10.5%	9.9%
Gross Revenue	28,191	25,805	4.5%	4.2%
Gross Revenue	6,300	4,500	1.0%	0.7%
Gross Revenue	5,000	5,000	0.8%	0.8%
Gross Revenue	11,000	15,000	1.8%	2.5%
Gross Revenue	600	480	0.1%	0.1%
Gross Revenue	51,095	40,876	8.2%	6.7%
Gross Revenue	4,000	2,500	0.6%	0.4%
Gross Revenue	2,000	1,500	0.3%	0.2%
Gross Revenue	1,200	850	0.2%	0.1%
Gross Revenue	20,000	63,000	3.2%	10.3%
Gross Revenue	9,000	9,000	1.5%	1.5%
Gross Revenue	3,375	3,375	0.5%	0.6%
Gross Revenue	5,300	5,300	0.9%	0.9%
Gross Revenue	40,083	32,066	6.5%	5.2%
Gross Revenue	6,100	7,100	1.0%	1.2%
Total Expenses	$619,721	$612,098	100.0%	100.0%
Net Income (Loss)	92,534	(42,294)	10.4%	-5.9%
Taxes	$30,536	0	33.0%	0.0%
Net Income After Taxes	$61,998	($42,294)	6.9%	-5.9%

Figure 27.4. Comparative and common-size income statement.

General reports help identify variances. Detailed information is often necessary to determine causal factors. Comparative and common-size reports are specifically designed to support variance analysis. Comparative reports present financial information from different sources or periods. A comparative report can be used to present budget and actual data or to compare budget to budget data or actual to actual data from one or more periods (Dillon and LaMont, 1983).

Financial Ratios

Another technique to compare financial performance over time, between elements, or between similar businesses is the use of **financial ratios**. Financial ratio analysis is use of the relation between two mathematical quantities. The idea behind the use of financial ratios is to summarize key financial data in a format that is easy to understand and evaluate (Berman et al., 1994). Liquidity, capital, and activity ratios are types used to evaluate financial performance.

Liquidity Ratios

Liquidity ratios are used to assess a business's ability to meet its short-term financial obligations (liabilities). Types of liquidity ratios are discussed next, beginning with the current ratio:

$$\text{Current ratio} = \frac{\text{current assets}}{\text{current liabilities}}$$

The **current ratio** is the ratio of current assets to current liabilities. It is a common index of liquidity. The higher the ratio, the better a business is positioned to meet its current obligations (Berman et al., 1994).

$$\text{Acid test ratio} = \frac{\text{cash + marketable securities}}{\text{current liabilities}}$$

The **acid test ratio** is the most rigorous test of liquidity. It takes into consideration only cash or assets that can be immediately liquidated for cash. The higher the ratio, the better the potential to meet current obligations (Berman et al., 1994).

$$\text{Days cash on hand} = \frac{\text{cash + short-term investment + funded depreciation reserve}}{\text{average daily operating expense} - \text{depreciation reserve}}$$

The **days cash on hand ratio** is the ratio of most liquid assets to average daily operating expenses. This ratio indicates the number of days a business can stay in operation without incoming cash receipts. This ratio is an indicator of performance but also reflects the cash management practices of the business. A higher number may decrease concern about a business's ability to cover day-to-day expenses. Too high a number may indicate a failure to maximize the potential for income in longer-term investments.

$$\text{Days in net accounts receivable} = \frac{\text{accounts receivable} - \text{deductions}}{\text{average daily operating revenue}}$$

The **days in net accounts receivable ratio** is a measure of how long it takes to collect money owed, that is, accounts receivable. A long or lengthening collection cycle can signal future liquidity problems.

Capital Ratios

Capital ratios help assess the financing structure of the organization. Financing structure refers to the mix of debt (liabilities) to equity. Potential creditors will review capital ratios as a way to determine the current level of debt. The greater the ratio of debt to equity, the less likely creditors are to provide additional credit or loans. The greater the debt, the greater the related interest expense (debt service expense). The higher the debt service costs of a business, the more liquid assets the business must maintain to cover current liabilities. High debt service limits resources that otherwise could be used for more productive purposes. Capital ratios include the following:

$$\text{Debt service ratio} = \frac{\text{net income + depreciation}}{\text{debt principal payment + interest}}$$

The **debt service ratio** is a measure of ability to pay principal and interest on its debt. The higher this ratio, the better able the business is to cover costs of current debt and to handle additional debt in the future.

$$\text{Long-term debt to fixed assets} = \frac{\text{long-term debt}}{\text{net fixed assets}}$$

The **long-term debt to fixed assets ratio** is the proportion of fixed assets that are financed through long-term debt. A higher ratio means that more fixed assets have been financed through loans or other forms of financing. Potential lenders use this ratio as an indication of ability to handle additional debt. Potential creditors become increasingly hesitant to extend credit as this ratio increases.

$$\text{Long-term debt to equity ratio} = \frac{\text{long-term debt}}{\text{equity}}$$

Long-term debt to equity is the ratio of both sources of long-term funding. The higher the ratio, the greater the amount of long-term funding from long-term debt. The higher this ratio, the more difficult it is to obtain additional long-term financing.

Activity Ratios

Activity ratios show the relationship between revenue and expenses. Using information from both the balance sheet and the income statement, activity ratios measure the use of assets to cover the expenses of the company (Berman et al., 1994).

$$\text{Operating margin} = \frac{\text{total revenue} - \text{total expenses}}{\text{total revenue}}$$

Operating margin is the ratio of net income to total revenue. Operating margin can be calculated for all or discrete parts of a business. Good financial performance results in a high operating margin. This ratio provides a basis for comparison of the economic performance of one business to industry standards, to previous performance, and to other investment opportunities. Operating margin can also help a business assess the relative contribution of one operating unit to another.

$$\text{Return on assets} = \frac{\text{income} + \text{interest expense}}{\text{total assets}}$$

Return on assets is the relationship of total income to the total investment (assets) of the business. Return on assets can be calculated for all or discrete parts of a business. A higher return on assets indicates good performance. This ratio provides a basis for comparison of the economic performance of one business to industry standards, to previous performance, and to other investment opportunities. Return on assets may be used as a criterion for selecting between alternative business strategies.

Performance Indicators

Financial ratios offer a set of standard assessment tools that allow for the comparison of current financial performance to past performance, current expectations, and the performance of similar businesses on an individual or industry-wide basis. Skula and Psetian (1997) suggest some additional financial **performance indicators** that may be particularly useful for assessing the performance of a physical therapy practice.

Volume
- Referrals
- Scheduled treatments
- Completed (billed) treatments
- Visits
- Case mix

Revenues
- Net revenue per referral
- Net revenue per visit
- Net revenue as a percentage of charge

Costs
- Labor cost per volume measure
- Nonlabor cost per volume measure
- Employee benefits as a percentage of salary

Efficiency
- Productive hours paid per billed unit of service

Nonproductive hours paid per billed unit of service
Visits per referral
Visits per referral by diagnosis, age, or other defining factor
Billed units of service per visit

Performance indicators can be used to create a report card for business performance (Chapter 12). Management should use performance indicators that are relevant to its success. Through careful selection, clear performance expectations, sometimes called performance benchmarks, can be established and communicated to members of the organization. Organizational performance indicators should be tracked, trended, and the outcome shared with everyone who has a role in meeting performance targets (Case, 1995).

There is an increasing trend in health care toward the use of industry performance standards to evaluate individual health care businesses. Industry performance standards can help management to assess performance in a rapidly changing environment when historical performance has relatively little relevance, to set reasonable improvement targets, and for competitive positioning. However, the use of external performance standards should be done only with a complete understanding of the source and applicability of the standard. Selected industry standards must be clearly applicable and represent comparable data, and regional and organizational differences must be identified. Benchmarks (Chapter 31) should be adjusted accordingly. Performance assessment as a part of marketing strategy was discussed in Chapter 21. Several variations of these performance indicators were used in the sample worksheet provided in Chapter 22.

Keeping the Books

To be good, financial information must be accurate. Accuracy is achieved when the recording of financial information consistently follows an understood set of guiding principles. These principles provide direction on how financial information is collected and recorded. The recording of business transactions starts with the chart of accounts.

Chart of Accounts

An **account** is a category of asset, liability, owner's equity, revenue, or expense. A **chart of accounts** is simply a list of all of a business's accounts. The chart of accounts is often arranged in financial statement order (Meigs, Johnson, Meigs, 1977) as is this list. The chart of accounts can be viewed as a set of files. A single file holds only specific types of information to be entered into the file at specific times. Each file is identified by a name and numeric code (Berman et al., 1994) that is used to classify and differentiate accounts.

The number and types of accounts depend on the size, type, and complexity of the business. Management's information needs will influence the number and degree of specificity of the chart of accounts. For example, management may wish to have one general account to record revenue from equipment sold. If it is important to know the sales revenue for each type of equipment sold, management may choose to have one account for each type or category of equipment. The total of these equipment revenue accounts are combined to determine total revenue from equipment sold. Figure 27.5 shows a chart of accounts at the primary classification level. Each of the major account types from the balance sheet and income statement is assigned a series of numbers that define the characteristics of the account. Within each numerical series, the major accounts are further defined by subgroupings of funds or subgroupings of accounts.

Figure 27.6 contains a more detailed example of numeric coding for salaries and benefits. The logic used to assign a numeric code to each of the subclasses, such as employee type, is provided. The chart of accounts is specific to a business. Once the logic of the numeric coding is provided, it should be easily understood.

Student Notes

Most students have limited opportunity to apply health care accounting principles at the outset of their career. What is important is that all practicing physical therapists have sufficient familiarity with accounting princi-

Do It All Therapy, Incorporated
Chart of Accounts
Primary Classification
September 30, 2008

Code	Type	Subcode	Fund
100-199	Assets	110	Operating Fund
		120	Capital Equipment Fund
		130	Other Funds
200-299	Liabilities	210	Operating Fund
		220	Capital Equipment Fund
		230	Other Fund
300-399	Capital Accounts	310	Operating Fund
		320	Capital Equipment Fund
		330	Other Fund
400-499	Revenue Accounts	410	Patient Service Revenue
		420	Deductions From Revenue
		430	Other Revenue
500-599	Expense Accounts	510	Patient Services
		520	Support Services
		530	Management Services
		540	Purchased Services
		550	Other Expenses

Figure 27.5. Chart of accounts.

ples to interpret financial statements and reports. Remember, accounting is the language of business. The ability to understand and use financial information will allow you to contribute fully to the operation of your organization. Interpretation of financial ratios will help you evaluate the financial health of your own organization and support personal investment decisions. The annual report of an organization is a good place to start to see where the organization stands financially. This can also be a good place to start when you are seeking information about potential employers.

Summary

This chapter discusses the importance of financial information to support management decisions. Financial services professionals are experts in the design and implementation of an information management system that records, summarizes, and analyzes financial transactions. The application of standard accounting practices ensures that financial reports have a consistent meaning between time periods and organizations. Reliable financial information is essential to efforts to maximize financial performance. To ensure consistency and understanding, the accounting concepts of entity, transactions, cost valuation, double entry, accrual, and matching are defined and related to health care accounting. The major accounting profession conventions are introduced to further the discussion of financial management, that is, relevance, reliability, neutrality, materiality, comparability, conservatism, cost and benefit, allowances, fund accounting, and funded depreciation. The standard financial reports, that is, balance sheet, income statement, and cash flow statement, are identified and examples provided. In the discussion of financial reports attention was given to differences in financial status at different points in time as well as differences from expectations called variances. Variances call for further examination of their

Do It All Therapy, Incorporated Chart of Accounts September 30, 2008			
500-599	**Expense**		
		Salaries	
531.10			Management
511.10			Therapist
511.12			Technical
521.10			Billing
521.12			Clerical
		Benefits	
532.10			Management
512.10			Therapist
512.12			Technical
522.10			Billing
522.12			Clerical
		FICA	
533.10			Management
513.10			Therapist
513.12			Technical
523.10			Billing
523.12			Clerical

Summary-Coding Logic

Digit	Meaning	Code	Technical Salaries
1st	Type of Account	5	Expense
2nd	SubGroup/Fund	1	Patient Services
3rd	Account Class	1	Salaries
4th-5th	SubClass/Department	.12	Technical

Figure 27.6. Chart of accounts logic.

INDIVIDUAL CASE STUDY

Well, now you have enough information to assess how well a hospital, a department, a clinic, or an individual is doing financially. Financially, students generally have more liabilities than assets. What financial report would you choose to demonstrate this statement? Ask yourself: How are you doing financially? Are you any better off financially today than you were a year ago? What is your debt to income ratio? What type of financial report would answer this question? What would be a reasonable FY for students? If you want competent personal financial advice, where will you go?

GROUP CASE STUDY

You are a member of a limited-liability corporation (see Chapter 7). Six physical therapists are members. Form a group and deal with the following case.

Situation

Everyone's Physical Therapy Clinic serves many patients who are uninsured or underinsured. Fewer than half of patients receiving treatment have insurance. Those who have insurance are generally unable to pay for deductibles or co-payments. (Medicare and Medicaid require providers to demonstrate that they have made reasonable effort to collect co-payments regardless of the patient's financial status.)

The clinic relies heavily on volunteers (professionals providing pro bono care and others) and contributions to make up the difference between revenue from services and expenses. Net losses have been averaging $3500 per month. With $15,000 in cash reserves, how long can the clinic continue to operate before it must cut back on services? What financial reports would this information come from?

Task

What options can you think of to keep the clinic in operation? Discuss your suggestions and determine the options that are likely to extend the duration that services can be provided at the current level. Do a reality check: SWOT the identified options (see Chapter 11). Chapters 21 to 23 offer additional suggestions on how to bring your thoughts together.

causes. Finally, the most common comparative ratios based on the financial reports introduced in the chapter are examined and discussed. This financial information is a necessary prerequisite for what comes next.

The importance of maximizing financial performance is the focus of the next chapter. How to maximize revenues and minimize expenses is addressed in depth. Particular attention is given to the various ways physical therapy and other services are paid for. For any business, the bottom line is that there has to be more revenue than expenses for the business to continue to exist. The next chapter provides financial management principles intended to sustain or enhance a health care business's financial position.

REFERENCES

Berman HJ, Kukla SF. Weeks LE. The financial management of hospitals, 8th ed. Ann Arbor, MI: Health Administration. 1994.

Case J. Open book management: the coming business revolution. New York: Harper Business. 1995.

Dillon RD, LaMont RR. Financial statement analysis: A key to practice diagnosis and prognosis. Clinical Management. 1983;35:36–39.

Financial Accounting Standards Board. Statement of financial accounting concepts. No. 1.

Meigs WB, Johnson CE, Meigs RF. Accounting, the basis of business decisions. New York: McGraw-Hill. 1977.

Nosse LJ, Friberg DG. Management principles for physical therapists. Baltimore: Williams & Wilkins. 1992.

Skula RK, Psetian J. A comparative analysis of revenues and cost-management strategies for not-for-profit and for-profit hospitals. Hospital and Health Service Administration. 1997; 42:117–134.

Weltman B. The big idea book for new business owners. New York: Macmillan Spectrum. 1997.

MORE INFORMATION RELATED TO THIS CHAPTER

Accounting concepts related to managed care can be found in several sections of Kongstvedt PR. Managed care: What it is and how it works, 2nd ed. Gaithersburg, MD: Aspen. 2002).

More depth is provided in Kongstvedt PR. Essentials of managed health care, 4th ed. Gaithersburg, MD: Aspen. 2001: 628–642.

The APTA Reimbursement Resource Book has a section that concisely presents what a physical therapist entering into private practice ought to know about accounting: American Physical Therapy Association.

The reimbursement resource book. Alexandria, VA: American Physical Therapy Association. 2000.

A very readable textbook on health care accounting is Finkler SA, Ward DM. Essentials of cost accounting for health care organizations, 2nd ed. Gaithersburg, MD: Aspen. 1999. This text has chapters on budgeting, assessing new services, productivity, and other topics discussed in this and related chapters.

An advanced textbook on health care financing that is informative and readable by non–business majors is: Cleverley WO, Cameron AE. Essentials of health care finance, 5th ed. Gaithersburg, MD: Aspen. 2002.

Chapter 28

Budgeting and Financial Planning

Learning Objectives

1. Summarize the budgeting and financial planning presented in this chapter: establish a financial plan, set performance targets, track performance, and conduct a variance analysis.
2. Understand management's role in revenue management.
3. Correctly use budgeting and financial planning terminology.
4. Compare payment methods common to physical therapy.
5. Examine methods for revenue enhancement.
6. Correctly use expense terminology.

Key Words

Accrued expense, allocated cost, annual budget, capital expense, capital lease, capitated payment, case mix, case rate, cost center, cost reimbursement, depreciation, discounted fee-for-service, expense management, fee-for-service, Financial Accounting Standards Board (FASB), financial management, financial modeling, financial planning, fixed per diem, full-time equivalent (FTE), indirect cost, labor expense, nonproductive, operating budget, operating expense, operating unit, overhead expense, payer mix, performance target, price insensitive, price sensitive, productive, productivity, productivity standard, professional service, purchased service, revenue center, revenue enhancement, revenue management, salary expense, supply expense, useful life, variance

Introduction

Financial management is the actions taken by an organization's managers to obtain and maximize the use of financial resources (assets). In Chapter 27 financial management was discussed in terms of gathering and general use of financial information. This chapter takes the next step, which is to use financial information to do short- and long-term financial planning. The context of this chapter is a health care organization that offers many services including physical therapy. However, the principles of accounting and financial planning are very much the same for smaller operations.

Financial planning is projecting financial performance through analysis of previous performance and projected changes that may cause performance to change. A financial plan is used to evaluate actual financial performance and project financial needs. Often considered a management activity, financial planning can benefit from the input of employees at all levels of the organization.

Managing Financial Performance

The goal of financial management is to maximize profit from operations. **Financial management** can be viewed as a four-step cycle:

Step 1. **Establish a management plan.** To do this, an organization uses information about past performance and current market trends to set targets for financial performance (profitability). Frequently covering a 3- to 5-year span, this is often called a long-range financial plan.

Step 2. **Set annual performance targets.** Set for each operating unit (department) of an organization, this short-term plan is the annual **operating budget**.

Step 3. **Track and report performance.** Financial reports are used to compare actual performance to budgeted **performance targets**.

Step 4. **Perform variance analysis and take corrective action if needed.** Actual performance deviating from targets is called **variance**. A variance may be positive or negative. A positive, or favorable, variance means that actual performance has exceeded the target. A negative, or unfavorable, variance means actual performance was less than the target. Variance analysis should determine what factors led to a specific variance and what resulted from the variance. Whether a variance is good for the company is determined by looking at the whole picture.

Figure 28.1 depicts financial planning as a continuous process.

Figure 28.1. The financial planning process.

The Financial Management Plan

As discussed in Chapter 27, profit is determined by the relative proportion of operating costs to revenues. Profitability of an entity can be affected by management of revenue or expenses (Shukla, 1997). When management undertakes to influence financial performance through operations, it involves some form of revenue and/or expense management strategy. The long-term financial plan is an effort to translate strategic directions into projections of financial performance. Just as strategic directions should be based on a sound knowledge of the business, customers, competitors, and other external factors (Chapters 11, 22, and 23), so should the long-range financial plan.

The number of years covered by a long-term strategic and financial plan is determined by each individual organization. Typically, health care organizations use a 3- to 5-year period. The accuracy of any long-term plan depends on an organization's ability to predict its future. The rate of change in the health care industry affects the accuracy of long-term plans. The longer the planning period, the less accurate the financial performance projections.

Financial modeling is the application of principles to develop projections that can be used to assess business strategies. Financial modeling is an essential part of the business plan. If an organization decides to move forward with a strategy, projections from the financial model are incorporated into its financial plan. Financial modeling can also be used to evaluate expense reduction strategies. Chapters 11 and 22 to 24 provide additional information on business planning that is applicable to either a new business or business development project.

Revenue Management

Revenue management is actions taken to increase total revenue and improve the collection of accounts receivable (Chapter 27).

Most of the approaches to managing revenue are directly related to the marketing process. These approaches take into consideration such things as product, place, price, and promotion (Chapter 21). Revenue can be enhanced by increasing revenue from current services or expanding service volume. Raising prices and/or improving the collection of accounts receivable can increase revenue. Pricing and service volume expansion strategies are used to demonstrate financial forecasting.

Forecasting the Financial Impact of Price Changes

Under the current health care reimbursement system, a price increase is likely to have a limited effect on net income. In a **price-sensitive** market, overpricing may result in a loss of volume and decrease in revenues. In a **price-insensitive** market, raising prices may increase revenue only if actual reimbursement increases in proportion to the price increase (Chapter 26). Chapter 23 has a detailed review of pricing strategy. The relation between price and reimbursement is determined by the organization's **payer mix**. Health care providers receive payment from patients (self-pay) and from a variety of third parties (for example, insurance companies, employers, government) (Chapter 2). There is great variation in payment method and rate between payers. Methods include the following:

Fee-for-service: Payment based on full charges.

Discounted fee-for-service: Payment based on full charges less a percentage discount.

Cost reimbursement: Payment based on the lower of charges or the health care provider's actual cost.

Fixed per diem or case rates: Payment based on a set fee schedule for an inpatient stay, outpatient procedure, or course of care.

Capitated payments: Payment at a set rate to cover all of the care or an aspect of care delivered to the entire population of patients covered by the third-party payer.

An additional perspective on payment methods is provided in Chapters 29 and 30 . Price increases affect revenues only under fee-for-service and discounted fee-for-service systems. Under cost reimbursement, fixed case rate payment, fixed per diem payment, and capitated payment systems, price increases have little or no effect on revenues. Cost-based reimbursement pays the provider the lower of cost or charges. A price increase will result in a reimbursement increase only if current charges are less than the provider's cost. Fee schedules, case rates, per diem rates, and capitated payments are generally fixed by contract terms. A price increase will not result in an increase in payment unless the increase is recognized under the terms of the contract. Figure 28.2 illustrates the effect of a 10% price increase in the reimbursement for Do It All Therapy, Inc. Using a baseline of FY 2008, a 10% price increase will result in an $89,282 increase in gross revenue (charges). However, when adjusted for payment method by payer type, the reimbursement effect of the price increase is reduced to $21,963. The actual reimbursement increase resulting from a 10% price increase was only 2.5% of the increase in gross revenue.

Financial Modeling to Assess Alternative Expansion Strategies

Strategies that seek to increase the number of customers, that is, increase market share (Chapter 23) are common, and in some reimbursement models they can be a successful **revenue enhancement** strategy. Service volume can be increased in two ways: (1) the number of customers served can increase or (2) the amount of service provided to each customer can increase. To determine whether a specific strategy will produce the desired financial results, the organization should ask the following key questions:

What are the clinical and payment characteristics of the customers the strategy targets?

What are the incremental operating costs required to provide services to the target group?

Will a capital investment be required?

Will the projected revenue after deductions cover the incremental costs including depreciation?

Will the new services be profitable?

Do It All Therapy, Incorporated
Revenue Impact Following 10% Price Increase
October 1, 2008

Payer Type	Percent Revenue	Percent Deduction	Gross Revenue Before Price Increase	Deductions Before Price Increase	Revenue After Deductions	Gross Revenue Following 10% Price Increase	Deductions Following 10% Price Increase	Revenue After Deductions	Revenue Impact Following 10% Price Increase
Medicare	33	30	$294,630	$88,389	$206,241	$324,093	$117,852	$206,241	$ 0
Medicaid	8	50	71,425	35,713	35,713	78,568	42,855	35,713	0
Managed Care	30	15	267,845	40,177	227,669	294,630	66,961	227,669	0
Commercial	20	5	178,564	8,928	169,635	196,420	9,821	186,599	16,964
Charity Care	1	100	8,928	8,928	0	9,821	9,821	186,599	0
Self Pay	8	30	71,425	21,428	49,998	78,568	23,570	54,998	5,000
Total	100%		$892,818	$203,563	$689,255	$982,100	$270,881	$711,219	$21,963

Assumptions
1. Price increase of 10% of FY 2007 prices produces an $89,282 increase ($982,100–$892,818) in gross revenue.
2. FY 2007 revenues are used as a baseline to calculate the impact.
3. Medicaid payment based on a fixed fee schedule and not affected by provider price changes unless previous pricing was below current Medicaid payment rates.
4. Managed care payment rate is fixed by contract and not affected by provider price changes.
5. Commercial payments are fee-for-service and will be affected by price increases. Patient may pay more out of pocket.
6. Charity care deduction will remain equal to gross revenue.
7. Self pay is based on fee-for-service and will change with provider price changes.

Figure 28.2. Price increase analysis.

The revenue effects of service volume, payer mix, and case mix are interdependent. When evaluating strategies for revenue enhancement, a review of the impact of each of these factors on the others is a good place to start.

Payer mix reflects the source of payment for services and products as a percentage of total charges. Assuming the discounts or allowance for each payer type is known, payer mix can be used to identify attractive target markets, evaluate the potential impact of new business, and project deductions from revenue.

Case mix refers to the mix of patients by diagnostic grouping. Case mix is used to estimate the volume of services required by patients based on historical service use patterns. For example, say that Do It All Therapy's demand forecast indicates that the clinic will receive approximately 100 referrals for adults complaining of acute back strain. Do It All Therapy follows a plan of care that includes on average five 45-minute treatment visits. Do It All Therapy charges $35 per 15 minutes of treatment. Total charges (gross revenue) for each patient would be $525 ($105 per visit times five visits).

To use case mix information, management must have in place a mechanism for tracking the use of services by diagnosis. Although this may sound simple enough, it requires the development of a method of sorting charges by diagnosis. Historically, the patient information and financial data of health care businesses have not been merged. Often a manual review of medical records has been required to obtain service use by case mix.

We use Do It All Therapy as our model to demonstrate strategy assessment and development of a 3-year financial plan. Figure 28.3 shows how Do It All Therapy assessed two alternative service expansion strategies. The first strategy is to enter an exclusive provider agreement with an HMO that subcontracts with the state Medicaid program (Chapter 2). The second strategy is to open a new clinic in a growing suburb. To begin the analysis of these expansion options, Do It All Therapy had to project new service volume, patient types (case mix) and payer mix. With this information in hand, Do It All Therapy management could predict:

- Services needed
- Amount and type of equipment needed
- Amount and type of supplies needed
- Revenue from new services
- Expenses related to the delivery of new services

In Figure 28.3 each option's overall effect on performance has been projected. Prior to the financial assessment, Do It All Therapy assumed that the HMO contract was the best opportunity. It was less expensive to implement, and expansion of the HMO would result in continued expansion. However, once payer mix, services capacity, and incremental costs were assessed, it became evident that the HMO contract would operate at a loss and would drag down the company's overall financial performance. This assessment showed regional expansion to be the better opportunity. Of course, the reliability of both financial assessments depends on the accuracy of the market assumptions (Chapters 21–23).

Expense Management

Expense management is control of operating and capital costs. Different strategies are required to manage labor and other costs. Strategies for labor cost management are particularly important for service organizations, whose labor costs account for a high percentage of total cost. Capital cost management focuses on controlling total fixed costs and interest expense and on maximizing the return on investment of capital assets. Cost management strategies can be modeled with the same incremental approach used to model revenue. The process starts with a strategy for cost reduction. The cost decrease is projected and the outcome incorporated into a financial model to determine the effect of the change on overall financial performance.

Types of Expenses

An organization can incur two types of expenses, **operating expenses** and **capital ex-**

Do It All Therapy, Incorporated
Financial Impact Analysis: Medicaid HMO Contract VS. Geographical Expansion
October 1, 2008

		Medicaid HMO		Regional Expansion	
	FY 2007	Projected Incremental Impact	Revised Income Statement	Projected Incremental Impact	Revised Income Statement
Work Statistics	23,795	10,000	33,795	10,000	33,795
REVENUE:					
Gross revenue					
Service	$832,818	$350,000	$1,182,818	$350,000	$1,182,818
Equipment	60,000	0	60,000	25,000	85,000
Total Operating Revenue	$892,818	$350,000	$1,242,818	$375,000	$1,267,818
Less:					
Deductions	203,563	192,500	396,063	63,000	266,563
Gross Rev Net Deductions	$689,255	$157,500	$846,755	$312,000	$1,001,255 0
Non–Operating Revenue	23,000	0	23,000	0	23,000
Total Revenue	$712,255	$157,500	$869,755	$312,000	0 $1,024,255
EXPENSES:					
Salaries	$361,421	$112,819	$474,240	$133,619	$495,040
Benefits	65,056	20,307	85,363	24,051	89,107
FICA	28,191	8,800	36,991	10,422	38,613
Education	6,300	1,935	8,235	1,935	8,235
Recruitment	5,000	0	5,000	500	5,500
Professional Services	11,000	0	11,000	2,160	13,160
Purchased Services	600	0	600	15,000	15,600
Supplies	51,095	21,514	72,609	21,514	72,609
Travel	4,000	300	4,300	600	4,600
Dues	2,000	0	2,000	0	2,000
Equipment	1,200	5,000	6,200	15,000	16,200
Rent/Lease	20,000	0	20,000	36,000	56,000
Utilities	9,000	500	9,500	6,000	15,000
Communication	3,375	650	4,025	2,500	5,875
Environmental Services	5,300	0	5,300	5,200	10,500
Accrued Expenses	40,083	3,616	43,699	3,616	43,699
Insurance	6,100	0	6,100	3,500	9,600
Total Expenses	$619,721	$175,441	$795,162	$281,618	$901,339
Net Income (Loss)	92,534	(17,941)	74,593	30,382	$122,916
Taxes	30,536	(5,921)	24,615	10,026	40,562
Net Income After Taxes	$61,998	($12,021)	$49,977	$20,026	$82,354

Figure 28.3. Financial impact analysis.

penses. Both are related to the production of goods and services. Operating expenses are associated with the cost of resources used in the production of goods and services in a specific period. Salaries are an operating expense. An hour worked this week will have no value for the organization in future weeks. Capital expenses are associated with the purchase of equipment, facilities, and other high-priced items that will contribute to the production of goods and services over an extended time. The purchase of a clinic building is an example of a capital expense. A building purchased in one period will continue to contribute to the production of goods and services over many years to come.

An organization will often use a dollar threshold, such as $500, to differentiate operating from capital expenditures. Equipment with an extended life and a value equal to or greater than the threshold is classified as a capital expense. The classification of expenses can affect reimbursement under Medicare and Medicaid cost-based payment programs.

There are many types of operating expenses. Figure 28.4 lists several types of expenses associated with the period covered by the income statement. All of the expenses listed in Figure 28.4 are operating expenses that are common to therapy practice. For financial planning and budgeting, some expenses must be calculated. Others are recorded over time and then transferred to the income statement. Some key categories are labor, supplies, and accrued expenses.

Labor expenses include costs related to personnel employment and compensation, including salary, benefits, recruitment, development, health, and safety. **Salary expense** is a function of work hours paid times the hourly rate of pay.

Salary expense = labor hours paid
× rate of pay

Salary expense management uses both the hours paid and expense dollars to track labor productivity. Hours paid are commonly expressed in terms of a **full time equivalent (FTE)**. A FTE represents the work hour equivalent of one full-time employee whose compensation is based on a 40-hour workweek. A FTE does not always mean one full-time employee. A FTE can be filled by one full-time employee or two or more part-time employees.

FTE = 40 worked hours per week
× 52 weeks per year

FTE = 2080 paid hours per employment year

Hours paid can be categorized into **productive** and **nonproductive**. Productive hours are those an employee spends performing work that contributes directly to the production of services or products (Chapter 15). The definition of productive and nonproductive hours comes from the organization. For example, a physical therapy practice might define productive hours as direct care hours or billable service hours. Nonproductive hours might include vacation time, education time, travel time, sick time, and holidays. These all represent time for which an employee may be paid but is not available to perform productive work. Productivity standards are projections of the amount of work that can be performed by a worker within a specific time.

Productivity standards are used to project the work hours and related salary expense required to perform the work (Chapters 15 and 17). The projection of work hours paid starts with the prediction of the demand for service or product volume for a period. Productivity standard is used to project the number of FTEs that will be required to fill the projected demand for services. Paid hours needed to fill the projected demand are multiplied by the rate of pay to reach an estimated salary expense. Management can then compare actual salary expense, FTEs, and volume of work produced to evaluate worker (Chapter 19) and organizational performance (Chapter 12).

Figure 28.5 demonstrates how productivity standards and the number of FTEs are used to determine the volume of work and related revenue that can be produced by Do It All Therapy's employees

Figure 28.6, *A* to *C* shows the FTE, salary rate, and annual salary schedules, respectively, for Do It All Therapy for the FY ending September 30, 2008. These schedules demonstrate how FTEs and salary expense are estimated during the budgeting process.

Other labor-related expenses (Chapter 14) that must be incurred by most organizations are employee benefits, employment payroll tax (FICA), recruitment, orientation, ongoing training and development, and bonus and incentive pay. Employee benefits include such things as vacation and sick pay, health, life, and disability insurance, tuition reimbursement, health and wellness program membership, retirement plans, matching programs for employee savings, and child care. The size and financial condition of a company will largely determine the benefits it can offer to employees. Generally, the larger the company, the greater the value of the benefits offered

Do It All Therapy, Incorporated Income Statement Year Ending September 30, 2008			
REVENUE:			
Gross Revenue			
Services		$832,818	
Equipment Sales		40,000	
Equipment Rental		20,000	
Total Operating Revenue			$892,818
Allowance for Deductions			
Medicare		$88,389	
Medicaid		35,713	
Managed Care		40,177	
Commercial		8,928	
Charity Care		8,928	
Self Pay		21,428	
Total Deductions			203,563
Gross Revenue Net Deductions			$689,255
Non–Operating revenue			
Interest Income		$3,000	
Education Offerings		20,000	
Total Non–Operating Revenue			23,000
Total Revenue:			$712,255
EXPENSES:			
Salaries			
Management	$70,096		
Professional	145,725		
Technical	33,280		
Support	49,920		
Clerical	62,400		
Total Salaries		$361,421	
Benefits		$65,056	
FICA		$28,191	
Education		$6,300	
Recruitment		$5,000	
Professional Services			
Legal	$2,000		
Accounting	3,000		
Marketing	6,000		
Total Professional Service		$11,000	
Purchased Services			
Storage	$600		
Total Purchase Service		$600	
Supplies			
Supplies, General	$4,595		
Supplies, Medical	10,500		
Supplies Sold	36,000		
Total Supplies		$51,095	
Travel		$4,000	
Dues		$2,000	
Equipment			
Small Tools	$500		
Repair	200		
Replace	500		
Total Equipment		$1,200	
Rent/Lease			
Equipment	$4,000		
Facilities	16,000		
Total Rent Lease		$20,000	
Utilities			
Gas	$4,200		
Electric	4,800		
Total Utilities		$9,000	
Communication			
Telephone	$3,000		
Pagers/Cellular Phone	375		
Total Communication		$3,375	
Environmental Services			
Maintenance	$500		
Grounds	1,200		
Cleaning Service	2,600		
Linen Service	1,000		
Total Environmental Service		$5,300	
Accrued Expenses			
Depreciation	$26,624		
Interest	13,459		
Total Accrued Expense		$40,083	
Insurance			
Malpractice	$1,200		
Property/Casualty	1,500		
Auto	800		
Personal Liability	200		
Workers' Compensation	2,400		
Total Insurance		$6,100	
Total Expenses			$619,720
Net Income (Loss)			92,535
Taxes			30,536
Net Income After Taxes			$61,999

Figure 28.4. Detailed income statement.

Do It All Therapy, Incorporated Productivity Schedule Fiscal Year 2008							
Position Category	**UOS* per Day**	**FTEs @ 2080 Hours**	**USO per FTE per Year**	**Annual UOS per FTE Type**	**Average UOS Charge**	**Potential Revenue Per FTE**	**Potential Revenue Per FTE Type**
Manager/Owner	0	1.00	0	0	35	0	0
Physical Therapist	24	1.60	5,688	9,101	35	199,080	318,528
Occupational Therapist	24	1.00	5,688	5,688	35	199,080	199,080
Speech Language Path	24	0.50	5,688	2,844	35	199,080	99,540
PTA/COTA	26	1.00	6,162	6,162	35	215,670	215,670
Billing Clerk	0	1.00	0	0	0	0	0
Rehab Aide	0	2.00	0	0	0	0	0
Secretary	0	3.00	0	0	0	0	0
Total		11.10		23,795	$35		$823,818

Assumptions
1. Days worked per FTE = 260 – (6 holidays, 3 education days, 14 vacation and sick days) = 237 days per year.
2. UOS per FTE per year = 237 days × UOS per FTE per Day.
3. Annual USO per position type = total FTE's per position category × UOS per FTE
4. Annual revenue per FTE = annual UOS × average UOS charge.
* UOS, Unit of Service

Figure 28.5. Productivity schedule.

employees. Do It All Therapy spends an amount equal to 18% of salary on employee benefits. Many companies are moving away from offering a standard benefit package. Instead, employees are given a dollar amount to spend and may select the benefits they want from a benefits menu. These are commonly referred to as flexible benefits plans.

Supply expenses vary greatly between organizations. In therapy practice, supplies are typically divided into four categories:

1. Office supplies
2. Medical supplies
3. Minor equipment
4. Supplies to be sold

Office and medical supplies are consumed during the delivery of care. Minor equipment has a low cost and usually a short life. Personal digital assistants and training orthotic devices are examples of minor equipment that might be used by a physical therapy practice. Supplies to be sold, such as walkers or home traction units, are purchased and placed in inventory until they are sold to customers. The inventory entry under the assets section of the balance sheet represents the value of supplies in inventory as of the balance sheet date.

Purchased services and professional services is the expense category used to account for services purchased to support the work of the organization. Purchased services can be clinical or support services. Fees paid for legal services, financial management and accounting services, consulting, contract clinical staff, and educators are accounted for under purchased or professional service.

Accrued expenses are incurred but not paid over a period (Chapter 27). Accrued expenses are paid either on a regular schedule or as requested by the creditor. Accrued paid sick time is an example of an accrued expense. An employee may earn sick time each pay period. Sick time is paid when the employee takes time off for illness. It may also be paid when an employee retires or leaves the organization or at the end of an absence-free period. Alternatively, the accrued expense may never be paid. Responsibility for payment is based on the terms of the accrual. The concept of accrual also applies when consulting services are provided with pay-

Do It All Therapy, Incorporated Fiscal Year 2008 FTE and Salary Schedule													
FTE Per Position Type	**Oct**	**Nov**	**Dec**	**Jan**	**Feb**	**Mar**	**Apr**	**May**	**Jun**	**Jul**	**Aug**	**Sep**	**Annual**
Manager/Owner	1.00	1.00	1.00	1.00	1.00	1.00	1.00	1.00	1.00	1.00	1.00	1.00	1.00
PT	1.60	1.60	1.60	1.60	1.60	1.60	1.60	1.60	1.60	1.60	1.60	1.60	1.60
OT	1.00	1.00	1.00	1.00	1.00	1.00	1.00	1.00	1.00	1.00	1.00	1.00	1.00
Speech	0.50	0.50	0.50	0.50	0.50	0.50	0.50	0.50	0.50	0.50	0.50	0.50	0.50
PTA/COTA	1.00	1.00	1.00	1.00	1.00	1.00	1.00	1.00	1.00	1.00	1.00	1.00	1.00
Billing Clerk	1.00	1.00	1.00	1.00	1.00	1.00	1.00	1.00	1.00	1.00	1.00	1.00	1.00
Rehab Aide	2.00	2.00	2.00	2.00	2.00	2.00	2.00	2.00	2.00	2.00	2.00	2.00	2.00
Secretary	3.00	3.00	3.00	3.00	3.00	3.00	3.00	3.00	3.00	3.00	3.00	3.00	3.00
Total Salary Expense	11.10	11.10	11.10	11.10	11.10	11.10	11.10	11.10	11.10	11.10	11.10	11.10	11.10

A

Do It All Therapy, Incorporated Fiscal Year 2008 FTE and Salary Schedule	
FTE Per Position Type	**Rate Per HR**
Manager/Owner	33.70
PT	22.60
OT	22.60
Speech	22.60
PTA/COTA	16.00
Billing Clerk	8.00
Rehab Aide	8.00
Secretary	10.00

B

Do It All Therapy, Incorporated Fiscal Year 2008 Salary Schedule													
Salary per Month per Position Type	**Oct**	**Nov**	**Dec**	**Jan**	**Feb**	**Mar**	**Apr**	**May**	**Jun**	**Jul**	**Aug**	**Sep**	**Annual**
Manager/Owner	5,841	5,841	5,841	5,841	5,841	5,841	5,841	5,841	5,841	5,841	5,841	5,841	70,096
PT	6,268	6,268	6,268	6,268	6,268	6,268	6,268	6,268	6,268	6,268	6,268	6,268	75,213
OT	3,917	3,917	3,917	3,917	3,917	3,917	3,917	3,917	3,917	3,917	3,917	3,917	47,008
Speech	1,959	1,959	1,959	1,959	1,959	1,959	1,959	1,959	1,959	1,959	1,959	1,959	23,504
PTA/COTA	2,773	2,773	2,773	2,773	2,773	2,773	2,773	2,773	2,773	2,773	2,773	2,773	33,280
Billing Clerk	1,387	1,387	1,387	1,387	1,387	1,387	1,387	1,387	1,387	1,387	1,387	1,387	16,640
Rehab Aide	2,773	2,773	2,773	2,773	2,773	2,773	2,773	2,773	2,773	2,773	2,773	2,773	33,280
Secretary	5,200	5,200	5,200	5,200	5,200	5,200	5,200	5,200	5,200	5,200	5,200	5,200	62,400
Total Salary Expense	30,118	30,118	30,118	30,118	30,118	30,118	30,118	30,118	30,118	30,118	30,118	30,118	361,421

C

Figure 28.6. **A.** FTE schedule. **B.** Salary rate schedule. **C.** Annual salary schedule.

ment to be made after a satisfactory conclusion to the project. An accrued expense must be kept on the books as a liability until it is paid or the organization is certain it will never have to be paid. If this is not done, expenses will be understated in the accrual period and overstated in the period they are paid.

Capital expenses are associated with the purchase of equipment, buildings, land, and large pieces of equipment. Most expenses directly related to the startup of a new business or business component may also be capitalized. Capital expenses are purchases that are expected to have an extended useful life. Useful life is the period over which an item will continue to be used in the production of goods or service. The definition of capital expenses may vary somewhat between organizations. This variance occurs because the acquisition value of the item is considered. Each organization has to set a minimum acquisition value for capital expenditures. For example, Do It All Therapy will capitalize any extended-life purchase or business startup with a value equal to or greater than $500. Capital expense should reflect all expenses related to the acquisition of a capital asset. That includes expenses that are incurred to get the equipment ready to use. The following is a list of expenses that should be considered for inclusion as part of a capital asset acquisition:

- Shipping
- Site preparation
- Installation
- Required staff training
- Consulting or legal services
- Interest if money was borrowed to make the purchase
- Land and buildings
- Real estate commissions
- Escrow and legal fees
- Titling costs
- Accrued property taxes
- Land preparation
- Surveys
- Clearing and landscaping
- Capital improvements, such as sewer and roads
- Removal of existing structures
- Building renovations
- Architectural and design fees
- Insurance during the renovation or construction phase

If an organization chooses to lease rather than buy a capital asset, it may enter into a **capital lease**. If the lease covers the projected life of the asset, the lease costs may qualify as a capital expense. Lease arrangements should be evaluated on an individual basis. The **Financial Accounting Standards Board** (FASB) sets the standards for accounting and financial reporting. The accounting standards related to capital and capital lease expense classification change over time. Up-to-date standards should be consulted when determining acceptable costs for inclusion in the calculation of capital costs.

In a financial plan capital expenses are treated differently from operating expenses. The matching principle requires that the capital asset value consumed during a period be reflected as an offset to revenue from the same period. To maintain the matching principle, capital expenses must to spread across an asset's **useful life**. The value consumed during a specific period is reflected in operating expenses as **depreciation**.

$$\text{Annual depreciation} = \frac{\text{capital expense}}{\text{useful life (years)}}$$

Land is an exception because it has an unlimited useful life. Land is not subject to depreciation (Pyle and White, 1975).

Figure 28.7 indicates that Do It All Therapy has $330,000 invested in capital assets: $40,000 in land, $90,000 in buildings, and $200,000 in equipment. Do It All Therapy has financed $225,000 of this asset value through long-term notes payable. Figure 28.4 shows an annual depreciation expense of $26,624. Figure 28.8 is the depreciation schedule for Do It All Therapy for FY 2008. Note that land holdings are excluded.

As assets are added at various times and have different useful life estimates, depreciation should be calculated on each item or group of items. Many organizations apply a first-year convention. When this is done, only half of the annual depreciation is expensed the first year. Following years list the full depreciation amount as an expense until the full value of the asset is expensed over its useful life.

A Multiyear Financial Plan

Long-range financial plans are projected from current revenues and expenses adjusted for projected changes in the base organization

Do It All Therapy, Incorporated
Balance Sheet
September 30, 2008

ASSETS		LIABILITIES AND OWNER'S EQUITY	
Cash	$ 45,000	Liabilities:	
Investments	60,000		
Prepaid Expenses	2,000	Accounts Payable	$ 50,000
Inventories	10,000	Accrued Expenses	5,000
Accounts Receivable	60,000	Notes Payable	225,000
		Total Liabilities	$280,000
Land	$ 40,000		
Buildings	90,000		
Equipment	200,000	Owner's Equity	$227,000
TOTAL	$507,000	Total Liabilities and Owner's Equity	$507,000

Figure 28.7. Balance sheet.

and future strategies targeted for implementation. For example, nonlabor expenses increase with inflation. Labor costs rise with annual wage adjustments and increased benefits costs. The cost of money continues to increase. Additional support staff may be needed because of business expansion. The rate of reimbursement may be projected to decline over time. The long-range financial plan must account for these factors as accurately as possible. Published indexes can be used to assist in making future projections. Support from financial management professionals is often necessary to develop a reliable

Do It All Therapy, Incorporated
Depreciation Schedule
Fiscal Year 2008

Asset	Booked Value	Useful Life (Years)	Annual Depreciation	Monthly Depreciation
Equipment:				
Clinic Furniture	$7,000	12	$583	$ 49.00
Office Furniture	13,000	12.5	1,040	86.67
Tx Equipment	110,000	11.75	9,362	780.14
Computer System	16,742	4	4,186	348.79
Billing Software	25,000	5	5,000	416.67
Transcription Equip	7,000	6	1,167	97.22
Car	21,258	7	3,037	253.07
Equipment Total	$200,000		$24,374	$2,031.17
Building				
1st Street Clinic	90,000	40	2,250	187.50
Total	$290,000		$26,624	$2,219

Figure 28.8. Depreciation schedule.

Do It All Therapy, Incorporated
Three Year Financial Plan
FY 2007 to FY 2010

	FY 2007 Actual	FY 2008 Actual	FY 2009 Actual	FY 2010 Actual
Work Statistics	23,795	34,985	48,483	54,301
REVENUE:				
Gross Revenue				
Service	$832,818	$1,224,459	$1,696,905	$1,900,533
Equipment	60,000	85,000	110,000	110,000
Total Operating Revenue	$892,818	$1,309,459	$1,806,905	$2,010,533
Less:				
Deductions	203,563	302,732	408,772	434,388
Gross Rev Net Deductions	$689,255	$1,006,727	$1,398,133	$1,576,145
Non–Operating Revenue	23,000	23,000	23,000	23,000
Total Revenue	$712,255	$1,029,727	$1,421,133	$1,599,145
EXPENSES:				
Salaries	$361,421	$534,600	$740,095	$844,124
Benefits	65,056	96,228	133,217	151,942
FICA	28,191	41,699	57,727	65,842
Education	6,300	8,672	11,995	13,490
Recruitment	5,000	5,638	6,803	6,974
Professional Services	11,000	13,489	13,040	10,000
Purchased Services	600	15,990	16,000	1,000
Supplies	51,095	77,043	108,888	125,003
Travel	4,000	4,715	5,448	6,199
Dues	2,000	2,050	2,101	2,200
Equipment	1,200	16,500	17,000	2,000
Rent/Lease	20,000	57,680	98,550	101,507
Utilities	9,000	15,375	21,909	22,457
Communication	3,375	6,042	6,304	6,611
Environmental Services	5,300	10,763	14,230	14,585
Accrued Expenses	40,083	44,791	53,513	58,928
Insurance	6,100	9,840	13,674	14,015
Total Expenses	$619,721	$961,115	$1,320,495	$1,446,877
Net Income (Loss)	92,534	68,612	100,638	152,268
Taxes	30,536	22,642	33,191	50,218
Net Income After Taxes	$61,998	$ 45,970	$ 67,448	$ 102,050

Assumptions:

The addition of one new suburban clinic location in FY 2008 and FY 2009 (See Financial impact Analyses).
A volume increase of 5% in 2008, 10% in 2009 and 12% in 2010
A 5% increase in all salary rates per year.
A 3% increase in existing rental expense per year.
A 2.5% increase in all other expense categories per year.
A 5% decrease in the commercial payment rate for FY 2008 and FY 2009
A 3% decrease in the commercial reimbursement rate for FY 2010.
A 1.5% increase in payment for Medicare and Medicaid payments per year.
A 5% payer mix shift from commercial to managed care for 2008 and 2009.
Prices will remain unchanged.

Figure 28.9. Three-year financial plan.

long-range financial plan (Chapters 21 and 34). Figure 28.9 is a 3-year financial plan developed for Do It All Therapy. The assumptions used to develop the plan are listed at the beginning of the plan. The financial projections follow. Other reports that should be prepared include projected balance statements and cash flow statements to ensure that cash flow requirements created by such a high growth rate can be met. As plans and circumstances change over time, the long-term financial plan should be adjusted accordingly. See Chapter 27 for an example of a balance statement and cash flow statement for Do It All Therapy.

The Annual Budget: Setting Performance Targets

In creating the **annual budget**, the financial performance targets for the current year are broken down into a more detailed plan that can be used to direct day-to-day activity. The overall financial plan is broken down by division, operating unit, department, service program, or any other subunit that the organization designates. The allocation of budgeted revenue and expenses should reflect the organization's structure and information needs. **Operating units**, or departments, should be recognizable as distinct operating segments. Organizational units should be designated as revenue or cost centers (Chapter 27). A **revenue center** has a budget that includes both direct revenue and direct expense. A **cost center** budget includes only direct expense. Answers to the following questions will help determine whether an organizational division should be designated as a revenue or cost center.

- Can the work of the unit be clearly separated from that of other units?
- Do the employees assigned to the unit share common knowledge and skills that distinguish them and their work from others?
- Does an individual or team have authority over and responsibility for the unit's performance?
- Is information sufficient and reliable enough to be used to separate the revenue and/or costs of the unit from those of the rest of the organization?
- Will separation of the revenue and/or costs of the unit increase management's ability to plan for and direct the work of the organization?
- Will separation of the unit make it easier to evaluate and improve performance?

If these questions can be answered yes, the operating unit should have its own budget. If the answer to one or more of these questions is no, the work of creating a budget is likely to outweigh any potential benefit. In fact, resources spent developing and maintaining a budget may decrease the performance of the company.

The owner of Do It All Therapy requires information about the total cost per unit of service for each revenue department. This information will improve the accuracy of cost projections for additional service volume and for price setting during managed care contract negotiations. Without this detailed information, Do It All Therapy would have to use the average cost for all visits. Using average cost places the company at risk for setting a price below actual cost. To make a profit, revenue after deductions must be greater than total cost. See the cost–volume–profit analysis in Chapter 27 .

To provide needed information, the financial information system must collect the right data in the right way (Chapter 13). How data are collected is tied to the way revenues and costs are budgeted and recorded throughout the year. In the case of Do It All Therapy, total revenues, and expenses have been divided between the clinics. Within each clinic, the budgeted revenue and/or costs are divided among general administration, office functions, physical therapy, occupational therapy, and speech therapy. Department-level budgets include all of the direct revenue and cost related to the department's operation. This budget structure will provide specific performance information for each clinic and each department within each clinic. Projected work statistics, revenue, and expenses are used to determine the portion of direct revenue and expense that is distributed to each clinic and department. This flow is depicted in Figure 28.10.

Projected expense and revenue are divided between the clinics based on total clinic work statistic projections. Revenue and expenses are divided among clinic departments in the same way. At the department level, revenues and expenses are allocated to the subaccounts according to projected use. An accurate division of resources depends on the availability of accurate performance history adjusted for any anticipated change.

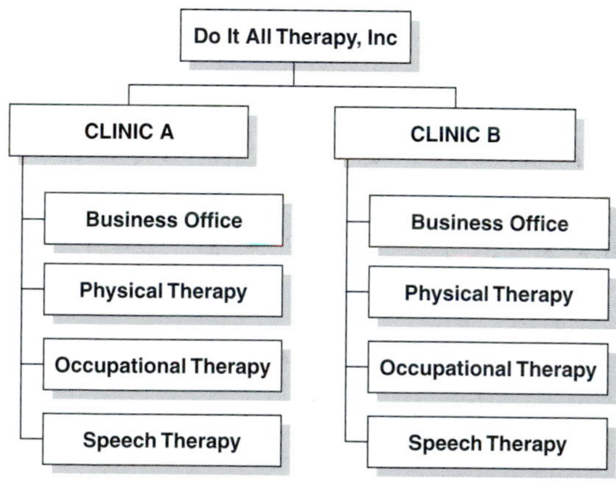

Figure 28.10. Organizational chart.

Indirect costs, which are incurred by the organization but cannot be directly associated with the production of any specific good or service, are allocated to departments. For example, administrative salaries, financial services, information service, grounds care, building services, and employee food service costs cannot be directly associated with the delivery of patient services but contribute to the overall operation.

Shared indirect costs are **allocated costs**. Allocated costs are not listed as department expenses but are allocated to departments as shared **overhead expense**. Indirect expense allocation uses a meaningful basis, such as the department's share of total square footage, revenue, expense, number of employees, or volume of service. A department is allocated a percentage of overhead expense equal to its determined percentage of the basis. For example, a department that occupies 5% of the square footage of a building is allocated 5% of the building utility cost. Indirect costs should be included in the calculation of the total cost of a unit of service.

In review, information needed for accurate budgeting of revenue and expenses at the department level includes the following:

- Charges per unit of service
- Equipment charges
- Volume of services and equipment to be sold
- Payer mix
- Case mix
- Percent of deductions from revenue by payer type
- Amount of anticipated non–operating revenue
- Salary increase planned for the FY
- Average hourly rates by job category adjusted by the anticipated salary increase
- Work statistic projections for each division and department
- Productivity standard per FTE by job category
- Variable cost per unit of service
- Direct and indirect fixed cost

Admittedly, few organizations can provide all of this information with complete confidence. Cost information is typically the most difficult to obtain. The larger and more complex the organization, the more difficult it is to determine the cost of services. In our experience, a poorly designed data collection system and lack of automation are frequently associated with unsatisfactory cost information (Chapter 13).

Unit-level budgets are presented in an income statement (profit and loss) format. Preparation of both monthly and annual budgets is common, although any time frame can be used. Monthly budgets provide periodic performance targets that are important for performance monitoring. Once set, the annual budget becomes a financial performance target for each operating unit of the organization.

Student Notes

Financial planning used to be considered a management function. Today's organizations recognize that opportunities to predict future trends and identify opportunities for improvement are enhanced when input is sought from all employees. Employees with a basic understanding of financial planning will be better prepared to make a useful contribution. If you have an idea for a program that you believe will benefit your department, one of the essential ways of marketing your idea to your manager is to include a reasonable cost and expense budget.

The principles of financial planning are equally applicable to personal financial planning. Would you have completed your education without financial planning? As you start job interviews, personal financial planning will become more important. You will confront questions such as these: What is the best way to manage your flexible benefits package? How long should you take to pay off education debt, given your longer-term goals? In the long term, it is possible that you will own your own business? The information presented in this chapter provides a foundation for you to plan for and manage a physical therapy business. It will at least help you understand financial consultants when you seek their services.

INDIVIDUAL CASE STUDY

Health care providers share many common challenges. One of the most concerning is a continual decline in reimbursement rates in the face of rising expenses. While labor expense rises about 3% per year and other expenses climb at the rate of inflation or higher, actual payment declines or stays flat. Growth in service volume is among the most common ways to maintain a positive total net income. What internal and external factors can interfere with a physical therapy practice's ability to grow its service volume? You may want to scan Chapters 21 to 24 to guide your response.

Summary

This chapter explores the concept of the financial management cycle. The first two steps of the financial management cycle, long-term financial planning and annual financial planning, are reviewed. Application to physical therapy practice is demonstrated through example. Revenue and expense budgets are discussed. Capital expenses are defined as high-cost items that often have their own budgetary category. Direct and indirect costs, that is, costs clearly related to providing service and costs shared by others in the organization, are discussed. Comparative examples that use different reimbursement methods are presented to demonstrate the key financial ramifications of fixed prepayment and other payment systems. Key aspects of fee-for-service, discounted fee-for-service, cost reimbursement (Medicare related), fixed per diem, case rate, capitated payment systems are discussed. The concepts of case mix and payer mix are elaborated upon through several physical therapy examples. The types of patients treated and the type of insurance the patients have are essential components of the information base

GROUP CASE STUDY

Form a group of six members: CEO, division head, section manager, department manager, assistant department manager, and senior physical therapist.

Physical therapy is a labor-intensive business. That means that a high percentage of total expense will be labor expense. Consider the case of a physical therapy practice with the following financial performance:

Gross revenue	$1,538,333
Net revenue	549,244
Labor expense	823,541
Nonlabor expense	130,023
Net income	35,525

A 25% decline in reimbursement rates translates into an $8881 reduction in income with no related reduction in expenses. Assume that nonlabor expenses are already at a minimum and that any reduction must be accompanied by a reduction in services.

Task

Identify three strategies to bring net income back to previous levels. Discuss your strategies in small groups and come to a consensus. As time permits, compare strategies with other groups and select the strategies that seem most likely to meet the objective of increasing net income. Keep track of the effect of the strategies on stakeholders (Chapter 6).

needed to staff, equip, and manage a service-based department and to guide decisions regarding entering into contracts to provide services.

In Chapter 29 , discussion of the financial management cycle will shift to use of the financial plan as a benchmark against which actual financial performance can be compared. Trend analysis will be used to set the stage for updating the financial plan as the cycle continues.

REFERENCES

Pyle WW, White JA. Fundamental accounting principles, 7th ed. Homewood, IL: Richard D. Irwin. 1975.

Shukla, RK. A comparative analysis of revenue and cost-management strategies of not-for-profit and for-profit hospitals. Health & Hospital Services Administration. 1997;42:117–134.

MORE INFORMATION RELATED TO THIS CHAPTER

A compact summary of health care budgeting, cost allocation, cost behaviors, and reports is provided in Longest BB, Jr, Rakich JS, Darr K. Managing health services organizations and systems, 4th ed. Baltimore: Health Professions. 2000:469–529.

Another view of budgeting that includes many of the topics covered in this chapter can be reviewed in McConnell CR. The effective health care supervisor, 5th ed. Gaithersburg, MD: Aspen. 2002.

Additional depth of information on budgeting, flexible budgeting, and variance analysis can be found in Finkler SA, Ward DM. Essentials of cost accounting for health care organizations, 2nd ed. Gaithersburg, MD: Aspen. 1999.

Periodically consult http://www.apta.org for continuing education courses, video and audio tapes, home study courses, and other resources relevant to budgeting and financial planning including personal financial planning.

Chapter 29

MAXIMIZING FINANCIAL PERFORMANCE

Learning Objectives

1. Summarize the major revenue and expense management methods suggested in this chapter.
2. Understand management's role in revenue and expense management.
3. Correctly use the terminology presented in this chapter.
4. Examine and compare methods for increasing payment for physical therapy services and controlling related labor and other expenses.
5. Examine the opportunities and risks associated with being a physical therapy provider under each of the payment methods discussed in this chapter.
6. Demonstrate the ability to apply methods aimed at increasing net income from operations.

Key Words

Accepting assignment, accounts receivable, allowable cost, capitated payment, carrier, case management, case mix, case rate, case rate payment, charge master, commercial health insurance, comparative and common-size report, copayment, cost cap, cost-based methodology, coverage guidelines, coverage limit, credit, days in net accounts receivable, deductible, deduction, diagnosis-related group (DRG), disability insurance, discounted fee-for-service payment, enrollee, expense management, external benchmark, fee-for-service payment, fee schedule, financial ratio analysis, flexible budgeting, full time equivalent (FTE), government program, gross revenue, group purchasing discount, health, indemnity health insurance, indemnity insurer, insurance carrier, intermediary, inventory control, inventory reduction plan, labor expense, malpractice insurance, managed care organization (MCO), Medicaid, Medicare, net revenue, noncovered services, opportunity cost, outlier, outsourcing, participation agreement, payer audit, payer mix, payment limit, payment reduction, per diem payment, personal liability insurance, point-of-service plan, payback period, preauthorization, preferred provider organization (PPO), price, primary care physician (PCP), prior authorization, productivity, productivity standards, property and casualty insurance, quick pay discount, request for proposal (RFP), return on invested funds (ROI), revenue management, revenue net deductions, sales volume, self-payment, skill mix, statement of assignment, third party administrator (TPA), third-party payment system, unit measure, usual and customary rate (UCR), use management, variance, willing provider, workers' compensation insurance

Introduction

Financial information is a management tool of incomparable value. To use this tool effectively, management at all levels of an organization needs a working knowledge of financial management principles. Application of financial management principles allows therapy managers to relate the delivery of patient care to the revenues and expenses of operating a health care business. Decisions about new or expanded services, staffing, and purchases that would otherwise be based on a manager's best guess will seem clearer. Application of objective information about the performance of a business as compared to what was planned and/or what competitors are doing will help the manager stay on target with performance objectives. The management of health care is too important and too complex to proceed without good information.

Once the principles of health care accounting and financial planning are understood (Chapters 26 and 27), financial management skills can be applied to health care operations to maximize an organization's financial performance. Financial performance is best when net revenue is maximized and expenses minimized (Chapter 27). To achieve maximum effectiveness health care managers must address some unique issues. In collecting payment for health care services, managers must consider the multiple customers (Chapters 21–25) and possibly multiple payers (Chapter 28) in most transactions. Most health care services are provided on credit. The patient pays some portion of the expense, while a third party (insurer) pays the rest (Chapter 2). The method and division of payment is different with every transaction. Expenses must be managed to limit the cost per unit of service when most expense is in salaries that are continually increasing to make it possible to recruit and retain qualified employees. Revenue and expense management is key to maximizing a health care organization's financial performance.

Revenue Management

The goal of **revenue management** is to maximize income from operations and investments. Payment for health care services may be collected in the form of cash at the time of service or provided on credit, with payment at a later date. Payment at the time of service simplifies revenue management but is often impractical under the **third-party payment system** (Chapter 2).

Gross revenue from operations is equal to volume of sales times the price of what is sold. **Revenue net deductions** is equal to gross revenue minus deductions for discounts and other payment allowances. **Net revenue** is a function of **price**, **sales volume**, **payer mix**, and **case mix**.

Gross revenue = units sold × selling price per unit

Net revenue = gross revenue – deductions from revenue

Deductions = discounts + payment allowances

For most health care organizations revenue management is the management of **accounts receivable**. Accounts receivable is an asset that represents money owed to the business for delivered products and services. **Days in net accounts receivable** is a measure of how long it takes to collect accounts receivable. A long or lengthening collection cycle can indicate future financial problems. Refer to Chapter 27 for additional information about accounts receivable and days in net accounts receivable. Effective revenue management maximizes income from operations. Revenue management is a long process that entails several activities:

1. Measuring services and products for sale
2. Setting prices (charges)
3. Identifying the payer or payers for each transaction
4. Establishing billing, credit, and collections policies and processes
5. Calculation of expected payment

6. Payment receipt, account reconciliation, and cash management
7. Financial reporting

Measurement of Services and Products for Sale

To assign a consistent price, a **unit measure** must be associated with each discrete increment of service or product for sale. A unit measure for service can be based on time or activity. A time-based unit can be a minute, an hour, a month, or any other specific increment of time. An activity measure can be a visit, a modality, a treatment, or a procedure composed of several discrete procedures. It can be an entire plan of care, often referred to as a **case rate** (Chapter 28). Products are measured by the amount of product sold. A dose, a pair, one, a package, an ounce are all measures of amount. Even a small business like Do It All Therapy, Inc., will use several types of measurements to define its services and products. In the case of Do It All Therapy, measurements are required to define increments of service, supplies, and equipment to be rented and sold. Units of measure vary between organizations. There is no one right way to select the units of measure a business will use. Some factors that should influence the selection process (Nosse and Friberg, 1992):

- The unit of measure should be a logical choice for the product or service. If a product is always used in pairs, it should be packaged and sold in pairs. If multiple discrete services are billed to the same customer, a common unit of measure, for example, all 15-minute units or all procedures, makes more sense to the customer.
- The unit of measure should allow for accurate cost allocation. If the largest expense of a service is to staff costs that are paid according to time, a time-based unit of measure may make cost allocation easier and more accurate.
- Units of measure for a given product or service should be standardized within the organization. If a service charge for therapy is based on 15-minute increments in one department, they should be based on 15-minute time increments in departments.

When selecting a unit of measure, consider what the customer is familiar with and what the competition is using. This is essential for price-sensitive services and products.

Setting Prices

A key element of the accounts receivable management system is the **charge master**, a listing of services and products that the business offers for sale to its customers. Each listing on the charge master, or **fee schedule**, is defined by

1. Numeric charge code
2. Description
3. Unit of measure for the product or service
4. Price

The charge master varies with the size and complexity of the business. It also varies with management's and customers' information needs. The more specific the information needs of management, the more specific the charges. For example, a therapy practice that sells equipment may need a single charge code or several codes for the items sold. Billing records are often used to track use of products and services by patient type. This information is important for managed care contracting.

The concepts behind market-driven pricing were discussed in Chapter 21. Unfortunately, in health care *the price charged is rarely the price paid.* This is because the payer for health care is seldom the patient. Rather than individual customers, health care providers receive the largest percentage of payment from the government and other large-volume customers. Size and control of the market allow third-party payers to negotiate or set payment rates that are standardized across payers and/or below the prices the health care provider charges others for their services. To maximize the amount actually paid, health care organizations must set charges to accommodate varying payment rates and practices.

A common question for managers new to health care finance is why you charge more than you know you are going to be paid. The reason is a practical one, to maximize revenue under the unique U.S. health care third-party payer system. Price is a management decision that should be determined by financial and marketing considerations. Decisions about price setting should balance the desire to maximize net income against business development strategies and market sensitivity to price, as discussed in Chapter 26. All businesses must be mindful of laws that govern pricing. The Robinson-Patman Act prohibits businesses from charging similar customers different prices unless the differences are based on differences in cost of production, transportation, or sale or quantities in which commodities are sold (Garrison, 1979). Differential pricing must be based on real cost differences. Businesses are required to charge all customers the same price for the same product or service unless there is a real difference in the provider's costs of delivery of service. As a result, the health care provider must set charges to maximize the potential payment from all sources while using one charge for all patients. All of these factors can be accommodated if the charge rate is set somewhere above the highest payment rate. Contract agreements can then be used to discount services to high-volume payers. Volume discounting is allowable because volume decreases the cost of a unit of service or product, assuming the provider's cost is lower than its charge.

Chapter 28 reviews a financial model for predicting the change in net income resulting from a price increase and the concept of price setting to maximize revenue less than third-party reimbursement. Management under varying payment models is discussed later in this chapter in the section on calculating payment deductions and allowances.

Who Pays for Health Care?

Payment for health care services comes from many sources (Chapter 2):

- Patients
- Patients' families
- Health care providers
- Charitable groups and individuals
- Employers
- Insurance companies
- Government

Each payment source has its own set of criteria to be met before a bill is paid.

Patients and/or their families may be responsible for payment of a bill for several reasons. Berman, Kukla and Weeks (1994) have identified five reasons:

- Insurance plan deductibles and co-payments
- Insurance coverage limits
- Insurance payment limits
- Lack of health insurance
- Patient's decision

Patients are commonly responsible for payment of all or part of their health care costs because of insurance **deductibles** and **co-payments** (Chapter 2). An insurance deductible is an amount that the patient or family has agreed to pay out of pocket for covered health care services before the insurer must pay any part of the bill. Deductibles are often amounts per person and/or per family per calendar year. A co-payment is an amount or percentage of the service cost a patient and/or family must pay after the deductible has been satisfied. Co-payments may be limited to a total dollar amount per person and/or per family per year. Co-payments are made by the patient directly to the service provider. Some insurers require providers to collect the co-payment at the time of service.

Coverage guidelines are established by insurance plans to identify which health care services are and which are not covered by the plan. Specific services, the amount of a specific service, **prior authorization** requirements, **payment limits**, or the source of service may be used to limit coverage. There are different types of **coverage limits**. Coverage limits may be applied to elective, experimental, and cosmetic procedures. Payment for outpatient therapy may be limited to a fixed number of visits per policy year. Coverage may be available only for services received from specific providers. Payment for any services received by the patient without prior approval may be denied or limited. Services excluded from coverage are called noncovered services. Patients and their families are responsible for payment of **noncovered services** unless an agreement between the insurer and the provider limits the patient's financial responsibility in some manner.

Payment limits are the amount the insurer will pay for a specific service (Chapter 2). Often, commercial **indemnity insurers** pay a fixed amount for services. What they pay is defined by a schedule of fees. Fee schedules vary between payers because there is no standard method for payers to arrive at what they consider a fair price. As with any private business, the insurer's goal is to maximize income by keeping the amount it pays to health care providers as low as possible. While this may sound fair, it actually places an extra burden on the patient and family, who are often responsible for payment of the difference between charges and insurer payment.

Payment may be the responsibility of a *patient and/or family* if they are uninsured or elect to receive a noncovered service. This category is self-payment. Because self-pay patients cannot negotiate special rates based on volume or other considerations, they ultimately are charged more for health care than most third-party payers. Health care providers are likely to have a higher rate of delayed payment and nonpayment of charges with self-pay.

Health care providers fund a portion of the health care service they provide. The provision of charity care, care that is funded below the cost of services, and provisions for bad debt are ways providers pay for care. Urban and not-for-profit teaching organizations commonly provide more unfunded care than their counterparts. It is this community service that qualifies health care providers for a tax-exempt status (Chapter 2). Also, those who provide a disproportionately high percentage of unfunded care may be eligible for governmental funding referred to as disproportionate share payments.

Charitable contributions, once a major source of health care funding, still pay for some services. Prior to the development of today's third-party payer system, not-for-profit community health care institutions relied on individuals and philanthropic foundations to fund capital equipment and facilities investments. As government funding of health and social service programs declines, the need for alternative funding sources increases. Once again, health care providers have turned to individuals and philanthropic foundations for funding. This is evidenced by the increased resources being devoted to formal fundraising activities. Money received from individuals and philanthropic foundations to fund health care may be targeted for a donor-specified use or given as a general contribution to a health care provider to fund expenses.

Employers and their employees pay the greatest amount, about 32%, of national health care costs (Berman et al., 1994). Employers may pay health care costs through the purchase of insurance. Alternatively, an employer may choose to self-insure. A self-insured employer is directly responsible for its employees' health care costs. Self-insured employers have the option of managing their self-insurance or outsourcing. Either an **insurance carrier** or **third-party administrator (TPA)** may be contracted for use management and/or claims processing for self-insured plans. Traditional insurance companies also offer the self-insured employer the option of purchasing stop-loss insurance, which limits the employer's financial risk to a dollar amount per case. The stop-loss insurer pays costs above the stop-loss limit. For example, the employer may be responsible all of an employee's health care expense up to $30,000. Any costs in excess of $30,000 become the responsibility of the stop-loss insurer.

*Health, **malpractice, personal liability, property and casualty, disability, and workers' compensation insurance*** all provide some level of payment for health care services. Health insurance plans are, of course, a primary source of health care payments. **Indemnity health insurance** provides comprehensive coverage for medical and hospital service. To enroll in an indemnity insurance plan the employer and/or subscriber pays a premium, and the subscriber agrees to pay any required deductible, co-payments, and amounts over the insurer's usual and customary rate for specific services. In return, the subscriber may receive medical and hospital services from the physician, hospital, or other qualified provider of his or her choice (Chapter 2). The subscriber can choose a level of coverage from a package that may include (Berman et al., 1994) the following:

- Hospital care benefits
- Outpatient care benefits
- Medical benefits
- Major medical (benefits paid after deductible is satisfied)
- Dental care

Coverage is usually restricted to services that are covered under the insurance plan, are considered to be medically necessary, and meet accepted standards of medical practice. Prior approval may be required. Experimental or other noncovered services may be negotiable under certain circumstances.

Managed care organizations (MCOs) started providing health care insurance in the early 1980s, when the federal government and other employers began to look for ways to control the costs of providing health insurance for their employees. The cost of insurance premiums had escalated to the point that the cost was threatening the financial health of businesses and the government-sponsored insurance plans. Many employers looked to the growing number MCOs for relief.

According to Berman and associates (1994), MCOs offered an identified set of medical and/or hospital services for a predetermined fixed premium. In return for this premium, the MCO is required to deliver all needed services within the cost limits of the fixed premium rate. To meet this requirement, MCOs restrict subscribers' choice of providers and control their access to health care through various forms of use management. A common method of control is the exclusive use of an employed or contracted panel of primary care physicians. Physicians specializing in family practice, internal medicine, general medicine, pediatrics, geriatrics, adolescent medicine, and obstetrics–gynecology are most often used in the role of **primary care physician (PCP)**. Each enrollee chooses or is assigned a PCP who acts as a gatekeeper for all other medical and hospital services. Services may be provided directly by the MCO or under contract with a limited number of providers (Chapter 2).

Providers may be required to accept significant discounts or capitated payment in exchange for an increased volume of business. MCOs need contracted providers who will support their cost containment efforts. **Payment reduction** and **use management**, made possible by limiting enrollee choice of providers, are the foundation of managed care cost reduction strategies (Chapter 2). Payment reduction largely consists of the discounts payers receive from contracted providers. Cooperation with use management strategies is generally a part of the payer–provider contract.

MCOs have continued to evolve in an effort to gain an increased share of the health insurance market. Plan options, which offer the subscriber a greater choice of providers, have become increasingly popular. Use of a **preferred provider organization (PPO)** is one approach. A PPO is a nonexclusive network of affiliated providers who contract with a MCO to provide care to the MCO enrollees. Use of a provider network broadens the enrollees' choice of providers but still allows the managed care insurer to operate at lower cost than an open choice indemnity insurer. In a network model, the insurer contracts with a panel of service providers in a specific area. Contracted providers are preferred providers. Enrollees pay less when they choose to receive care from a PPO member. They pay more out of pocket when they choose to receive care from a provider outside the system. In this way, the nonexclusive PPO is different from the exclusive MCO. Managed care plans that offer enrollees access to a broad choice of providers at different co-payment rates are called **point-of-service plans**.

From the provider perspective, contracting with an MCO provides the opportunity to maintain and/or increase market share. When considering such a contract, a provider must weigh the potential value of holding or gaining market share against the terms and conditions of the managed care agreement. A provider considering a managed care contract must be able to determine the financial outcome of the agreement. We are familiar with more than a few providers who entered into managed care contracts to capture the market, only to face a financial loss on the increased business.

Personal liability and other insurance plans are also sources of health care payment. Coverage under these types of insurance is limited to services provided for the treatment of an injury or illness related to the specific circumstances. Workers' compensation insurance provides payment for medical services necessitated by a work-related injury or illness. Workers' compensation plans are regulated by state governments and vary greatly from state to state (Chapter 2). Disability insurers may opt to pay for medical services if the services have the potential to decrease disability payments. Providers often have to pursue and negotiate with the insurer for this type of service payment. Disability insurance plans may pay for extended rehabilitation services that are not covered under a patient's health insurance plan. Personal liability, malpractice (Chapter 5), and property and casualty insurance pay for services needed for the treatment of injury or illness resulting from the circumstance subject to insurance coverage. An auto accident, an injury resulting from medical malpractice, or slip and fall injury in a store may be subject to coverage under these types of insurance.

Government programs that provide payment for health care services include Medicare, Medicaid, Tricare, Veterans Administration, and health services provided by state and local government programs (Chapter 2). It is estimated that the federal government pays for 29% of national health care costs, while state and local governments pay for an additional 15%. The largest of these government payers are **Medicare** and **Medicaid**. Medicare and Medicaid were initiated in 1966 under Title XVIII and Title XIX of the Social Security Act. It is estimated that 40 million people are eligible for benefits under Medicare and another 34 million are covered by Medicaid (Health and Human Services, 2002).

The Medicare program provides services to persons 65 years of age or over and those who meet special eligibility requirements. Special eligibility is provided for persons under 65 who have a long-term disability or chronic renal disease and to widows 50 or over who are eligible for disability payments. There has been some indication that the Medicare program's age of eligibility may increase from the current 65 years of age in the near future. Funding for the Medicare program comes from a variety of sources, payroll taxes, and the federal Medicare trust fund.

Medicare beneficiary deductible and co-payment amounts are set on an annual basis. Medicare is structured in two parts, Part A and Part B. The Balanced Budget Act of 1997 established the Medicare Choice option, sometimes referred to as Medicare Part C (Chapter 2). Each part provides coverage for a specific set of services under specified conditions and cost sharing (co-payment) requirements. Limits to coverage and the duration of coverage are also defined. For Part A, the Medicare program uses contracted **intermediaries** to administer services for defined regions. Intermediaries may administer the entire program for a region or only specific services. A large business providing several types of services, such as hospital, home care, and hospice, may work with three intermediaries. Intermediaries perform a variety of administrative functions, including claims processing, review and investigation, provider education, provider financial review, audit and provider certification review, and regulatory compliance. Periodic changes in payment levels and in the official interpretation of service coverage and benefits regulations make it necessary for health care providers to frequently obtain updated information. Medicare information can be obtained from industry publications, consultants, and industry representatives such as professional organizations. Participating providers can obtain this information from their Medicare intermediary through periodic advisory notices or direct contact with the intermediary provider services department. Medicare Part A helps pay for hospital care, services at a skilled nursing facility after a hospital stay, intermittent services from a home health agency for homebound patients, and hospice care.

For Part B, Medicare uses contracted fiscal agents called **carriers**. A typical carrier is a large insurance company that is already doing business in a large area. Providers work directly with their assigned carriers to obtain information and for claims processing. Part B is the medical insurance section of Medicare. It helps pay for physician services; outpatient services; medical equipment; some hospital, home health, and rehabilitation services; and supplies not covered under Part A. Part B is funded through beneficiary-paid monthly insurance premiums and co-payments. The premium rate is set each year to be effective in January. Annual premium increases must be at or under the annual percentage increase in social security payments (Berman et al., 1994).

Medicare Choice is a managed care option available to Medicare beneficiaries eligible for Part A and part B benefits. Under Medicare Choice, a beneficiary may join a Medicare-qualified managed care plan. Medicare pays a negotiated premium, and the managed care plan pays for the beneficiary's health care.

Medicaid was established by Title XIX of the Social Security Act of 1965 to provide for the health care needs of the poor. This program provides services to the blind, the disabled, families with dependent children, and the poor elderly. Responsibility for funding Medicaid is shared between state and federal governments. Each pays a percentage of the total cost. State participation in Medicaid is voluntary. Participating states are not required to implement the program with a standard set of benefits. States enter into an agreement with the federal government to furnish a minimum set of mandated health services to qualified persons as described earlier. To qualify as needy, a family's income level must be below the state poverty level. The percentage of federal funding received by a state is based on per capita income. A lower per capita income results in a higher percentage of federal payment (Chapter 2).

How Are Health Care Providers Reimbursed?

In the U.S. system, most health care payments come from private health insurance and governmental plans (Chapter 1). A minor but growing percentage of payment is **self-payment** by patients themselves. **Commercial** (private) **health insurance** plans typically use standardized payment schedules that determine the amount they will pay for a specific service. This is called the **usual and customary rate** (**UCR**). Often, commercial health insurance pays the provider charges up to the UCR. The patient is sometimes required to pay the difference. Governmental payers, such as Medicare, use a variety of systems that range from paying some percentage of the provider cost (expenses) to paying a fixed amount per service regardless of the provider's cost. Payments from government health insurance programs vary with type of service, type of provider. and patient's status (Chapters 28 and 30). With so many diverse payers involved, health care providers are challenged to follow the specific requirements of each type of payer. An example of multiple payers using different payment methods in one state is shown in Table 29.1.

These requirements may include prior authorization as well as specific coding, documentation, and billing formats. For transactions that involve more than one third-party payer, the requirements become even more complex. All of these requirements must be known at the start of service so that billing can proceed without delay.

Who Can Bill an Insurance Plan?

Participation agreements are also called managed care contracts, preferred provider contracts, or service agreements. As noted earlier in this chapter, a participation agreement is a contract between an insurer and a provider that allows the provider to participate in care of the plan's enrollees. Third-party payers may require businesses to have provider participation agreements before they will pay for services provided to the plan's enrollees (Chapter

Table 29.1 Reimbursement Mechanisms for Physical Therapy in Michigan (1/01/03)

	Payers					
Settings	***Medicare***	***Medicaid (MI)***	***Workers' Compensation***	***Commercial Insurance***	***Managed Care***	***Blue Cross/ Blue Shield (MI)***
Acute care hospital, inpatient	PPS/DRG	PPS/DRG	FFS/PD	FFS or negotiated	FFS or cap negotiated	DRG
Rehab hospital	PPS	PD	FFS/PD	FFS or negotiated	FFS or cap negotiated	CR or PD
Hospital, outpatient	FS (MPFS)	FS	FS	FFS or negotiated	FFS or cap negotiated	CR
Physical therapist, private practice	FS (MPFS)	FS (minimal)	FS	FFS or negotiated	FFS or cap negotiated	Per Visit
Rehab agency	FS (MPFS)	FS (minimal)	FS	FFS or negotiated	FFS or cap negotiated	Per visit
Comprehensive outpatient rehab facility	FS (MPFS)	FS (minimal)	FS	FFS or negotiated	FFS or cap negotiated	NA
Skilled nursing facility	PD (SNF PPS)	PD	FFS/PD	FFS or negotiated	FFS or cap negotiated	PD
Hospice	CR	PD	FS	FFS or negotiated	FFS or cap negotiated	N/A
Home care	PPS	FS	FS	FFS or negotiated	FFS or cap negotiated	FS

Cap, capitation; CR, cost reimbursement; FFS, fee for service (includes fee schedule); FS, fee schedule; MPFS, Medicare physician fee schedule; PPS, prospective payment system (includes diagnosis-related groups); DRG, diagnosis-related groups; rehab, rehabilitation.

2). Participation agreements set out the terms and conditions under which a health care business must operate if it wishes to provide services under the plan. Not all payers under all circumstances require participation agreements. For example, Medicare pays for physical therapy provided by a participating hospital, skilled nursing facility, home health care agency, rehabilitation agency, outpatient clinic, public health agency, comprehensive outpatient rehabilitation facility (CORF), and physical therapists in private practice (Chapter 30). Medicare also pays for physical therapy services provided in the office of a licensed physician. A participation agreement is not required for the physician to bill for these services. However, Medicare usually requires a participation agreement with a provider who wishes to serve its enrollees. A few managed health plans allow enrollees to receive service from nonparticipating providers if the enrollee is willing to pay a greater portion of the service charge (Chapter 2).

A health plan may take an open or restrictive approach to provider participation agreements. The least restrictive allows participation by any willing and qualified provider. Medicare, Medicaid, and most traditional indemnity health insurance plans accept any **willing provider**.

Managed health plans want to limit the number of providers in return for discounts. These plans take a competitive approach to awarding limited-term participation agreements. The competitive selection may be by invitation only or open to any qualified provider. During competitive selection, interested providers receive and respond to a **request for proposal** (**RFP**) to provide the specified services (Chapter 34). The RFP should spell out the services needed and delineate the information required from the provider who wishes to be considered for participation. The RFP may specify minimum requirements for participation. For example, a payer seeking to limit the number of providers may have requirements for the provider's service capacity and geographic coverage area (Beckley, 1997; Gill, 1995). If selected for participation, providers sign an agreement and become part of the plan's preferred provider panel. The most restrictive approach to provider participation is an exclusive participation agreement. Using competitive selection, the health care plan chooses one provider to deliver the specified care to an identified group of enrollees. This approach guarantees the provider a higher volume of patients. In return, the health plan expects to pay less for the services.

A participation agreement provides access to the market of patients requiring services. As managed care plans gain a greater share of the health insurance market, including Medicare and Medicaid beneficiaries, participation agreements become more important to both large and small providers. If 40% of the population in a market area is enrolled in a single managed care plan, the provider without a participation agreement lacks access to 40% of the market. Unfortunately, this is the type of market pressure that may force a health care business to accept unreasonable financial risk.

Access to the market should be a strategic initiative for any provider facing an increase in the use of restrictive provider contracting. Chapter 22 describes a market-oriented approach to business development. Marketing starts with an assessment of customer needs. The successful health care business can offer customers a service that meets their needs. Industry experts agree with this approach (Beckley, 1997; Gill, 1995). Gill (1995) notes that managed care plans are looking for three elements in contracting for rehabilitation services:

1. A reduction in cost
2. Geographic coverage
3. Quality service that satisfies enrollees

Proactive strategic and financial planning will help minimize the risks inherent in managed care contracting. As noted previously, to plan effectively, the health care provider must have access to reliable financial and outcome information.

Credit, Billing, and Collections

A high percentage of health care services are provided on **credit**. Credit purchasing occurs when the customer is billed for money owed after the services or products are provided. When this is the case, it is advisable to establish clear policies and practices regarding the extension of credit. Policies on charity care and discounts, financial counseling, patient self-pay obligations, coordination of third-party benefits, billing procedures, and cash receipts management should be considered.

Effective management of accounts receivable starts before admission or at the point of patient registration (Berman et al., 1994). Ideally, the source of payment should be established before service is provided. Patient self-pay obligations should be identified. Payment terms and conditions should be discussed before the patient receives services. If a patient is seeking emergency medical treatment, asking about payment prior to treatment may be a violation of the Emergency Medical Treatment and Labor Act (EMTALA), also known as the Emergency Medical Treatment and Active Labor Act (Centers for Medicare and Medicaid Services, 2002). Emergency services should be delivered as soon as the patient presents. Routine payment screening should be initiated as soon as the emergency has been resolved. When third-party benefits are available, the patient or a representative should be asked to sign a **statement of assignment**. This allows insurance payments to go directly to the provider. If the patient is unwilling to assign benefits, self-pay policies are applied.

When a third-party payer is involved, services should not be given until the payer authorizes them. This is called **preauthorization**. Preauthorization does not guarantee payment, but it may limit loss of payment for technical reasons. Usually it is the responsibility of the **enrollee** (patient or person who has the insurance plan covering the patient) to understand and comply with the terms of the insurance plan. In practice, it is in the provider's best interest to assist the patient with benefit verification and preauthorization compliance. Not only is it good customer service, preauthorization of service coverage has the potential to increase the speed and rate of payment.

A full review of insurance coverage requirements, credit, collections, and billing practices is beyond the scope of this text. Please refer to the references and suggested readings for additional resources.

What Will Be Paid?

Payer mix reflects by percentage of total charges the source of payment for services and products sold. Figure 29.1 shows payer mix and revenue deduction projections for Do It All Therapy, Inc. Assuming the discounts or allowance for each payer type is known, payer mix can be used to project deductions from revenue. In the case of Do It All Therapy, Figure 29.1 shows that for patients covered under managed care contracts, the business will collect 85% of what is billed. Continuing with the case of Do It All Therapy and the 100 adult patients with back strain, the method and effect of revenue deductions can be easily demonstrated. If all 100 of these had commercial insurance, net revenue per patient would be \$446.25 (\$525 per patient × 0.85 of billed charges). If all 100 of the patients were covered under the Medicaid program, net revenue per patient would be \$262.50 (\$525 per patient × 0.50 of billed charges).

Methods Of Reimbursement

Cost-based methodology has been used by governmental payers, such as Medicare. Under cost-based reimbursement, the health care provider is paid the lesser of charges or full allowable cost plus an additional amount to cover the depreciation of facilities and capital equipment. Allowable costs are defined by the payer but are generally limited to costs that can be shown to contribute directly to patient care. Under some cost-based reimbursement programs, total allowable cost is capped. Under a capped program, the provider is paid charges, allowable costs, or capped costs, whichever is least (Nosse and Friberg, 1992).

Under **fee-for-service payment** health care providers deliver, bill, and are paid for each discrete increment of service or product provided. Fees may be discounted, but payment is calculated for each increment billed and combined to create a total billed amount. Fee-for-service payment means that health care

Do It All Therapy, Incorporated **Payer Mix and Schedule of Deductions** **September 30, 2008**				
Payer Type	**Percent Revenue**	**Percent Discount**	**Revenue**	**Discount**
Medicare	33	30	$294,630	$88,389
Medicaid	8	50	71,425	35,713
Manage Care	30	15	267,845	40,177
Commercial	20	5	178,564	8,928
Charity Care	1	100	8,928	8,928
Self Pay	8	30	71,425	21,428
Total	100%		$892,818	$203,563

Figure 29.1. Payer mix and deductions from revenue.

businesses must define measurements for each discrete increment of service or product. The more diverse the care provided, the more extensive the charge master (fee schedule). Under fee-for-service payment the care provided to a patient with back strain is billed for each specific unit of evaluation, exercise, and modality provided. A single visit might result in several billed charges (Chapter 30).

Under the **case rate payment** method, the health care provider offers to provide at a preset charge (1) all of some service or product or (2) all services and products required for the management of a specific patient's case. If the cost of providing the required products and services is less than the case payment rate, the provider makes money. If the average case costs more than the case payment rate, the provider loses money. The broader the scope of services included in the case rate, the greater the variability in cost and the greater the provider's risk of incurring unexpected cost. To protect the provider and payer under case rate payment, both parties must agree to the definition of a case. Both must understand what is and is not included in the case rate. This understanding should be supported by a written definition of the case and included services. Important questions include these: When does service under the case start and stop? What products are part of the case? Because case rates cover larger increments of service and/or product, accurate definitions and pricing are essential.

Per case pricing is referred to as a risk arrangement. The risk occurs because the provider is responsible for the delivery of care *even if the case cost exceeds the case price.*

The importance of accurate definition and pricing can be demonstrated by returning to the case of Do It All Therapy and the 100 patients with back strain. Do It All Therapy has determined that it is paid an average of $446.25 for services per case after deductions. If asked to provide services to adults with back strain on a case rate basis, would $500 be a reasonable payment? The answer depends on what is covered. For the sake of discussion, assume the case rate covers only required physical therapy. According to that definition, a case rate of $500 may sound reasonable. But what if one patient of 100 who comes in with a diagnosis of back strain does not respond to the usual treatment? Instead, the patient requires extensive treatment and manual therapy over several months for a total of 36 treatments of 60 minutes each. The charges for this one case are $5040. If the average charge for all other 99 cases is at the expected $525, this one outlier raises the average charge to $565. At $565 per case the discount increases from the planned $2500 to an unplanned $6500 discount from charges. Such outlier cases have the potential to harm a small health care business.

What could have prevented this situation was a clearer definition of when the case coverage starts and stops. A major deviation from the routine course of care could have been defined as being outside of the case rate. Products that are to be included in the case rate should also be clearly defined.

The Medicare program reimburses hospitals for inpatient care using a case rate payment system. Hospitals receive a preset payment for providing inpatient care to a Medicare patient. Each Medicare inpatient is assigned by diagnosis to a **diagnosis-related group (DRG)**. The case payment rate is determined by the patient's DRG.

Per diem payment, applicable to inpatient and daily outpatient services, has more risk than fee-for-service but less risk than a case rate payment. Per diem payment uses a day as the increment of time for service delivery. Usually, the per diem rate stays the same through the course of the patient's care. This is important because the initial days of the patient's treatment are generally more service intense and costly than later days (Berman et al., 1994). Day therapy programs have been known to use a per diem rate charge structure.

Capitated payment, relatively new to health care, is used by managed care insurance plans whose design lets them direct all patients to the selected service providers (Chapter 2). Capitated payment allows the managed care insurer to shift some of the financial risk of care delivery from itself to the health care provider. Under capitation arrangements, the provider agrees to accept a set fee in return for the delivery of specified health care services to a specified group of enrollees. An enrollee is an individual who has paid a premium for coverage under a health insurance plan. Under capitation, payment to the health care provider should be based on two variables: (1) historical use of services by the enrollee group and (2) the provider's cost of delivering care. Managers rely on the use data to project the future volume and cost of service. The provider negotiates a set fee at a level that reflects projected cost plus a reasonable profit margin. Fees are generally structured as a set fee per enrollee per month.

In capitation payment arrangements, a provider makes money if the cost of providing services is lower than the capitation payment. The provider loses money if the cost of providing care exceeds the capitation payment. In practice, providers have had difficulty obtaining accurate use data and making accurate cost projections. If volume or costs are underestimated, the provider is likely to lose money. The managed care plan pays only the agreed rate per enrollee. This allows the insurer to do accurate financial planning and set premium rates at a level that covers its committed cost and provides for a profit margin. The provider takes the risk of loss in return for the potential of a profit and the guarantee of a larger market share.

Other payment practices that affect provider revenue are acceptance of assignment and application of UCR. Under UCR, patients may be asked by providers to sign an agreement that they will pay the difference between charges and the UCR payment made by their insurance carrier. Assignment is a term associated with charge reimbursement. When a health care business has agreed to accept assignment, it means that it has agreed to accept as full payment the UCR for that third-party payer. In that case, the health care business will not bill the patient for the difference between the UCR and its charge. The patient may still be billed for co-payments.

Maximizing Net Income With Third-Party Payment

Maximizing net income requires a working knowledge of the various third-party payment methods. It also requires the ability and willingness to manage the resources used in the care of the patient. The following discussion focuses on the relationships among payment methods, volume of services, cost, and net income. Any payment method carries the risk of provider abuse. Providers must be cautious and apply their knowledge of the third-party payment system in an ethical and legal manner. As providers assume more of the financial risk when they deliver health care services in fixed payment arrangements, they must be increasingly mindful that any and all efforts to maximize reimbursement are guided by applicable standards of practice.

Managing With Cost-Based Payment

In cost-based methods, the service provider is paid the lesser of charges or full allowable cost plus typically an additional amount to cover the investment in facilities and capital equipment. **Allowable costs** are defined by the payer and are generally limited to costs that can be shown to contribute directly to patient care. In some cost-based reimbursement programs, total allowable cost is paid up to a preset maximum amount. Costs in excess of the maximum are not covered by the payment. The maximum is called a **cost cap**.

Cost-based payment methods encourage increased service use and cost. Without a limit to allowable cost, the provider has no incentives to limit services or control cost. The use of cost reimbursement is decreasing, but it remains a significant payment method for outpatient rehabilitation services, children's hospitals, and long-term care hospitals that accept Medicare beneficiaries. Government and private health insurance plans have made and will continue to make changes that eliminate cost-based pay systems.

Assuming that a provider's charges are set reasonably above cost, net income is maximized under cost-based payment methods in these circumstances:

- More patients receive service.
- Individual patients receive more service.
- Increments of service cost more to provide.

When allowable costs to provide services are capped, net income is maximized in the same conditions as long as costs are kept under the cost cap. Some capped payment programs offer providers an incentive payment when their costs are kept significantly below the cost cap. In cost-based reimbursement the provider has limited financial risk (Berman et al., 1994).

Managing With Fee-for-Service and Discounted Fee-for-Service Payment

In a fee-for-service system, the provider delivers, bills, and is paid for each discrete increment of service or product provided. Payment is calculated for each increment billed and combined to create a total billed amount. Assuming the provider's charges are set reasonably above cost, net income is maximized in these circumstances:

- More patients receive service.
- Individual patients receive more services.
- Increments of service are provided in the least expensive manner.

Actual fee-for-service payment may be less than charges if payers apply the UCR schedule. If the health care provider has agreed to accept the UCR payment as payment in full, payment is usually less than charges. Medicare and Medicaid call this **accepting assignment**. If the patient is responsible for the difference between UCR and charges, payment may be delayed and/or the cost of collecting money owed to the provider may increase.

A health care business may desire to enter into discounted arrangements for two reasons: (1) to keep current market share controlled by third-party payers or (2) to increase market share. Provider risk is minimal in fee-for-service systems. Provider risk in **discounted fee-for-service payment** systems is minimal if discounts are based on good cost and use information. Cost and use information are required to set appropriate percentage discount rates. The provider must set a rate that keeps the total payment above total cost for services provided under the discount arrangement.

Managing With Per Diem Payment

In the per diem payment system, the health care provider is paid a set amount per patient per day. The amount usually covers all specified services provided in the care of the patient for the day. This method of payment can be applied to inpatient and outpatient care. The per diem rate is constant from start to finish. The length of treatment is also an important factor in evaluating per diem payment arrangements. The financial contribution from per diem services may be calculated on a case or contract basis. Net income (loss) is equal to the total payments for the case or contract minus total costs for the case or contract. In the per diem system, net income is maximized in these circumstances:

- More patients receive service.
- Average length of service per patient is longer.

- The health care provider who is at financial risk has control over service use.
- Individual patients receive only the services they require.
- Required services are provided in the least expensive manner.
- Care is coordinated between providers as applicable.
- Provider incentives are aligned to minimize per-day service use and cost.
- Care plans are standardized to minimize variations in care for similar patients.
- Common complications are managed proactively.

Note: Efforts to manage resource use is often referred to as **case management**.

An accurate definition of services covered by the per diem rate is critical to minimizing provider risk. Both parties must agree on the definition of the covered service. The covered services should be specifically documented and acknowledged in writing by all parties. The health care provider does share in the financial risk in the per diem system. The degree of risk depends on the setting, services to be provided, and potential for expensive variation from the standard plan of care. Anything that results in an increased need for services per day will decrease net income.

Managing With Case Rate Payment

In the case rate payment system, also known as case capitation, the health care business offers to provide (1) all of some service or product or (2) all services and products required for the management of a specific patient's case at a preset charge. For example, agreement by a provider to deliver for one inclusive price all health care services for a knee joint arthroplasty is a case rate.

The provider's goal is to set the case payment rate at a level that exceeds the average case cost. Net income (loss) equals the difference between case rate and average cost per case. The average case cost is used because some variation in service use (high and low) is expected. The more cases, the greater the potential net income (loss). Using the average case cost gives a better performance picture. Once the case payment rate is set, the health care provider is responsible for all costs of covered care. This is a risk agreement because the provider is responsible for the delivery of care even if the costs for the case exceed the case payment rate. Complex cases have more potential for variability in the plan of care. Variability in the plan of care between patients also increases the health care provider's risk of incurring unexpected cost. Assuming the case rate covers the average cost of providing the specified care (case cost), net income is maximized in these circumstances:

- More patients receive service.
- The health care provider at financial risk also controls service use.
- Individual patients receive only the services they require.
- Required services are provided in the least expensive manner.
- Care is coordinated between providers and settings as applicable.
- Provider incentives are aligned to minimize service use and cost.
- Care plans are standardized to minimize variations in care for similar patients.
- Common complications are managed proactively.

Accurate definition of the case, including covered services and pricing, is essential to minimizing provider risk. Both the provider and the payer must agree on the definition of the case. The definition should include what is and what is not covered under the case rate. A description of covered services should be written and accepted in writing by all parties. When do services under the case start and stop? How and by whom is the care plan determined? What products are included in the case rate? Is there a point at which the high cost of an individual case will trigger extra payment?

A case that falls well outside the norm for cost and service use is called an **outlier**. Outlier payment provisions are often included in case rate agreements. Outlier provisions act as stop-loss insurance. The outlier provision comes into play when the cost of a case exceeds a preset dollar amount. Outlier provisions limit a provider's financial risk.

Managing With Capitation Payment

Capitation, otherwise called full-risk capitation, is an arrangement in which the provider agrees to accept a preset dollar amount in return for accepting full financial responsibility for the delivery of specified health care services to specified enrollees during the contract period. Capitation is unique to managed health care insurance plans. Capitated payment rates are not based on the actual amount and cost of services used. Rather, capitated rates are based on estimations of the expected amount and cost of services used by the enrollees. Use projections are usually expressed in terms of the amount of service used by the members in a given period. For example, use projections for outpatient therapy services might be expressed as the number of visits or procedures per 1000 plan members per month. The cost of service is based on the average use and cost of services delivered in a managed care approach. The capitation method offers many technical challenges. In our experience, one of the greatest challenges is the accurate projection of service use and related costs when applied to small, self-selected populations of enrollees. According to Berman and associates (1994), without adequate correction for costly outliers, adverse population selection and unreliable use and cost data greatly increase the financial risk assumed by the health care provider. If the payment rate is inadequate, a capitation agreement can jeopardize the financial viability of the provider. Payment under capitation can be based on a set amount of payment per enrollee per month or as a percentage of the monthly premium (Beckley, 1997). Assuming that the payment rate is appropriate for the patient population, net income is maximized in these circumstances:

- Relatively few of the covered patients receive service.
- Access to and use of service is controlled by the at-risk provider.
- Individual patients receive only the services they require.
- Required services are provided in the least expensive manner.
- Care is coordinated between providers and settings as applicable.
- Provider incentives are aligned to minimize service use and cost.
- Care plans are standardized to minimize variations in care for similar patients.
- Common complications are managed proactively.

In capitation payment, the provider benefits when members covered under the plan receive relatively little care and/or services are provided efficiently (Gill, 1995).

Other Payment Practices That May Affect Net Income

Additional payment practices that can affect net income include **quick-pay discounts**, **payer audits**, and prior authorization requirements. An offer by providers to discount billed charges in return for quick payment and an agreement that there will be no audit of charges post payment is known as an offer for a quick-pay discount. This practice minimizes the cost of dollars sitting in non–interest-bearing accounts receivable and payer bad debt. It also improves cash flow (Chapter 27).

Payers audit bills against medical record documentation to verify charges. Documentation is reviewed to determine whether services provided were medically necessary, covered under the plan, and based on a physician-approved plan of care. Charges that cannot be verified or justified are not paid.

Many health insurance plans require the provider, the enrollee, or the enrollee's representative to obtain prior authorization for services. Payment is denied for services that were not authorized in advance of delivery. In this situation, the patient or the provider may be financially responsible for the charges. Responsibility for charges may be determined by a payment agreement signed by the patient, the patient's insurance plan coverage guidelines, and/or a provider participation agreement.

Expense Management

Health care providers are under increasing pressure to demonstrate the cost effectiveness of their services. They are challenged to demonstrate to customers that they provide a better value than the competition. Value, which is defined by the consumer, can be a tangible or intangible measure of the benefit received in return for resources expended (Chapter 26). Providers who produce good outcomes at a relatively low cost are positioned to get the business of customers looking for value. The goal of financial management is to maximize net income. To reach that goal, the spread between gross revenue and total cost must become wider. Armed with a working knowledge of cost characteristics and cost–volume–profit analysis (Chapter 26), managers should be able to predict the effects of their decisions regarding the purchase and use of resources on net income. The importance of efficiently managing resources has increased as payment cuts reduce the net income of most health care businesses. Health care payment rates, even when maximized, are expected to decline over the next several years. As payment rates decline, health care companies must continually improve revenue and/or decrease cost. It should be no surprise that cost management has become a priority for health care businesses. To manage expenses effectively requires knowledge of the types of expenses, what expenses can be controlled, how expenses are controlled, and how expenses behave in relation to volume of service and/or goods produced (Chapters 26 and 27). With this knowledge, expenses can be projected for any future volume of sales. The ability to project volume and related expenses is the foundation for financial planning and creating an operating budget (Chapter 28).

Effective Management of Operating Expenses

Expense management should start with a clear understanding of what the business wants to accomplish. What are the financial targets? Where is the organization in relation to its financial targets now and in the foreseeable future? What is the organization willing to sacrifice to reduce expenses? Clear expectations will guide management decisions about selection, acquisition, and use of resources.

Target time frame is another important aspect of cost management. Is there a need to control expenses for a short or long time? Cost management efforts that are meant to produce a long-term or progressive decrease in operating expenses will require fundamental and sustainable changes in the operating processes. For example, Do It All Therapy anticipated a cash shortfall for the first 3 months because of the opening of a new clinic. The shortfall is due to the large number of incremental expenses associated with opening the new clinic. To cover the payroll without taking out a high-priced short-term loan, the owner–manager has put a hold on all inessential expenditures for 4 months. Instead of using temporary staffing, the manager personally filled staff absences on two occasions. The strategy was to reduce total current expense for a short period. The goal was to preserve the company's short-term cash position. These strategies would be difficult to sustain over time.

Resource Productivity

Chapters 15 and 28 discuss productivity in relation to human resources. The concept of productivity applies to all types of resources. **Productivity** refers to the amount of a resource consumed in the production of a unit of output. As with any other aspect of organizational performance, an objective performance target will help direct management and staff efforts in the right direction. **Productivity standards** are performance targets. To offer maximum benefit, productivity standards should be

- Based on a measurable unit of output
- Objectively measured
- Readily available
- Understandable
- Achievable

Management is responsible for setting productivity standards (performance expectations) for resources consumed. Where productivity standards do not exist or are out of date, new standards should be set according to internal and whenever possible external use data. Internal data demonstrate how well the organization is performing in comparison to its historical performance. Comparison of **external benchmarks** to internal performance measurements will show how the organization is performing in comparison to other similar organizations. External benchmarks may be available through professional organizations, business associations, consultants, proprietary databases, or directly from similar businesses. Even if the organization exceeds external benchmarks, management may find opportunities to improve performance (Chapter 12).

For example, if a physical therapy treatment room must be scheduled for 1 hour per 30 minutes of billable treatment, productivity for the treatment room is 50%. If the time for patient preparation and cleanup could be reduced to 15 minutes per treatment, the productivity of the treatment space would increase to 66.6%. This calculation is a performance standard for operations, but it does not give an accurate representation of the financial productivity of this resource.

Financial productivity measures the total cost of the resource against the value of the output. It can be calculated for any resource used in the production of services and goods for sale. In the case of space, financial productivity can be measured by dividing annual facility expense by total billed treatments per year. This calculation yields the facility cost per treatment. Financial productivity must be known before the production cost of a distinct unit of service or product can be calculated.

Labor Expense Management

Typically, **labor expenses** are a high percentage of the total operating expense of a health care organization. Control of labor expenses can be approached in many ways because there are so many types of labor expenses. Compensation, benefits, recruitment, staff training and development, and employee recognition are the major categories. Examples of labor costs in those categories are listed in Table 29.2.

Labor costs are determined by management decisions such as the following:

- How to obtain needed human resources
- Number of **full time equivalent** (FTE) employees to hire
- Type of FTE employees (skill mix)
- How to recruit for employees
- Whom to hire
- Level and method of compensation
- Benefit package
- Amount of investment in staff training and development
- Type of staff training and development
- Funds available for employee recognition

Table 29.2 Categories and Types of Labor Expenses

Compensation	*Benefits*	*Training and Development*	*Employee Recognition*
Regular compensation	Auto allowance	Paid education time	Subsidized meals
Overtime	Club membership	Paid registration	Recognition events
Holiday differential	Subsidized child care	Travel expenses	Performance awards
Shift differentials	On-site health facility	Tuition reimbursement	
Recruitment bonus	Employee discounts	Continuing education	
Retention bonuses	Stock purchase plans	Professional dues	
Incentive bonus	Employee assistance		
Tuition repayment			
Profit sharing			
Early retirement pay			
Severance pay			

The first decision management must make is whether to hire or contract for needed services. This decision should weigh both cost and performance. The cost can be calculated with the comparative model presented earlier in this chapter. The incremental cost of hiring an employee is compared to the incremental cost of contracting for services. Calculation of performance is likely to be more complex. Performance of contract labor is situational (Chapters 8, 15, and 17–19). The performance of staff brought into a company under contract can be affected by their qualifications, familiarity with the work of the company, the company's ability to orient contract staff to the new environment, contract period, receptivity of employees, and the contracted employees' satisfaction with the arrangement. Contracted employees require the same orientation and training as any other employee if they are to be maximally effective.

Management must also decide the number of FTE employees to hire. Ideally, these decisions should be based on the projected use of the department's products or service and the productivity standards for each budget center. An FTE represents 2080 hours of paid time per year. The 2080 hours represents time when the employee is available to work (productive time) and time when the employee is paid but not available (nonproductive time). In calculating the amount of staff required to get the work done, the nonproductive time must be included in the equation. This process is demonstrated in Figure 29.2. Using this example, if Do It All Therapy projects the demand for 3500 units of physical therapy service, the owner should employ or contract for 0.60 FTE (based on 3500 UOS ÷ 5980 UOS per FTE physical therapist per year) of physical therapy time.

Skill mix is another area in which the manager will need to balance cost and performance demands. Skill mix refers to the types and combination of positions hired. Going back to the example in Figure 29.2, if a physical therapist assistant (PTA) is hired instead of a physical therapist, the lower compensation rate for the PTA will reduce the cost per unit of service. The therapy manager needs to weigh the cost savings that result from lowering the skill mix against the clinical performance requirements of the practice and the types of patients usually treated.

How employees are recruited and who is recruited affects labor cost. Advertising, mailing, exhibiting at conferences, attending career days, and use of recruitment agencies are all options for the recruitment of new staff. Some practices rely on student training programs to provide candidates. Each of these methods has an associated direct cost. Unmet demand for service because of staff vacancies can be associated with the **opportunity cost** of lost revenue (Chapter 26). Management decisions regarding recruitment should weigh the direct cost against the opportunity cost. The goal is to minimize both lost revenues and direct recruitment costs. Who is recruited affects costs of both recruitment and compensation. The more experienced and/or specialized the employee sought, the more likely the recruitment and ongoing compensation costs will be high.

Level and method of employee compensation are often driven by market practices and going rates (Chapter 14). Management must decide whether the organization should lead, keep up, or follow the market going rate for employees. Leading the market generally makes it easier to recruit and may reduce the opportunity cost of vacant positions. Keeping up with the market makes compensation a neutral issue in recruitment. If the market for employees is competitive, other job elements take on a more important role in getting a candidate to accept a position. When management chooses to lag behind a competitive market, recruitment is difficult. In this case, the therapy practice must rely on other employment incentives, such as significant staff development opportunities.

Employee benefits account for an increasing percentage of labor costs. As you can see in Table 29.2, a variety of benefits can be offered to entice employees to join and remain with an organization. The makeup of the benefit package determines its cost. While benefit offers are often driven by market practices, the makeup of the benefits package is a management decision.

Resource Cost Element	Physical Therapist	Physical Therapist Assistant
Amount	1.0 FTE	1.0 FTE
Hours Paid	2080	2080
Non-Productive Hours:		
Vacation	120	120
Holiday	56	56
Education	40	40
Sick/Personal	24	24
Total Non-Productive	240	240
Productive Hours	1840	1840
Billed Hours		
(6.5 Billed Hrs/8 Wrkd Hrs)	1495	1495
UOS (15 Min)	5980	5980
Resource Cost:		
Compensation	$47,008	$37,918
Benefits	8,461	6,825
FICA	3,596	2,901
Education	750	500
Human Resource	200	100
Employee Recognition	100	100
Total Annual Cost	$60,116	$48,344
Position Cost Per UOS	$ 10.05	$ 8.08
Productivity Per Hour Paid	0.72	0.72
Hours Paid Per Hour Billed	1.40	1.40

Figure 29.2. Calculating financial productivity.

Other discretionary labor expenditures include the amount and type of investment in staff training and development and funding for employee recognition. For therapists, funding of continuing education remains a standard benefit. Availability of continuing education funds may not induce a candidate to accept a job offer, but lack of education funding may induce him or her to decline it. Employee recognition can take the form of an awards dinner or a performance bonus. Employee recognition is for the most part discretionary and varies widely among health care businesses.

Nonlabor Expense Management

Although labor costs account for a large percentage of health care business costs, control of other costs is equally important. Watching what the company spends on nonlabor resources is the most obvious approach to controlling both fixed and variable costs (Chapter 27). Using financial modeling, management can and should project the effects of decisions that will change the amount of short-term or long-term fixed costs. Day-to-day decisions about the purchase of resources that make up the variable operating costs should be guided by the budget and volume of services.

The budget provides management with two performance measures to gauge spending patterns (Chapter 29). The first is the total budgeted amount of resource for the period under consideration. Any difference between budgeted and actual resource use shows up as a budget variance. The second performance measure is the expense per increment of service or product. Expense per increment can be viewed in total or broken down into fixed and variable components. If workloads fluctuate, expense per increment may be the only effective way to monitor operating expenses. When budgeted expense per increment is multiplied by the volume of service and product sold, it provides a volume-adjusted total expense performance target. **Flexible budgeting** refers to the use of updated budget expense targets to account for volume fluctuations.

In addition to controlling the use of resources, the health care manager should consider some other opportunities for cost reduction. Group purchasing discounts, **inventory reduction plans**, workload balancing, and service and product outsourcing may all offer cost reduction opportunities.

Group purchasing discounts may be available to high-volume buyers or buyer groups. Identification of opportunities for volume discounts should begin with a review of accounts payable. Management should investigate any expenditures or category of expenditures that show high numbers of purchases or high-dollar expenditures on a regular basis. For example, purchase of all types of office supplies can amount to a considerable annual expense. A volume discount may be available if the purchase of office supplies is consolidated with one vendor. If a single small business has insufficient purchasing power to warrant a discount, a buying group may be able to obtain a discount.

Inventory control is another opportunity for cost reduction that should not be overlooked. Expense is associated with stocking an inventory of supplies or products for sale. Every dollar in inventory is a dollar unavailable for productive investment in other activities of the business.

The use of resources may also be reduced through proactive workload balancing, that is, using a system to match capacity with demand. For example, a therapy practice that directs patients to one of two clinic locations based on availability of schedule openings is engaged in workload balancing. Decreasing the down time of available resources minimizes cost and maximizes productivity.

Outsourcing also offers opportunities for cost reduction. If some aspect of the work of the organization can be performed at a lower cost by an external contractor, outsourcing is an opportunity to reduce cost. Factors such as quality, customer perception, and management control of service all should be considered in the decision to outsource.

Maximizing the Contribution of Capital Expenditures

Because resources are limited, management should determine the potential contribution of a proposed capital purchase. Sometimes called a cost–benefit analysis, this is done to determine the short- and long-term financial effects of the purchase. The results of the cost–benefit analysis can help management make good purchasing decisions and/or set priorities for multiple capital purchase requests. Calculation of the payback period and the expected return on investment are two methods used to assess the desirability of capital purchases.

Payback period is the length of time it will take to recover the entire cost of a capital investment from the annual net cash flow that results from the investment. A shorter payback period means a better investment. Payback is calculated by dividing the capital investment by the projected annual net cash flow. Net cash flow equals revenue less deductions and operating expenses for the business or unit using the asset.

$$\text{Payback period (years)} = \frac{\text{amount to be invested}}{\text{projected annual net cash flow}}$$

Return on invested funds (ROI) is the ratio of the average projected net income from the investment divided by average investment. Average investment is calculated by dividing the total amount invested by two. The average projected net income is calculated for the life of the asset (Finkler and Ward, 1999).

$$\text{ROI} = \frac{\text{average projected net income}}{\text{average investment}} \times 100\%$$

A higher ROI means a better investment. A look at personal finance will help to show how ROI is used. If you were asked to choose between two savings accounts, one offering an interest rate (rate of return) of 5% and the other offering 6.5%, all other factors being equal, you are likely to pick the account that offers the higher rate of return. Use of the ROI ratio allows management to make the same type of decision about a proposed capital expenditure (Gill, 1995).

Monitoring Financial Performance

Financial performance monitoring techniques all have one thing in common: they look for deviations from what was planned to identify potential problems. When a company identifies such a variation, it can take action. Performance variation should be seen as a signal for management attention. If gross revenue and profit are above the target, these **variances** may indicate favorable performance. But until management knows the causes of the variation, its effects cannot be fully assessed. The assumption that a variation is understood without an analysis can cause management to miss future opportunities. If the variance is favorable, management needs to know what the company is doing right so it can keep doing it. If the variance is unfavorable, management needs to know where change is needed (Chapter 12).

A key to effective variance analysis is information presentation. Managers' time is limited. If financial information is difficult to obtain or presented in a format that requires extensive rework, management is less likely to identify performance variances. Variance analysis can also be complicated by lack of detail. Financial information systems should be flexible enough to provide more or less detail depending on the needs of management. General reports help identify variances. More detailed information is often necessary to determine causal factors. Chapter 27 introduces the use of financial reports and financial ratios. **Comparative reports** and **common-size reports** are specifically designed to support variance analysis. Comparative reports present financial information from different sources or periods. A comparative report can be used to compare budget to actual data, budget to budget data, or actual to actual data from one or more periods. Common-size reports provide information in dollars and as a percentage of the total category. Figure 27.4 presents a combined comparative and common-size financial report.

Financial ratio analysis is use of the relationships between two significant mathematical quantities. Financial ratios are used to summarize key financial data in a format that is easy to understand and evaluate. The use of financial ratios is well accepted. This makes it very easy for management and external parties to use ratios to evaluate business performance. Industry standards may be available for comparative analysis. Ratios can be used to assess change in performance over time or as performance benchmarks to compare a company's performance to the industry norm. In either case, the use of ratios is a form of variance analysis.

Student Notes

Some insurance plans hold the health care provider responsible for compliance with the plan's coverage guidelines. The insurer does not pay for services that are not covered, and the provider may not be allowed to bill the enrollee directly without an advance written agreement with the patient. Notably, Medicaid and Medicare typically operate in this manner. It is the responsibility of the provider to know and apply coverage guidelines and limits. A coverage determination for physical therapy requires the treating therapist to have a working knowledge of each payer's coverage guidelines.

Using Medicare as an example, the treating therapist is largely responsible for providing only services for which coverage provided. The therapist must know:

- Which services and products are covered under the Medicare program
- The conditions under which coverage is available and when coverage is restricted
- The specific services and equipment needed by the patient
- The criteria Medicare uses to determine whether services are considered to be reasonable and necessary for a specific patient

INDIVIDUAL CASE STUDY

Consider a small physical therapy practice. The owner knows the average cost per patient treatment is $45 and the average number of treatments per patient referral is six. Also, 45% of the owner's business comes from one managed care plan. The MCO that offers this plan wants to renew its physical therapy contracts at $43 per visit. If the owner does not renew, she will not have enough business to pay her bills. Should she renew? What should she consider in making that decision?

Under Medicare, to be reasonable and necessary, services and equipment must be expected to result in a reasonable level of improvement in a reasonable and generally predictable time. Finally, the therapist must document information in support of the clinical decision, including patient history, status, and improvement over time. Should Medicare dispute the therapist's decision and deny coverage, the therapist must be prepared to defend the decision during an appeal.

The example demonstrates the size of the responsibility of individual health care providers for the financial success of their employer or their own business.

Summary

Financial management principles are constant, which makes it possible for multiple internal and external users to interpret the financial information produced by an organization. The application of financial information and accounting principles to management of revenue collection and expense containment allow management to plan and implement strategies to maximize financial performance. This chapter reviews models for health care reimbursement. It discusses approaches to managing for maximum revenue, for example, payer mix, skill mix, and inventory control. The essential considerations for those examining managed care agreements are presented. The financial implications of providing services in various fixed-payment reimbursement systems are compared with each other and with fee-for-service arrangements. Expense management for operating expenses such as labor costs and the importance of careful assessment of prospective investment in capital equipment are reviewed. The prin-

GROUP CASE STUDY

Form a group of four members. Each of you are major stockholders of Do It All Therapy, Inc.

Situation

Do It All Therapy is faced with a 2.5% annual decline in reimbursement. To be competitive, it has offered its professional staff an annual increase of 5% and support staff an annual increase of 3%. Obviously, this trend cannot be sustained indefinitely. Develop four strategies to widen the narrowing gap between total revenue net deductions and expenses. Consider the relationships between volume, payer mix, case mix, and expense for each strategy.

Task

Each of you take on one of the strategies and bring your recommendation to the rest of your group for discussion. Come to a consensus on the best path to take based on your discussion.

ciples of revenue and expense management are demonstrated with examples throughout the chapter. Profitability is the goal. Financial planning and good management are both important for successful fulfillment of this goal.

Getting paid by third-party payers requires understanding and appropriately using alphanumeric codes. For payment to be issued, third-party payers often require the provider to note the diagnosis and treatment. This process is coding. The next chapter deals with diagnostic and service codes with an emphasis on those often used by physical therapists.

References

Beckley NJ. Reviewing contracts. Rehab 1997; April/May:128–129.

Berman HJ, Kukla SF, Weeks LE. The financial management of hospitals, 8th ed. Ann Arbor, MI: Health Administration. 1994.

Centers for Medicare and Medicaid Services. EMTALA. Available from http://www.cms.hhs.gov/faca/ppac/emtalaup.pdf. Accessed 12/28/02.

Finkler SA, Ward DM. Essentials of cost accounting for health care organizations, 2nd ed. Gaithersburg, MD: Aspen. 1999.

Garrison RH. Managerial accounting: Concepts for planning, control, decision making, Revised ed. Dallas: Business Publications. 1979.

Gill HS. The changing nature of ambulatory rehabilitation programs and services in a managed care environment. Archives of Physical Medicine and Rehabilitation. 1995;76:SC-10–15.

Health and Human Services. Overview of program management and financial performance FY 2001. Available from http.www.hhs.gov/of/reports. Accessed 11/1/02.

Nosse LJ, Friberg DG. Management principles for physical therapists. Baltimore: Williams & Wilkins. 1992.

More Information Related to This Chapter

A preview of accounting processes available in Excel spreadsheet software is available at http://www.iol19.com/murphy/excel/. The Code of Professional Conduct for Certified Public Accountants is available at http://www.aicpa.org/about/code/index.htm.

A recent readable and relevant text on financial management is Cleverly WO, Cameron AE. Essentials of health care finance, 5th ed. Gaithersburg, MD: Aspen. 2002.

For strategic financial planning see Ginter PM, Swayne LM, Duncan WJ. Strategic management of health care organizations. Malden, MA: Blackwell. 1998:314–340.

For several of the topics covered in this chapter, including costing out services and reimbursement incentives of various payment systems, see The reimbursement resource book. Alexandria, VA: APTA. 2000.

Chapter 30

Coding

Learning Objectives

1. Examine the unique purposes of the major coding systems.
2. Contrast the actual codes that make up the major coding systems.
3. Given the appropriate resources and data, correctly code for disease, services provided, and supplies used.
4. Analyze the relationship between Current Procedural Terminology and the Resource-Based Relative Value Scale.
5. Explore the consequences of underbilling as discussed in this chapter.

Key Words

Centers for Medicare and Medicaid Services (CMS), coding, Current Procedural Terminology, 4th edition (CPT-4), diagnosis-related group (DRG), Health Care Financing Administration (HCFA), Health Care Financing Administration common procedural coding system (HCPCS), International Classification of Diseases, 9th revision (ICD-9), International Classification of Diseases, 9th revision, Clinical Modification (ICD-9-CM), resource-based relative value scale (RBRVS), resource utilization group, version 3 (RUG-III), underbilling

Introduction

Coding is the health care industry equivalent of a barcode for payers. You must understand and be able to use several coding systems if you want to get paid for the services you provide. The coding system used depends on the type of setting in which services are delivered. Table 30.1 shows the variety of settings, mechanisms of reimbursement, categorization system, coding schema, and resources for more information.

The setting is the location or service type where the physical therapy services are provided. The reimbursement mechanism describes the manner in which payment for services is calculated (Chapters 21, 28, and 29). The categorization system is the way the services are classified so that the reimbursement can be applied. The coding schema is the tool or mechanism used to determine how to apply the categorization system to a specific patient. The final column shows resources for current information. The resources are provided because each of these coding systems has specific requirements and extensive guidelines. In addition, each coding system is specific to the settings and conditions of services indicated in the table.

The codes listed in Table 30.1 form coding systems. These systems are most often identified by their abbreviations rather than by their full names. A working knowledge of the

Table 30.1 Variables Associated With Coding Systems

Setting	*Reimbursement Mechanism*	*Categorization System*	*Coding Schema*	*Further Information*
Acute-care hospital inpatient	Prospective payment system	Diagnosis related groups (DRG)[ab]	DRG	www.AcutePT.org
Rehab hospital inpatient	Prospective payment system	PAI[c]-based groups, resource use	IRF[d]- PAI	www.cms.hhs.gov/providers/infpps
Hospital outpatient	Medicare physician fee schedule	HCPCS[e]/CPT[f]	CPT-4[g]	www.APTA.org www.PTManager.com
Physical therapist, private practice	Medicare physician fee schedule	HCPCS/CPT	CPT-4	www.APTA.org www.PTManager.com
Rehab agency	Medicare physician fee schedule	HCPCS/CPT	CPT-4	www.APTA.org www.PTManager.com
Certified outpatient rehabilitation facility	Medicare physician fee schedule	HCPCS/CPT	CPT-4	www.APTA.org www.PTManager.com
Skilled nursing facility, Medicare Part A	Prospective payment system	Minimum data set[h]	RUG-IIIi	www.APTA.org
Home health agency	Prospective payment system	Diagnostic category		www.APTA.org

[a]Diagnostic related group (CMS, 2003a, b).
[b]Patient Assessment Instrument (CMS, 2003c).
[c]Inpatient rehabilitation facility (CMS, 2003c).
[d]Health Care Financing Administration Common Procedural coding system (CMS, 2003d).
[e]Common procedural terminology (AMA, 2003).
[f]Common Procedural Terminology Manual, 4th ed. (AMA, 2003).
[g]Minimum Data Set 3.0 (CMS, 2003e).
[h]Resource Utilization Group, 3rd ed. (CMS, 2003f).

coding system associated with documenting what care was provided, to whom, the diagnosis and functional limitations is as important to being a competent professional as is rendering evidence-based care.

Physical therapists and physical therapy practices use many coding systems. They code to describe the diagnosis of the patient (typically ICD-9-CM) (American Physical Therapy Association [APTA], 2001a) and the clinical procedures provided (typically CPT-4) (American Medical Association [AMA], 2003).

Describing the Diagnosis: ICD-9

The ***International Classification of Diseases, 9th Revision, Clinical Modification*** (ICD-9-CM) is the World Health Organization's official classification of diseases (AMA, 2000). ICD-9 is designed for statistical classification of morbidity and mortality information, for indexing of hospital records by disease and operations, and for data storage and retrieval. The historical background of the ICD-9 may be found in the Introduction to ICD-9 of the Manual of the International Classification of Diseases, Injuries, and Causes of Death (World Health Organization, 1977).

ICD-9-CM is a clinical modification of ICD-9. The term *clinical* is used to emphasize the modification's intent: to serve as a useful tool for classification of morbidity data for indexing of medical records, medical care review, and ambulatory and other medical care programs, as well as for basic health statistics. To describe the clinical picture of the patient, the codes must be more precise than those needed only for statistical groupings and trend analysis. ICD-9-CM must be used by all hospitals receiving federal funds (Kovner and Jonas, 1999).

Guidance in the Use of ICD-9-CM

To code accurately, it is necessary to have a working knowledge of medical terminology and to understand the characteristics, terminology, and conventions of the ICD-9-CM. Transforming verbal descriptions of diseases, injuries, conditions, and procedures into numeric designations (coding) is a complex activity and should not be undertaken without proper training.

Originally coding was to provide access to medical records by diagnoses and operations for retrieval for medical research, education, and administration. Medical codes today are used to facilitate payment of health services, to evaluate use patterns, and to study the appropriateness of health care costs. ICD-9 codes provide the bases for epidemiologic studies and research into the quality of health care. Therefore, disease coding must be correct and consistent to produce meaningful data to aid in planning for the health needs of the nation. Questions regarding the use and interpretation of ICD-9-CM can be directed to any of the organizations listed in Table 30.2.

Example of ICD-9-CM Coding for a Common Physical Therapy Diagnosis

One common diagnosis for physical therapy is internal derangement of the knee. The following is an example of diagnostic coding that might apply to such a diagnosis. This information is excerpted from the ICD-9-CM manuals (AMA, 2000).

Table 30.2 Resources for Information on ICD-9-CM Codes

Centers for Medicare and Medicaid Services
Division of Prospective Payment System
1H1 East High Rise
6325 Security Blvd.
Baltimore MD 21207

Central Office on ICD-9-CM
American Hospital Association
1 North Franklin
Chicago IL 60606

National Center for Health Statistics
Centers for Disease Control and Prevention
Department of Health and Human Services
6525 Belcrest Road
Hyattsville MD 20782

ICD Code 717: Internal Derangement of Knee

Includes degeneration of articular cartilage or meniscus of knee rupture, old, of articular cartilage or meniscus of knee
Excludes acute derangement of knee (836.0–836.6)
Ankylosis (718.5)
Contracture (718.4)
Current injury (836.0–836.6)
Deformity (736.4–736.6)
Recurrent dislocation (718.3)

717.0 Old bucket handle tear of medial meniscus
Old bucket handle tear of unspecified cartilage
717.1 Derangement of anterior horn of medial meniscus
717.2 Derangement of posterior horn of medial meniscus
717.3 Other and unspecified derangement of medial meniscus
Degeneration of internal semilunarcartilage
17.4 Derangement of lateral meniscus
17.40 Derangement of lateral meniscus, unspecified
17.41 Bucket handle tear of lateral meniscus
17.42 Derangement of anterior horn of lateral meniscus
17.43 Derangement of posterior horn of lateral meniscus
17.49 Other
17.5 Derangement of meniscus, not elsewhere classified
Congenital discoid meniscus
Cyst of semilunar cartilage
Derangement of semilunar cartilage NOS
717.6 Loose body in knee
Joint mice, knee
Rice bodies, knee (joint)
717.7 Chondromalacia of patella
Chondromalacia patellae
Degeneration [softening] of articular cartilage of patella
717.8 Other internal derangement of knee
717.81 Old disruption of lateral collateral ligament

717.82 Old disruption of medial collateral ligament
717.83 Old disruption of anterior cruciate ligament
717.84 Old disruption of posterior cruciate ligament
717.85 Old disruption of other ligaments of knee
Capsular ligament of knee
717.89 Other
Old disruption of ligaments of knee NOS

Example of ICD-9 Codes for a Common Physical Therapy Practice Pattern From the Guide to Physical Therapist Practice

This list contains the current (at this writing) and most typical three- and four-digit ICD-9-CM codes for the example preferred practice pattern. Because patient diagnostic classification is based on impairments, functional limitations, and disabilities—not on codes—patients may be classified in the pattern even though the codes listed with the pattern do not apply to those clients (APTA, 2001b). This list is intended for general information only and should not be used for coding. The codes should be confirmed by referring to the ICD-9-CM, Volumes 1 and 3 (AMA, 2000) or subsequent revisions or by referring to other ICD-9-CM coding manuals that contain exclusion notes and instructions regarding fifth-digit requirements (for example Hart and Hopkins, 2002). The online draft version of ICD-10 PCS will be in field trials for several years (Centers for Medicare and Medicaid Services [CMS], 2003g).

The following are the common ICD-9 codes for common physical therapy practice pattern 5E: impaired motor function and sensory integrity associated with progressive disorders of the central nervous system (APTA, 2001c)

042 Human immunodeficiency virus [HIV] disease
191 Malignant neoplasm of brain
192 Malignant neoplasm of other and unspecified parts of nervous system
237 Neoplasm of uncertain behavior of endocrine glands and nervous system
237.5 Brain and spinal cord
303 Alcohol dependence syndrome
303.9 Ataxia
331 Other cerebral degenerations
331.0 Alzheimer's disease
331.3 Communicating hydrocephalus
331.4 Obstructive hydrocephalus
332 Parkinson's disease
333 Other extrapyramidal disease and abnormal movement disorders
333.0 Other degenerative diseases of the basal ganglia
333.3 Tics of organic origin
333.4 Huntington's chorea
333.9 Other and unspecified extrapyramidal diseases and abnormal movement disorders
334 Spinocerebellar disease
334.2 Primary cerebellar degeneration
334.3 Other cerebellar ataxia
334.8 Other spinocerebellar diseases
335 Anterior horn cell disease
335.0 Werdnig-Hoffmann disease
335.1 Spinal muscular atrophy
335.2 Motor neuron disease
336 Other diseases of spinal cord
336.0 Syringomyelia and syringobulbia
340 Multiple sclerosis
341 Other demyelinating diseases of central nervous system
341.8 Other demyelinating diseases of central nervous system
Central demyelination of corpus callosum
341.9 Demyelinating disease of central nervous system, unspecified
345 Epilepsy
345.4 Partial epilepsy, with impairment of consciousness
Epilepsy:
partial
secondarily generalized
345.5 Partial epilepsy, without mention of impairment of consciousness
Epilepsy:
sensory induced
348 Other conditions of brain
348.9 Unspecified condition of brain

780 General symptoms
780.3 Convulsions
781 Symptoms involving nervous and musculoskeletal systems
781.2 Abnormality of gait
Gait:
ataxic
781.3 Lack of coordination
Ataxia, not otherwise specified

These examples clearly show the applicability of ICD-9 CM diagnostic codes to physical therapists to link diagnosis and functional impairment. In addition to the diagnostic codes there are codes for treatment procedures, medical equipment, and related supplies.

Current Procedural Terminology Coding[1]

The reimbursement environment in physical therapy is a challenging one, with payment policies changing on a daily basis. **Current Procedural Terminology** (**CPT**) 4 is one of the many reimbursement tools that can help improve the efficiency in the management of patient accounts. When clearly understood and effectively applied to describe your clinical services, the CPT codes can convey clearly to the payer what services were provided to the patient. Payers, referral sources and even our patients rely on the coding system known as CPT-4 or Physician's Current Procedural Terminology—Fourth Edition for a description of their health care providers services (AMA, 2003). Following is a discussion of what CPT is, how it has developed since its inception in 1966, and an update of recent code revisions and additions that will most likely affect how your physical therapy services are reported. The scope of applications of the CPT codes is rapidly increasing, as the largest payer in the country (Medicare) requires CPT codes for all rehabilitation services provided in an outpatient setting. This includes hospital-based outpatient settings, comprehensive outpatient rehabilitation facilities, rehabilitation agencies, physical therapists in private practice, home care provided to the nonhomebound patient, and skilled nursing facilities providing outpatient services under Medicare Part B. Most private payers and workers' compensation carriers also require CPT codes for physical therapy services. It pays to know the codes!

What is CPT?

CPT is a comprehensive classification and nomenclature system used to identify services performed by health care providers. The CPT system includes more than 8000 five-digit codes, each of which is assigned to a description of a service or procedure. The physical medicine and rehabilitation section of the CPT manual has 44 codes that describe services a physical therapist can provide. More than 140 codes describe services within the scope of physical therapy practice as described by the Guide to Physical Therapist Practice. The other reimbursement tools were noted earlier, that is, ICD-9 CM, describing diagnoses, and the HCPCS, which Medicare uses to describe supplies and other ancillary services.

How Is CPT Used?

A CPT code's primary function is to provide a common language for communicating what services have been provided to a patient. The CPT system works to simplify claims processing by providing an abbreviated descriptor and code suitable for use on health insurance claim forms. Other uses of CPT codes include providing a comprehensive account of the health care services commonly performed. This alone can be a useful resource for both the provider and the payer to summarize what services different practitioners are performing and to develop an evolutionary perspective of health care delivery.

CPT codes can also provide a mechanism for therapists to gain valuable information about the services they provide in their own practices, such as tracking the use of CPT codes to quantify the use or volume of specific procedures. Links are also made between CPT codes and the diagnosis documented on the claim form. This valuable tool can be an efficient and effective way to perform practice forecasting or for reporting for credentialing purposes. Because of the current emphasis on medical fraud and abuse (Chapters 2, 3, and 5), it is even more important that CPT codes be used accurately to describe the services provided.

How Is the CPT System Maintained?

The CPT manual is updated annually to reflect the most current services provided. As new procedures and technologies are introduced

[1]Courtesy of Helene Fearon.

and other procedures become obsolete, the CPT manual is revised to reflect those changes through an organized and thorough process. APTA has been actively involved in this process since 1993 as a member of the AMA CPT advisory panel. The goal of this active involvement is to ensure that services provided by physical therapists are accurately described in the CPT manual.

The AMA publishes the CPT manual and owns the copyright to the CPT-4 system (AMA, 2003). The AMA facilitates the maintenance of the CPT system by providing for comprehensive review. Any proposals to add, modify, or delete codes go through several important steps, including research, consultation, and action by AMA coding experts, the CPT advisory committee, and ultimately the CPT editorial panel. APTA participates by appointing a representative to the CPT editorial panel's Heath Care Professionals Advisory Committee (HCPAC). This committee, which represents health care providers other than physicians, advises the editorial panel on proposed codes. The members of the HCPAC also develop and present coding proposals pertaining to their profession. APTA has proposed and achieved code additions, deletions, and revisions each year beginning with the initial review and revision of the 97000 series, Physical Medicine and Rehabilitation CPT codes, in 1995 and continuing with the most recent addition of a code describing the assessment for assistive technology (for 2004) and revision and addition of new codes describing active wound care management (for 2005).

Knowing how to describe your services and being as consistent as possible when doing so will be one of the most important tools you can use in achieving reimbursement for your services. The hands-on nature of what we do in physical therapy practice can be conveyed to others effectively for reimbursement purposes only when the codes come to life through their proper use and our effective documentation.

CPT Codes and Payment

CPT codes identify the services provided. Payment for the coded services is based on the resources used in providing the services. A national Medicare payment scale known as the **Resource-Based Relative Value Scale (RBRVS)** is related to CPT codes. RBRVS is calculated by applying a complex formula to set a base dollar value for services provided by physicians and other health care providers to Medicare beneficiaries. The resources considered in the computation include the time to provide service, training and skill needed to provide service, practice expense, and liability costs. The RBRVS assigns values to each service based on the resources associated with providing the service. To maintain the relative payment concept, geographic differences in expenses are recognized through adjustment factors. Other third-party payers also use the RBRVS to determine provider fees (Kongsvedt, 2002).

Table 30.3 lists common CPT codes used by physical therapists. This table includes the code and a short description of it, whether it is a timed code, and comments on the description and type of code. Timed codes, such as procedural codes, are typically counted as multiples of 15-minute interventions. Untimed codes are billed as single use regardless of duration of the intervention. Coding has been fraught with legal and ethical issues. Sometimes codes have been used illegally to maximize income. However, we find that therapists sometimes are reluctant to charge for the services they provided. There are consequences for the organization when this occurs.

Underbilling[2]

Therapists are often concerned with appropriately charging patients for the services the therapists perform. The federal government and commercial payers alike have been scrutinizing overbilling practices by providers. But has anyone shown concern for those who practice the underbilling of services? The Office of the Inspector General (Chapters 3 and 4) and other federal government agencies are starting to take notice, and so are the organizations and facilities for which you work. First, for the purpose of this discussion, let's define underbilling.

Underbilling is the conscious process of not billing for all of the services provided on a

[2]Adapted with permission from Lane DO, Kovacek PR. Underbilling: Advance for Directors of Rehabilitation. 2000;January: 14, 15.

Table 30.3 Common CPT Codes Used By Physical Therapists

Code	Description	Timed	Comments	Type
97001	Physical therapy evaluation	No		Evaluation
97002	Physical therapy reevaluation	No		Evaluation
97003	Occupational therapy evaluation	No		Evaluation
97004	Occupational therapy reevaluation	No		Evaluation
97005	Athletic training evaluation	No		Evaluation
97006	Athletic training reevaluation	No		Evaluation
97010	Hot or cold pack	No	Application of modality to one or more areas:	Modalities—supervised
97012	Traction, mechanical	No	Application of modality to one or more areas:	Modalities—supervised
97014	Electrical stimulation (unattended)	No	Application of modality to one or more areas:	Modalities—supervised
97016	Vasopneumatic devices	No	Application of modality to one or more areas:	Modalities—supervised
97018	Paraffin bath	No	Application of modality to one or more areas:	Modalities—supervised
97020	Microwave	No	Application of modality to one or	Modalities—supervised more areas:
97022	Whirlpool	No	Application of modality to one or more areas:	Modalities—supervised
97024	Diathermy	No	Application of modality to one or more areas:	Modalities—supervised
97026	Infrared	No	Application of modality to one or more areas:	Modalities—supervised
97028	Ultraviolet	No	Application of modality to one or more areas:	Modalities—supervised
97032	Electrical stimulation (manual)	Each 15 min	Application of modality to one or more areas that requires direct (1 to 1) patient contact by provider	Modalities—constant Attendance
97033	Iontophoresis	Each 15 min	Application of modality to one or more areas that requires direct (1 to 1) patient contact by provider	Modalities—constant Attendance
97034	Contrast baths	Each 15 min	Application of modality to one or more areas that requires direct (1 to 1) patient contact by provider	Modalities—constant Attendance
97035	Ultrasound	Each 15 min	Application of modality to one or more areas that requires direct (1 to 1) patient contact by provider	Modalities—constant Attendance
97036	Hubbard tank	Each 15 min	Application of modality to one or more areas that requires direct(1 to 1) patient contact by provider	Modalities—constant Attendance
97039	Unlisted modality	Each 15 min	Application of modality to one or more areas that requires direct (1 to 1) patient contact by provider	Modalities—constant Attendance

(continued)

Table 30.3 Common CPT Codes Used By Physical Therapists *(Continued)*

Code	Description	Timed	Comments	Type
97110	Therapeutic exercises to to develop strength and and endurance, range of motion, and flexibility	Each 15 min	Therapeutic procedure, one or more areas	Therapeutic proce dures 1 on 1 only
97112	Neuromuscular reeducation of movement, balance, coordination, kinesthetic sense, posture, and proprioception	Each 15 min	Therapeutic procedure, one or more areas	Therapeutic procedures 1 on 1 only
97113	Aquatic therapy with therapeutic exercises	Each 15 min	Therapeutic procedure, one or more areas	Therapeutic procedures 1 on 1 only
97116	Gait training, includes stair climbing	Each 15 min	Therapeutic procedure, one or more areas	Therapeutic procedures 1 on 1 only
97124	Massage, including effleurage, petrissage and/or tapotement (stroking, compression, percussion)	Each 15 min	Therapeutic procedure, one or more areas	Therapeutic procedures 1 on 1 only
97139	Unlisted therapeutic procedure (specify)	Each 15 min	Therapeutic procedure, one or more areas	Therapeutic procedures 1 on 1 only
97140	Manual therapy techniques (e.g., mobilization manipulation, manual lymphatic drainage, manual traction)	Each 15 min	Therapeutic procedure, one or more areas	Therapeutic procedures 1 on 1 only
97150	Therapeutic procedure(s), group (2 or more individuals)	No	Therapeutic procedure, one or more areas	Therapeutic procedures Not 1 on 1
97504	Orthotics fitting and training, upper or lower extremities	Each 15 min	Therapeutic procedure, one or more areas	Therapeutic procedures 1 on 1 only
97520	Prosthetic training, upper and/or lower extremities	Each 15 min	Therapeutic procedure, one or more areas	Therapeutic procedures 1 on 1 only
97530	Therapeutic activities, use of dynamic activities to improve functional performance	Each 15 min	Therapeutic procedure, one or more areas	Therapeutic procedures 1 on 1 only
97532	Cognitive skills development	Each 15 min	Therapeutic procedure, one or more areas	Therapeutic procedures 1 on 1 only
97533	Sensory integration	Each 15 min	Therapeutic procedure, one or more areas	Therapeutic procedures 1 on 1 only
97535	Self care/home management training (e.g., ADL and compensatory training, meal preparation, safety procedures, and instruction in use of adaptive equipment)	Each 15 min	Therapeutic procedure, one or more areas	Therapeutic procedures 1 on 1 only
97537	Community/work reintegration training (e.g., shopping, transportation, money management, avocational activities and/or work environment modification analysis, work task analysis)	Each 15 min	Therapeutic procedure, one or more areas	Therapeutic procedures 1 on 1 only

(continued)

Table 30.3 Common CPT Codes Used By Physical Therapists *(Continued)*

Code	Description	Timed	Comments	Type
97542	Wheelchair management/ propulsion training	Each 15 min	Therapeutic procedure, one or more areas	Therapeutic procedures 1 on 1 only
97545	Work hardening/conditioning, initial 2 hours	2 hours	Therapeutic procedure, one or more areas	
97546	Work hardening/conditioning, each additional hour	Additional hour	Therapeutic procedure, one or more areas	
97601	Wound care—selective debridement	No	Therapeutic procedure, one or more areas	
97602	Wound care—nonselective debridement	No		
97703	Checkout for orthotic/ prosthetic use, established patient	Each 15 min	Therapeutic procedure, one or more areas	Therapeutic procedures 1 on 1 only
97750	Physical performance test or measurement (e.g., musculoskeletal, functional capacity) with written report	Each 15 min		Tests and Measurements
97770	Development of cognitive skills to improve attention, memory, problem solving, includes compensatory training and/or sensory integrative activities	Each 15 min	Therapeutic procedure, one or more areas	Therapeutic proceedures 1 on 1 only
97780	Acupuncture, one or more needles, without electrical stimulation	No		Other procedures
97781	Acupuncture, one or more needles, with electrical stimulation	No		Other procedures
97799	Unlisted physical medicine/ rehabilitation service or procedure	Each 15 min		Other therapeutic procedures 1 on 1 only

Reprinted with permission from Kovacek Management Services (2003).

given date. For example, you are treating an ankle patient with commercial insurance who in the course of the treatment receives 30 minutes of therapeutic exercise, 15 minutes of gait training, joint mobilization, and ice at the conclusion of the treatment. When it comes time to charge for the treatment, you charge for two therapeutic exercises, one gait training, and one hot/cold pack. Based on the number of modalities that occurred in the treatment, you opt not to charge for the joint mobilization (manual therapy, 15 minutes).

The most likely reason for not billing for all services performed is the notion that the charges for those services are too high and therefore extremely expensive to the patient. Underbilling for services has the potential to affect many of your facility's internal operations and can lead to investigations into your billing practices by outside agencies. The following discussion will examine four effects, both internal and external, of underbilling.

Effect 1: Reimbursement

Underbilling of services affects reimbursement in several ways. First, billing for services rendered ultimately generates reimbursement to your facility. Should you elect not to charge for all of the services performed, you are leaving reimbursement money on the table. Your facility loses the reimbursement for services not billed. Second, if services are reimbursed on a per-visit rate, case rate, or capitated rate, services not billed still affect reimbursement. While the services may not be billed in units to the payer in these payment mechanisms, the number of units of care performed is used in negotiations for per-visit rates, case rates, and capitation rates. If the units of care are understated, the facility cannot demonstrate an accurate level of clinical activity. When a facility engages in contract negotiations with an insurance company, the facility needs to understand the cost of operations as it relates to charge activity. Simply put, they like to know the cost of operations for each charge rendered (for example, it costs the facility $8 for every procedure or modality charge). This ratio of costs to charges can be extrapolated into an average per-visit charge for patient care services. Armed with this information, the facility can properly negotiate reimbursement that is in its best interest. Third, if reimbursement dollars are affected by underbilling, so then is the use of that lost money in operations of the facility. If the reimbursed dollars are less than expected or budgeted, current and future operations are affected (Chapters 27–29). Operations may be affected in terms of facilities planning and improvement, equipment and supply purchasing and budgeting, and staffing and benefits budgeting. Health care facilities are already faced with streamlining and cutting operational expenses due to declining reimbursement. Underbilling of services only compounds the problem of lost dollars to the facility.

Effect 2: Collection of Co-payments

Many commercial insurers base the calculation of co-payments on either a percentage of charges or a percentage of a fee schedule (Chapter 2). For instance, Medicare requires that calculations of co-payments for outpatients be based on 20% of the Medicare fee schedule. Collected co-payments are a direct source of cash to the organization unless otherwise specified contractually. If the charges are underbilled, the co-payment is also low. The resulting effect is less cash for the organization. This is likely to affect operations (Chapters 27–29).

Effect 3: Productivity and Staffing

Many staff productivity measurement tools are based on the number of units generated by each clinician treating patients (Chapter 17). Each individual clinician may have an established productivity goal. Similarly, management bases staffing decisions on the total productivity of the department or facility. If therapists are appearing underproductive, the need for additional staffing may not be recognized. If you are a clinician in these types of productivity systems, underbilling directly affects you, your productivity, and potentially your peers as it pertains to department staffing.

In large facilities that use labor distribution systems, the number of productive FTE employees may be measured and monitored by unit production (Chapter 28). Underbilling will affect the interpretation of these measures as well. Typically the finance department uses these systems to track and forecast staffing needs. In this scenario, future budgeting of payroll will be affected by underbilling. If a department appears underproductive and a reduction in payroll appears warranted, the department may be hard pressed to request the same or a higher allocation for payroll.

So how do you identify underbilling? Recognition of underbilling fortunately is the easy part. Connect the dots. Whenever clinicians perform treatment, they must do two other things. They must document that treatment occurred and they must bill for that treatment. Your task is to gather these two pieces of documentation and audit them (Chapter 12). Use a suitably sized sample of patients for each clinician each month and gather the treatment notes or complete medical record and a corresponding sample of the bills for each patient for the dates of service that you are reviewing. Now, connect the dots. If the note says 30 minutes of therapeutic exercise, the bill should have two units of therapeutic exercise (two units of CPT code 97110 [Table 30.3]) for the same date of service. Continue this procedure for all of the dates you have chosen to review. Keep an audit worksheet for every clinician and every patient's documentation you review. It is highly recommended that you attach a copy of the treatment notes and bills reviewed. This establishes a viable set of working papers that supports your efforts, and it provides a quick and easy way of creating a set of documents that may be used as a feedback and corrective action plan document for each staff member reviewed.

Before you create an entirely new review process, consider the fact that most departments carry out some form of monthly peer review or quality assurance mechanism (Chapter 13). When this is true, the only pieces missing are the bill review and the audit tool to match the documentation to the bills and summarize your findings. This documentation and billing audit may be performed at the peer level, but to address the sensitive nature of this information, it is recommended that management review the results and work papers and give feedback to the staff member.

Effect 4: Positive Results

If billing is reviewed, addressed, and monitored by department or facility management, the results will be positive for all involved. The likely positive results for management:

- Reduced risk of governmental scrutiny
- Less reimbursement lost
- Greater co-payments accuracy
- Improved cash flow
- Improved accuracy of data for negotiating contracts with payers
- Improved accuracy of data for forecasting and budgeting internal operations
- Better data for staffing decisions
- Improved staff productivity measurement
- Improved reimbursement

Student Notes

There are at least three reasons to appropriately document what you do to patients. The first reason is legal. If you knowingly miscode the treatment given to a Medicare or Medicaid beneficiary, it can be considered abuse, fraud, or both. It may be a federal offense. The second reason is financial. If you are in a small practice and the therapists do nearly everything from scheduling to cleaning to patient care to coding, you must code accurately or you will probably place the business in financial jeopardy. If your organization contracts out coding, you have the moral obligation to know that the billing codes were correct to the best of your knowledge. If you work in a large institution, there is a billing department. However, you retain the professional responsibility to know that the codes used are accurate and within the law. The final reason has to do with research. The association between diagnosis and treatment is one way to determine which treatments are more effective and efficient than the alternatives. The assignment of diagnostic or treatment codes influenced more by financial motives than accuracy brings inaccurate information to databases used to identify preferred practice patterns. The bottom line is that understanding the codes associated with identifying your patients' diagnosis, what treatment you gave, and how long you treated them are important only if you want payment (in salary or directly) for treating the patient.

Summary

Payment in cash for services at the time services are provided is the best way to ensure that payment will be received. Few patients and clients pay cash. Services are mostly provided on credit, and the payer is a third party. Third parties need ways to verify that services were properly given to their policy owners, beneficiaries, or members and some way to compare treatments in terms of frequency, appropriateness, and efficacy. Requiring a diagnostic code allows grouping patients with the same main diagnosis and making comparisons with diagnosis as the common feature. A common diagnostic coding method is the World Health Organization's International Classification of Diseases, Clinical Modification. The link between this coding system and the practice of physical therapy is clearly demonstrated throughout the *Guide to Physical Therapist Practice*, 2nd edition. The coding system also describes health care services for third-party payers and others. The AMA's *Current Procedural Terminology Manual*, 4th edition, provides codes for physician and other outpatient procedures and services. For physical therapists the rehabilitation medicine codes, the 97000 codes, are most relevant. To attach dollar amounts to CPT codes there is an annual evaluation of the amount of work required to administer the procedure, the expenses associated with providing the service, and the risk of malpractice suits associated with the professionals who provide the service. A new base monetary amount is calculated each year, and coded services are assigned dollar amounts according to this base amount. Procedures that require more work and are riskier than base factors receive higher payments, and those that require less than the base factors are assigned lower pay-

INDIVIDUAL CASE STUDY

There is always a temptation to make more money. There is always an ethical obligation to be just in your interactions with stakeholders (Chapter 6; APTA, 2001a). And then there is law (Chapters 3 and 5). In the case of coding for treatment for Medicare beneficiaries, breaking the law by altering treatment codes to increase payment or billing for services that were not provided may well result in prosecution for fraud and abuse. The Offices of the Inspector General (OIG) are always watching. Take a look at the OIG site: http://fda.gov/oc/reform/OIG2/oig_guide_21292.htm.

ments. Because of regional cost differences there are regional payment differences for the same code.

To get paid for services assumes there are patients to treat. Ways people find information about what physical therapy provides are what they hear about the provider from their acquaintances (word of mouth) and what they read in ads and from Internet sources. Physicians may base their decision to refer a patient to a specific physical therapy provider or physical therapist on satisfactory prior experience with the provider organization or an individual therapist. In one way or another,

GROUP CASE STUDY

Form small groups based on the criterion that the members come from different states. If that is not possible, use the criterion of having a mix of people from rural and metropolitan areas.

Background

In addition to describing the body of physical therapy knowledge, the Guide to Physical Therapist Practice (APTA, 2001a) was "designed as a reference to help providers and third-party payers to make informed decisions about reasonableness of care and appropriate reimbursement" (Wynn, 1997, p. 62). ICD-9-CM diagnostic codes are well known in health care environments, so relating these codes to what physical therapists do makes sense. For example, if you had an outpatient with abnormal gait and a diagnosis of multiple sclerosis, what ICD-9-CM code is appropriate?

Task 1

Everyone, check practice pattern 5 D in the Guide (APTA, 2001d). Remember, the ICD-9-CM code describes the diagnosis; it is not a payment code. CPT codes are for payment. Suppose you provided the following services to the example outpatient: exercises for dynamic balance with and without assistive equipment, gait training, and lower extremity stretching. What codes are appropriate for billing? See Table 30.3.

Task 2

Use the same sites to determine the geographic payment rate based on the RBRVS. Use your permanent residence as the location. Assume you are a member of a preferred provider panel and the managed care organization pays on a discounted fee-for-service basis. The discount is 20%. What is the expected payment for the services you provided?

Task 3

Explore differences in the bottom line.

patient and physician impressions are influenced by the outcomes of prior services. Outcomes evidence to objectively or subjectively grade physical therapy services comes from multiple sources such as customer satisfaction measures, financial measures, and productivity measures. Discussion of the purpose, methods, and use of outcomes measures in physical therapy is the focus of the upcoming chapter.

References

American Medical Association. World Health Organization's International Classification of Diseases, 9th Revision, Clinical Modification (ICD-9-CM 2001), Volumes 1 and 3. Chicago: AMA. 2000.

American Medical Association. Physician's Current Procedural Terminology, 4th edition. Chicago: AMA. 2003.

American Physical Therapy Association. Guide to physical therapist practice, 2nd ed. Physical Therapy. 2001a;81.

American Physical Therapy Association. Guide to physical therapist practice, 2nd ed. Physical Therapy. 2001b;81:142.

American Physical Therapy Association. Guide to physical therapist practice, 2nd ed. Physical Therapy. 2001c;81: 384.

American Physical Therapy Association. Guide to physical therapist practice, 2nd ed. Physical Therapy. 2001d;81:365-382.

Centers for Medicare and Medicaid Services. Acute inpatient prospective payment system Available from http://www.cms.hhs.gov/providers/hipps/background.asp. Accessed 10/30/03a.

Centers for Medicare and Medicaid Services. List of diagnosis related groups (DRGs) FY 2001. Available from http://www.cms.hhs.gov/statistics/medpar/Drgdesc01.pdf. Accessed 10/30/03b.

Centers for Medicare and Medicaid Services. Inpatient rehabilitation facility patient assessment instrument (IRF PAI). Available from http://www.cms.hhs/providers/irfpps/irfpai.asp. Accessed 10/30/03c.

Centers for Medicare and Medicaid Services. Health care common procedure coding system (HCPCS). Available from http://www.cms.gov.medicare/hcpcs/default.asp. Accessed 10/30/03d.

Centers for Medicare and Medicaid Services. Minimum data set (MDS) 3.0. Available from http://www.cms.hhs/gov/quality/mds30. Accessed 10/30/03e.

Centers for Medicare and Medicaid Services. Description of the RUG-III classification system. Available from http://www.cms.hhs/gov/Medicaid/reports/rp1201-g.pdf. Accessed 10/30/03f.

Centers for Medicare and Medicaid Services. December 2002 final draft ICD-10 PCS coding system and training manual. Available from http://www.cms.hhs.gov/paymentsystems/icd9/icd10.asp. Accessed 10/30/03g.

Hart AC, Hopkins C, editors. ICD-9-CM: Professional for hospitals. West Valley City, UT: St. Anthony/Medicode. 2002.

Kongsvedt PR. Managed care: What it is and how it works, 2nd ed. Gaithersburg, MD: Aspen. 2002.

Kovacek Management Services. Common CPT codes used by physical therapists. Available from http://www.PTManager.com. Accessed 1/30/03.

Kovner AR, Jonas S, editors. Jonas and Kovner's health care delivery in the United States, 6th ed. New York: Springer. 1999.

Lane DO, Kovacek PR. Underbilling: Advance for Directors of Rehabilitation. 2000;January: 14, 15.

World Health Organization. Manual of the International Classification of Diseases, Injuries, and Causes of Death. Geneva: WHO. 1977.

Wynn KE. A guide to the guide. PT Magazine. 1997;5(11):58–69.

More Information Related to This Chapter

Coding and reimbursement are brought to the attention of APTA members as soon as they become news. Regularly check http://www.apta.org/gov_affairs and http://apta.org/reimbursement. These matters are also of interest to the Section on Health Policy and Administration. The section's Web site is http://www.aptasoa.org.

Information on Medicare payment systems can be found at http://www.cms.hhs/gov.

Many of the acronyms used in this chapter come from CMS. There is a glossary of CMS acronyms at http://www.cms.hhs/acronyms/listall. Substantial regulatory and reimbursement literature and requirements are available through Centers for Medicare and Medicaid Services at http://www.hhs.cms/gov and various professional organizations, including APTA at http://www.APTA.org.

Part VI

Measuring Up and Getting Help

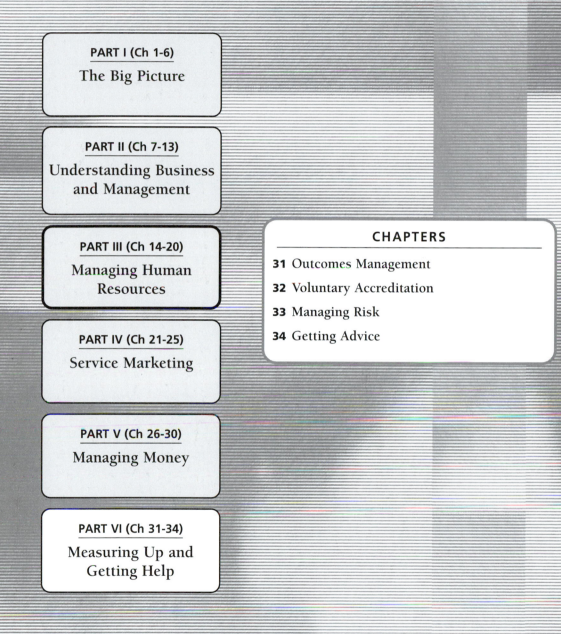

PART I (Ch 1-6)
The Big Picture

PART II (Ch 7-13)
Understanding Business and Management

PART III (Ch 14-20)
Managing Human Resources

PART IV (Ch 21-25)
Service Marketing

PART V (Ch 26-30)
Managing Money

PART VI (Ch 31-34)
Measuring Up and Getting Help

CHAPTERS

Chapter 31

OUTCOMES MANAGEMENT

Learning Objectives

1. Examine the purpose of measuring outcomes.
2. Contrast the terms *effectiveness* and *efficiency* as used in outcomes measurement.
3. Contrast satisfaction, clinical performance, functional, and financial outcomes.
4. Apply the nine-step outcomes management process to formulate a physical therapy–relevant outcomes program.

Key Words

Assessment, clinical performance outcome, effectiveness, efficiency, functional outcome, outcome indicator, outcome, risk adjustment, satisfaction outcome, technical outcome

Introduction

This chapter addresses the measurement and management of performance outcomes in clinical care. **Assessment** and measurement are synonymous. **Outcomes** are results of interventions (American Physical Therapy Association [APTA], 2001). Satisfaction, cost, and technical or functional are three types of outcomes that are important in management of clinical practices because they are ways to gauge results or performance. Use of performance outcome information is critical to an organization's success. This chapter provides a foundation for understanding why and how to incorporate outcome information into daily decision making. The role of a manager in interpreting data and the role of the entire staff in using the data to change practice behaviors is discussed.

Outcomes Management

Outcomes management includes data collection, analysis, and interpretation of the effectiveness and efficiency of treatment, that is, paying attention to the results of the process. Outcomes management in health care has been defined as determining the results of clinical interventions based on reliable measurement so as to identify the most efficient means to achieve a desirable result and to improve results over time (Dobrzykowski, 1997). The purposes of outcomes management include measurement of the effectiveness (assessment of the impact of treatment on a population) and efficiency (assessment of the outcomes in conjunction with the resources used) of health care (Dobrzykowski, 1997).

The Outcomes Management Imperatives: Values and Business

The United States today has relatively few health care markets whose service providers have the option not to measure their outcomes; outcome measurement is essential (Dobrzykowski, 1997). Even when outcomes data are not demanded, it is the responsibility of the professional to provide the highest quality of care feasible. Although the Code of Ethics of the American Physical Therapy Association (APTA) does not list its core values, ethical principles are identifiable, and from these principles values can be inferred (Chapter 6). Principle 4 of the code states, "A physical therapist shall exercise sound professional judgment" (APTA, 2003). Principle 5 requires that members achieve and maintain professional competence. These principles call for the exercise of sound judgment and clinical competence, which are predicated on appropriate knowledge, training, and supervision. Values that support these ends are to do no harm and to pursue excellence and competence (Chapter 6). Clearly, a key component of outcomes management is developing a system to monitor the efficacy of treatment, to revise treatment based on experience, and to pursue excellence and competence.

Principle 10 requires members to "endeavor to address the health needs of society" (APTA, 2003). Values that support these motives are enhancement of the profession, beneficence, service to the community, and social justice (Chapter 6). This principle assumes that physical therapists can evaluate the results of clinical intervention from the perspective of the public and know what is in the public's best interest. From a business perspective, it is a competitive advantage (Chapter 11) to provide customers with clear and accurate evidence of clinical efficiency and effectiveness. It is essential to have such evidence when negotiating with managed care organizations for access to the organization's covered patients (Chapter 2). The major uses of outcomes data for management and clinical decision making are shown in Table 31.1.

The foremost use of outcomes data is to improve practice. Outcomes data can also be useful to determine how to lower costs, demonstrate to external stakeholders the relationship between cost and functional outcome, and market services. The key to understanding outcomes management is to recognize the links between clinical management decisions, clinical treatment decisions, and clinical documentation (Portney and Watkins, 2000). Outcome measurement and the use of outcome information reflect the organization's ability and intention to achieve outcomes that meet the needs of their consumers (Lewis and McKerney, 1994).

Table 31.1 Goals of Outcomes Management

1. To improve practice
2. To document the results of clinical intervention
3. To examine and document practice patterns
4. To identify the most effective and cost-efficient practice patterns
5. To gain a better understanding of practice
6. To use the outcome information in daily clinical and business decision making

Modified from Kovacek P. Improving Productivity Without Sacrificing Quality. Harper Woods, MI: Kovacek Management Services. 1995:121.

Measuring Performance to Develop and Maintain Accountability

To develop the accountability of clinicians for the results of their work, it is necessary that **outcome indicators** reflect the health care goals of the organization (Goldfred, Pine, Pine, 1993). It is also important that these indicators reveal when and to what extent these goals have been achieved (Goldfred et al., 1993.) A typical rehabilitation center has three key areas from which to sample outcome information:

1. **Clinical performance outcomes**, often referred to as **functional outcomes**: The goal of clinical outcome management is to improve clinical care.
2. **Financial outcomes**: The goal of financial outcome management is profitability and cost effectiveness.
3. **Satisfaction outcomes**: The goal of satisfaction outcomes management is to understand customers' perceptions and to identify actions to improve customer satisfaction.

Each of these areas must be assessed in an outcomes management program.

Clinical Performance Outcomes

The measurement of **clinical performance outcomes** is often the most difficult of the three. However, its importance cannot be overemphasized. Clinical physical therapy performance is the single thing that truly and uniquely differentiates physical therapy within the health care system. If physical therapists are to continue to be important to health care, it is necessary to define the clinical scope and limitations of the profession and of its individual clinicians.

Clinical performance outcomes, or functional or **technical outcomes**, are the results in terms of the patient's level of recovery and function achieved as a result of clinical intervention and influences not under the control of the clinician. There are three prerequisites to acquiring useful data for this kind of outcomes management:

1. Adequate measurement, description, and documentation of the clinical and functional condition of the patient prior to intervention, that is, baseline status, clinical findings, demographics, psychosocial status (Kane, 1997).
2. Adequate measurement, description, and documentation of the intervention, including the type of treatment setting (Kane, 1997).
3. Adequate measurement, description, and documentation of the clinical condition of the patient after intervention.

To interpret these prerequisites, it is necessary to collect and analyze outcomes data on relatively large numbers of patients in each category of diagnosis so that patterns of outcomes can be identified.

Choices regarding data to be collected, data collection, and data analysis are addressed later in this chapter. First we discuss the second prerequisite, adequate measurement, description, and documentation of clinical intervention.

As previously stated, there are several excellent reasons to undertake outcomes management programs. In our opinion, the most significant reason to use outcomes management programs is to learn the most effective clinical behaviors and to improve clinical practice, that is, to improve patient care. To do this, it is necessary to define existing practice. This requires a significant level of standardization of care. Without this standardization, it is very difficult to improve practice. Without standardization of clinical care, too many variables can affect outcomes that may be attributed to clinical care. If you want to improve practice, you must define, document, and consistently carry out the baseline practices.

Such standardization of practice is often difficult for physical therapists to accept. Often, as highly trained professionals, they hold the misconception that with training, education, and a certain level of autonomy comes the right to deviate from the discipline that is needed to provide high-quality care in a structured and scientific manner. A research frame of mind is crucial. There is also an ethical obligation to provide the best possible care.

Many clinical practices are developing formal mechanisms to standardize care. These include critical pathways (often referred to as clinical pathways or care maps), protocols, clinical decision algorithms, and treatment guidelines. All of these mechanisms reduce variation in care. Adoption of standardized clinical programs is advantageous to the provision of high-quality clinical care. Standardization is also critical to understanding practice patterns and fully describing the therapeutic interventions as required in prerequisite 2. Standardization supports adequate measurement, description, and documentation of the clinical intervention.

Financial Performance

Chapters 27 and 28 review the measurement and management of financial performance on a macro level. To evaluate cost outcomes, it is necessary to assess financial performance on a much smaller scale, or at a micro level. Typical financial outcome measurements include the following:

- Average cost, revenue, or margin per case
- Average cost, revenue, or margin per visit

- Average cost, revenue, or margin per unit of service
- Average revenue collected per case, visit, or unit of service

Each of these financial outcomes is related to the financial resources devoted to the delivery of care. Each may be further analyzed for specific staff members, types of patients, clinical sites, or venues in the continuum of care.

In some clinical practices, personnel costs represent as much as 80% of operating expenses (Chapter 28). Because of this, it may be helpful to develop systems to analyze and manage personnel productivity as an indicator of costs and overall financial success.

Customer Satisfaction

As caregivers who frequently spend a significant amount of time in intimate physical and emotional contact with patients, physical therapists should be concerned about their customers' perception of their services. Given that physical therapists often function within a health care system that patients can easily perceive as less than friendly and accessible, one would expect that patients perceive physical therapists as warm, kind and talented professionals. Experience indicates that this is frequently the case.

Patients' satisfaction is the relationship between their expectations and their perception of the organization's success in fulfilling those expectations. To achieve higher levels of satisfaction, it is necessary either to lower patients' expectations or raise their perception of performance in relation to those expectations. Clearly, there are ethical considerations in inappropriately lowering or raising expectations. There is the potential to violate the ethical rules of truth telling, patients' autonomy, and veracity (giving information that is needed to make informed decisions). However, appropriate expectations and perceptions, especially when high-quality care is being delivered, are in the patient's best interest.

Elliot-Burke and Pothast (1997) suggest several ways patient satisfaction studies can assist clinicians:

1. Aid in developing a service-oriented culture.
2. Add an important component of a comprehensive outcomes measurement system.
3. Assist in predicting health-related behaviors and health care use.
4. Determine a patient's compliance with his or her treatment program.
5. Provide a better understanding of the patient's frame of reference.
6. Provide data for continuous process improvement.

A study of 19,834 physical therapy patients in more than 120 centers in 12 states identified key factors related to overall patient satisfaction (Elliot-Burke and Pothast, 1997). These five areas most frequently drove overall patient satisfaction:

1. **Communication**: This is the clinician's ability to communicate the treatment plan from the patient's perspective.
2. **Consistency** of clinician and other service providers: This includes dealing with the same staff members.
3. **Respect** for patient autonomy: This reflects the amount of input by the patient in setting treatment goals.
4. Respectful professional **attention**: The quality of time the clinician spends with the patient.
5. **Understanding**: The service provider has relevant personal knowledge of the patient and history.

There are many methods to measure satisfaction. APTA (1996) has produced a compendium of satisfaction instruments from clinics in diverse geographic and clinical settings that demonstrate the variety of tools that can be used to collect patient satisfaction data. Goldstein, Elliott, and Guccione (2000) formed and tested a patient satisfaction instrument based on selected questions in the compendiums' 36 example questionnaires and other sources. These investigators selected questions that were supported by other satisfaction studies and their own experiences. The patient satisfaction instrument had 11 domains:

1. Billing accuracy
2. Convenience of appointment time
3. Cost
4. Courtesy of all staff

5. Courtesy of physical therapists
6. Easy means of making appointments
7. Privacy respected
8. Satisfaction with the total experience
9. Scheduling quick and easy
10. Treatment satisfaction
11. Waiting time

Data from 289 patients were analyzed. Treatments were given in a variety of outpatient settings. Analysis showed that the questionnaire had high internal consistency of measurements. This is a form of reliability. Several validity measures were also computed. These analyses make this one of the few physical therapy satisfaction instruments with known psychometric properties (Goldstein et al., 2000).

Using Outcome Information

Some questions may help establish a patient satisfaction outcomes management system. Dobrzykowski (1997) recommends asking these questions:

- What is your place in the delivery system? (Who are we?)
- What are the most common diagnoses? (Who are our clients?)
- Who are the customers seeking outcome information? (Who wants information?)
- What are the typical questions? (What do they want to know?)
- Which outcomes do you wish to measure? (What will be measured?)
- What outcome measures or systems are already available? (What do we know now?)
- What is the data collection protocol? (How should we handle the data?)
- How will you train the staff? (How can we be sure we are good at this?)
- How will you process the data? (Will we handle the data correctly?)
- How will you analyze and interpret the results? (How do we make sense of the data?)

Each of these questions must be answered to establish a successful patient satisfaction outcome management program.

How to Measure and Manage Outcomes

Management of any project requires a process. One approach to managing an outcomes measurement project is to break it down into logical steps. Figure 31.1 is a general nine-step process using a physical therapy example.

Step 1: Identify the Population to Be Studied

The most likely patient population to study is the current one. Not all tools or processes work well with every population. It may be necessary to identify a subset of the entire population to get started. In the early stages of outcomes management program development, it may be best to limit the scope of the project to patients in the most frequently treated diagnostic groups. Starting on a smaller scale may increase the likelihood of success.

Step 2: Choose an Outcome Measurement Tool

A wide variety of tools are available. Each has its advantages and disadvantages with regard to the specific population to be studied and project limitations. Tools can and should be combined if necessary.

A specific outcome measurement tool must be selected. Tool evaluation must address several difficult issues. One is whether the chosen instrument should use clinician-measured or patient-measured data. Lewis and McKerney (1994) noted several advantages to clinicians measuring functional data:

- Excellent for showing validity of task being performed
- Greater reliability
- More sensitivity to change
- Measures usual activity versus maximal activity

Lewis and McKerney (1994) also identified disadvantages of clinicians' measurement of functional data compared to patients' reports:

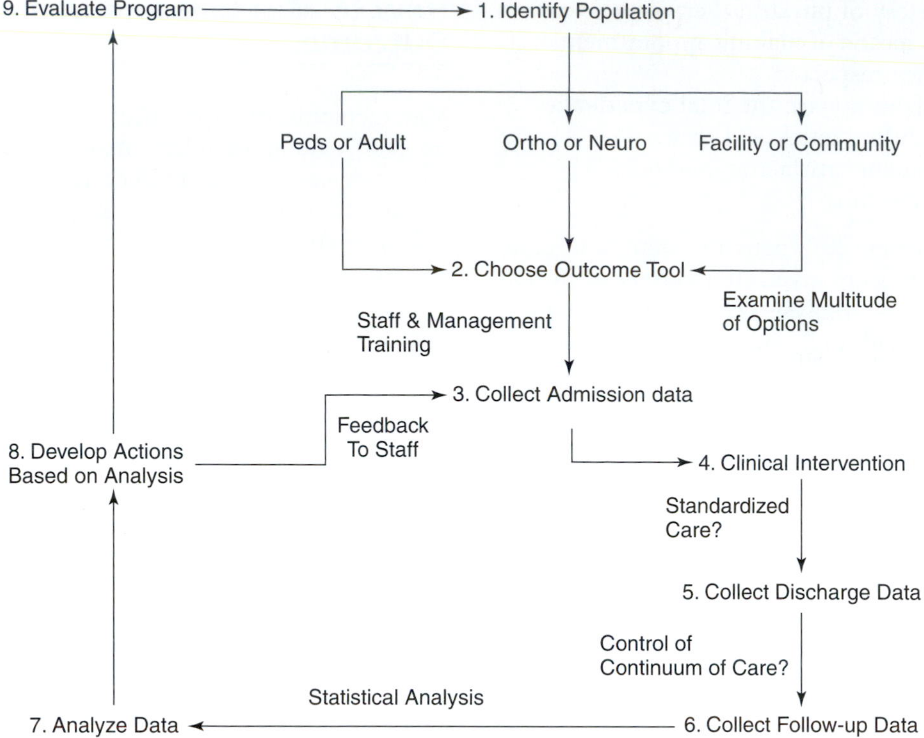

Figure 31.1. A nine-step outcomes management process.

- Influenced by language, culture, and education
- May need modification or different setting (that is, the home)
- May need special training of examiners
- Performance on standardized tests may not represent performance in real life
- Poor for cognitively impaired patients
- Potential for injuries
- Requires more time

To make usable measurements and appropriate comparisons across institutions and locations, it is essential to take into account the differences in types, severity, and complexities of illnesses among the populations treated at various institutions and location (Kane, 1997).

This **risk adjustment** accounts for factors beyond the control of the clinician that can influence outcomes (Dobrzykowski, 1997). Risk adjustment includes identification of confounding variables, including these:

- Comorbidity
- Ethnicity
- Gender
- Income
- Source and type of insurance
- Level of education
- Number of prior episodes of care
- Patient's acuity
- Severity of the patient's condition
- The patient's age

Correct interpretation of the data collected in an outcomes management program requires inclusion and consideration of these and other confounding variables.

To use any outcome measurement tool effectively, it is necessary to identify confounding factors and understand the appropriate use of the tool. As with any standardized instrument, each outcome tool should provide users with explicit instructions and substantive explanations regarding these factors:

Completion: How long the test takes to complete and score.

Interpretation: What do the scores mean? How will the examiner use the scores?

Mode of administration: How the tool is completed. For example, will the tool be self-administered by the patient with paper and pencil or will the therapist ask the questions or grade the activities?

Population: The specific type of person for which the tool applies.

Reliability: The degree to which the instrument produces consistent results when used under similar circumstances.

Validity: The extent to which a test measures what it was designed to measure. Validity cannot be directly assessed but must be evaluated through the use of the operational definition of the measure or through comparison to similar or dissimilar measures (Lewis and McKerney, 1994).

At this stage you should consider time. How much time is needed to carry out measurements, and how much time is available during treatment sessions to take reliable measurements? These are difficult questions whose answers can have a significant influence on staff productivity, morale, and the usefulness of data obtained.

Step 3: Collect Admission Data

Before you begin data collection, make sure the participating staff members are competent in the process. This will require substantial orientation and training, including a full explanation of the purpose and limitations of the study. The staff should also recognize the scope and limitations of outcomes management before undertaking what can be a substantial amount of extra work. Staff members should also understand that there will be delays between data collection and analysis and between analysis and the implementation of a plan. It may be necessary to view the staff as one of the customers of the outcomes management system.

At the time of initial data collection, the procedures to gather, validate, store, and access the data should have been established. All issues of information management discussed in Chapter 13 apply to outcomes data management.

Step 4: Clinical Intervention

At this stage, the actual treatment of the patients is not uniquely a part of the outcomes management system development. Treatment was going on before the clinic became interested in managing outcomes. Treatment will continue even if efforts at outcomes management fail. However, several key issues often arise at this stage of the outcomes management program. Among these issues is the realization by the staff and management that it will be difficult to interpret the outcomes of treatment when it is not possible to define a standardized treatment. During the later stages of developing the outcomes management process, discussions of treatment standardization are likely to arise. These discussions are important to the outcomes management educational process. Inability to define the initial status of the patient (baseline clinical status), the final status of the patient (outcome clinical status) or the treatment provided to the patient (clinical intervention) invalidates the outcomes data.

The three components are especially important if internal outcome comparisons are desired. The physical therapist chooses an intervention; the data are collected and pooled with similar information. The pooled data are analyzed and feedback is given regarding the most effective intervention. For example, one therapist may choose to use electric stimulation and ultrasound to treat a neck condition, while another may choose a hands-on approach with exercise. Patients in both groups are given a functional outcome evaluation initially and at discharge. If it is determined that the hands-on treatment and exercise group realized significantly more improvement on the measures of interest than those who received the electric stimulation and ultrasound, the therapist should be informed about the outcome of their treatments and encouraged to modify treatment strategies and programs appropriately.

As an example, consider several hands-on techniques and respond to these questions:

- Which hands-on technique is most helpful for specific kinds of patients?

- Which practitioners are most successful with this technique?
- How do frequency and duration of treatment affect clinical success?

Discussions among the staff on topics such as these are valuable and should be encouraged throughout the outcomes management process.

Step 5: Collect Discharge Data

Step 6 is a repetition of step 3, except it is done after the intervention. For a valid comparison of data, you must use similar data collection procedures. As in the initial data collection step, appropriate processes of information management (Chapter 13) apply to outcomes data management.

Step 6: Collect Follow-Up Data

Although it may be tempting to try to analyze data after admission and immediately upon discharge, it is best to consider the sustainable effects of therapeutic interventions. This requires collection of data at one or more points significantly after discharge from treatment; 90 days after discharge has been suggested (Dobrzykowski, 1997).

There are many reasons to collect postdischarge data. They include evaluation of sustainable effects of interventions, reduction of bias that person-to-person interaction between patients and staff may encourage, and assessment of the entire continuum of therapeutic care as opposed to a single venue in the continuum.

Step 7: Analyze and Interpret Data

This step may intimidate some managers and staff members. Use of a statistician as a consultant is a well-established practice in outcomes management. A statistical consultant can be helpful in overall program design as well as for analyzing the data. The potential for misinterpretation of statistical data is significant. The information is personal to both patients and staff. Clinicians may fear or believe that outcomes evaluation is an attempt to determine who the best clinicians are and who the worst are. Although this is often an inappropriate use of the data, staff frequently have that impression. Training and orientation to the limitations of outcome management should help alleviate these concerns. However, be careful not to extend the findings to different groups, settings, treatments, or diagnoses.

An additional area of concern regarding data analysis is the potential for high levels of energy and resources to be devoted to analysis, leading to commensurately lower levels of attention devoted to action plans to address problems or opportunities.

Step 8: Develop Actions Based on Data Analysis

Considering all the steps in the outcomes management process, this step is the most crucial. It asks the question, so what? The collection and analysis of data are of little value if nothing further occurs. Opportunities and problems may be identified during the interpretation of the data. A definitive plan to address these must be developed and implemented.

The most basic of action plans should include developing a mechanism to report summarized data to consumers and the clinicians who generated the data. Emphasis on the educational value of the outcome information may reduce concerns. This will be especially beneficial if there are opportunities to learn continuing education or from others who are achieving better outcomes.

Hopefully, outcomes findings are incorporated into many of the clinic's activities. Table 31.2 shows many of the activities that should use outcomes data as a guide.

Step 9: Evaluate the Outcomes Program

Periodic formal evaluation of the success of the program closes the outcomes management loop. If the organization is to improve clinical care, management must critically examine all programs in relation to the specific care improvement objectives. Since an outcomes management program is evolutionary, the more experience the managers and staff

Table 31.2 Using Outcomes Data in Daily Practice

Performance appraisal of staff
Cost/value decisions for managed care
Clinical research on treatment efficacy
Data-based decisions in a changing environment
Program development decisions
Program termination decisions
Staff assignment to specific programs

Modified from Kovacek P. Improving Productivity Without Sacrificing Quality. Harper Woods, MI: Kovacek Management Services. 1995:123.

develop in evaluating and using outcome information, the more they can refine the processes to meet the needs of their service environment.

In evaluating an outcomes management program, it is necessary to consider the feedback available from many sources, including patients, staff, referral sources, payers, and other stakeholders.

This model is consistent with what has been identified as essential strategies for the successful collection and management of outcomes (Dobrzykowski, 1997). The model in summary suggests:

- Begin with the most prevalent diagnoses
- Select a minimum number of measures
- Collect data at admission, at discharge, and 90 days after discharge
- Consider the data collection interface for customers entering data and minimize data gathering redundancy when feasible
- Train participants in outcomes management
- Secure and use data processing and analysis consultants
- To identify usual variations, a minimum of 1 year should be spent examining and monitoring outcomes information before implementing major changes in the delivery of the services being monitored

Student Notes

The development of an outcomes measurement program is similar to the development of a research project:

- Ask a question (which kind of performance indicator).
- Define variables of interest (definition of the construct).
- Select or develop one or more tools to measure changes over time (reliable measurement instruments).
- Use consistency in data collection methods (protocols and interrater and intrarater measurement reliability),
- Use analyses that make sense (statistical consultation).
- Make sure interpretations are in line with the findings (SWOT analysis).
- Disseminate your findings (share the information).
- Implement the suggested course (apply the findings to clinical practice and begin the next measurement cycle).

Start with http://www.apta.org/research. Access the Hooked on Evidence link. See what is available on outcomes for physical therapist mangers. Compare the processes and methods reported in the resources you found. Pay attention to what is said about the influence of outcomes measurement on those who were providing direct care to consumers.

Summary

This chapter addresses the measurement and management of performance outcomes in clinical health care. Outcomes measures for patient satisfaction, technical or functional results, and cost are considered. Benefits and pitfalls of outcomes research are addressed. A nine-step algorithm that includes initiating, conducting, and using clinical outcomes data for the management of clinical services is presented and discussed. The main uses of outcomes data include improvement of clinical practice, documentation of clinical interventions, assessment of practice patterns, increased understanding of practice variables, and assistance with business decisions. Pitfalls include infringement on treatment time, pressure to do more in the same time, and difficulties in ensuring reliability of treatment

INDIVIDUAL CASE STUDY

What are some sound criteria that a wise consumer could use in choosing the kind of doctor to see for treatment of a back problem? As you contemplate, consider all the kinds of doctors that might treat such conditions, for example, medical doctor, doctor of chiropractic, and doctor of physical therapy. If you were a doctor and provided back care, what kind of outcomes would you want your services to have? Do you have outcome data that would influence the consumer? Who might the consumer choose and for what reasons? Where would consumers get understandable outcome information?

methods, measurements, and other variables of data gathering.

Outcomes attained by similar practitioners using the same treatment methods on the same patients in the same clinical environments are obviously comparable. This allows members of a department and external stakeholders to draw conclusions about the quality of services. Another form of quality assessment is measurement against an external standard by an unbiased team of evaluators, that is, voluntary accreditation. The next chapter examines voluntary health care accreditation as it relates to various standards for health care organizations. Outcome measurement is an essential component of voluntary accreditation.

GROUP CASE STUDY

This case study is based on a 1999 article by Peter Kovacek. It is reproduced with permission.

First, read the following article. After you finish reading, pair up with a classmate and formulate answers to the questions at the end of the article.

The Quality Imperative

We all know how important it is to provide the highest quality care possible. That belief is at the core of physical therapists. It is one of the earliest things that we are taught in school and one of the things that we hold closest to our hearts. One of the reasons that we struggle so with managed care is that, at times, we believe that we are prevented from providing the quality of care we know that we can and should provide.

Being committed to the provision of high quality physical therapy is easy. Doing what we need to do so that we can state with confidence that we have lived up to that commitment is much more difficult.

The Quality Commitment

In order for us to walk the talk of quality, we need to develop skills to allow us to systematically evaluate the impact of our interventions on the patients we serve. That means that we need to subject our clinical activities to fairly intense review and inspection. We need to exert a significant degree of discipline into our analysis—we all know that. But we also need to exert a significant degree of discipline into our delivery of care—many of us struggle with that part.

Many of us are actively involved in the measurement of clinical outcomes in attempt to examine the issues related to providing quality care. Typically, outcomes programs measure certain clinical measures of well-being or impairment prior to treatment and then again after treatment. Differences in these measures are thought to be, at least in

GROUP CASE STUDY *(Continued)*

part, to the clinical intervention. By comparing the results of different therapists or clinics, we can come to some conclusions about what may be "better" therapists or clinics—at least based on the results they obtain with their patients.

This is all well and good. We should be actively reflecting on the work that we do. We owe it to our patients, our communities, and ourselves to pursue a thoughtful and intentional path in our clinical journeys. However, to draw any conclusions from our reflection, we require evidence—data. Also, we require enough data to provide for the variations that are inherent in treating patients who are individuals—not clones. The researchers among us can explain better the critical role that an adequate sample size plays in the proper interpretation of data.

What we also need to understand is that it is just not a case having a large enough sample size. The members of the sample population also need to share certain "controllable" characteristics. One of these characteristics that we need to make serious attempts to control is the clinical intervention itself. Somehow, we seem to resist controlling our clinical interventions. Somehow, we seem to lack the discipline to provide a consistent style and method of intervention with our patients. In short, we need to do a better job of standardizing our clinical interventions. This is not suggesting that we should routineize physical therapy. It is suggesting that we standardize, when possible, the technical interventions that we provide. This is not the same as "cookbook" therapy. At the heart of cookbook therapy is an unthinking, nonreflective clinician who does what [he or she is] told. Evaluation is more of a billing code than a practice component to the cookbook therapist. That is not good therapy. What I am suggesting is that therapists use the highest level of professional training, judgment, and decision making to determine the course of clinical intervention—then intervene using standardized, evidence-justified treatment techniques.

If we are to be able to interpret our quality data, we need some degree of confidence that there was consistent intervention for consistently assessed clinical conditions. Without that standardization, we will always be comparing apples and oranges. Valid conclusions will not be possible. Our quality programs will not be valuable—rather, they will merely consume our time and lead us to the wrong decisions about our actions.

To realistically compare post treatment status with pre treatment status in any logical manner, we need to be able to define clearly and concisely the essence of the treatment intervention. Without the discipline to consistently apply these treatments, we risk doing our patients and ourselves a disservice. The conclusions about our treatment that we will make will be based on a nebulous treatment concept no better defined than a mysterious black box.

Questions for Discussion

1. Do you think the author's assessments and statements are true today?
2. What, if anything, can be done within a typical practice to facilitate the development of outcomes management systems (Fig. 31.1.)?
3. What do you foresee as the major organizational obstacles to the successful development of outcomes management systems in organizations with which you are familiar?
4. Consider the clinical setting you know best. If you are aware of performance outcomes being measured there, what outcomes were measured? If you are not aware of performance outcomes being measured, which type of outcomes would you begin with and why?

REFERENCES

American Physical Therapy Association. Patient Satisfaction Instruments: A Compendium. Alexandria, VA: American Physical Therapy Association. 1996.

American Physical Therapy Association. Code of Ethics. Physical Therapy. 2001;81:685, 687.

American Physical Therapy Association. APTA guide for professional conduct. Available from http://www.apta.org/pt_practice/ethics_pt/pro_conduct. Accessed 10/11/03.

Dobrzykowski, Edward A, The Methodology of Outcomes Measurement. Journal of Rehabilitation Outcomes Measures. 1997; 1:8–17.

Elliot-Burke TL, Pothast L. Measuring patient satisfaction in an outpatient orthopedic setting, Part 1: Key drivers and results. Journal of Rehabilitation Outcomes Measures. 1997;1:18–25.

Goldfred N, Pine M, Pine J. Measuring and managing health care quality: Procedures, techniques and protocols. Rockville, MD: Aspen. 1993.

Goldstein MS, Elliott SD, Guccione AA. The development of an instrument to measure satisfaction with physical therapy. Physical Therapy. 2000;80:853–863.

Kane RL. Approaching the outcome question. In Kane RL, ed. Understanding health care outcomes research. Gaithersburg, MD: Aspen. 1997;1–15.

Lewis CB, McKerney T. The functional toolbox: Clinical measures of functional outcomes. Washington: Learn. 1994.

Kovacek P. Improving Productivity without Sacrificing Quality. Harper Woods, MI: Kovacek Management Services. 1995:121, 123.

Portney LG, Watkins MP. Foundations of clinical research, 2nd ed. Upper Saddle River, NJ: Prentice Hall Health. 2000.

MORE INFORMATION RELATED TO THIS CHAPTER

An excellent overview of the major issues for selecting outcome measurement tools and how the data from these tools may enhance the treatment of patients, along with more than 70 outcomes measurement tools covering 14 functional outcome domains are described and analyzed in Finch E, Brooks D, Stratford PW, Mayo NE. Physical rehabilitation outcome measures. A guide to enhanced clinical decision making, 2nd ed. Baltimore: Lippincott, Williams & Wilkins. 2002.

Several chapters in an evidence-based text deal with outcome measurement, including appendices with forms to guide reading various types of outcome reports, in Helewa A, Walker JM. Critical evaluation of research in physical rehabilitation: Towards evidence-based practice. Philadelphia: Saunders. 2000.

An Internet source with an extensive list of evidence-based links can be found at http://www.marquette.edu/library/sites/health.html#evidence. This site provides links to most major evidence-based sites worldwide. Access http://www.apta.org, click on practice, and then information for managers of physical therapy services. You will be able to find current literature categorized under outcomes/effectiveness and measurement.

Chapter 32

VOLUNTARY ACCREDITATION

Learning Objectives

1. Synthesize the concepts of oversight, certification, and accreditation as they relate to health care organizations and physical therapy educational programs.
2. Summarize the distinct purposes of major accreditation bodies for health care organizations, physical therapist managers, staff members, and student physical therapists.
3. Contrast the various major accreditation bodies in terms of their focuses, criteria, methods of measurement, and other areas important to those pursuing accreditation or certification.
4. Evaluate voluntary accreditation of health care organizations from the perspectives of consumers, payers, physical therapist managers, and accreditation bodies.
5. Analyze the relationships between accreditation or certification, marketing, and third-party payer requirements.
6. Know where to access current information about accreditation for health care organizations, accounting, and educational programs.

Key Words

Accreditation, American Institute of Certified Public Accountants, American Physical Therapy Association, CARF—the Commission on Accreditation of Rehabilitation Facilities, certification, Commission on Accreditation in Physical Therapy Education (CAPTE), Financial Accounting Standards Board (FASB), Health Plan Employer Data and Information Set (HEDIS), oversight, Securities and Exchange Commission, the Joint Commission on Accreditation of Healthcare Organizations (JCAHO), The National Commission on Quality Assurance (NCQA)

Introduction

Chapter 3 describes **oversight** of health care as the state and federal governments' legal authority to supervise, manage, direct, control, and provide surveillance. Nongovernmental bodies also provide oversight. Two terms are usually associated with oversight: **certification** and accreditation. To a point, certification is voluntary. It signifies that governmental and/or nongovernmental entities have recognized a health care provider as being compliant with certain requirements. Certification is mandatory for providers who want Medicare and Medicaid to pay for services. The responsibility for monitoring provider compliance with regulations lies with state departments of health and human services (Chapters 2 and 3). **Accreditation**, like certification, is generally voluntary. However, it has three features that differ from certification. The first difference is the ability to treat any type of patient. There is no restriction on who has access to an accredited health care provider's services. The second difference is that an accredited provider has the right to offer any type of health care service. Certification is often limited to specific kinds of services, for example, provision of services to individuals covered by Medicaid (Chapters 2 and 3). The final difference is that accreditation signifies conformity to standards that are more stringent than the minimums required for certification or licensure (Health and Administration Development Group, 1999).

Health care organizations and individuals voluntarily pursue external recognition and validation as evidence of their commitment to and achievement of quality. External oversight is used to improve quality, as an alternative to government inspections, and to promote the provider's services to prospective customers (Chapters 21–23). Recognition of the roles of governmental (Chapter 3) and nongovernmental oversight agencies is the first step toward preparing for regulatory compliance and voluntary accreditation. The following discussion is limited to accreditation. The focus is on identifying, comparing, and contrasting selected independent accrediting organizations and professional organizations and associations commonly encountered in health care. Attention is drawn to the relevance of these entities to physical therapist clinicians and managers.

Nongovernmental Oversight and Accreditation Bodies

Nongovernmental accreditation takes two general forms: (1) as a supplement to governmental regulations and (2) to fill a void in governmental regulations. Supplemental accreditation may be seen as a mark of excellence in addition to certification. There is no universal oversight of institutions of higher learning. Regional accreditation associations like the North Central Association fill this void. Likewise, individual disciplines such as physical therapy have independent accrediting bodies (discussed later in the chapter). These regional and individual discipline accreditation groups are the primary sources of oversight of higher educational settings and programs, respectively (Institute of Medicine, 2001).

Examples of oversight activities provided by health care accrediting bodies:

- Accreditation
- Certification
- Evaluation of organizations
- Standards setting

The listed activities are aimed at improving the quality and fiscal accountability of health care organizations and providers. Some health care organizations choose to submit to nongovernmental oversight as a substitute for governmental review. To be recognized as a quality accreditation body requires resources, expertise, respect, and a broad scope of influence. According to the Institute of Medicine (2001), an ideal accrediting entity must

- Be national in the scope of its interests and actions
- Be autonomous, that is, independent of any particular interest group
- Have stakeholder credibility
- Have deep and wide knowledge of stakeholders' needs

The Institute of Medicine (2001) has identified six processes that an accrediting body should use to meet the needs of its constituents:

1. Applications
2. Self-evaluations
3. Training for external observers who make on-site inspections
4. Appeals
5. Measurement of level of achievement of standards
6. Reaccreditations

Some Recognized Accreditation Groups

Accreditation is a rigorous and comprehensive evaluation used by external organizations to assess how well a health care organization manages all parts of its care delivery system. Accreditation is based on consensus quality standards. Therefore, organizations that seek accreditation are subjecting their outcomes, structure, and processes to scrutiny by external examiners (Sandstrom, Lohman, Bramble, 2003). Several important regulatory agencies affect physical therapy services. The most notable are the Rehabilitation Accreditation Commission (CARF), the Joint Commission on Accreditation of Healthcare Organizations (JCAHO), and the National Commission on Quality Assurance (NCQA).

CARF: The Rehabilitation Accreditation Commission

CARF—the Commission on Accreditation of Rehabilitation Facilities is an international, independent not-for-profit accrediting body. Its mission is "to promote the quality, value, and optimal outcomes of services through accreditation that centers on enhancing the lives of the persons receiving services and its purpose is to improve the quality of services that enhance the lives of the persons receiving services" (CARF, 2003a). These are CARF's purposes:

- To seek the input of stakeholders and be responsive to such input.
- To develop and maintain standards focused on improving the value and responsiveness of health care delivered to people in need of rehabilitation programs and other enhancement services.
- To recognize the organizations that meet standards for rehabilitation programs and services that focus on the needs and outcomes of the people served. Also to demonstrate a commitment to continual improvement in efforts to meet the needs and better the outcomes.
- To engage in accreditation research on outcomes measurement and management and disseminate the results to participating organizations and other stakeholders.
- To support organizations through consultation, education, training, and publications to assist them to achieve and maintain the accreditation of their services and programs.
- To inform and educate others of the value of accreditation (CARF, 2003a).

CARF's target markets are as follows:

- Adult day services
- Assisted living
- Behavioral health
- Employment and community services
- Medical rehabilitation

In 2003, CARF accredited more than 3700 health care facilities (CARF, 2003b). Recently CARF expanded the breath of its accreditation influence by the acquisition of Continuing Care Accreditation Commission. This latter commission accredits continuing-care retirement communities and other organizations. These two commissions merged function as CARF (CARF, 2003c). Accreditation service is offered by CARF in the United States, Canada, and Europe (CARF, 2003a).

CARF's standards are established to help health care providers measure and improve the quality, value, and outcomes of their services. To accomplish this, in the development of its standards CARF engages persons receiving services, rehabilitation professionals, and purchasers of services.

CARF uses peer review to evaluate the performance of an organization in serving its customers. Government and other third-party payers may require an organization to obtain CARF accreditation as a condition for licensure and/or reimbursement. The programs and services accredited by CARF have demonstrated that they substantially meet nationally recognized standards. The basis for meeting standards is an on-site survey conducted by knowledgeable, trained surveyors who are professionals in rehabilitation. The survey offers the organization's personnel an opportunity to consult with CARF surveyors to enhance the delivery of quality services. Input from consumers is obtained during the on-site survey. CARF accreditation acknowledges that an organization has made a major commitment to enhance the quality of its programs and services and to focus on positive outcomes. According to CARF, use of accredited organizations offers significant benefits to the consumer:

1. Consumers participated in the development of the accreditation standards.

2. The facility's programs and services met consumer-focused national standards of performance.
3. The facility is focused on obtaining the optimum outcome for each person served.
4. The accredited program actively involved stakeholders in decision making related to the planning and implementation of the services they received (CARF, 2003d).

CARF's fundamental purpose is the preservation and improvement of programs provided by organizations serving those with disabilities and others in need of rehabilitation. It provides organizations with an accepted blueprint for operations, a guide to organizational development, and an internal tool to evaluate and improve their programs on an ongoing basis.

The Joint Commission on Accreditation of Healthcare Organizations

The Joint Commission on Accreditation of Healthcare Organizations (JCAHO) is probably the best-known nongovernmental accreditation organization. The JCAHO evaluates and accredits more than 17,000 health care organizations in the United States. Its mission is "to continuously improve the safety and quality of care provided to the public through the provision of health care accreditation and related services that support performance improvement in health care organizations" (JCAHO, 2003a). The JCAHO is an independent not-for-profit organization that develops professional standards against which the compliance of health care organizations is evaluated. The JCAHO offers accreditation to health care organizations of many types:

- Ambulatory care
- Assisted living
- Behavioral health care
- Critical access hospitals
- Health care networks
- Home care
- Hospitals
- Laboratory services
- Long-term care
- Office-based surgery (JCAHO, 2003b)

The JCAHO is governed by a 28-member board of commissioners that includes a variety of clinical and administrative health care professionals including representatives of the American College of Physicians–American Society of Internal Medicine, the American College of Surgeons, the American Dental Association, the American Hospital Association, and the American Medical Association. JCAHO offers many benefits with its accreditation (JCAHO, 2003a):

- Patient care is improved.
- The organization has an opportunity to demonstrate its commitment to safety and quality.
- It facilitates and improves an organization's safety and quality improvement efforts.
- Accreditation may improve employee recruitment and retention.
- Accreditation may substitute for state certification surveys for Medicare and Medicaid.
- It is attractive to managed care plans.
- It offers the organization a competitive edge.
- It enhances the organization's public image.
- It may fulfill state licensure requirements.
- It strengthens consumer confidence.

A segment of health care providers not yet accredited by the JCAHO is the rapidly expanding managed care market (Chapter 2). The main accrediting organization is the **National Committee For Quality Assurance (NCQA)**.

The National Committee for Quality Assurance

The NCQA began accrediting managed care organizations (MCOs) in 1991 in response to the need for standardized objective information about the quality of these organizations. The NCQA accreditation program, which is voluntary, has been recognized by purchasers, consumers, and health plans as an objective measure of the quality of the MCO. The specific accreditation focus of the NCQA is managed care plans (Chapter 2) and managed behavioral health care organizations. Its mission is "to improve the quality of health care delivered to people everywhere" (NCQA, 2003a). The NCQA has a vision to become the most widely trusted source of information driving health care quality improvement. According to the NCQA, more than 50% of U.S. HMOs participate in voluntary accreditation and certification programs. Approximately 90% of health plans measure their performance using the NCQA's **Health Plan Employer Data and Information Set (HEDIS)** (NCQA, 2003b). HEDIS is a proprietary tool used to measure a managed care plan's performance in key areas such as immunization and mammography screening rates. The NCQA evaluates health care in three ways:

1. Accreditation (a rigorous on-site review of key clinical and administrative processes)
2. A comprehensive member satisfaction survey
3. HEDIS

HEDIS is a set of standardized performance measures designed to ensure that purchasers and consumers have the information they need to reliably compare the performance of managed health care plans. In combination with information from NCQA's accreditation program, HEDIS provides a view of health plan quality that can be used to guide choice. HEDIS 3.0 is intended to help purchasers and consumers both to evaluate the quality of health plans along a variety of important dimensions and to base their choice of plan on demonstrated value rather than simply on cost (NCQA, 2003c).

HEDIS has eight performance domains for which measures are in place:

1. **Effectiveness of care**: How well the care delivered by a managed care plan is achieving the clinical results that it should.
2. **Access to and availability of care**: Whether care is available to members when they need it and in a timely and convenient manner.
3. **Satisfaction with the experience of care**: Whether a health plan is able to satisfy the diverse needs of its members.
4. **Cost of care**: Economic value of services.
5. **Stability of the health plan**: Health plan stability is important, because consumers make enrollment decisions that generally bind them for a year. Should the plan's network of providers change significantly or should the plan become insolvent, the member's health care could be badly disrupted.

These are measures to help consumers estimate how likely these problems are:

- **Informed care choices**: How a managed care plan helps members become active partners in their decisions. This means the plan must equip members to make informed choices about their care.
- **Use of services**: How a plan uses its resources is a signal of how efficiently care is managed and whether or not needed services are being delivered; it may also provide some information about opportunities to improve both the effectiveness and efficiency of care. These measures assess patterns of service use across different plans.
- **Descriptive information**: A variety of elements of interest to consumers regarding plan management (including a description of selected network, clinical, use, and risk management activities).

While items 1 to 3 are not performance measures per se, the information has consistently been useful to purchasers and consumers.

HEDIS and NCQA are used primarily in the accreditation of health plans (Chapter 2), but they also affect providers, such as physical therapists. Because providers are interested in attaining NCQA accreditation, they are required to collect information in the HEDIS data set. A substantial component of the HEDIS data is clinical information that can best be collected at the provider (department or clinic) level. Health plans frequently require contracted providers, including physical therapists, to assist in such data collection. Therefore, it is necessary for the physical therapy manager and clinician to become familiar with these tools and organizations.

Another area of interest regarding accreditation is in the financial arena. Financial accounting practices are important to payers and providers alike.

The Financial Accounting Standards Board

The **Financial Accounting Standards Board (FASB)** is the designated organization in the private sector for establishing standards of financial accounting and reporting (Chapter 27). FASB's mission is "to establish and improve standards of financial accounting and reporting for the guidance and education of the public, including issuers, auditors, and users of financial information" (FASB, 2003). FASB standards govern the preparation of financial reports. Since 1973, the **Securities and Exchange Commission** (SEC) (Financial Reporting Release No. 1, Section 101) and the **American Institute of Certified Public Accountants** (Rule 203, Rules of Professional Conduct, as amended May 1973 and May 1979) officially recognized FASB standards as authoritative (Rutgers, 2003). The SEC has the authority to establish accounting and reporting standards for public companies under the Securities and Exchange Act of 1934. Accounting standards are necessary for the efficient functioning of the economy because investors, creditors, auditors, and others rely on credible, transparent, and comparable financial information. Questions about nongovernmental entity accounting may be answered by logging on to http://www.fasb.org.

Professional Associations

Professional associations are membership organizations established to represent the interests of specific types of businesses, professionals, or both. The **American Hospital Association** and the **American Association of Homes and Services for the Aging** are professional associations that represent the interests of similar businesses. The **American Medical Association** and the **American Physical Therapy Association** (APTA) both represent the interests of a group of professionals. Professional organizations provide a variety of services on behalf of or for the benefit of its membership. Products and services may include the following:

- Advocacy
- Buying groups
- Career management
- Consulting services
- Credentialing and certification
- Education
- Job search
- Networking
- Professional standards
- Publications
- Research
- Risk protection (e.g., insurance)

APTA is a national professional organization representing physical therapists and physical therapist assistants. Membership is voluntary. APTA's goal is to "foster advancements in physical therapy practice, research, and education" (APTA, 2003a). A step toward accomplishing this goal, according to APTA's vision statement, is that doctors of physical therapy will provide physical therapy. The essence of the vision is that physical therapists "will be recognized as practitioners of choice to whom consumers have direct access for the diagnosis of, interventions for, and prevention of impairments, functional limitations, and disabilities related to movement, function, and health" (APTA, 2003b).

The **Commission on Accreditation in Physical Therapy Education** (CAPTE) grants specialized accreditation status to qualified entry-level education programs for physical therapists and physical therapist assistants. The U.S. Department of Education and the Council for Higher Education Accreditation (CHEA) recognize CAPTE as an accrediting agency (CHEA, 2003). APTA and CAPTE have a cooperative relationship. CAPTE has representation from the educational community, the physical therapy profession, and the public. Accredited programs have met established and nationally accepted standards of scope, quality, and relevance (APTA, 2003c).

Student Notes

Involvement in the process of accreditation is necessary for physical therapist managers in organizations of any size. Concepts of certification and accreditation place the focus on compliance with a standard set of requirements. Furthermore, compliance with standards depends to a large degree on management's efforts to develop, maintain, and measure clinical competence of staff members (Chapters 14 and 17). Think about certification, accreditation, and compliance. Compare and contrast the likely activities of a physical therapist manager for accreditation and to support compliance with standards, that is, developing and measuring competence. Remember, compliance relates to meeting *minimal* standards for performance, whereas the driving forces for competence should be related to meeting the *optimal* standards for performance—the desire to be the best, to succeed, and to excel.

Summary

This chapter examines several key agencies that certify or accredit health care organizations delivering physical therapy and other services. Certification and accreditation are important symbols of quality. Recognition by external groups that specific standards for multiple areas of organizational and clinical care activities have been met is often essential to getting paid for services. Recognition by national certification or accreditation organizations may influence customer choices.

The major U.S. certification and accreditation groups are discussed. Comparative information regarding their characteristics, purposes, target markets, and other commonalities is presented. The health care organizations discussed are CARF, JCAHO, and NCQA. Physical therapists often work in CARF-accredited adult day care and medical rehabilitation organizations and programs. Physical therapists who work in hospitals are likely to work in ways that are congruent with the JCAHO standards. Those who work in managed care settings, the predominant model of health care delivery in the United States, need to understand and meet NCQA standards.

Examples of the types of data collected and used to meet the standards of the major accrediting bodies are presented. Meeting certification and accreditation standards is part of the daily responsibilities of most health care managers and clinicians. Certification and accreditation standards therefore are voluntary forms of oversight of health care.

Some accreditation bodies have an interest in setting standards for professional groups and educational programs. FASB sets standards for financial accounting procedures. For physical therapists three important accreditation entities affect student physical therapists and educational institutions: APTA, CHEA, and CAPTE. APTA is the recognized voice of physical therapists in the United States. Its influence on standards is exerted on members through its code of ethics, on legislation through lobbying efforts, and on education through its communication with CAPTE.

CHEA, a government agency, gives official recognition to CAPTE as the physical therapy education accrediting commission. CAPTE in turn establishes the educational standards for entry-level physical therapist education programs. Compliance with CAPTE standards is the requirement for earning recognition as an accredited entry-level physical therapy education program.

Seeking accreditation voluntarily is a strategic commitment to offering quality services as judged by external bodies. Among the major areas of interest to accrediting bodies is the welfare of patients, that is, safety, quality of care, continuity, and outcomes. Health care organizations are interested in these same factors for reasons other than accreditation. Injuries to patients, visitors, employees, and others in a health care organization can lead to financial losses and a damaged reputation. Risks that can harm a health care organization or practitioner are discussed next. Chapter 33 presents principles of risk management applied at the organizational, departmental, and personal level. Special issues related to risk in physical therapy environments are addressed.

INDIVIDUAL CASE STUDY

Medical rehabilitation is one of the areas accredited by CARF. Assume you have a family member in need of rehabilitation for spinal cord injury. Your relatives call and ask you how they might check on the quality of care provided at the facilities near them. What advice could you give them right now?

GROUP CASE STUDY

Form a group of six members and assume the roles of a first-level physical therapist manager, two senior staff, and three staff therapists with 1 to 3 years of experience.

Situation

JCAHO has a standard for the uniform performance of patient care. The key areas of the standard are timely access to services and location or setting. Timely access means patients receive the services they need within a defined time. Location refers to where the services are delivered, such as at bedside or in the main physical therapy department. The first concern of the standard is to have sufficient numbers of qualified professionals so patients are seen in a timely manner. The second concern is that treatments may not be equivalent if they are delivered in different locations.

Task

Develop a policy (Chapter 10) that addresses the issue of uniformity of care in an urban general hospital. In a small group, begin discussing types of patients, that is, those with various diagnoses and levels of acuity, and locations in which physical therapy services might be provided, such as at bedside, in a satellite unit, or elsewhere. Clarify the issues. Come to a consensus on a policy to address the uniformity of care standard. If time allows, merge with another group and compare your end products with the intent of improving the policy to meet the JCAHO uniformity standard.

REFERENCES

American Physical Therapy Association. Mission. Available from http://www.apta.org. Accessed 4/12/03a.

American Physical Therapy Association. APTA vision sentence and vision statement for physical therapy 2020. Available from http://www.apta.org/About/aptamissiongoals/visionstatement. Accessed 4/12/03b.

American Physical Therapy Association. Accreditation frequently asked questions. Available from http://www.apta.org/Education/accreditation/general_information/faq#11324. Accessed 4/18/03c.

CARF—The Rehabilitation Accreditation Commission. About CARF. Available from http://www.carf.org/About CARF/Mission Purposes.htm. Accessed 4/15/03a.

CARF—The Rehabilitation Accreditation Commission. What is CARF? Available from http://www.carf.org/consumer.aspx?content=content/About/about.htm. Accessed 4/15/03b.

CARF—The Rehabilitation Accreditation Commission. Consumers to benefit from merger of two leading accreditation organizations in a service field. Available from http://www.carf.org/consumer.aspx?content=content/About/News34.htm. Accessed 4/15/03c.

CARF. The value of accreditation to the provider. Available from http://www.carf.org/payers. Accessed 4/15/03d.

Council for Higher Education Accreditation. Specialized and professional accrediting organizations 2002-2003. Available from http://www.chea.org/Directories/special.cfm. Accessed 4/18/03.

Financial Accounting Standards Board. Facts. Available from http://www.fasb.org/facts. Accessed 4/18/03.

Health and Administration Development Group. Health care quality and outcomes management. Gulledge J, ex. dir., Haught LB, research ed. Gaithersburg, MD: Aspen. 1999.

Institute of Medicine. Preserving public trust. Accreditation and human research. Participation protection programs. Committee on Assessing the Systems for Protecting Human Research Subjects. Washington: National Academy. 2001.

Joint Commission on Accreditation of Health Care Organizations. Facts about the Joint Commission on Accreditation of Health care Organizations. Available from http://www.jcaho.org/about+us/index.htm. Accessed 4/18/03a.

Joint Commission on Accreditation of Health Care Organizations. What's new for accredited organizations. Available from http://www.jcaho.org/accredited+organizations/index.htm. Accessed 4/18/03b.

National Committee on Quality Assurance. About NCQA. Available from http://www.ncqa.org/about/about.htm. Accessed 4/18/03a.

National Committee on Quality Assurance. A letter from NCQA president Margaret J. O'Kane. Available from http://www.ncqa.org/about/president.htm. Accessed 4/18/03b.

National Committee on Quality Assurance. Solutions for employers and employees from the most trusted source of health care quality information. Available from http://www.ncqa.org/Programs/cr/hcbrochure.pdf. Accessed 4/18/03c.

Rutgers. FASB and IASB agree to work together toward convergence of global accounting standards. Available from http://accounting.rutgers.edu/raw/fasb/news/nr102902.html. Accessed 4/18/03.

Sandstrom RW, Lohman H, Bramble JD. Health services policy and systems for therapists. Upper Saddle River, NJ: Prentice Hall. 2003.

MORE INFORMATION RELATED TO THIS CHAPTER

The best source for additional information related to accreditation is from the specific accreditation agency. Web sites for the most common:

CARF—The Rehab Accreditation Agency: http://www.CARF.org

Joint Commission on the Accreditation of Health Care Organizations: http://www.JCAHO.org

National Committee on Quality Assurance: www.NCQA.org

An excellent additional resource for rehabilitation professionals is the Desktop Consultant—The Rehab Professional's Guide to JCAHO, by Angie Phillips, PT. Available at http://www.RehabBusiness.com.

Chapter 33

Managing Risk

Learning Objectives

1. Examine the purposes and processes of risk management in health care settings in general and in physical therapy environments in detail.
2. Analyze the components of the risk management process described in this chapter.
3. Explore options for dealing with risk in health care settings.
4. Explore the methods for dealing with risk in areas that have historically posed the greatest risks in physical therapy environments.
5. Discuss the role played by department managers and staff in dealing with risk.
6. Summarize a typical sequence of events for dealing with a reportable incident.

Key Words

Abuse, adverse patient outcome (APO), assault, asset, battery, boundary crossing, claim, Equal Employment Opportunity Commission (EEOC) incident, incident/occurrence report, liability, occurrence, occurrence screening, potential risk, professional liability, risk, risk avoidance, risk exposure, risk management committee, risk management program, sexual harassment

Introduction

Risk is the probability of suffering harm or loss. Chapter 5 introduces the concept of risk at the more personal level, as it dealt with professional liability. While we do not always think about it, we do deal with the probability of suffering harm or loss on a daily basis. For example, there is the risk of an auto accident when driving. To protect ourselves, our passengers, and other drivers, we reduce the risk of harm or loss by driving cautiously in poor weather, in the dark, and in heavy traffic. Another way to manage risk when driving is to buy auto insurance. This transfers some of the financial risk from the purchaser to the insurer. A third commonsense way to manage risk is to make protective adjustments, such as pulling to the side of the road during a heavy downpour. This is an example of **risk avoidance**.

Health care businesses are also interested in managing risk to protect the financial and other assets of the business and to enhance the quality of care by actions to minimize risks to patients, visitors, and staff. In health care organizations, risk management can be defined as "the process of systematically monitoring health care delivery activities in order to prevent or minimize financial losses from claims or lawsuits arising from patient care or other activities conducted in a health care facility" (Scott, 2000, p. 191). Risk management is an integral part of a health care organization's quality improvement (Chapter 12), communication (Chapter 16), accreditation (Chapter 32), and other systems.

This chapter concentrates on the principles of health care risk management and relates them to physical therapy circumstances. You will become familiar with a formal process and tools for managing risk at the organizational, departmental, and individual level. Familiarity with the process may enhance your consciousness of the need to minimize risk, the ability to anticipate risk, the willingness to follow established procedures, and the ability to participate in a formal risk management program.

This chapter also includes some general legal information. Use this information to familiarize yourself with the concepts of managing risks and the consequences of not managing them. This material is intended to give you a conceptual understanding of managing risk and the possible consequences of not doing so. The legal information in this chapter is *not intended* for use, nor should it be used, as a substitute for consultation with a qualified attorney or other professional specialists (Chapter 34).

Risk Management

Anyone who has read the latest newspaper or watched any of the weekly television hospital drama programs has seen some of the situations that can increase risk in a hospital, such as drug tampering, violence in the emergency room, impaired professionals, administration of the wrong medication, equipment failure, misdiagnosis, and falls. In the late 1960s and early 1980s, because of increasing frequency of suits, increasing amounts of the awards, and increasing costs for **professional liability** (Chapter 5) insurance, hospitals and other health care organizations began risk management programs (Monagle, 1985). These programs were intended to prevent, control, and monitor **risk exposures**. The desired outcomes of **risk management programs** are twofold: protection of the organization's assets and improvement in quality of care. These are the major categories of **potential risk** in health care organizations in alphabetical order:

- Confidentiality issues, such as failure to protect privacy of written records and verbal exchanges
- Employees
- Equipment not in good operating order or not correctly calibrated
- Finances
- Individuals with staff privileges, such as physicians and physical therapists
- Infection control
- Patients
- Physical plant
- Students and interns
- Visitors
- Volunteers
- Waste management, such as radioactive and infectious materials

General Risk Management Concepts

The goal of every health care provider should be to provide the highest possible quality of care as defined by evidence-based information and interpreted in light of clinical experience, patient satisfaction, and economic realities. This multipart goal is attainable with communication, coordination, cooperation, and integration of clinical, service, and administrative departments. The essential element of this collaborative process is a strategic commitment to quality care, of which managing risk is one part (Scott, 2000).

Responsibilities

Strategic commitment begins at the highest level of leadership (Chapters 8 and 11). A health care organization's board of directors and the chief executive officer are responsible for high-quality care being delivered in a safe, satisfactory, and fiscally acceptable manner (Chapter 10). To deal with actual and potential risks, large health care organizations have formal risk management programs with risk management personnel and other individuals from a variety of clinical and administrative disciplines. A risk manager or coordinator is responsible for implementing a coordinated process that minimizes the likelihood of the organization being harmed because someone was injured. To facilitate coordinated efforts, there is often a **risk management committee**. The formal membership of such committees varies, but it typically includes representatives of segments of the organization that have been or are most likely to be at risk for claims. A risk management committee may also have ad hoc members (temporary members to deal with certain issues). Representational membership helps ensure organization-wide perspectives on the issues and solutions to them. A common process risk management groups use has several steps:

- Identify situations that have resulted in harm to someone or financial loss to the organization
- Analyze the risk for level of severity, frequency of occurrence, and possible level of loss
- Pose solutions and implement the most appropriate ones
- Monitor the results

Risk Management in Health Care Organizations

Effective risk management protects **assets** from loss. An organization's assets include property, money, human resources (employees), and intangible items such as public opinion (Salman, 1986a). To manage risks that may result in the loss of any of these assets, a traditional problem-solving process should be used. Kavaler and Spiegel (1997) offer one version of this process with five overlapping steps (Fig. 33.1).

Identification of Exposure to Risk

Risk is often looked at in terms of certainty and uncertainty. In a health care organization, as in other types of organizations, risks can be real, having resulted in an **occurrence**, or probable, being likely to occur. Several areas of uncertainty are associated with making decisions about risks. For example, there is uncertainty estimating the following:

- The likelihood of harm occurring
- How severely someone will be harmed
- Whether the organization will be harmed
- Whether someone will sue
- Whether one course of action is better than another

Looking for exposure to risk should not be limited to occurrences associated with patient care. Every segment of the organization, from administration to the maintenance department, is a source of risk. Table 33.1 lists some general areas of interest to risk managers. Several of these areas are discussed later in this chapter.

The broad scope of the areas of concern in risk management necessitates that managers have access to records from all areas of operation. The authority for such access comes directly from the highest levels of administration (Fig. 33.2).

Anything that hinders or may hinder the delivery of quality care, diminishes customer satisfaction, or has the potential to harm the organization financially is a risk, so risk consciousness should be a priority. This logic is reflected in the upper portion of Figure 33.2. Administrative support makes it more likely that risk management will become part of the organization's culture.

Another means of stimulating risk consciousness is through an interdisciplinary risk

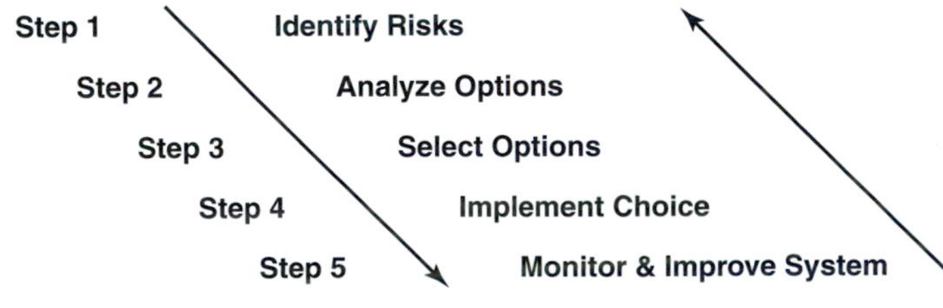

Figure 33.1. Process model for risk management.

Table 33.1 Some Areas of Interest to Risk Managers in Health Care

Abuse (child, elder, physical, sexual)	Insurance against all types of liability, damage, and loss
Antitrust violations	Noncompliance with Americans With Disabilities Act (1990)
Assault and battery (staff, patients, visitors and others)	Professional malpractice
Breach of contract	Property risks, damage, loss, maintenance
Credentials of medical staff	Quality assurance
Discrimination (age, race, religion, sex)	Recruitment and hiring practices
Embezzlement	Safety and security
Equipment risks, damage, loss, maintenance	Sexual harassment
Fraud	Theft
Failure to obtain informed consent	Workers' compensation
Incident reports	
Infection rates	

Adopted from Kavaler and Spiegel, 1997, pp. 5, 53–55, and Scott, 1997, pp. 85–105.

management committee that is represented near the middle of Figure 33.2. Representation on the risk management committee typically includes individuals from organizational units with the potential for incidents that can result in harm. The major focuses of the risk management committee are to manage risks and ensure that quality care is delivered. These two purposes can put the risk management and quality assurance functions in overlapping complementary roles. Risk managers typically are mainly concerned with the financial aspects of risk, and quality assurance managers are often more concerned with standards of care (Salman, 1986b). Major accrediting bodies require that risk management and quality assurance functions work collaboratively (Kavaler and Spiegel, 1997) to protect the organization and its patients. More information on accrediting agencies can be found in Chapter 32. Some examples of the categories of risk listed at the bottom of Figure 33.2:

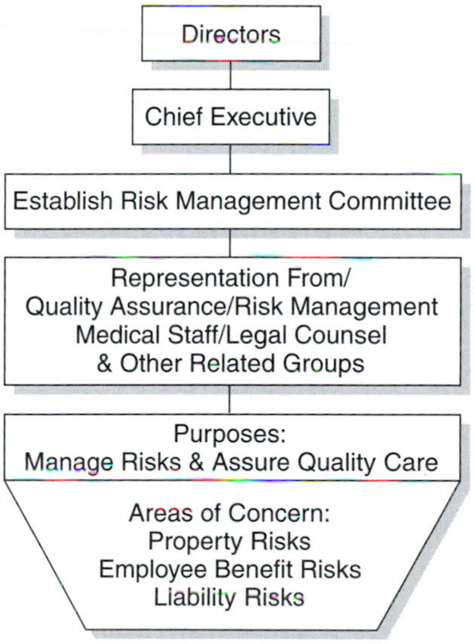

Directors

Chief Executive

Establish Risk Management Committee

Representation From/
Quality Assurance/Risk Management
Medical Staff/Legal Counsel
& Other Related Groups

Purposes:
Manage Risks & Assure Quality Care

Areas of Concern:
Property Risks
Employee Benefit Risks
Liability Risks

Figure 33.2. General structure of a risk management system in a large health care organization.

- **Property risks**: These include structural damage, such as a loose railing and broken or uneven sidewalks or curbs. In physical therapy, structural damage can be a rough edge on a mat table.
- **Employee benefit risks**: Long-term disability and retirement costs. In clinical departments, this may relate to pay equity.
- **Liability risks**, or **Casualty risks**: Professional negligence or malpractice, misbehavior by managers, e.g., embezzlement, failure of directors or officers to meet their fiduciary responsibilities (Kavaler and Spiegel, 1997)

These classifications of risk are helpful in grouping events; however, each organization also has a unique set of risks to fit into the classification system. Identifying risks has a subjective aspect. What is considered a risk is partly influenced by the organization's fundamental documents (Chapter 9). The values of individuals also come into play. The values of risk managers influence the determination

Table 33.2 Some Important Sources of Historical Information About Health Care Organization Risks

Internal Resources	
Committee reports	Previous claims
Incident reports	Quality assurance
Medical staff	Safety Inspectors
Patients records	Others
External Resources	
Expert consultants	
Insurance company representatives	
Industry publications	

of what a risk is and its significance to the organization (Troyer, 1986). For example, if the organization prizes patients' autonomy and dignity (Chapter 6), it is likely to support a restraint-free environment and accept some risk that slips and falls may occur. To counter this, however, staff might be added to supervise patients more closely and to respond more quickly, and training programs could be implemented to ensure that staff members meet patients' needs without restraints. In a different environment, say in a long-term care facility, honoring the values of autonomy and dignity while maintaining a restraint-free environment may present some unique challenges, solutions, and accompanying risks (Singleton, 1997). Examples of implementing this philosophy would be to have handrails on all patient room walls. Circular walkways could be developed to allow long walks (Singleton, 1997). Floors at selected doorways could be painted to look like deep holes. This may stop patients from wandering in areas with little supervision. Increased risks include falls due to fatigue, patients bumping into one another or staff, and patients wandering out of the designated safe areas. Architectural changes and new equipment add risk because of unpredictability of patient and staff responses to novel situations (Salman, 1986a). These examples show that each environment has idiosyncratic risks. The interpretation of the importance of these risks varies.

Information Needed to Manage Risk

The risk manager has numerous sources of information. Some data come from historical sources, such as previous claims against the organization, insurance records, incident reports, and other records. Other sources of information require more investigation but may be helpful in anticipating undesirable events. These additional resources are presented in Tables 33.2 and 33.3. Table 33.2 identifies resources that assist with identifying occurrences that have taken place in the past. Table 33.3 lists resources that may be useful in gathering information about potential risks.

Previous Claims

A **claim** is a demand for something that is alleged to be rightfully due. When a claim has been made against an organization or individual and the organization or person has been found liable, there may be an out-of-court or court-mandated financial settlement (Chapter 5). Typically, some form of liability insurance covers legal and settlement costs. However, all information related to settled claims must be available for review by risk man-

Table 33.3 Additional Sources of Information About Risks in a Health Care Organization

Administrators and department managers
Admissions personnel
Aides, orderlies, certified nursing assistants
Chaplain services director
Committee members (risk management)
Discharge personnel
Financial services managers
Maintenance personnel
Medical records manager
Quality assurance and safety committee members; case managers
Patient escorts
Public relations and marketing directors
Security officers
Social services manager
Students
Voluntarily terminating employees
Volunteers
Vendors

agers. If there was more than one incident or claim arising from the same cause, data on the frequency of occurrence in the industry can be consulted to see whether this is a common or uncommon problem. Consultant experts (Chapter 34) may be required to clarify the information.

Occurrence Reports

Most health care organizations have a system for reporting unusual events, or **incidents**. In health care environments an **occurrence report** or **incident report** (Fig. 33.3) is required whenever something unusual occurs in the care of a patient, operation of equipment, interaction with visitors, and so on. The system is activated by an incident. The reporting of an occurrence is essentially based on trust. Ideally, employees are trustworthy and follow policies and procedures (Chapter 11) for reporting unusual occurrences that they have participated in or witnessed.

For systemization purposes, an incident should be clearly defined so everyone in the organization recognizes one when it occurs. Anyone involved in or knowing of an incident is required to report it. Once completed, reports should be signed by the person making the report and given to a designated person within the specified time. Typically, the occurrence report is disseminated to one or more groups: quality assurance department, risk management department, and possibly the organization's attorney (Kavaler and Spiegel, 1997; Scott, 2000). A general recommendation is that incident report forms be kept separate from patients' records (Scott, 1997). Or-

ABC HOSPITAL (Automatic date and time of entry)

ABC Hospital System Log ID:_______________

PATIENT INCIDENT - OCCURRENCE REPORT (Form=RM1)

PERSON(s) INVOLVED: __________ LOCATION: __________

STREET: __________ PHONE: __________

CITY/STATE: __________ ZIP: __________ DEPT: __________

OCCURRENCE: DAY OF WEEK: __________ DATE: _____ TIME: __________

PATIENT/VISITOR CONDITION PRIOR TO OCCURRENCE: (01) ALERT
(02) AMBULATORY (03) ORIENTED (04) OTHER

AIDES: __________ OTHER: __________

PATIENT/VISITOR/EMPLOYEE ACCIDENT: (01) UNWITNESSED

DESC OF OCCURRENCE: __________ TYPE: __________

EXPOSURE TO: __________ OTHER: __________

BED HT: ____ BED RAILS: U D RESTRAINT IN USE: Y N TYPE: __________
BED CHECK IN PLACE: Y N SAFETY ALERT IN PLACE: Y N

BODY PART: (01) HEAD (02) NECK (03) SPINE (04) SHOULDER (ETC.)
EXTENT OF INJURY: (01) MINOR (02) MODERATE (03) OTHER

ADDITIONAL DETAILS: __________

PHYSICIAN: __________

PHYSICIAN NOTIFIED: __________

PATIENT SEEN BY MD: __________

NAME, ADDRESS, PHONE # OF WITNESSES: __________

DATE: __________

SIGNATURE OF PERSON PREPARING REPORT: __________

MANAGER SIGNATURE: __________

THIS INCIDENT REPORT IS TO BE COMPLETED AND ROUTED TO THE DIRECTOR OF RISK MANAGEMENT AS SOON AS POSSIBLE.

Figure 33.3. Computer incident report form.

ganizations should take steps to protect the information in incident reports from disclosure in case of litigation. How this information can be protected varies by state. In some states, reports sent to quality assurance are not necessarily accessible by third parties, while reports sent to legal counsel are (Scott, 1996). Occurrences that are likely to result in lawsuits should be forwarded to the organization's legal counsel. Once in their possession, the information may be considered privileged communication between lawyer and client and kept from a plaintiff's lawyer (Salman, 1986a). This is to the advantage of the named defendant (individual or organization) should a claim be made (Gaynor, 1995). Numerous states, including Arkansas, Colorado, Florida, Kansas, Maryland, Massachusetts, New York, North Carolina, Rhode Island, and Washington, require reporting of occurrences in health care facilities (Spiegel and Kavaler, 1997). Even if a patient does not make a claim against an organization, a state may require corrective action to protect future patients. For ease of tracking, an incident report form may be kept on an organization's computer system. However, internal access to the report must be strictly limited to those associated with managing quality and risk, and the system must be secure from unauthorized access. If computer security is in doubt, one hard copy should be kept in a locked cabinet or safe, with access limited to the organization's risk manager and legal personnel. Whether a computer-based reporting form (Fig. 33.3) or a written form is used, blank forms should be readily accessible to staff. Regardless of format, the basic information requested on an incident report is similar (Scott, 2000).

This is the usual information on an incident report form:

- The names of those involved, including witnesses
- What occurred
- When it occurred
- Where it occurred

The report should avoid interpretive information such as the cause of the occurrence or corrective actions that were taken (Gaynor, 1995). The person who responded to an adverse occurrence affecting a patient should follow established emergency procedures. Reiteration of this procedure is not needed on the incident report form. However, deviations from established procedures require written explanations.

Incident reports say what happened. What is done with this information is discussed more fully in the next section. In general, incident reports can lead to activities to prevent recurrence or reduce its likelihood. However, by themselves, incident reports are insufficient to reduce risks because they depend on employees complying with the requirement to complete and file reports. Compliance has been reported to be poor. It has been estimated that only 5% to 30% of adverse patient occurrences are actually reported in hospitals (Kavaler and Spiegel, 1997).

Reasons offered for failure to report occurrences include lack of understanding of what constitutes an incident, reluctance to implicate physicians, and fear of personal liability (Kavaler and Spiegel, 1997). Some employees believe that filing an incident report puts their job in jeopardy. Department managers need to make clear that not filing an incident report reduces the organization's ability to defend the employee if a claim is made.

With a minority of incidents being reported, for risk management and quality of care purposes it is necessary to consult additional records to identify actual or potential **adverse patient outcome** (APO) information. This broad search for risk-related evidence is called **occurrence screening**. Typical information sources used in occurrence screening are discussed next.

Treatment Records

In addition to what is recorded in a patient's chart, other records document what services were provided and other relevant information. The information in the patient's chart and in other records should match. It is the risk manager's responsibility to look for corresponding and discrepant information related to an adverse occurrence when a claim has been filed. Reviewing records can help prevent repeated occurrences as well as raise awareness (Kavaler and Spiegel, 1997). Some of the important records available to review for related information:

- Appointment cancellations
- Hospital readmissions
- Hospitalization for complications of prior care
- Medication records
- No-show rate
- Nosocomial (infections occurring after admission) infection rates and infection control reports
- Patients' medical records
- Records of emergency responses
- Records of patient transfers to more acute level of care
- Return to emergency services within 48 hours
- Transfer to another acute care facility
- Unscheduled returns to surgery and surgical reports

Committee Reports

The members of risk management committees should include representatives of diverse interested departments. The agenda of the committee is based in part on what concerns the members. Familiarity with the reports of the committees and departments represented by risk managers can help guide discussions, planning, and actions.

Insurance Company Representatives

Insurance companies pay out money when they settle claims against insured parties. It is to an insurer's benefit to help its policyholders minimize the number of claims filed against them. Insurance representatives called loss control consultants help reduce risks by sharing relevant information and experience with their company's policyholders (Kroft, 1992). These consultants have pooled data from similar organizations that help identify common trends, causes, successful remedies, and other information useful in preventing, minimizing, or eliminating compensable risks. Other sources of information on claims are listed at the end of the chapter.

Occurrence Screening

Incident reports are filed after an undesirable event, which makes them retrospective documents. Occurrence screening of such documents has both reactive and proactive purposes. The reactive purposes are to uncover causes and to determine what actions are needed to minimize harm to the patient, organization, and others that might result if no remedial action is taken. In occurrence screening, the event is investigated and evidence from multiple sources is pieced together. The proactive purpose is to prevent recurrences and to look for risks in similar categories. When occurrences are identified, corrective actions are initiated to stop, remedy, or minimize further complications. This can take place for patients still in the hospital. It is assumed that reactive and proactive actions will reduce the likelihood that patients will sue (Salman, 1986a).

Risk managers and others, including clinical department directors, actively look for signs of trouble for the organization. Looking for risks within the organization can lead to the discovery of risks before harm occurs and before a lawsuit is filed. Having foreknowledge of a potential claim allows time for the risk manager or department head to prepare to manage any suit and work with those likely to be named in it. This type of information is extracted from other routine records of patient care, emergencies, patients' comments, repair orders, security calls, and other activity reports. Occurrence screening requires more effort on the part of risk managers and department heads than is required in reviewing occurrence reports. This is because the information may not have been previously identified as an occurrence.

A risk manager or department manager screens many documents to get a broad perspective on past and potential risks. Some of the important documents, such as patient treatment records and committee reports, have been mentioned earlier. The basic question is whether you have any problems that should be considered further. The focus is on looking for possible evidence of adverse patient outcomes. In physical therapy, for example, perhaps a patient who has been using a cane with supervision for several days now requires a walker and physical assistance. Questions to consider include:

- What happened?
- Why?
- Did the person fall?
- Does the person have increased pain?
- Was there another incident?

A result of consulting multiple sources of information is the compilation of a fairly comprehensive list of APOs specific to the organization. Up to 85% of such occurrences can be identified through occurrence screening (Kavaler and Spiegel, 1997). In following up on APOs, risk management personnel may call upon representatives of departments identified in the occurrence screening to do a peer review of relevant cases to determine whether standards were upheld and whether changes should be made (Kavaler and Spiegel, 1997). Risk management involves all segments of an organization, and a close and coordinated working relationship between risk managers and quality assurance managers (Chapter 12) can protect the organization and its patients. The focus thus far has been on direct patient care occurrences and direct-care providers. Other people can provide useful risk management data. However, contacting these people may be time consuming.

Walking the Beat

To assess risk throughout an organization, risk managers should be a part of organizational thinking. This means that everyone from the board of directors and chief executive officer to student volunteers is a potential resource for identification of the organization's risks. For example, financial services may receive complaints written on bills but not say anything to anyone except that the bill was paid. Volunteers may know patients personally and may be told things that were not said to employees. The value of interviewing various employees and others is that common concerns may be identified prior to an undesirable occurrence. This information may not be found in the official databases or reports because no occurrence is associated with them. Such informal findings may alert the risk manager before risks materialize. The following list and comments identify additional resources for acquiring risk management information. The list and comments represent our thoughts and the writings of others, that is, Ashcroft, 1991; Kavaler and Spiegel, 1997; Melzer, 1995; Mittermaier, 1986; Salman, 1986a; Scott, 1997; and Young, 1991.

Administrators and **department managers**: Sometimes patients and others complain directly to the top. Concerns perceived to be trivial may be dismissed and not passed on to the risk manager. A system for centralizing and reviewing all complaints can help ensure a comprehensive view of the risks. Also, the scope of the issue may be beyond the department manager's responsibility. In these cases, the manager should involve those who have wider authority. Inquiries to other department managers may uncover the breath of the situation.

Admissions personnel are often the patient's first contact with an organization. The impressions they get of patients and their families may forewarn of risks.

Aides, **orderlies**, and **certified nursing assistants** may spend more time with patients than do some professional staff members. They may have useful information regarding a specific patient's level of expressed satisfaction. These individuals often do much of the physical labor of patient care. They may work with various pieces of equipment from pneumatic lifts to electric hospital beds. These front-line employees are a valuable source of information about patients' satisfaction, physical demands of work, and condition and availability of equipment not obtained from other sources.

Chaplain service director may offer unique insights regarding risks.

Committee members may be able to bring up situations that have not yet been addressed in interdisciplinary risk management committee meetings. There may be issues they would rather discuss on an informal or individual basis.

Discharge personnel may have comments regarding satisfaction. They are among the last members of the organization to interact with patients. A small hitch at discharge time may lead to comments by patient or family that were not voiced earlier.

Financial services managers may get notes with or on bills indicating dissatisfaction. Such complaints may also be made over the phone. Unless inquires are made, such comments may not be reported. If a patient or former patient gets no response from the organization, animosity may escalate and increase risk of a claim. Stakeholders may have concerns about financial resource management, such as questions about cash flow problems, large expense accounts, and suspicions of fraud, theft, or other serious matters that individual managers may bring up.

Maintenance personnel respond to requests for repairs, new installations, remodeling, and other services. They may see problems recurring, know of deteriorating conditions, and have insight into potential problems.

Medical records managers may have received requests for information about patients from unauthorized individuals. Knowing who is asking for the information may forewarn of a future claim.

Patient escorts may hear comments of patients and family members relevant to their feelings about the care they received, accidents that occurred, and observations that they were concerned about.

Public relations and marketing involve dealing with many individuals external to the organization. Such interactions may provide unique perspectives on the organization. This is particularly important in terms of public opinion, perceptions, and misperceptions. These departments may conduct customer satisfaction and visitor surveys. A visitor survey may be generated from visitor sign-in lists. These surveys may provide useful information regarding risks associated with specific departments and may alert staff to a future suit. Useful information may come from visitors because they may notice situations that patients do not. Visitors may be less stressed and more observant than patients and close family members.

Quality assurance, **utilization review**, and **safety and case managers** have frequent contact with patients and third-party payers. They may have heard concerns during these contacts. Interviews with case managers may lead to discovery of impressions that suggest further investigation.

Security officers are often called in emergencies. Discussions and reviews of their records may show patterns or areas of increased activities and may raise concerns about many areas, including theft, assault, and suspicious activities. Security records and records of emergency calls can be used for cross-checking.

Social services managers are often involved with the patient and the patient's family, third-party payers, employer, and so on. They may have an integrated view of a patient's environment and be able to pinpoint potential risks not obvious to others.

Students may have unique perspectives. They have not been fully acculturated to the organization. They may question why things are done as they are. They may raise issues based on experiences gained in other organizations or they may reflect on differences between what they have been taught and what they are doing or observe others doing.

Vendors may have information about risks associated with equipment or supplies they have sold the organization. They may also have published information about equipment or supplies from other manufacturers.

Voluntarily terminating employees are usually interviewed at their end of service by their department managers and human resource representatives. Employees leaving on good terms may be willing to express concerns about risks that they were reluctant to bring up while they were employed. Following up on these employees may uncover new risks.

Volunteers often converse freely with patients, because volunteers are perceived differently from employees. Volunteers overhear comments about care from patients, family members, and visitors that may imply a risk.

These sources may yield a representative list of APOs and other types of risks. Risk managers should assess the APOs and discuss possible solutions. These activities are part of the second step in risk management (Fig. 33.1).

Analysis

Risks are often assessed according to which have the most severe financial consequences for the organization (Rail, 1986). Risk managers consider the judgment of many people, including each other, risk management personnel, safety officers, utilization reviewers, and quality assurance committee members, to name a few. Identified occurrences and risks should be assessed so they can be managed in order of importance.

Asking and answering several questions can guide assessment. For occurrences, undesirable events that have happened, it is important to ask the following questions (Salman, 1986a):

1. What was the frequency of each specific occurrence?
2. What was the severity of the loss?
3. How severe could the loss have been?
4. What was the effect of past occurrences of this type on the organization?
5. What is the likelihood of an occurrence happening again?
6. What effect would a recurrence likely have on the organization?

A form such as is shown in Figure 33.4 may be helpful to organize the responses to these questions.

The analysis in Figure 33.4 requires integration of occurrence and risk information, comparison of occurrences and risks, use of actual data, and estimations of the relative importance of each of the listed criteria. The advantage of adopting a quantification method is that making comparisons is easier. Among the disadvantages of such a method is that it may not account for some special issues associated with certain occurrences and risks. The same questions can be asked for risks that have been identified but have not yet occurred, although the answers are necessarily more speculative.

Discussions of options for dealing with the risks may be carried on concurrent with the analysis of known risks. Once it is clear which occurrences and risks will be dealt with and what options are available (Table 33.1), the focus changes to selection of the most appropriate option.

General Risk Management Options

Selection of the most appropriate options for managing identified risks is the third step in risk management (Fig. 33.1). The general options for dealing with risk are presented in Table 33.4 and discussed next.

Loss Prevention

Ideally, risks are resolved so they no longer occur. Preventable risks are identified in the examination and analysis stage. Examples of corrective actions include educational programs, improved communication among involved parties, typed orders, and preventive maintenance. All of these procedures can be useful in physical therapy environments.

Loss Reduction

One way to describe loss reduction is to say it is a way to cover your back. It is being prepared in case there is a claim. Among the means of managing claims effectively are having all records completed in a reasonable time, informing staff about claims that have been filed, preparing staff for the possibility of legal action, and revising procedures that have led to occurrences. Each of these loss reduction suggestions is applicable to physical therapy departments.

Controlling Exposure

When you are faced with a pattern of repeated occurrences, one solution is to carry out a series of corrective actions. For example, one experiment could be spreading the

OCCURRENCE ANALYSIS SHEET Date: ______

Occurrence: Name ______________________ Description ______________________

Comments:

Frequency Code # ____ x Weighted Value ____ = ____

Severity Code # ____ x Weighted Value ____ = ____

Est. Correction

Cost Code # ____ x Weighted Value ____ = ____

Est. Correction

Time Code # ____ x Weighted Value ____ = ____

External Interest/Intangibles

Code # ____ x Weighted Value ____ = ____

Sum of Weighted Value: [ ]

Priority Rating: [ ]

Instructions: Descriptor code numbers range from a minimum of .5/5 to a maximum of 5/5. Weighted values are determined by the Risk Management Committee.

Frequency	#5 = Daily
Severity	#5 = Catastrophic
Correction Cost	#5 = Under $1000
Correction Time	#5 = Under a day
External Interest	#5 = Widespread

Figure 33.4. Occurrence analysis form for prioritizing risks. (Modified with permission from Salman SL. Risk management processes and functions. In: Troyer GT, Salman SL, eds. Handbook of health care risk management. Rockville, MD: Aspen Systems. 1986b;171–174.)

delivery of the service, say in a single physical therapy location, to several areas and rotating personnel through these locations to see whether a specific person or place is prone to the occurrences. Alternatively, an already decentralized procedure could be centralized to see what effect it has on frequency and severity of occurrences.

Risk Acceptance

Risk acceptance may occur by choice or oversight (Nelson and Gill, 1986). A risk that would cost more to insure against than the likely loss may be acceptable to the organization. This does not mean that nothing will be done to try to protect assets from harm or loss. It means that the organization will limit use of resources to reduce the risk. Risks accepted inadvertently are risks that were not considered (Nelson and Gill, 1986). Although risk acceptance is a risk management decision, physical therapy managers should seek clarifications regarding who and what is and is not covered by institutional insurance policies and the limits of applicable policies.

Table 33.4 General Options for Managing Risk

Control exposure	Risk acceptance
Loss prevention	Risk avoidance
Loss reduction	Risk transfer

Based on Kavaler and Spiegel, 1997, pp. 5, 6.

Risk Transfer

Risk can be shifted through contractual arrangements. This is frequently done for radiology services. The risk is transferred to the organization providing the service when the contract has a clause indicating that the contractor assumes responsibility for all risks. Such clauses do not, however, eliminate the organization's risk entirely (Kavaler and Spiegel, 1997).

Another form of risk transfer is through insurance. The insurance company assumes the risk of a suit in exchange for a premium paid by the health care organization. Over sufficient time, the premiums paid to the insurance company can increase to the point that the cost of insurance is greater than the risk being assumed by the insurer (Kavaler and Spiegel, 1997).

Avoidance

Certain health care services are associated with greater frequency of legal actions and large settlements. Neurosurgeons and obstetricians are notable examples. A health care organization may decide not to offer such services and thus avoid exposure to risks. In general, concentrating on the services at which the organization is most proficient reduces risk. Exposure avoidance in physical therapy might be the decision not to treat certain high-risk persons, such as premature infants.

The concepts of risk management have thus far been applied in an organizational context. Next we direct these concepts, the five risk management options, and suggestions for managing risk specifically to physical therapy environments. The next sections deal with risks to which departmental managers and individual practitioners are likely to be exposed. We include suggestions for self-protection against civil and criminal actions.

Risk Management Concerns in Physical Therapy

A comparison of Tables 33.1 and 33.5 shows many similar topics. However, the scope of the two tables differs. Table 33.1 relates to an entire organization. It was constructed from a risk manager's viewpoint. Table 33.5 has a limited scope. It focuses on areas of risk directly related to physical therapy. Physical therapy resources address many of the topics listed in Tables 33.1 and 33.5. Also see suggested resources later in this chapter.

Abuse, Assault, and Harassment

Abuse, in some form or degree, is associated with 10 of the topics listed in Table 34.5. **Abuse** means to misuse, hurt, or injure. Abuse typically involves neglect or harm of a minor or vulnerable adult (Rohman and Huber, 1996). Since physical therapists treat all diagnoses and age groups, awareness of the signs of abuse is important for the protection of patients. It is the moral, ethical (Chapter 2), and legal (Chapter 5) obligation of a physical therapist to protect those who are defenseless. While abuse is abhorrent no matter who is abused, it is particularly disturbing when it occurs within the context of health care.

Table 33.5 Some Important Areas of Risk In Physical Therapy Environments
Abuse (child, domestic, elder, sexual; police report may be mandatory)
Americans With Disabilities Act of 1990
Assault (fear of sexual or other type of harm)
Battery (unjustified offensive direct or indirect contact)
Civil Rights Act of 1964 (Title VII)
Civil Rights Act of 1991
Discrimination (age, race, sex, sexual preference)
Defamation (false communication about a person)
Employee discipline and termination
Equal Pay Act of 1963
Failure to obtain informed consent
False imprisonment (a form of abuse)
Invasion of privacy, public disclosure
Occupational Safety and Health Act of 1970
Pregnancy Discrimination Act of 1978
Recruitment and selection
Restrictive covenants in employment contracts
Sexual harassment (can be related to sexual assault or abuse)
Sexual misconduct (related to sexual abuse)
Theft, burglary

Abuse can cause emotional harm, physical harm, or both. For example, sexual abuse may have both physical and emotional consequences. Awareness of physical and behavioral patterns associated with abuse may aid the therapist in recognizing abuse cases when patients are interviewed and examined (Table 33.6).

Abuse Considerations and Risk Management

The risk management connection to abuse has four parts: situations involving individuals outside of the institution and three types of situations involving individuals within the institution. The external individuals include patients' acquaintances, caregivers, guardians, relatives, parents, or spouse. Individuals within the health care setting who may abuse patients include nonprofessional staff members, other patients, and professional staff members.

Table 33.6 Some Physical and Behavioral Signs Associated With Abuse

Physical Signs
Bruises in unusual areas or in areas inconsistent with history
Clothing dirty, torn, inappropriate
Crying
Easy startlement
Flinching when therapist makes unexpected movements
Poor hygiene
Recurring abrasions, bruises, burns, or cuts
Repeated touching of self in the genital area
Sunken eyes, cheeks; thin (malnutrition? lack of sleep? ill?)
Unexplained weight loss
Unwillingness to make eye contact
Withdrawal from touch
Behavioral Signs
Anxiety, nervousness
Emotional lability (emotional responses unusual for circumstances)
Hostility
Lethargy
Refusal to respond to reasonable relevant questions
Signs of depression

External Sources of Abuse

A physical therapist may be the first person to suspect abuse of a patient. Listening to a patient's comments may yield insight into the source of unreported abuse. In addition to unconvincing explanations for physical injuries, a physical therapist should listen for comments that might indicate the following (Rohman and Huber, 1996):

- Denial of basic essentials (e.g., clothing, food, medications, social contact)
- Exploitation (financial and other forms)
- Sexual abuse
- Unreasonable confinement (to room, restraints)

When abuse of a child is suspected, particularly sexual abuse, the physical therapist should be careful not to interrogate the child. Rather, write down what the child says using his or her words (Quaintance, 1996). Police or a child protective agency should be called. Until the authorities arrive, the therapist must ensure that the child is safe (Quaintance, 1996). The same general procedure should be followed if spousal abuse is discovered, but you must act only with the consent of the patient. Formal policies and procedures should be developed to authorize and guide staff actions in abuse situations. Assistance from legal staff may be required to assure the adequacy and legality of the adopted procedures.

Observations of interactions between the patient and others may also be informative. Watch how a patient reacts around certain family members or how a family member treats a patient when they are unaware that others are observing them. This may raise suspicions. This type of vigilance may be necessary because patients may be reluctant to implicate a family member on whom they depend for care or basic needs.

Internal Sources of Abuse

One internal source of abuse is patients. Patients are assigned to beds according to such criteria as surgical procedure, bed availability, and services needed. The compatibility of patients in a room is not typically a major consideration. Patients under duress may get angry, argue, and harm each other. They can bring ill feelings to the physical therapy area and squabble in wheelchairs or on adjacent mat tables. They can reach out and grab, swing, or shout at one another. This can distract other patients, who may become upset or lose balance and fall. When two or more patients do not get along, separate them. Treat them in different areas or at different times. Discuss the situation with nursing personnel to be sure that everyone is aware of the risk. Inquire whether psychological or social services have been or will be requested.

Another internal source of abuse is staff members. Use of controlled substances, personal problems, and stress are reasons a staff member might be rough, discourteous, abrupt, or rude in treatment of a patient. If these undesirable behaviors are intended to do harm and do result in harm, they may constitute a criminal act. If these behaviors are not intended to do harm but do have harmful consequences, professional staff, such as physical therapists, may be considered professionally negligent. This may be prosecuted as a civil wrongdoing rather than a criminal act. Personal and professional liability insurance covers the insured person for professional negligence but not for criminal acts. An employer is responsible for the acts of its employees. Proven misconduct in the form of abuse should be subject to disciplinary action. Failure to take action may increase an employer's liability.

A department manager needs to be aware of the level of care being provided by the professional staff and their extenders, such as aides. This necessitates more documentation review. Periodic observation of actual treatments being delivered is necessary to find out more than what has been written in reports or notes. Therapist extenders usually do not write reports. Observation of their performance is vital. For example, if behaviors become erratic or the person has unexplained absences, tardiness, and/or radical mood changes, one might suspect illicit drug use. It is appropriate to request drug testing following an accident resulting in serious injury to a patient or staff member to rule out impairment as a cause of the accident. If there is reasonable suspicion that an employee is using illicit drugs, to maintain a safe workplace, a manager may request that the employee submit to drug testing (Scott, 1997).

Assault Considerations and Risk Management

A distinction between abuse and **assault** is the status of the harmed individual. Abuse is done to individuals who are vulnerable or less able to fend for themselves than other people. Assault is defined as "any willful attempt or threat to inflict injury on a person when coupled with an apparent ability to do so, and any intentional display of force such as would give the victim reason to fear or expect immediate bodily harm" (Nolan and Nolan-Haley, 1990, p. 114). An assault can be committed with or without touching another person or doing bodily harm.

Assault and Battery

Assault is often coupled with the word *battery*, which means unjustified, offensive, unwanted intentional physical contact (Scott, 1997) (Chapter 5). The key element of battery is the injured party's lack of consent to physical contact (Schunk and Propas Parver, 1989). Together, assault (no physical contact) and battery (contact) mean any unlawful touching of another that is without justification or excuse (Nolan and Nolan-Haley, 1990).

An understanding of assault and battery is essential to physical therapists. Physical therapy necessitates physical contact. Accusations of assault and battery may stem from the handling of a patient in the course of treatment. In many situations patients may claim that they feared they were going to be touched for sexual purposes. This fear of contact or injury as discussed is legally considered an assault. For example, asking an opposite sex person to expose the clavicle or sacrum might frighten some patients. Palpating the pubic ramus to identify its location and mobilizing it prior to other activities to relieve a sacroiliac problem may seem inappropriate to a patient. This may be construed as sexual battery, or nonconsensual touching of another's body. If pain was increased by the maneuver, perhaps battery could be added to the charges. Patients may be concerned about unwanted touching or viewing of their genital area, breasts, thighs, or buttocks (Quaintance, 1996). To protect the patient, departmental personnel, and the institution, departmental policies must manage these types of contact risks. Some policy suggestions:

1. Require appropriate discussion before obtaining written informed consent from each patient. Consent is especially important from patients who will receive massage, manual therapy, or other physical agents applied to areas with sexual connotations. Consider cultural differences as well as gender differences.
2. Require patients to wear clothing appropriate for the activities in which they will participate.
3. Require draping of all patients.
4. Require informing patients that they can request a same-sex chaperone during treatment.
5. Require that a staff member of the patient's sex be present when a member of the opposite sex is treating a patient near the genitals or other areas usually considered private (Schunk and Propas Parver, 1989).
6. Require a knock-and-enter rule that allows a staff member to knock before entering and then to enter a private treatment area while it is in use.
7. Require treatment room doors be left partially open whenever the therapist senses a concern on the part of the patient or administer the treatment in a less secluded area, such as in a curtained booth (Schunk and Propas Parver, 1989).
8. Discourage social contact and dating between employees (all levels) and patients (Swisher and Krueger-Brophy, 1998).

Policies require procedures for their enactment. To ensure that these and other policies are carried out requires ongoing education and monitoring. The department manager must provide orientation and ongoing education to ensure that new staff develop appropriate skills and experienced staff maintain skills in obtaining informed consent and in carrying out procedures needed to enact policies intended to minimize risk.

Assault by a Physical Therapist

A final consideration is sexual assault of a patient by a physical therapist. A claim of assault may be the end result of a typical therapist–patient relationship. There is a reasonable option to terminate the relationship of a professional who has amorous feelings for a patient under his or her care or if the therapist believes a patient has such feelings. The most convenient action is simply to refer the patient to another therapist. However, this transfer may or may not alleviate the situation, especially if therapist and patient remain in the same treatment facility.

The physical closeness inherent in the practice of physical therapy and the long duration of treatment are two elements that facilitate building rapport with patients. This rapport may lead to more substantive thoughts and feelings. A progression of actions move from rapport building to sexual misconduct. This progression has been called **boundary crossing**, boundary violation, and sexual misconduct (Gutheil and Gabbard, 1993). The concepts of boundary and progression are clarified in the following questions (Wysoker, 1997):

1. Role of the therapist: Does it change over time?
2. Time together: Do treatments get longer? Are there extra treatment sessions?
3. Place: Are treatments administered in view of others?
4. Space: Is there less space between patient and therapist than what is needed or how similar patients are treated? Hugging? Touching in comforting ways? Hand holding?
5. Money: Are charges reduced or not made for treatment?
6. Gifts: Are gifts given or exchanged?
7. Services: Are additional services offered? Is non–physical therapy assistance offered?
8. Is the dress appropriate for the setting? Is clothing suggestive? Is either person's

clothing noticeably different when patient X and therapist Y work together?
9. Language: Are the language and content of the conversation appropriate for therapeutic needs? Is conversation personal? Is it intended to be just between therapist and patient?
10. Self-disclosure: Does one party tell the other very personal things? Is this self-disclosure reciprocal?
11. Physical contact: Is there touching that is not necessary for treatment? Is there touching for its own sake?

There can be no hard and fast rule regarding touching in physical therapy. Crossing boundaries is situational. If crossing one of these boundaries has a therapeutic purpose supported by evidence, it should be clearly noted in the patient's record. If it cannot be justified by evidence, it may be that a boundary has been crossed.

People's feelings for one another are not always subject to rational thinking. What can be done about therapist–patient social relationships? A guideline for psychiatric professionals is informative here. The guideline is that if a relationship is to occur, it is judicious to wait at least 6 months after treating a patient before having intimate relations (Stromber, Haggarty, Leibenluft et al., 1988).

A manager must be aware of developing relationships that may affect the organization. Relationships may be public or they may be divulged in private discussions with a staff member. If there is reason to believe that a therapist is abusing, assaulting, or battering a patient, for the welfare of patient, therapist, and organization, the therapist must be confronted and reported. After discussions, if suspicion remains, the suspicion should be reported to the organization's risk manager or other official. Needless to say, illegal acts like abuse and assault are unethical. The Guide for Professional Conduct of the American Physical Therapy Association (APTA) prohibits both abuse (Principle 1.1 C, 9.1.B) and sexual relationships with any patient (Principle 2.1.C) (APTA, 2002). Members of APTA are obligated to protect the public and report ethical and legal problems (Principle 9.1.C). Matters of ethical concern are to be reported by contacting the president of the identified individual's chapter. Matters of legal concern are to be reported legal authorities (many health care organizations have protocols; state laws may give mandates for certain kinds of circumstances).

Abuse and assault are criminal offenses punishable by imprisonment. Civil claims may also result from a sexual assault. The remedy for civil claims is payment of money. Since insurance policies exclude payment for criminal acts, the offender is obligated to pay the award from his or her personal resources. To complete the discussion of issues related in one way or another to sexual conduct, one more topic must be discussed. This is sexual harassment.

Sexual Harassment and Risk Management in Physical Therapy

Sexual harassment is distinct from abuse and assault in three major ways. First, it is considered a form of sex discrimination (Rubin, 2001). The Equal Employment Opportunity Commission (EEOC) can investigate complaints of sexual harassment in the workplace. This is the federal administrative agency responsible for administering and enforcing Title VII of the Civil Rights Act of 1964 and other federal regulations about equal employment opportunities (Scott, 1996). Second, sexual harassment is a civil wrong, not a crime. Third, all members of an organization are covered by sexual harassment regulations. Sexual harassment may occur between these types of persons:

- Supervisor and staff
- Coworkers
- Employees and vendors
- Employees and customers (including patients)
- People of the same or opposite sex

EEOC is the federal agency created by Congress in the 1964 Civil Rights Act. EEOC enforces all federal regulations, policies, and actions affecting equal employment opportunity. One of the areas EEOC deals with is sexual harassment. The EEOC definition of sexual harassment includes the following unwelcome acts:

- Demands for sexual favors in return for hiring, promotion, or tenure
- Leering or ogling
- Off-color jokes
- Patting, pinching, brushing against the body
- Physical assault or rape
- Pressure for dates
- Sexist remarks
- Verbal abuse

The 1990 EEOC guidelines made further clarifications regarding sexual harassment. "Harassment on the basis of sex is a violation of Section 703 of Title VII. Unwelcome sexual advances, requests for sexual favors, and other verbal or physical conduct of a sexual nature constitute sexual harassment" (Gamble, 1992, p. 291). Sexual harassment can occur in two scenarios. The first is called quid pro quo (something for something). This means that granting sexual favors are explicitly or implicitly a term or condition for initial or continued employment or other opportunities in the workplace. The second is the work environment itself. A hostile work environment is one in which conduct of the type Gamble describes unreasonably interferes with an individual's work performance or presents an intimidating or offensive working environment. The guideline goes on to state that the employer has an affirmative duty to maintain a workplace free from sexual harassment and intimidation (Gamble, 1992). If the harassment affects a person's work performance, it is an EEOC issue (Rubin, 2001).

Managing the Risk of Sexual Harassment

Sexual harassment can occur in stages or degrees of severity. A description of progressive sexually oriented behaviors is as follows:

1. Invited and reciprocal (this is not harassment)
2. Uninvited but welcome (a light gray area)
3. Offensive but tolerated (likely a legal matter)
4. Flatly rejected (clearly a legal matter)'

These comments and criteria are gender neutral. However, they have been interpreted to apply to women being harassed by men. The Supreme Court has recently begun deliberating about same-sex harassment being covered by the Civil Rights Act of 1964.

These criteria apply to all levels of personnel equally. This means an aide or executive officer of a health care organization may be a sexual harasser. It is the employer who is liable for quid pro quo and hostile environment harassment. Efforts by an employer intended to reduce the incidence of sexual harassment are called for by EEOC guidelines. For example, "to avoid liability, employers have to educate and sensitize their workforce" and "an employer is liable when it knew, or upon reasonably diligent inquiry should have known of the harassment" (Gamble, 1992, p. 291, 292). Table 33.7 contains several suggestions for reducing the incidence of sexual harassment and the risk of claims against the employer.

Table 33.7 Some Options to Combat Sexual Harassment

1. Establish a strongly worded written policy based on current EEOC guidelines.
2. Establish a grievance procedure for sexual harassment complaints. The procedures must ensure confidentiality and be directed by two organizationally powerful managers, one of each sex, who have credibility. The person making the complaint should be allowed to complain to someone outside of his or her supervisor's chain of command.
3. Establish a management response program that immediately starts an investigation. The investigation should check for trends and job changes and should go back to earlier records and contact past employees regarding sexual harassment.
4. Provide mediation between an employee and supervisor.
5. Teach all employees, especially managers, about sexual harassment as well as the organization's policy and procedures. This may be done through training programs to increase awareness of potentially undesirable attitudes, behaviors, stereotyping, and language.
6. Discipline offenders in accordance with the severity of the offense. Solid evidence is necessary for this. Keeping records of complaints, investigations, and actions develops an evidential database. It is important to conduct exit interviews with individuals who are terminating to clarify the reason for their leaving the organization.

Adapted from Wolkinsin and Block, 1996, pp.74, 75

An ideal complaint process provides anonymity to individuals making complaints of sexual harassment, is responsive to the complaint, and reflects concern for the person being harassed and earnestness about stopping sexual harassment. Risk to the organization due to sexual harassment is likely to be reduced when these actions are taken. However, not all complaint processes are ideal. Some individuals prefer to deal with such issues themselves. An individualized approach to dealing with sexual harassment involves saying no and putting it in writing. Clearly tell the person to stop the behavior soon after it occurs. If it continues, write a letter to the harassing party. In the letter, describe the offensive behavior, when it occurred and the circumstances, and the negative reaction the behavior caused; and say what should be done to rectify the situation in addition to ending the harassment. Deliver the letter in person in the company of a reliable witness.

This individualized approach keeps the matter private and it may solve the immediate problem. However, it bypasses data gathering. If the person engaging in the harassment does it habitually and complaints remain individualized, the problem is not solved. It is just passed on to the next person who is harassed.

Student Notes

Based on findings from a large study of a predominantly female physical therapists, you can expect to experience some form of sexual harassment from patients (deMayo, 1997). An individual option is to clearly let the other person know that he or she is out of line as soon as possible after the occurrence. If it continues, review departmental policy and procedures and act accordingly.

From an organizational standpoint, several options are available to reduce risk. A departmental policy regarding sexual harassment and a procedure for dealing with it is one way an organization can deal with the matter. This is a form of loss prevention. A second option is a combination of risk transfer and controlling exposure. If harassment has been com-

INDIVIDUAL CASE STUDY

You are ecstatic about being in your final clinical rotation. You have done well by every measure. Among the challenging and diverse patients you treat is an individual your age. This person was shot in the upper thigh, abdomen, and gluteal areas and had orthopedic, integumentary, and urological trauma. The patient wears a catheter and leg bag and has a long leg cast. He is to begin to stand and use a walker today. Treatment is done in the patient's room, as you have three patients to treat on this floor and it is already near 4:00 P.M. You enter the room and notice that the patient's wheelchair is not there and the bathroom door is closed. You knock on the door and are told to wait. As you stand there you smell what you believe to be cannabis smoke. The patient emerges and you see some smoke but nothing else. What options do you have at this point? You ask the patient if he is ready for gait training and he says yes. You remind the patient to lock the wheelchair and you attach a gait belt. You clearly smell smoke residue on the patient's clothing. What options do you have at this point? You give the appropriate instructions, grasp the gait belt, and the patient stands up. He says he can walk without help. You are about to stop him when he takes a couple of long steps away from you and falls. You are several feet from him. What do you do?

Use the recommendations offered in this chapter regarding completing an incident report and write up the report. What will you tell the risk management representative when you are interviewed? Are you at any risk? If so, explain (Chapter 5).

GROUP CASE STUDY

Read the case study and then form groups of three members. Two members will work on the case. The other member will act as a consultant (Chapter 34).

Situation

NFG is a part-time physical therapy technician in a general hospital. In addition, NFG is a student physical therapist. The context is as follows:

- Time: Late Saturday morning. Less than half an hour left before closing the department.
- Staff: One physical therapist, one physical therapist assistant, and one physical therapy technician (NFG).
- Patients: 1 person post total knee replacement yesterday (range and early strengthening), 1 person post stroke incurred a week ago (functional training), 1 person with acute low back strain admitted today (referred for exercise).
- Event: The physical therapist is called to the nurse's station for a short time (one floor up from the physical therapy department). The physical therapist assistant has been working with the person with the stroke. The assistant decides to treat the patient with the knee replacement concurrently. That leaves the patient with acute low back strain unsupervised for the moment. NFG, who is free, begins a no-hands-on gross assessment of this patient.

Task

The job of the paired class members is to identify and discuss the source or sources of risk in this scenario. Consider risks to employees (specify which employee and the source of risk), to patients (specify which patient and the source of risk), and the organization. The job of the consultant is to listen, and when asked, to give suggestions. The paired members may use the information or not. Be sure to answer these questions:

What information do you lack?
How will you deal with this need for more information?
Where will you get the information?
Was more than one reasonable solution formulated by group members?
What did you learn from this exercise?

mon and the characteristics of harassing parties have been identified, patients with these characteristics may assigned to experienced therapists. These actions, however, may just put someone else at risk. Patients have to be treated, so avoidance is of unknown benefit, particularly because someone else controls the initiation of sexual harassment behaviors.

Summary

Risk management is coordinated efforts to identify, assess, and minimize where possible risks to patients, visitors, staff, and the organization. Risk management programs aim to protect the patient as well as the organization.

An occurrence is an unusual event that may lead to a lawsuit. Any occurrence should be reported in a standardized way and sent to a central location for analysis. Individual occurrences or trends can lead to policies and procedures and other actions that will likely reduce the chance of similar untoward events happening in the future. Among the sources of risk are the environment, equipment, services offered, and employees. A plan to reduce risks in each of these areas has been discussed. Of particular pertinence to physical therapy is a discussion of abuse, assault, and sexual harassment. Recognition of the signs of abuse in vulnerable patients is also discussed. Abuse, assault, and sexual harassment are defined according to law. Suggestions for dealing with these situations are offered. To deepen thoughts about sexual issues, the discussion includes several perspectives. The focus is placed at different times on issues relating to a physical therapist examining and treating a patient, on a manager's responsibility for safeguarding patient and employee welfare, on the person being assaulted or harassed, and on the person committing the assault or harassment.

This chapter is an overview of risk management in the health care setting. We recommend consulting risk management and legal specialists in the organization before acting. How to deal with internal and external consultants is the focus of the next chapter. Chapter 34 presents the consultative process and how to select a consultant. External consultants are often contracted by health care entities for advice on law, accounting, and several subcategories of management. Individual physical therapists also dealt with consultants, for example, about career development, insurance, and financial planning. They too are often asked to be consultants. Chapter 34 provides background information on developing a consultative relationship, expectations from the process, and selection of a consultant.

REFERENCES

American Physical Therapy Association. APTA guide for professional conduct. Available from http://www.apta.org. Accessed 8/3/02.

Ashcroft C. Betting the odds: Risk management. Clinical Management 1991;11:12–13.

Civil Rights Act of 1964, Title VII, 42 U.S.C., 29 CFR. 1604.11(a–f).

deMayo RA. Patient sexual behaviors and sexual harassment: A national survey of physical therapists. Physical Therapy. 1997;77:739–744.

Gaynor E. Policies and procedures. In: Managing risk in physical therapy: A guide to issues in liability. Alexandria, VA: American Physical Therapy Association, 1995:III.1–III.34.

Gamble BS, ed. EEOC: Policy guide on employer liability for sexual favoritism under Title VII, January 12, 1990. In: Appendices, sex discrimination handbook. Washington: BNA. 1992:349–353.

Gutheil T, Gabbard GO. The concept of boundaries in clinical practice: Theoretical and risk management dimensions. American Journal of Psychiatry. 1993;150:188–196.

Kavaler F, Spiegel AD. Risk management dynamics. In: Kavaler F, Spiegel AD, eds. Risk management in health care institutions: A strategic approach. Sudbury, MA: Jones & Bartlett. 1997:3–25.

Kroft GG. Synopsis of an insurance company safety specialist. Preventing Injury. 1992;1:10–11.

Melzer BA. An introduction to risk management. In: Managing risk in physical therapy: A guide to issues in liability. Alexandria, VA: American Physical Therapy Association. 1995:I.1–I.11.

Mittermaier AJ. Organizing a risk management program: The smaller hospital. In: Troyer GT, Salman SL, eds. Handbook of health care risk management. Rockville, MD: Aspen. 1986:313–326.

Monagle JF. Risk management: A guide for health care professionals. Rockville, MD: Aspen. 1985.

Nelson RT, Gill WH. Alternative methods of risk financing. In: Troyer GT, Salman SL, eds. Handbook of health care risk management. Rockville, MD: Aspen. 1986:209–227.

Nolan JR, Nolan-Haley JM. Black's law dictionary, 6th ed. St. Paul, MN: West. 1990.

Pozgar GD. Legal aspects of health care administration. Gaithersburg, MD: Aspen. 1993.

Quaintance K. Sexual assault. In: Hauser BR, ed. Women's legal guide. Golden, CO: Fulcrum. 1996:85–98.

Rail R. Financial and risk management in hospitals. In: Troyer GT, Salman SL, eds. Handbook of health care risk management. Rockville, MD: Aspen. 1986:81–100.

Rohman LW, Huber PL. Health: Patient rights and policing the quality of health care. In: Hauser BR, ed. Women's legal guide. Golden, CO: Fulcrum. 1996:34–64.

Rubin PA. Civil rights and criminal justice: Primer on sexual harassment. In: Lewis JV, ed. Sexual harassment: Issues and analyses. Huntington, NY: Nova Science. 2001:1–12.

Salman SL. Risk management processes and functions. In: Troyer GT, Salman SL, eds. Handbook of health care risk management. Rockville, MD: Aspen. 1986a:149–182.

Salman SL. Quality assurance and risk management. In: Troyer GT, Salman SL, eds. Handbook of health care risk management. Rockville, MD: Aspen. 1986b:411–419.

Schunk C, Propas Parver C. Avoiding allegations of sexual misconduct. Clinical Management. 1989;9:19–22.

Scott RW. Incident reports: Protecting the record. PT: Magazine of Physical Therapy. 1996;4:24, 25.

Scott RW. Promoting legal awareness in physical and occupational therapy. St. Louis: Mosby. 1997.

Scott RW. Legal aspects of documenting patient care, 2nd ed. Gaithersburg, MD: Aspen. 2000.

Singleton JK. Identifying and controlling risks in long term care: Nursing homes and home health. In: Kavaler F, Spiegel AD, eds. Risk management in health care institutions: A strategic approach. Sudbury, MA: Jones & Bartlett. 1997:245–268.

Spiegel AD, Kavaler F. Regulatory environment. Standards and risk management. In: Kavaler F, Spiegel AD, eds. Risk management in health care institutions: A strategic approach. Sudbury, MA: Jones & Bartlett. 1997:26–46.

Stromber CD, Haggarty DJ, Leibenluft RF, et al. Physical contact and sexual relations with patients. The psychologist's legal handbook. Washington: Council for the National Register of Health Service Providers in Psychology. 1988:463.

Swisher LL, Krueger-Brophy C. Legal and ethical issues in physical therapy. Boston: Butterworth-Heinemann. 1998.

Troyer, G. The concept of risk. In: Troyer GT, Salman SL, eds. Handbook of health care risk management. Rockville, MD: Aspen. 1986:141–148.

Wolkinsin BW, Block RN. Employment law: The workplace rights of employees and employers. Cambridge, MA: Blackwell. 1996.

Wysoker A. Risk management in psychiatry. In: Kavaler F, Spiegel AD, eds. Risk management in health care institutions: A strategic approach. Sudbury, MA: Jones & Bartlett. 1997:225–244.

Young GJ. Home health: Special risks. PT Magazine. 1991;9:63–64.

More Information Related to This Chapter

The Associate in Risk Management credential is available to physical therapists and other health care professionals through the American Institute for Chartered Property Casualty Underwriters and the Insurance Institute of America (http://www.aicpcu.com).

The American Physical Therapy Association offers consulting services on risk management (http://www.apta.org) and a fax-on-demand service (800-399-2782) on insurance, financial planning, and women's issues.

A Web site of Canadian and U.S. sources for financial planning, insurance, and risk management is http://www.ucalgary.ca/uofc/faculties/mgm/inrm/ins_web.htm.

The International Risk Management Institute offers manuals, online courses, and audiotapes on a variety of topics for health care managers, including professional liability insurance, hiring, and human resources (http://www.irmi.com).

A comprehensive book about risk management that includes chapters on allied health professional credentialing, statutes, standards, regulations, and informed consent is Carroll R, ed. Risk management handbook for health care organizations, 2nd ed. Chicago: American Hospital. 1997.

Assault and battery are specifically covered in the professional liability insurance offered through the Health Providers Service Organization's professional liability insurance (http://www.hpso.com).

Public information regarding sexual contact between patients and therapists is available at http://www.psych.org/public_info/patient_&_fam.cfm.

Chapter 34

Getting Advice

Learning Objectives

1. Examine in detail the individual steps of the consultation process presented in this chapter.
2. Contrast consultation from the point of view of a perspective customer and a perspective consultant.
3. Summarize the six areas for which health care organizations typically seek external consultant advice.
4. Evaluate the concept of "managing the consultant."

Key Words

Consultant, letter of agreement, manage consultant, project proposal, request for proposal (RFP), retainer, screening question

Introduction

A consultant is one who confers and gives professional or technical advice (Webster's, 1984). When a practice or department is faced with problems that won't go away or an outside or fresh opinion would be welcome, a consultant may be the answer. In the long run, management can save time and money by funding the right assistance to help overcome a current obstacle or avoid costly mistakes in the future. A good consultant, looking at your situation objectively, should be able to identify and implement the solution to the problem more quickly and efficiently than internal personnel. After all, they would not seek a consultant if they were confident in their decisions. The trick is to know what types of problems warrant a consultant's services. This chapter examines the guidelines for getting help.

When to Hire a Consultant

Here are some typical situations that might merit engaging an outside consultant:

- When you need an objective point of view or when you are very close to a situation and have a tendency to favor a predetermined rather than creative solution
- When the problem or situation is short term, such as public relations around a special event
- When the problem requires special expertise, such as knowing how to buy a computer system, manage accounting, or address legal issues
- When your organization's financial situation is not favorable for hiring permanent staff with all the consequential financial obligations
- When your practice is facing a major crisis or when it seems to be operating in a crisis management mode

If your situation falls into any or all of these categories, a consultant's services may be a worthwhile investment. Of course, you will want to use all the financial tools discussed in previous sections of this book to determine whether the cost of bringing in an outsider will be justified by the rewards (Chapter 28).

Why Hire a Consultant?

Why you hire a consultant depends on what you are trying to accomplish. These are some examples:

- **To supplement staff time**. Your current staff may be productive in many areas but may not have the time to devote direct attention to new or expanding areas of work. Use of an outside consultant or adviser may be an excellent way to allow staff to continue to perform at a high level without the added distractions of new responsibilities.
- **To supplement staff expertise**. Your staff may not have the necessary education, experience, or expertise to undertake a new project or activity. Outside expertise and experience can be purchased to supplement or even train the staff in the new activities (Ginter, Swayne, Duncan, 1998).
- **To ensure objectivity**. Sometimes we all get too close to a concept or project. Using an outside expert who has not developed an attachment to the project can provide an unbiased opinion on strategy or procedure for the project.
- **To ensure credibility**. When you have to make a decision with a high degree of emotional content, it is often good to have an outsider give an opinion of the best course of action. This allows managers to benefit from both the second opinion and the ability to distance themselves from an unpopular decision.
- **To obtain a variety of skills**. No organization, no matter how large and complex, can possibly have all of the expertise it will ever need in the permanent employees and associates it hires. Specialized expertise may be needed for special projects or topics.
- **To deal with legal requirements**. Legal issues almost always require input from attorneys with expertise in the specific topic. Examples include employment law, real estate law, Medicare and reimbursement law and regulations, and in some states, certificate of need requirements.

Types of Consultants in Physical Therapy

Consultants are available in more than 800 specialized categories, offering assistance on everything from absenteeism to copiers. To identify the type of consultant you need, you must first accurately define your problem. In a physical therapy practice, the most common types of consultants are accountants, attorneys, risk management, and rehabilitation consultants, for example, HIPAA and coding (Chapter 4). Information technology (Chapter 13), real estate, personnel, and financial advisers (Chapter 27) are also quite common for physical therapy practices. Less common are specific treatment specialists, for example, aquatic therapy or incontinence programs.

Defining the Problem

Managers often mistake symptoms for problems. Such an error can interfere with the consultant's ability to help. The consultant may be misled by statements that point him or her in the wrong direction. However, looking at the symptoms is a necessary step in discovering the source of the problem.

In preparation for a discussion with a consultant, start with a review of symptoms (George and Cristiani, 1990). Outline the organization's or department's needs in relation to the present outcomes. For instance, let's say the organization is consistently over budget on campaigns to raise awareness of the mission. You have identified the symptom, that you are over budget, and are ready for the next seven steps:

1. Clarify your expectations.
2. What work do you need to have accomplished? Will there be a report, new system in place, a new person hired?
3. What skills are required? Do you need a facilitator, someone with specific technical skills, a generalist who can achieve agreement?
4. Establish a project committee to scope out the work, develop a request for proposal (RFP), and identify and screen potential consultants.
5. Establish a time frame. How much time will you allocate to this project? How quickly must it be performed?
6. Determine who will be responsible for the project. Who will be the lead contact for the consultant? Who will make decisions? Who will do the work? Who will be involved? How many staff members will be allocated to this project, and how will they be supervised?
7. Seek out resources, that is, where to find information about specific consultants.

Common Tasks Suitable for Consultants

Consultants, like any group of professionals, have common and unique experiences, backgrounds, and areas of special interest. Common tasks a typical consultant might be expected to be able to deal with:

1. **Board development**: Help you identify goals for your board, plan to recruit new members, and train the board to meet goals.
2. **Contract services**: Plan and execute high-skill tasks of limited duration.
3. **Diagnosis and assessment**: Identify your problems and state them.
4. **Executive search**: Locate candidates to fill key staff positions.
5. **Facilitation**: Help set goals for an important meeting, such as an annual retreat or membership meeting, and lead group members through a series of structured steps to meet the goals.
6. **Fund development**: Assist board and staff in developing strategies for fundraising or carrying out fundraising plans.
7. **Mediation**: Help resolve disputes with or within your organization.
8. **Organizational process**: Help identify and resolve problems in communication, personnel conflict, and collaboration that hinder you from attaining your organizational goals.
9. **Planning**: Work with the board to devise and complete a strategy for the organization's future.
10. **Problem solving**: Suggest ways of solving your problems.
11. **Research and analysis**: Investigate the trends, events, obstacles, and opportunities affecting your organization's goals.
12. **Systems development**: Devise reliable methods for conducting daily business or concentrate on providing the best available equipment to accomplish important tasks.
13. **Training**: Teach your board and staff essential skills.

In practice, consultants rarely take on just one of these tasks. A good consultant can work on several fronts simultaneously and comfortably.

How to Hire a Consultant

The process, from preparing to hire a consultant to the evaluation of the outcomes, has numerous steps. Each of these steps is discussed in order.

Preparing to Hire

Develop objectives that answer the following questions:

- What are the problems? Define both symptoms and causes.
- What are the expectations? What are the group needs?
- What should be accomplished?
- What skills are required? What type of consultant do you need?
- Who will be the consultant's contacts?
- What time frame will be used?

The Request for Proposal

Once the problem has been isolated, a **request for proposal** (**RFP**) must be developed. The RFP explains, among other things, the type of work to be done and its objective. It should also establish a general format for the proposals to be submitted by the prospective consultants. This format allows a comparative evaluation of consultants on the same criteria.

The RFP should include the following information:

- A brief description of your organization: mission, history, programs, facilities, sources of funding
- A copy of your organization chart and relevant brochures
- Your requirements, identified in an introductory statement that briefly explains the need and desired response from the consultant
- A statement of work that provides detailed information concerning the problem you expect to rectify
- Type of contract: scope of the work, time commitment involved, and payment parameters if desired
- The names and positions of the people within your organization that the prospective consultant might need and sources for additional information
- The end result of the work (for example, a new system design, a manual, a report on staff response to a training program)
- The desired format of the proposal
- Any special information or regulations pertaining to your sector that may affect the proposed work
- The need for progress reports on the other interim products and an explanation of how the proposal will be evaluated

Developing a Useful RFP

The purpose of the RFP is to offer prospective consultants as much useful information as possible so they can develop relevant proposals and accurate bids (Nosse, Friberg, Kovacek, 1999). At the same time, the format should not require an excessive amount of time and work from the respondent. Remember that consultants are not paid for developing their proposals. If the RFP entails a huge time commitment, it may deter qualified but busy prospects who simply lack the time to respond. The best strategy is to create a format that allows prospects to answer in a two- or three-page proposal.

Also, make sure the design allows for flexibility in the response. This will make it easier for respondents to present their ideas and avoid a design that solicits conclusions from the consultant. The purpose of the proposal is to specify how the consultant will approach the problem.

Finding Consultants

Once the RFP is developed, a mailing list of candidates for the job and/or places to publish the RPF must be compiled. There are many ways to go about finding consultants for your mailing list. The best is to ask friends, associates, and other nonprofit organizations for recommendations. The Nonprofit Consulting Directory (see additional resources section) is a good source. Professional and technical associations, foundations, and organizations that support nonprofit organizations may also be useful.

When asking for recommendations on consultants, determine whether the prospects have demonstrated the following capabilities:

- Ability to diagnose problems
- A track record of presenting workable solutions to clients
- The ability to implement those solutions (e.g., installing equipment, training personnel, revamping a budgetary procedure)
- The ability to facilitate consensus and commitment to the plan of action among staff

Sending the RFP

Once a consultant list is formed and reviewed, send the RFP to the most promising candidates and/or publish it in a place that is likely to attract the attention of the type of person you seek.

Screening Candidates

After you build the bid package and send it out to the consultants, you have to screen the respondents. This process should allow you to evaluate the respondents' qualifications for submitting their proposals, establish their dependability as contractors, and most important, assess the soundness of their plans.

In the first phase of screening, eliminate proposals that are obviously unsuitable, those that show lack of understanding of the problem, and those that do not provide the necessary information or tend to ramble.

In the second phase, look at the proposed actions. Will the respondent's strategy work for your organization? You need change, but are the stated techniques appropriate?

The third phase should be the careful selection of proposals that adequately address your needs. (At this stage, top management should be reviewing the proposals.) Make sure the respondent understands what is expected. Both management and the respondent should have a clear picture of the outcome of the work (Nosse et al., 1999). Also check to see whether the respondent's plan of action is supported by the specific techniques proposed to rectify the problem. Has the respondent given you a time line?

Check the respondent's references. Is he or she capable of delivering as promised? Is the person dependable? Asking for samples of previous work is appropriate.

Cost is an important factor when hiring a consultant, but do not allow price to eliminate a bid too quickly. You might be able to negotiate an acceptable fee with the respondent when it comes to the interview. You want to avoid eliminating a good plan, maybe the best plan, based solely on an estimate of cost. One way to avoid negotiation is to include budget parameters in the RFP. (If you choose to state these parameters, expect the fee for services to equal the amount you have to spend.)

Before you reach the final phase, personal interviews, you might want to give promising respondents the opportunity to rewrite their proposals. This allows them to improve their proposal to give it a better chance of being accepted.

Meeting the Candidates

When those final few proposals are chosen and you are ready to conduct interviews, consider the following thoughts. Consultants can sometimes be in your organization for weeks or even months. You will want to take into account the applicant's personality as well as the proposal in the interview.

The Interview

Decide who will initiate the interview by outlining the situation. Then develop a list of questions and decide who will ask them. As with any process, define how the candidates will be evaluated.

During the Interview

Begin by outlining the problem; then ask how the consultant would proceed. Review the RFP objectives. Add any relevant new information.

If this is a consulting firm, ask whether the presenters will be the ones doing the work. Ask what the consultant expects of you and what you can expect in return. Evaluate the candidate's personality, chemistry, and working style by observing his or her listening skill (Chapter 16). Listening skill is an important attribute for everyone but particularly important for a consultant. When talking with the candidate, determine the following:

- How well does the candidate listen?
- What questions does the candidate ask?
- How well does the candidate analyze the situation?
- What solutions are presented, and how realistic they are?

Discuss fee estimates and project time lines in the interview. Be sure you and the candidate agree on the type of interim materials you will be expecting.

Final Selection and Agreement

You will want to get a commitment from the chosen consultant to stay on track with the project and prove that the work was effective.

These and all terms and conditions of performance of the consulting should be specified in a written contract. Once you have conducted all of the interviews and made your choice, write a letter of agreement that covers the following:

- Services to be provided by the consultant
- Specific reports or presentations that are anticipated
- The beginning and estimated end date of project
- The fee for the service and hourly rate
- Whether a **retainer** is to be paid

Have both a representative of your organization and the consultant sign the letter.

As you begin working with the consultant, be sure that you agree upon the objectives of the project and the method of evaluation to be used at its completion. Allow for changes in the approach if reasonable and necessary.

Formalize the Arrangement

Seek a **project proposal** or outline. This should include the expectations of work due and fees expected. Expect that agreement on price will take negotiating. One of the key points in any agreement or contract is the financial terms. For short-term projects (a few days), write a **letter of agreement**. The letter should include the following points:

- Description of the work
- The expected date of completion
- Details regarding fees and how they will be paid

For long-term projects, a formal contract is recommended. This protects both parties from the common complaints of cost overruns and missed deadlines. A contract usually includes the following:

- Work plan: Tasks to be completed, outcomes expected, timetables.
- Fees: Hourly or daily rate. Billing monthly, on completion, or retainer basis; determine type of invoice required.
- Direct costs: Determine how to bill travel, long-distance phone and fax, subcontracted services.
- Workplace: Where will the consultant work? What administrative support, equipment, and supplies are expected?
- Contract dates: Define when contract begins and ends. Consider how the time line will be amended or extended.
- Termination clause: Under what conditions does one or both parties walk away from the work before completion? Notification may be 30 days, 60 days, or less. If disputes arise, arbitration may be needed.
- Rights to data: If proprietary information is collected, determine conditions under which data can be used and who has access once work is completed. If confidentiality is involved, consultant must be informed.

Assuming your staff is committed to making a positive change, the consultant should be able to effect permanent improvement in your organization.

Suggested Screening Questions for Consultants and References

Screening questions to use in discussions with consultant candidates are usually centered on determining their experience with the matters of interest to you and their understanding of your circumstances. Here are examples of screening questions:

- What are your areas of expertise? (For example, strategic planning, board development, fundraising analysis.)
- How long have you been in business?
- How large is your organization?
- What experience do you have working with nonprofit organizations?
- What other projects have you worked on that are similar to this? How are they similar; how different?
- Who would work with us on this project? Can we interview that person?
- Can you give references, including the type of projects and outcomes you provided?
- Can you provide samples of your work? (For example, if the project is marketing or public relations, a brochure.)
- What types of reports will we receive?

- What are your expectations of our involvement in this process?
- What can we expect from you? What do you require of us?
- What does a typical session with you look like in terms of time and work? How many sessions typically?
- What follow-up is there after the job?
- How would you describe the way you go about a job?
- Will your written scope of work include a time line and statement of fees?
- What is your fee structure? Is it hourly or a lump sum? What is included? (For example, travel, photocopying.)
- Will the invoice include a rate breakdown by task and an allocation of the number of hours per task? How do you relate costs to work completed?
- What is the average size project that you prefer? How many hours? Cost?
- Are you willing to take on short-term projects and projects that would be $2500 or less?
- What is your project workload at present? How long will it take to complete our project?
- Why do you think you're the best suited for this project? Why should we hire you?

Sample Questions to Use in Screening Consultant References

The next step is to verify candidate's background by thoroughly checking with those named as references. These are essential questions:

Did the project stay on budget?
Did he or she offer solid recommendations?
How well did the consultant prepare for and follow up meetings?
How well did he or she interact with the agency representatives?
How well was the agency's mission understood?
Was the consultant's analysis of the problem accurate?
Were deadlines met?
What evaluation process was used?
Who did the work? Who was expected to do the work?

How to Manage a Consultant

Consultants are hired. As with any other temporary worker, they have to be managed so goals are met. To facilitate the work, you should keep track of the agreed-upon tasks and get what is needed from the consultant's efforts. Ball (1991) gives recommendations to **manage consultants:**

1. Compile one or more preliminary reports.
2. Give the consultant sufficient information to get up to speed.
3. Insist on a work plan.
4. Outline the methodology used.
5. Request that the consultant provide progress reports on the project at specified times and when you need such information.

Final Report and Evaluation

Communicate regularly with the consultant to review timetables and responsibilities. As the project progresses, establish a process for any necessary changes in its scope. Throughout the consultation period, maintain control over the process and product.

If you are unclear about or not pleased with the work in progress, ask for a meeting to address the situation. Discuss your agreed-upon objectives, the work to date, and/or problems met. Reach consensus on how to proceed from there. Be prepared for resolution of disputes or changes required by a relationship that sours.

Pay the consultant's invoices promptly. Periodically evaluate the consultant's work. One way to conduct this evaluation is focus on four key components of the interaction:

1. Input: what your organization put into the consulting relationship.
2. Process: the relationship between the organization and the consultant.
3. Output: Comparison of the product to expectations.
4. Outcomes: Evaluation of the contribution to the organization's goals.

At the end of the project, hold a final debriefing to discuss the results of the project. The report should consider how the process can be improved the next time a consultant is used.

INDIVIDUAL CASE STUDY

You will pass the licensure examination and be a licensed physical therapist within the next few months. You will be traveling outside of the country right after graduation. You also need a job when you return. One solution is to use a job placement agency to seek out positions for you to investigate upon returning. There are two agencies you know of through mailings to students.

Your task is to develop the RFP for selection of an agency to represent you to potential employers. A quick scan of Chapters 21 and 25 may help you develop specifics for your RFP.

Student Notes

A soon-to-be licensed physical therapist can use paid and unpaid consultants. Some common consultant needs of new graduates include finding a job or apartment, loan or debt consolidation, financial planning advice, insurance information, wedding planner, and legal adviser. The RFP may be less formal, presented over the phone or in an e-mail, but the questions and observation of the responses are essentially the same.

Summary

The use of consultants can significantly improve the performance of your organization. This chapter examines some of the most typical considerations for engaging an outside

GROUP CASE STUDY

Two actors are needed for this case. Gender is not important. Each actor should take on the role of one of the characters.

Situation

Over the past 3 months Big Bucks PT, Inc., a national for-profit rehabilitation company, has repeatedly approached Dale and Chris, the owners of a private practice. Big Bucks PT is interested in purchasing the practice. Although Chris and Dale are satisfied with the practice and the manner in which they have structured their professional and personal lives, they both think it would be prudent to listen to the proposal from Big Bucks PT.

Before entertaining the sales pitch from Big Bucks PT, Chris feels strongly that they should determine the market value of the practice. Dale agrees, but neither of them is sure how to do so.

1. What factors should Chris and Dale consider as they attempt to determine the sale value of their practice? They decide to engage a consultant who is experienced in valuing physical therapy private practices for sale. They decide to develop a RFP to send to consultants who provide these types of services.
2. What information will Chris and Dale want to include in the RFP to help candidate consultants understand the services Dale and Chris desire?
3. What resources are available to develop a distribution list of candidate consultants for this RFP?

consultant. The process is described from the perspective of a manager or organization seeking a consultant, starting with preliminary tasks, such as developing an RFP, then finding candidates, interviewing them, negotiating the terms of the arrangement, hiring them, managing them, assuring accountability, and assessing the results.

REFERENCES

Ball EE. Maximizing the benefits of using consultants. In Ball MJ, Douglas JV, O'Desky RI, eds. Health care information management systems. New York: Springer-Verlag. 1991:326–330.

George RL, Cristiani TS. Counseling: Theory and practice, 3rd ed. Englewood Cliffs, NJ: Prentice-Hall. 1990.

Ginter PM, Swayne LM, Duncan WJ. Strategic management of health care organizations. Malden, MA: Blackwell. 1998.

Nosse LJ, Friberg DG, Kovacek PR. Management and supervisory principles for physical therapists. Baltimore: Williams & Wilkins. 1999.

Webster's II new Riverside university dictionary. Boston: Riverside. 2003.

MORE INFORMATION RELATED TO THIS CHAPTER

Sometimes organizations seek external help to restructure the way they work, from structure and planning to proposal writing. There are consultants to fit most organizations' needs. These resources have lists of nonprofit consultants and books and articles on consultants.

For self-directed searches, start with Literature of the Nonprofit Sector Online (LNPS) (http://www.lnps.fdncenter.org) for an extensive bibliographic database. Another key term is consultants or consultants—directories. Recommended books with information on consultants:

AFP Directory of Consultants and Resource Partners. Alexandria, VA: Association of Fund Raising Professionals, annual. A networking tool that provides contact information for AFP members and details the Association's various services and programs.

Kibbe B, Setterberg F. Succeeding with consultants: Self-assessment for the changing nonprofit. New York: The Foundation Center. 1992. Provides nonprofit administration and boards with a step-by-step method for working with consultants to diagnose and address organizational problems.

Kihlstedt A, Schwartz C. Capital campaigns: Strategies that work. Frederick, MD: Aspen. 1997. Covers the entire process of planning a capital campaign including how to select, hire, and use consultants strategically.

Articles from consultant trade journals:

The 2001 Consultants Guide to Non-Profits. Chronicle of Philanthropy. 2000;14 (October): 1–12.

Iaquinta L. Selection savvy: Seven steps to hiring a campaign consultant. Currents. 1999; (May):36–39. A step-by-step guide to finding a consultant for a capital campaign.

Klein K. Hiring a fundraising consultant. Grassroots Fundraising Journal. 1999; (June): 10–11. Discusses how to decide when a consultant is needed, what consultants can and cannot do, how to choose a consultant, and compensation issues.

Lipman H. Experts offer tips for charities on hiring a commercial fundraiser. Chronicle of Philanthropy. 2001;13 (April):29.

Temkin T. In search of the white knight: Finding the perfect consultant. Nonprofit World. 1999;17 (November-December): 37–39. Includes questions to ask a prospective consultant during an interview and questions an organization should ask itself to clarify its goals before beginning the search for a consultant.

Tempel ER. Choosing a consultant: Make sure you get what you really need. Nonprofit Times. 1999;13 (November): 63, 64, 66. Discusses the difference between consultants and intermediaries, how to decide when a consultant is needed, how to find a consultant, and how compensation should be determined.

Understanding fund raising: A guide for beginners. Giving U.S.A. 1999;Update 4:1–21. Introduction to fundraising, including the selection of a consultant.

Vaughn ET. Outsourcing in the nonprofit sector: A strategic approach to the challenges of growth and staffing. Nonprofit World. 1997;15 (September-October):50–52. Discusses issues of hiring outside specialists to address operational needs that the current organization cannot meet.

Zola I. Do you need a proposal writer? Nonprofit World. 1999;17 (January-February):15–17. Offers tips on hiring and working with a professional proposal writer.

Author Index

Subject Index

Page numbers in *italics* denote figures; those followed by a "t" denote tables.

F

G

J

K

L